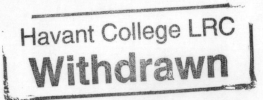

# The Royal
# Horticultural Society
# GARDENING
# MANUAL

# The Royal Horticultural Society
# GARDENING MANUAL

TED SMART

## A DORLING KINDERSLEY BOOK
www.dk.com

**Senior Editor** Gillian Roberts
**Senior Art Editor** Alison Lotinga

**Senior Managing Editor** Mary-Clare Jerram
**Senior Managing Art Editor** Lee Griffiths

**Principal Editors** Annelise Evans, Simon Maughan, Lesley Riley

**Principal Art Editors** Roger Daniels, Martin Hendry, Miranda Kennedy,
Kevin Ryan, Ann Thompson

**Media Resources** Neale Chamberlain, Rachel Hilford, Charlotte Oster

**Picture Research** Sean Hunter

**DTP Designers** Louise Paddick, Louise Waller

**Production** Ruth Charlton, Julian Deeming

First published in Great Britain in 2000
by Dorling Kindersley Limited
9 Henrietta Street, London WC2E 8PS

This edition produced for The Book People LTD.,
Hall Wood Avenue, Haydock, St. Helens WA11 9UL

Copyright © 2000 Dorling Kindersley Limited, London

A CIP catalogue record for this book is available from the British Library

ISBN 0 7513 0364 X

Text film output by Graphical Innovations, London
Reproduced by Colourscan, Singapore
Printed and bound by MOHN media and Mohndruck GmbH, Germany

### CONTRIBUTORS

**PART ONE: PLANNING YOUR GARDEN**
David Joyce

**PART TWO: MAKING AND LOOKING AFTER YOUR GARDEN**

**Patios and Paths**
Lin Hawthorne

**Lawns and Ground Cover**
Alison Copland

**Boundaries, Divisions,
and Structures**
Pamela Brown, Claire Calman,
Joanna Chisholm

**Beds and Borders**
Alison Copland, Lin Hawthorne

**Containers and Raised Beds**
Claire Calman, Alison Copland

**Ornamental Trees in the Garden**
Claire Calman, Alison Copland

**Water Gardening** Lin Hawthorne

**Herbs in the Garden and their
Uses** Claire Calman

**The Edible Garden**
Louise Abbott, Lin Hawthorne

**Looking After the Garden**
Alison Copland

**Dealing with Weeds and
Plant Problems**
Louise Abbott, Lin Hawthorne

**PART THREE: WHAT LOOKS GOOD WHEN**
Louise Abbott, Fiona Wild

**PART FOUR: WHAT TO DO WHEN**
Annelise Evans

**GLOSSARY**
Joanna Chisholm, Lin Hawthorne

**INDEX**
Lynn Bresler

# CONTENTS

## DEALING WITH WEEDS AND PLANT PROBLEMS

## PART THREE
# WHAT LOOKS GOOD WHEN

## PART FOUR
# WHAT TO DO WHEN

## SEASONS

In this book, the gardening year is divided into twelve seasons that correspond to calendar months, as shown below.

Early spring: March
Mid-spring: April
Late spring: May
Early summer: June
Midsummer: July
Late summer: August
Early autumn: September
Mid-autumn: October
Late autumn: November
Early winter: December
Midwinter: January
Late winter: February

## SYMBOLS

The hardiness symbol indicates the minimum temperature at which plants can survive, unprotected, outdoors. The categories of hardiness used in Part Three of this book, and corresponding minimum temperatures, are shown below.

❊❊❊ Fully hardy, down to –15°C (5°F)
❊❊ Frost hardy, down to –5°C (23°F)
❊ Half hardy, down to 0°C (32°F)
❀ Frost tender, down to –5°C (23°F)

Ultimate height is shown as ↕ and spread as ↔

## PART ONE

# PLANNING YOUR GARDEN

# A GARDEN OF YOUR OWN: CHOICES AND CONSIDERATIONS

## WHAT MAKES A GARDEN?

SO POWERFUL ARE THE impressions made by flowers and foliage, it is tempting to think of the garden as essentially a place in which plants grow. Gardens are, however, first and foremost for people, whose preferences and requirements can be very different. You might relish the idea of honing your gardening skills and making a special collection of plants. But creating a pleasant, low-maintenance setting for outdoor living is an equally legitimate ambition. At its most rewarding, a garden is a highly personal creation, and one that happily reconciles your idea of what is best for you with the potential of the plot that is available.

## WHAT YOU NEED TO THINK ABOUT

The way you want to use the garden affects the way you organize the space within its boundaries. This will be reflected in the relative weight given to hard landscaping, such as paving and walls, and the planted areas or soft landscaping. If, for example, you want the garden to be an outdoor room for entertaining, you will probably need a large area of paving or decking. If your passion is plants or you want to grow fruit or vegetables, you might make do with narrow paths criss-crossing planted areas. A pool might be high on your list if you wish to attract wildlife to your garden.

Once you have thought through how you want to use your garden, and how best to exploit the site, you can start planning how you want it to look.

△ THE BALANCED GARDEN
*A garden, screened by a hedge and with an interesting water feature as a focal point, is laid out with a balanced mixture of variously textured hard surfaces — brick, gravel, slabs, and timber — and planted areas. Flowers, including those grown in containers, are colourful, but foliage also plays an important role in this planting scheme.*

◁ A GARDEN WITHIN A GARDEN
*The approach to the screened compartment in this garden is marked by a change in level and a row of planted containers. Screens and dividers clothed with plants can be used to make the most of the three-dimensional space in a garden and also to create distinct areas that are sheltered and intimate.*

⊲ **THE RESTFUL GARDEN**

The garden as a place of rest and relaxation is summed up by this simple bench surrounded by colourful and scented flowers. The use of hard surfaces and simple planting helps to create a garden requiring only a little maintenance.

△ **A PLANT LOVER'S GARDEN**

The mix of shapes, textures, and colours in this garden shows that it has been created by someone with a broad love of plants. Choosing plants with good shape and form adds interest to the garden well beyond the flowering season.

△ **A MEANS OF SELF-EXPRESSION**

There are many ways in which the garden can declare the taste and interests of its creator. The layout, the choice of built features, and the way they are decorated can all bear the gardener's personal stamp. So, too, can the choice and arrangement of foliage and flowering plants.

△ **A SOURCE OF PRODUCE**

Some gardeners value above all the chance to grow vegetables, fruit, and herbs. Even when the operation is scaled down to a few containers, the output can be worthwhile. With imaginative planting and design, the productive garden can be ornamental as well as practical.

△ **THE CHALLENGE OF SCALE**

There is no need to think you need a vast amount of space to create a successful garden. Some designs do extend over broad landscapes, but rewarding gardens, such as this arrangement of container-grown plants, can be made on a minute plot, or even aloft, on a balcony or roof terrace.

# FINDING YOUR OWN STYLE

As well as reflecting the uses you are going to make of your garden, the design should be developed in a style with which you feel comfortable. Your choice, even in a small garden, can range from severe order to jungle effect, while in between taking in ideas from gardens of different cultures and climatic regions.

A distinction is often made between formal and informal styles of gardening, but in effect the difference is not clearcut. The cottage garden, the inspiration of many highly sophisticated 20th-century gardens, appeals because of its happy jumble of plants, many of them remarkable survivors of changing fashions. The plants obscure the fact that the traditional cottage garden often has a simple geometric layout, which also underpins classically formal designs.

You need to weigh up carefully the pros and cons of the style you think might suit your garden. You may be drawn by the austere beauty of a minimalist garden, but is it suitable for a growing family? The idea of a wild garden is seductive, but it cannot be achieved simply by throwing seeds of pretty plants on the lawn. The best solution may be a style that you find sympathetic but that is also labour-saving.

△ MINIMALIST APPROACH
*Carefully chosen rocks set in gravel, a smudge of moss, and a background of trees and shrubs of varying foliage qualities make a powerfully designed garden despite its spare content. Modern gardens such as this have their origins in traditional Japanese designs.*

◁ NATURALISTIC PLANTING
*An informal planting style using herbaceous perennials suited to the growing conditions is an environmentally friendly approach to gardening that takes its inspiration from plant communities in the wild. The textures of plants such as grasses count for as much as flower colour. In contrast to the more rigid herbaceous border, this makes for relatively low-maintenance gardening.*

◁ A WILDFLOWER GARDEN
*The loss of natural habitats and the wild flowers that make them beautiful has encouraged conservation-oriented gardening. A meadow effect can be created with wild flowers growing in turf on soil that is low in fertility. The mowing regime must allow the wild flowers to seed before being cut.*

COTTAGE-GARDEN INSPIRATION ▷
*The bright flowers of poppies (Papaver) crowding in on a brick path convey the style of a traditional cottage garden. This relies on the use of familiar flowers tightly packed together, often in close company with herbs and vegetables, but can be interpreted in many different ways.*

# THE FORMAL VOCABULARY

For its enduring appeal the formal garden relies on calm order. This is usually expressed in a balanced treatment of space, with symmetry in the details. The most common symmetrical arrangement is simple pairing, for example of matching containers of plants flanking a doorway or seat. An avenue, often of trees, is an extension of pairing, and gives a strong formal structure to a drive or path.

Clipped plants, as hedges or as topiary, reinforce the formal tone of a garden, as do trained plants of many kinds, including fruit trees in restricted shapes. A much gentler approach to formality can be created simply by establishing rhythms in the garden, with a conspicuous planting repeated at intervals.

*FORMAL TONE ▷*
*The neat lawn and matching paved areas at either end, clipped bushes, and symmetrical arrangement of details give this garden a spruce — but not forbidding — formal tone.*

# MOOD AND THEME

The character of the hard landscaping and the planting both influence the mood of the garden. Colourful containers and mosaics, for example, make a much bolder impact than simple shapes in terracotta or stone.

A garden filled with foliage in subtle shades of green will have a very different feeling from one in which strong colours dominate. Yet another effect, one of airy lightness, could be achieved using white and very pale shades in a narrowly defined colour scheme.

The choice of plants can also convey the idea of a garden from another climate. An impression of Mediterranean heat or a jungle effect with bamboos and other leafy plants can be created even in cool temperate gardens.

△ **SCULPTURE IN THE GARDEN**
*Sculpture and interesting objects, including pieces of driftwood, unusually shaped rocks, and items of scrap, can help to establish a mood or tone. They are usually placed prominently at focal points, but can also be effective in a more discreet location.*

◁ **STRONG COLOURS**
*The tulip season lasts from late winter to late spring, and the wide range of single and mixed colours makes these bulbs useful for bold effects. A fence, painted blue-green, intensifies a powerful colour scheme contrasting orange and near-black tulips.*

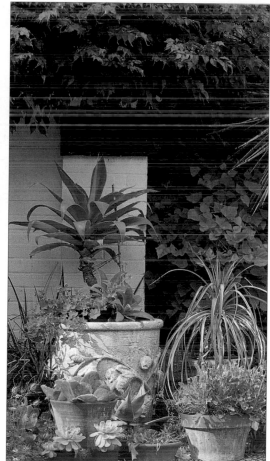

△ **A MEDITERRANEAN THEME**
*In a tableau that suggests a Mediterranean garden, the trumpet creeper (Campsis), with tubular orange flowers, makes a canopy over a collection of foliage and flowering plants, most of which are in containers.*

# THE CONTAINED GARDEN

AN ENCLOSED SPACE, separated by walls from the surrounding landscape, and made distinct inside by its planting and design, is one of the oldest types of garden. Its original appeal may have been as a well-watered, cool, and green retreat from a harsh natural world. Now the harsh world outside is much more likely to be urban, and the relief that is needed is from the bustle and noise of the city. The typical modern version of this garden is contained by the walls of neighbouring properties, or lodged above ground, on a balcony or rooftop. The scale is small, but this can be made into a virtue by plantings that create a sense of privacy and intimacy. At its most extreme, the contained garden has no open ground, but is simply a space magically transformed by container-grown plants.

## A COURTYARD GARDEN
**Although walls hem in a courtyard, an ingenious layout and well-chosen plants can help to create a sense of space. Here, exuberant planting disguises the proximity of the walls and makes a lush green setting for an intimate retreat.**

### CORNER DETAIL ▽
Small corners that are not needed for access can be filled with plants requiring little maintenance. Another attractive solution is to use the corner as a setting for an ornament. Here, a pair of pleasingly shaped vessels, raised on a platform, is complemented by minimalist planting.
SEE ALSO: Focal Points, p.29

## A WALLED GARDEN
**An arched opening in a brightly coloured, rendered wall gives a glimpse of a brick-paved garden with low, clipped hedges and generous planting. This is a variation on the traditional walled garden in mellow brick. The epitome of the warm and sheltered garden is often laid out formally, with fruit trees, wall shrubs, and climbers planted to take advantage of reflected heat.**

### CONSERVING WATER

In areas of low rainfall, or when growing lots of plants in containers, watering can be a major task. Many problems can be overcome by selecting plants that tolerate drought. Other steps should be taken to make the most of the available water.

■ When watering, give priority to new plants and to plants in containers.

■ Cover the surface of soil or potting compost with a mulch to slow water loss: grit is an effective topping in containers.

■ Add water-retaining crystals or granules to compost in containers.

■ When it is impossible to water regularly by hand, install a trickle or drip-feed irrigation system that incorporates a timing device.

### ORNAMENTAL FEATURES △
Two pieces of metal sculpture — a wall-mounted relief and a free-standing head — make arresting focal points in this courtyard, despite their sober colouring. In small gardens, ornaments such as masks and reliefs that can be fixed to walls have the advantage of leaving the limited ground surface uncluttered. Here, the almost two-dimensional giant profile, looming out of richly textured foliage, takes up surprisingly little space and adds a surreal touch.
SEE ALSO: Focal Points, p.29

## OUTDOOR FURNITURE ▽

Even in this small and densely planted courtyard, there is space for a weatherproof circular table of generous size. It almost fills the seating area by the pool, but there is enough room to accommodate five or six people comfortably. Lightweight folding chairs can easily be stored away when not in use.

SEE ALSO: Leisure Elements, pp.34–35

## PLANTING FOR PRIVACY ▽

Containers packed with colourful busy Lizzies (*Impatiens*) provide bright splashes of colour, but the emphasis in this garden is on foliage. Wall-trained shrubs, bamboos, and palms, including a paddle-leaved banana (*Musa*), create the impression of an intimate and private zone carved out of lush greenery.

SEE ALSO: Plants for a Purpose, pp.38–41

## HANGING BASKETS △

Hanging baskets suspended from wall-mounted brackets are a useful way of introducing colourful planting to courtyard gardens where there is little ground space for containers. Once the initial display is over, they can easily be replanted, providing interest through much of the year — even in winter in mild climates.

SEE ALSO: A Place for Plants, pp.42–43

## ◁ WATER FEATURE

To underline the tropical character of this courtyard, cooling water overflows from a raised pool, to trickle over large stones in the lower basin. The water, circulated by a submersible electric pump, provides a constant and soothing murmur.

SEE ALSO: Water Features, pp.32–33

## ◁ HARD SURFACES

The clean, hard surfaces that cover a relatively small proportion of the garden's area give access from the house to the space furnished for outdoor entertaining. The seating area is defined by stone paving slabs, the access route by lengths of wooden decking.

SEE ALSO: Surfaces, pp.24–27

## A ROOFTOP GARDEN

An L-shaped arrangement of benches makes a pleasant corner that is lightly sheltered and screened by plants growing in containers attached to the balustrade. The informal planting sets a relaxed tone; wooden decking makes a neat and clean surface under foot; and the benches are made more comfortable by padded cushions covered in weather-resistant fabric. The weight-bearing capacity of flat roofs and balconies may make it necessary to use lightweight materials such as plastic and fibreglass for standing containers. To prevent their being dislodged by wind, all containers must be well secured.

# THE FAMILY GARDEN

A SUCCESSFUL FAMILY GARDEN is a happy compromise between the competing claims of adults and children. The ideal is a garden with secure boundaries where plants have their place, but where there is also room for children to be boisterously active and for adults to relax. Although practical and safety considerations may be paramount, the garden can be attractively laid out and imaginatively planted. Needs change as the family grows up. From the outset it is worth thinking about how you might develop the garden, perhaps with more ambitious planting, when children's interests have expanded beyond play equipment.

## ONE GARDEN FOR ALL

A "borrowed" background of leafy trees makes an attractive setting for a garden designed to balance the interests of adults and children. A furnished paved area near the house leads to a utility lawn flanked by plant-filled borders with ornamental features and a set of swings. At the far end, the gazebo, sitting on the centre line, emphasizes the garden's underlying symmetry and its unifying and bold colour scheme.

### ROBUST PLANTING ▷
Tough perennials, bulbs, shrubs, and climbers fill the borders either side of a hard-wearing lawn, which serves as a play area. A Chusan palm (*Trachycarpus fortunei*), with distinctive fan leaves, makes an off-centre focus. The vibrancy of the container plantings on the patio stands up to the strong colours of both furniture and features.

### SUNKEN SANDPIT △
This timber-framed sandpit has been positioned so that playing children can be easily observed from the house or from the outdoor seating area. The rim helps to prevent sand being scattered and also provides a safe seat.
SEE ALSO: Leisure Elements, pp.34–35

### ◁ PLAY EQUIPMENT

Climbing equipment and play areas that offer children an enjoyable challenge must be solidly built and designed with safety in mind. The footings should be on well-drained ground. A thick topping of shredded bark gives a relatively soft landing, when needed.
SEE ALSO: Leisure Elements, pp.34–35

### ◁ SWINGS

Swings, here matching the garden's bright colour theme, are a strong draw for young children. They can be removed later on, when they are no longer required, without leaving a serious gap in this garden's design.

### ◁ PATIO AREA

Quarry tiles, decorated and laid with two contrasting patterns, provide an easily cleaned and firm surface for family activities, including eating outdoors. Planted pots soften the effect of the large tiled expanse.
SEE ALSO: Surfaces, pp.24–27

SEE ALSO: Leisure Elements, pp.34–35
SEE ALSO: Surfaces, pp.24–27

## PLAYING SAFE

Special precautions have to be taken to ensure a garden is safe for children.

• Make boundaries secure, to prevent youngsters straying onto busy roads.

• Site play areas where they can be easily supervised from house windows.

• Avoid growing plants with sharp thorns and those known to be toxic.

• Be aware of the danger of open water, even when it is shallow.

• Store tools and garden chemicals securely out of reach of inquisitive hands.

### ◁ FLOWER PATCH

Children feel they have a stake in the garden when they are allocated a decent piece of ground to themselves. To sustain their delight they usually need some unobtrusive help in growing plants that give quick results. Phenomenal growth and large flowerheads make sunflowers (*Helianthus annuus*) firm favourites for a child's patch. Easy vegetables, such as radishes and loose-leaf lettuces, are also good choices.

## A PLAYGROUND GARDEN

As children grow older, their play tends to become more exuberant, and it often pays to dedicate a part of the garden to them. This sheltered activity area consists of a broad expanse of hard-wearing grass. Brightly coloured play equipment is arranged so that there is still plenty of room in which to run about without the risk of collisions. The structures are light enough to be moved to different positions should patches of grass wear thin. In time, when the equipment becomes redundant, the area could revert to uncluttered lawn, or it could be transformed by beds planted with ornamentals.

# THE LEISURE GARDEN

FOR MANY WHO lead busy lives, juggling all manner of demands on their free time, the ideal garden is one that provides a pleasant setting for the house without presenting too many challenges. It is a matter of finding the right balance, between the time you spend enjoying the garden – whether relaxing in it or simply viewing it from inside – and the hours you take to maintain it. Hard surfaces are less effort to look after than beds and borders, but even these can be planted with resilient ground-covering ornamentals needing little care and attention to keep them looking good.

## A GARDEN FOR RELAXATION

A long narrow garden has been divided lengthways to create three distinct areas, needing varying degrees of attention. Nearest the house is a paved outdoor room. At a higher level, at the far end, is an area laid to lawn. The terraced section in the middle of the garden, with formal beds and containers, is the most labour intensive but is small enough to make it manageable.

### SIMPLE PLANTING ▷

Trees, shrubs, and climbers soften the boundary walls, but most of the planting is concentrated in the terraced central section of the garden, some of it in containers. The matching lower beds are outlined in dwarf box (*Buxus sempervirens* 'Suffruticosa'), reinforcing the garden's formal tone, but the low-maintenance planting at the next level is more naturalistic.

SEE ALSO: Plants for a Purpose, pp.38–41; A Place for Plants, pp.42–43

### △ SWIMMING POOL

A terraced site has here been used to accommodate a boldly designed swimming pool of irregular outline that has shallow and deep areas. Above the white retaining wall is a terrace for sunbathing, which is surrounded by neat planting and dominated by a giant amphora. The pump house, painted blue, circulates the pool water via a waterfall.

SEE ALSO: Leisure Elements, pp.34–35

### SEATING AREA △

Two benches are set at right angles to one another, making the most of sun throughout much of the day. The crisp white of the furniture and its neat arrangement help to define the garden's formal style. A looser arrangement of tables and chairs would give a garden with this structure a quite different, more relaxed appearance.

SEE ALSO: Leisure Elements, pp.34–35

## PROVIDING SHADE

To be enjoyed when the weather is hot, a garden needs areas of cool shade. It may take years for trees to grow large enough to cast useful shade, but purpose-built structures can be quickly covered by climbers.

• Train climbers over pergolas and arbours to create shady walks and seats.

• Plant trees with light foliage such as the Mount Etna broom (*Genista aetnensis*) to provide areas of dappled shade.

• Use sun umbrellas to shade furniture that is moved about.

## ◁ QUALITY LAWN

Here, the lawn will not be subjected to heavy wear, but can be enjoyed for its soft, springy texture under foot and, when viewed from the upper windows of the house, as a calm, green extension of the garden. Regular cutting, a task made simple by the rectangular shape, will help to ensure the lawn stays in good condition.
SEE ALSO: Surfaces, pp.24–25

## ◁ STAGED CONTAINERS

Two flights of steps invite a leisurely walk to explore the different areas of the garden. They can also serve as a tiered stage for plant-filled containers, to give an unchanging display or one that reflects the seasons.
SEE ALSO: Surfaces, pp.26–27

## BARBECUE ▽

Although its purpose is utilitarian, a built-in barbecue can be an attractive feature if constructed of materials that match other hard surfaces in the garden.
SEE ALSO: Leisure Elements, pp.34–35

## △ THE PATIO AS THOROUGHFARE

As well as providing a clean, hard surface where tables and seating can be set out for relaxation and entertaining, a patio also usually serves as a thoroughfare from the house to other areas of the garden. Using the same flooring material – such as quarry tiles – throughout helps to strengthen the link between indoor and outdoor areas.
SEE ALSO: Surfaces, pp.24–27

## A SECLUDED GARDEN

The most important function of your garden may be to provide a haven, somewhere to escape from the outside world. A backdrop of dense foliage and crowded planting makes this garden seem a magically secluded place, especially when viewed from an inner compartment and framed by the uprights of a delicate pergola.

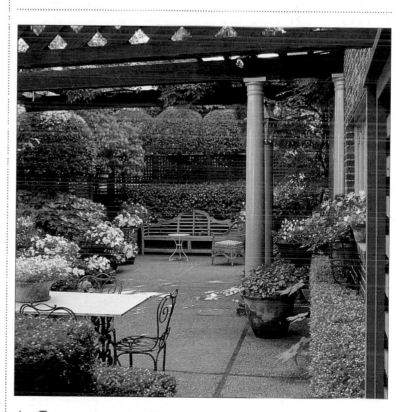

## A GARDEN FOR ENTERTAINING

This paved area adjoining a house conveys the impression of an outdoor salon about to be filled by a bright and chattering crowd. The tone is set by the architectural framework, partly consisting of clipped hedges and trees, and the space for people to circulate with furniture thoughtfully arranged about it. Container-grown plants, as perfect as meticulous flower arrangements, add to the air of elegance.

# THE EDIBLE GARDEN

A PRODUCTIVE GARDEN, providing seasonal supplies of vegetables, fruit, and herbs for the home, can take many forms. The traditional kitchen garden laid out on a generous scale, with beds separated by a grid of paths, can meet all your needs, but requires space and is labour intensive. An attractive solution where space is limited is a potager, a garden of edible plants – even fruit trees trained in restricted forms – arranged to make the most of their decorative qualities, perhaps with a few ornamentals to boost the colour. Patches of vegetables can be set among the flowers in a mixed border, and many edible plants grow well in containers so that even a tiny garden, a patio, or a windowbox can be a source of fresh produce.

## SUPPORTS FOR CLIMBERS ▽

Temporary supports are needed for climbing vegetables such as runner beans, and for plants such as sweet peas (*Lathyrus odoratus*), grown to provide cut flowers for the house. Here, frames are made of paired bamboo canes inserted into the ground at a steep angle and strengthened by horizontal canes. Where space is at a premium, the supports can consist of a wigwam of bamboo canes or a tapered column of brushwood.

## A KITCHEN GARDEN

**Mown paths separate the large beds of a kitchen garden, in which vegetables are planted in regimented rows, with the ground between kept clear of weeds. Comparable quantities of food can be produced in a smaller area using narrower beds with more deeply cultivated soil, and access paths on each side. Crops are then close-planted in blocks, rather than in rows.**

### PLANTS IN ROWS ▷

In the traditional system of orderly planting, vegetables are grown in rectangular beds with wide spacing between rows, a method that allows easy access for cultivation. To make the best use of the space, fast-maturing salad crops can be sown between rows of slow-growing vegetables while these plants are still small.

### △ PEAR ARCH

Most fruit trees are very decorative and some can be trained into compact shapes. Pears and apples are commonly grown as espaliers, with several tiers of branches trained horizontally either side of the trunk, or – as the pear trees here – grown over a series of metal arches.

## A Decorative Edible Garden

Herbs, vegetables, and a compact apple tree are here grown together in a way that is as attractive as it is productive. The mauve globes of alliums, members of the onion family, top red chard — one of the most colourful vegetables on account of its stems — and yellow and orange pot marigolds (*Calendula officinalis*). Pot marigolds are herbs, now often grown as ornamentals; they self-seed freely. The traditional cottage garden, with its casual mixtures of decorative and edible plants, can be a useful source of ideas for your own plot.

### ◁ Mown Paths

Grass paths are an attractive way of dividing up the beds of a large kitchen garden, but they need regular cutting, and can soon become reduced to mud in wet weather. Where paths get heavy use, particularly in a small garden, a hard surface, for example of brick, is a better choice.
SEE ALSO: Surfaces, pp.24–27

### ◁ Aromatic Edging

Plants with aromatic leaves make a delightful edging to beds and borders, releasing their scent when brushed against; they are useful also for picking. Suitable herbs include hyssop, lavender, rosemary, and thyme. Here, rows of the purple-leaved sage (*Salvia officinalis* Purpurascens Group) run along each side of a grass path.
SEE ALSO: Plants for a Purpose, pp.40–41

### Herb Corner △

Herbs can be grown formally, in a bed of their own, or informally, among other plants. Many thrive in a sunny position with well-drained soil. They include garden thyme, seen above covered with purple flowers in early summer.

### Good Management

Keeping a kitchen garden healthy and productive depends on good management.

• Maintain soil fertility, condition, and capacity to hold moisture by working in plenty of well-rotted organic matter, such as garden compost.

• In a dedicated vegetable garden prevent the build up of pests and diseases by rotating crops from one area to another each year.

• Burn diseased plants, and compost fallen leaves and other soft plant material.

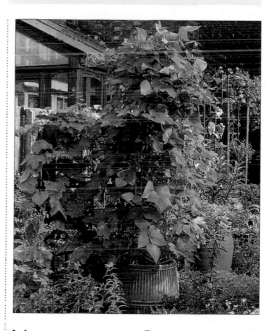

### Vegetables in Containers

Climbing beans do well in deep containers, provided they have support, such as a wigwam of canes. For containers in exposed positions, for example on a balcony, salad leaves and early bush tomatoes are among the most suitable edible plants.

# THE ENTHUSIAST'S GARDEN

THE ENTHUSIAST'S GARDEN has many interpretations, reflecting the interests and tastes of the individual gardener and the challenges of the site. What makes it stand out is almost invariably the quality of the planting. The gardener's enthusiasm is often shown by a passion for collecting rare, unusual, or even obvious kinds of plants (such as roses), but most imaginatively when it brings into the garden plants suitable for all its growing conditions. Plants are grouped according to their needs, in a way that is pleasing to the eye, the standard of cultivation is high, and there is a sense that the garden is not static, but ever evolving.

## A HIGH-MAINTENANCE BORDER

The enthusiast's commitment, from ground preparation and planning to staking and deadheading, shows in this well-staged border, with a late-summer display of pink dahlias. A border in such a state of perfection is deeply satisfying, while for the dedicated gardener the work involved is also a source of pleasure.

### ◁ DUAL-PURPOSE GREENHOUSE

A greenhouse can be costly, but it is a considerable asset to – and excellent investment for – a keen gardener. Unheated greenhouses are mainly used to raise and grow on plants so that they are well advanced by the time you plant them out in the open garden. A heated greenhouse offers greater versatility, and its protected environment can be a permanent home for tender plants.
SEE ALSO: Garden Maintenance, pp.36–37

## A GARDEN ON THE WILD SIDE

Labour-saving design and planting allows the keen gardener to make the best use of limited time. Naturalistic associations of plants requiring similar growing conditions – the sedums and grasses here are tolerant of drought – can make the most of foliage qualities as well as of flower colour. Mulches of gravel or of well-rotted organic matter help to keep down weeds and retain moisture.

### CONTRASTS OF FORM ▷

In a naturalistic association of plants, forms interlock as they do in wild plant communities. In this garden, a low skirt of silver-leaved plants, including *Senecio cineraria*, outlines clumps of grasses, mounds of sedums, and a spiky yucca.

### EXTENDED SEASON ▷

The garnet and tawny colours of autumn, or the spare and graphic contrasts of winter, play just as important a part in the enthusiast's garden as the fresh and dazzling combinations of spring and summer.

### FOLIAGE FOR TEXTURE ▷

A garden of rich and subtle effects relies on the interplay of different textures found among foliage, as well as on flower and foliage colour. A stiffly jagged yucca framed by softly arching grasses stands out in this autumn garden against rigid vertical stems.
SEE ALSO: Plants for a Purpose, pp.38–39

## STOCKING THE GARDEN

Filling a garden with plants bought from a nursery or garden centre can be expensive, but raising them yourself – from seed or cuttings for example – is a way of increasing stocks at very low cost.

• Join local and national horticultural societies to take advantage of exchange schemes for seeds and plants and to participate in shows, where specialist nurseries usually sell interesting plants.

• Set aside a nursery area in which plants raised from seed or from cuttings can be grown on before being planted out into their final positions.

• Use cold frames as well as a greenhouse to increase the number of plants you can raise from cuttings or seeds.

## A WATERSIDE GARDEN

Special sites such as the margins of still or moving water and areas of boggy ground provide scope for imaginative associations of plants that have similar needs. Well-chosen plants that are thriving in conditions to which they are suited create the impression of a natural plant community, and yet the constituent members will often come from areas that are geographically far apart. This waterside planting, in which foliage plays a major role, includes a maple (*Acer*) and hostas from Japan, Asiatic primulas, a large-leaved *Lysichiton* from North America, a hybrid of Himalayan rhododendrons, and a New Zealand tree fern.

# SURFACES 1

SURFACES ARE KEY ELEMENTS in gardens, even in those that are almost covered by ornamental planting. The structure of a garden is commonly defined by hard surfaces such as gravel paths and paved courtyards, which are clean underfoot, even in wet weather. Their function is to provide routes through the garden and tidy surrounds to utilities, as well as to floor outdoor rooms used for relaxation and entertaining. Colour, texture, and pattern can make much hard landscaping an attractive component of the garden.

Most soft surfaces, for example turf, are planted. Some are suitable for areas that are used for play or recreation. Few stand up to heavy wear, particularly in wet weather, but their functional value is often less important than their appearance.

## SOFT SURFACES SEE ALSO: LAWNS AND GROUND COVER, PP.74–89

### FINE LAWN

Lawn grass grown principally for its appearance consists of a mixture of fine-leaved species, commonly bents and fescues.
**Advantages** The uniform green is restful to the eye; the velvet sward a luxury surface to walk on.
**Disadvantages** Suitable only for an open, scrupulously prepared site. Needs very frequent mowing (roller needed for classic striped effect), and a high level of maintenance, including watering in dry weather. Expensive as turf; slow to become established if sown from seed.

### UTILITY LAWN

Lawn grass that provides a hardwearing surface consists of a mixture of resilient species, often including perennial ryegrass.
**Advantages** Pleasing appearance and yet tough enough for a family garden. Less demanding to maintain than a fine lawn.
**Disadvantages** Ground must be thoroughly prepared. Appearance always inferior to that of a fine lawn. Requires frequent mowing and, in dry weather, watering. Fairly expensive as turf and slow to become established if sown from seed.

## GARDEN STEPS

Steps are an architectural and theatrical way of linking different levels in a sloping site. They invite movement, but are unsuitable for taking equipment such as wheelbarrows.

• Safe steps have firm foundations, generous treads that are level, with a non-slip surface, and risers of a manageable height.

• Cost depends on the nature of the site, the scale of the steps, and the choice of materials.

• Materials, which can be mixed as in the timber and brick steps below, are best matched to other built features.

## HARD SURFACES SEE ALSO: PATIOS AND PATHS, PP.56–73

### TIMBER DECKING

Lengths of timber – rot-resistant such as western red cedar, or pressure-treated with preservative – are supported on joists to make a level surface, even over sloping or uneven ground.
**Advantages** Timber readily available in panel form. Good for linking the garden to indoor living space. Versatile material. Design possibilities with colour, texture, and pattern.
**Disadvantages** Construction and weight-bearing requirements may be governed by local or national regulations. Structure needs regular maintenance to prolong life.

### GRAVEL

Gravel consists of stone fragments and pebbles, graded according to size, which make a crunching sound when walked on. Colour varies, depending on the original stone. It is usually laid over plastic to discourage weeds.
**Advantages** Relatively cheap; easy to lay, even in irregular shapes. Suitable for informal and formal settings. Mixes well and unifies planted and open areas. Crunchy noise deters intruders.
**Disadvantages** Scatters unless restrained by a firm edging, and is frequently carried indoors on shoes. Weed control often necessary.

## ROUGH GRASS

Grasses, particularly native species, often combined with flowers that grow naturally in grassland, are allowed to flower and seed. Paths and patterns can be created by mowing.

**Advantages** Few cuts needed annually. Suitable for awkward areas, including rough and sloping ground, and poor soils. Can help conserve wild flowers. Sympathetic to wildlife.

**Disadvantages** Cut grass needs to be removed. Control of pernicious weeds necessary. Small areas of rough grass can look untidy.

## CHAMOMILE LAWN

Plants other than grass used to create lawns include aromatic perennials such as chamomile (*Chamaemelum nobile*). The low-growing and non-flowering 'Treneague' is especially suitable.

**Advantages** Provides a contrast of texture to other areas of the garden. When bruised by light treading, the leaves release a pleasant apple-like scent. Needs only occasional trimming.

**Disadvantages** Tolerates only very light wear and is best limited to small areas where there is no regular traffic. Requires frequent renovation.

## BARK CHIPPINGS

Mechanically chipped or shredded bark, widely used as a mulch among plants, is also suitable as a surface for footpaths and around children's play equipment.

**Advantages** Relatively inexpensive and easily applied material. Soft under foot and an appropriate surface in a woodland garden.

**Disadvantages** Effect can be overpowering when used over large areas. Needs replenishing every two to three years because chippings break down and scatter unless retained by edging.

## POURED CONCRETE

Concrete, prepared from cement, sand, and aggregate mixed with water, is laid over a foundation of hardcore. To prevent cracking, large areas must have expansion joints.

**Advantages** Relatively cheap and durable material, versatile enough to be laid in almost any site, however oddly shaped. Provided access is adequate, often possible to have ready-mixed concrete delivered. Can be coloured and there are various ways of texturing the surface.

**Disadvantages** Harsh appearance of large areas is difficult to disguise, even with colour.

## CONCRETE SLABS

Pre-cast concrete slabs are readily available in a range of sizes, shapes, and colours. They can be smooth or textured, some simulating stone. They are usually laid on strips of mortar on sand over a hardcore base or, for heavy-duty areas such as drives, on a concrete base.

**Advantages** Relatively inexpensive and easily laid. Both versatile and durable. Weathering improves appearance.

**Disadvantages** When first laid, slabs look raw. Some of the brighter colours never really blend with plants or other materials.

## GRANITE SETTS

These roughly rectangular blocks of granite need to be bedded in mortar or sand. They provide a more even surface than cobblestones, which are naturally rounded stones selected for uniformity of size and laid in the same way.

**Advantages** Very durable and maintenance-free. Mix well with other materials and small unit size makes for flexibility. Pleasing colour variations. Attractive in formal and informal areas.

**Disadvantages** Expensive both to buy and have laid. Surface is slightly uneven. Slippery when wet, but no more so than other hard surfaces.

# SURFACES 2

## MORE HARD SURFACES SEE ALSO: PATIOS AND PATHS, PP.56–73

### STONE SLABS

Regular slabs of quarried stone are usually bedded in sand that has been spread over a hardcore base. The slabs are levelled, and the gaps between them filled with mortar or sand.

**Advantages** Wide range of colours and textures available. Very durable and require little maintenance. Create impression of quality in formal areas.

**Disadvantages** Expensive to buy and have laid. Heavy work to lay and skill required to achieve a highly finished surface of interlocking shapes.

### CRAZY PAVING

Irregularly shaped fragments of quarried stone, bedded in sand that is laid over hardcore, are fitted together to cover the available area. A mixture of different kinds of stone can be used, as here. The joints are usually filled with mortar.

**Advantages** Broken fragments of stone are cheaper than whole slabs. Usually lighter work to lay than whole stone slabs. Durable.

**Disadvantages** Time-consuming to fit pieces together. Over a large area, the effect of the irregular joints can be irritatingly eye-catching.

### CONCRETE STEPPING STONES

Pre-cast concrete slabs that are spaced to match an average walking pace are bedded in sand to create an easy route through plants or gravel.

**Advantages** Relatively cheap, easy to lay, and durable. Versatile material that has many utilitarian applications, making paths that are easily modified and clean under foot. Appearance may improve with weathering.

**Disadvantages** Harsh appearance when first laid and often never weather sufficiently to blend in with their surroundings.

## MIXED PAVING SEE ALSO: PATIOS AND PATHS, PP.56–73

### STONE, GRANITE, AND GRAVEL

An unusual feature, such as an old grinding stone, here composed of fitted elements, forms the centrepiece of a design incorporating granite setts and gravel.

**Advantages** Impressive when laid out with style, as here. Mix of materials creates a strongly textured and patterned effect. Suitable for a formal area. Durable.

**Disadvantages** Expensive. Can be difficult to combine materials satisfactorily when more than two are used. Control of weeds in the gravel probably necessary.

### CUT BRICKS AND TERRACOTTA

Bricks cut to fit and laid around a series of rings composed of terracotta flowerpots, sitting one inside another, make an unusual circular design. The flowerpots are bedded in sand and the bricks in mortar.

**Advantages** A distinctive and eye-catching feature made from relatively modest materials. Suitable for a focal point in a larger brick surface.

**Disadvantages** Even if the flowerpots are frostproof, the terracotta centrepiece is less durable than the brick surround. Skill needed to cut the bricks to shape. Weed control necessary.

### LARGE STONES AND PEBBLES

Large fragments of stone are bedded in sand and laid, surrounded by pebbles, so that the upper surface is approximately level.

**Advantages** Naturally occurring pieces of stone are cheaper than shaped stone and may even be available free on site. Pleasing contrasts of textures, shapes and, in some cases, colour. Suitable in an informal setting. Durable.

**Disadvantages** Not suitable for formal parts of the garden and appropriate only for secondary paths. Uneven surface of stones a potential hazard. Weed control may be necessary.

## BRICKS

Weather-resistant bricks of various colours and textures used for flat surfaces are usually laid on a bed of mortar and pointed. Clay pavers, which are thinner than bricks, are laid in a similar way.
**Advantages** Sympathetic materials, particularly near brick buildings. Mix well with most other forms of paving. The various bonding patterns can be highly decorative in formal areas. Small unit size makes them flexible paving materials.
**Disadvantages** Because time-consuming to lay, work done by contractors likely to be expensive.

## TILES

Quarry tiles, which are of clay fired to a high temperature, and frostproof glazed ceramic tiles are laid on levelled concrete. Quarry tiles are usually bedded in mortar but ceramic tiles are fixed with a tile adhesive.
**Advantages** Scope for colourful and decorative effects. Useful for linking indoor and outdoor areas. Mosaics can be made from tile fragments.
**Disadvantages** Glazed tiles can be slippery when wet. Cutting tiles often proves difficult and wasteful. Not suitable for informal areas.

### PATTERNS IN PAVING

Patterns made from paving materials are traditional elements in garden design but, as this illustration shows, there is still scope for using them in original ways. Here, the spirals are filled with contrasting light and dark pebbles set in cement.

• Many patterns, such as the various brick bonds, provide a simple and pleasing way of bringing order to small units of paving

• Interlocking patterns strengthen surfaces.

• The use of contrasting materials heightens the effect of pattern.

## BRICKS AND GRAVEL

Frostproof bricks bedded in mortar on a firm base form a strong design and act as an edging for gravel infill.
**Advantages** An economical way of creating a strongly patterned design that exploits contrasts of texture and colour. Mix of materials is suitable for a formal part of the garden.
**Disadvantages** Gravel tends to scatter and needs topping up from time to time. A buffer zone of brick between mixed paving and house is advisable to stop gravel being taken indoors on shoes. Weed control may be necessary.

## STONE SLABS AND LAWN

Stones slabs of various sizes bedded on sand are laid as a surround to neatly trimmed turf.
**Advantages** Pleasing contrasts of texture, colour, and shape. The stone slabs provide a surface that can be walked on in wet weather. Suitable for formal settings. Effect can be achieved with only small patches of turf, so can be successful in even a tiny garden.
**Disadvantages** For maximum effect, careful and regular mowing of the grass and trimming of the turf edge are essential. Control of weeds between paving stones necessary.

## STONE SLABS AND PEBBLES

Loose pebbles of varying size surround regular or irregular stone slabs that are bedded in sand.
**Advantages** An economical way of using a relatively small quantity of paving stone, which provides an even surface for walking. Attractive contrasts of texture and, in some cases, colour. Combination suitable for informal areas of the garden. The pebbles can be treated as a mulch, with plants growing through it.
**Disadvantages** Weed control of the area covered by pebbles may be necessary. Pebbles may scatter unless retained by an edging.

# BOUNDARIES AND DIVISIONS 1

WALLS, FENCES, AND HEDGES form barriers and screens that mark out the boundaries of a garden and create divisions within it. They can also make an area secure, keeping in children and animals and, if the barriers are high enough, keeping out intruders. Even when the security is not total, they create the intimate atmosphere of a place apart by blocking views into the garden and controlling what is seen of the world beyond. Open structures such as arches and pergolas can also play some of these roles.

. By providing shelter, trapping warmth, casting shade, creating dry spots, and filtering wind, barriers and screens influence growing conditions in different parts of the garden. They also help to muffle noise and keep out traffic fumes.

## FREE-STANDING WALLS SEE ALSO: BOUNDARIES, DIVISIONS, STRUCTURES, PP.90–121

### BRICK WALL

Walls of brick are built on a footing of hardcore and concrete, with the bricks laid in a bonding pattern and topped by a protective coping.
**Advantages** Durable and requires little maintenance. Good for security and privacy. Bricks available in many colours and textures. Attractively patterned bonds. Heat retained by wall creates warm microclimate on sunny side.
**Disadvantages** Expensive to have built; for DIY, needs some skill. Acts as a solid barrier to wind, creating turbulence on sheltered side.

### RENDERED WALL

Rendering is a coat of plaster or mortar applied to walls that lack a good natural finish, such as those of concrete blocks. The rendered surface is usually painted.
**Advantages** Solid and durable wall with good finish possible using relatively cheap materials. Render can be textured in many ways, such as by brushing or combing or with pebbledash.
**Disadvantages** Forms a solid barrier to wind, creating turbulence damaging to plants and unpleasant for people. Requires maintenance.

## FENCES SEE ALSO: BOUNDARIES, DIVISIONS, STRUCTURES, PP.90–121

### WOODEN PICKET FENCE

Vertical stakes or posts set in the ground are connected by horizontal rails, to which upright pales are fixed at regular intervals. The fence may be left plain but is often painted or stained.
**Advantages** Attractive, light barrier. Can be given individual character by varying spacing and width of pales, shaping the tops of the pales, and by giving a colour finish. Because of gaps between pales, the fence filters wind, lessening the risk of turbulence near it.
**Disadvantages** Requires maintenance. Offers limited security and privacy.

### WOODEN PANEL FENCE

Wooden panels consisting of a frame and slats or boards are supported by wooden or concrete posts to make screens and fences.
**Advantages** Relatively inexpensive. Easy to erect. Good for creating privacy. Closeboard fencing, which consists of overlapping vertical feather-edged boards, can also be built on site and is reasonably solid.
**Disadvantages** Basketweave panels, with interwoven slats, and waney-edged panels, with overlapping horizontal planks, as illustrated here, are lightweight and not long-lived.

### POST AND RAIL FENCE

Upright timber posts spaced at regular intervals support usually two or three horizontal rails or poles. Chestnut and oak split lengthwise and treated with a preservative are the timbers commonly used. A more finished effect can be achieved using sawn timbers that are painted.
**Advantages** Relatively inexpensive boundary marker. Allows the garden to be part of its landscape setting.
**Disadvantages** Does not provide shelter or security against intruders. Will not keep children or small animals in — or out.

# RETAINING WALLS SEE ALSO: BOUNDARIES, DIVISIONS, STRUCTURES, PP.90–121

## DRY-STONE WALL

Dry-stone walls are constructed from local stone, laid in courses or randomly, without the use of mortar. Planting pockets can be created by filling gaps with soil.

**Advantages** Where local stone freely available, a relatively cheap material. Durable. Attractive when colonized by desirable plants.

**Disadvantages** Requires skill to erect. Some maintenance eventually required. Can be difficult to control pernicious weeds once they have become established.

## WALL WITH SLEEPERS

Old railway sleepers are heavy and therefore stable when laid to make low walls or a series of tiers, as here. If there are more than two courses, the sleepers need to be held in position, for example with metal rods.

**Advantages** Durable material that provides a good backdrop to plants. Suitable for raised beds.

**Disadvantages** Sleepers, once cheap, no longer are. Suitable only for low retaining walls. Heavy to handle. Often leak tar and may have been treated with a preservative that is toxic to plants.

## FOCAL POINTS

When carefully placed in the garden, built structures, furniture, ornaments, containers, and plants act as focal points of the design.

• They create an inviting goal beyond a division or boundary.

• They arrest the eye, drawing attention to a particular area of the garden.

• Framing, as here, intensifies the magnetism of focal points.

## BAMBOO FENCE

Various bamboos, cut to length either as canes or as brushwood, are lashed together vertically with wire or cord and supported by posts to form screening panels and fences. Thicker canes may, as here, be used as horizontal rails.

**Advantages** Excellent screens. Variety of textures and colours, all of which are sympathetic to plants.

**Disadvantages** Skill required to construct, unless bamboo bought as ready-made panels. Relatively lightweight barrier. Requires regular maintenance and renewal.

## WATTLE HURDLE

Strips of wood or stems are interwoven to form panels that are usually of slightly irregular shape. When erected, they are supported by stakes or posts.

**Advantages** Relatively inexpensive ready-made panels available. As a short-term measure, excellent for creating shelter and privacy, for example while hedges develop. Colours and textures pleasing and associate well with plants. Rustic but versatile.

**Disadvantages** Difficult to make on site. Relatively short-lived.

## IRONWORK FENCE

Fences of wrought and cast iron usually consist of vertical and horizontal railings set close enough to form a barrier against animals and, when high enough, against human intruders. They allow a view, decorated by their own tracery, in and out of the garden. A paint finish is necessary to prevent rust.

**Advantages** Durable. Good for security. Many highly ornamental designs possible.

**Disadvantages** Quality ironwork expensive. Does not provide privacy or shelter. Requires repainting from time to time.

# BOUNDARIES AND DIVISIONS 2

## HEDGES SEE ALSO: BOUNDARIES, DIVISIONS, STRUCTURES, PP.90–121

### FORMAL EVERGREEN HEDGE

Evergreen shrubs and trees suitable for formal hedges, making dense surfaces when trimmed regularly, include box (*Buxus*), shown above flanking the path, and yew (*Taxus*), either side of the opening.

**Advantages** Strongly architectural and long-lived. Uses range from low edging to tall and secure barriers. Sympathetic to other plants.

**Disadvantages** As with all hedges, takes time to reach required height. Needs clipping annually, fast-growing kinds several times a year.

### FORMAL DECIDUOUS HEDGE

A number of deciduous shrubs and trees (which lose their leaves in winter) respond to regular trimming by forming a dense surface and are therefore suitable for formal hedges. With beech (*Fagus*) and hornbeam (*Carpinus*), the dead leaves, attractively russet, are retained until spring. This purple-leaved hedge is of *Prunus cerasifera* 'Nigra'.

**Advantages** Textures and colours different from those provided by evergreen hedges.

**Disadvantages** Most suitable plants are leafless in winter. (*See also left,* formal evergreen hedge.)

### HEDGES AND TOPIARY

Topiary shapes, usually trimmed from evergreen hedging plants, are used to create accents and focal points, here in combination with hedges. They may be simple geometric figures or representations of animals or birds.

**Advantages** When mature, give the garden an apparently timeless and dramatic structure.

**Disadvantages** Limited range of plants, most of slow to moderate growth, suitable for long-lived topiary. Shapes take time to develop and require regular trimming with care and precision.

## ARCHES AND PERGOLAS

### PLEACHED TREES

Pleaching is a method of forming a raised screen by training trees so that their stems and foliage become intertwined. Limes are most commonly used (especially *Tilia platyphyllos* 'Rubra'), but any tree that has flexible branches is suitable.

**Advantages** Creates unusual perspectives. Unlike a barrier to ground level, allows cold air to drain away. Can be underplanted or combined with a conventional hedge or wall.

**Disadvantages** Rigorous initial training required, for which a wire or timber framework is needed. Annual maintenance necessary.

### INFORMAL HEDGE

Shrubs that are naturally dense and bushy, including, as here, some roses, can be planted in rows to form effective barriers. When left unclipped or only lightly trimmed, so that they produce flowers and fruits, these hedges can be very ornamental.

**Advantages** Often highly colourful at certain seasons. Little trimming required, and it does not have to be precise.

**Disadvantages** Hedges tend to be thick and space-consuming. Any trimming needs to be timed to avoid loss of flowers or fruit.

### METAL ARCH

Metal arches are frames, usually of ironwork, spanning paths and consisting of uprights and crosspieces, often hooped. They can be bought in kit form or made to order. Like other arches, such as timber, they are placed to create accents, or to mark transitions in a garden, and usually support climbers.

**Advantages** The material is strong and versatile, making elegant structures in many styles.

**Disadvantages** Relatively expensive to have made. Some in kit form are flimsy. Usually needs painting from time to time.

## HEDGE WITH OPENING

Arched openings and windows in hedges are normally planned from the outset to relate to main pathways and views through the garden. Stems are initially trained on supports, in some cases an arch rising above the hedge.

**Advantages** Underlines the architectural character of boundaries and helps define the garden's structure. Guides the eye to vistas and focal points, sometimes introducing surprises.

**Disadvantages** Care needed to train and clip. Completion depends on growth rate of hedge.

## TAPESTRY HEDGE

A tapestry hedge, composed of a mixture of plants, makes a virtue of contrasts in foliage. In a hedge of plain- and purple-leaved beech (*Fagus*), as here, it is colour that counts, but using more than one species, with different leaf surfaces and sizes, can create additional contrasts of texture.

**Advantages** Striking effects, changing with the play of light.

**Disadvantages** Some mixtures create a restless effect. Tendency for uneven development because plants grow at different rates.

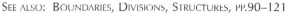

SEE ALSO: BOUNDARIES, DIVISIONS, STRUCTURES, PP.90–121

## TIMBER ARCH

Sawn timber and rustic poles make arches that are more conspicuous than those of ironwork (*see left*, metal arch), but the structures, spanning paths and often framing vistas or focal points, fulfil the same function.

**Advantages** Versatile material, which can be painted or stained, making it possible to build arches that match other garden features. Timber treated with preservative widely available.

**Disadvantages** Decorative finish needs renewing from time to time, and all timbers eventually need replacing.

## RUSTIC PERGOLA

The structure, consisting of linked arches made of poles, spans a walkway, creating shade and supporting ornamental climbers. Other materials used to build pergolas are sawn timber, brick, masonry, and metal.

**Advantages** Relatively cheap pergola and not difficult for an amateur to construct. Is useful for providing shade in a new sunny garden while slow-growing trees and shrubs develop.

**Disadvantages** Even treated timbers need replacing. Structure is less durable and sturdy than pergolas made of other materials.

## A VARIETY OF EDGING

Edgings, usually functional and often decorative, define where a surface such as a lawn or paving meets a bed or border. The edging may be a low barrier of a hard material such as bricks or tiles; it can be little more than an outline, a timber surround for example, framing a paved surface; or it may consist of a row of low plants.

• A narrow band of paving edging a lawn and set just below its level (*see above* combined with tile edging) simplifies mowing.

• Loose surfaces such as gravel require a firm edge to hold them in place.

• Surfaces that are composed of small units such as bricks or granite setts need an edging, often laid level with the main surface, to hold the bond together.

• Low trimmed hedges, for example of dwarf box (*Buxus*), make neat enclosures for looser planting, including vegetables, as above.

• Informal low hedges, aromatic in the case of the lavender (*Lavandula*) illustrated below, soften the lines where paving and steps meet beds and borders.

# WATER FEATURES

THERE WERE POOLS and streams in the earliest gardens, and water remains almost universally fascinating. Still water pleases with its brilliant or darkly reflective mirror surface. Moving water catches the eye with its lively play of light, accompanied by murmuring or rushing sound.

Thanks to modern materials and equipment, water can be a feature of virtually any garden, where it will play an important role in attracting wildlife. The ready availability of liners makes it easy to create pools of any size, and a flow of water can be maintained with a submersible pump.

Two warnings are necessary. Unless properly installed, electrical equipment can make a lethal combination with water. Open water is also a potential attraction and danger to young children.

## POOLS SEE ALSO: WATER GARDENING, PP.198–223

### FORMAL POOL

Pools with a geometrically regular outline can be built of concrete or made with rigid or flexible liners. They may be sunken, or raised above ground level, as here. The pool can be a simple mirror, or its surface can be partly covered by plants or broken by water from a fountain.

**Advantages** Works well with a wide range of paving materials. Successful on any scale, so suitable even for a very small garden.

**Disadvantages** May be difficult to marry formal shape with informality of marginal planting.

### INFORMAL POOL

Pools with an irregular outline are usually constructed with a flexible or rigid liner, but they can also be made in a traditional way using puddled clay. To look natural they need to be set in a low-lying part of the garden and made with shelving edges that provide homes for moisture-loving plants.

**Advantages** Easy to make with a liner. The most suitable kind of pool to attract wildlife.

**Disadvantages** On a small scale, particularly when made with a rigid liner, can look contrived.

## FOUNTAINS SEE ALSO: WATER GARDENING, PP.198–223

### FORMAL FOUNTAIN

The simplest formal fountain consists of a single jet throwing up a short column of water in the centre of a pool. It is usually powered by a submersible pump, which recycles the water, and the height of the fountain depends on the size of the pump. More elaborate effects can be created with multiple and angled jets, which may be incorporated in statues.

**Advantages** Gives an extra dimension to a formal pool. Simple to install and operate.

**Disadvantages** Need to camouflage cable to pump. Flow may have to be stopped in winter.

### WALL FOUNTAIN

A conventional wall fountain consists of two parts. A small stream of water issues from a simple spout or ornamental feature such as a mask. Beneath it, a pool, usually in the form of a raised basin, catches the water and spray. The water is recycled by a submersible pump.

**Advantages** Relatively inexpensive; available in a range of different styles. Easily accommodated in a patio or courtyard.

**Disadvantages** Feeble dribbling can be more irritating than pleasing. Cable and pipes from basin to spout need to be concealed.

### NOVELTY FOUNTAIN

The jets and spouts of fountains can be incorporated in a wide range of improvised items, such as this metal watering can, as well as in conventional sculptures. Fountain heads and extension tubes to create a variety of effects are often supplied as attachments to submersible pumps, or they can be bought separately.

**Advantages** An unusual fountain helps to give a garden individual character. Improvisation with inexpensive materials not difficult.

**Disadvantages** Needs to be chosen with care since the novelty may quickly lose its appeal.

# FLOWING WATER SEE ALSO: WATER GARDENING, PP.198–223

## CONTAINER POOL

Small water features that are suitable for a patio or conservatory can be made from a variety of watertight containers, including half-barrels, tubs, and old sinks. Wooden containers may have been impregnated with substances harmful to plants and fish and need to be lined.

**Advantages** Relatively inexpensive. Simple way of bringing water into even the smallest garden.

**Disadvantages** Water needs frequent topping up in hot weather. May have to be drained in winter since small volumes of water tend to freeze solid.

## CHANNELLED WATER

Channels for flowing water can have a soft edge, bordered by naturalistic planting, or their character can be strongly architectural, as here, where they flow at right angles in and out of a pool surrounded by granite setts. The stream can be one that occurs naturally or an artificial one, with the water circulated by a pump.

**Advantages** Interesting effects of light and sound possible with a modest flow of water.

**Disadvantages** Requires skill to create; expensive to have built professionally.

## WATER CASCADE

Waterfalls and cascades are natural or artificial steps made by water descending a slope. The flow itself can be natural or be driven by a pump. In the example illustrated, a series of simple channelled steps, each with a stone lip, makes an extended water staircase through a sloping meadow garden.

**Advantages** Lively effect of movement, light, and sound. Materials not necessarily expensive.

**Disadvantages** If there is no natural stream, a powerful surface pump needed to recycle water.

# BRIDGES SEE ALSO: WATER GARDENING, PP.198–223

## COBBLE FOUNTAIN

A low jet of water flowing gently over a bed of cobbles forms a simple but effective feature. Here, a large stone, with a hole drilled through the middle, is used as a centrepiece and conceals the sunken water tank and electric pump.

**Advantages** Safe for children and suitable for a small garden. Relatively inexpensive in kit form or easily constructed from cheap materials.

**Disadvantages** If the flow is stopped, as may be necessary in winter, the feature looks dull. Needs to be surrounded by sympathetic planting to remain attractive all year.

## PLANK BRIDGE

A rudimentary bridge consisting of a plank placed across a stream can be elaborated, as here, to make a stylish timber walkway. Texturing the surface, by carving shallow grooves into the wood or roughening it with a wire brush, helps to stop the planks becoming slippery when wet.

**Advantages** Materials relatively inexpensive and construction not difficult. Well suited to an informal, wildlife pool.

**Disadvantages** Unsuitable for a main route in the garden. Requires regular maintenance to prolong life and keep surface safe under foot.

## BRIDGE WITH HANDRAILS

Arched or level bridges with handrails and with firm footings on either bank can be built from treated timber, as here, or from more expensive materials, such as brick or masonry. Small-scale timber bridges are available in kit form.

**Advantages** Makes a safe and picture-book feature to span small or medium-sized streams. Can be used to support trained plants. Timber bridges in kit form are not expensive.

**Disadvantages** Purpose-built bridges relatively expensive. If made of timber, regular maintenance required.

# LEISURE ELEMENTS

A RANGE OF FIXED and movable features helps to make the most of the garden by transforming it into a place for outdoor living.

Playhouses and sandpits keep young children happy and occupied, but will eventually be outgrown and need to be replaced. A swimming pool, which appeals to older children and adults alike, is a lasting, if ambitious, feature.

Some form of seating is essential. A summerhouse with comfortable chairs is delectable, but a few folding chairs may be sufficient. Permanent furniture is certainly practical if there is regular dining al fresco and, to many people, a barbecue is essential for authentic outdoor meals.

Lighting makes the garden a friendly place at night, and magically different from the garden in daylight.

## BUILT FEATURES See also: Patios and Paths, pp.56–73

### BUILT-IN BARBECUE

A simple barbecue built from bricks, as here, concrete blocks, or stone incorporates a bed for the fire and a cooking grid. There should also be storage space for fuel and surfaces for stacking plates and assembling food.

**Advantages** A focus for family meals and entertaining. Relatively easy to build.

**Disadvantages** Location critical to get good draught and to avoid smells and smoke being a nuisance. Needs strict supervision because of fire risk, and use may be controlled in some areas.

### SUMMERHOUSE

Small ornamental buildings, usually of timber construction and often open on at least one side, provide a shaded area for seating away from the house. They need to be sited where they please the eye while giving a good view of the garden.

**Advantages** An opportunity for a modest, but characterful, architectural feature.

**Disadvantages** Purpose-built or off-the-peg model that is well designed is likely to be expensive. Wooden summerhouses need maintenance to prolong life.

## SEATING See also: Patios and Paths, pp.56–73

### WOODEN BENCH

Wood is a classic material for garden benches and is suitable for a wide range of designs, from plain and functional to boldly decorative, as this example. The wood can be stained or painted to suit the overall scheme of the garden, or oiled to give a natural finish. With hardwood furniture, check the timber is from a sustainable source.

**Advantages** Sturdy and eye-catching styles available. Can be long-lived.

**Disadvantages** Good-looking designs usually expensive. Comfort often secondary. Requires maintenance. Best stored under cover in winter.

### SLATTED METAL BENCH

Some of the most elegant garden furniture is made of metal. The simple bench illustrated here is of wrought iron with galvanized slats. More ornate metal furniture, often based on 19th-century designs, is usually cast in iron or in aluminium alloy and given a painted or enamelled finish.

**Advantages** Elegant designs available. Can have a long life.

**Disadvantages** Usually expensive. Can be uncomfortable and cold to the touch. Requires maintenance. Best stored under cover in winter.

### WOODEN SWING SEAT

Informal garden furniture, designed for comfort and relaxation, comes in an infinite variety of forms. The swing seat shown above has a fixed frame but the seat itself can be taken down for storage in winter. Items that can be moved about and stored easily include hammocks, deckchairs, cushioned loungers, and collapsible swing seats.

**Advantages** Comfortable. Sets a relaxed tone.

**Disadvantages** Takes up more space than a comparable bench set on the ground. Cannot be moved to take advantage of sun and shade. Requires maintenance.

## SWIMMING POOL

Various methods are used to construct swimming pools but the basic material is normally concrete, which is often lined and edged with tiles.

**Advantages** Can be glamorous and beautiful.
**Disadvantages** Space-consuming and visually dominating. Best installed with professional advice and this is costly. Structures needed for changing rooms and to house filtration equipment. Potential danger to unsupervised children. Maintenance required.

## PLAYHOUSE

The traditional material for a child's playhouse, as in this highly individual example, is wood, although many commercially available models are made of plastic, in bright, cheerful colours. Any playhouse needs a sunny position, where children can be supervised.

**Advantages** A source of pleasure to children, encouraging creative play.
**Disadvantages** As children grow up, will probably become redundant. A wooden playhouse requires maintenance.

## SANDPIT

Young children are almost always pleased to play in a bed of clean silver sand. A site in view of the house is required, ideally in a sunny spot. The sand, contained here by a timber frame, should be laid over a water-permeable membrane, which is itself laid on a base of hardcore topped with gravel. A cover keeps out debris and pets.
**Advantages** A safe focus for the outdoor activities of young children. Inexpensive, easy to build, and can be converted later, say, to a pool.
**Disadvantages** Redundant after a few years.

# LIGHTING See also: Patios and Paths, pp.56–73

## TABLE AND CHAIRS

For planned and impromptu entertaining and dining outdoors a table and chairs are indispensable. Garden furniture is made of wood, plastic, and metal, some lightweight and weather-proof, as this metal table and chairs. The furniture needs to be set on a level hard surface, ideally with an umbrella for shade.

**Advantages** Practical and make the garden, or part of it, look like an outdoor room. Wide range of designs available.
**Disadvantages** Usually expensive. Space-consuming. Best stored under cover in winter.

## ELECTRIC LIGHTING

Electric lighting in the garden can be used to illuminate paths and areas for entertaining, to create striking effects, particularly with spotlighting and uplighting, and to floodlight areas around the house to deter intruders. Soft lighting can be provided by low-wattage systems. Stronger lights need a mains supply, installed by a qualified electrician.

**Advantages** Easy to use. Makes walking in the garden safer when it is dark. Dramatic night-time transformations. Improved security.
**Disadvantages** Cost of installation can be high.

## FLAME LIGHTS

The various light sources based on burning wax or paraffin (either in liquid or solid form) include flares, lanterns, candles, and night lights. In some cases, as with the night lights illustrated here, the flame is sheltered by glass.

**Advantages** Inexpensive, and a flexible method of lighting that is easily rearranged according to need. Provides pleasant, soft light. Some forms include an insect repellent.
**Disadvantages** Weak source of light, more for decorative effect than practical use. Possible fire risk. Material burned has to be renewed.

# GARDEN MAINTENANCE

GOOD BACK-UP FACILITIES help in the efficient running of a garden. A greenhouse makes it possible to keep frost-tender plants over winter and to start others growing early, giving flowers and produce over a longer period. Even without a greenhouse, much can be achieved using the modest equipment of cold frames and cloches.

With a good-sized compost bin, whether homemade or a proprietary model, garden and kitchen waste can be recycled; once rotted down, it makes an excellent soil conditioner, improving both fertility and texture.

Neat storage of equipment under cover saves time and prolongs the life of tools. It must be borne in mind, however, that while locked sheds do offer some security, they also attract the attention of thieves.

## GREENHOUSES SEE ALSO: LOOKING AFTER THE GARDEN, PP.274–287

### FREE-STANDING GREENHOUSE
One of the most widely used greenhouse designs consists of a framework of metal or, as here, wood, with vertical sides topped by a span roof, one that slopes evenly each side of a central ridge. The walls can be part solid or all glass.
**Advantages** Many models available in different price brackets. Allows economic use of space, with plenty of bench area. Headroom adequate. Many fittings available.
**Disadvantages** May let in less light than greenhouses with all glass surfaces sloping.

### LEAN-TO GREENHOUSE
The structure, with either a metal or a wooden frame, is set against the wall of a building and is often used as a garden room.
**Advantages** Many models available. Good solution where insufficient space for a free-standing greenhouse. Insulation provided by wall reduces heat loss. Cheaper to put in services, such as water supply and electricity, than to a free-standing greenhouse.
**Disadvantages** Solid wall reduces amount of light admitted. Ventilation often inadequate.

## CLOCHES AND TUNNELS SEE ALSO: THE EDIBLE GARDEN, PP.234–273

### GLASS CLOCHE
Traditional cloches consist of sheets of glass that are held in place with metal clips or a metal frame. They form a protective cover that can be lowered over plants or seed that is sown early. Rigid plastic cloches are increasingly common.
**Advantages** Easily moved about so a versatile means of protecting a single plant or a small group of plants. Glass allows better light penetration than does plastic.
**Disadvantages** Relatively expensive to use on a large scale. Glass easily shattered if not handled with care.

### PLASTIC TUNNEL CLOCHE
A continuous tunnel of flexible plastic is supported by wire hoops over crops such as early carrots and salad vegetables grown in rows. The plastic should be heavy-duty and treated with an ultra-violet inhibitor. When not in use should be stored out of sunlight. Models made with rigid plastic are also available.
**Advantages** Relatively cheap way of protecting early crops.
**Disadvantages** In comparison with glass, plastic lets in less light and does not retain heat as well. Relatively short life.

## COMPOST BINS SEE ALSO: LOOKING

### WOODEN COMPOST BIN
Wooden bins provide a means of storing relatively large quantities of plant waste from the kitchen and garden in conditions that encourage it to break down. Removable front panels make emptying easy. If two bins are used, one heap can decompose while the other is assembled.
**Advantages** Materials fairly inexpensive and construction within the competence of many gardeners. Available in kit form.
**Disadvantages** Difficult to accommodate in a small garden. Unless covered, compost can dry out in summer and may need watering.

# COLD FRAMES SEE ALSO: LOOKING AFTER THE GARDEN, PP.274–287

### ORNAMENTAL GREENHOUSE

Free-standing greenhouses designed as attractive garden features can have frames of plastic-covered steel, as here, plain aluminium, or wood. This model is essentially a traditional span greenhouse with part-solid walls of brick.
**Advantages** Can be as effective as other kinds of greenhouse in providing a protected environment for plants, but also makes a highly ornamental feature. Steel very strong.
**Disadvantages** Models of stylish design more expensive than utilitarian greenhouses.

### HOMEMADE COLD FRAME

The traditional cold frame, a cabinet for protecting plants in cold weather, has wooden sides supporting sloping "lights" (the glass-paned tops), which are hinged or slide open. Commercial production of wooden frames has declined but they are simple to make at home from railway sleepers or other timber.
**Advantages** Wooden sides retain heat well.
**Disadvantages** When available, commercial models are expensive. Not easily moved about, as aluminium frames can be.

### ALUMINIUM ALLOY FRAME

Light frames of aluminium alloy and glass are available in a wide range of designs. The top panels, the "lights", normally slide open.
**Advantages** Readily available in kit form, easily assembled, and relatively inexpensive. Let in more light than brick or wooden frames. Can be moved to take advantage of changing conditions of light and shade.
**Disadvantages** Less robust than brick or wooden frame and in cold weather has greater need of additional insulation.

# STORAGE UNITS SEE ALSO: LOOKING AFTER THE GARDEN, PP.274–287

AFTER THE GARDEN, PP.274–287

### PLASTIC COMPOST BIN

Many plastic models are available, most of which are designed for small and medium-sized gardens. Some have a mechanism for turning the compost, which speeds up decomposition.
**Advantages** More efficient than wooden bins at maintaining heat and moisture levels, necessary to break down waste. Tidy, compact, and of a subdued colour. Generally sturdy.
**Disadvantages** Can be relatively expensive and price an unreliable guide to performance. The amount of compost produced, governed by bin size, often small.

### WALK-IN SHED

Garden sheds are made of a variety of materials, including wood, concrete, metal, and glass fibre. Whether individually designed, assembled from a kit, or bought ready-made, a wooden shed is best built from naturally rot-resistant cedar or from pressure-treated timber.
**Advantages** Moderate cost. Provides weather protection for tools, including large items such as lawnmowers. Provides all-weather protection for jobs such as potting.
**Disadvantages** Not for prominent position. Requires maintenance. Limited security.

### ORNAMENTAL TOOL LOCKER

A tool locker can be purpose-built, assembled from a kit, or bought ready-made. In a small garden, it can be given a decorative finish and be treated as a design feature.
**Advantages** Relatively inexpensive and compact. Provides protection from weather. If sited carefully, can make a focal point.
**Disadvantages** Requires maintenance. Even with skilful arrangement of the interior, difficult to accommodate large items of equipment. Some commercially produced lockers of poor design. Limited security.

# PLANTS FOR A PURPOSE 1

WHATEVER THE BALANCE between planting and hard landscape, it is plants that bring a garden to life through all seasons of the year. Colour counts for much and the palette available in foliage and flowers is infinitely varied. The texture of foliage and all the other parts of plants that reflect light or create complex patterns of shadow adds another layer of interest to the garden. Of the many other plant qualities to exploit, one of the most valuable is scent, spicy and pungent as well as sweetly perfumed. Some plants come into their own when used for specific reasons, including those with which it is possible to create a low-maintenance garden, handsome specimens for accents and focal points, and those that are suitable for clothing vertical surfaces.

## FOR SEASONAL EFFECT SEE ALSO: BEDS AND BORDERS, PP.122–165

### SPRING

This is the high point in the year for colourful bulbs, which may be combined with annual or biennial bedding plants, as here, and set against a delicate background of burgeoning foliage. More subtle bulbs go well with leafy woodland plants and the numerous spring-flowering rock garden plants. Many trees and shrubs reach their flowering peak at this time, among them magnolias, *Prunus*, and rhododendrons. For house fronts and pergolas there are flowering climbers such as wisteria and several clematis.

### SUMMER

The leafiest time of the year is also the main flowering season for many plants. In the first half of summer, roses that flower once produce a tremendous burst, but those that repeat will go right through to autumn. Lupins, delphiniums, and pinks (*Dianthus*), shown here, are just a few of the border plants that follow one another into bloom, running parallel with summer bulbs. For beds and containers there are long-flowering petunias and verbenas and numerous colourful but shorter-lived annuals.

## FOR COLOUR AND TEXTURE SEE ALSO: BEDS AND BORDERS, PP.122–165

### THEMED COLOUR

A colour theme is one of the most reliable ways of giving a planting scheme coherence. It is a matter of choosing flowers that blend or contrast with one another and combining them with compatible foliage plants. Single colour themes are often more complex than they seem at first glance, as with this cool planting of white spring flowers with silver and cream-variegated foliage. Harmonies are based on closely related colours, but contrasts are just as important. The occasional shock, say of clashing purple and orange, wakes up the garden.

### FLOWER COLOUR

Although far from being the only ornamental feature of plants, flowers have a special value: choosing and combining their colours presents one of the most exciting challenges of gardening. The range extends from white and pastel shades to brilliant and saturated colours, some of fiery intensity, as in the Maltese cross (*Lychnis chalcedonica*) above, others of near-black depths. Flower colour is rarely bland and uniform. Individual flowers or clusters are often a mixture of subtle shades, and sometimes a startling combination of base colour and bold markings.

### FOLIAGE COLOUR

Except in autumn, the colours of foliage rarely match those of flowers in brilliance or variety, but leaves are long lasting – even those that are deciduous. We take for granted the green of foliage as the reassuring and restful background colour of natural landscapes. In the garden there is the chance to exploit an infinite range of green shades and even more dramatic variations in colour. Among the most conspicuous are variegations in white and yellow, golds, a range of silvers, greys, and blues, and weighty tones of bronze and purple, as in this berberis.

SEE ALSO: ORNAMENTAL TREES IN THE GARDEN, PP.184–197

## AUTUMN

The illusion that summer continues is sustained by many long-flowering plants, among them roses, fuchsias, pelargoniums, and numerous small-flowered clematis. These overlap with plants that are more authentically autumnal, perennials such as asters, Japanese anemones, and heleniums, and bulbous plants ranging from delicate cyclamen and true autumn crocuses to colchicums. What gives the show away is the colouring foliage of deciduous trees and shrubs, bright berries and, finally, leaf fall.

## WINTER

Plant activity seems arrested in winter, when graphic qualities, dramatic when highlighted by frost or snow, count for more than flower colour. Grasses as well as skeletal deciduous trees and shrubs have a subdued but often intricate beauty against the solid shapes of evergreens. Yet there are signs of movement, betrayed in the unexpectedly penetrating scent of several flowering shrubs, and in the flowers of precocious bulbs and perennials, such as snowdrops (*Galanthus*) and hellebores.

SEE ALSO: BOUNDARIES, DIVISIONS, STRUCTURES, PP.90–121

## FOLIAGE TEXTURE

Foliage provides the major contrasts of texture in the garden. The richest textures rely on the interplay of several characteristics. One element is the quality of the leaf surface, which might be shiny or matt, waxy, or woolly. Crinkled and puckered leaves and those with wavy or serrated outlines contrast with those that are smooth and have a regular profile. Leaf shape and size are also important. Here the large leaves of a bergenia are set against deeply fretted fern fronds, but would look equally effective paired with the slender blades of grasses.

## MIXED TEXTURE

As well as foliage, many other parts of a plant bring texture to the garden. Flowers can be of markedly different textures, soft and velvety as in bearded irises, or bright and glistening, as in many tulips. Among the most striking effects are those produced by leaf-like parts surrounding flowers. Here the jagged bracts encircling the flowerheads of a sea holly (*Eryngium*) stand out from a background of love-in-a-mist (*Nigella*), whose flowers have a ruff of fine threads. Bark, twigs, seedheads, and fruit also add pleasing textures to the garden.

## PLANT CATEGORIES

The following terms describing plants are those most commonly used by garden centres, nurseries, and plant catalogues.

• **ANNUALS AND BIENNIALS** Short-lived plants. Annuals complete their life span within one growing season, biennials within two.

• **BEDDING PLANTS** Plants, usually annuals, biennials, or tender perennials, used to create a temporary display.

• **BULBS** Strictly, bulbs are modified buds, usually underground, which store food during a rest period. Loosely, refers to plants growing from any kind of swollen underground storage organ, such as bulb, corm, rhizome, and tuber.

• **CLIMBERS** Plants with lax stems that grow upwards by twining round supports or by attaching themselves with tendrils, special roots, or hooks.

• **CONIFERS** Usually evergreen trees or shrubs with needle-like, strap-shaped, or scaly leaves. Most bear woody cones, but yew (*Taxus*), for example, has fleshy fruits.

• **FERNS** Non-flowering plants that reproduce by means of spores that are borne in clusters on the leaf-like fronds.

• **GRASSES** Plants with jointed stems, normally sheathed by long narrow leaves, and flowerheads in plumes or spikes. Usually form tufts, clumps, or carpets. Bamboos are woody grasses.

• **GROUND-COVER PLANTS** Mainly evergreen and low-growing plants with ornamental foliage that forms a dense, weedproof cover over the soil.

• **PERENNIALS** Plants that live for more than two years. Usually refers to herbaceous perennials, non-woody plants that die down in winter, but grow again in spring.

• **ROCK PLANTS** Low-growing shrubs, perennials, or bulbs (not necessarily alpines, which are natives of mountainous terrain) suitable for a rock garden or raised bed.

• **SHRUBS** Evergreen or deciduous woody-stemmed plants, smaller than trees and with main branches growing from near the base.

• **TREES** Evergreen or deciduous woody-stemmed plants, larger than shrubs, usually with a clear trunk supporting the branches.

• **WATER PLANTS** Very broad term used to describe plants that grow rooted, floating, or submerged in water; also plants that grow at the water's edge, and in boggy conditions.

# PLANTS FOR A PURPOSE 2

## FOR FRAGRANCE SEE ALSO: ORNAMENTAL TREES, PP.184–197; HERBS IN THE GARDEN AND THEIR USES, PP.224–233

### SCENTED TREES AND SHRUBS

Trees and larger shrubs with fragrant flowers create magical effects in the garden by perfuming the air over considerable distances. The scent, wafted by a breeze, often comes as a delicious surprise. This is particularly true of several fragrant but subdued winter-flowering shrubs, among them wintersweet (*Chimonanthus*). In summer, lime trees (*Tilia*) can be a similarly mysterious source of fragrance. Spring-flowering azaleas (*Rhododendron*), seen here, are more showy, as are lilac (*Syringa*) and mock orange (*Philadelphus*).

### FRAGRANT BORDER PLANTS

There is a wide range of smaller shrubs, perennials, and bulbs that can add a scented dimension to borders. Plants such as daphnes, pinks (*Dianthus*), and several lilies, like the Madonna lilies (*Lilium candidum*) shown here, have perfumes that carry well. Strongly scented annuals and biennials, such as stocks (*Matthiola*) and wallflowers (*Erysimum*), planted in blocks are an effective way of boosting the fragrance of borders. These plants are also suitable for bedding schemes and containers.

### AROMATIC PLANTS

Aromatic herbs have long been grown as flavourings for food and for medicinal use. As with other aromatic plants, a light bruising of the leaves is often all that is needed to release the volatile oils from which their fragrance comes. Whether grown in a herb garden or mingled with other plants, they need to be thoughtfully positioned: at the front of a border where they will be brushed against in passing, among paving where they get lightly trodden, or in containers close enough for the leaves to be gently pinched.

## PLANNING PLANTING

Planting that defines and underlines the garden's structure and keeps it interesting throughout the year can be broken down into three broad categories.

• Plants for the framework of the garden come first. Trees and shrubs for windbreaks are not always necessary, but they belong here with hedging and large shrubs and trees that are meant to frame and divide the garden or to play key roles as focal points. Lawns are an almost two-dimensional component of the framework, while climbers are indispensable for disguising or decorating vertical surfaces such as walls and fences.

• The major plants filling in the framework are shrubs, perennials, and bulbs. Several specimens of the same plant can be used, best in odd numbers, to create informal groups or drifts. A more natural effect comes from mixed plantings that mimic the tapestries and tiered groupings of plants in the wild.

• Temporary planting offers a means of creating colourful displays or of filling a new garden. Annuals give almost instant results; fast-growing shrubs and perennials, close-planted as fillers, eventually need thinning.

## FOCAL POINTS AND ACCENTS SEE ALSO: BOUNDARIES, PP.90–121

### TOPIARY

Shrubs or trees clipped into formal geometric or representational shapes make a strong impact in the garden as a form of living sculpture. They can be used singly as focal points or accents or grouped, for example in avenues or walks. Evergreens are most often used. The relatively slow rate of growth of classic topiary plants such as bay (*Laurus nobilis*), box (*Buxus*), and yew (*Taxus*), shown above, is initially frustrating but becomes a significant advantage when the shapes are complete, since a single annual trim is usually sufficient to maintain them.

### DISTINCTIVE TREES AND SHRUBS

The combination of interesting natural shape and one or more other characteristic – it could be striking foliage, distinctive bark, or heavy crops of fruits – can make a tree or shrub a splendid eye-catcher. A specimen can be positioned to draw the eye to the end of a vista or to mark an important intersection in the garden. Good shapes include narrow columns and heads of weeping branches. The silver-leaved pear (*Pyrus salicifolia*) shown here makes a good focal point, and is also available in a weeping form that is equally suitable for this purpose.

# FOR EASY MAINTENANCE SEE ALSO: LAWNS AND GROUND COVER, PP.74–89; BEDS AND BORDERS, PP.122–165

## VIGOROUS GROUND COVER

Evergreen plants that are naturally dense can be planted to form a thatch of vegetation that gives weeds little opportunity to develop. Suitable plants require minimal care and are quick to spread and knit together with their neighbours to form an uninterrupted cover. To create a pleasing effect they must themselves be decorative. Ivies (*Hedera*) are popular for their leaf shapes and colours. Periwinkles (*Vinca*), as shown above, produce attractive flowers in spring and early summer.

## DENSE FOLIAGE

Not all plants that look after themselves and produce dense foliage will knit together to form their own exclusive leafy cover. When, however, they are planted closely with other perennials and shrubs of similar constitution they can provide an effective and highly ornamental cover that gives weeds little chance to get established. Despite the delicacy of their fronds, many ferns are tough and long-lived plants that are particularly well suited to this purpose in shady parts of the garden.

## SELF-SEEDERS

Plants that seed themselves provide a labour-saving way of filling gaps in a border, so discouraging weeds. Self-seeders give the garden an assured casualness, and any unwanted seedlings are easily removed. Careful selection of plants is needed, however, for some seed so freely they become weeds themselves. Good annuals and biennials include the poached egg plant (*Limnanthes*) and honesty (*Lunaria*). Welcome perennials include lady's mantle (*Alchemilla*) and aquilegias (the white flowers shown here).

# FOR CLOTHING BOUNDARIES AND DIVISIONS SEE ALSO: BOUNDARIES, DIVISIONS, STRUCTURES, PP.90–121

## CLIMBING AND RAMBLING ROSES

Roses with ascending and sprawling stems are suitable for training on a wide range of supports. The most vigorous are ramblers, which usually bear small fragrant flowers in large clusters in early to midsummer. They are ideal for pergolas and for training into trees. The less vigorous climbers, many with large flowers in small clusters, can be tied to structures such as metal arches or trellis, or to wires strung on walls. Some of the climbing roses are fragrant and many produce more than one flush of flowers between early summer and autumn.

## SELF-CLINGING CLIMBERS

A number of highly ornamental climbers attach themselves to surfaces by aerial roots or suckers and the most vigorous kinds are capable of covering very large areas. The ivies (*Hedera*) are outstanding evergreen examples, many of them small-leaved but some with large and handsomely variegated foliage, as the example above. Virginia creeper and its close relatives (*Parthenocissus*) are deciduous and the foliage colours brilliantly in autumn. Provided the supporting wall is sound, the roots of self-clinging climbers are unlikely to cause damage.

## TWINING CLIMBERS

Many climbers, among them honeysuckles (*Lonicera*), pull themselves up by twining their stems round supports. Others, such as most clematis, including the large-flowered hybrid illustrated here, rely on twining leaf stalks to get a purchase. Flowering climbers that twine are suitable for arches, and can be trained on walls that are fitted with strained wires or trellis. If grown through trees or shrubs, twining climbers can produce happy coincidences of flower — or a succession of blooms, when the supporting plant and the climber flower at different times.

# A PLACE FOR PLANTS

THERE CAN BE two, apparently very different, approaches to organizing the planted areas of a garden. At one extreme, geometrically regular plots are allocated for planting, with the plants arranged in patterns that are precise and symmetrical. At the other extreme, the aim is to create a garden that seems to be a naturally occurring community of plants. In such a layout, a contrived grouping of plants is as out of place as straight lines and right angles.

The apparent distance between these two approaches is misleading. Whether plants are marshalled formally, arranged in casually organic groupings, or even displayed in containers, the underlying principle of successful planting is the same. Success comes by choosing plants to suit the growing conditions.

## BEDS AND BORDERS SEE ALSO: BEDS AND BORDERS, PP.122–165

### MIXED BORDER

The term "border" is sometimes used strictly for a plot of regular outline, planted ornamentally and running along the edge of a garden. A broad strip at the base of a wall or hedge fits in with this definition and with a notion of ordered space and methodical working of the soil. In reality borders can be much less regular in shape and lie in almost any part of a garden. A mixture of shrubs, bulbs, and perennials, including grasses, rather than an herbaceous border of perennials only, gives interest year-round.

### SEASONAL BED

In its most general sense a bed is a plot of worked ground in a garden, but the term is often qualified. When used of an ornamental plot, it suggests an open area, often but not necessarily in the centre of a garden, where the planting is temporary, changing with the season. The year might begin with winter-flowering pansies (*Viola*) and spring bulbs such as tulips, the bed then being filled with flowers, such as petunias and verbenas, that give a long-lasting summer display.

## NATURALIZED PLANTINGS SEE ALSO: LAWNS AND GROUND COVER, PP.74–89; BEDS AND BORDERS, PP.122–165

### PLANTING IN GRAVEL

This apparently casual and naturalistic method of planting is particularly suitable in a dry garden that is stocked with drought-tolerant plants. The top-dressing of gravel improves surface drainage, allowing moisture to drain away quickly from the plants, but it also helps to conserve moisture by slowing evaporation from the soil. The gravel acts as insulation and should not be laid over ground that is cold or frozen. Gravel discourages the growth of weeds, but perennial weeds must be eradicated before the gravel is spread.

### PRAIRIE AND MEADOW

Ornamentals can be naturalized in grass to create the effects of wild plant communities in prairies, as above, and in meadows. Success depends on introducing plants that grow well together in the local conditions, either natives of the area or of areas with similar soil and climate. Establishing a stable and self-perpetuating community of naturalized plants may be slow. In the early stages it is necessary to control competitive weeds and, in the case of meadows, to reduce soil fertility to prevent the flowers being swamped by vigorous grasses.

### WOODLAND

Many plants thrive in the dappled light of deciduous woodland, although the main flowering season usually occurs in spring, before the foliage of the canopy unfurls. True woodland can be transformed into a naturalistic garden by large-scale planting, rhododendrons doing well under a canopy where the soil is acid. An impression of woodland can be achieved with the remnants of an old orchard, even a solitary tree, underplanted with bulbs and shade-tolerant perennials such as hellebores, ferns, and perhaps a shrub or two.

SEE ALSO: CONTAINERS AND RAISED BEDS, PP.166–183; THE EDIBLE GARDEN, PP.234–273

## HEDGED BEDS

Beds surrounded by low hedges were a characteristic feature of 16th- and 17th-century gardens and are familiar components in modern formal designs. The most widely used low hedging for beds, as in this garden, is the evergreen dwarf box (*Buxus sempervirens* 'Suffruticosa'). The bed might be planted for seasonal displays or more permanently, for example with roses. The loose growth in the bed often makes a pleasing contrast with the firm lines of the hedge.

## RAISED BED

Beds raised above the level of surrounding paths are used in ornamental and kitchen gardens. A common reason for creating raised beds is to provide specific growing conditions, particularly for plants such as numerous bulbs and rock garden plants that do well only where the soil drains freely. The extra height also makes beds easier to work and helps to show off small plants that might be overlooked in a border. The walls of the beds can be made with a variety of materials, including bricks and railway sleepers.

## KITCHEN BED

The kitchen garden can be divided into several large beds, with the crops planted in long rows, as here. Crops are readily accessible in this arrangement, but the soil between rows is unproductive and becomes compacted by treading. As an alternative, a vegetable plot can be laid out in small permanent beds or strips and the ground worked only from paths running along each side. The soil is constantly improved, allowing plants to be grown much closer together, resulting in increased yields.

SEE ALSO: WATER GARDENING, PP.198–223

# CONTAINERS SEE ALSO: CONTAINERS AND RAISED BEDS, PP.166–183

## WATERSIDE

Few gardens have the advantage of a natural stream or pool where aquatic and marginal plants can be naturalized, but it is not difficult to create bodies of water and boggy areas using flexible liners. A bog garden can form a margin to a stream or pool or stand as a feature in its own right. To look convincing as an isolated feature, it must be set in a low-lying position. The liner for a bog area, unlike that for a pool, has some perforations in it, but the soil it contains holds enough moisture, topped up in sunny weather, for waterside and bog plants.

## POTS, TUBS, AND PLANTERS

Growing plants in containers increases the scope of any garden. Treated as either a permanent feature or a seasonal planting, used singly or in groups, containers can brighten a dull corner, provide a focus of attention, or bring colour and greenery to a patio or terrace. The many different kinds of purpose-made container include plastic and terracotta pots, wooden tubs and windowboxes, fibreglass planters, and metal urns. Almost any receptacle is suitable, however, providing it is stable and holes can be made in the base to allow excess moisture to drain away.

## HANGING CONTAINERS

Containers that can be suspended increase the opportunities for displays in the garden and allow plants to be grown where there is neither ground nor the possibility of setting out pots and tubs. Like all other plant containers, those that are suspended must have drainage holes and be large enough to hold compost that will supply the plants with sufficient nutrients and moisture. Before containers are put in position it is necessary to work out how to water them. Fixtures for hanging baskets and brackets for pots must be securely fastened.

# WORKING OUT WHAT YOU WANT

WHETHER YOU ARE PLANNING a garden from scratch or modifying something that already exists, created either by previous owners or by yourself, you need to have a clear idea of what you are aiming for. This does not mean that you have to work out all the details right from the start. What you must do, though, is bring into focus your own ideas about the style and mood the garden should have and the kind of features that really matter to you. It is expensive and time-consuming to make yet more changes later on, so it is worth taking the trouble to order your thoughts and work through what is involved in creating the garden that you really want.

## FINDING OUT WHAT YOU LIKE

The information and ideas in books and magazines and on television are all useful when sorting out the way you would like your garden to develop. You can also get ideas from model gardens featured in garden shows, but remember that these have been specially staged and are unlikely to reflect the year-round practicalities of maintenance and plant care.

REAL-LIFE INSPIRATION Real gardens, those of friends and neighbours as well as those open to the public, are by far the best source of ideas. Even when a garden is on a grand scale, you can often find in it something that could be adapted to your own more modest plot. It might be the treatment of a slope, or a particular approach to planting, or the arrangement of features such as raised beds.

FLORAL DREAM ▷
*For some, this is an idyllic garden — borders filled with flowers, a mown grass path, an old sundial, and a cast-iron gate giving a view of a distant landscape. But do you have the time and money to create and maintain this dream?*

△ LOW-MAINTENANCE PLANTING
*The green heads of* Euphorbia characias *and a subtle combination of green and grey foliage make virtually care-free ground cover along the path to a wooden summerhouse.*

## THINKING ABOUT WHAT YOU NEED

Whenever you are visiting gardens, it is worth carrying a notebook. Jotting down points on layout, style, and mood, as well as more specific information on features and planting, helps to crystallize ideas that you might want to apply in your own garden. For this there needs to be a debate, whether it is simply in your own mind or with partner and family. The best way to sift through the options open to you is to draw up a list. The checklist (*opposite*) makes a useful starting point.

The difficult decisions often involve matching short-term needs with long-term ambitions. At an early stage, because of lack of time, you may have to rely on broad effects, using low-maintenance planting; but you might hope to provide conditions, later on, for a specialist group of plants — for example a raised bed in which to grow bulbs and rock garden plants. It is worth marking on your plan any future adaptations you would like to make.

You must also resolve conflicts between the style you are seeking and the features you want. A barbecue fits naturally on a patio that is laid out in a relaxed way as an outdoor room, but it may not sit so comfortably with the stark simplicity of a Japanese garden. These issues are matters of taste, and only you and those with whom you share the debate can resolve them.

# PLANNING CHECKLIST

## PRIORITIES

The point of this checklist is to help you rank the components of a garden according to the importance they have for you. Your priorities should reflect what is useful and desirable for you now and also, say, in 10 years' time, when you may have children to cater for, or when you may have more time, but also may be less mobile.

■ CHILDREN'S PLAY AREA  ■ FACILITIES FOR ENTERTAINING  ■ FRUIT
■ HERBS  ■ LOW COST  ■ LOW MAINTENANCE  ■ PARKING  ■ PETS
■ PRIVACY  ■ ORNAMENTAL PLANTS  ■ SPECIALIST PLANTS  ■ SUITABLE
FOR ELDERLY PEOPLE OR PEOPLE WITH DISABILITIES  ■ VEGETABLES

## STYLE AND MOOD

Recognizing the style and mood you want to evoke will help you to decide what elements to include in your garden. Structures such as arbours and gazebos help to create a romantic atmosphere, while obelisks and topiary can play important roles as accents in formal gardens. There are, however, many components that are perfectly at home in gardens of very different kinds.

■ COTTAGE  ■ EXPANSIVE  ■ EXUBERANT  ■ FORMAL
■ MEDITERRANEAN  ■ MINIMALIST  ■ NATURALISTIC  ■ PEACEFUL
■ PRODUCTIVE  ■ ROMANTIC  ■ SECLUDED  ■ SUBTROPICAL

## PLANTS

■ BORDER PLANTS
  ■ Colourful flowers
  ■ Fragrance
  ■ Good shape and texture
  ■ Interesting foliage
  ■ Long-term (perennials)
  ■ Quick-growing (annuals)
■ CLIMBERS
  ■ Colourful flowers
  ■ Decorative fruit
  ■ Evergreen
  ■ Interesting foliage
■ FEATURE PLANTS
■ FRUIT
  ■ Soft fruit
  ■ Tree fruit
■ GROUND COVER
■ HERBS
■ LOW-MAINTENANCE PLANTS
■ NATURALIZED PLANTS
■ PLANTS TO ENCOURAGE WILDLIFE
■ PLANTS FOR ALL-YEAR INTEREST
■ SHRUBS
  ■ Colourful flowers
  ■ Decorative fruit
  ■ Evergreen
  ■ Interesting foliage
■ TREES
  ■ Colourful flowers
  ■ Decorative fruit
  ■ Evergreen
  ■ Interesting foliage
■ VEGETABLES

## SURFACES

■ BARK CHIPPINGS
■ BRICKS AND PAVERS
■ COBBLESTONES
■ CRAZY PAVING
■ GRANITE SETTS
■ GRAVEL
■ LAWN
  ■ Aromatic lawn
  ■ Rough grass
  ■ Traditional lawn
■ PAVING SLABS
■ PEBBLES
■ POURED CONCRETE
■ TILES
■ TIMBER DECKING
■ SURFACES FOR PLAY AREAS
  ■ Bark chippings
  ■ Grass
  ■ Rubber granules

## LEISURE

■ BARBECUE
■ GARDEN FURNITURE
  ■ Bench
  ■ Hammock
  ■ Loungers
  ■ Swing seat
  ■ Tables and chairs
■ PLAY EQUIPMENT
  ■ Basketball net
  ■ Games area
  ■ Play frame
  ■ Sandpit
  ■ Slide
  ■ Swings
  ■ Playhouse
  ■ Tree house
■ SWIMMING POOL
■ TENNIS COURT

## BOUNDARIES AND DIVISIONS

■ DIVIDERS
  ■ Arch
  ■ Pergola
  ■ Trellis
■ FENCES
  ■ Bamboo
  ■ Iron railings
  ■ Chain link
  ■ Picket
  ■ Post and chain
  ■ Post and rail
  ■ Wattle hurdle
  ■ Wire mesh
  ■ Wooden panels
■ HEDGES
  ■ Breached
  ■ Clipped
  ■ Deciduous
  ■ Evergreen
  ■ Flowering
  ■ Laid
  ■ Mixed
  ■ Pleached
  ■ Topiary
■ WALLS
  ■ Brick
  ■ Concrete block
  ■ Dressed stone
  ■ Dry stone
  ■ Glass brick
  ■ Imitation stone
  ■ Screen block
  ■ Sleepers

## DECORATIVE FEATURES

■ ARBOUR
■ BIRD BATH
■ BIRD TABLE
■ CONTAINERS
  ■ Hanging baskets
  ■ Pots and tubs
  ■ Windowboxes
■ GAZEBO
■ RAISED BEDS
■ ROCK OR GRAVEL GARDEN
■ STATUES AND ORNAMENTS
■ SUMMERHOUSE
■ SUNDIAL
■ VERTICAL ACCENT FEATURES
  ■ Cane wigwams
  ■ Obelisks
■ WATER FEATURES
  ■ Bog garden
  ■ Cobble fountain
  ■ Container pool
  ■ Flowing water
  ■ Formal fountain
  ■ Formal pool
  ■ Informal pool
  ■ Wall fountain

## STORAGE AND UTILITIES

■ COLD FRAME
■ COMPOST BINS
■ GREENHOUSE
■ LIGHTS
  ■ Electric
  ■ Candles and flares
■ POTTING SHED
■ RUBBISH BINS
■ STORAGE BENCH
■ TOOL SHED
■ WASHING LINE

# ASSESSING WHAT YOU HAVE

BEFORE YOU CAN draw up a realistic plan for your garden, you need to make a proper assessment of your site. It is a good idea to spend some time over this. You need to get an impression of what the garden is like at different times of the day – which parts get the most sun; how much shade is cast and where. If at all possible, it is worth waiting to see it at different seasons of the year so that you discover its warmest and coldest corners, its wettest and windiest spots. Every plot has its good and bad points – yours may be very small, have impoverished soil, or be on steeply sloping ground – but a challenging site can be the making of an interesting and highly individual garden. In the light of what you discover, you may find yourself abandoning preconceived ideas of your ideal garden – or at least adapting them to suit the scale and conditions of your own particular plot.

## MATTERS OF SIZE

There are various ways of making the best of the space in your garden, no matter how small or large the site.

**LARGE SITES** These are often best treated as a series of compartments, the partitions formed by hedges and other screening devices. Vistas, focal points, and the occasional surprise feature all help to give the garden coherence. There may be opportunities for planting trees and large shrubs (perhaps adding to specimens already on the site). Plants that need a lot of attention may have to be concentrated in a few small areas, with much of the garden planned for low maintenance.

**SMALL SITES** Many small gardens are rich in possibilities, despite the limitations of size. Concealing the boundaries by planting around the edges and "borrowing" the trees and shrubs of neighbouring gardens helps to create a sense of space. A slight change of level and a few large plants lend dramatic touches, while the exclusive use of dwarf plants has a dull, miniaturizing effect.

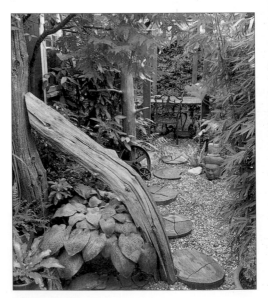

◁ **GREEN COURTYARD GARDEN**
*The intimate character of this tiny garden is emphasized by the curious tree-trunk barrier and the log sections making stepping stones across gravel to a small outdoor dining area. A cool, green atmosphere has been created using foliage plants.*

△ **SMALL PATIO GARDEN WITH DECKING**
*Although this garden is small, the decked area for outdoor entertaining, partially screened from the house, has given an impression of space. The depth of the garden is emphasized by the lengthways run of the timber. The container-grown plants can be moved about to alter the shape of the garden room.*

# THINKING ABOUT SHAPE

The shape of the site is just as important as its area and has implications for the way the garden is designed.

**NARROW GARDENS** On a long and narrow site of the kind common in suburban areas, a straight path running from end to end is likely to draw the eye immediately to the far boundary, making the garden look smaller than it really is. To avoid revealing all at a single glance, it is worth introducing one or two screens that run partway across the garden, in effect subdividing it and forcing the path off a direct track.

**WIDE GARDENS** The broad spaciousness of a wide garden along the front of a house will often be welcome and might be designed with organic shapes and flowing lines. An interesting garden might also be made with a broad central path hedged on either side, with openings in the hedges giving access to separate compartments. Lighter barriers running from front to back, perhaps consisting of plants trained on ropes, offer a means of giving a short, wide plot more pleasing proportions.

**AWKWARD SHAPES** A design that masks the boundaries can overcome some of the disadvantages of an awkward site. In the case of a triangular garden, for example, the best solution may be to fill in the angled corners with planting, perhaps with a shed tucked behind, and to turn the rest into one or two spaces of regular shape, each surrounded by planting.

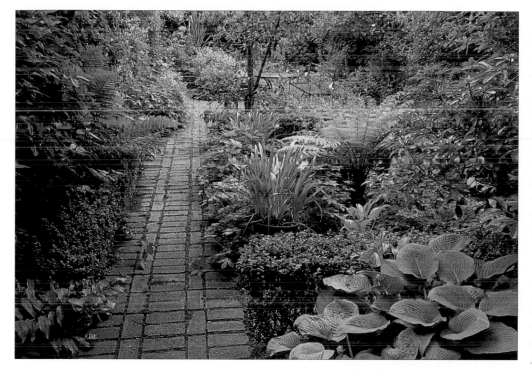

◁ **A PAUSE IN A LONG GARDEN**
*In this long and lushly green garden, a place for pausing and resting to one side of the main pathway is a welcome diversion. The way the design opens out at this point creates a sense of space without contradicting the private character of the garden, resulting from the lavish use of foliage plants on the boundaries as well as in the beds.*

# DEALING WITH SLOPES

On a sloping site there are opportunities to make the most of different views and to create areas of distinctive character at different levels. Even a slight change of level can make a flat site more interesting.

**TERRACING AND STEPS** The most ambitious way to deal with a sloping site is to build a series of terraces supported by retaining walls and connected by steps. Terracing often involves having to move considerable quantities of soil, and retaining walls may need to be reinforced if they are to withstand the pressure of soil and moisture.

**RAMPS** Gentle slopes or ramps as alternatives to steps may take up more room in the garden, but they are easier for the elderly to negotiate and give access for equipment such as wheelbarrows and lawnmowers as well as wheelchairs. Slopes are more fun for children, too, allowing them an uninterrupted trackway for bikes, cars, and other wheeled toys.

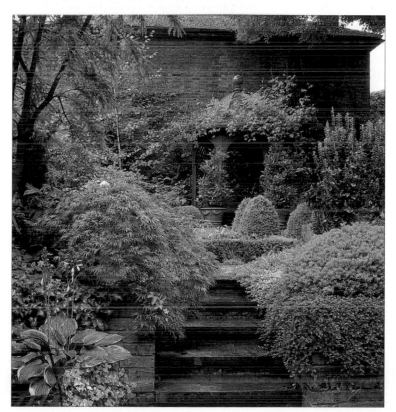

◁ **TERRACING**
*A short flight of steps connects two levels in a terraced garden. The structure of the retaining walls has been deliberately obscured by planting along the top and at the base. Enough of the upper terrace is hidden for it to retain an element of surprise.*

## LOCATION AND VIEW

If there is a good view from the site of the garden, it is worth taking it into account in the design. It is, however, much more common to have to block out unsightly views and to screen for privacy.

**VIEWS** To make the most of a good view, it needs to be framed. This principle applies to views beyond the garden and to those within it. Sight lines from windows and doors deserve special attention. Paired shrubs and trees, avenues, and arches are the most common framing devices.

**PRIVACY** If your garden is overlooked, you may want to consider increasing the height of walls and fences. Training climbers on trelliswork fixed to the top is one of the quickest ways to create an effective screen. Carefully chosen shrubs and trees planted on the boundary may give you enough privacy, but will take some time to reach the required height.

**NOISE POLLUTION** Traffic noise is a common problem in gardens near busy roads. A hedge or other thick barrier of foliage can help to deaden the sound.

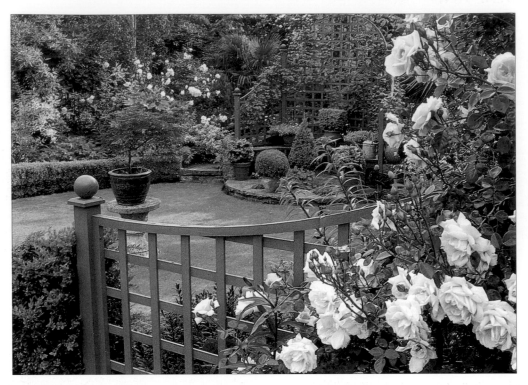

△ **SHELTER AND PRIVACY**
*Hedges and open fences act as wind filters and can be used to create areas of the garden that are relatively calm and sheltered. Solid walls and close fences, though, tend to cause wind turbulence. Trees, large shrubs, and structures such as trellis screens clothed with climbers can block views into a garden and help to make it private.*

## CLIMATE AND MICROCLIMATE

The range of plants you can grow and the way you can make use of your garden are greatly influenced by climatic factors such as rainfall, temperature, and wind.

**CLIMATE** You need to find out about the broad pattern of weather in the area where you are gardening, the effects of altitude and the proximity of the sea, and, in particular, when frost, cold winds, and low rainfall might be expected. Talking to local people is perhaps the easiest way of getting this information. Looking at other gardens in the locality will also give you a good idea of the kind of plants you can hope to grow well.

**MICROCLIMATES** Within any garden there may be several different microclimates, where conditions vary to some extent from those generally prevailing. Some parts of the site may be in a frost pocket, where cold air lingers longest, or may be particularly warm and sheltered, at the base of a sun-baked wall, for example. You can take advantage and make the most of a garden's patchwork of microclimates by matching plants to existing conditions.

△ **SUNNY SPOTS**
*Many plants will retain their naturally compact shape and thrive only if they are given an open, sunny position. If grown in shade, almost all annuals, including Shirley poppies (Papaver rhoeas) and cornflowers (Centaurea cyanus), shown here, become drawn and straggly and produce few flowers.*

◁ **SHADY CORNERS**
*The understorey of woodland provides a model for shady parts of the garden — not just areas under trees and shrubs, but also where there is shade from walls and buildings. Many spring bulbs that in their natural habitat flower before the tree canopy develops do well in these conditions. In summer, good foliage cover is provided by many perennials, including hostas.*

# SOIL AND DRAINAGE

The nature of the soil in your garden greatly affects what will thrive in it. There are five basic types – clay, silt, sand, chalk, and peat – and most plants grow better in one type than another.

**SOIL STRUCTURE** The ideal soil consists of a balanced mixture of clay, sand, and silt, and is rich in organic matter (decaying remains of plants and animals). A well-structured soil, with plenty of air pockets but also retaining water well, is crumbly and moist. When you rub a small sample between your fingers, it will hold together, making a cylindrical shape, but without being sticky. The structure of any soil can be improved by digging, and by incorporating well-rotted organic matter.

**ACID AND ALKALINE SOILS** Soils vary in the degree to which they are acid or alkaline, depending on how much lime they contain. This is known as the pH level and, since some plants prefer alkaline conditions and others acid ones, it is worth testing your soil, using a simple kit.

**DRAINAGE** The rate at which water drains from the soil has a bearing on the plants you can grow. Some tolerate very dry soil; others survive in waterlogged ground. You can install irrigation or drainage systems, but it makes more sense to choose plants that like the natural conditions you have.
SEE ALSO: BEDS AND BORDERS, PP.122 165

◁ **ACID SOIL**
*The plants best known for needing lime-free, acid soil are shrubs and trees belonging to the heath family. They include rhododendrons, azaleas, and heathers. There are in addition a number of perennials, many of them woodland plants, as illustrated here, that are really happy only on a neutral to acid soil.*

◁ **ALKALINE SOIL**
*Many lovely gardens have been made on thin, alkaline soils over chalk. Unlike acid-loving plants, those that prefer alkaline soils generally tolerate conditions outside their ideal range. This is true for red valerian (Centranthus ruber), of which the white flowered form is seen here. However, it often shows its preference by self-seeding freely over old limy walls.*

**WET PLANTING** ▷
*Rather than draining a low-lying wet area, it may be less expensive and more practicable to transform it into a bog garden. Moisture-loving plants, such as the colourful marsh marigold (Caltha palustris) shown here, thrive in permanently boggy conditions at the margins of a pool.*

◁ **DRY PLANTING**
*Successful gardening in areas with low rainfall and where the soil is free-draining depends on choosing plants that tolerate drought. An attractive form of dry gardening is to plant in a gravel mulch, which helps to reduce water loss, grouping plants in the manner of naturally occurring communities. In fact, the plants used may come from regions geographically far apart.*

# PLANNING CHANGES

IF YOU ARE TO DEVELOP your garden in a coherent way, you need to make a careful survey and prepare a plan, drawn to scale, of how you want it to be. Allowing the garden to develop in dribs and drabs, or haphazardly, tends to be less satisfactory than a planned approach, and in the long run usually proves more expensive.

◁ **WAITING TO BE TRANSFORMED**
*Despite its neglected state, this walled site has great potential. The photographs on pp.52–53 show how clearing unwanted trees and shrubs and imaginative planning have transformed it into a beautiful and varied garden.*

## MAKING A SURVEY

The first impressions of a site, sometimes discouraging, can give a very false idea, particularly of scale. Gathering accurate information will help to give the correct perspective, and form the basis of the plan that you eventually put into action.
**SKETCH AND NOTES** Making a rough ground plan (*see right*) is essential to get a grasp of the garden. Use this plan as the basis for notes, assembling information on anything that affects the way the garden grows: the site's exposure to prevailing wind, how much shade is cast throughout the day, the quality of the soil and how well it drains. Note good views and those that need screening. Record the condition of built features, including walls, fences, and hard surfaces.
**PHOTOGRAPHS** A camera is a valuable tool when you are surveying your site, and the photographs you take will provide a fascinating record when the garden is mature. Take photographs from different angles, looking to and away from the house and from doorways and windows, including views from upstairs. The same shot taken at different times of the day and, if possible, at different seasons, will reveal a lot about the way shadows fall.
**ESTIMATING SLOPES** You need a clear idea of the levels and slopes on your plot, since they affect drainage and the position of features, as well as the damp-proofing of the house. In a small garden it may be enough to know there is a slight slope away from the house. You need more precise information if the slope is more marked. Make the calculation over a fixed distance, say 2m (6ft). Lay a level plank (testing with a spirit level) between two vertical pegs. The difference in height above ground of the two pegs gives the slope over the 2m (6ft) distance.

▽ **BEDS AND BORDERS**
*The rigid pattern of the existing beds and borders, now overgrown with shrubs and weeds, could be reinstated, but there is no compelling logic to these vestiges of the garden's design and the best course is to make a fresh start.*

▽ **OVERGROWN SHRUBS**
*Hard pruning might make these shrubs vigorous and shapely again, but they are not well placed and it is better to take them out.*

## DRAWING A ROUGH PLAN

Draw a rough plan of your existing garden on site, pacing out distances to enable you to plot measurements approximately. Note the points of the compass and record all the built features, including paved areas, and the position of beds, borders, trees, and shrubs. Identify, if possible, any prominent plants. You may have to do additional research to establish the position of drains, the run of sewers, and the underground route of gas, electrical, and water services.

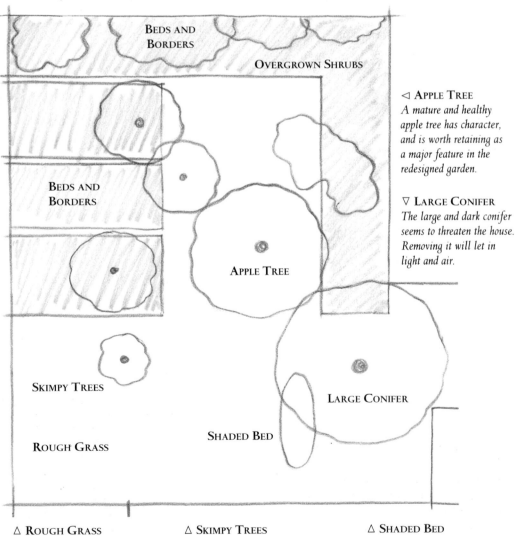

BEDS AND BORDERS

OVERGROWN SHRUBS

BEDS AND BORDERS

APPLE TREE

SKIMPY TREES

LARGE CONIFER

SHADED BED

ROUGH GRASS

◁ **APPLE TREE**
*A mature and healthy apple tree has character, and is worth retaining as a major feature in the redesigned garden.*

▽ **LARGE CONIFER**
*The large and dark conifer seems to threaten the house. Removing it will let in light and air.*

△ **ROUGH GRASS**
*There is no paving around the house and the lawn has become rough, weedy grass.*

△ **SKIMPY TREES**
*The poorly shaped fruit trees dotted randomly about the garden are not worth keeping.*

△ **SHADED BED**
*A mysterious bed where little would thrive in the shade of the conifer is best abandoned.*

# WORKING OUT YOUR NEW DESIGN

You may have a good idea of the way you want to develop your garden, but it is still worth looking at the information you have gathered with an open mind. An accurate scale drawing recording the features you want to retain (*see below*), as well as the changes you want to make, allows you to review the options and to make realistic assessments of the materials and plants required.

**TESTING IDEAS** In the initial stages, you can treat your scale drawing as a base plan, and use overlays of tracing paper to test out different ideas.

**VISUAL AIDS** With your plan in hand, go back to the garden and try to visualize how your ideas would work. Marking the outlines of beds and borders and other features with hosepipe, with garden line strung between stakes, or with a trickle of sand can help you assess the proportions. Canes can be used to give an idea of the position of upright features such as trees.

**PLANTING AND STRUCTURAL PLANS** Once you have established the broad outlines of your garden, you may find it helpful to make detailed planting plans for particular areas, as well as to draw up cross-sections of specific features, for example pools or pergolas.

### MAKING A SCALE DRAWING
In the first instance, the scale drawing should record the position of the features of the garden, both old and new. Make the drawing accurately, on graph paper, basing it on the measurements you have taken on site (*see below*, Plotting Boundaries and Features). Use a scale relating to the size of the grid on the paper and one that allows the plan to fit comfortably on the sheet, ideally with space at the margins for notes or an explanation of any codes used.

**ARBOUR AND GRASS WALK ▽**
*The narrowing perspective of the grass walk leading to an arbour helps to make the garden seem larger than it is.*

**▽ LIME WALK**
*The avenue of lime trees is intended to create another vista and to provide a screen higher than the garden wall.*

**▽ POND AND VEGETABLE PLOT**
*Screening adds mystery to the pond area and sets the productive part of the garden apart.*

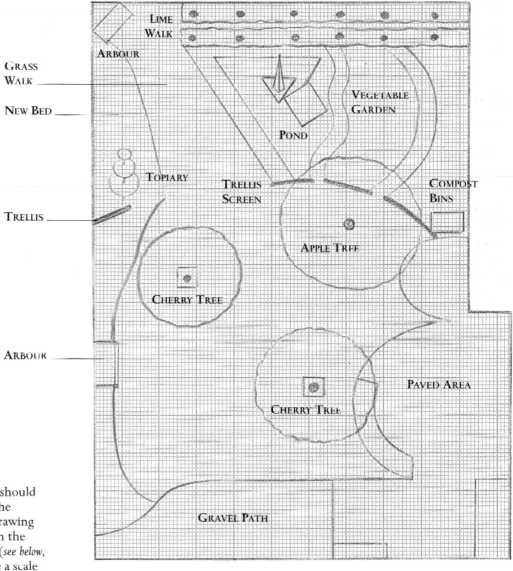

**△ HARD SURFACES**
*Much of the garden is lawn and planting, but access areas around the house have hard surfaces.*

**△ APPLE TREE AND TRELLIS**
*The mature apple tree has been retained as a key feature and given extra weight by the trellis curve.*

---

## PLOTTING BOUNDARIES AND FEATURES

Work methodically, taking measurements of all buildings, trees, and planting areas and marking them on your rough plan.

• If the garden is a simple rectangle or square, take measurements, at right angles, from a base line such as a boundary.

• Triangulation is a useful way of pinpointing features or establishing the boundaries if the shape of the garden is irregular.

**1 MEASURING UP**
Measure to the junction of two boundaries from two fixed points, here two corners of the house. Note the measurements (a and b) on your rough plan. Take measurements in the same way for each of the other boundary corners.

**2 DRAW TO SCALE**
On graph paper draw the house to scale. Set a compass to the scaled down measure (a) and draw an arc from the first fixed point. Repeat with (b) from the second fixed point. Where the arcs intersect marks the boundary corner.

# PUTTING THE PLAN INTO PRACTICE

It is difficult not to be impatient when at last you have decided on the way ahead for your new garden. Before rushing in to order materials, it is worth shopping round, particularly for paving and for large quantities of plants. You may want to get most of the work done between autumn and spring, but it is wise to delay if the ground is sodden. The compaction caused by treading and machinery can result in serious drainage problems.

## A GARDEN IN THE MAKING

The garden illustrated in the rough plan on p.50 provides a case study of garden making. The three-dimensional plan (*right*) of the new garden shows that the mature apple tree was retained, while the photographs record how new features were created either side of the lawn's strong diagonal.

### △ SPRING BORDER
*Early in the garden's development, autumn-planted tulips were combined with forget-me-nots (Myosotis) to create a colourful effect in spring.*

### △ SUMMER BORDER
*Blue-flowered perennials play an important role in this summer border, but late-flowering annuals such as cosmos are used to extend the season into early autumn.*

### △ WINTER BORDER
*The stems of deciduous shrubs such as dogwood (Cornus) give texture and colour in autumn and winter, but here the glowing focus is a cluster of ornamental cabbages.*

### ◁ LAYING PAVED AREAS
*In an ideal sequence, the paving would have been laid first to avoid damaging the lawn. Fortunately, there was access from one side in this garden so that the paving operation had little effect on the established lawn, which otherwise would have needed to be protected with planking.*

△ **A WALK OF PLEACHED LIMES**
*Two rows of limes (Tilia) along the far boundary have been pleached, the branches above a height of about 1.8m (6ft) trained horizontally to form an avenue on stilts. A pergola clothed with climbers would create a similar effect.*

△ **TRELLIS SCREENS**
*See-through trellis panels, which cast unusual shadows, help to create separate but interrelated spaces within the garden and reinforce the barrier formed by the old apple tree. The screens have now been painted deep green.*

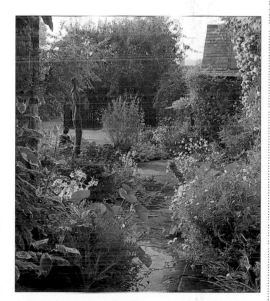

△ **FROM THE KITCHEN DOOR**
*The kitchen door provides the most frequently used access to the garden, and this corner serves as a gentle introduction to the whole. Colourful flowers and foliage plants are clustered close to the door before the paving opens out to a generous circular area.*

## ESTABLISHING PRIORITIES

You or your contractor may not be able to carry out work to an ideal timetable, but you must fix an order of priorities and think through the implications of the schedule you adopt.

■ **Boundaries** Build boundary walls and fences early to provide shelter and security and before the development of the garden makes access difficult.

■ **Services** Lay underground cables, pipes, and drains before putting down hard surfaces, creating lawns, or planting. Keep a plan of all underground services.

■ **Hard landscaping** Put down paving and other hard surfaces while it is still easy to move materials about and stack them. If you decide to lay quality paving little by little, as funds become available, work out how you will store materials and dispose of rubble.

■ **Lawns** Lawns sown from seed in spring or autumn take many months before they can withstand heavy wear, and even a turf lawn needs several months to settle down. Establish lawns when you know that the area can be left undisturbed.

■ **Renovation** The best time to carry out drastic pruning of overgrown and neglected trees and shrubs is between mid-autumn and early spring, but cutting back may be necessary at other times so that other work can be carried out.

■ **Planting** The main planting season is between mid-autumn and early spring, but see PLANT PRACTICALITIES below.

## LEGAL MATTERS

It is important to be aware of the legal dimension to every garden.

■ **Boundaries** Recognize that boundaries are the most sensitive areas, where there is the potential for conflicts of interests with neighbours, and where regulations and responsibilities may be laid down by local authorities.

■ **Building work** Familiarize yourself with building and planning regulations before undertaking any construction work, including putting up a greenhouse.

■ **Removal and demolition** Check planning regulations before felling trees, removing hedges, or demolishing structures such as walls or buildings.

## PROFESSIONAL HELP

Even if you enjoy the practical side of gardening, use professionals for tasks that are potentially dangerous, require the use of specialized equipment, or are too heavy for you to undertake on your own. Use professionals, too, if you need legal advice and help on planning or engineering (for example, if building retaining walls). A personal recommendation counts for a lot, but in any case use a member of a trade or a professional organization.

■ **Electrics** Use a qualified electrician for all electrical work in the garden.

■ **Tree surgery** Employ a qualified tree surgeon to take down whole trees and remove large branches, and for pruning where the work has to be carried out above ground level.

## PLANT PRACTICALITIES

Plants can be bought from a wide range of outlets, including specialist nurseries and garden centres, and also by mail order.

■ **Container-grown stock** This can be planted outside the traditional period, which is between autumn and early spring, but attention to watering is essential until plants are well established.

## TIPS FOR AN INSTANT GARDEN

Staged development of a garden, beginning with short-lived but colourful, fast-growing plants, is less expensive than trying to create an immediate mature effect using quality paving and well-grown trees and shrubs.

• For hard surfaces use gravel, combined with paving or decking for seating and access areas. Plant into the gravel.

• Screen, shelter, and compartmentalize the garden using trellis covered with fast-growing climbers such as Canary creeper (*Tropaeolum peregrinum*).

• Create vertical accents with arches, pergolas, and cane wigwams, training up climbers such as ornamental gourds and sweet peas (*Lathyrus odoratus*).

• Fill beds and borders with bedding plants, placing taller annuals (eg cleomes) and fast-growing shrubs (eg shrubby lavateras like 'Rosea') at the back.

• Create height in the foreground with standard bushes of marguerites (*Argyranthemum*) and fuchsias in containers.

## PART TWO

# MAKING AND LOOKING AFTER YOUR GARDEN

# PATIOS AND PATHS

## SITING PATIOS

A PATIO THAT LINKS house and garden is both a practical and decorative means of enjoying outdoor living – a haven for simple relaxation or dining. Siting in the usual way, close to and foursquare with the house, is most convenient, with the advantage that a power source for lighting is readily accessible. If the site does not offer warmth and shelter or afford privacy, however, consider some alternatives. An angled or corner site, for example, might receive sun for much of the day, perhaps with views across the garden or to the landscape beyond. Or two smaller areas could provide a choice of warmth or cool shade, a welcome retreat on a hot, sunny day.

### SITING A PATIO AREA

A site that is warm and sheltered will be enjoyable both earlier and later in the year than one that is exposed to wind. Create wind shelter for comfort by using trellis screens or pergolas – both also provide planting opportunities for a range of fragrant plants to enhance the ambience.

Avoid sites too close to large trees; they may cast excessive shade, drip rain from their canopy, cause nuisance with falling leaves and insects, and may even dislodge paving with their questing roots.

#### GOOD IDEAS

• Size is important. Allow 3.3sq.m (4sq.yd) for each person likely to use the patio, and make room for seating and tables. Take into account the size of house and garden, too: the patio needs to be in proportion with both.

• Keep it simple. Furniture and plantings in ornamental pots usually look best against an unobtrusive surface. Simple materials are also easier to lay – important if you do it yourself.

△ **SHOWING OFF**
*The neutral colours of paving do not detract from the clean lines of elegant patio furniture; textural interest is gained from the simple contrast of smooth stone flags and gravel.*

◁ **THE PERFECT SITE**
*A small patio sited away from the house receives maximum sunshine. High walls with trees behind lend shelter and privacy and the resulting still air is pervaded by perfumes from surrounding plantings.*

### MEASURING UP

The first task when building a patio is to measure the area in order to calculate quantities of materials needed. Given accurate measurements, a good DIY store or builders' merchant will be able to advise on quantities.

Area is calculated simply by multiplying length by width. If the site is irregular, mark it out on graph paper, using one square per sq.m (sq.yd). Counting all full squares and any more than a third full gives a sufficiently accurate estimate of the area.

### TAKING THE STRAIN

Patios and paving must be built with appropriate load-bearing paving laid on firm foundations if they are to be stable in use. Decide whether the surface will take only foot traffic or may occasionally have to bear vehicular weight. Consider also the climate; areas that suffer summer drought or severe winters usually need deeper foundations. Seek the advice of your local authority building officer.

CAST SLAB      PRESSED SLAB

**CHOOSE THE RIGHT COURSE**
*Cast slabs are designed to bear light to medium-weight traffic, while pressed slabs, though lighter, are stronger. Cast slabs are ideal for patios that take only foot traffic, but if a patio is integrated with a driveway, for example, you must use a material that will take the strain.*

SEE ALSO: Doing the Groundwork, pp.58–59; Using Lighting in the Garden, pp.70–71; Enhancing Patio Areas, pp.72–73; Garden Styles, pp.122–123

# CHOOSING PAVING MATERIALS

While appearance is often a matter of taste, the best results are had by taking a cue from the colour and materials used in the house and its setting, and by reflecting the mood and style of the garden.

The selection of pavers, with shapes, sizes, colours, and costs in bewildering variety, is daunting. Focus on structural factors first to narrow the possibilities. The finished surface must bear the expected loading and be durable and weatherproof in the given climate, which may also include being non-slip when wet.

**BELGIAN BLOCKS**

**RED BRICK PAVERS**     **CLAY PAVERS**

△ **SMALL UNIT FLEXIBLE PAVERS**
*Small units are ideal where a fine-textured or patterned surface is desired. In irregularly shaped areas, they can often be laid without wasteful cutting. Many are designed for easy laying on a compacted sand base without mortar.*

**TERRACOTTA SQUARES**

Terracotta lends Mediterranean warmth to paved surfaces but must be frostproof for outdoor use

**TERRACOTTA TILES**

**CONCRETE PAVING SLABS**

Strong and durable, concrete is available in many attractive finishes, which belie its utilitarian image

Pointed slabs provide a fine-textured, non-slip surface that makes pattern work simple

**POINTED SLABS**

**NATURAL STONE**

**ARTIFICIAL STONE**

△ **LARGE UNIT PAVERS**
*Large units are available in a wealth of shapes, sizes, and finishes, with a wide colour range that allows selection to match local architecture and materials. They come in natural and reconstituted stone, or cast concrete and are usually laid on mortar on a prepared sub-base.*

# EDGING MATERIALS

Edging serves practical functions, as well as making a decorative finish to delineate and separate a path or patio from surrounding lawns and borders. Mortared in place, edging acts as a restraint for flexible surfaces, such as small unit pavers, and, if higher than a loose gravel surface, it is an effective means of keeping it in place. Suitable materials include pressure-treated wood, bricks, and clay tiles.

△ **MODERN STYLE**
*Small unit pavers make a neat patio edge, and they make mowing easier set just below the level of the lawn.*

**TRADITIONAL STYLE** ▷
*Suitable for both informal or formal styles of garden, a rope edge is especially useful for keeping gravel off surrounding surfaces.*

**TERRACOTTA ROPE EDGING AND POST**

**PRE-CAST DIAGONAL BRICKS**

◁ **COTTAGE STYLE**
*A pretty edging that is simple to install as pre-cast units; individual bricks on edge are difficult to lay level and true.*

**SEE ALSO:** Doing the Groundwork, pp.58–59

# DOING THE GROUNDWORK

THOROUGH PREPARATION of a firm foundation that takes into account the load-bearing requirements and existing soil conditions is essential if the finished surface is to be stable, durable, and long-lasting once in use. Accurate measurement and attention paid to making corners square and surfaces level are key to a professional finish.

Keep safe at work. Wear stout gloves if using concrete and mortar; use goggles if dealing with loose materials; if using machinery, wear ear defenders and close-fitting clothing, and keep head, limbs, and shovels well clear of moving parts. Never overestimate your strength when lifting; share the load with a helper whenever you can.

## PREARING THE SUB-BASE FOR A PATH OR PATIO

Before excavating, locate all underground pipes, cables, and drains. Remove all plant material, including tree roots. Dig out the topsoil until you reach firm subsoil. For non-load-bearing areas, a 10cm (4in) layer of compacted hardcore covered with a 5cm (2in) layer of sand makes an adequate foundation. On heavy clay or peaty soils, which shrink when dry and expand when wet, use 15cm (6in) of hardcore and top

with sand or ballast. If the surface is to bear a car's weight, prepare a sub-base of at least 10cm (4in) of compacted hardcore, with a 10cm (4in) layer of concrete on top; increase the concrete layer to 15cm (6in) on peat or clay soil. Concrete may form the finished surface, or it may be used as a base for pavers bedded on mortar. In areas with severe winters or very dry summers, take expert advice on foundations.

> ### GOOD IDEAS
>
> • Plate compacters can usually be hired by the half- or whole day; to reduce costs, prepare in advance so the machine can be used promptly.
>
> • Make sure you get clear instruction in the safe use of all hired machinery and that it works properly. Check on fuel type and have adequate supplies at hand. A good hire shop will advise you on these points.

### PREPARING A SUB-BASE

**1 MARK OUT THE AREA**
*Use pegs and string lines to mark out the area accurately, setting the strings at the desired level of the finished surface. Make right-angled corners, and use a builder's square to check that they are straight and true.*

**2 COMPACT THE BASE**
*Dig out the topsoil to firm subsoil. Level and compact the subsoil with a plate compacter. Allow for a 10cm (4in) depth of hardcore and a 5cm (2in) layer of sand (or deeper if appropriate), plus the thickness of the intended surface layer.*

**3 INSTALL LEVEL GUIDES**
*Drive in levelling pegs at 2m (6ft) spacings each way. For a patio, incorporate a slight slope for drainage (see below). Use a straight edge and spirit level to make sure that the tops of the pegs are level with the strings. Adjust as necessary.*

**4 ADD HARDCORE**
*Add a 10cm (4in) layer of hardcore to the entire area and level roughly. Compact until completely level, using pegs as a guide. Top with sand and compact again. The level, compacted surface is now ready to receive a surface layer of pavers.*

## DEALING WITH DRAINAGE

When building a patio, you must include a drainage slope – a fall of 2.5cm (1in) every 2m (6ft) usually suffices. If a wall borders the patio, it must slope so water runs away from the wall. Mark and dig out the patio area, and compact the base (*see above*). Work out the depth of the sub-base plus surface material, then mark this depth on several long pegs, measuring down from their tops. Next to the wall, drive in a row of these pegs, 2m (6ft) apart, so the marks are level

with the bottom of the hole; the peg tops now indicate the final level of paving, which must be at least 15cm (6in) below the damp-proof course. Insert a second row of marked pegs 2m (6ft) away from the wall, with a 2.5cm (1in) thick offcut of wood on top of each one. Level the tops of the two rows of pegs. Remove the offcut and repeat the procedure down subsequent rows of pegs. Dig and rake soil so it is level with the marker lines on each row of pegs.

Do not breach the damp course

The two pegs are levelled with offcut in place

△ **BUILDING IN A FALL**
*Use a spirit level and straight edge to level adjacent rows of pegs then remove the offcut and repeat the process for ensuing rows. The excavated base and the surface of the finished paving, as shown by the dotted line, should be parallel.*

SEE ALSO: Marking out a Bed, p.145

# LAYING PAVING SLABS

First establish a straight edge to start from, called a base line. A string line is best, even if you choose to start from a house wall, which may not be as straight as it looks. In this case, also consider whether the paving will be flush with the house, or if you want a planting gap between wall and paving. To save cost and reduce the need for cutting slabs, make the dimensions of the area divisible by the dimensions of whole slabs. Most standard slabs are 45 × 45cm (18 × 18in) or 45 × 60cm (18 × 24in). Prepare bedding mortar with a mix of 1 part cement to 5 parts sharp sand, the same mix can be used for jointing, but with less water to give a dry, crumbly texture. When the pavers have been laid, avoid walking on them until the mortar is dry. After jointing, brush surplus mortar off the slabs immediately and, to avoid staining, spray with water and sponge off excess mortar from the pavers.

## HOW TO LAY PAVING SLABS

**1 PREPARE MORTAR BASE**
Mark out the area and prepare sub-base. Start at a corner of the base line (see above). Lay strips of mortar, 3–5cm (1½–2in) high, in a square just smaller than the slabs. Add cross strips for slabs 45cm (18in) square or larger.

**2 MAKE IT LEVEL AND TRUE**
Lower slabs into place. Tap gently with the handle of a club hammer to level. Check levels in both directions. Use 0.5–1cm (¼–½in) wide offcuts of wood as spacers between the slabs. Check levels in each direction after every 3 or 4 slabs.

**3 MORTAR THE JOINTS**
Remove spacers before the mortar sets and without standing on the paving. After about 2 days, when the mortar is fully set, fill the joints with stiff mortar. Firm mortar down with a dowel or rounded piece of wood.

**4 FINISH OFF USING A JIGGER**
A jigger is a board of wood with a central slit, 0.5–1cm (¼–½in) wide. It allows joints to be mortared without staining the slabs. Simply align the slit above the joint and apply mortar through the slit; the mortar must be recessed by 2mm (⅛in).

# LAYING FLEXIBLE PAVING

Small unit pavers are bedded onto sand of a total compacted depth of 5cm (2in) for normal garden use; on unstable soil or for heavy use, increase the sub base to 20cm (8in) deep. Since they can be lifted and relaid if they sag in use, this type of paving is called flexible paving. It is laid with a firm edge restraint to prevent creepage of sand or blocks after laying. The top surface of the compacted sand layer should be 4.5cm (1¾in) below the level of finished paving if using 6cm (2⅜in) blocks, or 5cm (2in) for 6.5cm (2½in) blocks. Keep sand dry and do not walk on it while laying pavers; work from a kneeling board. Most manufacturers of flexible pavers offer telephone helplines or websites, which are good sources of expert advice.

## HOW TO LAY FLEXIBLE PAVING

**1 LAY THE EDGE RESTRAINT**
Prepare a sub-base of 8cm (3in) of compacted hardcore on firm subsoil. Lay edging strips around the entire area and bed them in concrete. Use a spirit level and the handle of a club hammer to tap the edges level.

**2 LAY THE SAND BASE**
Divide area into 1m (3ft) wide strips, with 5cm (2in) thick battens. Fill to top of battens with sharp sand. Compact with a plate compacter. Add more sand to top of battens. Strike level with a piece of wood. Remove battens, and fill voids with sand.

**3 LAY PAVERS**
Begin at one corner, and lay blocks in required pattern. Proceed along the edge restraint and complete one course before laying the next. For a herringbone pattern, with blocks at 45°, lay whole blocks at this stage; cut blocks to fill any spaces last of all.

**4 COMPACT AND FINISH**
Vibrate pavers into place by running over the area 2 to 3 times with a plate compacter fitted with a rubber-faced vibrating plate. Brush fine, dry sand over the surface and make another 2 or 3 passes with the compactor to vibrate sand into the joints.

**SEE ALSO:** Laying Concrete, pp.60–61; Laying Gravel, pp.62–63

# LAYING CONCRETE

CONCRETE IS ONE OF the least costly ways to make large areas of hard surface and is easy and quick to lay. Valued for its strength and durability, it is far more versatile than its utilitarian image suggests. Concrete forms an excellent base for a variety of inlaid decoration, or it can be brushed, pressed with patterning tools, or scored to produce a variety of surface textures. Avoid laying concrete if the temperature is above 32°C (90°F) or close to freezing, and never lay it onto frozen ground. Dry, windy days are also best avoided: they can create problems with surface drying. Wet concrete is caustic, so always cover up your skin when working.

## HOW TO LAY CONCRETE

The standard mix for poured concrete is 1 part cement to 1½ parts sharp sand to 2½ parts 2cm (¾in) aggregate (by volume). Heap sand and aggregate onto a board or into a barrow and place dry cement on top. Mix well by turning with a spade. Make a hollow in the dry mix and almost fill it with water. Push dry mix into the hollow bit by bit, adding more water gradually until you have a firm mix that has absorbed all of the water. Smooth the surface and make a row of troughs with a spade; the concrete is ready to pour if it holds peaks without slumping.

When levelling, a film of water appears on the surface; let it evaporate before smoothing further. Do not overwork concrete once poured, as this weakens it.

### GOOD IDEAS

- Hiring a concrete mixer saves a good deal of time and hard labour and makes mixing thoroughly to the required consistency much easier.
- If you are mixing by hand, don't try to mix too much at once. About six buckets full at a time is an easily manageable quantity.

### LAYING AN AREA OF CONCRETE

**1 MARK OUT AND INSTALL LEVELLING PEGS**
*Mark out the site with pegs and string, and excavate to about 20cm (8in) into firm subsoil. Drive in levelling pegs at 1m (3ft) intervals, using the string as a guide. Level pegs with a straight edge and spirit level.*

**2 INSTALL THE FORMWORK**
*Remove the string lines and nail wooden planks to the inner side of the pegs, joining the planks at the corners end-to-face. This formwork holds the concrete in place until it is fully set or "cured".*

**3 LAY THE SUB-BASE**
*Divide large areas into sections, no more than 4m (12ft) long, using formwork. Spread a 10cm (4in) layer of hardcore and compact it using a roller, or firm it down with a stout timber post.*

**4 POUR THE CONCRETE**
*Starting with the first section, pour in the concrete and spread it level so that it stands just proud of the formwork. Work the concrete well into the edges using a spade or shovel with a chopping motion.*

**5 LEVEL OFF THE CONCRETE**
*Use a wooden beam that spans the width of the formwork to compact the concrete with a downward chopping motion. Then slide the beam from side to side to level the surface at the height of the formwork.*

**6 FILL AND SMOOTH**
*Stroke the surface smooth with a builder's float. Fill any hollows with fresh concrete and level again. Protect concrete with plastic sheeting until set, which takes about 10 days. Remove the formwork only when concrete has set hard.*

SEE ALSO: Doing the Groundwork, pp.58–59; Making Paths, pp.66–67

# READY-MIXED CONCRETE

Ready-mixed concrete is a labour-saving solution for large areas, but you must prepare the sub-base and have the formwork in place on delivery. Give the supplier the dimensions and information about the intended use of the surface, so that the correct mix and quantities are delivered. The site must be accessible to a large vehicle, on firm ground, and with room to manoeuvre, as the delivery chute needs to be repositioned several times as the formwork fills. Otherwise, recruit a team of helpers and several barrows to move, firm, and level the concrete quickly, before it sets.

## ALWAYS REMEMBER

### BE PREPARED!

Ready-mixed concrete shoots rapidly down the chute and must be firmed and levelled before it hardens. If necessary, ask the delivery driver to slow down the delivery rate. Make sure you have enough helpers — equipped with gloves, goggles, stout boots, and tough clothes that cover all bare skin.

# EXPOSING AGGREGATE

If you use an attractively coloured aggregate in the concrete mix, it can be exposed to give a decorative finish, and different textures are created according to the size of aggregate used, ranging from coarse grit through different grades of gravel to water-worn pebbles. Choosing a locally sourced material will ensure that it blends well with its surroundings.

◁ **BRUSH AND CLEAN**
*After pouring the mix, do not smooth with a float. Let dry for about six hours, and brush the surface with a stiff-bristled brush. After a further 36–48 hours, clean remaining cement residue from the aggregate with a high-pressure hose.*

△ **WATER-WORN PEBBLES**
*Pebbles give an attractive, subtly coloured but rough-textured finish. It can be uncomfortable to walk on, so use it for edging or deterrent barriers.*

△ **PEA SHINGLE**
*Choose 6–8mm (¼–⅜in) shingle or standard aggregates up to 2cm (¾in) in diameter for a comfortable, non-slip walking surface.*

△ **FINE-GRADE GRAVEL**
*The finest grades of gravel give a finely textured, natural-looking surface, which is especially useful where a non-slip surface is required.*

# APPLYING COLOUR

Concrete can be coloured during mixing with a mineral pigment or with powder pigment dry-sprinkled onto the wet surface after it has been smoothed with a float. Other types of colour are applied when it has set fully, after about a month.

■ Patio sealants add colour pigment and an extra protective layer.

■ Stains can be applied about six weeks after laying concrete.

■ Semi-transparent wood stains take well on concrete.

■ Specially formulated concrete paints offer the widest choice of colour. Water-based, latex ones are the most effective. Apply two or three coats.

◁ **APPLYING COLOUR**
*Apply paints, stains, or sealants — as shown here — with a clean, dry brush, and follow the manufacturer's instructions. Make the application on a clear and dry day when no rain is forecast, and when winds are light.*

# DECORATIVE FINISHES

Concrete and mortar both make an ideal matrix in which to set more decorative materials. Provided the inlaid material is pushed in to at least two-thirds of its depth, they will be securely fixed once the matrix is dry. This method can be used for pebbles, cobbles, glass nuggets, or pottery shards to create intricate patterns. Bear in mind that large inclusions will be difficult to walk on.

If your ambition is to create a large-scale mosaic, plan ahead. Lay the sub-base first, graph out the design, and sort materials by size and colour. Divide the area into square sections. Lay a topping of mortar or concrete onto one section, and push in the mosaic fragments. Complete each section before moving onto the next, or the concrete or mortar may be dry before you finish.

△ **PEBBLE MOSAIC**
*Bed pebbles by pressing into bedding mortar to two-thirds of their depth. Level with a presser board.*

**MIXED MEDIA** ▷
*A broad band of cement with inlaid pebbles borders concrete slabs with finer textured, exposed aggregate.*

SEE ALSO: Making Steps, pp.68–69

# LAYING GRAVEL

A SMOOTH SWEEP of raked gravel has everything to recommend it aesthetically, especially if it is locally sourced. Few other materials blend so seamlessly with brick and stone, while at the same time making a fine-textured foil for plants. Lay it around the house and its crisp crunch under foot will also be a subtle deterrent to intruders. Gravel is also relatively inexpensive and easy to install. There are downsides, however: gravel needs regular replenishment and continuous attention to weed control, but if a modern geotextile fabric is used as a weed-suppressing underlay, gravel replenishment becomes the only regular chore involved.

## TYPES OF GRAVEL

Gravel comes in two main types: angular chippings from parent rock, and water-worn, rounded shingle that is obtained by dredging. The sizes vary from fine grits to fairly chunky chippings 2cm (¾in) or more in diameter. The smaller the size, the finer the finished surface texture.

In practical terms, finer grades are the easiest to walk on. Fine grits, however, are picked up readily on shoe soles, and tracked into the house or onto the lawn. Coarse grades make for an uncomfortable walking surface, but are hardwearing under regular use. Grades in the 6–10mm (¼–½in) range suit most garden uses.

△ PEA SHINGLE
*Rounded stones give a fine-textured surface for comfort and suit formal and informal garden styles.*

△ GRANITE CHIPS
*Granite chips are available in a range of colours; use a local source to blend well with the surroundings.*

△ LIMESTONE CHIPS
*Chippings give a more formal effect than shingles; a local source is nearly always the cheapest.*

△ COARSE GRAVEL
*Use coarse-gauge gravel as a deterrent barrier to foot traffic, or as a hard-wearing surface for vehicles.*

## SITE CLEARANCE

To make the most of this versatile and practical medium, and to reduce later maintenance to a minimum, thorough preparation is essential.

■ The site must be level. Gravel will work its way down even the slightest of slopes.
■ The site must be cleared of all weeds and roots. Take off fertile topsoil to reduce re-growth and to remove the reservoir of weed seeds, or simply lay gravel over an impermeable geotextile fabric.
■ The sub-base must be firm and well compacted. Gravel gradually but surely works down into loose surfaces. A geotextile membrane helps prevent this.
■ Rake and roll laid gravel to provide a firm surface for walking and to make pushing barrows and other wheeled machinery easier.

## EDGING GRAVELLED AREAS

Since gravel is a loose material, it needs some form of edge restraint to prevent the nuisance it can cause when scattered under foot onto lawns and borders and to reduce the frequency of replenishment.

A wide range of materials can be used. Inexpensive but utilitarian timber gravel boards are simply nailed to pegs sunk into the ground; they are effectively disguised once the adjacent plantings grow. Reclaimed wooden sleepers are expensive, but practically maintenance free and last a lifetime if laid on a modest foundation of compacted hardcore. Edgings of stone, clay, concrete, cobbles, or bricks must be mortared in place in a shallow foundation trench on firm subsoil or hardcore, deep enough to hold a laying base of 5cm (2in) of compacted sand.

## GRAVEL PATIOS AND PATHS

Unlike harder, more solid materials that need cutting and shaping to conform to awkward shapes, the loose nature of the material means that gravel will flow easily into the most intricate corners and the tightest of curves. It is the easiest material to use to create winding or zig-zag paths, patios of irregular organic forms, or experimental geometric outlines.

### ALWAYS REMEMBER

**SAFE PRACTICES**

Where a patio or path butts up to a lawn, the restraining edge must be sufficiently proud of the gravel to prevent it from being kicked onto the lawn, yet low enough to avoid mower blades. Loose gravel is a potential hazard during mowing, as it may be thrown into the air and may also damage the mower.

△ A PAVER RETAINER
*A broad band of pavers is complementary in colour and texture and makes an effective retainer.*

◁ THE ROPE TRICK
*Rope edging reinforces the crisp lines of a formal knot garden and keeps gravel firmly in place.*

SEE ALSO: Edging Materials, p.57; Preparing the Sub-base for a Path or Patio, p.58

## LAYING A GRAVELLED AREA

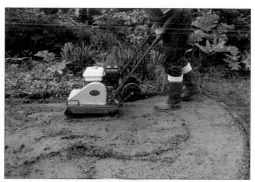

**1 PREPARING THE GROUND**
*Clear the ground of weeds and remove a 10cm (4in) layer of topsoil from the entire area so that it is fairly level. Mortar edging bricks in place or install treated timber edging to keep the gravel in place.*

**2 LAYING A SUB-BASE**
*Rake the surface level, then fill the excavated area with a layer of unprocessed gravel, hoggin, or hardcore almost back up to the original soil level. Rake the surface completely flat.*

**3 COMPACT THE SUB-BASE**
*Use a hired plate compacter or heavy garden roller to compact the base and remove air pockets. This provides a stable base. Compress the base to at least 2cm (¾in) below the original ground level.*

**4 LAY THE GRAVEL**
*When the base is firm and compacted, add the surface layer of gravel. Start at one side and rake level as you go. If using geotextile fabric, lay it before adding gravel and peg it in place with small wire hoops or staples.*

**5 RAKE AND ROLL**
*Rake over the entire surface to produce a level finish of uniform depth. The gravel depth will be about 2.5cm (1in) and the finished surface just below the edging material. Use a garden roller to bed the gravel down.*

**6 FINISHING OFF**
*The freshly laid gravel will be dusty, so wash it down by spraying with a hose pipe fitted with a rose. Watering while rolling will further compact the ground. Alternatively, let natural rainfall do the work.*

# PLANTING IN GRAVEL

Gravel is an ideal substrate for a range of plants, but its free drainage and light- and warmth-reflecting qualities make it especially suited to robust alpines and natives of Mediterranean climates, both of which are vulnerable to winter wet.

Planting in gravel is essentially the same as in open ground; gravel is scraped away to dig out a planting hole and pushed back after planting up to the plant neck. If a geotextile fabric is used, cut two crosswise slits wide enough to hold the root ball, fold back in place and top off with gravel.

**ALL THE ADVANTAGES ▷**
*Not only is gravel an elegant foil for architectural plants, but it is also a great way of ensuring excellent drainage at their necks in winter, which reduces the risk of rot. Structural plants, such as this verbascum, will also help to break up an expanse of gravel.*

△ **A LIVING FOUNTAIN**
*The feathery plumes of this grass, Stipa tenuissima, rise above a sea of gravel to lend summer-long textural contrast and dynamic movement as the delicate plumes shimmer in the slightest breeze.*

**SEE ALSO:** Beds for Drought-tolerant Plants, pp.132–133; Establishing Plants in the Border, pp.148–149; Gravel Herb Garden, p.229

# INSTALLING DECKING

TIMBER DECKING IS ONE of the most modern and practical of design elements and brings the natural beauty of wood into the garden in ways that appear perfectly at home in a diversity of garden styles. Whether used for dining and entertaining, or for simple relaxation, decks can be a magnificent way of extending your living space.

Depending on climate, they may be sited to receive full sun or cool shade; you should also consider how their location might affect privacy and security. In some areas, building regulations apply, which stipulate load-bearing requirements and inspection of work; you may also need to obtain approval from the relevant authority.

## WOOD FOR DECKING

Local timber merchants give helpful advice when choosing timber for decking, and specialist deck companies may even send a representative to your home. Timber is graded for its durability and suitability for outdoor use. Some wood is naturally rot-resistant, but most is pressure-treated with preservative. Treat all wood regularly with preservative after installation to extend its

life. Seek out decking timber with a reeded surface for a non-slip finish, and use brass screws and fittings where possible, because they do not rust or stain the wood.

USING READY-MADE TIMBER PANELS ▷
*Ready-made panels, which are sometimes available with a non-slip finish, are the simplest way of achieving surface detail on a deck. The supporting joists (see below) must be spaced to ensure that each panel is securely supported.*

CHEQUERBOARD PANEL   HERRINGBONE PANEL   PARALLEL-SLATTED PANEL

## LAYING A TIMBER DECK

This simple, free-standing deck is 2.5m (8ft) square and uses elementary building methods and a design that is easily adjusted for size and shape.

All simple decks are constructed in a similar way, with a foundation at the base and a framework of bearers and joists to support the surface. To ensure structural strength, the joists must be fixed on top of, and at right angles to, the bearers. Decking planks run parallel with the line of the bearers. Here, concrete blocks are used as bearers. For elevated decks, joist shoes (*see opposite, top*) make construction simple, and the bearers would be made of timber in this case. The surface planks are laid with small gaps to allow room for the planks to swell when wet without warping.

### GOOD IDEAS

• You can find specialist suppliers, plans, and specifications for decks on the Internet; many have details that are specific to a given region and climate.

• Use the construction method shown here to create a staggered series of decks or perhaps to enframe a corner site. Joist shoes make it simple to build stepped decks by varying the height of the support posts.

### HOW TO LAY A TIMBER DECK

**1 MARK OUT THE SITE**
*Lay out 4 planks in a square; check that corners are at right angles using a builder's square. Mark the outline with a spade on the outside of the planks. The final area will be 15cm (6in) larger than the 2.5m (8ft) square platform.*

**2 LOCATE THE JOIST FOUNDATIONS**
*Put 3 of the planks aside and align 4 joists at even spacings along the remaining plank. Ensure the end joists lie flush with the ends of the plank. Mark a 15cm (6in) wide border around the length of each joist.*

**5 BACKFILL THE TRENCH**
*Backfill each trench with sand, treading it down firmly to compact it. Do this thoroughly, otherwise the blocks will shift and the decking will warp. Level off the sand so that it is flush with the level of the soil.*

**6 LAY THE JOISTS**
*Lay and centre the joists across the blocks; check that the first and last joists are exactly 2.5m (8ft) apart, using one of the planks. Check that all the ends are in line with each other.*

SEE ALSO: Using Lighting in the Garden, pp.70–71

## USING SHOE SUPPORTS

Steel joist shoes bolted on to concrete to make a firm underpinning for bearers and joists and are especially useful for elevated decks. Each needs a foundation, 30cm (12in) square, filled with 10cm (4in) of hardcore topped off with a 10cm (4in) layer of concrete.

◁ **HOW IT WORKS**
*Space joist shoes 1.2m (4ft) apart. Level timber uprights and nail the bearers in place, flat side down. Fix joists at right angle to bearers, 45cm (18in) apart, with nails at an angle of 45°. Then fix slats or panels on top.*

Shoe is bolted on to cured concrete with 5cm (2in) wall bolts in pre-drilled holes

## JOINING TIMBER SUPPORTS

Ideally, a single length of joist timber should be used to span the bearers, but where this is not possible two lengths can be joined safely and securely using a simple lap joint. The two lengths are nailed together with two vertical nails and to the bearer with skewed nails.

△ **MAKING A LAP JOINT**
*A lap joint is a strong and simple way of joining joists. Make a 5cm (2in) horizontal cut and a 10cm (4in) vertical cut in the end of each joist. Half-lap them where they cross the bearer and nail in place as shown.*

## MAINTAINING DECKING

Check all timbers annually for splits or cracks and replace any that are damaged. If the chosen finish wears thin in areas of heavy foot traffic, clean the surface and reapply. Keep surfaces free of algae and moss. Sweep away fallen leaves and other plant debris regularly.

### ALWAYS REMEMBER

#### KEEP DECKING SAFE

In damp climates, the inevitable algal and/or fungal growth on wood makes surfaces dangerously slippery. Make sure that any proprietary cleaners are safe for use near plants and non-toxic to wildlife; if not, take steps to protect them, or choose the safer alternative – a stiff broom with a scrub of water and sharp sand or household bleach.

## FINISHING TIMBER

Pressure-treated timber needs only occasional preservative treatment. The range of finishes that protect wood is extensive and many both colour and preserve. Check with the supplier that the treatment you buy will give the desired effect and is suitable for outdoor use. Translucent wood stains penetrate wood and darken or colour it while enhancing the grain; dyes offer more intense colour. Non-penetrating finishes should be microporous to allow wood to breathe and reduce risks of flaking or peeling.

**3 DIG OUT FOUNDATION TRENCHES**
*Using the marker lines as a guide, dig out the trenches 10cm (4in) deeper than the depth of the concrete bearers. Line each trench with sand and compact it to produce a total compacted depth of 5cm (2in).*

**4 LAY CONCRETE BEARERS**
*Lay the concrete bearers, 3 to a trench, placing one at each end and one at the centre of each trench. They should stand proud of the soil by 1cm (½in) so that the joists do not come into contact with the soil. Level and adjust.*

△ **NATURALLY STYLISH**
*Most outdoor timber is pressure-treated with a green-tinted preservative. For a more natural effect, as shown here, seek out naturally rot-resistant timbers or specialist landscaping timber treated with colourless preservative. Use shoe supports.*

**7 SECURE JOISTS AND INSTALL PLANK PANELS**
*Secure joists in place using metal brackets on both ends of each joist, screw them to joist and block (see insert). Fix the first plank in place with its ends flush with the joists; use 2 countersunk screws per joist.*

**8 FINISH PLANKING AND FIT FASCIA BOARDS**
*Position remaining planks, 5mm (¼in) apart, and screw in place. Fit 4 more 2.5m (8ft) planks as fascia boards by nailing them into joist ends; 2 of the fascia boards must be 4cm (1½in) longer, so they overlap neatly at the corners.*

**SEE ALSO:** Enhancing Patio Areas, pp.72–73; Containers, pp.166–179

# MAKING PATHS

THE PRIMARY PRACTICAL reason that our gardens have paths is, of course, to get from A to B, taking the most convenient route on a clean, hard-wearing surface. But there are legions of other, less prosaic roles that paths play in the scheme of things. The wealth of available materials allow paths to enhance a garden design and can make beautiful features in their own right. A meandering route can ensure that all the garden's beauties are not seen at once, often lending the illusion of greater space, while intersecting linear paths lend possibilities of vistas in variety. Not least, paths form a vital element of unity that ties a design together.

## ROUTING A PATH

When planning paths, identify the most travelled routes in the garden, from gate to door, from house to utility areas, or down to the compost heap, for example. These paths form the main framework. Take account of desire lines — usually the shortest distance between two points — an inconvenient route is seldom used. To avoid trampled lawn or border edges, make corners curve across right-angled bends — they will also be much easier to negotiate with a barrow.

With a main framework defined, decide on secondary routes that might lead to a view or a secluded arbour, or simply meander amongst favourite plants.

## DESIGN CONSIDERATIONS

In every well-designed garden, pathways form a major element in the architectural skeleton that underpins, frames, and enhances the plantings that clothe it. When planning, easy access is obviously a high priority, so bear in mind the natural tendency to take the shortest route from point to point. But consider also the role paths make to dividing a garden into areas of different use, or how they might delineate and shape planting areas.

You could consider combining purely functional paths with secondary ones for other purposes. For example, a side branch that is hidden from view until you stumble upon it creates an exciting element of surprise. Or how a narrow path that opens out before a view will invite a pause to stop and stare. Use a change of surface texture to proclaim a change of direction, or define the boundaries of different garden rooms.

### ALWAYS REMEMBER

**FORM FOLLOWS FUNCTION**

Access paths need to be level, smooth, and wide enough for walking and wheel-barrowing. A width of 1.2–1.5m (4–5ft) allows two people to walk side by side, even where plants spill over the edges. Secondary paths, intended to gently meander around the garden, can be narrower and less even.

## PATH STYLES

Since the essence of formality is geometry and precision, and the converse sinuous irregularity lends informality, the line of a path and the materials used in its construction define its style. Natural materials, perhaps in the form of slabs of tree trunk set in bark chippings or stone slabs used as random stepping stones through gravel, are perfect in an informal setting. Formal gardens positively demand the use of elements with clean, straight edges laid out in strong, crisp lines; here, pavers or dressed stone might be the materials of first choice. Gravel is the obvious exception to the general rule, since this versatile material can be used in almost any style of garden.

**BREAKING THE RULES** ▷
*It is satisfying to use reclaimed materials, not least in terms of cost. Old bricks can lend an aged charm, but usually flake during freeze-thaw cycles. If they disintegrate entirely (they seldom do), chisel out and replace them.*

**BASKET WEAVE**

**INTERLOCKING**

**HERRINGBONE**

△ **PATTERNWORK**
*Bricks or pavers can be laid in various formal patterns. Choose bricks that are suitable for exterior use and resistant to wetting and freezing. In a herringbone pattern, bricks are laid at an angle of 45° and a great deal of cutting is required.*

SEE ALSO: Surfaces, pp.24–27; Laying Paving Slabs, p.59; Laying Gravel, pp.62–63

# A Crazy-paving Path

Crazy paving is a relatively inexpensive way of constructing an informal path. It can be laid on sand or, for a safer, firmer and more durable surface, on mortar. To make bedding mortar, mix 1 part cement to 5 parts sharp sand and add water to give a dry, crumbly consistency.

Prepare the sub-base with a slight slope for drainage. Loose lay the slabs, in areas about 1m (3ft) square, without mortar. Lay large slabs first, and infill with smaller ones, fitting together like a jigsaw. You may need to trim to size with a bolster chisel and hammer (wear goggles). Make gaps as small as possible. When satisfied with their placement, bed them in. Adjust the levels by lifting slabs and removing or adding more sand or mortar, as necessary.

## GOOD IDEAS

- If using a dark-coloured stone, like slate, add a concrete dye powder to the mortar mix to make the cracks less conspicuous.

- If you wish to grow plants in paving cracks, bed crazy paving on sand. For a firmer, more durable surface, bed the paving on mortar.

## HOW TO LAY CRAZY PAVING

**1 LAY EDGING PIECES**
*Use string lines and pegs to mark out the area and prepare a sub-base of compacted hardcore. Lay edging pieces first, on either side of the path, with straight edges outermost. Mortar edges in place to form a firm edge restraint, even if you bed the remaining pieces on sand.*

**2 FILL THE CENTRE**
*Lay large slabs in the centre and infill with smaller ones. Lay them on sand or blobs of mortar, using a timber offcut and club hammer to bed them in. Check that central slabs are level with edge pieces using a straight edge and spirit level. Lift and adjust as necessary.*

**3 FINISHING OFF**
*If bedding on sand, brush dry sand into the cracks. If using a mortar finish, fill the cracks with crumbly, almost dry mortar. Bevel the mortar with a pointing trowel so that surface water drains quickly away from the slabs (see inset).*

◁ **GRAVEL PATHS**
*Gravel paths are very simple to lay and, if laid on a geotextile membrane, need little maintenance. Here, an edge restraint of gravel boards is completely hidden by the billowing growth of lavender. A clear case of minimum effort, maximum effect.*

△ **COBBLED PATH**
*Visually pleasing, but seldom smooth and even, cobbles are best reserved for informal secondary paths.*

**STEPPING STONES** ▷
*Here, informality meets practicality, stepping stones keep feet dry, lead the eye on, and invite exploration.*

**SEE ALSO:** Doing the Groundwork, pp.58–59; Laying Gravel, pp.62–63; Herbs for Cracks and Crevices, p.229

# MAKING STEPS

IF YOU GARDEN on a sloping site, steps are the obvious way of negotiating a change in level, but don't think of them simply as a utilitarian device — they can add an attractive element of interest, perhaps to replace a previously bland, grassy incline or to allow other focal points in the garden to be viewed from another angle. Wide, shallow steps invite a pause to enjoy a view, and they make plinths to display pots filled with plants. Narrow, steep steps move you faster to a different area of the garden. Safety is paramount, so where winters are icy and wet, use textured, non-slip surfaces for treads, and make sure that they are wide enough for safe use.

## TREADS AND RISERS

The width of treads and the height of risers must be in the correct proportion to each other for safety and comfort. Treads must be a minimum of 30cm (12in) from front to back, and the height of risers will vary between 10–18cm (4–7in).

As a rule-of-thumb, the width of the tread plus double the height of the riser should equal about 65cm (26in). First, choose the height of the riser, double it, then subtract it from 65cm (26in) to give the width of the tread.

To calculate the number of steps, divide the slope height (*see step 1, right*) by the height of one riser. You may need to adjust the height of the riser to fit the slope.

If you want to check the maths, plot the run and rise of the steps to scale, on graph paper, and sketch out risers and treads to fit comfortably with the given proportions.

The riser height is usually between 10–18cm (4–7in), and is adjusted to suit the overall rise

The tread must be at least 30cm (12in) wide; you may wish to add 2.5–5cm (1–2in) as an overhang

Concrete footing over a hardcore base supports the first, or "base" riser

△ **HOW IT WORKS**
*This construction detail illustrates principles that can be used for a wide range of materials in any number of combinations. You could substitute stone or concrete flags for the brick risers, for example. The dimensions can be adjusted to avoid having to cut bricks or stone.*

## BUILDING STEPS UP A BANKED SLOPE

Measure the height and run of the slope to calculate the number and proportions of the steps needed (*see left*). The height of each riser includes slab and mortar.

Mark out the width of the steps and the position of the risers with wooden pegs, and excavate soil to form a series of earth steps. Make a concrete footing using a mix of 1 part cement to 2½ parts sharp sand to 3½ parts 2cm (¾in) aggregate; or use 5 parts combined aggregate to 1 part cement. Construct risers using masonry mortar (1 part masonry cement to 3 parts soft sand). Check that bricks are level using a straight edge and spirit level.

After laying the first tread, mark the position of the next riser on the tread and mortar it into position.

### HOW TO BUILD THE FOUNDATIONS

The run, or length, of the slope is the distance between the peg at the top of the slope and the post at the bottom

**1** **MEASURING UP**
*Measure the height and run of the slope to work out how many steps are needed. Drive a peg into the top of the slope and a post into the base. Tie a string between them and measure the height between ground level and the string (the height).*

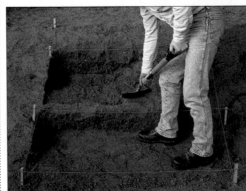

**2** **EXCAVATING THE TREADS**
*Mark out the width of the steps using pegs and string line, then run string lines to mark the front of each tread. Calculate the number of steps, the depth of the risers, and width of the treads. Dig out the steps and compact the earth at each tread position.*

**3** **MAKE A FOOTING FOR THE RISER**
*Dig out a trench for the footing, 15cm (6in) deep and twice the width of the riser bricks. Pack the base with a 8cm (3in) layer of hardcore and fill to the top with concrete. Leave it to set hard for a few days before laying the riser bricks.*

### ALWAYS REMEMBER

**PROPORTIONS ARE VITAL FOR SAFETY**

The technique shown here can be adapted to suit a range of materials, but it is vital when planning steps to keep safety and ease of use in mind. The most important factor is to ensure that the height of the risers are uniform — if shallower or deeper than expected they will, sooner or later, cause someone to trip or stumble. The treads must also be deep enough so that they can be stood on easily: they should be a minimum of 30cm (12in) from front to back, and the overhang should be no greater than 5cm (2in).

SEE ALSO: Doing the Groundwork, pp.58–59; Laying Concrete, pp.60–61

## LAYING THE BRICKS AND SLABS

**4 LAYING THE RISERS**
Lay the first riser on the footing, using a single course of bricks, making sure that the joints between bricks are staggered in subsequent courses, as shown. Use a string line stretched between pegs to ensure that bricks are straight and level.

**5 LAYING THE TREADS**
Backfill behind the riser with hardcore and compact it well, using a post as a tamper. Set the paving slabs on a 1cm (½in) bed of mortar, leaving a small gap between the two slabs. The slabs should make an overhang of 2.5–5cm (1–2in), and have a slight forward slope for drainage.

**6 LAYING THE SECOND STEP**
Mark the position of the second riser on the slabs and mortar the bricks in place. Backfill the void with hardcore as before, compacting it well, and lay the second set of treads. Continue for the remaining steps and then mortar the joints between each slab.

# STYLES OF STEPS

Brick and slab steps are easy and practical because these materials come in standard sizes, making calculations relatively simple. The same basic methods of construction apply even if you choose railway sleepers or concrete or stone flags as the risers, with a gravel infill or patterned bricks for the treads. Lay gravel over a compacted base of unprocessed gravel with a 5cm (2in) layer of firmed sand to fill any voids.

Long, shallow slopes might be better traversed by single risers separated by long landings, or pairs of equal-height steps and landings. Such arrangements are often more visually impressive and encourage a more leisurely ascent than a short run of steps. As long as the risers are uniform and no more than 10–18cm (4–7in) high, and the treads are a minimum of 30cm (12in) wide, the variations are infinite.

**△ HERRINGBONE**
In this case, the steps are constructed without an overhang. The bricks are laid lengthways at the edge of each tread, with a double course of brick risers beneath. The treads are laid on a full mortar bed.

**SLEEPER STEPS ▷**
Here, sleepers form a generously broad sweep of curving, shallow steps. The sleepers are bedded in a shallow trench, onto firmed soil topped off with a 5cm (2in) layer of compacted sand.

**◁ NATURAL STONE**
A short flight of natural stone steps with a broad platform on top uses elevation to great effect. It almost demands that you pause to enjoy the sweeping view across the garden.

**△ DECKING PANELS**
Here, decking panels form a series of shallow landings with a rhythmic repetition of alternating diagonals. It is ideal for dry climates, where slippery algal growth is seldom a problem.

**SEE ALSO:** Choosing Paving Materials, p.57; Installing Decking, pp.64–65; Using Lighting in the Garden, pp.70–71

# USING LIGHTING IN THE GARDEN

IT IS OFTEN THE NEED for safe access and security that first prompts consideration of garden lighting, but this is seriously to underestimate its potential for bringing the garden to life at night and creating striking features of interest after sundown. Furthermore, lighting can be enjoyed from within or without the home. With a little applied imagination, a variety of functional and beautiful effects can be created. Detail lighting, used primarily to highlight a feature, also scatters light to illuminate its surrounds for safety, with incidental effects of providing a degree of security and deterrence to intruders. So why settle for utility only, when you can have beauty too?

## WHY USE LIGHTING?

One of the best reasons for installing garden lighting is to extend the use of the garden at night, especially if busy working days limit daytime enjoyment. Consider installation at the garden's planning stage, rather than as an afterthought, and it can be sited to achieve specific ends: to provide for atmospheric evening dining or to light a meandering path, perhaps fitted with movement-activated sensors, where you can wind down after work, wine glass in hand. Use lighting to set a mood, lend theatrical shadows to favourite features, or, most practically, to provide a safe route to the door on dark nights.

▽ **SUBTLE DIFFUSION**
*Several light sources above ground level provide subtle illumination for evening dining. Diffusion through frosted glass shades eliminates glare, and strategic placement, at points where levels change, increases safety.*

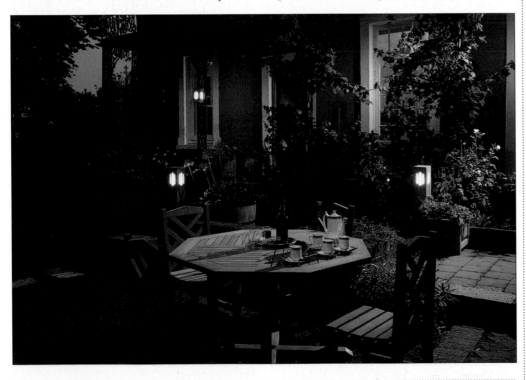

## LOW-TECH SOLUTIONS

Low-tech solutions – hurricane lamps, flares, and candle lights – are a cheaper alternative to permanent systems, ideal if cool summers lend few opportunities to use the garden at night. They cast the most atmospheric light for a midsummer party; a string of candle lanterns among the trees can be enchanting. Use citronella candles in pretty, open jars to scent the air and keep biting insects at bay.

SHINE ON... ▷
*Position lamps, naked flames, or other heat-producing sources, well away from foliage to avoid damage. Attach hanging lights with wire, not string. Take sensible precautions with flamed lights and be sure to extinguish them at the end of the evening.*

## FIXTURES AND FITTINGS

All exterior light fittings and fixtures must be robust and purpose-made for outdoor use. Exterior lighting units are sealed and specified as waterproof – never use internal fittings outdoors. Site the lighting system so that it can be turned on from indoors and out. Make sure that surface power points have a screw-fit or lockable cap and site them out of reach of children.

## ELECTRICAL SAFETY

Outdoor lighting is powered by a mains or low-voltage source. Low-voltage systems are safest and many are suitable for DIY installation. Ideal for small gardens, it uses only short cable runs and small lighting units and may be run off the mains with a transformer. For higher intensities and long cable runs, use mains electricity and have it installed professionally. Cables, in armoured conduits, must be buried at least 45cm (18in) deep, along a wall, path, or other marked site, safely out of harm's way when cultivating. All systems should include a circuit breaker (RCD).

◁ **ATTEND TO DETAIL**
*There is a huge range of lighting styles available, so finding a style that fits with home and garden will not be difficult. They may be wall-mounted, as here, post-mounted, recessed into walls or floors, or set on fixed or adjustable spikes.*

SEE ALSO: Enhancing Patio Areas, pp.72–73; Safety First, p.199; Always Remember box: Out of your depth?, p.209

# LIGHTING EFFECTS

For security and safety, area lighting in the form of a downlighter, usually a high-output flood- or spotlight, is most often used. Crosslighting with two floodlights gives excellent coverage over a wide area and installing below eye level helps reduce dazzle. For dining and entertaining, a softer glow is more comfortable, so choose a diffuse form of area lighting rather than a strongly directional beam. Detail lighting is closely focused and may be used for safety, close to steps for example, yet it is also the type to use to create the special effects shown below.

◁ **MOONLIGHTING**
*A high-level, downward-pointing source provides soft-shadowed highlights for a focal point; at the same time, the scattered light provides a measure of safety and security.*

**SPREADLIGHTING** ▷
*A hooded light source casts its beam downwards and outwards, here creating safe and practical lighting for a flight of steps without the potential danger of blinding glare.*

◁ **SHADOWING**
*A light angled towards a flat surface creates impressive shadows when used with architectural plants. Effects vary with light intensity and the distance from the object.*

**SPOTLIGHTING** ▷
*Spotlighting uses a highly directional, low-level and full-frontal beam for the dramatic highlighting of important focal points or features, such as a piece of sculpture or fine tree.*

◁ **UPLIGHTING**
*Use a ground-level source that casts an upward beam to create plays of shadow and light. Angle it away from the viewer to avoid glare; remember it may be a source of light pollution.*

# SPECIAL LIGHTING EFFECTS

Lighting brings an added dimension to water features, perhaps intimating that a pool has hidden depths, or lending a vital spark to the sound and movement of cascades or spouts. Safety is paramount. It is important when lighting water features to make sure that the lighting units and all cabling and connectors are sealed, waterproof, and specified as suitable for submersion. Ordinary exterior lighting is waterproof, but it is not submersible and regulations stipulate that it should not be installed within 2m (6ft) of a pool or water source.

◁ **ELECTRICAL SUPPLY**
*Supply is installed during building, by a professional if it uses mains electricity. All equipment must be specified for submerged use.*

Cabling runs through armoured ducts and lighting is plugged into a waterproof connector

▽ **SON ET LUMIÈRE**
*An underwater light source can lend a sense of magical enchantment, elevating an already beautiful feature to new heights. The spurting fountain spouts hit the light-suffused water beneath, making it gleam like quicksilver.*

# HINTS AND TIPS

Bear in mind that thoughtlessly placed lighting may be irritating to neighbours and disturbing to wildlife – site with care.
■ For safety and comfort, site and angle lighting to avoid direct glare at eye level.
■ Choose frosted or translucent glass shades for soft, diffused, glare-free effects.
■ Use white light, like that from a halogen source, to reveal true natural colours, of foliage for example; tungsten sources give a softer, yellow-tinted light.

## GOOD IDEAS

• Use long-life, low-energy bulbs to reduce running costs and maintenance. Seek out solar-powered units to conserve energy.

• Achieve different colour tones by using lamps with tinted bulbs, and vary intensity with lamps of different wattage. Colour filters may be used, but effects lack subtlety.

• The effects of detail lighting often work best if the source is concealed.

SEE ALSO: Enhancing Patio Areas, pp.72–73; Safety First, p.199; Always Remember box: Out of your depth?, p.209

# ENHANCING PATIO AREAS

A NEWLY CONSTRUCTED PATIO is a blank sheet which, like an empty room, awaits decoration and furnishings to turn it into an inviting living space. The design principles that apply to interiors are equally applicable outdoors — thinking about the flooring, lighting, and how to arrange furniture for dining or relaxing is as essential in creating comfort and pleasure on the patio as it is in the home. And outdoors, you have the additional element of planting to consider. Plants not only play a vital role in creating shelter, shade, and privacy, but they also lend their fresh scents and heady perfumes to turn simple outdoor living into a sensory delight.

## LINKING HOME INTERIOR AND GARDEN

The key to tying in the house and garden successfully lies in paying the same detailed attention to outdoor materials, furnishings, and their spatial arrangement as you do when considering interior decor. You might choose, for example, outdoor flooring to tone with indoor carpeting, or to echo a colour theme of interior soft furnishings with those of outdoor

upholstered seating and plantings. Time spent seeking out the right textures, colours, and furnishings — and the fun you have doing it by visiting shows, gardens, and websites, for example — pays off as well in the finished effect of outdoor rooms as it does in interior ones.

Glazed doors or French windows are an obvious and psychologically inviting way to link house and garden. They allow obvious physical access, and they act as a picture frame for the outdoor composition, whether the doors are open or shut. So when planning the planting, remember to take a view from indoors too.

> ### GOOD IDEAS
>
> • Pots, containers, and lighting details, made of natural materials such wood, wicker, metalwork, or terracotta, look equally at home indoors and out. Use them as a unifying element between the two areas.
>
> • Use awnings or pergolas to lend a room-like quality outdoors and reinforce the sense of enclosure, if you wish, with screening plants, chosen and placed where their fragrance can waft indoors.

**A PERFECT FRAME** ▷
*An open doorway, framing a long-flowering composition that includes fuchsias, Japanese anemones and crocosmias, provides an irresistible invitation onto the patio and into the garden beyond, while the garden's sweet verdant scents and the sound of birds drift gently into the house.*

## COMBINING PATIO AREAS AND WATER FEATURES

The idea of enhancing an area for peaceful repose with water has long held special appeal for garden makers, whether used for the contemplative beauty of its still reflections, or the somnolent murmur of a bubbling rill or splashing fountain. Even the smallest patio may have room to add a wall-mounted spout, a bubble fountain, or a container pool. Still more ambitious effects — incorporating a raised pool, or building out over a body of water with decking, for example — can be achieved if they are well thought out at the planning stage. And what better way of appreciating plantings, or observing visiting wildlife at close quarters, than from the comfort of a recliner, with Pimms in hand?

◁ **GONE FISHING**
*An overhanging deck is the perfect site from which to observe ornamental fish or wildlife, like bathing birds and darting dragonflies.*

△ **CLASSICAL CANAL**
*A simple canal lends cool humidity for comfort on hot days, and is kept safe after dusk in the ethereal glow of submerged lighting.*

SEE ALSO: Installing Decking, pp.64–65; Moving Water in Small Spaces, pp.212–213

# COMPLEMENTING WITH PLANTING

With careful selection, patio plantings can perform a number of functions. Tall and climbing plants lend shade and shelter while enclosing the space and screening it off for privacy. Choose wisteria, jasmine, honeysuckle, and climbing roses for their sumptuous perfume, or a luxuriant grape vine for fruit and ornament. Grow smaller plants — selected for colour and scent — in open soil or in containers. Try lilies, like *Lilium regale*, nicotianas, or a scattering of night-scented stock (*Matthiola longipetala* subsp. *bicornis*) — all have scents that are delightfully pervasive in still evening air. And underfoot, use creeping thymes and chamomile to release a heady fragrance when brushed by passing feet. If you cook outdoors, consider having aromatic herbs, like rosemary, thyme, and sage, close at hand to add a stroke of culinary brilliance to barbecued food and scent the night air with fragrant smoke.

**HOME COMFORTS** ▷
*A pergola clothed with scented climbers and beautiful pots filled with aromatic plants provide sensory delights as well as shelter, shade, and a feeling of seclusion.*

△ **POCKET PLANTING**
*Planting pockets can be built into the patio at the design stage, or flags may be lifted later and the space filled with good topsoil or potting compost to provide a home for low-growing, preferably fragrant plants.*

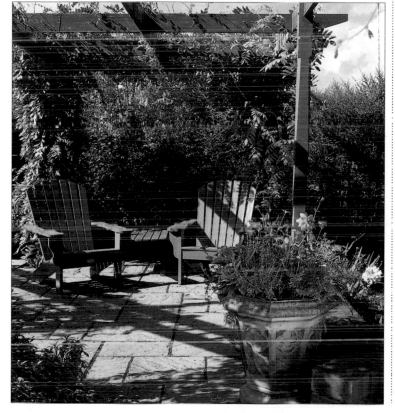

# PATIO FURNITURE

Taste, comfort, and expense aside, patio furniture must be tough enough to withstand the elements or, if upholstered, light enough to bring under cover. Timber furniture is sympathetic to a wide range of settings, ages gracefully, and lasts for years if properly maintained, but if you choose tropical hardwoods, like teak or iroko, make sure that it comes from sustainably managed sources. Metal furniture is durable, strong, and often surprisingly comfortable. Plastics are widely available and inexpensive, and although resistant to wet, they often become dingy and sometimes brittle after prolonged exposure to sunlight.

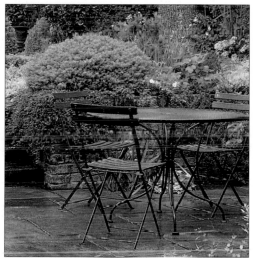

△ **FUNCTIONAL ELEGANCE**
*This lightweight furniture has a durable and weatherproof finish and folds flat for easy winter storage — the perfect combination of elegant appearance with practicality.*

# BARBECUE AREAS

Food undeniably tastes better when eaten outdoors, especially so if taste buds are primed by the delicious odours that arise from food cooked on a barbecue.

Whether you choose an in built or a portable barbecue, plan the cooking area with easy access to the kitchen indoors — impromptu meals are infinitely more enjoyable if you don't have to ferry ingredients down the garden. Give the chef plenty of elbow room and a weather resistant, easy-clean work surface. Site with shelter from the prevailing winds so that diners are not engulfed in smoke.

## ALWAYS REMEMBER

### SAFE AND HAPPY COOKING!

Be sure to place the barbecue far enough away from timber fences, trellises, and pergolas to avoid damage and risk of fire. Keep a fire blanket or extinguisher on hand. Be considerate of neighbours by siting, if possible, to avoid smoke drift into nearby gardens (or invite them to share the feast).

**A MOVABLE FEAST** ▷
*Portable barbecues are ideal for small spaces, especially if unreliable summers do not justify a built-in one, and siting to account for wind direction is almost infinitely adjustable.*

**SEE ALSO:** Lighting in the Garden, pp.70–71; Herbs in the Garden and their Uses, pp.224–233

# LAWNS AND GROUND COVER

## A LIVING CARPET

MANY GARDENS HAVE at least one area, large or small, that is ideal for carpeting with low-growing plants to create a gentle, pleasing, and lasting surface for walking, sitting, or playing on. Grass is the obvious choice for most gardeners, but spreading plants, such as chamomile or thyme, offer an attractive alternative on a small scale. Grass lawns can vary from an exquisitely tended showpiece to a hard-wearing play area for children and may be planted with bulbs or wild flowers to provide fragrance and colour. Where an area is unlikely to be walked upon, the choice widens to include ground-cover plants such as prostrate conifers, heathers, or flowering shrubs and perennials.

## WHY A LAWN?

Make absolutely sure that a grass lawn is the right option before embarking on seeding or turfing. If you have unlimited enthusiasm and time to spend in the garden, creating a beautifully manicured lawn fit for a bowling green may be a challenge you will relish. If, on the other hand, you would prefer to keep the maintenance to a minimum, first think hard about the area you intend to surface:

■ Is it really suitable for grass? If there is not much sunlight, for example, which is essential if grass is to thrive, it might be better for you to choose either a hard surface, such as gravel or paving, or one or more of the ground-cover plants that grow well in shade.

■ How easy will the lawn be to mow and maintain once established? If the area to be covered is on a steep slope, creeping plants may be far easier to look after.

◁ **ATTRACTIVE INFORMALITY**
*The sweeping curves of this informal grass lawn enhance the bold use of flowers and foliage in the adjoining borders. The curves are continued in the winding gravel path beyond, combining a delightful visual effect with hardwearing practicality.*

### TELL ME WHY

**WHY IS GRASS SO POPULAR IN GARDENS?**

Grass has many advantages: it grows close to the ground and has tough, narrow leaves that are stimulated by regular cutting, making it resilient to a range of conditions and uses. It is also relatively cheap to create a lawn with turf or seed, and increasingly easy to maintain an established lawn with the help of modern lawnmowers and other specialist equipment.

△ **LARGE LAWN**
*For a large area, grass often proves the cheapest option, and it can be easier to maintain than a network of paths and flower borders.*

**SMALL LAWN** ▷
*Where space is restricted, a formal grass lawn, edged with bricks and surrounded by a profusion of flowers and foliage, looks stunning.*

SEE ALSO: Patios and Paths, pp.56–73; Planning a Lawn, pp.76–77; Alternative Lawns, pp.88–89; Using Ground Cover in Shady Areas, p.131

# CHOOSING THE RIGHT SURFACE

Think about the activities for which the area will be used – games, relaxing, entertaining, for example – and also assess the position and conditions of the site.

■ Grass needs sunlight and good drainage; some ground cover plants, however, are tolerant of shady and damp conditions.

■ There are several types of grass, from coarse "family lawn" mixtures, ideal for play areas, to high-quality fine grasses suited to formal, less-used lawns.

■ If you live in a warm climate, you will need a grass that is tolerant of drought and long periods of hot sunshine.

### WEAR AND TEAR ▷
*Children playing, especially on a small area like this one, make great demands on the grass, so choose coarse, creeping grasses that are able to withstand constant use. They are available as both turf and seed mixtures.*

**FINE GRASS**　　　　**COARSE GRASS**

**WHAT WILL THRIVE?**
*High quality fine grasses (see above) need good growing conditions, regular and careful maintenance, and little use. Coarse grasses (see above right) are less fussy in their requirements and extremely hardwearing. Ground-cover plants that tolerate shade such as dead nettle, (see right) need little attention once established.*

**SHADE-LOVING PLANTS**

# LAWNS WITH ADDED INTEREST

Grass lawns can occasionally be a little dull visually, but you can provide more interest by planting spring bulbs in the grass to cheer up the garden early in the season. Wild flowers, available as seed mixtures, can also add summer colour to the grassed area and attract beneficial insects such as butterflies and bees, but these plants can be invasive and should be treated with care. Small areas can also be brought to life with low-growing herbs such as chamomile, creeping thymes, and mints, which produce delightful scents when they are trodden on.

▽ **NATURALISTIC WILDFLOWER MEADOW**
*If you have the right setting – such as a larger, more rural garden with an area that is not in constant use – creating a thoroughly informal meadow full of colourful wild flowers can be a joy. Remember to use plants and grasses that are native to your area and therefore more likely to put on a good show.*

# GROUND COVER

Any plant with a low, quickly spreading habit can be used to cover patches of ground, suppressing the growth of weeds, and usually requiring little maintenance. Most will withstand the occasional tread, but are not as likely as grass to survive if they are constantly being walked over. They are best for small, less-used areas, and should be matched carefully to the conditions of the site. Combining ground-cover plants creates even more interest.

### WOODLAND EFFECT ▷
*Fill the shady area beneath the canopy of a tree with a combination of low-growing plants that will thrive there and create the impression of a natural woodland floor.*

△ **CARPET OF PACHYSANDRA**
*This plant has all the qualities of the perfect ground-cover alternative to grass: it is low-growing, evergreen, tidy, and easy to look after all year round.*

**SEE ALSO:** Choosing Seed Mixtures, p.77; Alternative Lawns, pp.88–89; Daffodils, p.137; Planting and Cultivating Herbs, pp.228–231

# PLANNING A LAWN

YOU MAY THINK that it is simply a matter of buying some seed or turf and getting on with the job as quickly as possible, but your lawn will benefit greatly from careful planning before you embark on creating it. Only after considering all the relevant factors and options should you start to make important decisions about site, shape,

paths, edges, type of grass, and whether to use seed or turf. Remember also that in warm climates, plugs and sprigs will establish better than either seed or turf. A little thought and effort put in at this planning stage will help to avoid problems occurring later, when they may turn out to be very difficult and expensive to solve.

## SITING AND SHAPING

There may not be any choice about where you put your lawn, especially if your garden is quite small, but it will pay you to analyse the site anyway. Is it sunny or shady? What is the soil like? Is the area well-drained or prone to retain moisture to any degree? If there is not likely to be enough sunlight or adequate drainage, consider whether there is a better site for the lawn than the one you first chose.

When it comes to shape, squares and rectangles may be practical, but visually unstimulating. Resist the temptation, however, to make the shape of the lawn too fussy, as this may cause you problems when mowing and trying to keep the edges tidy. Ovals and circles can look very

attractive in some settings. Narrow strips are better avoided, as they can quickly start to look messy.

When you have laid the lawn, you may wish to create "island" beds for shrubs and flowers, or plant specimen trees in the lawn. It is a good idea to take such features into consideration early in the planning stages so that you can make sure the siting and conditions will be suitable.

**NARROW LAWN** ▷
*For plant enthusiasts, borders may take priority, greatly reducing the lawn area. This size and shape of lawn will need a lot of attention to look good.*

△ **CHANGING ASPECT**
*With an interesting shape of lawn, you can view the garden from different angles by moving the seat.*

**GENTLE CURVES** ▷
*For easier mowing and edging, keep the shape of the lawn simple, and the curves wide and sweeping.*

**SEE ALSO:** Plugs and Sprigs, p.81; Using Ground Cover in Shady Areas, p.131; Marking out a Bed, p.145

## A Variety of Lawn Shapes

*The shape of your lawn should blend in with the style and formality of the rest of the garden, or at least the area immediately surrounding it. In general, straight edges complement formal gardens and curves create a more relaxed effect. Tight curves and complicated angular shapes will require more effort to keep tidy.*

### △ WIDE CURVES
*Choose this type of shape if you are looking for informality, perhaps surrounding it with tumbling plants.*

### △ CLASSICAL ELEGANCE
*The right angles in this shape create an instant formality, but will need regular attention to keep the edges crisp.*

### ∧ A DIVIDED LAWN
*A large area of grass, formal or informal, can be bisected by a path to give a greater degree of visual interest.*

### △ ISLAND BEDS
*An island bed is an ideal way of breaking up a large lawn, but should reflect the overall style of the area.*

# SEED OR TURF?

Both methods of creating a general-purpose lawn have their advantages (*see below*), but for a specialist lawn requiring a particular species of grass, seed will probably be the only choice. Only you can make the final decision, because it depends on a large number of factors.

■ Are you fit and able to transport and lay turf, bearing in mind that it must be laid as soon as it is delivered or collected?

■ Do you have friends or family members who can help you lay turf? If not, seed may be a better option.

■ Is the area to be grassed large or small? If small, turf may be more suitable.

## SEED

The advantages of using seed are:

■ It is relatively economical.

■ It requires no heavy, physical work.

■ There is a choice of seed mixtures.

■ It is easy to transport.

■ It can be stored without harm.

■ You can re-sow bare patches with the same seed mixture.

### EASY SOWING ▷
*Scattering seed by hand can result in unevenness, so try using a pot that has several small holes in the base. When the pot is shaken, the seed is distributed evenly.*

---

## TELL ME WHEN

### WHEN SHOULD I LAY OR SOW THE LAWN?

If you have opted for turf, it can be laid at any time except when the weather is very hot and dry, very cold, or if the ground is frozen. Autumn or early spring are preferable because the lawn will not be subject to much use before it has had a chance to establish as it might be in summer, when it is also difficult to keep it moist. For seed, the best times to sow are mid-spring or early autumn, when the soil is moist but not wet. Autumn is often the better option, because the new lawn will be advanced enough in the following summer to take light use; if sown in spring, the new lawn will need watering in dry weather and may not be ready before autumn.

---

## CHOOSING SEED MIXTURES

Many seed mixtures are available; avoid unspecified ones. For quality lawns, you will need a fine-leaved mixture with fescues and bents, which can be very closely mown. Rye grasses are coarser and resilient, but some also have attractive, fine leaves. Single species, suited to warm climates, include bents (*Agrostis*), carpet grass (*Axonopus*), and red fescue (*Festuca rubra*). Special mixes for light shade include meadow species that should not be closely cut.

### ▽ BUYING TURF
*Before you part with any money, inspect the turf closely for quality. Check that the grass is uniform in habit and has a good system of roots and leaves, that there are no bare or brown patches, and that all the pieces of turf are of similar quality. Buy more than enough to cover the whole lawn, so that all the turf will be from the same batch.*

The major disadvantage of seed is that it looks sparse for a time and cannot be used in the first season. Furthermore, diseases and weeds lurking in the soil, unless rigorously prepared, may stunt or choke the grass seedlings.

## TURF

Turf can be inexpensive, but be sure to inspect it before buying, in order to be satisfied that it is cultivated, seeded turf of good quality rather than meadow turf. Although it is cheap, meadow turf may include a mix of coarse grasses and weeds that have the potential to cause many problems later on.

The advantages of using turf are:

■ It gives fast results – an instant lawn that can soon be used.

■ The edges are well-defined.

■ No weeding is necessary while the lawn establishes.

■ It can be laid at almost any time of year;

■ You can fill in any bare patches with pieces of new turf.

---

**SEE ALSO:** Creating a Lawn, pp.78–79; Laying Turf, p.80; Repairing Damage, p.86

# CREATING A LAWN

ONCE YOU HAVE decided exactly where and what shape your lawn should be, your next task is to level and prepare the ground thoroughly to remove any lumps, stones, or weeds. This will give the grass a good chance of establishing successfully without developing any bare or weedy patches. You may need to install a drain if the area is likely to become waterlogged. Then you are ready to sow the lawn seed or begin laying the turf. If you live in a warm climate, however, alternative methods of planting the grass, such as plugs and sprigs, may give far better results than either seed or turf. Your final task will be to finish off the edges of the lawn neatly.

## PREPARING THE SOIL

Dig over the soil, removing all perennial weeds, and level if necessary (*see right*). Firm and rake the soil to clear it of unwanted matter such as leaves and large stones. The area may also require a drain (*see opposite*) or the addition of organic matter to improve the soil quality.

For seed, leave the prepared ground alone for two to three weeks; in this time any annual weed seeds that are still in the soil will have germinated, and you can then remove them by hoeing or spraying.

### △ FIRMING THE SOIL
*If the area for your lawn is already fairly level, begin preparation by firming the ground. This can be achieved by treading the soil carefully and evenly in a methodical manner over the whole area to be sown or turfed. Alternatively, you can use the back of a rake to firm down an area of soil. Repeat this process until the entire site has been consistently and well firmed.*

### ◁ RAKING
*Rake the soil very finely, removing any debris or weeds. For seed sowing, leave the area until annual weeds have appeared, then apply a weedkiller or hoe them off.*

## LEVELLING THE GROUND

How level the ground needs to be depends on the type of lawn you are creating. If it is to be rough grass or a meadow area, exact levelling is not critical, but if you are looking for a more formal lawn or an area for ball games, you will have to be much more precise. Rough levelling by eye can be achieved by raking soil from mounds into hollows and then firming. More accurate levelling will require the use of marked pegs, a wooden plank, a spirit level, and a hammer. Insert the pegs to the desired level (*see below*) and then rake the soil to the marks on the pegs. This method can also be used to create smooth slopes with a gentle gradient (*see right*).

### △ USING LEVELLING TOOLS
*Mark some pegs 5cm (2in) from the top. With a hammer, knock in a peg so that the mark sits at the desired ground level. Insert the rest so that the tops are level, using a plank and spirit level.*

### CREATING A LEVEL BASE

**1 MARKER PEGS**
*Insert a row of pegs along the edge of the site. The marks on the pegs should sit at the desired final level of the ground.*

**2 CHECKING THE LEVEL**
*Add a second row of pegs about 1m (3ft) from the first. Using levelling tools, adjust until the tops are level.*

**3 MOVING THE SOIL**
*Repeat to create a grid of pegs. Rake the soil to the level of the marks, filling in any hollows with topsoil. Remove the pegs.*

### ▽ MAKING A SLOPE
*If you want to create a gentle slope, maybe leading away from a paved area, mark the pegs (see right) at increasing distances from the top, using standard increments. Knock the pegs into the soil at constant intervals across the area, and check with a plank and spirit level (see below) that the tops are level. Rake the soil to the marks to provide a gradient for the area to be grassed.*

PEGS

### △ LEVELLING METHOD
*Knock in the pegs in a grid. Then use the plank and spirit level in every direction to make sure they align at the top, adjusting the pegs as necessary.*

SEE ALSO: Seed or Turf?, p.77; Plugs and Sprigs, p.81; Improving Soil Types, p.142

# SOWING GRASS SEED

Having prepared the ground thoroughly, you are ready to sow. Calculate how much seed is needed, depending on the mixture:

- For **fine-leaved grasses**, use 25–30g (1–1⅛oz) per sq m (sq yd).
- For **coarser grasses**, use 35–40g (1⅜–1⅖oz) per sq m (sq yd).
- For **single species**, check the rate for the particular species you have selected when buying – rates vary from about 2g (⅛oz) per sq m (sq yd) for centipede grass (*Eremochloa ophiuroides*) to about 30g (1⅛oz) for perennial rye grass (*Lolium perenne*).

Weigh out the correct amount of seed for the entire lawn, and sow evenly using either a hand-held pot or a purpose-built spreader. Rake the soil lightly to cover the seed. Keep the soil moist, and you should witness the first signs of growth in one or two weeks. The lawn will need its first mow in spring when the grass is about 5cm (2in) tall; set the mower blades high.

## GOOD IDEAS

- Choose a dry, still day for sowing so that the seed does not blow away.
- Do not sow seed too thickly – there is no advantage to be gained.
- Divide the area into sections, and measure and sow the seed for each section; this will help you to sow evenly.
- Keep birds off the seed once sown. To do this, use seed treated with a repellent, cover the area with fine chicken wire, suspend strips of foil from sticks or a line over the soil, or attract them to another part of the garden with food.

## SEEDING A LAWN

△ **USING MARKERS**
*When sowing grass seed over a small area, you can mark out measured squares with pots or sticks and scatter the correct quantity of seed evenly between them. Repeat the process until the whole area has been seeded consistently.*

△ **MAKING A GRID**
*For larger areas, it is better to mark out a grid system before sowing, using canes to divide up the site into many equal squares. Weigh out each portion of seed, scattering half of it up-and-down and the other half side-to-side.*

△ **CREATING A CURVE**
*Attach a length of twine to two sticks; the length depends on the size of the desired curve. Insert one stick in the ground and use the other to mark the curved line.*

◁ **USING A SPREADER**
*To ensure that you get even distribution, you can use a purpose-made seed spreader. Lay down a plastic sheet where you want the edge to be. Sow half the seed in one direction and the other half at right angles to the first*

◁ **FINAL TOUCHES**
*Once you have finished sowing, lightly rake over the surface of the soil across the whole area to cover the seed. In the following days and weeks, if the weather is dry, water the site regularly to encourage germination of the grass seed.*

# MAKING A DRAIN

Depending on the site of your lawn, it may be a good idea to install a soakaway – a simple drain – at the lowest point, before laying turf or seeding. This will counteract any potential problems caused by a build-up of moisture in wet periods. Make sure that the soakaway is sited well away from any house walls in order to prevent damp entering the building. If drainage is a real problem, grow plants better suited to moist conditions or consider creating a bog garden.

Slope away from house

Trench

Topsoil

Drain at lowest level

Hardcore

Gravel

Pipe (optional)

◁ **LAYING A SIMPLE DRAIN OR SOAKAWAY**
*Dig a trench and fill the base with rubble and course gravel so that excess water can drain away. Cover this with topsoil to the level of the rest of the prepared area. The pipe or perforated tube is an optional feature, and it is only necessary if drainage is a serious problem.*

SEE ALSO: Seed or Turf?, p.77; Mowing, p.82; Bog Gardens, pp.204–205; The Moisture Lovers, pp.218–219

# LAYING TURF

The best aspect of using turf rather than seed is that it gives an instantly pleasing effect. You must resist the temptation to walk on it straightaway, however, as the grass roots must be given time to penetrate the soil and get a good foundation before the lawn is used. You must also keep the turves moist to stop them turning brown and curling up at the edges. Although you can lay turves at any time, it is advisable to avoid rainy or frosty conditions, as well as hot, dry spells during which it will be hard to keep the new grass sufficiently watered.

Be sure to plan thoroughly before you start. Calculate how many turves will be needed, allowing extra for wastage, and make sure you have time to prepare and level the soil thoroughly before the turf is delivered. Also ensure that you have allowed enough time to lay it. If you cannot lay the turves as soon as they arrive, for example if it is raining or if there is a ground frost, you can store them (see right) for up to three days; if kept any longer, they may start to dry out and turn yellow.

If there are any turves left over when you have completed the lawn, stack them upside-down in a little-used place. After a while, they will break down into a fine soil that can be used for lawn top-dressing.

△ **HOW TO KEEP TURF FRESH**
*If you cannot use the turves as soon as they arrive, lay them out flat, but not touching or overlapping, on some plastic sheeting or soil, and water them well every day.*

## TURFING A LAWN

**1 MAKING A START**
*Begin by laying the first row of turves using a straight edge, such as a path or plank, as a guide, making sure that each new piece of turf lies flush against the next one.*

**2 USING A PLANK**
*Once the first row is complete, place a plank on top of it and kneel on the plank. Lay the second row of turves, remembering to stagger the joints against those of the previous row. Repeat this process until you have covered the entire area. Try not to walk on the bare soil at any time.*

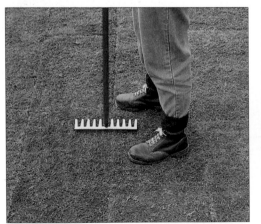

**3 SETTLING IN**
*With the back of a rake, firm down the turf to get rid of any air pockets and to create good contact between the grass roots and the soil. Alternatively, use a light roller.*

**4 FINISHING OFF**
*First apply a light top-dressing of sieved, sandy loam, and brush it into any gaps between the turves. Soak the lawn, and continue to keep it moist if the weather is dry.*

## GOOD IDEAS

• Begin to lay the turf at the part of the lawn that is closest to where the turves are being stored.

• Use a plank to spread your weight as you work, to avoid compacting the turf.

• If you have any small pieces of turf, lay them in the middle of the lawn rather than at the edges, where they may be prone to drying out and shrinking.

• In each new row of turves, stagger the joints with those in the previous row.

• Extend the turf beyond the final desired area and trim it afterwards.

• When making the first cut in late spring, set the mower to its maximum height.

**SEE ALSO:** Seed or Turf?, p.77; Preparing the Soil, p.78; Levelling the Ground, p.78; Mowing, p.82

# PLUGS AND SPRIGS

In warm, dry climates it can be difficult to establish a traditional lawn. In these areas, it is best to use warm-season, spreading grasses that are capable of tolerating extreme conditions, or cool-season bent grass. In order to prevent the lawn having a patchy appearance, use just one type of grass for the whole area.

Small pieces of these plants, known as plugs and sprigs, are used to get the lawn established. The best time to do this is spring or early summer. Plugs are small pieces or tufts of rhizomatous grass, and these should be planted in individual holes (*see right*). New shoots will grow outwards from the joints and quickly mesh together. Sprigs are rooting stems

or rhizomes that should be strewn evenly over the soil surface (*see right*), covered with a thin layer of soil, and then watered in well. With both of these methods, the grasses should have rooted after a couple of months and grown together to produce a smooth, even lawn.

### ALWAYS REMEMBER

Lawns created from plugs or sprigs of tough, drought-tolerant grass species will never exactly resemble their cool-climate counterparts, but they are resilient, practical, and easy to maintain. As with all lawns, the soil must be well prepared in advance, because plugs and sprigs are living plant material that cannot be stored for long.

△ **SCATTERING SPRIGS**
*Distribute the sprigs over the surface of the soil and then cover them with top-dressing of fine soil. Water well.*

△ **PLANTING PLUGS**
*Space the plugs evenly over the area, 15–30cm (6–12in) apart. Apply a top-dressing of soil and keep well watered.*

# FINISHING THE EDGES

Once the main task of creating the lawn has been completed, it is time to turn your attention to the edges. Far from being an afterthought, the way you edge your lawn is one of the most important aspects from both a practical and an aesthetic point of view. Even if the grass in the main part is not absolutely perfect, well-kept edges give a fine impression of neatness and good care. Whether you choose hard or soft edging, remember that ease of mowing is a vital consideration. Mowing strips or raised edging with holding strips (*see below*) and hard edging (*see right*) reduce the need to trim the edges with shears or a lawn edger.

△ **CURVED EDGE**
*After turfing, mark out a curve using string attached to a peg and a funnel of fine, dry sand. Then trim off the excess turf.*

**STRAIGHT EDGE** ▷
*Use a taut string, a plank, and a lawn edger to create a true, straight edge.*

△ **SOFT EDGING**
*Plants in the border will need staking and the lawn edges regular trimming if you prefer this soft look.*

△ **HARD EDGING**
*Narrow stone pavers and terracotta edging tiles make a practical and attractive finish to the lawn.*

**RAISED EDGING** ▷
*The lawn may be raised above the level of the path and attractively edged with wood (see right) or plastic holding strips (see far right).*

**MOWING STRIP** ▷
*Separate the grass from the borders (see right) with a row of bricks on a layer of mortar (far right) to slightly below the level of the lawn for ease of mowing.*

**BRICK APRON** ▷
*To avoid the mowing problems that would arise if a step (or other raised feature) immediately adjoined the lawn, try surrounding it with an area of brick paving. This brick apron allows trouble-free mowing as well as providing a hardwearing surface just below the step.*

**SEE ALSO:** Edging Materials, p.57; Making Steps, pp.68–69; Lawncare, pp.82–85

# LAWNCARE

YOUR LAWN WILL only look good and stand up to wear if you spend a little time caring for it properly. Mowing and keeping the edges neat are the most obvious jobs to many people, but there are a few other important seasonal tasks. In the main growing season, spring and summer, the grass will need feeding and watering in hot, dry spells, as well as mowing; in autumn, it will benefit from scarifying, aerating, top-dressing, and raking or sweeping up dead leaves that have fallen onto it. If these are left on the grass, they will shade it and slow its growth, and maybe even encourage disease. Carrying out these tasks will help prevent many common problems.

## MOWING

The act of mowing should stimulate the grass to produce more shoots and therefore a denser cover, inhibiting weeds. To achieve this, you should mow little and often (*see below*). For a formal look, work to a pattern (*see right*), but remember to vary the direction of the pattern each time so that ridges do not build up. If possible, always use a grass box to prevent a build-up of clippings at soil level.

◁ **IRREGULAR SHAPE**
*For an asymmetrical lawn, first mow around the edges and then work across in parallel lines.*

**REGULAR SHAPE** ▷
*Start by mowing down the edges of opposite sides and then work across the lawn at right angles to them.*

## WHEN TO MOW

Start in early spring and set the cutting height on your mower to the maximum. During the summer, you can reduce the height a little. In autumn, revert to the maximum cutting height, and stop mowing altogether in late autumn. Overcutting or "scalping" the lawn will result in unsightly bald patches.

■ For high-quality lawns, mow once or twice a week in spring and autumn to 1cm (½in) height; in summer, mow up to three times a week to a minimum of 8mm (⅜in) in early summer.

■ For utility lawns, mow once a week from spring to autumn, to about 2.5cm (1in) in spring and autumn, and to a minimum of 1.5cm (⅝in) in summer.

**LAWNS WITH BULBS** ▷
*If you have planted some spring-flowering bulbs in your lawn, you can still cut the grass until late autumn, but do not start mowing again until at least 6 weeks after flowering has finished. This will enable the bulbs to build up stores of food for the following year's flowers.*

## CHOOSING A MOWER

There is a huge array of lawnmowers to choose from – so which is best for you? For small lawns, a manual cylinder mower may be sufficient; it is cheap, quiet, and needs no cables. It will, however, require some effort on your part. If you have a larger area, or prefer to expend less energy, you will need a mower powered by either electricity or petrol. Electricity is cleaner and more efficient than petrol, but not suitable for powerful engines.

Powered mowers come in various types:

■ **Cylinder mowers** give the finest cut, and produce good stripes, but can tear the grass if incorrectly adjusted, and they are quite heavy to manoeuvre.

■ **Rotary mowers** are easier to handle, especially in longer grass, but will not produce stripes.

■ **Hover mowers** are the lightest and easiest to use, and they are ideal for gentle slopes.

For all types, check that the height of cut is adjustable, and choose a model with a grass-collecting box, if possible.

▽ **POWERED, CYLINDER MOWER**
*This is probably the best choice if you have a high-quality lawn. It will provide a fine, close-cut finish with distinct stripes. The blades are set along a cylinder that rotates forward and cuts against a fixed blade. The blade cylinder is driven by a rear roller – the heavier the roller, the more pronounced the stripe will be. Petrol-driven cylinder mowers often have broader cutting widths than electric ones, but this makes them harder to manoeuvre. Ride-on or tractor-hauled petrol models are ideal for extensive lawns.*

**CYLINDER BLADES**

**SEE ALSO:** Lawncare, pp.84–85; Planting Bulbs in Grass, p.89

# TRIMMING EDGES

Keeping the edges of your lawn neat and tidy will greatly enhance the appearance of the whole garden. During the growing season, clip the edges regularly with shears (*see below*), using an angled cut that is hard against the turf edge, or with a nylon-line trimmer (*see below, right*). Collect the clippings so that they cannot root in adjoining beds or paths. Also make sure that border plants do not spill over onto the lawn, causing areas to brown and die. If you trim regularly in this way, you will only need to re-cut the edges once a year in early spring to retain the lawn's shape and create definition. This task involves removing a small strip of turf manually with a half-moon edger (*see below*) or with a power edger, which can be hired. Do not use a spade, because the concave blade will produce a scalloped effect.

△ **TRIMMING AN EDGE**
*After mowing, tidy edges with long-handled edging shears or a nylon-line trimmer.*

△ **RE-CUTTING AN EDGE**
*Use a sharp half-moon edger and a plank to achieve a well-defined, straight edge.*

◁ **NYLON-LINE TRIMMER**
*Electric trimmers have a flexible nylon cutting line, which rotates at high speed. Some have an adjustable head that may be turned into a vertical position for trimming edges. They are ideal for a large lawn.*

△ **CUTTING GUIDE**
*This keeps the line off the ground for an even trim.*

▽ **ELECTRIC HOVER MOWER**
*Hover mowers ride on a cushion of air and have replaceable plastic blades that cut the grass with a scythe-like motion as they rotate horizontally. They are ideal for cutting grass on small lawns and difficult places, such as next to paths and beneath overhanging plants. They can be easily moved over both flat surfaces and gentle gradients, but may flip over and cut out if used on steep slopes. Most models do not have boxes to collect the grass, so you will have to rake up the clippings afterwards. They will not cut particularly close, but are good for long or uneven grass.*

**PLASTIC BLADE**

▽ **PETROL-DRIVEN ROTARY MOWER**
*For very large areas of lawn, including rough and long grass, this is a good option because the petrol motor provides more power than electricity. The mower rides on wheels and employs a replaceable metal blade that rotates horizontally, meaning that it is unlikely to "scalp" uneven areas, but equally it cannot cut very low. Most rotary mowers do not have rollers, but are fitted with large grass collectors that do not require frequent emptying. Petrol mowers have no cables to worry about, but are more expensive than electric ones to buy and maintain.*

**METAL BLADE**

**SEE ALSO:** Finishing the Edges, p.81

# WATERING A LAWN

New lawns should be kept moist by regular watering until they are well established. Thereafter, the grass will look after itself quite well, except during prolonged dry spells of weather when growth slows down and the turf turns brown. It is therefore necessary to water the lawn thoroughly in dry periods. As soon as the grass fails to spring back up after being walked on, it is time to water.

To avoid wasteful evaporation, the best times to water are either early morning or evening. Make sure you give the lawn enough water (*see right*); if the soil is heavy, do not allow pools to form on the surface because this inhibits the intake of oxygen and minerals by the roots. To check if you

have watered sufficiently, dig a small hole to the required depth, and see whether the soil is damp all the way down. Electric moisture meters are also available.

For small areas, you can use a watering can, but for larger lawns you will probably need either a hose or a sprinkler. Before using either of the latter, check that there are no restrictions in force preventing their use in your area. Extensive grassed areas that are likely to need repeated watering will benefit from the installation of a built-in, pop-up, underground sprinkler system, but these are expensive. When the water supply is turned on, the pressure lifts the sprinkler heads above the surface and water is released.

△ **LACK OF WATER**
*Shallow watering, where the soil is only moistened to a few centimetres below the surface, as shown in the dark-coloured soil above, may make the lawn vulnerable to drought by encouraging the grass roots to remain near the surface of the soil.*

△ **SUFFICIENT WATER**
*After watering, remember to check that the soil has been moistened to a depth of about 10–15cm (4–6in), as shown above. This will encourage the roots to grow strongly and will help them to find water more easily during parched spells.*

# FEEDING A LAWN

To avoid problems of disease, patchiness, moss, and weeds, supply your lawn regularly with a special lawn feed or fertilizer to stimulate dense, healthy, bright green growth. For most lawns, two applications a year are sufficient: one in late spring or early summer and the other in late summer or early autumn.

Most lawn fertilizers come in granular or powder form. Only small amounts are needed for lawns on heavy, clay soils that are rich in nutrients; greater quantities will be required for those on light, sandy soils. Spread the feed evenly either by hand for small areas or with the use of a spreader for large areas (*see right*).

SPREADER FOR LARGE AREAS

◁ **APPLYING LAWN FEED WITH A SPREADER**
*The spreader's hopper releases feed evenly. Apply half one way, and then the other half at right angles.*

△ **SCORCH**
*This area of scorch, where the grass has died off, has been caused by an over-lapping, double application of lawn feed. Using the application methods shown on the left and below should help to eliminate this.*

△ **FEEDING BY HAND**
*When feeding a small area, divide the lawn into equal-sized squares and measure the fertilizer into portions. Scatter it evenly one way and then the other, using a pot.*

## TELL ME WHY

### WHY ARE LAWN FEEDS BENEFICIAL?

Lawns flourish when they have access to high levels of the essential nutrients that grass requires for good growth – nitrogen, phosphorus, potassium, and iron. Lawn feeds are specially formulated to provide these nutrients. The formulations vary at different times of year: in spring, more nitrogen is included to replace what has been lost over the winter; in autumn, there is more potassium to toughen the grass for winter. Some lawn feeds are also combined with chemicals to control weeds.

SEE ALSO: Repairing Damage, p.86; Watering Equipment, p.280

# AUTUMN MAINTENANCE

After summer, when the lawn has been well used and the soil has become compacted, it is beneficial to let air into the lawn by creating holes and channels. This alleviates compaction, which chokes the grass, and it encourages deep roots for healthy growth. Top-dressing helps further by improving drainage. These two tasks are best carried out in early autumn after vigorous scarifying to remove excess thatch (*see below*). Together, they give the lawn an excellent chance of coming through strongly in the following spring.

There are several ways of aerating a lawn (*see right*). The simplest is spiking with a garden fork. You can also remove cores of soil with a hollow-tining tool or machine, or use a rotary aerator. After aerating, the lawn will benefit from top-dressing (*see below, right*) to fill the holes left by aerating, to keep the passages open, and to level small hollows in the lawn.

**HOLLOW-TINING ▷**
*In order to improve surface drainage, use a specially designed tool to remove cores of grass and soil up to 2cm (¾in) wide. Work methodically over the area so that you do not step on the cores. Brush the cores away and compost them.*

**SPIKING ▷**
*If you have only a small area of grass to aerate, you can do it with an ordinary garden fork. Insert the fork into the ground, at 15cm (6in) intervals across the lawn, and then rock it back and forth gently to allow more air to enter the soil.*

△ **SLITTING**
*For large lawns, it may be a good idea to hire a rotary aerator, which will create deep slits in the turf.*

Channel created by fork tine
Fill channel with top dressing to improve drainage

◁ **ADVANTAGES OF AERATION**
*The channels created by aeration allow moisture, air, and fertilizer to reach the roots of the grass more easily, discouraging moss. The soil next to each channel expands slightly, reducing the chance of compaction. This, in turn, creates better drainage, especially if the channels are filled with top-dressing.*

---

## GOOD IDEAS

• Before aerating, mow the lawn to its normal summer height. After aerating, apply a low-nitrogen autumn feed.

• Aerate when the soil is moist; it is easier and the lawn will be less vulnerable to drought.

• Apply top-dressing on a dry day so that it does not get washed away.

• Use top-dressing at a rate of about 3kg (7lb) per sq m (sq yd).

## TOP-DRESSING LAWNS

**TOP-DRESSING MIX ▽**
*You can create your own top-dressing by mixing together 6 parts of medium-fine sand (top), 3 parts of garden loam (below right), and 1 part of either peat or peat substitute (below left) or leafmould. Pass the mixture through a 5mm (¼in) sieve to remove any stones.*

◁ **APPLYING A TOP-DRESSING**
*For small areas, you can use a shovel or spade to apply the top-dressing; for larger areas, however, you may prefer to use a mechanical spreader. Apply evenly over the lawn, then use a brush to work it into the grass.*

---

# SCARIFYING

This is another job for early autumn. Scarifying serves to remove thatch (*see below, right*) and dead moss, and it lets air enter the surface of the lawn, thus allowing the grass to breathe. The lawn will look worse after you have finished than it did before, but you will reap the benefits in the following spring when plenty of new, healthy shoots appear.

Scarifying is best undertaken when the soil is just moist. It is advisable to kill off any moss before you start, or it may be spread to other parts. For small areas, you can use a rake to scarify the grass.

An ordinary wire or spring-tined rake will be effective, but a sharp-toothed scarifying rake is specially suited to the job. With large areas, you may find it easier to use a mechanical or powered scarifier. Work the machine back and forth across the lawn, just like using a lawnmower.

**THATCH ▷**
*By autumn, there may be a build-up of dead material, known as thatch, in the lawn. If left, this will choke the grass and result in brown or bare patches.*

◁ **USING A SPRING-TINED RAKE**
*Pull the rake vigorously over the lawn, making sure that the tines are pushed well down into the surface.*

◁ **SCARIFYING RAKE**
*This rake has rigid, metal tines that are designed to cut deeply into the thatch and even the turf itself.*

**SEE ALSO:** Mowing, p.82; Repairing Damage, p.86; Hollows and Humps, p.87; Rakes, p.279

# DEALING WITH PROBLEMS

UNLESS YOU ARE very lucky, your lawn will incur a few problems from time to time. These can include damage caused by wear and tear, the appearance of hollows or humps, moss, weeds, and even some pests and diseases. Most are fairly minor and sometimes you may even choose to tolerate them. Repairing damage is fairly easy to do, as is rectifying a hollow or hump. For moss, weeds, pests, and diseases, always consider remedying the cause of the problem or employing organic methods of control before resorting to chemicals. Some diseases can be eradicated by improving drainage, for example. Early treatment of problems is strongly recommended.

## REPAIRING DAMAGE

Uneven wear can cause parts of the lawn to become damaged and unsightly. This is easily rectified by removing the affected piece and then re-turfing or re-seeding. The best time to do this is in mid-spring or mid-autumn. It is essential to use the same type of seed or turf as was used originally for the rest of the lawn; if you do not know the turf or seed type used, swap a piece of turf from a little-used part of the garden with the damaged patch. If the lawn repeatedly becomes damaged, you could replace it with a more durable surface such as paving or gravel.

To repair a damaged edge, remove the affected piece and fill in the gap with new turf or with soil for re-seeding (*see right*). Alternatively, cut out a section containing the damaged edge, and simply turn it so that the damaged edge now butts up to the lawn. Firm it into place, then add some sandy loam to bring the damaged edge up to the level of the rest of the lawn. Sow grass seed over the loam, and water in. To repair a patch, remove the affected turf, fork over the soil, fertilize it, and then re-turf or re-seed as necessary (*see below*).

### REPAIRING A DAMAGED EDGE

**1 REMOVING A SECTION**
*Cut a square of turf including the damaged area. Undercut the turf with a spade and slide it forward.*

**2 TRIMMING THE EDGE**
*Using a plank aligned along the lawn edge, trim the turf with a half-moon edger so that it is level.*

**3 FILLING THE GAP**
*Now cut a new piece of turf and ease it into the resulting hole. Trim it until it forms a perfect fit.*

**4 ADJUSTING THE LEVEL**
*Remove or add soil beneath the new piece of turf until it sits exactly level with the rest of the lawn.*

**5 FIRMING IN**
*Press the new turf firmly into place with the back of a rake, or use a medium-weight roller.*

**6 FINISHING OFF**
*With a trowel, apply some sandy top-dressing over the repaired area, especially on the joins. Water well.*

## REPAIRING A DAMAGED PATCH

**1 REMOVING THE PATCH**
*Cut out a square around the damaged area using a half-moon edger, then undercut the turf with a spade and remove it.*

**2 PREPARING THE SOIL**
*Loosen the soil to encourage rooting, by lightly forking or raking it over. Apply a dressing of a liquid or granular fertilizer.*

**3 FIRMING THE SOIL**
*Carefully tread over the prepared soil to consolidate it and firm the surface before inserting new turf.*

**4 RE-TURFING**
*Cut a new piece of turf to fit the space, trimming it with a half-moon edger to match the exact size and shape of the hole.*

**5 FINISHING OFF**
*Check the turf is level with the rest of the lawn, adjusting the soil level if necessary. Firm in the turf and water it well.*

SEE ALSO: Patios and Paths, pp.56–73; Seed or Turf?, p.77; Sowing Grass Seed, p.79; Laying Turf, p.80

# HOLLOWS AND HUMPS

After a while, you may find that your lawn develops a few hollows or humps, or both. The grass in a hollow will become unevenly long, and the grass on a hump will be mown too closely, resulting in scalping. On a small scale, these problems may be quickly and easily rectified by cutting a cross in the affected turf, peeling back the corners, and levelling the soil underneath (*see right*).

Where a large area is affected, it may be better to remove entire sections of turf. Store them on one side, making sure they do not dry out. Then level the soil over the whole area, using a spirit level (*see p.78*), before carefully re-laying all the pieces of turf in their original positions.

## LEVELLING A HOLLOW OR HUMP

**1 CUTTING A CROSS**
Using a half-moon edger, cut a cross through the hump or hollow. The cuts should extend to a little beyond the problem area. Then undercut the resulting triangles of turf with a spade.

**3 LEVELLING**
Fill in a hollow with good, sifted, sandy topsoil, firm it, and make sure it is level. For a hump, remove some of the soil and check that the rest is firm and perfectly level.

**2 LIFTING THE TURF**
Fold back the triangles of turf from the centre of the cross. Take care not to pull them too vigorously or they may crack.

**4 REPLACING THE TURF**
Fold back the triangles of turf. Lightly firm, and check that the level is correct. If necessary, re-adjust the soil level beneath the turf. Top-dress and water well.

# CONTROLLING WEEDS

Some lawn weeds, such as daisies and clover, can look attractive and, unless you have a very high-quality lawn, you may wish to leave them alone. Others, however, if left, will cause the grass to suffer, and even on a utility lawn it is better to control them. Most lawn weeds are creeping or rosette forming plants that are not affected by mowing, such as plantains and dandelions. Some of the most common examples are shown here. Others that may cause problems are couch grass, ground ivy, crab grass, goose grass, annual blue grass and oxalis.

Regular mowing, feeding, and watering should discourage weeds. If they do appear, however, it is possible to cut out individual weeds by hand using either a special tool known as a "daisy grubber" or a kitchen knife. Remember that some weeds have long tap roots that must be completely removed. On large lawns, you may need to employ chemical weedkillers.

Weedkillers come in various forms:
■ **Liquids** are diluted and watered onto the lawn with a rose or dribble bar.
■ **Powders and granules** are applied to the lawn when the soil is moist, and they can be spread either by hand or with a wheeled spreader.
■ **Spot weedkillers**, usually a gel, are applied to individual weeds.

## CONTROLLING MOSS

Moss can be a problem even in the best-kept lawns, but is commonly found in wet lawns in shade and in underfed lawns. Treat it with a chemical moss-killer or lawn sand, preferably in spring, and rake out the dead moss. If done in autumn, scarifying may spread the problem. If the soil is poor and acid, try applying lime. Feed the lawn regularly to encourage strong grass growth.

If the moss keeps reappearing, try to identify the cause and take steps to rectify the problem. This may involve improving soil aeration, drainage, and fertility. In dense shade where moss recurs repeatedly, it may be sensible to replace the grass with ground-cover plants, or even to create a moss lawn.

△ **FIELD BINDWEED**
Spreading by underground shoots, this can be quite a problem in poor soils.

△ **SLENDER SPEEDWELL**
On moist soil, this weed is difficult to control. Lawn sand may weaken it.

△ **CREEPING BUTTERCUP**
This is a fairly common weed on moist, clay soils.

△ **BROAD-LEAVED PLANTAIN**
A weed that forms broad, grass-smothering rosettes.

△ **YARROW**
This weed thrives on poor, dry soils. Small areas may be forked out.

△ **DANDELION**
These have long tap roots, form rosettes that smother grass, and self-seed.

△ **LESSER YELLOW TREFOIL**
An annual weed that is spread in grass clippings.

△ **COMMON WHITE CLOVER**
This plant will spread quickly in dry weather.

**SEE ALSO:** Levelling the Ground, p.78; Alternative Lawns, pp.88–89; Dealing with Weeds, pp.290–291

# ALTERNATIVE LAWNS

THERE ARE SEVERAL options open to you if you are not keen on a traditional grass lawn, such as using ground-cover plants or herbs, or brightening up grass with wild flowers or bulbs. These are best suited to small areas that are not subject to heavy use, because not only are they more expensive than grass, but also the plants cannot withstand being walked on regularly. A lawn with flowers or bulbs in it is more likely to thrive if left alone during flowering. The occasional tread, however, on a herb lawn will release delicious scents. Mowing is not required for a non-grass lawn, but you will still need to care for it by watering, feeding, weeding, and trimming.

## GROUND-COVER PLANTS

Popular choices for non-grass lawns include pachysandras (*see p.75*), the non-flowering chamomile (*Chamaemelum nobile* 'Treneague', which cannot be grown from seed), and herbs like the creeping Corsican mint (*Mentha requienii*), and low-growing, fragrant thymes, such as *Thymus serpyllum*. These can also be combined (*see below*).

Other ground-cover plants useful for filling awkward places are:
■ Creeping plants, such as acaenas, cotulas, dichondras, or periwinkles.
■ Dwarf, spreading conifers, such as *Juniperus squamata* 'Blue Carpet'.
■ Low-growing shrubs or climbers, such as euonymus, heathers, and ivies.

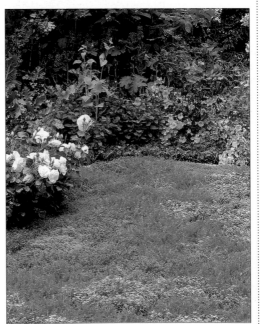

△ SCENTED LAWN
*Ideal for a little-used area, this mixture of chamomile and thyme has created an attractive carpet that looks good all through the year, suppresses weeds, and has the bonus of colourful flowers in summer. Walking lightly over the herb lawn every now and again will stimulate the release of a variety of delightful fragrances.*

## CREATING A NON-GRASS LAWN

A non-grass lawn can be costly to create, unless you raise your own plants to start it off with. To do this, you will need room to care for seedlings and small plants. Most chamomiles and thymes may be grown from seed, and larger plants may also be divided into smaller sections and replanted. Cuttings may also be rooted from thymes and other herbs. Otherwise, you will have to buy enough plants for the area to be covered. Always choose plants that suit your soil and conditions.

Prepare the ground thoroughly as for a grass lawn, removing all perennial and annual weeds, and space the plants 20–30cm (8–12in) apart. Water regularly until established, and weed around the plants until they have begun to form a weed-smothering mat. Apply a general fertilizer in spring, and trim the plants in early spring or late summer. Remove any weeds that appear by hand. After a few years, the whole lawn may need to be replaced and the soil enriched.

SINGLE-HANDLE SHEARS

LONG-HANDLED SHEARS

△ TRIMMING TOOLS
*Because you will have to trim your ground-cover plants by hand, purpose-made tools such as one-handed or long-handled shears have been designed to make the job easier.*

◁ MINIMUM MAINTENANCE
*It is best to keep the area of a non-grass lawn quite small, so that weeding and trimming by hand will not become too onerous. The lawn should then flourish.*

SEE ALSO: Ground Cover, p.75; Creating a Lawn, p.78; Dividing Perennials, p.148; Increasing Border Plants, pp.162–163

# NATURALISTIC EFFECTS

Grass never grows in isolation in nature; it mingles with meadow flowers or woodland-type plants. The simplest way to re-create a natural effect is to plant bulbs or corms in the turf (*see below*) and enjoy a colourful show of daffodils, snowdrops, or crocuses in spring. More effort is needed to create a wildflower meadow from seed, but the rewards can be exciting. Wild flowers thrive on poor soil, so stop feeding and remove all mowings for a season or two before sowing. Choose plants native to your area, or they may not survive. In general, a meadow should be cut in early spring and late autumn with a nylon line trimmer.

△ CROCUSES
*Spring flowers liven up the lawn before the grass begins to grow strongly.*

◁ MEADOW FLOWERS
*A meadow seed mixture may include poppies, corn-flowers, and corn cockles.*

# PLANTING BULBS IN GRASS

Bulbs and corms suitable for planting in grass include most spring-flowering ones, and some autumn-flowering crocuses and colchicums. Once you have taken the trouble to plant some bulbs in an area of grass, they will naturalize and multiply each year, providing even more colour for no extra cost. It is vital to remember, however, not to cut their foliage down by mowing the grass too soon after flowering has finished, because this will inhibit the growth and flowering potential of the bulbs. Leave the first mowing until at least six weeks after flowering, or until the foliage is turning yellow.

## PLANTING LARGE BULBS IN GRASS

**1 MAKE A HOLE**
*Clean the bulbs (here, daffodils) and scatter them on the grass. Make a hole 10–15cm (4–6in) deep for each one with a bulb planter or trowel.*

**2 PLANT THE BULB**
*Mix a pinch of bone meal with soil from the core of turf and place it in the hole. Put the bulb on top, with the growing point uppermost.*

**3 REPLACE THE CORE**
*Loosen the soil from the bottom of the core over the bulb, and replace the turf lid in the hole. Firm in gently, and fill in any gaps with soil.*

## PLANTING SMALL BULBS IN GRASS

**1 CUTTING THE TURF**
*Using a half-moon edger or spade, cut the shape of an "H" in the turf. Make sure the cut penetrates the soil.*

**2 FOLDING BACK**
*Carefully undercut the turf and fold back the 2 flaps to expose the bare soil beneath. Try not to tear the turf.*

**3 PREPARING THE SOIL**
*Loosen the soil with a hand fork to at least 8cm (3in) deep; mix in a small amount of slow-release fertilizer.*

**4 PLANTING THE BULBS**
*Place the bulbs (here, crocuses) on the soil, at least 2.5cm (1in) apart, with the growing points uppermost.*

**5 SCORING THE TURF**
*Score the back of the turf with a hand fork to allow the bulbs easily to grow through. Fold back the turf and firm.*

### GOOD IDEAS

• Plant bulbs randomly for a more natural effect by scattering them over the grass or soil and planting them where they land.

• Make sure that large bulbs are planted at least their own width apart.

SEE ALSO: Lawns with Added Interest, p.75; Daffodils, p.137; Planting Bulbs, p.149

# BOUNDARIES, DIVISIONS, AND STRUCTURES

## BOUNDARIES AND DIVISIONS

A BOUNDARY NOT ONLY establishes the edges of a legally defined area, it also creates an immediate visual impact, setting the atmosphere in a garden. Together with any internal divisions, boundaries form an integral part of the design, and, when coordinated with the surrounding planting schemes, they provide a vital link through the whole garden and with the house, too. Different materials create different impressions: low walls and fences and open trellis allow for extensive views outwards or across a garden, while dense hedges and high solid boundaries and screens provide intimacy and a sense of seclusion from the outside world.

### DESIGNING WITH BOUNDARIES

When considering the suitability of a boundary, it is important to note what safety, security, and privacy it provides. Does it need to keep in small children? Will it deter intruders? Are you worried about neighbours overlooking your garden? You may need to keep pets in and other animals out. To deter deer, a fence needs to be at least 2m (6ft) high. Chicken wire buried to 30cm (1ft) should prevent rabbits burrowing underneath.

Open gardens, with low-key boundaries, often have a relaxed, informal ambience. Boundaries made from light, airy trellis look stunning covered in climbers such as honeysuckle (*Lonicera*). This lightweight material is also excellent on a rooftop garden, where greater privacy can be provided by canvas screening. The relative costs of different materials and their durability will inevitably influence your choice. A brick wall is extremely expensive but will last for decades. A much cheaper, more temporary option might be a mesh fence covered with climbers.

You should discuss any boundary changes with your neighbours and your local authority because you may need planning permission. As a rule, fences and walls should be no more than 2m (6ft) high, except when they adjoin a public path, when they may have to be lower.

◁ **NATURAL BARRIER**
*A homemade wooden fence such as this is reasonably easy to erect and makes a pleasing yet sturdy boundary. Suitable for rural areas, it is strong enough to keep out animals such as horses and cattle.*

▽ **ORIENTAL TOUCH**
*Bamboo fence panels provide privacy as well as an attractive background for this eye-catching mix of foliage plants.*

◁ **MELLOW BACKGROUND**
*A high brick wall provides complete privacy and makes an effective foil for a wide range of planting in this colourful herbaceous border.*

**SEE ALSO:** Boundaries and Divisions, pp.28–31

## DESIGNING DIVISIONS

Even in a modest-sized garden you may want to create different areas of interest using constructed or planted screens. Trellis panels will separate off a vegetable plot or a children's play area, or hide the dustbins or compost heap. A difficult long, narrow garden can be split into a series of small, more easily designed areas, and an enclosing screen or trellis around a patio provides shelter and seclusion, especially if it is clothed in climbing plants. On a timber screen, paint or wood preservative will introduce colour, but it needs to blend with the planting schemes as well as your garden furniture. In exposed sites, screens of trellis, bamboo, hessian, or mesh, can be positioned to protect small areas or vulnerable plants.

Pergolas can sometimes form a division when covered with leafy climbers, and arches can be incorporated into screens, drawing the gaze to the area beyond. A tantalizing glimpse of another part of the garden can also be highlighted by creating a "window" in a fence, wall, or even a hedge (*see p 116*). Much grander in scale, a pleached hedge creates a similar effect, but it will take skill and time to achieve – anything up to 15 years. The branches of young trees are trained by tying them in horizontally to a strong wooden framework. Then they are gradually woven together to form a hedge on stilts.

△ **FOLIAGE SCREEN**
*Pleached lime trees have here created a leafy arch over the meandering pathway. Such a raised division delineates different areas within the garden and enticingly frames the view beyond.*

**VARIED DIVISIONS** ▷
*Three different types of screening – a hedge, trellis, and bamboos – have been effectively used together to create a gap in an enclosure, with the trellis allowing glimpses through to another area.*

## USING ORNAMENTAL PLANTS ON BOUNDARIES AND SCREENS

Boundaries and divisional screens can be made all the more decorative by planting with colourful climbers and wall shrubs. In a small garden or courtyard, you can make the planting around the edges so luxuriant that the boundary gets lost and you instead create a feeling of space or restful seclusion (*see p.14 and p.19*). Use a mixture of evergreen and deciduous plants: ivies, grasses such as *Miscanthus*, ferns, and bamboos, for example, and architectural *Fatsia japonica* and cordylines.

◁ **INTEGRATED PLANTING**
*This pink climbing rose successfully links the border planting of California tree poppy (*Romneya coulteri*) and variegated iris with the hard boundary wall behind.*

Depending on the materials used, screens and boundaries can be formal and elegant, or informal and rustic. To create an informal atmosphere, allow roses and clematis to mingle unrestrained. For a more formal effect, fan-train a peach or cherry tree against a wall. Easily grown pyracantha makes a good evergreen choice, with its white flowers followed by berries.

Pergolas and arches, sometimes used to form a screen, can usually be viewed from all sides, and this should be reflected in the choice of planting. All such structures must be strong and durable enough to carry the weight of the plants, which is often considerable.

**SEE ALSO:** Grasses, Bamboos, and Ferns, pp.140–141

# FENCES AND TRELLIS

FENCES AND TRELLIS provide one of the quickest and cheapest ways of marking boundaries or forming screens or windbreaks. They can supply instant privacy and security, and make an excellent support or background for climbers or wall shrubs. When chosen well, they can also play their own decorative role in the garden. They do, however, need maintenance to prevent rot. Fences and trellis are available in an extensive and versatile range of designs and qualities, so choose according to your purposes. Although simple styles are relatively inexpensive, unusual or ornate designs inevitably cost more because of their complex construction.

## TYPES OF FENCES

There are two main styles of fencing: solid or open, both of which may be stockproof. Solid or closely woven fences provide greater privacy than open styles but also have greater resistance to wind. Since they are therefore subjected to increased stress, the support posts need especially secure foundations. Open fencing allows light and rain onto nearby plants, and protects them by filtering the wind. Interesting patterns can be created by fixing boards on the diagonal or to create a chevron design. In an open fence, this can make a dramatic feature in winter when low sun casts long shadows on a lawn or patio.

All fencing and fence posts must be within your own garden if the fence acts as a boundary marker between two properties. Choose a style sympathetic to your garden (*see pp.28–29*). Types of fencing include:

- **Bamboo** (*solid*): Available as panels of canes woven or lashed together; filters wind well but may deteriorate quickly.
- **Chain-link** (*open*): Wire mesh, fixed to concrete, wooden, or iron posts; stockproof, cheap, and quick to put up long lengths.
- **Picket** (*solid or open*): Wooden or plastic vertical boards (pales) fixed to horizontal rails; good for fronting suburban gardens.
- **Post-and-rail** (*open*): Two or more wooden horizontal rails fixed between posts; a strong and inexpensive boundary.
- **Railings** (*open*): Usually cast or wrought iron; expensive and not usually an option unless available from a reclamation yard; best suited to fronting small gardens.
- **Wattle hurdles** (*solid*): Panels of woody woven stems, often hazel or willow; offers interim protection for young shrubs and hedges; not long-lasting.
- **Wooden panel** (*solid*): Interwoven or overlapping boards or slats, usually larch or pine, are attached to a frame easily fixed to posts; boards may be arranged vertically or horizontally; available in a range of heights and qualities; affords privacy but is not especially strong.

△ **CHANGING ROLES**
*While the hedge is growing, the post-and-rail fence behind it marks the boundary and provides a barrier that will keep out farm animals from the meadow beyond.*

△ **DOUBLE DUTY**
*An open picket fence allows views beyond the boundary as well as enabling plants to grow through and over it. White paint, used to preserve the wood, also complements the flower colours.*

**NATURAL SHADE** ▷
*The soft colour of this vertical featherboard fence provides an excellent foil for the clematis flowers and foliage in front.*

SEE ALSO: Boundaries and Divisions, pp.28–29

# TYPES OF TRELLIS

Trellis can be used as a freestanding, light boundary marker or to delineate divisions within a garden, or it can be fixed against a wall or fence or secured on top. It is available in a range of sizes, weights, and materials, including curved and more complex designs for arches and arbours. Some diamond-lattice trellis can be expanded to fit a space exactly but should be nailed to timber supports before fixing. Opt for a close-patterned design if the trellis is to act as a windbreak. Custom- or homemade trellis of bamboo or willow gives a garden an individual air, but beware

if you use willow since the stems may take root. Then you will need to weave in and prune the sideshoots as they grow.

Check that the trellis is sufficiently sturdy to support the plants you have in mind, and choose a stout quality if it is to be freestanding. Planed hardwood is stronger and more expensive than sawn softwood but is much more durable and, if it is to play an important role in the garden's design, may be worth the extra cost. Wooden battens are more pleasing than plastic and plastic-coated wire trellis but need more maintenance and should be treated regularly with a non-toxic wood preservative. Some of the eye catching new shades have instant impact, but shades of brown or sage green merge satisfyingly into the background.

## DESIGN IDEAS

• Create a decorative feature by fixing trellis panels to the top of a fence or wall.

• Conceal ugly buildings, unwanted vistas, or utility areas in the garden behind trellis.

• Frame a special view by fitting a trellis "window" between solid-fencing panels.

• Surround a rooftop garden with sturdy trellis to provide a degree of privacy as well as to help shelter plants from wind.

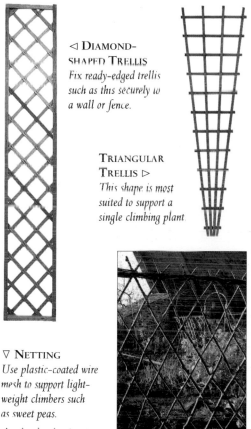

◁ **DIAMOND-SHAPED TRELLIS**
Fix ready-edged trellis such as this securely to a wall or fence.

**TRIANGULAR TRELLIS** ▷
This shape is most suited to support a single climbing plant.

**SHAPED TRELLIS** △
A convex or concave trellis introduces an informal note to an otherwise formal boundary or screen.

▽ **TACKED TRELLIS**
Concertina-style trellis such as this is held together with tacks and is much less sturdy than jointed trellis.

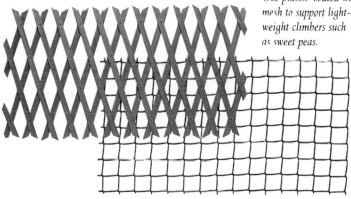

▽ **NETTING**
Use plastic-coated wire mesh to support light-weight climbers such as sweet peas.

△ **HOMEMADE TRELLIS**
This charming screen of interwoven willow wands adds character to the garden as well as helping to shelter the plants in the vegetable patch.

# GARDEN GATES

The style and condition of your garden gate or gates are important because they are likely to make an instant impression on visitors, and they set the tone for the garden and house within.

When choosing a new gate, consider the practicalities:

■ How wide does it need to be, and will you hang it yourself? Any gate needs posts set securely in the ground, usually using concrete, and the wider the gate the more difficult it is to hang.

■ Does it need to be kept shut, to keep in small children or pets? If so, choose a latch that is reasonably toddler-proof and remember that small animals can easily squeeze through a gap at the bottom.

■ Do you want privacy? A tall, solid gate, of similar height to the surrounding boundary, may be the answer.

Most gates are in constant use. As well as choosing an appropriate style that blends well with the boundary on either side, make sure that the materials and construction will be able to withstand everyday wear-and-tear.

△ **WOODEN GATE**
The strong geometric lines of this square timber gate echo the shape of the formal clipped hedges on either side. Although a rather heavy-looking, austere design, the way in which it offers glimpses of the garden within and the countryside beyond prevent it from seeming intimidating.

**SEE ALSO:** Ways of Supporting Plants, pp.108–109

# ERECTING A WOODEN FENCE

A wooden fence should be placed on your side of any boundary, with the best side facing outwards. The easiest type to erect is panel fencing, which is widely available in a range of styles, often in ready-to-assemble kits, complete with brackets.

Each panel is held in position by wooden or concrete posts. The latter are less attractive but last considerably longer than wooden posts, which need metal supports to prevent them rotting, or a footing of concrete with a base layer of hardcore to allow drainage. To prolong a fence's life further, use pressure-treated timber and fix protective coping to each post top. A replaceable wooden gravel board (also available in concrete), at the bottom of each panel, saves having to replace a whole panel if damp soil causes rot. The panels should fit tightly against the posts, which must be checked with a spirit level at all stages of construction.

◁ **METAL POST-SUPPORT**
*To prolong the life of wooden posts, insert them into metal post-supports. These are driven into the soil by hitting a steel or wooden post-driving tool, inserted into the support, with a sledgehammer or mallet. Using this type of tool protects the metal edges of the support.*

## PUTTING UP PLAIN LARCHLAP PANELLED FENCING

### TOOLS AND MATERIALS

- Metal post-supports
- Fence panels
- Post-driving tool
- Sledgehammer
- Spirit level
- Timber posts
- Mallet
- Metal panel and trellis brackets
- White crayon
- Screwdriver
- Galvanized screws and nails
- Gravel boards
- Metal gravel-board brackets
- Trellis and coping
- Hammer

**1 MEASURE POST POSITIONS**
*Insert the first metal post-support into the ground (see above). Locate the position for the second post-support by laying the panel against the base of the first one.*

**2 CHECK POST-SUPPORT LEVELS**
*Drive in the second post-support. Then check that it is level by laying a board and spirit level over the top of both post-supports. Put in other post-supports in the same way.*

**3 SECURE POST**
*Set the first post in its metal support, knocking it to the base with a mallet. Check that it is vertical on all sides, then secure in position by tightening the clamping bolt firmly.*

**4 PANEL BRACKET**
*Mark a central white line down the post and two or three evenly spaced horizontal lines for the tops of the metal panel brackets. Screw the panel brackets in position.*

**5 GRAVEL BOARD**
*Place one end of the gravel board centrally into a gravel-board bracket. Nail the bracket to the gravel board and the panel. Repeat at the other end of board and panel.*

**6 INSERT PANEL**
*Slide the panel into the brackets and hammer into place using a wood offcut and mallet. Screw brackets to one side of second post, put it into the ground and fit panel into its brackets.*

**7 INSERT TRELLIS**
*Position metal brackets for trellis on both posts and screw them into place. Slide the trellis into the brackets. Repeat these steps to complete the length of fence.*

### ALWAYS REMEMBER

#### TO KEEP FENCES IN GOOD CONDITION

- Clear soil and debris away from the base of posts and wooden gravel boards to prevent premature rot, or use concrete gravel boards.
- Every 3–4 years treat all exposed timber with a non-toxic wood preservative.
- Fix any loose panels or boards with nails, or replace with pieces in a matching style.

**8 WOODEN COPING**
*Secure some flat wooden coping over each post top, using 5cm (2in) galvanized nails. Then screw on the decorative top, if required. Such a top sheds rainwater even more effectively than flat coping.*

**9 FINISH OFF**
*Secure each panel and piece of trellis firmly in position by screwing into them through the holes on each metal bracket. Do this on both front and back surfaces of the panels and trellis.*

SEE ALSO: *Types of Trellis, p.93*

# PICKET FENCING

The easiest way to put up picket fencing is using ready-assembled panels supported by concrete or timber posts. A wider range of styles is available if you style and attach the pales (vertical boards) yourself. Using a template, the top of each pale can be rounded or cut to a point so that it readily sheds rainwater, or you can create more distinctive outlines, using a jigsaw. The length of the pales can also be varied, for example by alternating long and short pales, as can the spacing between pales. For a decorative fence, pales are generally spaced at their own width apart, but for greater privacy fix them closer together. If you want a rustic picket fence, make it from rough, unplaned timber, but if you prefer a more sophisticated style, or want to paint the fence, choose planed wood.

If you decide to make your own fence – perhaps because you want an individual style – determine the position of the posts and put in the post-supports and the posts (*see facing page, Steps 1–3*). Then, to make your own panels of the appropriate size, lay the pales on the ground between the posts, with their bases aligned against a straight board. Place two horizontal crossrails across the pales at a suitable distance from the top and bottom, checking with a set square and using a spacer to give an even distance between pales. Fix the crossrails by driving two nails diagonally into each rail. Drill holes at the ends of the crossrails and screw them to the posts.

∧ **VERSATILE PALETTE**
*A fence stained or painted to complement the surrounding planting will not only look professional but will also help to keep the timber in good condition. A different preservative shade can be used if you change your planting scheme.*

# PUTTING UP TRELLIS PANELS

Freestanding trellis panels can be erected and fixed to posts in the same way as wooden fence panels (*see facing page*), but often they are to be attached to a wall or fence to provide support for plants.

Any flat garden, house, or garage wall or fence in good condition should be suitable, but for safety reasons, if in doubt, seek professional advice, and have any necessary repairs done before you start work. To minimize the chances of causing damage to a wall, fix horizontal wooden battens between it and the trellis panel. This also benefits plants trained to the trellis, since it allows a little more air to circulate around the foliage, reducing the risk of disease, especially mildew. Trellis panels can be fixed permanently in position, using galvanized nails, but it is often wise to attach them to the battens with hinges and hooks so that the panel, plus the plants it supports, can be lowered whenever you need to reach the surface for maintenance work.

## GOOD IDEAS

- Paint the trellis in a contrasting colour to the wall or fence if you would like to make a feature of it.
- Colour the trellis to match its support if it is to blend into the background.
- Water-based, non-toxic wood preservative is less harmful to plants than creosote, so use it on trellis that is to support climbers.
- To ensure even colouring of the trellis, apply the paint or stain only on dry timber.

## FIXING TRELLIS ONTO A WALL

### TOOLS AND MATERIALS

- Trellis panel
- Pencil
- Drill with wood and masonry bits
- 2 pieces of 3.5×2.5cm (1⅜×1in) wood batten, as long as the trellis panel is wide
- Metal tape measure
- Bradawl
- Hammer
- 6 rawlplugs
- Screwdriver
- 6 size-8, 50mm (2in) galvanized screws
- 2 hinges, plus galvanized screws
- 2 hooks and eyes

**1 MARK OUT**
*Hold the trellis panel in position against the wall and make a pencil line on the wall at the top and bottom of the trellis panel. Drill three evenly spaced holes in each batten. Aligning the battens against the wall marks, pencil in the position of the screwholes on the wall. Drill the holes in the wall and tap in the rawlplugs.*

**2 FIX THE UPPER BATTEN**
*Screw the top batten to the wall, aligning its upper edge with the appropriate positional marks for the trellis. Screw the hinges to the lower batten.*

**3 ATTACH THE TRELLIS PANEL**
*Align the lower batten on the wall and screw in position. Then screw the hinges attached to the batten to the bottom edge of the trellis panel.*

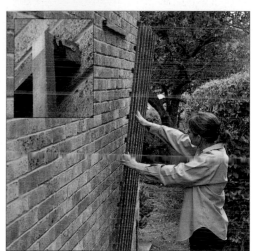

**4 SECURE THE TRELLIS TOP**
*Carefully swing the trellis panel up against the wall, checking that it aligns correctly at the top. Then fix a hook into each end of the upper batten (see inset) and an eye into an adjacent part of the trellis panel.*

**SEE ALSO:** Designing with Climbers and Wall Shrubs, pp.102–103; Choosing Climbers and Walls Shrubs, pp.104–107

# WALLS

THE HEIGHT, TEXTURE, AND COLOUR of a permanent hard structure such as a garden wall must always harmonize with its surroundings. A retaining wall near a house, for example, should be built from the same or similar materials, so that it forms a satisfying visual link between house and garden. A well-built wall, although initially much more expensive than other types of boundary or screening, fortunately needs almost no maintenance and will last for decades. It may, however, require planning permission, because there may be local restrictions as to its maximum height. The deeds of your property may similarly impose special conditions.

## DESIGNING WITH WALLS

When building either a boundary or a retaining wall (to terrace a slope or create a raised bed), it is important to select appropriate materials. Since colour and type of brick can vary from area to area, try to match new bricks to existing nearby buildings. The same goes for stone. Golden sandstone, for instance, will look completely out of place in an area where the local material is grey-white limestone. Even reconstituted stone is available in different shades. This can be a useful substitute for prohibitively expensive natural stone but shop around for the best because it varies greatly in quality.

Stone walls can be constructed with evenly laid courses or in a random style depending on how the stone is cut (*see facing page*). Dry-stone walls, often used as retaining walls, contain no mortar at all, and need patience and skill to fit together. A solid retaining wall will need weepholes to provide drainage. All walls need a top row of coping, or capping, bricks or stones. These can be decorative as well as functional, and often have a sloping shape or are wider than the rest of the wall to shed water easily. Check that bricks are frostproof or they may crumble when moisture inside freezes.

Any substantial length of walling, even of local materials, will create impact in a garden and needs choosing with care. A wall with a rendered surface can be useful for introducing unexpected colour or decorative elements such as mosaic.

Pierced blocks can be used to build semi-permeable screens. In exposed areas, these will reduce wind speed and help to protect plants on the leeward side. Solid barriers often tunnel wind, and instead create turbulence. Glass blocks can make an interesting screen in a contemporary design but, if they become grimy, cleaning them may prove a chore.

△ **MULTI-PURPOSE MARKER**
*This low stone wall cleverly defines the boundary between two areas of the garden while at the same time allowing extensive views. The broad coping doubles as a seat.*

△ **STRONG CONTRAST**
*The white colouring of this reconstituted-stone wall contrasts starkly with the black-metal built-in seat, but it tones in well with the white-flowered planting in the foreground.*

▽ **CURVED WALL**
*The possible monotony of a long, plain wall has been avoided here by giving it gentle curves, a brickwork base, and stylish coping. The neutral colour prevents it from being obtrusive.*

SEE ALSO: Planting against a Wall, p.110

# WALLING MATERIALS

The materials for a garden wall need to be frostproof and capable of preventing moisture penetration from both sides. They also need to be strong enough for the purpose in hand. Low retaining walls do not require professional expertise, but remember that if they are of any length, the pressure exerted by damp soil behind can be considerable. Building regulations generally apply to retaining walls over 1m (3ft). All walls need firm foundations (*see right*). A wall can be built of single-brick thickness up to 65cm (26in). A wall higher than this requires much greater skill and should be of double-brick thickness or have supporting piers. Screens also need firm foundations.

Types and styles of walling include:

■ **Adobe:** traditionally made from clay but now more likely to be concrete blocks covered with a clay render; moderately priced and fairly strong.

■ **Breeze block:** lightweight and cheap; not very strong; can be faced with brick or stone or rendered and painted.

■ **Brick:** colour and weather resistance will depend on the source of the clay and firing – not all bricks are frostproof; expensive, strong, and long-lasting.

■ **Concrete block:** available in a variety of finishes and styles but often utilitarian-looking; reasonably cheap, strong, and easy to use; can be faced with brick or rendered and painted.

■ **Flint:** traditional material in areas where it occurs naturally; expensive, and setting the stones in mortar requires skill.

■ **Glass block:** made from reinforced glass; can form an unusual screen.

■ **Natural stone:** can be cut into uniform blocks or left undressed; colour varies with type; strong and extremely costly.

■ **Reconstituted stone:** made from crushed rock and cement; it is much cheaper but not as strong as natural stone.

△ **PERFECT BACKDROP**
*Weathered and attractively colonized by lichens, an old high brick wall retains and radiates warmth, encouraging a rose to thrive and bloom profusely.*

◁ **COURSED BRICK**
*The arrangement of bricks (bonds) within a wall, and the wall's thickness, define its strength. This wall is Flemish bonded, that is, the bricks are laid alternately lengthways and sideways within each row.*

◁ **COURSED STONE**
*This limestone wall has been laid dry, in rows, without mortar jointing Such a wall is often topped with a coping set in mortar. The crevices can be filled with soil and planted with rock plants.*

◁ **RANDOM STONE**
*Stones of all shapes and sizes are used in a random stone wall, so they need to be secured in place with mortar. Such a wall can be expensive, since fitting and matching the various shapes is time-consuming.*

## ALWAYS REMEMBER

### SAFETY AND SECURITY

For a wall 45–65cm (18–26in) high, concrete footings should be 10–15cm (4–6in) deep and 20–30cm (8–12in) wide. Walls up to 1m (3ft) need footings 23–30cm (9–12in) deep and 45–60cm (18–24in) wide. For a wall any higher than this, you should almost certainly call in a professional builder.

# MIXING WALLING MATERIALS

◁ **SYMPATHETIC MATERIALS**
*Bricks provide a wall of knapped flints set in mortar with a secure, weatherproof edging, as well as softening the rather harsh texture of the flints.*

Traditionally, materials are often mixed. An edging of brick makes a wall of soft local stone weather resistant as well as adding to its aesthetic appeal. Red brick enhances grey flint. Mixing modern materials can create some superb effects, too, and frequently helps to reduce costs.

Concrete or breeze-block walls can be disguised by rendering with a mix of masonry cement and fine sand, finished with a coat of masonry paint. White and cream are effective in shade since they reflect light; earthy tones are warm and mellow and induce a feeling of relaxation; or in urban areas, you may be tempted to try a more vibrant colour. While the cement is still drying, you could also score or stamp patterns into it, or embed pebbles, seashells, or broken crockery or tiles. Work on a small area at a time, embedding the pieces of decoration to at least two-thirds their depth. The same idea could be applied to an old brick or stone wall that needs renovating. Fill gaps or small crumbling areas with cement and sand and stud them with a suitable decoration.

**SEE ALSO:** Boundaries and Divisions, p.28; Laying Concrete, pp.60–61; Building a Raised Bed, p.181

# ORNAMENTAL ARCHES

EVEN THE SMALLEST OF GARDENS may be enhanced by the careful positioning of an ornamental arch, which can be used in many ways: for example, over the gate to provide an appealing entrance or to outline a doorway; to make an opening through divisions within the garden; or to partition the garden into separate areas without the solidity of a wall, hedge, or fence. An arch can be ornate or simple, to suit your garden's style, and can be bought in kit form, in an extensive range of styles. It is also comparatively easy to build your own simple structure, or you could have one custom-made professionally, especially if you want an intricate design.

## DESIGNING WITH ARCHES

Before you introduce an arch into your garden decide on its purpose. It will not look right unless it has a function to serve, whether it is to guide you along a path, or perhaps act as an inviting entrance to another part of the garden.

A freestanding arch is likely to be made of timber or metal. For a bold statement, select an eye-catching design and think carefully about what sort of climbers to grow up it. Arch and plants need to complement one another. For a subtle effect, choose a style that will blend with the surrounding planting, for example a simple rustic arch that can be covered with traditional rambling roses.

Any arch will usefully add height. It can also act as a focal point, drawing the eye

◁ **MATCHING LOOK**
*The style of this rustic-poled, homemade arch attractively complements its surroundings, but it would look totally out of character if set in a formal garden.*

△ **ELEGANT SUPPORT**
*An iron arch and a rose make ideal partners. The rose does not hide the arch's slender shape yet its profusion of flowers are displayed to perfection.*

to a feature such as a pool, steps, or seat at the end of a path. It can also serve to distract the gaze from a less glamorous part of the garden. Skilful designers sometimes create a *trompe l'oeil* effect by placing an arch at the boundary and a mirror within it. The reflected view makes the garden appear larger but arch and mirror need careful placing and the mirror should be angled downwards slightly to avoid catching the sun.

## BUILDING A WOODEN ARCH

A homemade arch of unpeeled poles or pressure-treated timber is generally cheaper to make than a kit. Treat any cut ends and areas where the bark has flaked with preservative before assembly. Insert the uprights securely into the ground using metal post-supports or concrete and a base layer of hardcore. Fix the roof and crossrails with galvanized nails or screws. Allow a minimum height of 2.2m (7ft) to give adequate head clearance.

### SIMPLE WOODEN ARCH

This plain arch is relatively easy to build from a kit. The crossrails on the roof add strength. For additional rigidity secure diagonal struts on each side, between the uprights.

Housing joint secured with galvanized nails

Crossrail helps to stabilize arch

Pitched roof provides extra height for safe passage below

Sawn upright post, 10x10cm (4x4in), is sturdy enough to support climbers

Strong, deep, metal post-supports prevent base of timber post from rotting and give arch a secure footing

SEE ALSO: Covering Arches and Pergolas, p.103

# ERECTING A METAL ARCH

Metal arches are available in a wide variety of styles, some much sturdier than others, so ensure that you select one capable of taking the weight of your chosen plants when they are fully grown.

Fortunately the components of most kits readily slot together with the aid of only a few basic tools. Before you start to assemble the pieces, read the instructions thoroughly and check that you have all the pieces. Moisture seals, slid over the joints, keep out rain, while crossrails help to prevent the structure from twisting. Accurately mark the arch's position on the ground and make the post holes. If the hole-maker in the kit is not pre-marked, make your own depth indicator on the tube 30cm (12in) from the base. Finally, the whole structure must be carefully checked with a spirit level.

| ALWAYS REMEMBER |
| --- |

**STRUCTURES MUST BE SECURE**

The slender but strong uprights of the arch below are easily inserted into the ground to a secure depth. Heavier, timber structures may need their posts setting into concrete, with a base layer of hardcore to prevent rot. Timber kits often use metal post-supports. Security is doubly important in windy sites.

## PUTTING UP A METAL ARCH

### TOOLS AND MATERIALS

- Metal arch kit
- PVC moisture seals, as supplied
- Nuts and bolts, as supplied
- Screwdriver
- Hole-maker, as supplied
- Club hammer
- Spirit level

**1 JOIN UPRIGHTS**
Place a moisture seal along one upright section, then slot a second upright into the first section. Drag the moisture seal back over the join. Repeat to make all the other uprights.

**2 FIX CROSSRAILS**
Starting 60cm (24in) from the base, evenly space three T-joints down two sets of joined uprights. Insert three crossrails into the T-joints and screw tight, to form an arch side.

**3 ERECT SECOND SIDE OF ARCH**
Repeat Step 2 for the other arch side. To ensure that the crossrails on the second side are similarly positioned to those on the first, lie the second side beside the completed one.

**4 ASSEMBLE TOP**
Slot two curved pieces together and loosely secure with a T-joint. Repeat with the other two curved pieces. Insert and secure the crossrail between the two top sections. Then add the decorative finials.

**5 MAKE POST HOLES**
To complete the arch, set the top section into the sides, then cover the joins with moisture seals. Make four holes where the arch is to stand, by hammering the hole-maker into the ground to the marked depth.

**6 CHECK ALIGNMENT**
Set the completed arch in the holes and then check on all sides that it is vertical. Tighten all nuts and bolts.

# PLANTING AGAINST AN ARCH

To transform the arch, plant one or two climbers on either side that will grow up and eventually cover it. To help the plants reach the top, fix large-mesh plastic netting to the arch sides and fan out the young, pliant shoots. Most climbers will flower more readily if their stems are spiralled around the supports. When they reach the top of the arch, prune the stems as necessary so that the plants do not outgrow their position or become too heavy for the structure.

**1 NETTING SUPPORT**
Using ratcheted plastic ties, secure large-mesh plastic netting to both sides of the arch.

**2 PLANTING ANGLE**
Plant the climber at an angle of 45° towards the arch. Tie the main stems to the crossrail.

**3 INITIAL TRAINING**
As soon as the stems are long enough to reach the netting (and have all been untied from the stake) spread them out evenly across the side of the arch. Using figure-of-eight knots, loosely secure them to the crossrail and tie them in to the netting. Keep training and tying as the plant grows, until it starts to twine or cling.

SEE ALSO: Annual Climbers, p.106

# PERGOLAS AND ARBOURS

COVERED IN A VINE, WISTERIA, or other climber, a pergola provides shade and welcome refuge from hot, bright sun. It can make a refreshing place to eat and relax or a cool spot to linger on a path. Pergolas may be freestanding or fixed to the walls of a building. Attached to a house they may also shade the rooms inside. Arbours, usually smaller and enclosed on three sides, and sited near the garden's boundary, also offer retreat and a sense of seclusion. Both can be invaluable in a new garden for they will also provide an immediate focal point. In a more mature garden, a pergola can act as a link that binds the whole garden together year-round.

## DESIGNING WITH PERGOLAS

If a pergola is to shade a sitting or eating area, its position is most likely to have already been decided, but if it is to cover a path, where it will immediately become the focus of attention, it needs very careful siting. It might, for instance, also be used to act as a screen between two distinct areas of the garden.

Thought must also be given to its design. It is essential that the style and materials used are in sympathy with the surroundings. A straight pergola, for example, would look out of place in a garden filled with gentle curves; nor would a formal, elegant pergola fit a rustic, country-style garden. Wood or metal would suit an informal setting, whereas brick, concrete, or stone columns conjure up a formal atmosphere.

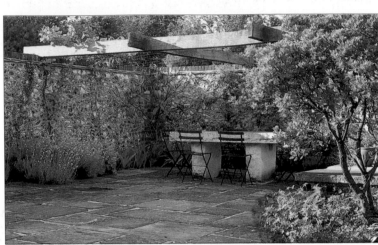

◁ SHADE AND SECLUSION
*A difficult corner, bounded by three walls, has been transformed into an interesting eating area by bolting the beams of a pergola on to the top of each wall. Its solid design is in keeping with the somewhat monumental look of the stone table.*

Pergola proportions are notoriously difficult to get right, so you may decide to seek the services of a professional for all but the most simple designs. A pergola must itself be a balanced structure as well as being in scale with the rest of the garden. The spacing between the uprights should be roughly equal to the pergola's width. Its height will depend on whether it is over a path or sitting area.

◁ NATURAL SHADOW
*Strong sunlight piercing this terrace balustrade produces a striking honeycomb pattern on the ground, similar to the pergola roof above. In summer the flowers of a wisteria hang gracefully through the beams.*

△ SUMMER GLORY
*This rose-covered wooden pergola forms an inviting tunnel for a fragrant, leisurely stroll. Not only does such a planting soften the outlines of the pergola, it also provides welcome shade during the summer months.*

## TELL ME WHY

**WHAT SHOULD I TAKE INTO ACCOUNT WHEN CHOOSING AND SITING A PERGOLA?**

- Simple designs are usually most satisfying, plants will add to the decorative quality.
- The size and scale must be appropriate to the size of your house and garden.
- Materials and construction must be sturdy enough for the plants you have in mind.
- If the pergola is to cover an eating area, make sure it is large enough to comfortably accommodate table and chairs.
- A pergola might be useful if your garden is overlooked, because the canopy can offer privacy from neighbouring windows.
- If it is to be attached to one side of the house, make sure the pergola and will not make the rooms inside too dark.
- A pergola will draw attention to a path. Check that the path is definitely in the right place, that it is wide enough, and that the pergola will frame a suitable view.

**SEE ALSO:** Autumn and Winter Interest, p.107; Fragrant Climbers and Wall Shrubs, p.107; Ways of Supporting Plants, pp.108–109

## ARBOURS

These climber-clad structures inject a feeling of intimacy and privacy into an otherwise open space. They generally house a seat, from where you can enjoy views out across the garden.

Where an arbour should be sited depends on when it is most likely to be used. If it is to provide a leafy retreat on hot summer evenings, for example, it will need to be placed where it catches the sun's fading rays. It should be at least 2.2m (7ft) tall so that the seating area does not feel claustrophic, especially when screened by trailing plants.

The structure itself must be robust enough to support the ornamental plants trained over it, yet open enough to admit any fragrances they exude. Wrought iron and wood are the most popular materials, but how they are used depends on the style that fits your garden.

A simple wooden shelter, made from sawn or rustic poles with trellis on three sides, would suit an informal setting, whereas extravagantly moulded and carved timber would be more appropriate in a formal garden. Delicate wrought ironwork or wirework might suit a small garden, while an ornate Italianate style needs spacious surroundings to look right.

△ **CLASSIC SIMPLICITY**
*The clean lines of this wrought iron arbour rise elegantly above the sea of colourful plants, and it provides a spectacular focal point enhanced by the evergreen backdrop.*

## BUILDING A PERGOLA

Pergolas are available in kit form or you can build your own. A simple design of rustic poles nailed together will support lightweight climbers, although with untreated wood it will not be long-lasting. For heavier plants the pergola should be much sturdier and, unless you are confident of your DIY skills, it is better to have one professionally designed and built.

A pergola is generally at least 2.5m (8ft) high, so that people can walk under it unhindered, even when it is covered with mature trailing plants. A pergola over a seating area may be slightly lower.

If you do decide to build your own wooden pergola from a kit, you should

### WOODEN PERGOLA WITH TRELLIS TOP
An all-wood pergola with trellis top, such as this, is quite cheap to buy and straightforward to construct from a kit. It would look pleasing painted with a soft green or blue preservative.

**SECURING THE TOP**
*Rest the trellis on the top of the uprights and crossbeams. Then, using brass screws, attach the trellis framework firmly to the uprights.*

**POSITION CHECK**
*Insert each upright post into a metal post-support and secure in position, constantly checking on all sides, with a spirit level, that each post is vertical.*

find that the manufacturers have made its assembly reasonably simple. Kits come with timbers planed and pre-notched, so that crossbeams can be gently hammered into place. Check that you have all the necessary nuts, bolts, and screws or nails. Metal post-supports are generally supplied for securing the uprights in the ground. If you have any doubts about the structure's security, you can set the posts in a footing of concrete with a base layer of hardcore to help prevent rot.

Put up the endposts first, then the remaining uprights, and finally fix the crossbeams and other supports. If one or more sides of the pergola is to be supported by a wall, use metal, L-shaped joist shoes or timber plates to attach the crossbeams to the masonry.

### ALWAYS REMEMBER

**MAKE CONSTRUCTION EASY**
On unpacking a kit, check that you have all the pieces, plus all the tools for the job. A spirit level is essential to ensure the uprights are vertical. Follow the instructions carefully. It will help to have someone to assist. Do not fully tighten any nuts or bolts until satisfied that the pergola is complete.

Trellis roof supports only lightweight climbers, which should be pruned regularly

Crossbeams shaped at ends to reflect overall styling of garden

Upright posts cut so that they house the crossbeams securely

Pressure treated timber

Metal post-supports protect timber uprights from rot. Or sink them into concrete footings

Horizontal galvanized wires strung between upright posts provide support for plants and allow even coverage

**PLANT SUPPORTS**
*Attach galvanized wires vertically on all sides of each post, using vine eyes every 30cm (12in), to support twining and tendrilled climbers.*

SEE ALSO: Covering Arches and Pergolas, p.103

# DESIGNING WITH CLIMBERS AND WALL SHRUBS

MANY GARDENS CONTAIN VERTICAL SURFACES that would look much more attractive if they were decoratively clothed with climbers or wall shrubs. Such plants help to soften hard structures such as walls, fences, and pergolas, integrating them into the garden as well as adding height to a planting scheme. More vigorous climbers, such as honeysuckle and *Clematis montana*, are also excellent at masking functional buildings or ugly expanses of wall. Many climbers and wall shrubs produce marvellously scented flowers or brightly coloured berries, while some of the most spectacular results can be produced by training climbers into suitable trees.

## COVERING WALLS AND FENCES

In order to make the most of the hard surfaces in your garden, it is important to understand how climbers and wall shrubs differ and why this affects the way they are used in a planting design.

Most climbers need other plants or a support to gain height while they grow. They have developed various means of anchoring themselves to their support, for instance by using adhesive pads, twining stems, tendrils, or hooked thorns (*see p.108*). Wall shrubs, however, have no such devices. They may simply look their best or benefit from being grown against a wall because of the protection it gives. For example, many less hardy shrubs such as flannel bush (*Fremontodendron*) will thrive against a sunny wall because they respond to its reflected warmth and shelter.

Climbers can be allowed to scramble attractively over a wall or fence, given a support system of trellis or wires to which they can be loosely tied at strategic points. Use evergreens which provide year-round cover to camouflage eyesores. The stems

△ CONCEALED FENCE
*This crisp, architectural boundary marker has been created by training* Muehlenbeckia complexa, *a tiny-leaved, vigorous climber over a stepped, wiremesh fence.*

of some wall shrubs can be trained into a tiered or fan shape, so that flowers and fruit are displayed to advantage. Stiff, woody-stemmed wall shrubs are difficult to detach from their supports for maintenance and must be trained against supports secured only to sound walls or fences that do not need frequent attention.

△ TRELLIS FENCE
*One advantage of open fencing such as this is that the stems of climbing plants, such as roses here, can be supported by weaving the young stems through the holes.*

△ FLORAL BEAUTY
*The surface of this mellow wall has been softened by a ceanothus, which has been trained to display its glorious crop of spring flowers.*

◁ GREEN CURTAIN
*New fencing or other stark surfaces can be entirely clothed by interestingly textured evergreens, such as variegated ivy here, for year-round interest.*

SEE ALSO: Ways of Supporting Plants, pp.108–109

# COVERING ARCHES AND PERGOLAS

Arches and pergolas bring height to a design, especially if there are no mature trees, and can link or separate two areas of the garden. When covered in lush foliage, they create private, refreshingly shaded spaces. Choose climbers with fragrant flowers and the stark lines of a large new pergola can be wonderfully transformed into a cool, scented tunnel, inviting you to explore the area that lies beyond.

△ **ABUNDANT CLIMBER**
*This arch laden with hops (Humulus lupulus) charmingly frames the view beyond. Such a well-planned feature anchors the arch into the surrounding planting.*

It is vital to select climbers and wall shrubs whose growth habits are appropriate to the site and their intended supports. A vigorous evergreen such as Persian ivy (*Hedera colchica*), for example, would soon swamp a fine wrought iron arch. Pergolas, on the other hand, often need a tall, strong-growing climber. A rose such as 'Seagull' or 'Albéric Barbier' will produce sufficient growth to cover the top generously with its cascading flowers.

Plants of different vigours may also be mixed and matched successfully. Fast-growing *Clematis montana* var. *rubens* will provide spring interest, while its pink tones could be picked up later in summer by *C.* 'Mrs N. Thompson' and *C.* 'Nelly Moser'. Think, too, about using foliage to introduce colour and texture. The leaves of the golden hop (*Humulus lupulus* 'Aureus') are brighter than many a flower, while those of vines such as *Vitis coignetiae* and *V.* 'Brandt' turn stunning red or purple in autumn. In summer they also cast particularly refreshing shade.

All wall shrubs and climbers naturally grow towards the light and so may blossom on only one side of the arch or pergola. It is worth trying to position them so that their flowers and fruits are displayed to maximum effect.

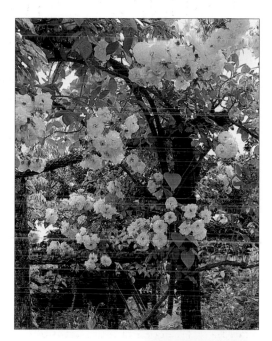

△ **LINKED DIVISIONS**
*Two separate structures — a pergola and an arch — are connected by a planting of glorious white roses.*

**SUMMER SCREEN** ▷
*The trailing flowers of a wisteria create an alluring summer partition on a metal pergola. When mature, its woody twining stems can make maintenance of a wooden structure difficult.*

# OVER HEDGES AND TREES

Trees with only one season of glory can be made to work harder by growing climbers into them. In a small garden particularly, where space is limited, such double use of an area can produce displays of fragrant flowers or colourful leaves from spring to autumn. Or you might be able to train a herbaceous climber up a hedge. Neatly clipped yew dramatically sets off the scarlet flowers of flame creeper (*Tropaeolum speciosum*), although this can be a tricky plant to grow.

A climber or shrub and its host must be compatible not only in the type of soil each requires but also in their habit of growth. Plant vigorous climbers, such as the splendid honeysuckle *Lonicera* × *americana*, into large trees, and smaller, lighter weight

◁ **FRAGRANT TREAT**
*Rampant rambling roses such as 'Wedding Day' look marvellous trailing through a large tree.*

**HELPING HAND** ▷
*A cane may be needed to guide a newly planted clematis, such as 'Comtesse de Bouchard' here, up into a tree fork, from where it will naturally grow through the branches.*

climbers such as annual morning glory (*Ipomoea*) over hedges or shrubs. Pruning regimes must also be complementary. Both plants should be accessible for maintenance, and the host must not need pruning while the climber is at its peak.

**SEE ALSO:** Ornamental Arches, pp.98–99; Hedges in the Garden, pp.116–119

# CHOOSING CLIMBERS AND WALL SHRUBS

IF CLIMBERS AND WALL SHRUBS are to provide long-lasting pleasure, select those that suit the conditions in your garden. You will need to ascertain how much sun a particular wall or fence receives, and at what time of day. Avoid acid-loving plants if the soil is alkaline; if dry, choose those with some tolerance to drought. If the space will not allow plants to grow freely, find out their vigour first. Take account of climate and the risk of strong, possibly salt-laden, winds or harsh winters, although some plants that are not completely hardy may survive against a warm wall or fence. Some planting suggestions are given below and on the following pages.

## PLANTS FOR A DRY SUNNY SPOT

The soil at the base of a sunny wall or fence is likely to be dry, because of the rainshadow, and is best suited to climbers like actinidia that tolerate such conditions. A clematis will grow well only if its roots are kept cool and moist by placing paving slabs or tiles over the surrounding soil.

Many wall shrubs positively need a sunny wall to thrive: the heat absorbed by the wall is reflected back, helping to ripen their wood so that they are better able to withstand cold. Aromatic Mediterranean shrubs such as rosemary benefit from such a site, and some shrubs, ceanothus for example, may grow taller than when planted in open ground. Early morning sun, however, will damage frosted shoots and blooms of winter- and spring-flowering plants by thawing them too fast.

### OTHER RECOMMENDATIONS

*Abutilon megapotamicum.* Evergreen or semi-evergreen shrub with bell-shaped yellow flowers in summer.
*Actinida kolomikta.* Deciduous climber with variegated pink, white, and green leaves when mature.
*Buddleja crispa.* Deciduous shrub with mid- to grey-green leaves, white-woolly young shoots, and, from mid- to late summer, fragrant, lilac-pink flowers.
*Clematis* 'Bill MacKenzie'. Deciduous climber with bell-shaped, yellow flowers, from midsummer to late autumn, and large, fluffy seedheads.
*Cytisus battandieri* (pineapple broom). Vigorous, tree-like, Mediterranean shrub with silver leaves and yellow flowers smelling of pineapple.
*Fremontodendron* 'California Glory'. Evergreen wall shrub. Deep yellow blooms, late spring to autumn.
*Lavatera maritima.* Shrubby evergreen with saucer-shaped, lilac-pink to white flowers. Late summer.
*Rosa banksiae* Vigorous climbing rose with scented, double flowers in late spring.
*Vitis vinifera* 'Purpurea'. Deciduous climber. Grey-hairy leaves turn plum-purple, then dark purple in autumn. Bears purple unpalatable grapes.

◁ **PASSIONFLOWER**
Passiflora caerulea *is the hardiest passionflower but still needs a sunny, sheltered site. It may climb to 10m (30ft), but often loses some of its top growth during winter.*

△ **LEMON BOTTLEBRUSH**
Callistemon pallidus, *a shrub which grows to 4m (12ft) tall, is prized for its grey-green leaves and, from late spring to mid-summer, its abundant spikes of flowers.*

△ **SOLANUM CRISPUM 'GLASNEVIN'**
*The Chilean potato tree (a relative of the more down-to-earth vegetable) needs a sheltered site, where it will quickly scramble to 6m (20ft) and produce its flowers in summer.*

△ **VITIS COIGNETIAE**
*This vigorous vine needs space to display its brilliant autumn colours. It can be pruned heavily in spring but it rapidly makes new growth and can reach 15m (50ft).*

## IVIES

Evergreen climbers such as self-clinging ivy provide year-round cover in cool temperate areas. Ivies are easy to grow and, when mature, their green autumn flowers provide a late source of nectar for insects, while the black midwinter berries supply food for the birds. In heavy shade, an all-green ivy such as *Hedera colchica* 'Dentata' gives interesting texture. Some variegated ivies such as *H. helix* 'Goldheart' colour best in reasonable light. Always match the mature size of an ivy to its planting site, because ivies vary greatly in their vigour.

△ **HEDERA HELIX 'EVA'**
*One of the smaller-growing types, this pretty white-variegated ivy grows to only 1.2m (4ft) tall. It prefers a sunny position in the garden.*

△ **HEDERA COLCHICA 'SULPHUR HEART'**
*Growing to 10m (30ft) tall, this ivy's yellow-variegated foliage provides a welcoming wall of colour in a dark corner, especially during long bleak winters.*

### OTHER RECOMMENDED IVIES

*H. colchica.* Almost oval, leathery, dark green leaves, 8–12cm (3–5in) long; to 10m (30ft) tall.
*H. helix* 'Glymii'. All-green leaves take on purple or bronze tints in winter; 2m (6ft) tall.
*H. helix* 'Green Ripple'. Mid-green leaves with five jagged, veined lobes; 2m (6ft) tall.
*H. helix* f. *poetarum.* Shiny, mid-green leaves, 8cm (3in) long, and orange-yellow fruits; 3m (10ft) tall.
*H. helix* 'Pedata'. Dainty, mid-green leaves that resemble the shape of a bird's foot; 4m (12ft) tall.

**SEE ALSO:** Planting Climbers and Walls Shrubs, pp.110–111

# PLANTS FOR SHADY WALLS

As long as a wall or fence receives some light, there are climbers and wall shrubs that will tolerate, and often thrive in such cool conditions. In the wild, many such as jasmine grow naturally in woodland or similarly shaded places. Some plants, such as silk-tassel bush (*Garrya elliptica*), tolerate the dry soil in the shade of a tree or beside a moisture-absorbent brick wall, while others, such as hops (*Humulus lupulus*), prefer damp shaded areas, at the bottom of a slope for example. A few plants such as honeysuckles can be grown in shade or sun, although, like shrubby flowering quince (*Chaenomeles speciosa*), they may flower or fruit less reliably in shade. Chinese virginia creeper (*Parthenocissus henryana*) also tolerates sun, but it tends to produce better-coloured foliage in shade.

### CHEERFUL PYRACANTHA ▷
*Pyracantha berries — here orange but also yellow or, more commonly, red — are produced in great abundance. They bring vivid colour to a dull wall for several months, persisting well beyond the middle of winter.*

### CHILEAN BELLFLOWER ▷
*This climber, Lapageria rosea var. albiflora, is a tender acid-lover needing a sheltered spot. It produces its showy white flowers from summer to autumn amid dark green leaves.*

## OTHER RECOMMENDATIONS

*Clematis.* Large-flowered hybrids with pale flowers, 'Nelly Moser' and 'Bees' Jubilee' for example, are less inclined to fade in light shade.
*Euonymus fortunei* cultivars. Evergreen shrub. Foliage is often variegated white or gold.
*Lathyrus latifolius.* Climbing perennial sweet pea, but not scented. Bears pink to purple or white flowers in summer and early autumn.
*Lonicera × tellmanniana.* Deciduous twiner with bright copper-orange flowers that appear in late spring to midsummer. Not scented.
*Mitraria coccinea.* Evergreen shrub with tubular, scarlet flowers borne from spring to autumn.
*Parthenocissus tricuspidata.* Deciduous climber, potentially rampant, so keep out of gutters. Bright green leaves turn bright red and purple in autumn.
*Rosa* 'Mme Alfred Carrière'. Repeat-flowering climber with fragrant white flowers tinged pink. Suits a cool wall.

### ◁ CLIMBING HYDRANGEA
*A deciduous climber (H. anomala subsp. petiolaris) that bears its lacy flowers in late summer. During winter, the bare stems are attractively cinnamon-coloured.*

# FAST-GROWING CLIMBERS

To cover a large expanse of wall or quickly camouflage a boring shed you need vigorous climbers such as *Muehlenbeckia complexa* or *Clematis* 'Perle d'Azur'. Exceptionally rampant plants, however, such as mile-a-minute vine or Russian vine (*Fallopia baldschuanica*), should be avoided in confined areas, where they may smother plants as well as neighbouring gardens. Always match a climber to its support. Many fast-growing climbers eventually grow very large. A huge rambling rose such as 'Kiftsgate', for example, needs a large garden and large forest tree for support. For lightweight structures that need fast cover, an annual climber such as morning glory (*Ipomoea tricolor*) is often a good choice (*see also* p.106). In sheltered sites, some tender perennials, often grown as annuals elsewhere, may survive, and, even if cut to the ground in winter, will quickly reshoot to give good but lightweight cover. Try yellow- or red-flowered Chilean glory flower (*Eccremocarpus scaber*), for example.

### ◁ CLEMATIS MONTANA
*This vigorous clematis can reach anything from 6 to 10m (18 to 30ft) depending on conditions. Some of the pink-flowered types are shorter-growing*

### ▽ AKEBIA QUINATA
*The chocolate vine, so called because of its scent, is not as speedy as some but will reach 10m (30ft). It is a useful climber because it will grow in light shade as well as sun.*

### ◁ AMPELOPSIS BREVIPEDUNCULATA
*A tendrilled climber that will quickly cover a wall or pergola or clamber into a tree. The small green flowers are insignificant but are followed by unusual berries that turn gradually from pink to blue.*

## OTHER RECOMMENDATIONS

*Ampelopsis megalophylla.* Deciduous. Dark green leaves, glaucous beneath, and black fruits in autumn.
*Campsis × tagliabuana* 'Madame Galen'. Deciduous. Orange-red flowers from late summer to autumn.
*Clematis montana.* Deciduous. Single flowers are borne in late spring and early summer.
*Cobaea scandens.* Evergreen perennial usually grown as an annual. Scented, bell shaped, creamy green flowers mature to purple. Summer to autumn.
*Jasminum polyanthum.* Evergreen with very fragrant, pink-budded, white flowers in spring–summer.
*Lonicera × americana.* Deciduous. Has strongly scented, yellow flowers, flushed red-purple, in summer.
*Rosa* 'Paul's Himalayan Musk'. Deciduous. Bears masses of double, pale pink flowers in summer.
*Vitis coignetiae.* Vine with large sculptural leaves that turn vivid shades of yellow and red in autumn.

SEE ALSO: Maintaining Climbers and Wall Shrubs, pp.112–115

# COMBINING CLIMBERS AND WALL SHRUBS

To create a tapestry of different plants, grow wall shrubs and climbers together. Textures and colours should blend harmoniously. In autumn, the yellow flowers of *Clematis tibetana* look good winding through a yellow- or orange-berried pyracantha. Or team the white-margined leaves of the shrub *Euonymus fortunei* 'Silver Queen' with the plain green foliage and lacy white flowers of climbing hydrangea for a handsome partnership.

When combining plants in this way, you should ensure that a plant grown for its berries, such as cotoneaster, does not have these covered by the leaves of its partner.

Nor must the vigour of one plant dominate the other. Clematis and roses are a classic combination, because their cultivation and pruning needs are similar. They work particularly well up pergolas and tripods, where they are less likely to be affected by mildew (*see p.296*) than against a wall. Two clematis can also be planted together: try combining spring-flowering *Clematis alpina* with a later-blooming large-flowered hybrid for a long display. Or put a clematis with a vine. The mauve flowers of *Clematis* 'Jackmanii' look lovely intertwined with the dusky leaves of a purple vine (*Vitis vinifera* 'Purpurea').

**EFFECTIVE COVER ▷**
*Two walls of this tiny courtyard garden have been transformed by the imaginatively combined planting of a scarlet-flowered honeysuckle with a white-flowered climbing hydrangea* (Hydrangea anomala *subsp.* petiolaris), *and deep red climbing roses.*

△ **TRIPLE BENEFIT**
*Evergreens, such as long-flowering Japanese honeysuckle* (Lonicera japonica), *combine well with deciduous climbers, such as roses here, to give year-round interest, greater variety of planting, and extended flowering season.*

## ALWAYS REMEMBER

### PRUNING REGIMES

If two or more climbers are to grow harmoniously together their pruning needs must not conflict. Does only one of the climbers need cutting back hard each year? If so, is this at a time when its partner is past its best? If both plants need regular care, their pruning times should coincide.

# ANNUAL CLIMBERS

These fast-growing plants are invaluable in a garden for giving quick, colourful cover, especially over new, bare arches or pergolas, and for training over tripods and obelisks in a border.

Because annual climbers are temporary, you can experiment with different colours and varieties, and try out combinations, perhaps with perennial climbers. Sweet peas, climbing nasturtiums, and runner beans can all be grown against trellis (they will need some tying in) and make effective screens in summer. Canary creeper (*Tropaeolum peregrinum*), black-eyed Susan (*Thunbergia alata*), Chilean glory flower

(*Eccremocarpus scaber*), and the cup-and-saucer plant (*Cobaea scandens*) are usually grown as annuals although they are in fact perennials. Many, including sweet peas and nasturtiums, will also grow through shrubs, as long as they receive sufficient water and light. Some have rather fleeting blooms. Those of morning glory fade by afternoon and sweet peas need regular cutting to flower over a long period.

**BLACK-EYED SUSAN ▷**
*The eye-catching flowers of this twining climber* (Thunbergia alata) *are produced from summer to autumn. A perennial that is usually grown as an annual, it can be raised from seed on a warm windowsill.*

SEE ALSO: Sowing Seed in Pots, p.162

# AUTUMN AND WINTER INTEREST

For a garden to look good all year round, it must include plants that are peak performers in autumn and winter. Herbaceous borders, which will have died down, now need an interesting backdrop, especially if they can be seen from the house. The flowers, leaves, and fruits of many climbers and wall shrubs fill this role admirably.

In autumn, the vigorous trumpet vine (*Campsis*) produces a welcome display of showy, trumpet-shaped flowers in warming oranges and reds. In winter, wall shrubs such as fragrant wintersweet (*Chimonanthus praecox*) scent the air, while the drooping grey-green catkins of the silk tassel bush (*Garrya elliptica*) look striking with a powdery dusting of frost.

Ivies provide a useful but unvarying year-round background for other plants, although a couple, 'Tricolor' and 'Glymii', turn deep pink and purple respectively in cold weather. Vines offer some of the most spectacular autumn colour, especially the huge, yellow and scarlet leaves of *Vitis coignetiae*. The fluffy seedheads of *Clematis tibetana* are delightful when they catch the fading autumn sun. They often appear while the yellow nodding flowers are still on the plant. The shrub *Berberis thunbergii* 'Dart's Red Lady' provides a double attraction in autumn with its orange and red leaves and glossy red fruits. For long-lasting winter colour, plant yellow-, red-, or orange-berried forms of pyracantha.

◁ WINTER CHEER
*Throughout winter and into early spring, the bright yellow flowers of winter jasmine (Jasminum nudiflorum) adorn many gardens, but regular tying back is needed.*

△ FIERY FOLIAGE
*The bright green leaves on this virginia creeper (Parthenocissus tricuspidata 'Veitchii') gradually change to dark red-purple in autumn, before they finally drop.*

# FRAGRANT CLIMBERS AND WALL SHRUBS

Many climbers and wall shrubs bear such beautifully fragrant flowers that, to appreciate them fully, it is worth taking time to find the best position for them in the garden. Delicately scented ones such as *Clematis armandii* should be planted closer to a path or house than more heavily perfumed honeysuckles, whose heavy fragrance will carry farther.

Arches, pergolas, and gates can become doubly attractive to walk through when surrounded by richly scented roses such as thornless 'Zephirine Drouhin'. Plant wisteria or *Actinida kolomikta* near a doorway or train it around a window, so that you can enjoy the fragrance indoors and out.

Some plants are at their most fragrant at a specific time of day, and this may affect where you site them. Those that release their scent during the day, for example chocolate vine (*Akebia quinata*), are best by arbours or arches, while patios or other sitting areas that tend to be used later in the day – are excellent sites for common jasmine (*Jasminum officinale*), which is at its most fragrant in the evening. Shrubs with aromatic leaves, such as rosemary, help to make a patio a more relaxing place.

△ RICH FRAGRANCE
*The heady scent of the late Dutch honeysuckle (Lonicera periclymenum 'Serotina') travels for many metres. It is especially strong in the evening.*

◁ PERFECT PERFUME
*Stiffly branched old glory rose ('Gloire de Dijon') produces its glorious, fully double flowers repeatedly during summer and autumn, filling the garden air with its delightful fragrance.*

## GOOD PLANT CHOICES

CLIMBERS AND WALL SHRUBS RECOMMENDED
FOR THEIR SCENTED FLOWERS
NH = not hardy

Actinida kolomikta
Akebia quinata (chocolate vine)
Chimonanthus praecox (wintersweet)
Clematis armandii, C. montana 'Elizabeth',
    C. rehderiana
Cytisus battandieri (Moroccan broom)
Honeysuckles Lonicera x brownii 'Dropmore
    Scarlet', L. x heckrottii,
    L. periclymenum 'Serotina'
Itea illicifolia
Jasminum azoricum (jasmine), J. officinale
    (esp. 'Argenteovariegatum'),
    J. x stephanense  NH
Prunus mume (Japanese apricot)
Roses 'Albertine', Bobbie James', 'Climbing
    Etoile de Hollande', 'Compassion',
    'Gloire de Dijon', JACQUELINE DU
    PRÉ ('Harwanna'), LAVINIA ('Tanklawi'),
    'Mme Alfred Carrière', 'Meg',
    'Wedding Day'
Schizophragma integrifolium  NH
Solanum jasminoides 'Album' (potato vine)  NH
Sweet pea Lathyrus odoratus, esp. 'Jayne
    Amanda', 'White Supreme', and
    old-fashioned types such as 'Painted
    Lady' and 'Matucana'
Trachelospermum asiaticum  NH
Wisteria sinensis (Chinese wisteria)

SEE ALSO: Ivies, p.104; Planting Climbers and Wall Shrubs, pp.110–111

# WAYS OF SUPPORTING PLANTS

CLIMBERS ARE BASICALLY plants with long, flexible stems, which, left to their own devices, trail over neighbouring plants – at times smothering them. In a garden they generally benefit from artificial support so that they and the surrounding plants can all flourish and flower freely. The correct type of support depends on how the climber grows. A lightweight annual or herbaceous perennial, with stems that die down in winter, is unlikely to cause a problem, but a large climber that develops a woody framework may, when mature, prove too heavy a burden for an arch or trellis screen. For safety's sake, it is essential that such structures are sturdy and strong.

## HOW CLIMBERS GROW

Climbers grow in one of three ways: clinging; twining or using tendrils; and scrambling. This influences the way they are trained but not how they are pruned. Some are self-supporting, while others may need initial assistance to reach a support but thereafter will climb by themselves. A few require frequent tying in to a permanent support.

■ **Clinging climbers** are all self-supporting. Some, such as ivy, use aerial roots to adhere to walls, fences, and tree trunks; they also make good ground cover. Others, such as Virginia creeper (*Parthenocissus*), develop touch-activated adhesive pads to stick to any hard surface. All clingers may need initial guidance towards a support.

■ **Twining and tendrilled climbers** are all self-supporting once they have something to wrap their stems or tendrils around. Twiners grow upwards in a spiralling motion – some, such as honeysuckle, twine in a clockwise direction while others, such as wisteria,

wrap their stems anticlockwise around any support. They can be grown into a strong host tree or shrub or tied to supporting wires, netting, or trellis against pillars, fences, and walls. Climbers such as vines and passionflower have true tendrils – modified shoots or leaves – which they use to twine around the stems of other plants or a suitable support. In others, such as clematis, it is the leaf stalks that act as twining tendrils.

■ **Scrambling climbers** all need fully supporting when grown in a garden. Some, such as winter jasmine (*Jasminum nudiflorum*), produce a mass of arching stems which make good ground cover if left to sprawl informally over a bank. Against a wall or fence, however, they should be secured to wires or trellis. Others, particularly brambles (*Rubus*) and climbing roses, have developed thorns to hook on to a host plant. When planted in a border, without the support of a tree or shrub, they too need tying to supporting wires or trellis at regular intervals.

### SOME TYPES OF CLIMBER

△ **TRUE TENDRIL**
*These modified shoots or leaves develop on plants such as passionflower (here). The climber uses them to coil tightly around any thin support.*

△ **LEAF STALK**
*The leaf stalks on plants such as clematis (here) act as twining tendrils, which curl tightly around a nearby support, for instance wire or plant stems.*

△ **TWINING STEM**
*Plants such as common jasmine and runner beans have stems that coil around their support. The direction in which they coil depends on the species.*

△ **HOOKED THORN**
*Some climbers use thorns as a kind of grappling hook to attach themselves to a support, even if it is not secure. Roses and brambles are typical examples.*

△ **AERIAL ROOT**
*These adhesive aerial roots form along the stems on plants such as ivy when the stem comes into contact with a fence, wall, or other rough surface.*

△ **ADHESIVE PAD**
*Small adhesive suckers, or pads, develop on the tendrils of plants such as Virginia creeper (here) once they come into contact with a supporting surface.*

△ **INITIAL TRAINING**
*Support stems of tendrilled and twining climbers (here a hop) by gently weaving them between crisscross wires or mesh while they are still young and flexible.*

### TELL ME WHY

**WILL CLIMBERS DAMAGE HOUSE WALLS?**

If the mortar is sound, plants should not cause problems as long as you keep them clear of gutters, window frames, and roof tiles or slates. Avoid growing climbers against tile-hung walls, where their shoots may get under the tiles and dislodge them. Plants with aerial roots and adhesive pads – ivies and Virginia creeper – are generally the only possible trouble-makers. Usually the rewards outweigh the problems. Climbers can help to insulate house walls against extremes of temperature, and they offer food and roosting sites for birds.

SEE ALSO: Planting Climbers and Wall Shrubs, pp.110–111

# ORNAMENTAL SUPPORTS

Introduce some ornamental supports into the garden to provide a focal point or to add a strong vertical element. Solitary pillars will form eye-catching features but for a more formal effect, erect a row of single pillars linked by chain or thick rope (swags) and train climbers along them. Flexible-stemmed climbers such as 'New Dawn' rose or 'Etoile Violette' clematis, which produce glorious displays of cascading flowers, are ideal for training up the pillars and along the swags. For the best effect, select plants that are sufficiently vigorous to cover the support generously with their flowers and foliage.

Tripods, obelisks, and wigwams are among the easiest and cheapest ornamental structures to introduce into a garden. They instantly add height, can be used for any climber that is not too tall or vigorous, and encourage good plant health because they allow easy air circulation around the stems. Many are attractive in their own right. Plant them with annual or other herbaceous climbers and their architectural outline will be a great asset in the winter garden.

Tie the stems at regular intervals

Wind a stem in the appropriate direction, depending on the plant

◁ **ROSE PILLARS**
*Training up pillars and along ropes is a traditional way of growing climbing and rambling roses. In this large kitchen garden, they also provide cut flowers.*

◁ **SWAG TRAINING**
*Carefully guide and secure the stems along a rope swag. Such horizontal training will encourage the formation of more abundant flowers than the same plant trained vertically.*

△ **ORNAMENTAL BEAN**
*Scarlet runner beans look attractive in a border (as here) or in a vegetable plot 'Painted Lady' has pretty pink and white flowers. You can buy or make your own cane tripod.*

# FIXTURES AND FITTINGS

Most climbers can be trained against trellis (*see p.93*), mesh netting, or taut lengths of galvanized wire. Use sheep or pig wire-netting for twining climbers; many with tendrils (sweet peas, for example) are light enough for plastic netting. Strands of heavy-duty wire are not too obvious and suit many climbers and wall shrubs. Soft garden twine can be used to tie in most stems. Fixtures and fittings must be resistant to corrosion and, in areas with high air pollution, use plastic or non-ferrous metal fixings.

Trellis and netting should preferably not be allowed to rest directly against a wall or fence, because air needs to circulate around a plant to prevent disease. Wooden 5cm (2in) battens can be fixed to the surface, and the trellis or netting hooked, hinged, or screwed to the battens (*see p.95*). Wires are best held 5–8cm (2–3in) away from the supporting surface and secured between vine eyes or galvanized nails. Tighten them with pliers – or attach tensioners at 2m (6ft) intervals, to prevent the wires sagging. Space wires 23–30cm (9–12in) apart, vertically and horizontally for maximum coverage, with the lowest wire 30cm (12in) above ground level.

△ **REGULAR MAINTENANCE**
*To encourage healthy, attractive growth, climber stems should be trained to their supports regularly, throughout the growing season. At the same time, cut out any dead or damaged shoots and check that old ties are not too tight.*

## HOW TO SECURE STEMS

◁ **FIGURE-OF-EIGHTS**
*Support stems against trellis or strong wire using garden twine tied in figures-of-eight. This kind of knot will be loose enough to allow for expansion of the stems while the plant matures and to prevent them chafing against any hard surfaces on the supporting structure.*

◁ **FENCE CLIPS**
*Support thin stems against wooden surfaces with plastic fence clips. One end of the clip should be pushed into the fencing panel, and then the other end is looped over the plant stem and pressed firmly into the wood so that the stem is held securely in position.*

SEE ALSO: Maintaining Climbers and Wall Shrubs, pp112–115

# PLANTING CLIMBERS AND WALL SHRUBS

MOST CLIMBERS AND WALL SHRUBS make long-lasting features in a garden, and, if they are to fulfil this role, must be carefully chosen to suit the intended site. Before planting, the ground must be thoroughly prepared (*see p.142*). The choice of support is important, too. If planting by a wall or fence, fix any wires or trellis in place before you prepare to plant. Walls, fences, and whatever support you use all need to be in good condition, because, once the plant is growing well, they will be difficult to repair. After planting, the plants should be well watered until they are established, carefully trained to their supports, and regularly checked for pests and diseases.

## PLANTING AGAINST A WALL

Autumn or spring is the best time to plant wall shrubs. Bare-rooted climbing and rambler roses should be planted from late autumn to midwinter or in early spring, and other climbers in autumn and mid- to late spring. Have your trellis or other system of support ready in place (*see p.95 and pp.108–109*) and prepare the planting area well, digging in plenty of well-rotted organic matter (*see p.142, also p.147 and p.150*). To avoid the rainshadow, the dry area beside the foot of a wall or fence, make the planting hole at least 30cm (12in) away from the base. Such an area, sheltered from the prevailing wind, receives little or no rain, and the wall itself may absorb moisture from the soil.

The plant should be angled towards the wall, and, if grafted, as with many roses, the graft union should be set 6cm (2½in) below soil level. This discourages the production of suckers from the rootstock. When refilling the planting hole, work the soil around the roots so that no air pockets remain. Any weak stems should be removed and, if only one main stem is desired, all but the most vigorous should be cut away. The addition of a thick, weed-suppressing mulch after watering well will speed the plant's development (*see p.152*).

All newly planted climbers and wall shrubs should be tied to their supports at once, to prevent wind damage to their young stems. If necessary, angle a bamboo cane between the stems and their support. Initially stems may require tying in but, once established, twining and tendrilled climbers will attach themselves. Wall shrubs and scrambling climbers will always need securing to their support.

## PLANTING NEAR A TREE

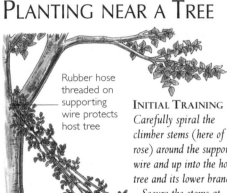

Rubber hose threaded on supporting wire protects host tree

**INITIAL TRAINING**
*Carefully spiral the climber stems (here of a rose) around the supporting wire and up into the host tree and its lower branches. Secure the stems at intervals with twine tied in figure-of-eight knots.*

A climber should be planted about 1–1.2m (3–4ft) away from the base of its host tree, beyond the edge of the tree canopy, to avoid competition for nutrients and moisture. This distance should be even greater if the host tree has a low crown or dense foliage that will restrict light. If planting in grass, clear a generous area around the planting site so that the climber is not competing with the grass.

To help a climber grow into a tree, its stems should be trained to a supporting wire or rope stretched between an angled peg in the ground and a low branch in the tree. When planting, angle the climber towards the tree, spreading out the roots (if bare-rooted) behind. Tie the stems to the guide. Winding the stems around the support will encourage flowering.

Never choose a climber that might swamp its host. *Clematis montana*, for example, needs a large tree. Small trees can support less vigorous large-flowered clematis or annuals such as morning glory.

### PLANTING A CLIMBER AGAINST A WALL

**1 CHECK LEVEL**
*Prepare a hole at least 30cm (12in) away from the wall. Insert the plant at a 45° angle, spreading the roots away from the wall. Use a horizontal cane to ensure the old soil marks on its stems are at ground level.*

**2 TRAIN STEMS**
*Fill in around the plant, firming the soil well. Then carefully untie the plant's original stake. With clips or soft twine, attach a cane to the base of each strong stem. Fan out and secure each cane top to the lowest wire.*

**3 INITIAL PRUNING**
*Using secateurs, cut out any remaining, unsupported stems — those that were spindly, damaged, or even dead. If strong stems are sparse, pinch out the tip of each supported stem to encourage new growth.*

**4 MULCH WELL**
*Now that the initial framework of the plant has been established, water well. Then cover the soil with an 8cm (3in) layer of well-rotted garden compost or manure to conserve moisture and discourage weeds.*

SEE ALSO: Fences and Trellis, pp.92–93; Walls, pp.96–97; Fixtures and Fittings, p.109; Preparing the Ground, pp.142–143

# PLANTING CLEMATIS

Clematis planted in spring or autumn, when the soil is warm and moist, are likely to establish the most successfully. Position them at least 30cm (12in) away from a wall or fence, to avoid dry soil. The planting hole should be deep, with the base of the stems buried well below soil level. This encourages plenty of new shoots to grow from the base, important if clematis wilt strikes and the stems need to be cut back; it may survive (*see p.301*).

Clematis prefer cool roots, so, after planting, shade the soil with stones, slabs, or roof tiles, or introduce low-growing plants in front. A deep mulch of well-rotted manure or garden compost will also help. Once established, clematis should flourish without extra water.

◁ **A GOOD BEGINNING**
*For fine flowers and foliage, give clematis (here C. montana 'Warwickshire Rose') a good start by adding plenty of organic matter, making a deep planting hole, and keeping the roots cool and moist.*

## PLANTING CLEMATIS BY A WALL

Most clematis need plenty of moisture, so at planting time bury a flower pot or piece of plastic pipe alongside the plant. This will channel the water down to the plant roots.

Bamboo cane supports plant until it reaches the trellis

Pipe slopes in same direction as cane

Water is poured into pot or pipe

Base of stems are below ground level

Cooling mulch of stones

Water seeps out of drainage holes

Trellis spaced from wall

Moisture is directed towards roots in base of hole

Stones prevent pipe from blocking

# GETTING THE BEST FLOWERS

Climbers need good training in their first season or two. Start by tying in shoots after planting and keep tying in as they grow to form a well-spaced, attractive framework. Spreading out stems allows flowers to be produced over a larger area. The closer stems are to the horizontal, the more sideshoots are likely to develop, all of which may be capable of producing flowers. Train plants in this way to create a tunnel of blooms on a pergola. For the

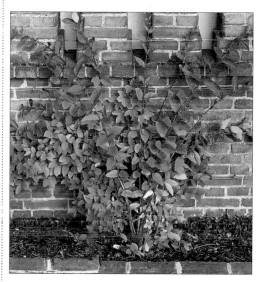

best wisteria flowers, prune an established plant by cutting back long growths and shortening sideshoots in late summer to form spurs, and reducing these spurs again in midwinter to two or three buds.

Although many climbers prefer their roots to be shaded, they flower best at the top, in light and sun. Training shoots horizontally helps, but extra support such as trellis is often needed at the top of a wall to prevent flowering stems flopping over and giving your neighbour the benefit. Wind climber stems around obelisks and tripods (*see below*), rather than letting them shoot straight up the supports.

**MORE FLOWERS ▷**
*On a tripod, obelisk, or similar structure, wind the stems (here of a rose) around the supports, tying them at intervals to horizontal wires. Such training will induce flower buds to form at all levels.*

◁ **GOOD COVERAGE**
*The stems of a young climber should be fanned out across a wall or fence while they are still flexible. Any gaps at the base can be difficult to fill once the framework is set.*

# AVOIDING PROBLEMS

When grown by a wall or fence, plants are sometimes more likely to suffer from certain problems. Powdery mildew (*see p.296*), is usually the worst, striking where air circulation is poor, especially if the soil is also dry. Avoid roses that are susceptible to mildew, black spot, and rust (*see pp.296–297*). Even if you are willing to use chemical control, climbers are difficult to spray once they have reached any height. Clear away affected leaves to prevent disease lingering from season to season.

The shelter of a warm wall may help pests to survive as well as plants. Keep a watch for greenfly on young shoots from early spring, and nip out tips, if necessary.

Clematis wilt (*see p.301*) may attack large-flowered hybrids but the smaller-flowered clematis (*see box, right*) are resistant.

Keep plants growing well. Check ties, feed after pruning, and mulch regularly. Soil must be damp when a mulch is laid.

**TELL ME WHY**

**WHY ARE CHOICE OF PLANT AND PLANTING METHOD IMPORTANT?**

Choosing a disease-resistant variety and giving it the best possible start will produce a plant that is best able to withstand attacks by pests and diseases.

**Some roses** are more susceptible to disease than others. Avoid mildew-prone types such as 'American Pillar', 'Handel', and 'Dorothy Perkins'. 'Aloha' and 'Golden Showers' are reasonably disease-free.

**Small-flowered clematis,** such as spring and early summer *Clematis alpina*, *C. macropetala*, and *C. montana*, plus late summer-flowering *C. tibetana* and *C. viticella* types, are resistant to clematis wilt.

**Soil at the base of a wall** is usually poor and dry and needs the addition of plenty of organic material before planting, to help retain moisture and nutrients. Keep roots moist until a plant is well established (*see illustration, left*) and mulch regularly.

SEE ALSO: General Border Maintenance, pp.152–153; Dealing with Weeds and Plant Problems, pp.288–311

# MAINTAINING CLIMBERS AND WALL SHRUBS

THE TIME SPENT LOOKING AFTER a climber or wall shrub will be amply rewarded by a healthy plant that puts on a handsome display of flowers, foliage, and possibly berries. Pruning and training is important for some, but not all. A climber such as ivy can largely be left to its own devices. Cut out dead or diseased stems, or variegated shoots that have reverted to plain green whenever you see them, but time other pruning according to the type of plant and its flowering season. Tie in stems promptly, while still pliant, and check that ties are not too tight, and that supports are sound and secure. Feed after pruning and mulch to conserve moisture in the soil.

## HOW AND WHEN TO PRUNE

Pruning helps to keep a shrub to an attractive shape, but remember that the harder you cut a stem back, the more vigorously it will regrow, so prune strong-growing stems lightly and weak ones more vigorously to achieve a balanced shape. Many shrubs, especially those with a lax habit grown in an informal fashion, simply need tidying up after flowering.

Pruning at the wrong time is unlikely to kill a plant, but it could result in losing a whole season's flowers or fruit if you cut away the stems that would have borne them. Prune shrubs and climbers that flower on stems produced in the current season, such as abutilon, *Campsis*, and *Solanum crispum*, in late winter or early spring, and those that flower on the previous year's growth, such as actinidia, flowering quince, and evergreen ceanothus, from early to late summer, after flowering.

Prune vines grown for their foliage in winter; *Prunus* in midsummer. Evergreens are best left until mid-spring. Pruning, combined with training, especially in the early years, is necessary for most climbers if you are to develop a good framework that will display flowers well and keep the plant to a suitable size. Vigorous climbers can ramble freely in a suitable site. A few climbers, such as clematis (*see p.114*) and wisteria (*see p.111*), have specific needs.

### WHAT TO PRUNE

△ **CROSSING BRANCHES**
*Cut any crossing or straggly stems back to their point of origin, to prevent them rubbing each other and eventually becoming damaged and diseased.*

△ **CROWDED STEMS**
*Thin areas of congested stems to open out the climber or wall shrub, so that light and air can circulate around it. Such pruning also prevents the plant becoming very heavy.*

◁ **PRUNING SIDESHOOTS**
*To fill a gap in the framework, shorten an adjacent sideshoot to encourage new growth. If possible, cut to an up- or downward-pointing bud, so that the new shoot does not grow away from the fence.*

---

### TELL ME WHY

**WHY IS IT NECESSARY TO PRUNE WALL SHRUBS AND CLIMBERS?**

**Creates a pleasing shape**: when combined with training, stems can be encouraged to grow in a desired direction so that they cover a surface evenly and the plant develops an attractive shape. Some wall shrubs can pruned and trained to form a specific shape such as a fan or tiered espalier, which can be useful where space is restricted.

**Improves flowering**: pruning stimulates new shoots to form that will in turn bear more flowers than old wood. Vigorous new stems often produce fewer but fatter buds that open into larger flowers.

**Restricts size**: climbers, such as vines, roses, and honeysuckles, can be kept within the available space on an arch, wall, or pergola.

**Promotes health**: cutting out dead, diseased, or damaged stems removes potential entry points for infection and helps to prevent its spread to the plant.

---

## WHERE TO PRUNE

Pruning cuts should be made as close to a bud or sideshoot as possible. Angle the cut where possible, so that moisture runs off, but avoid too steep an angle. A large wound that is slow to heal can easily become infected. Take care, too, not to leave a budless stub, which will die back and be vulnerable to disease.

Make clean cuts using sharp tools. Bruised or damaged wounds create a potential entry point for infection. Most pruning can be done with secateurs, but thick branches are best tackled with loppers or a pruning saw. Use shears on a climber with a mass of twiggy stems.

△ **ALTERNATE BUDS**
*Where the buds or shoots alternate on a stem, always cut just above and parallel to their angle of growth. Choose a bud that points in the same direction as the required new shoot.*

△ **OPPOSITE BUDS**
*Climbers and shrubs with buds that grow opposite each other should be cut squarely across the stem just above a pair of plump, healthy buds or young, vigorous shoots.*

◁ **CUTTING TO REPLACEMENT SHOOT**
*When needing to shorten a stem, always assess the shape of the whole plant before making any pruning cuts and then, using secateurs, cut just above a healthy stem pointing in the required direction.*

**SEE ALSO:** Using Mulches to Suppress Weeds, p.145; Deadheading, p.155

# SHAPING WALL SHRUBS

After planting, evergreen shrubs generally require little or no pruning, nor do those with a lax habit that are to be grown informally. Space out and tie in the stems to create an even, well-shaped framework, pruning out any ill-placed or weak shoots.

Shrubs that are to be kept flat to a wall, such as flowering quince (*Chaenomeles*) and pyracantha, or trained in a fan, for instance Japanese apricot (*Prunus mume*), need to have all outward-facing shoots removed, as well as any growing towards the wall. Space out the other shoots, gently pulling them down towards the horizontal, as appropriate, and tying them in.

◁ **ORNAMENTAL BUSH**
*Pyracanthas can look particularly effective when the flexible young stems are trained in horizontal tiers against a wall. They can even be shaped around windows. A strong support is needed, as are gloves to protect against the thorns.*

## INITIAL STAGES

△ **TYING IN**
*Using twine, secure all selected stems (here, of an evergreen ceanothus) to their support, spacing them out evenly*

△ **UNWANTED STEMS**
*Remove at its point of origin any stem that is growing directly away from the support or towards it.*

△ **PINCHING OUT**
*Nip, or cut back with secateurs, soft, young forward-pointing shoots, to encourage more branches to grow sideways.*

△ **CUTTING BACK**
*Lightly prune back the longest stems by two or three buds in order to keep the shrub balanced and within its allotted area.*

# KEEPING IN SHAPE

Tie in new shoots to fill gaps in the framework while they are still young and flexible, and, at the same time, loosen old ties before they can begin to restrict stems. Prune out dead, dying, or diseased wood whenever you see it, but wait to cut out frost-damaged shoots until frosts are over. The time for pruning other stems depends largely on when the shrub flowers (*see facing page*). Do not remove shoots that have just flowered on a shrub grown for its berries. Continue to prune out shoots growing into or away from the wall.

Some shrubs need minimal pruning, for example the "fishbone" cotoneaster, *C. horizontalis*, and *Garrya*. It is possible to prune flowering quince twice a year to produce more flowering spurs: shorten long summer shoots in midsummer by two thirds, then shorten these again in late winter to three or four buds. Avoid letting evergreen ceanothus get out of hand by pruning old flowering stems each season. Old wood will not reshoot.

## PRUNING A DECIDUOUS CLIMBER

◁ **UNWANTED STEMS**
*Remove weak stems, those that cross over another stem, and any growing directly towards or away from the support.*

**SPACING STEMS** ▷
*Tie in new growths, filling in any gaps in the main framework of the climber. Stimulate new growth by pruning if necessary*

◁ **OLD WOOD**
*Cut unproductive stems back to ground level. Then tie new growths into the resulting gap.*

**SPUR PRUNING** ▷
*Shorten long sideshoots to 3–6 buds to encourage the development of flowering shoots the following season.*

SEE ALSO: Renovating Climbers, p.115

# PRUNING CLEMATIS

The many types of clematis vary in their pruning requirements, depending on when they flower and age of wood they flower on. They can, however, be divided into three convenient pruning groups.

Group 1 clematis flower in spring and need minimal pruning, although occasional thinning will reinvigorate them. Most can be cut hard back if they need rejuvenating, but *Clematis montana* may not recover from pruning into old wood. If this gets too big, or the stems become heavy and tangled, cut away the old, dense growth but leave a few strong stems intact.

The clematis in Group 2, which start to flower in early summer, should be lightly pruned in late winter or early spring to thin the plant down to a framework of well-spaced one- or two-year-old stems.

Alternatively, these clematis can simply be cut back hard every three or four years, thus losing the first flush of flowers.

Late summer-flowering Group 3 types are pruned in late winter or early spring down to a pair of healthy buds within 30cm (12in) of the ground, but can be cut back in autumn if the dead stems will mar a host tree, shrub, or other climber.

◁ **LIGHT PRUNE**
*In late winter or early spring, shorten stems of Group 2 clematis back to strong growth or a pair of healthy buds, leaving a framework of one- or two-year-old stems to encourage flowering.*

◁ **OLD GROWTH**
*Remove old growth with a clean cut just above the point of origin. Tangled top-growth can also be sheared away, and the remaining stems unravelled, cut back to a healthy pair of buds, and spaced out against the support.*

◁ **HARD PRUNE**
*In late winter or early spring, once growth has just started, cut back all stems on Group 3 clematis to within 30cm (12in) of soil level. Remove any stems that are not shooting, to stimulate new growth from below ground level.*

# CLEMATIS PRUNING GROUPS

Clematis in Pruning Group 1 include the evergreens that flower in winter, *Clematis alpina* types with nodding bells, dainty *C. macropetala*, and vigorous *C. montana*. The double-flowered clematis all belong to Group 2, as do the large-flowered hybrids that bloom in early summer, sometimes with a later second flush. The later summer large-flowered hybrids belong to Group 3, as do the easily grown smaller-flowered *C. viticella* types like 'Alba Luxurians', plus *C. tibetana* and *C. tangutica*.

△ **GROUP 2, FOR EXAMPLE 'VYVYAN PENNELL'**
*In late winter or early spring, remove any weak laterals on these clematis, to stimulate new shoots and more blooms. Prune congested or damaged growth back to a branching point or to the soil level. To prolong flowering, make your pruning cuts over a period of weeks.*

△ **GROUP 3, FOR EXAMPLE 'GRAVETYE BEAUTY'**
*In late winter or early spring, remove all dead, damaged, or diseased stems. Hard prune the remaining stems back to plump, healthy buds about 30cm (12in) above the soil level. To extend the flowering season, shorten some of the stems again, in early summer.*

◁ **GROUP 1, FOR EXAMPLE *CLEMATIS MONTANA***
*These clematis require only minimal pruning because any cuts will remove potential flowering stems. They do, however, benefit from occasional thinning and shortening of some stems to healthy buds or shoots after flowering. Also remove dead, weak, and diseased stems.*

## THE THREE PRUNING GROUPS

Some of the most popular clematis and their groups:

### GROUP 1
*Clematis alpina*, 'Frances Rivis', 'Pink Flamingo', 'Ruby', 'White Moth', *C. armandii*, *C. cirrhosa*, *C. macropetala*, 'Maidwell Hall', 'Markham's Pink', *C. montana*, 'Elizabeth', 'Marjorie', 'Picton's Variety'.

### GROUP 2
'Arctic Queen', 'Beauty of Worcester', 'Bees' Jubilee', 'Dr Ruppel', 'Elsa Späth', 'Fireworks', 'Guernsey Cream', 'H.F. Young', 'Henryi', 'Lady Northcliffe', 'Lasurstern', 'Marie Boisselot', 'Miss Bateman', 'Moonlight', 'Mrs Cholmondeley', 'Multi Blue', 'Nelly Moser', 'Niobe', 'Royalty', 'Silver Moon', 'Sugar Candy', 'The President', 'The Vagabond', 'Vyvyan Pennell', 'Wada's Primrose', 'W.E. Gladstone', 'Vino'.

### GROUP 3
*Clematis rehderiana*, *C. tangutica*, *C. tibetana*, *C.viticella*, 'Alba Luxurians', 'Ascotiensis', 'Bill MacKenzie', 'Comtesse de Bouchaud', 'Ernest Markham', 'Etoile Rose', 'Etoile Violette', 'Gipsy Queen', 'Gravetye Beauty', 'Hagley Hybrid', 'Huldine', 'Jackmanii', 'Jackmanii Superba', 'Mme Edouard André', 'Mme Julia Correvon', 'Minuet', 'Pagoda', 'Perle d'Azur', 'Polish Spirit', 'Princess Diana', 'Rouge Cardinal', 'Royal Velours', 'Venosa Violacea', 'Ville de Lyon'.

**SEE ALSO:** Tools for Cutting and Pruning, p.279

# CLIMBING AND RAMBLING ROSES

Deadhead roses, to encourage more blooms on repeat-flowering types, and tie in new growths throughout the season. Feed plants immediately after pruning.

Ramblers and modern climbing roses differ in their growth and flowering habits and so are pruned in different ways. In fact ramblers often flourish without pruning, but look much better in a garden if cut back regularly and trained over a wall or to form a screen.

Rambling roses flower most prolifically on wood produced in the previous season. They are therefore pruned once their single flush of flowers is over, in summer. Ramblers make more new growth from the base of the plant than climbers, and this should be encouraged by taking out old stems at ground level. Flowers develop on the same sideshoots for several years, so these need not be cut every year.

### SEASONAL CARE
*At the end of the growing season, in autumn, long, arching stems on climbing roses should be carefully tied in, cutting them back slightly if necessary.*

Many modern climbing roses are repeat flowering so are pruned in autumn, when leaves begin to fall. Long shoots should be tied in or shortened to avoid wind damage. Reduce flowered stems by two-thirds, and cut out less productive shoots.

## PRUNING AND TYING IN RAMBLERS

**1 MAIN STEMS**
*Cut back one in three old main stems down to the ground. This will stimulate fresh basal growth. Remove each long, thick stem in sections, to prevent damage to adjacent stems.*

**2 EXCESS GROWTH**
*Thin some leading shoots and shorten others by 5–8cm (2–3in), and their sideshoots by two-thirds, to encourage branching and more flowers for the following season.*

**3 SECURING NEW SHOOTS**
*Throughout the growing season, tie in new shoots as they develop. Use proprietary ties or soft garden twine in a figure-of-eight knot, and aim to maintain a well-balanced framework.*

## PRUNING AND TYING IN MODERN CLIMBERS

**1 FLOWERED SHOOTS**
*Shorten stems that have produced flowers by two-thirds of their length. Tip-prune stems that have outgrown their allotted space.*

**2 UNPRODUCTIVE SHOOTS**
*Completely remove any leafless, weak, diseased, or damaged shoots back to a healthy stem. If necessary, cut main stems near ground level.*

**3 ADJUST TIES**
*Gradually loosen or replace ties, such as this ratcheted plastic one, as the stems expand. Prune or reposition and retie any stems that are rubbing.*

# RENOVATING CLIMBERS

A few climbers, such as passionflower and Chilean bellflower (*Solanum crispum*), are best replaced by new plants once they have become old and congested, or outgrown their space. Many, however, can be saved by renovation, but some are better suited to hard pruning than others.

Evergreens are usually the least likely to respond well to severe pruning. Ivy will shoot readily from old wood: cut it back to within about 1m (3ft) of the base. Honeysuckle, vines, *Campsis*, and oriental bittersweet (*Celastrus orbiculatus*) usually reshoot well if pruned to about 60cm (24in) above soil level. All the renovation can be undertaken in one operation, during winter while the plant is dormant, except for evergreens, which are best pruned in mid- to late spring.

Other climbers will recover best if renovation is staged over two or three seasons. This is the preferred method for climbing hydrangea. If in any doubt about a plant's ability to withstand hard pruning, renovate gradually in this way, taking out a few stems at a time. It may help to shear away tangled top growth, then sort out the main stems or detach the plant and lay it on the ground. Cut each stem back to a healthy bud. Keep most stems to a reasonable length, but prune one or two close to the ground. Rearrange the stems over their support and tie in. Mulch but do not feed heavily. Repeat this procedure over the next year or two, until all old stems have been removed.

### △ DRASTIC PRUNING
*Some climbers, such as this honeysuckle, quickly reshoot and flower well after cutting back to 60cm (24in) above ground level. Others such as wisteria and common jasmine (J. officinalis) may take several seasons to recover.*

**SEE ALSO:** Applying Mulch, p.152; Maintaining Roses, p.160

# HEDGES IN THE GARDEN

HEDGES COMBINE A PRACTICAL and an aesthetic role within the garden, where they establish its basic style and framework. Although generally used to form a legal boundary, they also make excellent internal divisions as well as being architectural features in their own right. Because most hedges are permanent features, it is important to link such living boundaries with the landscape beyond. The right choice of hedging material is vital to success: it must suit the soil, site, aspect, and climate, and grow at a suitable rate. Hedges are cheaper and more environmentally friendly than walls and fences, but are slower to create effective screens.

## DESIGN CONSIDERATIONS

Choice and style of hedge are a matter of personal taste. Any hedge needs to suit the style of planting in a garden, but there are no rules. A dense, precision-clipped hedge of yew not only suits a formal design, it will also provide the perfect background to a naturalistic or cottage-garden style planting. In rural areas, native species blend attractively into the surrounding countryside. Informal hedges provide the opportunity to introduce flowers and berries which in turn attract wildlife. Choosing the type of hedging plant goes hand in hand with deciding on

the style. If you opt for a formal hedge, remember that the faster it grows the more frequently it will need trimming. No plant grows quickly to 2m (6ft) then stops. In the long term, a slow-growing hedge is a lot less work and much more rewarding. Informal hedges are easier to manage, but will still need some pruning and often have a wider spread. Low aromatic hedges of lavender, box, or santolina look marvellous within a garden, lining paths and edging beds.

Taller internal hedges can be used to screen one part of the garden from another. If you want to create an arch, let some stems on either side of the opening reach a length where you can tie them together in the centre, at an appropriate height. Prune out the tips regularly to encourage bushy growth, tying in more shoots whenever necessary. Once the arch is growing thickly, carefully cut it to shape. Although it is more difficult, you can also create a "window" in a similar way by cutting and tying and training stems, using canes as a guideline if necessary to form the desired shape. A pleached hedge (*see p.91*) also offers glimpses to areas beyond.

Hedges are usually of a single species, but different plants can be combined for a tapestry effect. For formal hedges they need similar growth rates but this is less important for informal styles. Given plenty of space, you could imitate country hedgerows and plant a mixture including holly, hazel, hawthorn, or field maple.

◁ **FOLIAGE CONTRASTS**
*The colour and dense texture of this formal yew hedge is highlighted by the much lighter, looser, and longer leaves on the adjacent informal bamboo screen.*

△ **SQUARED EDGES**
*The solid, geometric framework of this garden has been cleverly interrupted by use of some wooden screening and by the "window" trained in one of the boundary hedges.*

▽ **RICH BACKDROP**
*This solid, dark green conifer hedge makes an excellent foil for the pink sidalceas and poppies, the golden yellow Spanish broom, and the grey-leaved plants in the foreground.*

SEE ALSO: Boundaries and Divisions, pp.30–31

# PRACTICAL CONSIDERATIONS

Before selecting what plant to grow, you need to consider the hedge's function. Some plants stand up well to wind (*see p.119*), and dense hedges muffle noise. Prickly plants such as hawthorn can form an almost impenetrable barrier (*see list, right*).

Take into account a shrub or tree's height when mature. If this is higher than you want, the hedge will need regular, time-consuming clipping, and if it is to form a garden boundary, it will have to be trimmed on your neighbour's side, too. You must keep fast-growing trees such as Leyland cypress under control and consider the effects on those around you. The conifer *Thuja plicata* is a good alternative; it is easily kept to 2m (6ft) or lower if clipped twice a year, in spring and early autumn. A wiremesh or hurdle fence makes a useful short-term boundary until slow-growing plants reach a reasonable height.

Cost is likely to be all important. Bare-rooted hedging plants, especially of native species, cost a lot less than container-grown plants. Specialist suppliers often advertise in gardening magazines. You may have time to produce your own rooted cuttings (*see pp.164–165*), especially useful when planting long hedges of box and lavender, both of which root easily. The planting distances below will produce a good, thick hedge. A slightly wider spacing is acceptable for a tall hedge.

Avoid planting hedges in very dry soil or beside narrow borders because they will take up nutrients and moisture to the detriment of surrounding plants.

## GOOD CHOICES

### RECOMMENDED PRICKLY HEDGES

Many plants that bear prickles or thorns on their stems or leaves make excellent hedges. Both evergreen and deciduous species are suitable – the choice depending on the style of hedge and whether it is to act as a uniform backdrop to the garden.

*Berberis*: especially *B. × stenophylla*
Flowering quince (*Chaenomeles*: lots to choose from)
Gorse (*Ulex*)
Hawthorn (*Crataegus monogyna, C. laevigata*)
Holly (*Ilex aquifolium, I. × altaclerensis*)
Japanese bitter orange (*Poncirus trifoliata*)
Pyracantha
Roses: especially 'Complicata', *Rosa eglanteria, R. rugosa*
Sloe/blackthorn (*Prunus spinosa*; try 'Paul's Scarlet')

◁ **SPIKY DETERRENT**
*Sharp spiny hedges, such as this berberis, will help to deter intruders and create an effective stockproof boundary. In autumn, the colourful leaves and berries vie with one another for attention in the garden.*

△ **HEDGE FOR WILDLIFE**
*The colourful fruits in this mixed informal hedge of red- and yellow-berried pyracanthas not only look good but also provide a source of food for birds.*

# PLANTING DISTANCES AND CLIPPING OR PRUNING FREQUENCY

## FORMAL HEDGES

| EVERGREEN | PLANTING DISTANCE | HEIGHT | CLIPPING TIMES |
|---|---|---|---|
| Box (*Buxus sempervirens*) | 30cm (12in) | S | 2 or 3 times in growing season |
| Escallonia | 45cm (18in) | M–L | Once, immediately after flowering |
| Holly (*Ilex × altaclerensis, I. aquifolium*) | 45cm (18in) | M–L | Once, in late summer |
| Lawson cypress (*Chamaecyparis lawsoniana*) | 60cm (24in) | M–L | Twice, in spring and early autumn |
| Lavender | 30cm (12in) | S | Twice, in spring and after flowering |
| Leyland cypress (*× Cupressocyparis leylandii*) | 75cm (30in) | L | 2 or 3 times in growing season |
| *Lonicera nitida* | 30cm (12in) | S–M | 3 or 4 times in growing season |
| Privet (*Ligustrum ovalifolium*) | 30cm (45in) | M–L | 3 or 4 times in growing season |
| Yew (*Taxus baccata*) | 60cm (24in) | M–L | Once or twice in growing season |
| DECIDUOUS | | | |
| Beech (*Fagus sylvatica*) | 30–60cm (12–24in) | M–L | Once, in late summer |
| *Berberis thunbergii* | 45cm (18in) | S–M | Once, in midsummer |
| Hawthorn (*Crataegus monogyna*) | 30–45cm (12–18in) | M–L | Twice, in summer and autumn |
| Hornbeam (*Carpinus betulus*) | 45–60cm (18–24in) | L | Once, in mid- to late summer |

*S (small) 30cm–1m (1–3ft); M (medium) 1–2m (3–6ft); L (large) 2m (6ft) or taller

## INFORMAL AND FLOWERING HEDGES

| EVERGREEN | PLANTING DISTANCE | HEIGHT | WHEN TO PRUNE |
|---|---|---|---|
| *Berberis × stenophylla* | 45cm (18in) | M–L | Immediately after flowering |
| *Cotoneaster lacteus* | 45–60cm (18–24in) | M–L | After fruiting |
| Escallonia | 45cm (18in) | M–L | Immediately after flowering |
| *Garrya elliptica* | 45cm (18in) | M–L | Immediately after flowering |
| Holly (*Ilex × altaclarensis, I. aquifolium*) | 45–60cm (18–24in) | M–L | In late summer |
| Lavender | 30cm (12in) | S | After flowering |
| Pyracantha | 60cm (24in) | L | In mid-spring |
| DECIDUOUS | | | |
| *Forsythia × intermedia* | 45cm (18in) | M–L | After flowering, remove old stems |
| *Fuchsia magellanica* | 30–45cm (12–18in) | S–M | In early spring, remove old stems |
| Hawthorn (*Crataegus monogyna*) | 45–60cm (18–24in) | L | In winter, remove selected vigorous shoots |
| Hazel (*Corylus avellana*) | 45–60cm (18–24in) | L | After flowering, in mid-spring |
| *Potentilla fruticosa* | 30–45cm (12–18in) | S–M | In mid-spring |
| Roses 'Roseraie de l'Haÿ', *Rosa rugosa* | 45–60cm (18–24in) | M–L | In spring, remove thin twigs |
| Sloe/blackthorn (*Prunus spinosa*) | 45–60cm (18–24in) | L | In winter, remove selected vigorous shoots |

*S (small) 30cm–1m (1–3ft); M (medium) 1–2m (3–6ft); L (large) 2m (6ft) or taller

SEE ALSO: Planting and Maintaining Hedges, pp.120–121

# FORMAL HEDGES

Plants used for formal hedges must produce dense growth and tolerate repeated close trimming. They are often small-leaved and slow-growing. Classic choices include yew, *Thuja plicata*, privet, holly, and, where there is sufficient space, large-leaved Portugal laurel (*Prunus lusitanica*). When frequently clipped, beech and hornbeam, although deciduous, attractively retain their dead, russet-coloured leaves in winter.

Formal hedges usually contain a single species, but mixed hedging of contrasting foliage can provide variety throughout the year. The plants used, however, should have compatible growth rates if over-vigorous species are not to dominate. A favourite combination mixes green and copper beech (*see p.31*). Combining shrubs with different-sized leaves creates an

◁ **LARGE LEAVES**
*Evergreens with handsome large leaves, such as Portugal laurel and this Elaeagnus × ebbingei 'Gilt Edge', should be trimmed using secateurs. Leaves that are sheared in half turn brown at the edges, spoiling the appearance of the hedge.*

interesting effect, for instance *Lonicera nitida* and privet. Add in their golden-leaved forms to make it all the more striking. A mosaic hedge of evergreen and deciduous species, such as hornbeam and holly, also looks attractive.

Box, lavender, *Santolina*, and *Berberis thunbergii* all make good low hedges. As well as using them to line beds and paths, try them above low retaining walls.

SEE ALSO: Bamboos, p.141

◁ **ELEGANT BOUNDARIES**
*Yew* (Taxus baccata) *makes some of the best-looking, dense formal hedging, but it may take six to ten years to become fully established. During this time it needs precise, regular cutting to develop an even shape and density.*

# BAMBOOS

The woody, arching stems and ornamental foliage of these evergreens make them useful for hedges, screens, and windbreaks, if close-planted. They are good at muffling noise as well producing their own soothing rustle.

Many bamboos have invasive root-runs so choose carefully. One of the most striking is slow-growing *Chusquea culeou*, which may eventually reach 6m (20ft). It bears graceful, olive-green stems. A slow-spreading dwarf bamboo, with green-striped, golden yellow leaves, is *Pleioblastus auricomus*. It grows to 1.5m (5ft) tall. *Phyllostachys flexuosa* makes a good screen up to 3m (9ft) high, although its wavy green canes, sometimes noticeably zigzagged, will in time form large thickets.

**YEAR-ROUND SCREEN** ▷
*The copious leaves on this* Phyllostachys nigra var. henonis *filter wind effectively, and this bamboo has the bonus of attractive, lustrous yellow stems, when mature.*

# INFORMAL FLOWERING AND BERRYING HEDGES

Left unclipped, some foliage shrubs make delightful informal hedges (*see list, facing page*) but often part of the charm of an informal screen is its flowers or berries.

For spring and summer interest, plant hedges of flowering quince (*Chaenomeles*), hypericum, and species and hybrid shrub roses, for example. For the best value, select scented flowered roses such as 'Roseraie de l'Haÿ'.

For reliable autumn colour, introduce cotoneaster, for its cheerful, usually red berries, or snowberry (*Symphoricarpos*), for its dense clusters of white fruits that last well into winter. Among good informal hedging plants with fine flowers as well as fruits are thorny pyracanthas, which have white flowers and yellow, orange, or red berries, while the carmine red flowers of *Rosa rugosa* are followed by large red hips.

In gardens with young children, beware of planting a hedge that bears tempting but toxic berries. The berries of hawthorn, cotoneaster, berberis, and viburnum may cause stomach upsets if eaten.

## PLANT LIST

### HEDGES RECOMMENDED FOR THEIR FLOWERS

Some plants in this list of flowering hedge shrubs are also of interest for their berries, and vice versa.

Berberis darwinii, B. × stenophylla
Escallonia 'Apple Blossom', E. 'Langleyensis',
E. 'Pride of Donard' some *
Forsythia × intermedia
Fuchsia magellanica, F. 'Phyllis', F. 'Riccartonii'
Garrya elliptica *
Hypericum forrestii
Lavender: especially Lavandula angustifolia 'Hidcote'
Potentilla fruticosa
Ribes sanguineum
Tamarix ramosissima

### HEDGES RECOMMENDED FOR THEIR BERRIES OR NUTS

Cherry plum (Prunus cerasifera 'Pissardii')
Cotoneaster horizontalis, C. lacteus, C. simonsii
Hawthorn (Crataegus monogyna)
Hazel (Corylus avellana)
Lonicera nitida 'Yunnan'
Myrtle (Myrtus: especially M. communis subsp. tarentina) *
Pyracantha
Roses: Rosa canina (dog rose), R. rugosa, R. 'Schneezwerg'
Sloe/blackthorn (Prunus spinosa)
Snowberry (Symphoricarpos × doorenbosii)
Viburnum tinus 'Eve Price'

\* not hardy

△ **FLORAL ASSET**
*Flowering hedges such as potentilla (here) will often be studded with a seemingly endless display of flowers, from spring until autumn.*

**AUTUMNAL GLOW** ▷
*The orange-red berries on this* Cotoneaster simonsii *are offset by the glossy, rich green leaves, creating an eye-catching combination.*

# HEDGES IN EXPOSED AND COASTAL SITES

△ **WINDBREAK**
*The arching stems of this graceful* Tamarix ramosissima *flex readily and will not break in strong winds.*

◁ **HARDY HEDGE**
*Among the most tolerant plants of coastal exposure is spiny-stemmed sea buckthorn (*Hippophae rhamnoides*), which has persistent, bright orange berries on female plants.*

Hedges can provide invaluable shelter for gardens in exposed sites where wind may desiccate foliage or scorch shoot tips. Plants growing near the tops of hills are especially vulnerable to gusting winds. By the coast, the wind may also carry damaging salt spray, causing leaves to turn brown. Any build-up of salt in the soil may harm roots as well.

Since hedging plants can suffer in just the same way, it is important to choose shrubs or trees able to withstand wind or salt spray (*see list, left*). Many of them share certain characterisitics: for instance, small, tough leaves, as on holly and hawthorn. Deciduous hedges can make the most effective wind filters. Thick evergreens may cause strong winds to "jump" the hedge and create turbulence.

In seaside gardens, the choice of hedging is greater. Frost is seldom a problem, especially on the west coast, and plants can be chosen that would not be hardy elsewhere. For example, flowering shrubs such as hebes, the daisy bush (*Olearia*), and tree lupins (*Lupinus arboreus*) can be used to make attractive informal hedges.

To help a hedge to establish in a windy site, erect a temporary, semi-permeable windbreak on the windward side, and perhaps support with wires (*see overleaf*).

## PLANT LIST

### HEDGES RECOMMENDED FOR EXPOSED AND COASTAL GARDENS
c = hedges especially suitable for coastal sites

Although many hedges will tolerate coastal winds, few flourish in frequent salt-laden gales.

Daisy bush (Olearia nummulariifolia) c
Elaeagnus: all, for example E. angustifolia (oleaster) c
Escallonia (see list above, some *) c
Griselinia littoralis c *
Hawthorn (Crataegus monogyna)
Hornbeam (Carpinus betulus)
Holly (Ilex × altaclerensis, I. aquifolium)
Juniper (Juniperus communis) c
Sea buckthorn (Hippophae rhamnoides) c
Tamarix ramosissima c
Tree purslane (Atriplex halimus) c *

\* not hardy

**SEE ALSO:** Preparation and Planting, p.120

# PLANTING AND MAINTAINING HEDGES

BECAUSE HEDGES ARE potentially long-lived, their site and soil must be thoroughly prepared before planting. The success of a newly planted hedge also depends on how it is pruned during its first two or three years – deciduous hedges, in particular, need formative pruning to ensure dense growth from the base to the top. Thereafter, the amount of trimming or pruning needed, or any other maintenance, depends on the type of hedge: evergreen or deciduous, formal or informal, flowering or berrying. All hedges, however, should be top-dressed with a balanced fertilizer each spring, and then mulched, in order to maintain strong, even growth.

## PREPARATION AND PLANTING

Container-grown plants are best planted from autumn to spring, and root-balled and bare-root plants from late autumn to late spring. Do not plant in frosty ground. If necessary, keep bare roots moist until conditions are suitable by planting temporarily in a frost-free spot. Prepare the planting site well. It must be free from perennial weeds such as ground elder, brambles, and bindweed. These will be impossible to eradicate once the hedge has grown. Weed regularly while plants are getting established.

A couple of weeks before planting, mark the line of the hedge with a string guideline and dig a trench, deep and wide enough to accommodate the plants' roots comfortably. Add plenty of well-rotted manure or garden compost (*see below*), and leave the soil to settle.

■ **Water the plants well** the day before planting. Keep bare roots wrapped until planting to prevent them from drying out.

### PREPARING THE GROUND

**1** **DEEP DIGGING**
*Dig a trench 30–60cm (12–24in) deep, 60–90cm (24–36in) wide along the guideline, and remove the topsoil. On heavy, poorly drained ground break up the subsoil.*

**2** **FEEDING THE SOIL**
*Alternate 8cm (3in) layers of organic matter and topsoil in the trench. Finish with 110g (4oz) of general-purpose fertilizer such as blood, fish, and bone meal per metre/yard.*

**STRAIGHT PLANTING △**
*Most hedges are planted in a single row, with 30–60cm (12–24in) between plants (see also p.117). Tiny plants for dwarf hedges can be set 10–15 cm (4–6in) apart.*

**STAGGERED PLANTING △**
*Only for a particularly thick barrier, 90cm (3ft) or more wide, alternate the plants between two rows 45cm (18in) apart. Space plants 90cm (36in) apart in the row.*

■ **Lay the plants** along the string line, at the appropriate spacing, alternating any weak plants with stronger, healthier ones.
■ **Dig holes and plant** one by one, removing each plant from its pot or wrapping only when its hole is dug and you are ready to plant. Set the plant in the hole at the same level as it was in its container or in the open ground. There is usually a mark on the stem indicating the previous soil level. Lay a cane across the top of the hole to check alignment. Backfill with soil, firming in stages to prevent air pockets.
■ **Water well** once you have planted the whole row. Apply a 5–8cm (2–3in) layer of mulch over the entire trench.
■ **In very exposed sites** support plants with a couple of wires strung between posts on the windward side. Tie in plants loosely to the wires so that they do not rub against the wire, damaging the bark.

## FORMATIVE PRUNING

Do not try to make the shoots on all plants an even length on planting. Most evergreens need minimal pruning and shrubs in informal hedges are pruned as specimens (*see p.158*). Prune strong shoots on beech and hornbeam by one-third, weak shoots by two-thirds. Cut back hawthorn and privet to 15–30cm (6–12in) above ground level in late spring, then cut back side-shoots in late summer; the next winter, remove half the previous season's growth.

### INITIAL STAGES

**1** **BEFORE PRUNING**
*Some vigorous evergreens, such as this Lonicera nitida, require formative pruning to encourage dense growth from the base.*

**2** **AFTER PRUNING**
*The strong laterals have been pruned lightly and the weak ones hard. The leaders are trimmed lightly once the hedge is the desired height.*

### HEDGE SHAPES

**ROUNDED TOP △**
*In heavy snowfall regions, shape a hedge so that it has a rounded or pointed top, which sheds snow more easily than a flat one.*

**SLOPED SIDES △**
*In areas prone to high winds or gales, shape a hedge so that it is narrower at the top, to deflect the wind and so reduce damage.*

SEE ALSO: Preparing the Ground, pp.142–143; Planting Shrubs, p.150; Planting with Sheet or Mat Mulches, p.151; Perennial Weeds, pp.292–293

# TRIMMING AND PRUNING

The aim of clipping a formal hedge is to ensure healthy, vigorous, dense growth from base to top, and to maintain a neat outline. Diseased or damaged growth needs to be removed whenever it is seen, otherwise trimming frequency depends on the rate at which a plant grows, plus the height it would normally reach when mature (*see p.117*). Aim to produce a shape with gently sloping sides that is narrower at the top than the base (*see facing page, below*). To keep the top level, use string stretched between canes as a guide. Evergreens are trimmed from spring to early autumn; deciduous hedges are usually clipped after midsummer. Always avoid clipping while there are birds

nesting in a hedge. The shrubs in an informal hedge are pruned in the same way as freestanding specimens (*see pp.158–159*), usually after flowering or berrying, or in spring. At the same time, they can be given any additional pruning needed to maintain an attractive shape.

Use electric hedge trimmers or shears for formal hedges, and secateurs, or a pruning saw if necessary, for an informal hedge. Prune or trim shrubs with large evergreen leaves with secateurs (*see p.118*). After trimming, feed, water, and mulch.

△ **USING ELECTRIC HEDGE TRIMMERS**
*Most small-leaved formal hedges are cut with electric hedge trimmers, which should be worked with a wide, sweeping action, keeping the blade parallel to the hedge. Do not cut with the trimmer raised above shoulder height.*

▽ **USING SHEARS**
*When trimming, hold the blades of shears parallel with the line of the hedge at all times. To get a straight, consistent shape, use a string line tied between canes as a guide.*

## ALWAYS REMEMBER

### GOLDEN SAFETY RULES

Never use an electric hedge trimmer in damp conditions. Always ensure that it is fitted with a residual current device (RCD or "circuit breaker"), and never allow the flex to trail dangerously. Protect yourself with goggles, ear defenders, and gloves, and check any staging or stepladders are stable.

# RENOVATING HEDGES

Overgrown, untidy, hedges can often be renovated by phased pruning, but success depends on the type of plant. Few conifers respond to severe pruning, apart from yew, which will readily resprout from old wood. Both height and width of a hedge can be drastically reduced, but separate the two operations by allowing at least a growing season in-between. If only the sides are to be cut back, it is also best to cut them in alternate years (*see below*). Renovate deciduous hedges when dormant, in winter; evergreens respond best in mid-spring. To encourage vigorous regrowth, feed and mulch the hedge well the season before renovation is to start, and again after each pruning session.

∧ **SECTION THROUGH A CONIFER HEDGE**
*Even if trimmed regularly on the outside, conifer hedges eventually lose all their leaves inside, because most are unable to produce new shoots from old wood. Ultimately such a hedge usually needs replacing although yew responds excellently to phased renovation.*

# TOPIARY

The tops of hedges, as well as freestanding shrubs, can be used for topiary. Spheres and cubes are the simplest shapes to create, while animals and birds allow scope for the imagination. Dense, slow-growing, small-leaved evergreens are the most suitable plants – yew and box are ideal. Round shapes can be cut freehand; canes and wire make a good guide for straight-sided shapes. Complex designs generally require a wire frame to be secured in place as a permanent cutting guide. Take time clipping and shaping, standing back frequently to assess the effect, especially in the formative stages.

∧ **TEMPORARY GUIDE**
*After clipping a young box roughly into shape, use canes and wire to achieve an even, symmetrical cone.*

△ **FINISHED CONE**
*Clip regularly to keep in shape. Use whichever tools – shears or secateurs – you feel most comfortable with*

△ **YEAR ONE**
*To reduce the width of a neglected or overgrown hedge, prune side growth almost to the main stem on one side only (here, the right side). Trim the other side less drastically. Then feed and mulch the hedge.*

∧ **YEAR TWO**
*A year later, provided the hedge is growing vigorously, cut back the other side (here, the left side) almost to the main stem, to match the previous severe pruning. Lightly trim the opposite side; feed and mulch.*

SEE ALSO: Pruning Established Shrubs, pp.158–159

# BEDS AND BORDERS

## GARDEN STYLES

OVER THE CENTURIES, the design of flower gardens has swung from artful formality to relaxed informality and back again, with a variety of styles in-between. Each has its virtues, and gardeners today can either draw on aspects they like from former eras or throw away the instruction book to create their own individual, modern patterns. Beds and borders may be completely formal, with structured planting, or more natural looking with intermingling plants; alternatively, you could try mixing the two. Height, shape, texture, and colour of the plants are just as important as the site and shape of a bed or border, and should be considered at the planning stage.

### THE FORMAL LINE

Geometry, pattern, and symmetry, expressed in strong lines and bold shapes, are the essence of formality. The style relies heavily on hard landscaping in the shape of bricks and pavers, which form both a frame for plantings and a unifying element between house and garden.

Plantings, too, may follow a geometric template, as with close-clipped hedges or knot gardens. Symmetry, in which each planting has its echoing mirror image, can be relaxed for emphatic contrast or restrained to reinforce design unity.

### AN INFORMAL APPROACH

The informal style tries to emulate nature by favouring irregular shapes. It uses sweeping curves and undulating forms as a framework for plantings of apparently undisciplined abundance and, if hard materials are used, they are usually of natural origin, such as stone or wood.

For the plant enthusiast, informality is the style of choice. If formality demands restraint and simplicity, informality has variety and exuberance at heart – new plant acquisitions can be added without fear of spoiling line or symmetry.

∇ **INFORMAL PROFUSION**
*Drifts of plants that weave together to create a natural-looking tapestry are the essence of an informal flower bed, but this is the result of much planning and hard work.*

> #### GOOD IDEAS
>
> • Garden visiting is a prime source of ideas and inspiration; observe, borrow, and build on other gardeners' successful ideas.
>
> • Look at books and magazines to identify appealing styles and features. Make a list of "wants" and "must haves" to help define the style and content of your own designs.

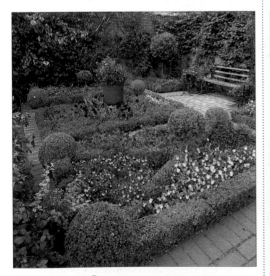

△ **GEOMETRIC SHAPES**
*Rectangles, triangles, and squares formed by low, clipped box hedges create an instant impression of formality, but this can be softened by flowering plants contained within the pattern. Brick paving adds to the effect.*

SEE ALSO: Border Types, pp.124–125; Raised Beds, pp.180–181

# ON THE WILD SIDE

Wild gardening may be regarded as the ultimate expression of the informal style. Bringing native plants into the garden may stem from a desire to conserve plants threatened by habitat loss, or from simple appreciation of their natural charms. Some can be grown in traditional borders, but most do better in areas that imitate habitats like a sunny meadow or shady woodland. Such areas provide special conditions, influencing the range of plants that thrive. They are an ideal solution for exposed sites or those with poor, dry soils. Native plants can also provide food and refuge for local birds, animals, and insects.

## TELL ME WHY

### WHY GO WILD?

Wild flowers native to your region are a rich source of nectar, for bees and butterflies, and food for insect- and seed-eating birds. Attracting wildlife brings its own fascinations and, as many of these creatures prey on garden pests, they can contribute to ecologically friendly forms of pest control.

**A WILDFLOWER BORDER ▷**
*Wild flowers usually prefer to grow in impoverished soils, and therefore can be used to give a spectacular display in an area of the garden where cultivated plants are likely to fail. They should also attract a variety of insects.*

# MAKING THE MOST OF SPACE

Beds and borders constitute one means of shaping and dividing up the garden in visually interesting ways that will provide privacy and enclosure as well as a setting for your favourite plants. The human eye perceives scale differently indoors and out, because, in the open, scale is reduced by the comparison with broader horizons. Be bold when deciding on the size of beds and borders. Make them as large as possible, but aim for a balance of open space and planting mass, making the latter of sufficient substance to allow contrasts of form and graduation of height. Make lines clean and strong, to draw the eye into the distance, or form broad, sweeping curves to hide – and invite exploration of – what lies beyond

**◁ ISLAND BEDS**
*Seen from all sides, an island bed allows planting compositions that vary depending on the standpoint of the observer. This is an excellent way to maximize plant variety in a relatively small space.*

**△ NO WASTED SPACE**
*The tiniest space can be made to work hard for its living. This shady corner is enlivened by a range of foliage textures that gives interest through the growing season, forming a verdant backdrop for a seasonal succession of flowers.*

**△ LINEAR SPACES**
*Long, narrow borders let you play with perspective. They lead the eye onwards, and, punctuated with tall, architectural plants, reward the observer with a series of interesting focal points.*

**CURVING EDGES ▷**
*A curved line between two points is always longer than a straight one. This is a trick that designers often use to gain more space for planting in small and confined gardens.*

SEE ALSO: Principles of Design, pp.126–127; Raised Beds, pp.180–181

# BORDER TYPES

BORDERS MAY BE CLASSIFIED according to the plant groups they contain — herbaceous borders and shrub borders, for example. Each has different attributes, but all are designed to provide maximum interest through the year. This is especially true in small gardens, where every plant must work hard to justify inclusion. While favourites always deserve a place, however short their season, the best approach uses plants that give value over prolonged periods: ones that bloom long or often, or flower early, producing fruits later on. Try to exploit foliage to the full; it may offer glorious tints in spring or autumn, as well as forming a textural backdrop for other features.

## SHRUB BORDERS

Woody-stemmed shrubs, both deciduous and evergreen, are valued for a wide range of ornamental virtues, and with careful selection their flowers, fruit, foliage, or stems can provide elements of interest in every season of the year. Shrub borders are particularly useful for creating a permanent and fairly low-maintenance framework for the garden.

### GOOD IDEAS

• A shrub border can make a peep-proof, sound-muffling, and relatively labour-saving alternative to clipped hedging, with the added advantage of seasonal variety.

• Make use of the permanence of a shrub border. Create a barrier to divide the garden into spaces for different activities, form an intimate and sheltered enclosure, and screen off any unappealing features that may lie beyond the garden's perimeter.

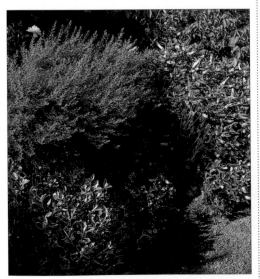

△ A FLOWER-COVERED BARRIER
*Shrub borders make ideal barriers, especially where formal hedging is out of keeping. Here, roses, hebes, and senecios combine long-lasting flowers with attractive foliage.*

## MIXED BORDERS

The mixed border is the most versatile of border types, since it exploits the virtues of all the plant groups. Shrubs lend height and structure, and they form an attractive backdrop for other plants. If chosen well, they add colour and variety with their foliage, seasonal flowers, and fruit.

Spring bulbs enliven the early months, dying back to make way for summer-blooming perennials, with summer bulbs as highlights. Gaps are filled with annuals and biennials, while late blooms are staged against a backdrop of seedheads, dried flowerheads, and tinted autumn foliage.

▽ COMBINING PLANT TYPES
*Here, long-blooming* Geranium endressii *interacts with the late-summer blues of hydrangeas and towering plumes of giant reed grass (*Arundo donax*).*

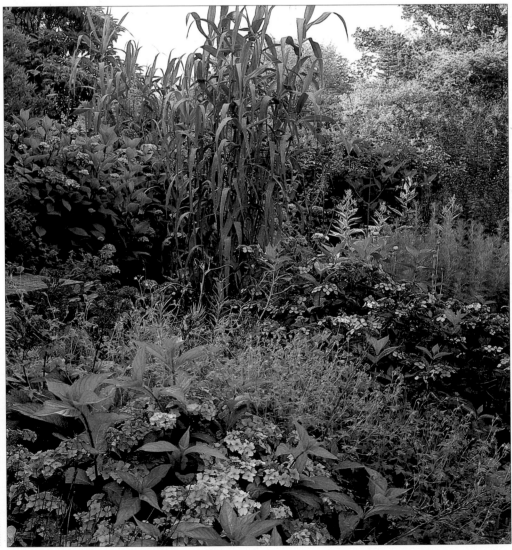

SEE ALSO: Forming a Structure, p.126; Raised Beds, pp.180–181

# HERBACEOUS BORDERS

The traditional herbaceous border is one of the highlights of the garden during the summer months, when most perennials are at their peak. Herbaceous perennials die back to a rootstock in winter and produce new growth and flowers each year. This is the main drawback of a perennial border, for dormant plants leave vacant areas of soil during the darkest months, when spirits are most in need of cheer. If the promise of the new season's regrowth and coming profusion does not satisfy you, extend interest with early-flowering spring bulbs, and into autumn with late bloomers and seedheads that lend sculptural beauties of their own.

### ▽ PROLONGED PERFORMANCE
*Long-serving alchemillas and astrantias provide a foil for the more transient campanulas; the sword-shaped leaves of crocosmia hint at late summer and autumn glories to come.*

# SEASONAL HIGHLIGHTS

For designing borders, the living palette of flowers, fruits, foliage, and stems has enormous potential for creating a year-long succession of ornamental highlights. Every border, however, has low points, so planning for additional features to cover seasonal gaps makes good sense, especially in small spaces where voids are especially noticeable. Bulbous plants offer a simple solution; their showy, highly seasonal flowering supplies vibrant colour, while their disappearance during dormancy is rapidly masked by the burgeoning growth of their companion plants.

## BULBS FOR SEASONAL INTEREST

**WINTER**
Snowdrops (*Galanthus*)
Winter aconite
  (*Eranthis hyemalis*)
Spring snowflake
  (*Leucojum vernum*)
Squilla (*Scilla*) (some)
Tulips (most)

**SPRING**
*Anemone blanda*
Chionodoxas (all)
Crocuses (most)
Daffodils (*Narcissus*)
*Erythronium* (most)
Grape hyacinths
  (*Muscari*) (most)
Hyacinths (*Hyacinthus reticulata*)
*Iris histrioides*
*Ornithogalum montanum*
Puschkinia
Spanish bluebells
  (*Hyacinthoides hispanica*)

**SUMMER**
Agapanthus
*Allium cristophii,*
  *A. giganteum*
Cannas (most)
*Galtonia candicans*
Gladiolus (most)
Lilies (most)
Montbretia (*Crocosmia*)

**AUTUMN**
Autumn snowflake
  (*Leucojum autumnale*)
Colchicums (most)
*Cyclamen hederifolium*
*Sternbergia lutea*

# USING ANNUALS AND BIENNIALS

Annuals and biennials are, by their very nature, short-term plants: annuals germinate, flower, set seed, and die within a single growing season; biennials produce leafy growth in their first year then flower, set seed, and die in the second.

Used alone, such short-lived, but rapidly growing, plants can provide instant colour in new gardens, in anticipation of more permanent plantings. They are also useful as fillers of spaces left to accommodate the mature spread of longer-lived plants. Since many will self-sow if conditions suit, they can also add pleasingly unexpected associations to permanent schemes.

### ANNUAL EXPERIMENTS ▷
*Short-lived plants are ideal for experiments in colour and form. Here, a complementary theme of yellow Ionas and blue ageratums proves a success that would bear repeating.*

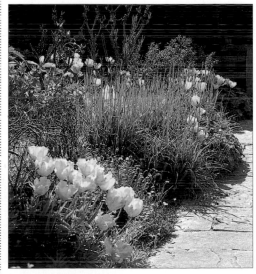

### △ SPRING INTO SUMMER
*The backlit brilliance of 'Texas Gold' tulips illuminates this border in late spring; as they fade, golden-flowered daylilies (Hemerocallis) continue the theme into summer.*

SEE ALSO: Natural-born Fillers, p.127; Raised Beds, pp.180–181

# PRINCIPLES OF DESIGN

ORIGINAL, INNOVATIVE IDEAS serve to distinguish some of the best borders as the work of individual designers, but there are basic principles that underly all good design, whatever the scale or site. They are similar to those used by a painter when composing a picture, so that separate elements are united to create a harmonious whole.

Good compositions embrace a balance of mass and space, unity and contrast, with all elements in proportion to each other and in scale with the surroundings. Although decorative qualities are obviously important, designers choose plants primarily for their function — the part they play in forming a layered and cohesive composition.

## FORMING A STRUCTURE

The structural elements in a garden may be likened to a skeleton that forms the bones beneath the flesh. In the broadest sense, these include the hard landscaping materials such as walls and paving, which define the garden's layout. Architectural plants, however, may also be used within the beds and borders to help in the creation of the garden's "skeleton".

Woody plants, chosen from a wealth of shrubs and trees, are key elements in building up planting schemes. They serve to enclose, to give shelter, and to provide a backdrop for other plants. They constitute a permanent frame for a composition, but at the same time are part of it. While structure plants can be very attractive in their own right, garden designers usually choose them first and foremost for their functional contribution to a scheme.

> ### TELL ME WHY
>
> #### WHY TRY TO COPY NATURE?
>
> Look at a woodland fringe and you will see distinct layers of plants. In sun, low grasses lie at the feet of taller perennials, some in dappled shade, which are themselves succeeded by a shrub layer and, finally, a tree canopy. This multi-layered composition is not only functional for the plants but also very pleasing to the human eye, which commends its use to the garden designer.

## FOCAL POINTS

A focal point acts as a visual "reward" as the eye moves along a planting scheme. Like a punctuation mark in a sentence, it tells the viewer where to pause, creating a striking contrast to the basic rhythm and flow of a design. Plants used as focal points must have distinctive presence by virtue of sheer size or strength of form. They may be used to terminate a vista, but gain greater value when viewed from more than one angle. One plant may form the focal point of adjacent compositions.

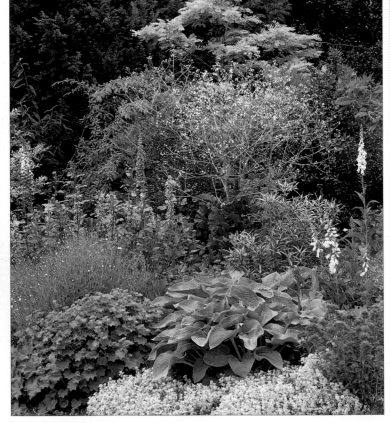

**NATURAL LAYERS ▷**
*This layered planting, with* Robinia pseudoacacia *'Frisia' as its golden focus, employs a framework of hollies, pittosporums, and olearias against a dark backdrop of cypress.*

△ **ARCHING ROSES**
*Flexible-stemmed roses, like 'Mme Isaac Pereire', can form an enclosure just with arching branches. Other climbers or ramblers will do so more formally, if trained on a pillar, arch, or pergola.*

△ **STAR PERFORMER**
*The pale, metallic hue and strong, spiky form of* Eryngium giganteum *demands full attention as it rises above a contrasting low carpet of dark leaves.*

**STRONG LINES ▷**
*Providing height and distinct, vertical lines,* Eremurus robustus *may be used to dramatic effect as a focal plant, especially against a plain, dark background.*

**SEE ALSO:** Shape and Form, p.128; Borders with Special Conditions, pp.130–131

# PLANTING IN DRIFTS

The plants that form the most significant mass in a planting scheme should also be the most decorative. The designer relies on these, in contrast with the framework plants, to provide both flower and foliage interest throughout the growing season. When planning their arrangement, the aim is to link individual groups with an underlying rhythm that leads the eye on in a smooth visual flow, in which nothing appears out of place. Planting in swathes, or drifts, is the technique used to achieve this. There are several methods, each lending a different feel and style, formal or informal, to the finished effect (see below).

△ **MASSED BLOCKS OF PLANTING**
*For strongly architectural effects, structured masses of planting form a patterned collage providing contrasts in colour, texture, and form. Here, white sedums and pink dahlias and mallows highlight a background of detail.*

△ **INFORMAL DRIFTS**
*Irregular, interlocking drifts, elongated and layered in height are punctuated with more upright groups to provide a more informal effect. Here, a drift of pale pink phloxes contrast with the upright form of salvias.*

△ **RANDOM DRIFTS**
*Mimic the randomness seen in nature by setting large plants singly among groups of smaller ones, and allowing them to spread by seed or runner. Here, foxtail lilies and delphiniums are dotted around smaller pink poppies.*

# GRADUATING HEIGHTS

Using drifts of plants increasing gradually in height from the front of the border to the back, or along its axis, is traditional, but it is not an unbreakable rule. It gives a layered effect, meaning that no plant is obscured by its neighbours. The occasional use of taller plants of open, "see-through" habit, such as *Crambe*, at the border's edge simply emphasizes the graduated effect.

△ **LEADING THE EYE**
*The tiered effect of graduated planting lends an illusion of depth to a border and generates a line that leads the eye smoothly onwards and upwards. If height increases along the border's length, it enhances perspective and the highest point obscures what lies beyond, thus inviting exploration.*

# USING GROUND COVER

Most ground-cover plants are dense, mat-forming or creeping plants, which smother weeds by excluding light and thereby preventing seed germination. Their low-growing habit also makes them ideal plants for the first layer at the front or edge of the border. There, they form a strong horizontal line that provides a good foil for taller vertical plants and more rounded forms. As they grow, their spreading habit enables plants of similar vigour to weave together to form a carpet, which also helps to soften any harsh edges.

## LOW-GROWING PLANTS

*Alchemilla conjuncta.* Lobed, blue-green leaves; sprays of lime-green flowers all summer.

*Anthemis punctata* subsp. *cupiana.* Mat former; feathery, silver-grey leaves; white flowers in early summer.

*Anthyllis montana.* Silky, divided, grey-green leaves, and pink, red, or purple flowers in early summer.

*Geranium renardii.* Mounds of velvety, grey-green leaves; white or lavender flowers in early summer.

*Heuchera micrantha.* Grey-marbled leaves, and sprays of pink-tinted white flowers in early summer.

*Nepeta* × *faassenii.* Aromatic, silvery grey-green leaves, and spikes of lavender-blue flowers all summer.

*Stachys byzantina.* Mounds of densely silver-hairy, grey-green leaves, and white-woolly spikes of pink-purple flowers throughout summer.

# NATURAL-BORN FILLERS

Annuals and biennials are perfect short-term gap fillers with the added benefit that they often self-seed to give naturally random effects in following years. If the results are not pleasing, the plants can be removed without great loss. If you choose colours initially to blend within a scheme, any seedlings will later produce flowers in the same range of complementary hues.

△ **UNEXPECTED EXCITEMENT**
*Many annuals and biennials will self-seed with abandon where conditions suit them, but there is no telling where their offspring will arise. Here, poached egg plant (Limnanthes douglasii) sprawls across a path below sweet rocket (Hesperis matronalis).*

**SEE ALSO:** Ground Cover, p.75; Colour, Form, and Texture, pp.128–129; Using Ground Cover in Shady Areas, p.131

# COLOUR, FORM, AND TEXTURE

WHILE STRUCTURAL PLANTINGS and the creation of a layered composition form the bones of a design, it is the varied shapes and textures of the mass of plants that provide its finish and colour. The form of plants provides potential for contrasts of line — verticals, horizontals, and dynamic diagonals — and between rounded, spiky, or arching shapes. Line and shape are linking elements, which can tie the whole design together, especially if repeated. Foliage texture may be used to form a verdant backcloth against which the more transient qualities of flowers will be highlighted, and the use of colour dictates the mood of a planting perhaps more than any other factor.

## VARIETY OR UNITY?

The degree of variety that is desirable in a design varies with the size of the site. Too much gives an impression of clutter and compromises the unity of a scheme; too little is simply boring. Contrasts are most telling if composed simply. Too many conflicting elements vie for attention — the eye darts restlessly about, unable to find a focus or follow a line.

Unity is the quality that ties a design together. It may be expressed in the use of patterns, shapes, or textures as repetitive motifs. A definite planting theme, perhaps in terms of colour or type of plants used, is one of the best ways to create unity.

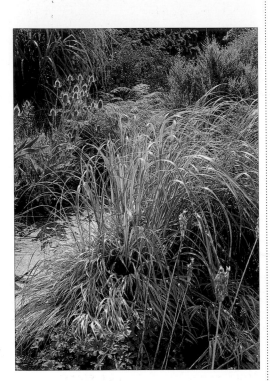

**VARIATIONS ON A THEME ▷**
*Ornamental grasses provide the unifying theme for this unusual border, but it does not consist of grasses alone. Their architectural forms are both separated and highlighted by plants of contrasting shapes.*

## SHAPE AND FORM

Designers like to compose schemes so that the shapes and forms of the plants contrast and link together in a balanced and visually pleasing way. A successful composition might juxtapose, for example, two junipers: the vertical *Juniperus scopulorum* 'Skyrocket' with the horizontal form of *J. procumbens*, and join the two with a more rounded form, such as *Hebe rakaiensis*. Try playing with ideas at the planning stage by sketching shapes and outlines on paper, and rearrange them until satisfied with the overall balance.

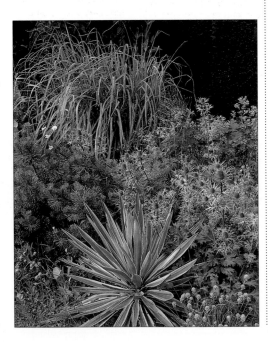

**STRENGTH IN UNITY ▷**
*The strong, spiky* Yucca gloriosa *'Variegata' forms a focus and sets the theme, which is echoed, but not overwhelmed, by the dark-needled pine,* P. mugo, *and metallic-blue mounds of* Eryngium × oliverianum.

## TEXTURAL ELEMENTS

Changes in texture form a subtle but vital element in a composition, especially in terms of foliage. Leaves form the greatest mass in a border and their textural qualities far outlive the more ephemeral delights of flowers. Texture depends on both leaf size and surface finish. Try contrasting the fine texture of small-leaved plants with large leaves of bold, simple outline, or offset matt and silky leaves with light-reflecting, glossy ones.

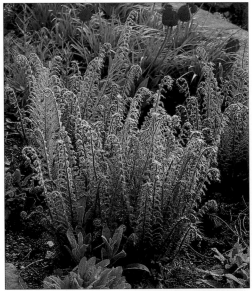

△ **FINE FRONDS**
*Backlit by spring sun, the fronds of a soft shield fern unfurl. Their feathery texture is offset by foliage of simpler shape.*

**SOFT AND SMOOTH ▷**
*The downy, quilted feel of the large leaves of some hostas, such as this* Hosta sieboldiana, *is a textural feast. Hostas form a good foil for finer-leaved plants.*

**SEE ALSO:** Perennials, pp.134–135; Grasses, Bamboos, and Ferns, pp.140–141

# COLOUR THEORY

The primary colours of red, yellow, and blue can be mixed, in pairs, to give the secondary colours of green, violet, and orange. With the exception of green, these intense hues can assault the eye if used in excess, but lend brilliant and dramatic contrast in small masses, if set against a backdrop of more subtle tones. Tertiary colours are formed by mixing secondaries and they *always* harmonize, since those next to each other on the colour wheel share "components". Conversely, colours opposite each other on the wheel form complementary contrasts.

## TELL ME WHY

### "FETTERS FOOLISHLY SELF-IMPOSED"

Volumes have been written on colour theory and its application in gardens, but colour purists often overlook personal taste and the subjectivity of colour perception. Some people adore hot, bright, and even clashing colours, while others find the cool restraint of pastels more restful. The theory of harmonics and complementary contrasts has been used by artists for centuries and it *does* work in practice but, if rules don't give the effects you desire, don't feel bound by them — experiment freely instead.

# COLOUR IN PRACTICE

Light intensity affects colour perception enormously, and it varies with latitude, season, and time of day. Pastels that appear washed out at midday acquire luminosity at twilight; a brilliant mass of magenta, as with bougainvilleas, achieves perfection in the bright subtropics, but appears strident in the blue-tinted light of duller climes. Personal taste, tones of hard landscaping, and any views beyond the garden should also be considered in colour associations.

Blue, indigo, violet, and their pastel tints provide cool sophistication; they appear to recede, so they can enhance the effects of perspective

Greens hold a scheme together and are used to separate strong or clashing colours

Colours next to each other on the colour wheel form close harmonies, whether they are true hues or muted tints

Complementary colours (any pair directly opposite to each other) used together enhance each other's effects, if used as contrasts

Hot shades of yellow, orange, and red supply a mood of exuberant warmth, and appear to advance, foreshortening perspective

## THE COLOUR WHEEL ▷

*Primaries in mixed pairs produce secondary hues; both have an intensity that is best used in small masses. Mixed secondaries produce tertiaries, which reflect the subdued colours of nature and can be used in greater masses.*

In general, the more intense the colour, the smaller its mass needs to be within the scheme to give striking, but not overwhelming, effects

△ **HARMONY**
*An opulent harmony, here cerise and purple, is made from colours that lie next to each other on the wheel.*

△ **CONTRAST**
*Grape hyacinths and tulips contrast primary blue with secondary orange, which are opposites on the wheel.*

△ **HARMONIOUS SHADES**
*This pastel palette uses mainly harmonizing colours from the same third of the colour wheel; monotony is avoided by including stronger hues such as the purple of salvias and the hot orange of daylilies to provide welcome contrast.*

# SEASONAL AND SUCCESSIONAL INTEREST

The advancing seasons bring a panoply of changing colour and texture. The fresh greens of spring, often tinted with pinks and reds, revert to a darker, more uniform backdrop in summer, before firing up in autumnal splendour. Short-lived flowers may give rise to ornamental seedheads or lustrous, often persistent fruit, which in many woody plants will decorate a stark and architectural winter outline. To gain maximum value throughout the seasons, try to choose reliable, long-flowering performers as well as plants that offer more than one season of interest.

△ **MELLOW FRUITS**
*Crab apples with their plentiful blooms and fresh green foliage in spring, assume renewed brilliance in autumn with foliage tints and fruits.*

△ **RIPE SEEDHEADS**
*Many poppies produce ornamental seedheads. The blue capsules of* Papaver somniferum *follow a succession of pink, mauve, or white flowers.*

## PLANTS FOR ALL SEASONS

*Amelanchier laevis.* Small tree or shrub with white spring flowers, blue fruits, and fine autumn colour.

*Cotinus* 'Grace'. Purple-leaved shrub with clouds of tiny pink flowers and brilliant red autumn tints.

Honesty (*Lunaria annua*). Annual or biennial with white or purple spring flowers and silver seedpods.

Japanese maple (*Acer palmatum*). Small trees or shrubs renowned for autumn foliage.

*Pyracantha.* Evergreen shrubs with early summer flowers and persistent autumn fruits.

*Rosa rugosa.* Emerald green leaves, pink or white flowers in summer, and red hips in autumn.

Teasel (*Dipsacus fullonum*). Biennial with emerald leaves and thistle-like, winter-persistent seedheads.

SEE ALSO: Oriental Poppies, p.135; Shrubs for Foliage Colour, p.139

# BORDERS WITH SPECIAL CONDITIONS

MOST PLANTS ADAPT well to a range of soil conditions if their needs for sun, shade, and temperature are met. Some gardens, however, are located in sites with special conditions, and these are often considered less than ideal. The optimistic gardener, however, is not deterred, but sees them as an opportunity to grow a different range of plants. In all gardens, the key to success is to select plants to suit the prevailing conditions; if conditions are special, the plants must be too. Throughout the world there are groups of plants adapted to various tough habitats, such as deserts, mountainous regions, waterlogged areas, and coastal sites — let these make up your planting palette.

## DRY, SUNNY BORDERS

In dry, sunny sites, remember to make the soil more moisture retentive (*see p.133*) and to choose plants with an inherent tolerance of drought and heat. Plants native to sun-baked habitats, such as the Mediterranean maquis, or South African veldt, should fit the bill. Many of these have leathery leaves that reduce water loss, or leaves that have white hairs to reflect ultra-violet rays. Some, like tulips, have bulbs to store food and water, and retreat below ground in the summer heat.

△ **FRENCH LAVENDER**
*From dry, rocky maquis, this aromatic, grey-leaved perennial (Lavandula stoechas) needs hot, arid conditions to thrive.*

### PLANTS FOR DRY, SUNNY SITES

| TREES AND SHRUBS | |
|---|---|
| Ceanothus thyrsiflorus var. repens | Dictamnus albus |
| Cistus ladanifer | Eremurus robustus |
| Helianthemum | Erigeron karvinskianus |
| Juniperus communis | Ferula communis |
| Lemon verbena (Aloysia triphylla) | Golddust (Aurinia saxatilis) |
| Perovskia atriplicifolia | Gypsophila repens |
| Vitex agnus-castus | Houseleek (Sempervivum) |
| Yucca | Osteospermum jucundum |

| PERENNIALS | HERBS |
|---|---|
| Acaena novae-zealandiae | Lavender (Lavandula) |
| Agastache mexicana | Oregano (Origanum vulgare) |
| Anthemis cupiana subsp. punctata | Rosemary (Rosmarinus officinalis) |
| | Thyme (Thymus) |

◁ **HEAT-LOVING PLANTS**
*Helianthemums, verbascums, and sisyrinchiums are typical plants of hot and dry, stony habitats. Such plants dislike wet soil at their stem base in winter; apply a top-dressing of gravel to aid rapid drainage and avoid waterlogging.*

## SEASIDE AND EXPOSED SITES

Coastal and exposed sites impose testing conditions, owing mainly to strong winds. Wind can obviously cause mechanical damage to plants, but also scorches leaves; a rapid air flow makes them lose water more quickly than they can replenish it from the roots. In coastal zones, salt-laden winds exacerbate this effect.

Mountain, moorland, and maritime native plants are the best choice here, and consider deep-rooting plants of creeping habit, such as *Dryas octopetala*, which are less affected by wind. Plants with leathery leaves, such as *Griselinia littoralis*, are often wind- and salt-resistant. The Latin epithets *montana* (of mountains), and *littoralis* and *maritima* (coastal natives) indicate likely survivors.

### PLANTS FOR COASTAL SITES

| TREES AND SHRUBS | |
|---|---|
| Blue daisy (Felicia amelloides) | Leucanthemum × superbum |
| Brachyglottis | Lobularia maritima |
| Cytisus × praecox | Phlomis russeliana |
| Genista hispanica | Phormium |
| Griselinia littoralis | Red hot poker (Kniphofia) |
| Pinus contorta, P. mugo | Red Valerian (Centranthus ruber) |
| Pyrus salicifolia 'Pendula' | Sea holly (Eryngium maritimum) |
| Rosa rugosa | Sea lavender (Limonium latifolium) |
| Rowan (Sorbus aucuparia) | Sea kale (Crambe maritima) |
| Sea buckthorn (Hippophae rhamnoides) | Sea thrift (Armeria maritima) |
| Whitebeam (Sorbus aria) | Stock (Matthiola incana) |

| PERENNIALS | |
|---|---|
| Anchusa azurea | |
| Antennaria dioica | SUCCULENT |
| Arenaria balearica | Hottentot fig (Carpobrotus edulis) |
| Geranium sanguineum | |
| Lavatera arborea | |

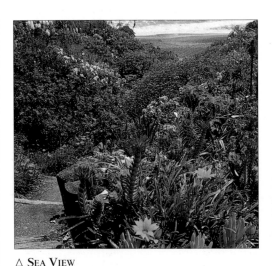

△ **SEA VIEW**
*Red hot pokers, blue daisies, and Hottentot figs feature among the thriving contributors to this exuberant planting, sited within reach of salt-laden winds that would be harmful to many common garden plants.*

SEE ALSO: Beds for Drought-tolerant Plants, pp.132–133; Preparing the Ground, pp.142–143

# SHADY SITES

Far from being a problem, the presence of some shade in the garden greatly increases the range of plants that can be grown; those native to woods and forests need shade to give off their best. Flowers last longer and hold their colour better out of the bleaching sun, and foliage stays fresh for longer periods. Slow to warm in spring, a shady site delays growth and provides a little shelter from frost. Shaded soil retains more moisture than that exposed to sun, reducing the need for watering, but this also means that some areas will be permanently damp. In the shade beneath the branches of large trees, however, the soil may be quite dry.

## PLANTS FOR MOIST SHADE

| TREES AND SHRUBS | FERNS (MOST) |
|---|---|
| Daphne laureola | |
| Gaultheria mucronata | PERENNIALS |
| Japonica (Chaenomeles) | Alchemilla mollis |
| Mahonia (most) | Anemone × hybrida |
| Skimmia japonica | Cardamine pratensis |
| Witch hazel (Hamamelis × intermedia) | Chelidonium majus |
| | Bleeding heart (Dicentra) |
| BULBS | Foxglove (Digitalis purpurea) |
| Iris foetidissima | |
| Lilium chalcedonicum, L. henryi, L. martagon | Primrose (Primula vulgaris) |
| Snowdrop (Galanthus) | Solomon's seal (Polygonatum × hybridum) |
| Spanish bluebell (Hyacinthoides non scripta) | Woodrush (Luzula sylvatica 'Marginata') |

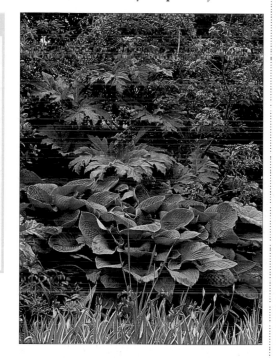

**LUSH FOLIAGE ▷**
*This moist, marginal border in partial shade has been thoughtfully planted with Iris laevigata 'Variegata' at the front with hostas and heracleums behind.*

# ACID SOIL

If you discover that your soil type is acid, there are many attractive plants that you can grow. These include camellias, flowering in winter and early spring, rhododendrons, with blooms often succeeded by downy new leaves, such as in *R. yakushimanum*, and azaleas. Heathers offer year-round foliage interest: callunas with late summer or autumn flowers, and ericas with spring blooms. Shrubs noted for their autumn tints, such as fothergillas or witch hazels, colour intensely on acid soil.

## PLANTS FOR ACID SOIL

| TREES AND SHRUBS | |
|---|---|
| Arbutus andrachne, A. menziesii, A. unedo | Pieris |
| | Rhododendrons |
| Arctostaphylos | Stewartia pseudocamellia |
| Azaleas (Rhododendron) | Vaccinium |
| Camellias | Witch hazel (Hamamelis) |
| Dogwoods (Cornus) (some) | |
| Embothrium coccineum | FERNS (MANY) |
| Fothergilla major | Regal fern (Osmunda regalis) |
| Gaultheria | |
| Heathers (Calluna, Daboecia, Erica) | PERENNIALS |
| Japanese maples (Acer japonicum, A. palmatum and cultivars) | Corydalis cashmeriana |
| | Gentiana asclepiadea |
| | Moltkia doerfleri |
| | Sanguinaria canadense |
| Spruce (Picea) (most) | Trillium |

# USING GROUND COVER IN SHADY AREAS

Gardening in shade relies greatly on variations in foliage form and texture, since the majority of shade lovers flower only in spring or early summer. Ground-cover plants, often natural inhabitants of the forest floor, can be used to make a low-level backcloth for the short-lived, seasonal flowers. This not only extends visual interest, but also helps minimize the amount of maintenance required in the area by smothering weeds and reducing moisture loss from the soil surface.

△ **WALDSTEINIA TERNATA**
*This creeping, semi-evergreen perennial, covered with flowers from late spring to early summer, is valued for its tolerance of dry shade.*

△ **LIRIOPE MUSCARI**
*Dense clumps of grass-like evergreen leaves make this drought-tolerant perennial a useful weed excluder. Its autumn flowers look good next to Cyclamen hederifolium.*

## GROUND COVER FOR SHADE

| SHRUBS/CLIMBERS | Heuchera cylindrica |
|---|---|
| Cotoneaster horizontalis | Hostas (most) |
| Ivy (Hedera helix) | Lily-of-the-valley (Convallaria majalis) |
| Sarcococca | |
| | London pride (Saxifraga × urbium) |
| PERENNIALS | Maianthemum bifolium |
| Bergenia | Pachysandra terminalis |
| Bugle (Ajuga) | Periwinkle (Vinca) |
| Brunnera macrophylla | Shortia galacifolia |
| Cyclamen hederifolium | Sweet woodruff (Galium odoratum) |
| Dead nettles (Lamium maculatum cultivars) | Tiarella wherryi |
| Epimedium | Tolmeia menziesii |
| Euphorbia amygdaloides var. robbiae | Vancouveria hexandra |
| Galax urceolata | Violets (Viola odorata) |

△ **SPOILT FOR CHOICE**
*The regal fern (Osmunda regalis) thrives in neutral to acid soils. The rhododendron in the background, 'May Day', is spring-flowering, but there are hundreds to choose from that will give flowers from midwinter to late summer.*

**SEE ALSO:** Clearing Weeds and Marking-Out Beds, pp.144–145; Buying Good Plants, pp.146–147

# BEDS FOR DROUGHT-TOLERANT PLANTS

MANY GARDEN SOILS are quite dry in summer and, if this is combined with hot, sunny weather, plants originating from Mediterranean regions and subtropical climes will flourish. This is why many aromatic herbs, silver-foliaged plants, and succulents can provide the answer for a sunny border. These plants are adapted to conserve moisture, however, so they cannot withstand the cold and wet of a temperate winter; if your garden is sunny and dry in summer, it is well worth producing special conditions so that such drought-tolerant plants can survive the winter. Improving drainage is the key, and this can be achieved in either a raised or gravel bed.

## GROWING SUN-LOVING PLANTS

Drought-tolerant plants come from areas where soil moisture is hard to get – for example, semi-desert regions, mountain sides, rocky scree, or cliff faces where rainwater drains away very rapidly. They develop long, penetrating root systems both for anchorage and to seek moisture and nutrients. Many are noted for their often white- or silver-hairy foliage, and brilliant, gem-like blooms. Planting sun-lovers in gardens reflects the increasing need to conserve water. Many are cold-hardy, but excellent drainage is essential, since the combination of winter cold and wet can be fatal to them.

### GOOD IDEAS

• Use field guides – or holidays in the sun – to help you spot plants that grow well in dry, hot places; these, and plants bred or selected from them, usually exhibit a good tolerance of dry conditions.

• Experiment with plants that show typical adaptations for conserving water – hairy, waxy, leathery, fleshy, silver, or narrow leaves and swollen stems or bulbs all give clues to likely tolerance of drought.

**SOAKING UP THE SUN** ▷
*A sunny, gentle slope may easily be adapted to suit sun-loving plants that enjoy good drainage. Most are compact and flower freely – therefore ideal for small gardens.*

## GRAVEL BEDS

Drought-tolerant plants, including alpines or rock plants, are vulnerable to rots or freeze-thaw damage at their necks (the junction of stem and root) in cold, wet conditions. To avoid this occurring in winter, and killing off your prize plants, the best method is to create a gravel border or bed in your garden. This will provide much better drainage than a normal bed of moisture-retentive soil, and gives the plants a good chance of survival. Choose a gently sloping, open, sunny site, and cover it with loose, variably sized rubble, some inverted turves, light topsoil, and a deep layer of gravel or shingle. If raised above ground level, the gravel bed will be a form of raised bed (see pp.180–183).

### CREATING A GRAVEL BED

**1 THE BASE LAYER**
*Remove the top layer of fertile soil and fork over the ground. Add coarse rubble, to a depth of 15cm (6in), to form a low mound. This will ensure that drainage is excellent in the base layer.*

**2 RETAINING LAYER**
*Cap the rubble with a layer of inverted turves, either removed from the area earlier or brought in specially. This will prevent the soil mix from being washed down to the layer of rubble at the base.*

**3 ADDING SOIL**
*Cover the upturned turves with a layer of light soil mix (see opposite, top), 15–25cm (6–10in) deep. Rake the soil to an even depth, and firm it down by treading gently over the whole area.*

**4 TOP-DRESSING**
*After firming, water the area to settle the soil, and top up with more to fill any voids. Prick over the surface with a hand fork. Top-dress with 10cm (4in) of gravel or shingle, and rake level.*

SEE ALSO: Laying Gravel, pp.62–63; Plants for Dry, Sunny Sites, p.130; Establishing Plants in the Border, pp.148–149

# THE SOIL MIX

If your topsoil is heavy or rich in clay, lighten it by mixing as given below:

- one part topsoil (removed from bed);
- one part garden compost or leafmould;
- 2 or 3 parts coarse grit or stone chips.

Sharp sand or gravel may also be added.

▽ **MODIFYING THE RECIPE**
*The basic recipe can be altered to suit soil conditions or different plants. Poor soil will need enriching with organic matter in the form of rotted compost or rotted manure, for example. A more moisture-retentive mix would consist of 1 part loamy soil to 1 part leafmould or garden compost to 2 parts stone chips or coarse grit.*

| TOPSOIL | SHARP SAND | GRAVEL | COARSE GRIT | GARDEN COMPOST |

# BUYING SUITABLE PLANTS

A healthy plant has compact growth, and no discolouration or pest damage evident on foliage or flowers (if present). Avoid any with weak, yellowed growth or straggling stems; they may have been kept in poor light or starved of water. Always check the eventual spread before you plant; vigorous plants can quickly overwhelm others.

Compact growth and clean, well-coloured foliage, with no dead or dying leaves

**A HEALTHY PLANT** ▷
*Check that the plant appears vigorous and healthy and the compost is weed-free, as for this saxifrage. Roots should almost fill the pot, without congestion.*

# HOW TO ESTABLISH PLANTS IN A GRAVEL BED

Plants in a gravel bed may need a little more care in the early stages, because the gravel, or shingle (which has rounded rather than sharp pieces), dries out before the roots can penetrate the moist soil below. Water regularly until the plants are established. One way of retaining soil moisture in especially dry areas is to lay a sheet of landscape or geotextile fabric and top it with gravel. Plant through slits in the fabric.

### PLANTING IN GRAVEL OR SHINGLE

**1 DIG A PLANTING HOLE**
*Scrape the gravel or shingle surface to one side. Dig a planting hole slightly larger than the plant's root ball in the soil mix. Make sure the root ball is evenly moist; water it thoroughly and allow to drain.*

**2 LOOSEN THE ROOT BALL**
*Tease out the roots gently and put the plant in the hole with its neck level with the gravel surface. For alpines, shake the potting compost off the roots; they establish better and root more widely in a light soil mix.*

**3 FIRM IN AND FINISH OFF**
*Backfill around the roots with more soil mix. Firm the root ball gently in place with your fingertips. Replace the gravel or shingle, and water in thoroughly. Keep well watered until new growth appears.*

## PLANTS FOR A GRAVEL BED

| MAT-FORMING PLANTS | |
| --- | --- |
| Alpine pink (*Dianthus alpinus*) | Rock cress (*Arabis*) |
| | *Saxifraga burseriana* |
| *Alyssum montanum* | *Silene acaulis* |
| *Anacyclus pyrethrum* var. *depressus* | |
| *Androsace sarmentosa* | OTHERS |
| *Antennaria dioica* | *Aethionema* |
| *Ballota pseudodictamnus* | *Allium akaka,* |
| California poppy (*Eschscholzia*) | *A. neapolitanum* |
| | Alpine toadflax (*Linaria alpina*) |
| *Campanula cochleariifolia* | *Anemone coronaria* |
| *Dianthus erinaceus* | *Artemisia stelleriana* 'Boughton Silver' |
| *Erinacea anthyllis* | *Cistus creticus, C. × cyprius* |
| *Gypsophila aretioides* | *Convolvulus cneorum* |
| *Jovibarba* | *Erinus alpinus* |
| *Oenothera acaulis* | *Hypericum olympicum* |
| *Papaver burseri, P. rhaeticum* | *Narcissus cantabricus* |
| | *Parahebe catarractae* |
| *Petrorhagia saxifraga* | *Viola cornuta* 'Minor' |

# CARE AND MAINTENANCE OF A GRAVEL BED

Once established, a gravel bed will be essentially a low-maintenance feature. Gravel and shingle both make a weed-suppressing mulch, and new weeds may be pulled easily from the loose surface if dealt with as soon as they are seen; they are difficult to extract if they gain a hold in the foliage mats of ornamentals.

Mat-forming or spreading plants will benefit from being lifted and divided (*see p.163*) every few years.

◁ **RENEWING GRAVEL**
*Gravel or shingle gradually washes away, especially on slopes. Top up bare patches as seen, and check again in mid-autumn and spring.*

**KEEPING TIDY** ▷
*In spring, when the danger of frost has passed, remove any dead or winter-damaged growth. Deadhead regularly throughout the season.*

**SEE ALSO:** Laying Gravel, pp.62–63; Using Mulches to Suppress Weeds, p.145; Maintaining Border Plants, pp.154–155

# PERENNIALS

HERBACEOUS, OR NON-WOODY, PERENNIALS make up the most diverse of all plant groups. Trees and shrubs are technically perennials too, but the term normally refers to those non-woody plants that live for two years or more and, once mature,` produce top-growth and flowers annually. Some are evergreen, with potential for winter interest, but most die back in autumn and overwinter beneath the soil. There are perennials to suit each and every garden, whether large or small, sunny or shady, sheltered or exposed, damp or dry. Over the years, plant breeders have developed species to extend the colour palette, increase flower size, and flowering period.

## PERENNIALS FOR THE BORDER

Few other plant groups offer the gardener such a range of form and texture, or spectrum of colour and fragrance, as the herbaceous perennials. They range in size from the lowest of ground-cover plants to architectural giants. Many gardeners are happy to endure their absence during the winter, simply to experience the joy of their re-emergence, heralding the return of spring. Others prefer to use them in mixed borders, which has greater potential for extending interest on either side of the perennials' midsummer peak.

While most perennials are valued for their flowers, many also offer value in terms of their foliage. All of the plants recommended here (*see right and below*) are chosen for a long season of interest and ease of cultivation; all they need to thrive is a sunny site and moderately fertile, well-drained soil. Such plants are the stalwarts that form the basic framework of a border. Remember there are uses, too, for plants whose beauty fades quickly, such as Oriental poppies. Their effects can be all the more intense for being brief.

Before you plant, analyse the site in terms of soil, light, moisture, exposure, and climate (*see pp.46–49*). To get the best results from your plants, select them to suit prevailing conditions; the aim is to establish a healthy, thriving population.

### OTHER PERENNIALS

**Cardoon** (*Cynara cardunculus*). An architectural giant with silver-grey, deeply cut leaves, and large thistle-like flowerheads from summer to autumn.

**Daylilies** (*Hemerocallis*). Narrow leaves and trumpet-shaped flowers from mid- to late summer.

*Echinacea purpurea*. Dusky, purplish red flowers with golden-brown, cone-shaped centres, borne from midsummer to autumn.

*Helenium*. Sunny, golden daisy flowers produced from late summer to autumn.

*Lavatera*. Funnel-shaped, purple-pink flowers throughout summer.

*Sedum spectabile*. Grey-green leaves and flat heads of deep pink flowers in late summer and autumn.

*Tradescantia*. Grass-like leaves, and blue, purple, pink, or white flowers throughout summer.

△ *ACHILLEA* 'MOONSHINE'
*Flat heads of pale yellow flowers are borne above divided, grey-green leaves from summer to autumn. At 60cm (24in) tall, ideal for mid-border placement.*

△ *DIANTHUS* 'DORIS'
*Neat mounds of narrow, grey-green leaves, with several flushes of clove-scented blooms in summer. Grow at the border front, especially with roses. They are 30cm (12in) tall.*

△ *LEUCANTHEMUM* × *SUPERBUM* 'WIRRAL PRIDE'
*Pure white double daisies on 75cm (30in) stems are borne in mid- to late summer above low mounds of glossy, dark green leaves. Tough and reliable. The flowers are good for cutting for indoor displays.*

△ *GERANIUM HIMA-LAYENSE* 'GRAVETYE'
*Forming dense mats of foliage, 30cm (12in) tall, this plant bears several flushes of bright blue flowers in summer, and colours well in autumn.*

△ *GEUM* 'LADY STRATHEDEN'
*Semi-double, rich yellow flowers adorn clumps of divided leaves throughout summer. To 60cm (24in) tall, but with an airy habit that suits the border front.*

◁ LAMB'S EARS
(Stachys byzantina)
*A tough, densely silver-hairy perennial that, at 45cm (18in) tall, is ideal for the border front. Forms low, spreading masses, which bear white-woolly spikes of pink-purple flowers through summer.*

◁ *SCABIOSA* 'CLIVE GREAVES'
*Soft lavender blooms, which make good cut flowers, are borne from mid- to late summer above low mounds of grey-green leaves. It is 60cm (24in) in height, but its open habit looks fine at the border front.*

◁ *ARTEMISIA LUDOVI-CIANA* 'SILVER QUEEN'
*Clumps of jagged, silvery leaves, 75cm (30in) tall, produce few flowers, but lend fine textural interest throughout the season and form a spreading foil for neighbouring plants of more intense colour.*

**SEE ALSO:** Assessing What You Have, pp.46–49; Herbaceous Borders, p.125; Borders with Special Conditions, pp.130–131

△ *ANEMONE × HYBRIDA* '**HONORINE JOBERT**'
*A star performer, this anemone blooms from late summer into autumn, for two months or more. The pristine white flowers, on 1.5m (5ft) stems, appear luminous at dusk. It prefers to be in sun or light shade.*

△ *ACANTHUS SPINOSUS*
*Arching mounds of glossy, deeply cut leaves and spires of white and purple flowers in early summer make a lovely architectural specimen, 1.5m (5ft) tall, especially against the purple-leaved backdrop of Cotinus 'Grace'.*

## ORIENTAL POPPIES

The many forms of *Papaver orientale* are the early summer mainstay of herbaceous borders. Clumps of divided leaves, clothed in bristly hairs, catch the light, especially if spotted with dew, and sumptuous flowers, crumpled at first, open to reveal satiny petals and a boss of dark, velvety stamens.

Their only fault is that the leaves die back after flowering to leave a gap in the border, but this is easily remedied; fill in with annuals or disguise with arching stems of plants like *Gypsophila paniculata*, with clouds of tiny white flowers. Grow in deep, fertile, well-drained soil in full sun. Divide in mid-spring, taking care not to damage the fleshy roots.

### OTHER ORIENTAL POPPIES

*P.* 'Allegro'. Brilliant, glossy, orange-scarlet flowers marked boldly with black at the base.

*P.* 'Indian Chief'. Large, unmarked flowers of an unusual shade of rich mahogany-red.

*P.* 'May Queen'. Double, orange-red, unmarked flowers with unusual, inrolled (quilled) petals.

*P.* 'Mrs Perry'. Pale pink blooms with a black blotch.

*P.* 'Picotee'. Large white flowers with crinkled petals, which have frilled margins flushed with orange-pink.

*P.* '**BLACK AND WHITE**' ▷
*The satin-textured, pure white flowers have a dark crimson-black blotch at the centre. This robust poppy, to 90cm (36in) tall, is an excellent choice for a monochromatic, grey- or white-themed border.*

◁ *P.* '**CEDRIC MORRIS**'
*With grey, hairy leaves, and very large, soft pink flowers, this associates well with the rambling rose 'Albertine'. The poppy hides the often bare lower stems of the rose during its flowering time.*

*P.* '**BEAUTY OF LIVERMERE**' ▷
*Large, glossy flowers, up to 20cm (8in) across, are a fabulously rich shade of crimson-scarlet with a black basal blotch. A vigorous plant that reaches a height of 1.2m (4ft).*

## HERBACEOUS PEONIES

Herbaceous border peonies are mostly cultivars of *Paeonia lactiflora* and variants of *P. officinalis*. Their saucer-, cup-, or bowl-shaped flowers are single, semi-double, or fully double, often globe-shaped at first. They come in reds and pastel colours and bloom in early summer. Grow in full sun or light shade in deep, fertile soil that is well-drained, but humus-rich and moisture-retentive. Propagate by division in early spring or early autumn, cutting the fleshy roots into pieces with a knife. They are long-lived and, contrary to popular belief, mature plants can be moved safely. Keep the root ball intact and keep the plants well watered until re-established.

### OTHER BORDER PEONIES

*P.* 'Bowl of Beauty'. Anemone-like, carmine-pink flowers with a central boss of creamy petals.

*P.* 'Festiva Maxima'. Very large, fragrant, double white flowers with frilled petals, the innermost flushed crimson at the base.

*P. mlokosewitschii*. Blue-green leaves and single, lemon-yellow flowers in late spring to early summer.

◁ *P.* '**SARAH BERNHARDT**'
*A sturdy and reliable peony, about 90cm (36in) tall, with upright stems bearing very large, double flowers of soft rose-pink, the inner petals ruffled and tinged with silver at the margins.*

△ *P.* '**DUCHESSE DE NEMOURS**'
*The pristine white flowers, tinted green in bud, are large and fragrant, and packed with many central petals that are flushed pale yellow at their base. To 80cm (32in) tall.*

△ *P. OFFICINALIS* '**RUBRA PLENA**'
*In early and midsummer, bowl-shaped, fully double flowers of rich crimson with ruffled, satin-textured petals are borne. Quite compact in growth, to 75cm (30in) tall.*

SEE ALSO: Borders with Special Conditions, pp.130–131; Establishing Plants in the Border, pp.148–149

# ANNUALS, BIENNIALS, AND BULBOUS PLANTS

ANNUALS AND BIENNIALS are the group of plants that are most valuable for extending interest when used as fillers in a mixed border or for creating masses of colour in bedding schemes. Many have pretty seedheads that may scatter seed with abandon, resulting in informal and pleasingly unpredictable effects, where conditions suit.

Bulbous plants provide seasonal features that come and go, providing the added dimension of dynamic change in a planting scheme. With careful selection, bulbs will kick-start the flowering season in late winter and early spring, illuminate the border throughout summer, and provide the season's glorious finale in autumn.

## ANNUALS AND BIENNIALS

Annuals and biennials are short-term plants, although they may bloom for long periods. Annuals flower, set seed, and die in the space of one year, but the flowering period is prolonged if they are deadheaded regularly or harvested as cut flowers. Biennials make leafy growth in the first year and die after flowering in the second.

There are annuals and biennials to suit most conditions – sun, damp, or dry – and seed packets give concise cultivation requirements. They can be used in borders devoted to them, which is a good idea for creating almost instant colour in new gardens, giving you plenty of time for planning more permanent plantings. They are also invaluable when used as spot colour, or to prolong seasonal interest, in mixed borders of shrubs and perennials.

### OTHER ANNUALS & BIENNIALS

*Begonia* Semperflorens Group. Low-growing, with glossy leaves, and a long succession of bright flowers.

Busy Lizzies (*Impatiens*). Glossy foliage and masses of bright flowers all summer, in red, pink, or white.

Godetia (*Clarkia amoena*). Silky, funnel-shaped, fluted flowers in pastel colours, all summer.

Larkspur (*Consolida ajacis*). Feathery foliage and spires of blue, pink, purple, or white flowers in summer.

*Moluccella laevis*. Shell-like, green bracts. Late summer.

*Onopordon acanthium*. Tall, architectural, grey-leaved, spiny biennial with purple thistles in summer.

Painted daisy (*Chrysanthemum carinatum*). Masses of daisy flowers zoned in red, yellow, white, or purple.

*Papaver somniferum*. Greyish leaves, white to purple flowers in summer, and blue-green seedpods.

*Silybum marianum*. Biennial with white-marbled, dark green leaves, and thistle-like flowers in summer.

Sweet peas (*Lathyrus odoratus*). Climber with sweet-scented, pea-like, bright-coloured flowers.

## BULBOUS PLANTS

The term bulbous plants includes true bulbs as well as plants with corms, tubers, or rhizomes. Most have highly seasonal blooms. They look jaded only for a short time, before they become dormant below ground. Allow the foliage to die down naturally, or leave it at least until yellow. Most demand only sun and well-drained soil; those of woodland habitats prefer moister soil and partial shade.

**GALTONIA CANDICANS** ▷
*An elegant, summer-flowering bulb, with spires of waxy white flowers in summer, and blue-green leaves. At 1.2m (4ft) tall, it is best placed in the middle of the border.*

◁ **ALLIUM GIGANTEUM**
*This ornamental onion reaches 1.5m (5ft) or more when flowering in summer, and it makes an excellent addition to a sunny border. It associates nicely with roses, and it is offset well by grey foliage.*

△ **VERBASCUM OLYMPICUM**
*White-woolly leaves and candelabra flower spikes all summer make this biennial useful as a focal point, growing to 2m (6ft) tall. It thrives in sun and tolerates poor, dry soils.*

△ **DIGITALIS PURPUREA 'SUTTON'S APRICOT'**
*Apricot flowers associate very well with many types of rose and all flowers of deep blue. This biennial reaches 1.5m (5ft) or more, and prefers to grow in sun or light shade.*

△ **COSMOS BIPINNATUS 'SEA SHELLS'**
*This cosmos has quilled petals and a colour range from white through pink to carmine-red, rising above feathery green leaves. At 90cm (36in) tall, this annual makes a colourful filler in mixed or herbaceous borders.*

◁ **SUNFLOWER**
*(Helianthus annuus)*
*All sunflowers are valued for their bright, sunny flowers; they range from rapidly growing giants, 5m (15ft) tall, to mid-border ones at 60cm (24in). They make excellent cut flowers.*

△ **CROCOSMIA 'LUCIFER'**
*This crocosmia, to 1.2m (4ft) tall, is valued for the brilliance of its flowers during mid- to late summer. The pleated, bright green leaves provide a strong vertical presence throughout the season, in sun or light shade.*

SEE ALSO: Using Annuals and Biennials, p.125

# DAFFODILS

With thousands to choose from, there are daffodils (*Narcissus*) to suit any border, and they can also be naturalized in grass. Careful selection will provide colour from late winter to late spring. Plant bulbs at one-and-a-half times their own depth in autumn, in sun or partial shade, in moist, fertile, well-drained soil. Deadhead faded flowers, but after flowering leave the foliage in place for at least six weeks.

△ *N.* 'ACTAEA'
*A late-spring delicacy with scented flowers that fill the air around them with fragrance. Pure white petals surround a flattened, yellow cup, rimmed with red. 45cm (18in) tall.*

## OTHER DAFFODILS

*N.* 'Cheerfulness'. Very fragrant, double, rounded white flowers in mid-spring. 40cm (16in) tall.

*N.* 'Hawera'. Diminutive, with slender, small-cupped, golden-yellow flowers. 18cm (7in) tall.

*N.* × *odorus*. Strongly scented, golden, trumpet-shaped flowers in early spring. 25cm (10in) tall.

*N. poeticus*. Scented white flowers with tiny, yellow, red-rimmed cups in late spring. 50cm (20in) tall.

**N. 'ARKLE'** ▷
*A vigorous daffodil with very large golden trumpets in mid-spring. It is equally at home in borders or naturalized in grass, and it reaches 40cm (16in) in height.*

# TULIPS

Lending unrivalled brilliance to the spring border, there are several different groups of tulips, which can provide colour from late winter to late spring, either as annual bedding or as groups in borders. Grow in fertile, well-drained soil in sun with shelter from strong winds. Plant bulbs, 10–15cm (4–6in) deep, in late summer or autumn. Lift the bulbs as the foliage fades, and ripen in a cool, dry place, or discard.

△ *T.* 'QUEEN OF NIGHT'
*A robust tulip with velvety, deep maroon flowers. One of the deepest coloured of all, it flowers very late in spring and is perfect among grey-leaved plants.*

## OTHER TULIPS

*T.* 'Artist'. Salmon-pink flowers, flushed green and purple, in late spring. 45cm (18in) tall.

*T.* 'Estella Rijnveld'. Fringed, white-flamed, red flowers in late spring. 55cm (22in) tall.

*T.* 'Plaisir'. Carmine-red and sulphur-yellow flowers in early spring. 15cm (6in) tall.

*T.* 'White Triumphator'. Elegant tulip with pure white flowers in late spring. 45–60cm (18–24in) tall.

**T. 'PEACH BLOSSOM'** ▷
*The double flowers are rich rose-pink, often flushed green at the base at first. This tulip blooms in late spring, and it associates well with blue forget-me-nots.*

# LILIES

Lilies (*Lilium*) are usually tall-growing and bear showy, often fragrant summer flowers, occasionally into autumn. The flowers are bowl-, trumpet-, funnel-shaped, or "turkscap" (where the petals curve back over themselves). Grow in well-drained soil enriched with organic matter; most prefer acid to neutral soils and a sunny position. Plant bulbs in early autumn to a depth of two or three times their size on a bed of grit to ensure good drainage.

△ *L. MARTAGON*
*A woodland lily that bears turkscap flowers on stems to 2m (6ft) tall in early and midsummer. It is so versatile that it thrives in almost any well-drained soil in sun or partial shade.*

## OTHER LILIES

*L. canadense*. Nodding, trumpet-shaped yellow flowers in mid- to late summer. 1.6m (5½ft) tall.

*L.* 'Fire King'. Bright orange-red flowers in midsummer. 1.2m (4ft) tall. Good in pots.

Madonna lily (*L. candidum*). Fragrant white trumpets. 1.8m (6ft) tall. Needs neutral to alkaline soil.

*L.* 'Sterling Star'. Upturned, slightly scented white, brown-speckled flowers in summer. 1.2m (4ft) tall.

**L. REGALE** ▷
*Midsummer elegance and fragrance make the regal lily invaluable. It flowers best in sun, but tolerates light shade. In favourable conditions, it reaches 2m (6ft) in height.*

# IRISES

Most irises bloom for relatively short periods between spring and early summer, but their bold fans or clumps of foliage, variegated in some instances, last through the season. There are several different types. The bearded irises, the most familiar of border irises, and bulbous irises, need fertile, well-drained soil in full sun. The Siberian irises, more slender and delicate in appearance, prefer slightly moister soil and tolerate sun or light shade.

△ *I. PALLIDA* 'VARIEGATA'
*A bearded iris bearing blue-mauve flowers in early summer and creamy yellow, striped leaves through the growing season. It reaches 1m (3ft) tall.*

## OTHER IRISES

*I.* 'Blue-eyed Brunette'. Warm brown flowers, with a violet flash and yellow beard. 90cm (36in) tall

*I. germanica*. Vigorous, with yellow-bearded, blue-violet flowers. 60–120cm (24–48in) tall.

*I.* 'Golden Harvest'. Bulbous iris with yellow flowers, mid-spring to midsummer. 70cm (28in) tall.

*I. sibirica*. Dainty, blue-violet flowers with paler, dark-veined falls. 50–120cm (20–48in) tall.

**I. 'ARNOLD SUNRISE'** ▷
*A beardless iris, which, at 25cm (10in) tall, is ideal for front-border placement. The white petals have a crystalline texture, the lower ones blotched with pale yellow-orange.*

SEE ALSO: Establishing Plants in the Border, pp.148–149; More Tulips, p.330; More Irises, p.336

# SHRUBS AND ROSES

DECIDUOUS AND EVERGREEN SHRUBS are essential elements in providing a permanent framework for the garden, whatever its size or style. They range from low-growing ground-cover plants to tall, almost tree-like plants, although most are considerably smaller in stature. The choice available is huge and, since they occur in all manner of situations throughout the world, there are shrubs to suit all aspects and soil types. They can offer architectural forms, often fragrant flowers, decorative fruits, and a great diversity of foliage in terms of size, shape, and colour. Their woody stems, frequently with textures and tints of their own, also make a contribution.

## SHRUBS FOR THE BORDER

By definition, shrubs are woody-stemmed plants that usually branch freely from the base, with many stems arising at or near ground level. Although distinguished by this feature from trees, which more often grow with a single stem, there is a degree of overlap between the two groups.

The shrubs described here are all easily grown, widely available, and most have an extended, or more than one period of interest. These are vital aspects to consider as you begin to stock your garden. As your interest and experience grows, you will discover many more that fit the bill, but never discount the common ones – many shrubs are popular *because* they are robust and reliable. It is the associations that you can create with them that will lend your own individual and creative style.

Before buying, always research a plant's individual needs and take account of its size at maturity. Allow adequate space to develop its natural form, filling gaps in the meantime with temporary plantings.

### OTHER SHRUBS

*Chaenomeles speciosa* 'Moerloosii'. Vigorous, spiny shrub, with dark, glossy leaves, white, pink-flushed spring flowers, and yellow-green autumn fruits.

*Cornus alba* 'Sibirica'. Vigorous shrub with white flowers in late spring, red-orange autumn colour; cut back every spring for bright red winter stems.

*Exochorda macrantha* 'The Bride'. Graceful, with white flowers in late spring and yellow autumn colour.

*Hibiscus syriacus* 'Red Heart'. Upright shrub, with red-centred white flowers from summer to autumn.

*Leycesteria formosa*. Upright, suckering shrub, bearing white flowers and red-purple fruits in late summer.

*Pyracantha* 'Soleil d'Or'. Spiny evergreen with glossy, dark green leaves, white flowers in spring, and a mass of winter-persistent, bright yellow berries.

Red chokeberry (*Aronia arbutifolia*). Small shrub with white spring flowers, red berries, and autumn tints.

Winged spindle (*Euonymous alatus*). Shrub with tiny flowers, red-purple, toxic fruits that split to reveal orange seed coats, and crimson autumn leaves.

**KOLKWITZIA AMABILIS 'PINK CLOUD'** ▷
*Graceful, medium-sized shrub with arching branches smothered in early summer with yellow-throated, soft pink flowers. Lovely with Geranium macrorrhizum grown as ground cover beneath.*

**VIBURNUM OPULUS 'XANTHOCARPUM'** ▷
*Large, bushy deciduous shrub with creamy white, lace-cap flowers in late spring and early summer, followed by persistent, glossy yellow fruits. The maple-like leaves blaze red in autumn. An excellent all-rounder.*

△ **RIBES SANGUINEUM 'PULBOROUGH SCARLET'**
*Vigorous, medium-sized deciduous flowering currant with dark red flowers in spring, blue-black fruit, and autumn tints of yellow and red.*

△ **BUDDLEJA DAVIDII 'WHITE PROFUSION'**
*Medium-sized deciduous shrub with very long sprays of tiny, yellow-eyed white flowers from summer to autumn. The fragrant flowers are attractive to bees and butterflies.*

△ **FORSYTHIA × INTERMEDIA 'LYNWOOD'**
*Medium-sized deciduous shrub bearing many rich yellow flowers in spring. Try underplanting it with sky-blue grape hyacinths (Muscari).*

△ **SYRINGA MEYERI 'PALIBIN'**
*Neat, slow-growing lilac that is ideal for small gardens. It produces dense clusters of tiny, delightfully fragrant, lavender-pink flowers in late spring and early summer.*

△ **PHILADELPHUS 'BOULE D'ARGENT'**
*Compact deciduous shrub that bears scented, creamy white flowers in early or midsummer. The colour and fragrance make this, and other mock oranges, an ideal companion for roses.*

△ **WEIGELA 'EVA RATHKE'**
*Neat deciduous shrub of upright habit, reliably producing crimson flowers over long periods in late spring and early summer. Use it as a support for later-flowering clematis.*

SEE ALSO: Plants for Acid Soil, p.131; Buying Good Plants, pp.146–147; Maintaining Shrubs, pp.156–157; Pruning Established Shrubs, pp.158–159

# SHRUBS FOR FOLIAGE COLOUR

Coloured foliage, beautiful in its own right, adds interest to a backdrop of framework planting. The colour of grey or purple leaves often lasts a whole season. Many golden-leaved plants turn green by midsummer, so use companion plants to pick up the interest and carry it on.

*AMELANCHIER LAMARCKII* ▷
This upright shrub has bronze leaves that turn dark green, then orange and red in autumn. It also has white spring flowers, followed by purple-black fruit.

◁ *BERBERIS THUN-BERGII* 'ROSE GLOW'
Red-purple, white-speckled leaves form a fine backdrop for grey or bright green foliage, and this spiny, medium-sized deciduous shrub makes an ideal host for Clematis 'Alba Luxurians'.

◁ SOUTHERNWOOD (Artemisia abrotanum)
This small, aromatic, semi-evergreen shrub with finely divided, grey-green leaves makes an eye-catching foil for flowers of intense colour such as blue, crimson, and purple, and it associates well with old-fashioned roses.

## OTHER FOLIAGE SHRUBS

*Choisya ternata* 'Sundance'. Medium-sized and evergreen, with bright yellow young foliage.

*Cornus alba* 'Aurea'. Medium-sized and deciduous, with persistently yellow foliage, and red winter stems.

*Cotinus coggygria* 'Royal Purple'. Medium-sized, with deep purple leaves that turn red in autumn.

*Elaeagnus × ebbingei* 'Gilt Edge'. Evergreen and medium-sized, with yellow-margined, dark green leaves.

*Pittosporum tenuifolium* 'Tom Thumb'. Small evergreen, with glossy, bronze-purple, wavy-margined leaves.

*Santolina chamaecyparissus* 'Lemon Queen'. Compact evergreen, with finely divided grey leaves, and a profusion of soft lemon-yellow flowers in summer.

*Weigela florida* 'Foliis Purpureis'. Compact and deciduous, with purple-flushed, bronze-green leaves, and funnel-shaped pink flowers in early summer.

# ROSES

No other single group of plants offers such a profusion of flowers with such exquisite scents and colours. In many roses, flowering lasts right through summer until the first frosts. Roses vary from low ground-cover plants to tall, arching shrubs and rampant scramblers. Use them in a border devoted to roses or exploit their versatility to the full in a mixed border. Ingredients for successful flowering are a sunny site, fertile, moist but well-drained soil, and appropriate pruning (*see p.161*). Add fertilizer in early spring and after the first flush of bloom. If possible, choose disease-resistant cultivars and deal with pests and diseases as soon as they are seen.

△ *R.* HAMPSHIRE
A ground-cover rose, which, at 30cm (12in) high by 75cm (30in) across, is ideal for path or border edging, or for decorating a patio in pots. It bears masses of flat, single scarlet flowers from summer to autumn.

◁ *R.* 'WHITE PET'
Polyantha rose with sprays of pompon-like white flowers that open from red buds from summer to autumn. A pretty border rose, or suitable for pots on the patio. 60cm (24in) tall and as much across.

*R.* QUEEN MOTHER ▷
A patio rose, 40cm (16in) tall, 60cm (24in) across, producing clusters of semi-double, clear soft pink flowers from summer to autumn. Very pretty with the deep purple flowers of Lavandula 'Hidcote'.

## OTHER ROSES

*R.* 'Cornelia'. Arching shrub, with soft, coppery pink, rosette-form flowers throughout summer.

*R.* Graham Thomas. Vigorous shrub, with fragrant, clear yellow flowers throughout summer.

*R.* Kent. Low, ground-cover shrub, with semi-double, creamy white flowers from summer to autumn.

*R. moyesii.* Tall, upright shrub, with waxy red flowers in early summer and flask-shaped, scarlet hips.

*R.* Rosy Cushion. Spreading shrub, with scented, single, pale pink flowers from summer to autumn.

*R. rugosa.* Prickly shrub, with bright pink flowers all summer and red hips in late summer and autumn.

*R.* Swany. Low, ground-cover shrub, with double, creamy white flowers all summer.

*R.* 'White Wings'. Large-flowered bush, with single white flowers with red stamens all summer.

△ *R.* 'BLESSINGS'
Vigorous, large-flowered bush rose with dark green leaves and fully double, fragrant, salmon-pink flowers from summer to autumn. It grows to 1m (3ft) tall, and spreads to 75cm (30in) across.

△ *R.* JACQUELINE DU PRÉ
Modern shrub rose with arching stems wreathed in musk-scented, ivory-white blooms with red stamens from early summer to autumn. 1.5m (5ft) tall by 1.2m (4ft) across.

△ *R.* 'MME ISAAC PEREIRE'
Flexible-stemmed Bourbon rose with fragrant blooms in several flushes from summer to autumn. At 2m (6ft) tall, by as much across, it can also be trained as a climber.

△ *R.* AMBER QUEEN
Cluster-flowered shrub with shiny, dark green leaves and fragrant flowers from summer to autumn. It associates well with blue larkspur or belladonna delphiniums. 50cm (20in) tall, 60cm (24in) across.

SEE ALSO: Establishing Shrubs and Roses, pp.150–151; Maintaining Roses, pp.160–161; More Roses, pp.334, 337, 339, 348, 362

# GRASSES, BAMBOOS, AND FERNS

GRASSES, BAMBOOS, AND FERNS can bring an unrivalled sophistication to a planting scheme, for this group relies heavily on form and texture rather than on floristic brilliance. The uninitiated often consider their colour range limited, but this is not so — they offer a rich palette of greens, including tints of emerald and lime, as well as blue and grey, silver and gold. The flowerheads of grasses provide delicate textures, the whole plant often lending an extraordinary element of rippling movement in the slightest of breezes. Ferns offer no flowers at all, but their statuesque fronds provide eye-catching texture in shady areas of the garden where flowers may fail.

## GRASSES

Grasses, including bamboos, are deciduous or evergreen perennials characterized by their narrow, usually linear leaves that come in a surprisingly wide range of colours, sometimes striped or variegated. Some are valued for their stately habit and delicate flowerheads, which shimmer gracefully in the breeze. Use them as specimens, or in mixed borders, in gravel, or create dedicated grassy borders. Others, such as *Elymus* and *Festuca*, are low-growing and good for ground cover.

Most thrive in full sun, in moist but well-drained soil that is not too fertile. They are best planted in spring. Once established, they need little maintenance other than cutting back to ground level in mid-autumn to early winter. Those with attractive winter flowers or foliage, which often colours well in autumn, are lovely when rimed with frost; cut these and tender grasses back in early spring as buds begin to break.

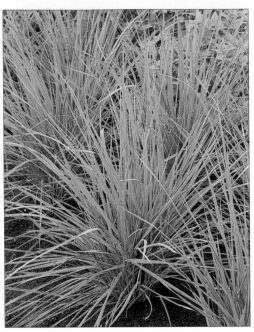

△ *ELYMUS MAGELLANICUS*
*This low, mound-forming lyme grass is 15cm (6in) tall with intensely blue leaves. It bears almost prostrate flower spikes throughout summer. Use it at the front of a mixed border, especially one based on a theme of grey leaves.*

△ *CORTADERIA SELLOANA*
'SUNNINGDALE SILVER'
*This pampas grass forms a majestic clump, 3m (10ft) or more tall, with silver plumes in late summer. The leaves are very sharp, so wear gloves when handling this plant.*

### OTHER GRASSES

*Alopecurus pratensis* 'Aureovariegatus'. Perennial foxtail grass with narrow, yellow and green-striped leaves. To 1.2m (4ft) tall.

Feathertop (*Pennisetum villosum*). Tufted annual or perennial, with green leaves, and plume-like flower-heads that are purplish when mature. 60cm (24in).

*Festuca glauca* 'Blaufuchs'. Evergreen perennial, with very narrow, bright blue leaves, and violet-flushed flowerheads in summer. 30cm (12in) tall.

*Holcus mollis* 'Albovariegatus'. Mat-forming and soft-textured, with flat, blue-green leaves with creamy white margins. 30cm (12in) tall.

Job's tears (*Coix lachryma-jobi*). Annual, to 90cm (36in) tall, with bright green leaves, and arching flower-heads bedecked with pearly grey seeds in autumn.

*Stipa tenuissima*. Upright and deciduous perennial feather grass, with thread-like, bright green leaves, and feathery, buff-coloured flowerheads. To 60cm (24in) tall.

△ *HAKENOCHLOA*
*MACRA* 'AUREOLA'
*The bright yellow leaves of this deciduous clump former are striped dark green and take on russet hues in autumn, which persist into winter. It reaches 35cm (14in) in height.*

△ *STIPA CALAMAGROSTIS*
*A feather grass with clumps of arching, blue-green leaves, decorated in summer with clouds of purple-tinted, silver-buff flowerheads. Although 1m (3ft) tall, the open, airy habit is well suited to the front of a border.*

△ *ZEBRA GRASS*
(Miscanthus sinensis
'Zebrinus')
*The fountain-like clump of broadly arching leaves with bands of creamy yellow looks good in mixed borders or by water. It reaches 1.2m (4ft) in height.*

SEE ALSO: Establishing Plants in the Border, pp.148–149

# SEDGES AND RUSHES

A large group of grass-like, usually evergreen perennials valued for their foliage – often a firmer, more leathery texture than true grasses – and for their flowerheads. They tolerate a range of conditions, but the majority thrive in damp or wet soils, in sun or shade. They provide strong verticals and dynamic diagonals within a planting scheme.

## OTHER SEDGES AND RUSHES

Bowles' golden sedge (*Carex elata* 'Aurea'). Deciduous sedge with arching, bright golden yellow leaves finely margined with green.

*Carex conica* 'Snowline'. Low, tufted, evergreen sedge with dark green, white-margined leaves

*Luzula sylvatica* 'Aurea'. Evergreen, tussock-forming woodrush with leaves that are yellow-green in summer and bright, golden yellow in winter.

# BAMBOOS

Plants in this group form elegant screens or clumps in dappled shade, often rustling in the breeze. They thrive in damp soil rich in organic matter, with shelter from strong or drying winds. Some spread rapidly by rhizomes, even more so in warmer climates, but they can be planted in bottomless barrels to restrict their spread. Check before you buy.

## OTHER BAMBOOS

Black bamboo (*Phyllostachys nigra*). Clump-forming, 3–5m (10–15ft) tall, with slender green canes that turn lustrous black in their second or third year.

*Chusquea culeou*. Elegant, to 6m (20ft) tall, with arching, glossy, yellow-green canes bearing clusters of narrow green leaves at each cane joint.

*Pleioblastus variegatus*. Compact, 75cm (30in) tall. Pale green canes and dark green, cream striped leaves

# FERNS

If you have a damp, shady, and sheltered corner, you have the ideal conditions for most ferns — shade plants *par excellence*. Gain maximum textural contrast by associating them with bold-leaved shade lovers, like hostas. If the soil is rich in organic matter and reliably moist, most will tolerate a little sun early or late in the day, but not when it is at its hottest.

## OTHER FERNS

*Athyrium niponicum* var. *pictum*. Creeping Japanese painted fern with silver-grey fronds flushed purple-red and red-purple stalks. 30cm (12in) tall.

Ostrich fern (*Matteuccia struthiopteris*). Forms "shuttlecocks" of lance-shaped green fronds. 1m (3ft) tall.

Sensitive fern (*Onoclea sensibilis*). Creeping fern with almost triangular, pale green fronds, flushed pink in spring. 45cm (18in) tall.

△ *CAREX OSHIMENSIS* 'EVERGOLD'
Low evergreen clumps of dark green leaves with a broad central band of gold. Brown flower spikes are borne in spring. It prefers any moist but well-drained soil, and it is suited to the front of a mixed border. 30cm (12in) tall.

△ *PLEIOBLASTUS AURICOMUS*
A textural feast of subtle colour, the canes of this upright bamboo are purple-green, and the leaves are striped bright yellow and green. It is about 1.5m (5ft) tall and wide.

△ *PHYLLOSTACHYS BAMBUSOIDES* 'ALLGOLD'
A spreading bamboo with golden yellow, sometimes green-striped canes; the leaves, usually green, may repeat the theme. It is 3m (10ft) or more tall.

△ *POLYSTICHUM SETIFERUM* DIVISILOBUM GROUP
An evergreen fern with arching, lance-shaped fronds that are very finely divided into narrow, leathery, mid- to dark green segments. It reaches 70cm (28in) tall, by as much across, and is invaluable for areas of light or deep shade.

△ SNOWY WOODRUSH (*Luzula nivea*)
This rush flowers best in a sunny site in damp soil, although it will tolerate dappled shade. The early summer flowers are good for cutting. It forms loose clumps, 60cm (24in) tall.

△ DROOPING SEDGE (*Carex pendula*)
A large, clump-forming sedge to 1.5m (5ft) tall that thrives in wet or moist soil in sun or partial shade. Catkin-like flowerheads appear in early summer and persist into winter

△ *SASA VEITCHII*
Slender bamboo that is suitable for ground cover, with purple canes and rich green leaves margined with white. It needs good wind shelter to prevent scorched leaf margins. 1.2m (4ft) tall with a spreading habit.

△ *SHIBATAEA KUMASASA*
A compact evergreen bamboo with fresh green, elegantly tapered leaves. At 1m (3ft) tall, and spreading slowly to 75cm (30in) across, it can be clipped to shape.

△ *ASPLENIUM SCOLOPENDRIUM* CRISPUM GROUP
Smooth, leathery fronds, about 50cm (20in) long, have crisped, undulating margins; it contrasts well with more feathery ferns in a damp, shady border

△ ROYAL FERN (*Osmunda regalis*)
Deciduous fern that has bright green fronds and, in summer, brown tassels appear, which hold the spores. It tolerates sun if the soil remains moist. To 2m (6ft) tall.

SEE ALSO: Shady Sites, p.131; Establishing Plants in the Border, pp.148–149; More Ferns, p.320

# PREPARING THE GROUND

THE SUCCESS OF ANY worthwhile activity depends on good preparation. In gardening, the first and most important task is to understand the soil in your garden and to learn how to prepare and care for it. The soil is a living eco-system that provides plants with anchorage, air, water, and nutrients. Care taken to keep it healthy, fertile, and friable, replenishing the nutrients taken out by the plants, will be clearly reflected in the continuing health and productivity of plants that grow in it. Few gardens are naturally blessed with the perfect fertile, moist but well-drained loam, but most soils can be satisfactorily improved — some just take more work than others.

## IMPROVING SOIL TYPES

All soils are improved by the addition of organic matter; this is broken down by soil organisms to provide nutrients and humus, which not only improves drainage, but also improves soil fertility and water retention. The ideal soil, known as loam, is a balanced mix of clay, silt, and sand particles.

■ Clay soils are heavy, sticky when wet, hard when dry, poorly aerated, and heavy to work. They are slow to drain and to warm in spring, but are very highly fertile.

■ Silty soils are moisture-retentive and fairly fertile, but can be easily compacted, becoming heavy, cold, and poorly drained.

■ Sandy soils are dry, light to work, and quick to warm in spring, but drain rapidly, so nutrients are quickly washed out.

■ Chalk soils are alkaline, drain freely, and are often shallow and lack organic matter; they lose nutrients and water rapidly.

■ Peat soils occur where wet conditions prevent the breakdown of organic matter. Prone to waterlogging, they make a good growing medium if drained. You can reduce acidity by liming, and remedy nutrient deficiencies with fertilizers.

This upper layer of topsoil includes organic matter and is fertile, unlike the poor subsoil beneath; never mix subsoil with topsoil

△ THE ANATOMY OF THE SOIL
*Most soils are formed by weathering of rock, and they form distinct layers. Topsoil, from which roots extract nutrients and water, is made fertile by the presence of soil organisms and organic residues. The poorer subsoil layer lies below it.*

## FORKING THE SOIL

In well-established gardens, forking over is often all that is needed. Forks are good for rough digging, turning the soil, and for clearing deep-rooting weeds for new plantings, particularly in established beds. Ideal for relieving surface compaction, forks do less harm to soil structure than spades; they break clods up along natural fracture lines rather than slicing them.

### HOW TO FORK OVER

**1 BREAKING UP THE SOIL**
*At a time when the soil is moist, but not waterlogged, work methodically over the area, inserting the fork and then turning it over (see inset) to break up the compacted soil into a crumbly structure.*

**2 ADDING ORGANIC MATTER**
*After breaking up the surface, you can improve the structure and fertility of the soil by incorporating into it with the fork some organic matter, such as well-rotted garden compost, rotted manure, or spent mushroom compost.*

## CULTIVATING SOIL

The aim is to introduce plenty of organic matter, such as rotted compost, manure, or spent mushroom compost, to produce a crumbly structure that will allow air, water, and dissolved nutrients to reach the plant roots. The best time for digging is autumn, since winter frosts help break up clods; but, for light, sandy soils, spread organic matter over the bare soil in winter and fork over in spring. Never dig or walk on soil when it is very wet or frozen; this compacts it and damages its structure.

### ALWAYS REMEMBER

#### TAKE IT EASY!

Digging can either be a back-breaking chore or, if you use common sense, healthy exercise. Use a spade or fork that is the correct size for you, and wear strong shoes. Take spadefuls of a size that you can lift comfortably. Take your time — if you have large areas to dig, plan ahead. Adopt a methodical approach and find your rhythm. Warm up gradually and use thigh muscles, not the lumbar region, to take the strain.

SEE ALSO: Nourishing your Crops, pp.238–239

# SIMPLE DIGGING

This involves lifting a spadeful of soil, inverting it, and dropping it back in its original position, where clods are chopped up with the spade blade. It is useful for clearing the soil of debris and non-persistent weeds, or for incorporating small amounts of fertilizer and organic matter or grit. It is a good option when working in established borders or irregularly shaped beds.

### ONE "SPIT" DEEP ▷
*The instruction to cultivate the soil "one spit deep" refers to digging to the depth of the spade blade. The blade of a standard digging spade is 25cm (10in) long*

A "spit" is the depth of a spade blade, about 25cm (10in) long.

## SIMPLE DIGGING TECHNIQUE

**1 INSERTING THE SPADE**
*Drive the spade blade vertically into the ground to its full depth. Wearing strong shoes, exert pressure on the top of the blade with the ball or heel of the foot. Do not use the arch of the foot, since this will cause tension, which soon results in discomfort.*

**2 LIFTING THE SOIL**
*Pull back on the handle and lever soil onto the blade. Bend knees and elbows to lift the spade. Try to minimize bending at the waist as this strains the lower back. Do not try to lift too much soil at once, especially where the soil is heavy.*

**3 TURNING THE SOIL**
*Twist the blade to turn the soil over. This allows air and water to penetrate and is beneficial for soil organisms. Work methodically (along an imaginary line) to ensure that all soil is turned over. If sowing seeds, rake over to produce a fine tilth.*

# SINGLE DIGGING

Single digging is a methodical and labour-efficient approach, which ensures that all of the soil is turned over to a uniform standard and depth. The technique can be adapted so that organic matter is forked in to the bottom of each trench, improving both quality and depth of topsoil.

### HOW IT WORKS ▷
*The bed is marked out into a series of trenches. The soil from the first trench is dug out and placed on one side, and then the soil from each subsequent trench is moved into the empty one. The last trench is filled with the set-aside soil.*

The soil from the first trench is set aside and then used to fill the last trench

Work backwards, so that you do not stand on, and so compact, soil that has been dug

## HOW TO SINGLE DIG

**1 THE FIRST TRENCH**
*Dig out the first trench, 30cm (12in) wide and one spit deep. Lift soil onto the ground in front and keep it in reserve. If you need to incorporate organic matter, place it on the trench base and fork it in lightly.*

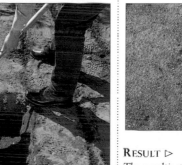

**2 SECOND AND SUBSEQUENT TRENCHES**
*Work backwards, digging out soil from the second trench and turning it into the one in front. Invert it to bury annual weeds and weed seeds. Repeat for all subsequent trenches. Put the reserved soil into the last trench.*

# THE NO-DIG TECHNIQUE

Digging increases the breakdown of organic matter, reducing fertility unless replenished, and brings weed seeds to the surface, stimulating their germination. The no-dig technique relies on earth-worms and micro-organisms to aerate the soil and uses an organic mulch on the surface to preserve soil structure, conserve water and nutrients, and suppress weeds. It works best following one thorough, deep digging, when all perennial weeds must be removed. Before sowing, remove the mulch and hoe or rake the surface.

◁ **EXPERIMENT**
*The soil on the right has been dug over, but that on the left is undisturbed. Digging introduces air that speeds the decomposition rate of organic matter and exposes weed seeds to light needed for germination.*

**RESULT ▷**
*The uncultivated soil on the left shows little weed growth, but many more have germinated on the dug soil on the right. The no-dig method can reduce the amount of preparation needed for seed beds.*

SEE ALSO: The Deep Bed Method, p.237; Dealing with Weeds, pp.290–291

# CLEARING WEEDS AND MARKING OUT BEDS

THE NEXT STEP IN CREATING your new bed or border is to clear out all weeds and mark out the shape. Weeds are vigorous, opportunistic plants that will compete with ornamentals for light, air, and nutrients. Many are also alternative hosts to a range of pests and diseases that infest ornamental plants. Borders should be completely cleared of weeds, especially deep-rooting and perennial ones, before planting, so that new plants have the best possible chance of establishment. New borders look much better if accurately rather than roughly marked out, and extra care needs to be taken with ground clearance if creating beds in a lawn or neglected area.

## CLEARING WEEDS ORGANICALLY

Non-chemical weeding methods remove weeds physically from the soil, and are ideal for organic gardeners. Hoes, hand forks, border forks, and digging forks are the main tools used. In most cases, the whole weed is removed, and this method causes little disturbance to existing plants. On very overgrown sites, you can use a strimmer, scythe, or brushwood cutter to slash down top-growth. Then remove all debris and dig out roots by hand. Rotary cultivators, or rotavators, are useful for large areas, but they chop weed roots into pieces, each of which may develop into a new plant. After rotavating, therefore, remove weed fragments promptly by hand-digging, and rake all debris out of the soil to prevent re-rooting.

DUTCH HOE

DRAW HOE

△ **THE RIGHT TOOL FOR THE TASK**
*The Dutch hoe, easiest to use and most versatile, cuts surface weeds off at ground level. The draw hoe can be used for chopping weeds, but is more useful for earthing up or creating channels, known as drills, for seed sowing.*

**USING A DUTCH HOE** ▷
*A Dutch hoe can be used for weeding between border plants. It will destroy annual weeds, but deep-rooting ones need repeated hoeing. Keep the blade parallel with the soil surface and move forward on or just below the surface.*

◁ **USING A FORK**
*Use a hand fork or border fork to dig out weeds in a border; both create minimal disturbance to established ornamentals. Tease out the roots, tracing them back as far as you can. Remove as much root as possible; any left in place will re-sprout to form new plants. Use a digging fork for larger areas and for deep-rooted weeds.*

## USING WEEDKILLERS

Clearing weeds with a chemical weedkiller is the fastest and most effective method, because it also kills the roots. Once it has taken effect, either cultivate the soil by mixing in organic matter, such as rotted compost or manure, or plant directly into the treated soil. Remove and dispose of dead woody material. Tough weeds, like brambles, may need a second application.

### ALWAYS REMEMBER

**STRICTLY FOLLOW INSTRUCTIONS**

Safe and effective use of chemicals demands that you follow the manufacturer's instructions to the letter. Weedkillers work best if applied on a warm and still, sunny day when the weeds are in active growth and with sufficient leaf area to absorb chemicals fully. If you time it correctly, only the toughest weeds are likely to need more than one application.

**NEGLECTED SITES** ▷
*A neglected or weed-infested site must be cleared thoroughly before planting. Chemical weedkilling is the most effective method for such a job; if you prefer to use organic methods, it is a good idea to apply a sheet mulch after clearance to suppress further growth.*

◁ **APPLICATION**
*For small areas, apply chemical weedkillers using a watering can with a dribble bar. Keep a clearly marked can for the purpose, as residues may affect border plants if the can is later used for watering. For larger areas, use a backpack sprayer.*

SEE ALSO: Dealing with Weeds, pp.290–291

## SPOT WEEDING

In areas of established planting, it is not a good idea to apply weedkillers with a sprayer or a can and dribble bar. Most will kill a broad spectrum of plants – they are not specific to weeds – and any spray drift or splash on the foliage of border plants will be damaging or even fatal.

Where small numbers of weeds occur in an established border, it is a simple matter to spot treat them with a "weed wand" or to apply a gel-based proprietary weedkiller with a brush. This technique is also useful for weeds growing in gravel, in paving crevices, or in lawns. For organic gardeners, a non-chemical alternative is to use a flame-weeder, which directs a narrow flame onto the growing point. The drier the soil, the better the result. A few seconds of intense heat will kill small annual weeds; perennials need repeated treatments.

**TREATING INDIVIDUAL WEEDS ▷**
*Spot-weeding chemicals are usually gel-based weedkillers that act on both the foliage and the roots. The gel gives good adherence, thereby minimizing the risk of drips or splashes. Brush it onto the leaves of the offending plant; wash your hands thoroughly after use.*

## USING MULCHES TO SUPPRESS WEEDS

Weed suppression by mulching is used for two main purposes: to clear weeds before planting, and to keep cleared areas free of weeds. It is a good method of clearance for organic gardeners. A light-excluding sheet mulch, such as black polythene or old carpet, kills most weeds if left in place for a season, or two seasons for tough weeds like horsetail. In reliably sunny areas, clear plastic sheeting is effective; temperatures rise rapidly beneath it and "cook" weeds to death.

Once the soil is completely clean of all weeds, sheet or loose mulches can be used to suppress further weed growth. Sheet mulches are effective but unattractive, but can be topped off with a shallow layer of more presentable, loose materials.

### GOOD IDEAS

• If you are averse to using chemicals, using sheet mulches is a good way to clear the ground, but you do need to plan well ahead.

• A combination of sheet and loose mulches is a cost-effective and attractive means of weed control. A 2–3cm (1–1¼in) deep layer of loose material is adequate to disguise the weed-suppressing sheet – half the depth (and cost) of using loose mulch alone.

• Local authorities or forestry enterprises often recycle and sell wood or bark chips; this is an ecologically sound and economical source of mulch material.

△ **LOOSE MULCHES**
*A 5–8cm (2–3in) layer of loose material, such as granulated bark, wood chips, coconut shells, or gravel, makes an effective weed suppressant. They can be laid on clean soil or over a geotextile membrane. Garden compost and manure are less efficient as they may contain weed seeds, but they still make valuable, soil-improving mulches.*

Weed seedlings cannot penetrate the membrane; deprived of light, they die quickly

The permeable material allows water and air to pass through it

△ **A GEOTEXTILE SHEET MULCH**
*For the mulch membrane, a material called geotextile is better than plastic; it is permeable to air and water, and fertilizers can be washed down by rain. The life of gravel or bark top-dressing is extended, since it does not become incorporated into the soil. To plant through it, make two slits cross-wise, and dig the planting hole beneath.*

## MARKING OUT A BED

To mark out curved beds or borders, use a length of twine or hosepipe laid on the ground, and adjust to the required shape. For best effect, make curves strong and sweeping. Wiggly lines are less pleasing to look at and harder to maintain. For formal beds, use pegs and twine to mark out straight lines. To make corners true, check with a builder's square. To make a circle, attach some string or twine to two pegs – the length of the string should equal the radius (not the diameter) of the desired finished circle. With the string taut, draw one peg around the other.

△ **STRAIGHT LINES**
*A straight line can be created with a length of twine and two pegs. To achieve accurate right angles at the corners of a formal bed, use a builder's square as a guide.*

Non-stretch string or twine

**CREATING CIRCLES ▷**
*Use two pegs, joined with string, to draw a circle on the ground. Drive one into the soil in the centre and move the other around it.*

**SEE ALSO:** Planting with Sheet or Mat Mulches, p.151; General Border Maintenance, pp.152–153

# BUYING GOOD PLANTS

ONCE THE GROUND HAS BEEN CLEARED, get planting schemes off to the best possible start with good, healthy, vigorous plants chosen to suit the soil, aspect, and climate of the position in which they will grow. It pays to be able to recognize, and therefore avoid buying, plants that have been produced in less than ideal conditions, since these are less likely to establish successfully. Poorly raised plants may also bring new pests and diseases into the garden. If you learn what to look for, however, and buy your plants only from a reputable supplier, the risks will be minimized, and you can look forward to a thriving garden that will give years of trouble-free pleasure.

## PERENNIALS

Most perennials are sold as container-grown plants throughout the growing season, and they can be planted in full growth if kept well watered until established. It is best, however, to buy in spring; plants then have a whole growing season to establish before the onset of winter. If buying early, check that the plants have some healthy buds. In warmer areas, you can buy and plant perennials in autumn when the soil is still warm and less likely to dry out.

When buying, check that the compost is evenly moist, and that its surface is free of weeds and mosses; these indicate that the compost may be poorly drained, or that the plant has been in its container too long and may have suffered nutrient starvation.

Strong growth and healthy green leaves with no evidence of pests or diseases

Stout, healthy stems, and plant is well clothed with foliage to the base

Compost surface is evenly moist and free of weeds, liverworts, and mosses

Well-established system of healthy roots retains compost to form a good root ball

△ **GOOD EXAMPLE**
*The example above is a healthy, vigorous lupin with fresh green foliage that shows no signs of discolouration, which may indicate nutrient deficiency or virus infection. Check the foliage for obvious signs of pests or eaten leaves, and make sure that it exhibits no sign of wilting; this may indicate root pests, root damage, or lack of water. If possible, remove the plant from its pot to inspect the roots.*

### GOOD IDEAS

• When buying clump-forming perennials, choose large specimens that have several strong shoots; these can be divided before planting to yield two or three plants for the price of one (*see p.148*).

• With planning and forethought, you can raise many perennials from seed (*see p.162*). This yields many plants at a fraction of the cost and you will have enough to give away or to swap with your gardening friends.

◁ **POT-BOUND PLANT**
*Plants that have been in their containers too long may be pot-bound; that is, the roots have filled the pot and begun to spiral around upon themselves, or they have rooted into the standing area beneath the pot. They may be starved of water and nutrients and suffered a severe check to growth.*

Dry compost has resulted in a poorly developed root system

Top-growth is weak and stunted by dry conditions

**POOR EXAMPLE** ▷
*Plants with sparse, spindly, or woody top-growth often have a poorly developed root system and do not establish well. As a result of erratic watering, the compost has dried out. Peat-based composts are difficult to re-wet, so growth is checked and the plant may not recover.*

## BULBS

Most bulbous plants are sold in a dry, dormant state and are best bought fresh, as soon as available – from late summer for spring bulbs; spring for summer bulbs; and from early summer for autumn ones. They deteriorate if kept dry for too long. Bulbs should be plump and firm, with a strong growing point. Choose the largest ones you can find. Check that outer coverings and roots are entire and mould-free, with no damaged or diseased areas.

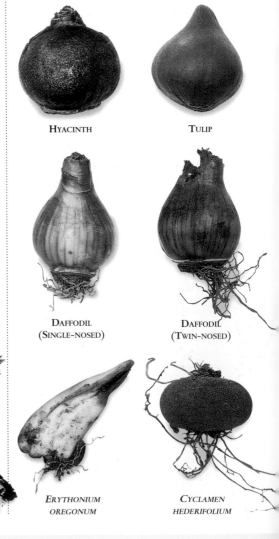

**HYACINTH**

**TULIP**

**DAFFODIL**
(**SINGLE-NOSED**)

**DAFFODIL**
(**TWIN-NOSED**)

*ERYTHONIUM*
*OREGONUM*

*CYCLAMEN*
*HEDERIFOLIUM*

**SEE ALSO:** Establishing Plants in the Border, pp.148–149

# SHRUBS

Shrubs are usually sold in pots and are either container-grown or field-grown and containerized in the season before sale. Container-grown shrubs usually have a better-established root system and can be planted at any time, except in very wet, cold, or dry periods. Containerized shrubs are best planted in winter; they are slow to establish at other times unless their root system is particularly well-developed.

Deciduous shrubs may be offered bare-rooted when dormant. Buy and plant these in late autumn to early spring; check that each fibrous root system is well-developed and not dried out.

◁ **GOOD EXAMPLE**
*Foliage is healthy, of good colour with no yellowing or signs of pests or diseases. Branch framework is evenly balanced and well clothed to the base. The root system is well-developed, with healthy white tips, and forms a firm ball that retains compost when removed from the pot.*

Vigorous, well-balanced top-growth clothed to ground level

A well-established system of fine, fibrous roots makes a compact root ball that almost fills the pot

Sparse, twiggy stems show little sign of new growth and some have died back

◁ **ROOT-BALLED**
*Root-balled shrubs, sold in autumn and early spring, are grown in open ground, then lifted with a compact ball of roots and soil. They are wrapped in net or hessian. The root ball must be firm and the wrapping intact, otherwise roots may dry out and die back.*

◁ **RENOVATION**
*If top-growth is promising, with plenty of plump new buds to come, but roots are crowded, a little renovation will ensure recovery and good establishment. Tease out pot-bound roots and cut any that are dead, very long, or damaged, back to clean, healthy growth.*

Pot-bound roots spiral around pot and have used up compost nutrients

△ **POOR EXAMPLE**
*Avoid plants with die-back and sparse, leggy, uneven top-growth that has few or no visible new growth buds; they are likely to be pot-bound and will have suffered a severe check from lack of water and nutrients.*

# ROSES

Roses have long been sold bare-rooted for planting in the dormant season, in late autumn, early winter, or early spring; if planted as soon as possible after buying, they will establish perfectly well. You may have to seek out old or uncommon roses from specialists who supply by mail order. These are often bare-rooted, but will be packed well in plastic to avoid desiccation.

Container-grown roses can be planted at any time except when the soil is very wet, dry, or frozen. Unsold, bare-rooted plants that have been potted up at the end of their season may be satisfactory; but if they have dried out or been exposed to cold, they are not likely to establish well. Check before buying that the plant is well-rooted by shaking the main stem gently.

Strong bud union and an evenly spaced framework of sturdy, healthy stems

◁ **BARE-ROOTED ROSE**
*Look for a good network of fibrous and main roots and 3–5 strong stems. Check that the roots have not dried out and that the stems show no premature growth; this indicates poor storage and such a plant will seldom establish well.*

**CONTAINER-GROWN ROSE** ▷
*A well-grown specimen has a well-balanced set of strong stems, clothed in an abundance of vigorous, healthy foliage of good, deep colour. There is no evidence of pests or diseases, such as rust or black spot. The compost is evenly moist and its surface is free of weeds and mosses.*

◁ **POOR EXAMPLE**
*Avoid buying bare-root roses that have spindly shoots with evidence of die-back or fungal disease. A stunted, desiccated root system with few fibrous feeder roots will never sustain healthy growth and development.*

Evenly moist compost with a system of plump and healthy roots

**POOR EXAMPLE** ▷
*Stems are sparse and spindly; leaves have black spot, and some have fallen. A weedy compost surface suggests the plant has been in its container for too long.*

**SEE ALSO:** Establishing Shrubs and Roses, pp.150–151

# ESTABLISHING PLANTS IN THE BORDER

THE PERIOD BETWEEN planning and planting or sowing can seem unending, but, having prepared the soil and researched and chosen suitable plants, it is worth taking a little more time to establish your border plants – perennials, bulbs, and annuals or biennials – correctly. Planting and sowing techniques, and their timing, must be suited to individual plants and to the climate you are working in. Once in the soil, keep young plants watered and free of weeds until well established. Thereafter, they usually need watering only in prolonged dry spells. They will always need weeding, but a dense foliage canopy of well-grown plants will help to discourage weed growth.

## PLANTING PERENNIALS

Container-grown perennials may be planted out at any time of year when the soil is workable – not too wet, too dry, or frozen. The best seasons, however, are spring and autumn. In autumn, the soil is still warm and unlikely to dry out – ideal conditions for good root growth before the onset of winter. In cold areas, spring is better, especially for plants that need drier conditions or are not fully hardy. It gives them a full growing season to become established before their first winter. Spring or summer plantings are likely to need watering until they are established. Perennials always look better when planted in odd-numbered groups.

### PLANTING A CONTAINER-GROWN PERENNIAL

**1 MAKE A HOLE**
Dig a planting hole with a border fork or hand trowel in a prepared bed. The hole should be 1½ times deeper and wider than the root ball of the plant.

**2 REMOVE PLANT FROM POT**
Water the pot thoroughly, let the excess drain away, and then gently slide the plant out, taking care not to damage either the roots or the growing points.

**3 TEASE OUT ROOTS**
Gently scrape off the top 3cm (1½in) of compost to remove weeds and their seeds. Tease out the roots gently with the fingers or a hand fork. This will speed up root establishment.

**4 FIRM IN GENTLY**
Put the plant in the hole at the correct depth (see below), and back-fill with soil. Firm in with your fingertips. Loosen the soil surface with a hand fork, and water in well.

## DIVIDING PERENNIALS

Large, clump-forming, fibrous-rooted perennials, such as asters, phlox, and sedums, are easy to divide, instantly providing you with bonus plants. Remove the plant from its container, and gently prize the root ball apart, creating two or three sections of equal size. Plant out all the new divisions straightaway.

◁ **GOOD VALUE**
This aster is well-grown, with a large number of healthy shoots that have not yet become so crowded as to weaken the plant's growth. It will consequently yield 2–3 good-sized divisions.

**HOW TO DIVIDE** ▷
Gently tease plant roots apart to form equal sections, each with a healthy root system. Keep plenty of soil around roots and plant out immediately.

## PLANTING DEPTHS FOR PERENNIALS

As a general rule, most perennials are planted at exactly the same depth as they were in the pot, but a number will grow better if planted a little higher or deeper, depending on their individual preferences. Rhizomatous plants, like bearded irises, may rot if planted too deeply, and some variegated plants revert to green if planted at ground level. Tuberous and moisture-loving plants both enjoy the added protection of deeper planting.

### HOW DEEP TO PLANT PERENNIALS

△ **DEEP PLANTING**
Plant perennials with tuberous root systems (here, Solomon's seal) so that their crowns are about 10cm (4in) below the surface of the soil.

△ **SHALLOW DEPTH**
Perennials that need a moist environment (here, a hosta) should be planted with their crowns at about 2–2.5cm (¾–1in) below ground level.

△ **GROUND LEVEL**
The vast majority of perennials should be planted with their crowns at ground level, that is at the same depth as they were when in the pot.

△ **RAISED UP**
Plants that are prone to rot, or variegated plants (here, Sisyrinchium 'Aunt May') that tend to revert, are planted with the crown just above ground.

SEE ALSO: Maintaining Border Plants, pp.154–155; Clearing Weeds and Marking Out Beds, pp.144–145; Increasing Border Plants, pp.162–163

# PLANTING BULBS

As a rule, spring-flowering bulbs should be planted in late summer or in autumn, summer-flowering bulbs in spring, and autumn-flowering ones in early to mid-summer. Plant most bulbs their own width apart, at two or three times their own depth (four or five times in sandy soils and very frosty areas). A few, such as nerines, need their tips to be at ground level.

**◁ SINGLETONS**
*If you wish to produce a scattered effect, for example among other plants, plant singly in separate holes of the right depth. Dig holes with a trowel or bulb planter.*

**IN THE GREEN ▷**
*Some bulbs, like snowdrops, benefit from being planted or divided, when in growth, or "in the green". Make a hole wide enough to spread out the roots, and plant the bulb at the same depth as it was growing before.*

## PLANTING BULBS IN OPEN GROUND

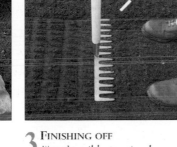

**1 MAKE A PLANTING HOLE**
*Excavate a hole in well-prepared soil to the appropriate depth. Place bulbs, growth points uppermost, on the base. Set bulbs that need good drainage on a layer of grit.*

**2 COVER WITH SOIL**
*For a natural effect, space the bulbs randomly, at least their own width apart. Draw soil over them gently by hand to minimize any risk of displacing or damaging them.*

**3 FINISHING OFF**
*Firm the soil by tamping down with the back of a rake. Avoid treading on the soil surface, because this might damage the growing points. Mark the position of the bulbs.*

**◁ NATURALIZING LARGE BULBS**
*Scatter large bulbs (here, daffodils) and plant where they fall. Make individual holes with a bulb planter. Place the bulb in the hole, growth point uppermost, cover it with loose soil, replace the cap of turf, and firm gently in place.*

**◁ NATURALIZING SMALL BULBS**
*For small bulbs like crocus, make an H-shaped cut in the turf with a lawn edger or spade blade. Roll back the flaps, and set the bulbs in place randomly. Score the turf flap to loosen the soil. Replace it carefully and pat gently to firm.*

# SOWING SEEDS OF ANNUALS AND BIENNIALS

Annuals and biennials are always grown from seed. In spring, annuals can be sown direct or in pots for planting out later. Broadcast sowing gives natural effects when filling gaps in borders, but weeding must be done by hand. Biennials should be sown in pots, or in nursery rows for bedding, from late spring to midsummer.

**◁ THINNING**
*With broadcast sowing, when seedlings appear they are often growing too close together. Encourage the healthiest seedlings to flourish by thinning; press gently on either side, and pluck out the weaker ones.*

**◁ TRANSPLANTING SEEDLING GROUPS**
*A dense patch of seedlings seldom thrives. Carefully lift out small clumps, with plenty of soil around their roots, and transplant these to another area to grow on. Then thin as normal later.*

## BROADCASTING ANNUAL SEEDS

## RAISING BIENNIALS

**1 PREPARE AND SOW**
*Rake the soil into a fine tilth (fine, crumbly texture) and scatter, or broadcast, seeds thinly over the area, by hand or straight from the packet.*

**2 COVER OVER**
*Very lightly, to avoid disturbing the seeds, rake the area at right angles to cover them. Water them in using a fine-rosed watering can, and label.*

**1 LIFT SEEDLINGS**
*To raise sufficient biennials for a bedding scheme (here, wallflowers), sow seeds in rows in a prepared seed bed in late spring to midsummer. Lift the seedlings when they reach 5–8cm (2–3in) tall and place on a tray.*

**2 TRANSFER TO NURSERY**
*Plant out the seedlings in a nursery bed, 15–20cm (6–8in) apart, in rows that are 20–30cm (8–12in) apart. If using biennials less formally, plant directly into their flowering site and grow on there.*

**3 PLANT OUT**
*In autumn, when the new plants are established and growing well, give them a thorough watering if dry. Lift each one carefully to avoid damaging the roots. Plant out in well-prepared soil in the final flowering site.*

SEE ALSO: Clearing Weeds and Marking Out Beds, pp.144–145; Increasing Border Plants, pp.162–163

# ESTABLISHING SHRUBS AND ROSES

SHRUBS AND ROSES ARE POTENTIALLY long-lived plants, so thorough preparation of the soil before planting is essential. Autumn and spring are the best times to plant shrubs. In autumn, residual soil warmth allows good root growth before the onset of winter, so that the shrub is well established before the following summer's dry weather occurs. Spring planting avoids winter exposure, but extra watering may be needed if the top-growth emerges before the roots have developed properly. Roses should be planted late in the season and pruned carefully to stimulate new growth. Mulching will help new plants establish by suppressing weeds and conserving moisture.

## PLANTING SHRUBS

Container-grown shrubs may be planted at any time the soil is workable, but need careful watering in the early stages if planted in full growth. The best times, however, as for all shrubs, are autumn or spring. Clear the ground of weeds, and work well-rotted organic matter into the top 30–45cm (12–18in) of soil. Cultivate the entire bed, if possible; otherwise prepare an area larger than the planting site. For bare-root shrubs, make the planting hole wide enough to spread the roots out fully. For root-balled and container-grown shrubs, make it at least twice the width of the root mass. Plant the shrub at the same level as it was in its pot or in the ground.

### HOW TO PLANT A CONTAINER-GROWN SHRUB

**1 DIG OUT THE HOLE**
*Water the plant well, and set aside to drain. Dig a planting hole, twice the width of the root mass, or wider on heavy clay soils, and the same depth as the pot.*

**2 PREPARE THE SOIL**
*Use a fork to loosen the soil at the bottom and sides of the hole, to relieve compaction and aid good root penetration. On one side, mix the excavated soil with organic matter.*

**3 REMOVE THE PLANT**
*Place a hand over the top of the compost and around the stem base to support it; slide the plant carefully out of its container. Place the root ball in the prepared hole.*

**4 ADJUST THE DEPTH**
*Lay a cane across the top of the hole to check that the soil level is the same as before. Adjust level, if necessary, by adding or excavating more topsoil beneath the shrub.*

**5 BACKFILL WITH SOIL**
*Use the mixed soil to backfill around the plant. Firm gently with your fingers or a trowel handle to remove air pockets and ensure close contact between roots and soil.*

**6 WATER AND MULCH**
*Firm the soil gently with your foot, and water in. On light soils, mound up soil to form a watering "basin" (see inset). Apply a loose mulch, leaving the stem clear.*

### TELL ME WHY

**WHY PLANT EVERGREENS IN SPRING?**
Broad-leaved evergreens and conifers retain their leaves in winter, so they are especially vulnerable to desiccation in cold, dry, winter winds; the effect is exacerbated if they do not have a well-established root system. Spring planting allows them a full growing season to develop a good root system before the onset of the following winter.

## STAKING SHRUBS

Shrubs do not normally need to be staked, except for large, root-bound specimens and standards. The former, which ideally should not have been bought in the first place, will need some support in their first year or two at least, until their roots begin to spread out and they become stable.

The best method for any shrub that branches from near ground level is to secure it with ties fixed to three stakes spaced evenly around the shrub. To prevent bark damage, cover the ties where they touch the branches with rubber or padding.

For standards, insert the stake in the planting hole before planting to avoid damaging the root system. The top of the stake should be just below the first branches. Secure the stem to the stake, using a tie with a spacer or a homemade figure-of-eight tie to prevent chafing.

### ALWAYS REMEMBER

**PROTECT NEWLY PLANTED SHRUBS**
Newly planted shrubs, especially broad-leaved evergreens and conifers, may suffer from desiccation or cold if not protected. A screen of hessian or mesh greatly reduces water loss from the foliage. To protect the roots from frost, spread a thick layer of mulch (*see p.153*) around the shrub.

SEE ALSO: General Border Maintenance, pp.152–153; Mulching Materials, p.153; Maintaining Shrubs, pp.156–157; Planting in Containers, pp.176–177

# PLANTING ROSES

Plant bare-root roses in late autumn or early winter at the beginning of, or just before, their dormant period. In areas with severe winters, plant in early spring. If soil is too wet, dry, or frozen, delay planting until conditions improve; keep the roots moist in the meantime. If the delay is prolonged, heel plants in by burying roots in a shallow trench on spare ground. Container-grown roses may be planted at any time. Roses need good, fertile soil to flower well, especially those that repeat throughout summer. Prepare the soil well and add extra fertilizer before planting.

## HOW TO PLANT A BARE-ROOT BUSH ROSE

**1 PREPARE THE ROSE**
*Soak the roots in water for an hour or so, until moist. Cut out diseased, damaged growth and remove crossing and straggly stems at their base, aiming for a balanced framework. Trim thick roots by a third of their length*

**2 DIG THE PLANTING HOLE**
*Dig a hole that is wide enough to hold the roots and deep enough for the "bud union" (a bulge at the stem base where the rose to flower has been grafted onto a more vigorous rootstock) to be 2.5cm (1in) below ground level.*

**3 CHECK PLANTING LEVEL**
*Fork half a bucketful of garden compost and a small handful of general fertilizer into the base. Set the rose centrally in the hole and spread the roots evenly. Use a cane to check that the bud union is at the correct depth.*

**4 BACKFILL AND FIRM IN**
*Refill the planting hole with soil, in stages. Firm firstly by hand to remove air pockets and then gently with your toes. Rake over the soil and water the plant in well. Apply a layer of mulch in the following spring.*

# PRUNING AFTER PLANTING

A compact and healthy shrub needs no, or minimal, pruning on planting, but minor defects are easily remedied when plants are young (*see below*). Most roses are also pruned immediately after planting to remove weak, damaged, or dead growth and any overlong shoots that spoil the general shape of the bush. In the case of container-grown roses that have been planted when in full growth, carry out initial pruning to shape in the first spring after planting.

△ **PRUNING A SHRUB ON PLANTING**
*Prune any dead, diseased, or damaged branches back to a healthy bud, and cut back any crossing or inward-growing shoots to an outward-facing bud. Remove weak or straggly stems, and shorten any very long shoots and those that spoil the overall balance of the branch framework.*

**SPRING PRUNING ▷**
*For container-grown roses, in the first spring following planting, remove any frost-damaged, weak, or dead shoots. Cut remaining stems back to an outward-facing bud, about 8cm (3in) above ground. For climbers, just remove weak, dead, or damaged growth.*

# PLANTING WITH SHEET OR MAT MULCHES

Using a sheet mulch (*see p.145*) can help newly planted shrubs to establish. Lay the sheet over the soil and secure it at the sides with metal pegs. Make a slit in the sheet with a knife or spade and plant through the hole. Alternatively, you can use a circular mulch mat; this has a ready-made planting hole, and it is slit from centre to edge so it is easily laid on the ground around the newly planted shrub.

## GOOD IDEAS

• Thoroughly water dry soil before applying a sheet mulch or mulch mat, or wait for waterlogged soil to drain; once in place, the mulch is impermeable to water.

• If necessary, incorporate organic matter or fertilizer in the soil before laying the mulch.

• Add extra nutrients to the soil, as required, through small holes in the mulch.

The mulch will help create better conditions for growth while the plant establishes

◁ **PLANTING THROUGH SHEET MULCH**
*Lay the sheet of plastic mulch over the soil and secure it. Make a cross-shaped slit in the sheet, dig a hole beneath, and plant the shrub as normal.*

SEE ALSO: Maintaining Shrubs, pp.156–157; Pruning Established Shrubs, p.158–159; Maintaining Roses, pp.160–161

# GENERAL BORDER MAINTENANCE

WHILE GOOD PREPARATION reduces the amount of aftercare required, beds and borders need a degree of maintenance if they are continue to look their best. Weeds will appear, but their numbers will fall over the years if always removed before they produce any seeds. In well-prepared soils, established plants seldom need watering, except in prolonged dry spells, but new plantings may need watering until established. In fertile soils, if plants are growing and flowering well, they will need little in the way of fertilizers, although they should be mulched annually with organic matter. If pruned regularly or heavily, they will need an annual top-up of nutrients.

## WEEDING ESTABLISHED BEDS

Always remove weeds as soon as they are seen. Weed little and often, rather than blitzing periodically. Hand pulling or forking are the safest methods around ornamental plants. Hoe carefully and not too deeply between the plants, so as avoid damaging nearby roots or stems.

**ROUTINE WEEDING ▷**
*To remove weeds from borders, hoe carefully and not too deeply between the ornamental plants in order to avoid damaging their roots or stems. Any stubborn weeds not removed by hoeing should be lifted out with a hand fork.*

## WATERING TECHNIQUES

It is vital to water thoroughly if moisture is to percolate deeply enough to reach the roots. Watering little and often is wasteful and potentially damaging; if only the surface layers of soil are moistened, plant roots tend to stay near the surface and are then more vulnerable to heat, cold, and drought. Hand watering by can or hose, fitted with a fine rose for seedlings or a coarse one for established plants, is practical for small gardens and individual plants. For larger areas, sprinklers or drip-feed systems, which deliver a gentle trickle to the plant base from a perforated pipe or seep hose, are useful, but both should be fitted with a timing device to avoid waste.

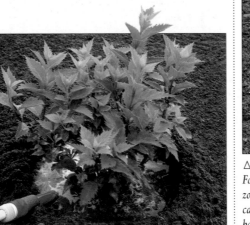

**△ BASIN WATERING**
*On light, sandy soils and sloping sites, make a ridge of soil around the root zone to create a basin and fill it slowly with water. This technique prevents water run-off and ensures that it seeps directly downwards to the plant roots.*

**◁ AVOID PUDDLING**
*Applying water at too fast a rate, or under pressure, causes puddling at the soil surface and may wash soil away, exposing roots and damaging the soil structure. If using a hose, keep the pressure low, fit a fine rose, and move the spray gently back and forth.*

**◁ POT WATERING**
*On silty or clay soils, which are prone to capping (compaction of the soil surface by wetting), sink a large pot into the soil near to the plant roots and fill it with water. Water seeps down to the roots through the drainage holes without damaging the soil structure.*

## APPLYING MULCH

Mulches are multi-functional; they help prevent germination of weed seeds, keep roots cooler in summer and warmer in winter, reduce evaporation of water from the soil surface, and prevent erosion by improving soil structure and fertility. Apply a mulch in autumn or spring, each or every other year, when the soil is moist. Never mulch dry, waterlogged, cold, or frozen soil. A 5–8cm (2–3in) layer helps to control weeds; a 10–15cm (4–6in) layer provides winter insulation in cold areas.

**△ MULCHING SHRUBS**
*For woody plants, apply a mulch to cover the entire root zone; this usually equates to the full extent of the foliage canopy. Leave a 10–15cm (4–6in) gap around the stem base; mounding mulch onto woody stems may cause rotting.*

**△ MULCHING PERENNIALS**
*Perennials, like peonies, that prefer rich, moist but well-drained soil, benefit from a 5cm (2in) mulch of loose organic matter. Apply in autumn, or in spring before new shoots emerge, so they are not damaged in the process.*

SEE ALSO: Clearing Weeds and Marking Out Beds, pp.144–145; Making Compost, p.236

# MULCHING MATERIALS

As well as helping with weed control, soil temperature regulation, and water retention, organic mulches improve soil structure and fertility as they are broken down or incorporated by soil organisms. There is a wide range of suitable materials available. Coconut shells and shredded or granulated bark have ideal characteristics and are free of weed seeds. Bark products are best if composted, since they may contain natural chemicals that can cause damage to susceptible plants. Garden compost, leafmould, and well-rotted manure add low levels of nutrients and are good soil improvers, but they often contain weed seeds. Spent mushroom compost improves soil and supplies nutrients, but it may contain low levels of lime, making it unsuitable for acid soils where lime-hating plants like rhododendrons grow.

**ORGANIC MULCHES ▷**
*Material suitable for use as organic mulches range from well-rotted garden compost or spent mushroom compost to shredded or granulated bark and pieces of coconut shell. All may be used to form a protective layer around border plants.*

**GARDEN COMPOST**      **SHREDDED BARK**      **COCONUT SHELLS**      **SPENT MUSHROOM COMPOST**      **GRANULATED BARK**

# DECORATIVE MULCHES

Some mulches, such as gravel, pebbles, or bark chips, provide an attractive finish to the surface of a bed, as well as performing the soil-protecting functions of a mulch. Lay the mulch on its own, 5–8cm (2–3in) deep, or at half that depth on top of a sheet of landscaping fabric. Such mulches are particularly useful in protecting the surface of clay or silty soils from problems caused by overwatering or heavy rain.

**COMBINING LOOKS AND PRACTICALITY ▷**
*This gravel mulch serves to protects the flowers and leaves of plants (here, hellebores) from soil splash. It also ensures good drainage around plant stems, and it looks attractive.*

△ **USING PEBBLES AS A DECORATIVE MULCH**
*Golden creeping jenny (Lysimachia nummularia 'Aurea') and bugle (Ajuga) growing through a pebble mulch. This looks particularly good next to a stream or pool.*

# USING FERTILIZERS

An annual application of a balanced fertilizer gives plants an adequate supply of nitrogen, phosphates, and potash. Fertilizers come in different formulations, but all should be applied to moist soil; if conditions are dry, water the soil first. Apply slow-release fertilizers in spring as, or just before, growth begins. If needed, use quick-release powders to provide a boost to growth in late spring or early summer. Liquid formulas, some of which are foliar feeds, act rapidly and are best used as an aid to ailing plants in full leaf.

△ **APPLYING FERTILIZER**
*Sprinkle fertilizer around the plant at the recommended rate, and lightly fork it in. Solid fertilizers should not touch the leaves or stem, as they may cause scorch damage.*

**SEE ALSO:** Clearing Weeds and Marking out Beds, pp.144–145; Nourishing your Crops, pp.238–239; Dealing with Weeds and Plant Problems, pp.288–311

# MAINTAINING BORDER PLANTS

TO GIVE A GOOD SHOW, most perennials need only a top-dressing of general fertilizer in spring, but a little extra attention will produce even better results. Thinning, stopping, and deadheading will all increase flower production. Taller perennials, annuals, and biennials, or those of arching growth, may need support to display their flowers to best advantage or to prevent them from flopping over. As perennials grow older, they should be rejuvenated by dividing and replanting to give them a new lease of life. At the end of each season, try saving seeds of annuals and biennials, and in autumn clear up any dead material that may harbour pests or diseases.

## THINNING AND STOPPING PERENNIALS

These two techniques are used to increase both the quality and quantity of flowers. Perennials that form clumps, such as delphiniums, phloxes, and asters, make a mass of stems in spring, some of which are weak and spindly. If these are removed at an early stage, the remaining shoots grow more strongly and produce larger flowers. Some perennials, like Michaelmas daisies, heleniums, and rudbeckias, often produce flowering sideshoots. If the growing tip is pinched out, or "stopped", plants branch more readily. If plants in a group are stopped a few days apart, this has the effect of prolonging the overall flowering display.

◁ **THINNING**
*In mid- to late spring, when plants reach a quarter to a third of their final height, trace weak shoots back to their base and pinch or cut them out. Remove no more than 1 shoot in 3. The sturdier shoots will produce larger flowers and are also less likely to need staking.*

**STOPPING** ▷
*When shoots reach a third of their final height, pinch out the top 2.5–5cm (1–2in) of the growing tip. This encourages buds in the lower leaf axils to grow out and bloom, and it promotes bushier growth.*

## SUPPORTING AND STAKING

Perennials, annuals, and biennials that are tall and fragile, and those that tend to flop, may need supporting, especially in exposed and windy areas. It is best to put supports in place early in the season; then the plants are more likely to disguise the support completely as they grow. Take care when inserting stakes not to damage the root system of the plant. For stability, stakes should be inserted to about one-third of their height. Proprietary supports are costly, but can often be reused. It is also possible to improvise, using large-gauge wire mesh either attached to canes, for supporting taller plants, or formed into a dome or cone for shorter ones.

### GOOD IDEAS

• Twiggy "pea-sticks" are unobtrusive and cheap. Push several in around a clump, arch over the centre, and secure.

• Insert one stout cane at the centre of a small group of plants or stems, with ties radiating out to loop round each stem.

◁ **CANE AND TWINE**
*For tall, single-stemmed plants, insert a cane to two-thirds of the stem's final height when the plant is 25cm (10in) tall. Tie twine loosely in figure-of-eight loops as the plant grows.*

**RING OF CANES** ▷
*For low, weak-stemmed plants, place a ring of split canes around the margins of the plant, and circle the canes and plant with soft twine. Loop it around each cane to secure it in place.*

△ **LINK STAKES**
*For tall clump-formers, like Michaelmas daisies and some campanulas, push link stakes deep into the soil and gradually raise them as the plant grows.*

△ **GROW-THROUGH SUPPORTS**
*These are ideal for tall, floppy plants. Set in place early in the season. As the stems grow through the mesh, they will hide it.*

**SEE ALSO:** Using Fertilizers, p.153; Dividing Perennials, p. 163

# DEADHEADING

Unless ornamental seedheads are wanted, or you wish to collect your own seed, plants should be deadheaded as soon as flowers fade. This diverts energy from seed production into new growth and helps to prolong the flowering season. With plants that produce sideshoots on their flowering stems, such as *Phlox paniculata*, removing the central flower encourages the sideshoots to bloom. In those that flower on a single stem, like delphiniums and lupins, removing the flowered stem at the base may encourage a second, though less profuse, blooming later in the season. Remove dead flowers with sharp secateurs to make a clean cut.

### △ PHLOX
*Trace back the stem below the central flowerhead, and remove the faded cluster with a straight cut just above a pair of sideshoots. This induces new sideshoots to break into growth and flower later in the season.*

### △ DELPHINIUM
*Tall delphiniums produce a main flower spike with a few small sideshoots in early and midsummer. Cut the entire spike back to the base as it fades, then the plant may flower again in autumn as a result.*

### △ LAVENDER
*Trimming back the midsummer flowers of lavender seldom induces a second flush, but by preventing seed production, energy is diverted into producing compact and bushy growth. The cut flowers can be dried for use in pot pourri.*

# AUTUMN CLEARANCE

Some perennials, such as grasses, have attractive winter flowerheads; others gain a little protection from cold if top-growth is left in place. Most perennials, however, are best cut back in autumn; remove dead leaves and stems at the base. Also take out any annuals or biennials that have finished flowering, and weed and mulch the bed.

### CUTTING BACK PERENNIALS ▷
*Use secateurs or a pair of hand shears to remove all dead and faded growth at the base of the stem. With most perennials, all top-growth should be removed to avoid the risk of diseases being harboured over winter.*

# RENOVATING PERENNIALS

Most perennials benefit from division every three to five years, or every other year for vigorous mat-formers such as *Stachys* and *Ajuga*. If allowed to become woody and congested, they will grow and flower less freely. Lifting and dividing (*see p 163*) rejuvenates the plant and allows the soil in the planting site to be dug over, improved, fertilized, and weeded.

Old, woody, and congested stems produce few new leaves or flowers

Top-growth becomes sparse and stunted

### △ RIPE FOR DIVISION
*This woody, congested Heuchera has deteriorated in vigour and appearance, and has produced few, sparse flowers. Lifting, dividing, and replanting in fresh soil restores health and vigour.*

### ▽ LIFT AND STORE
*Plants that are ripe for division can be lifted and put into temporary storage while their planting site is dug over and organic matter is incorporated to improve the quality of the soil.*

Moist bark or compost over roots prevents drying out

New, divided plants are ready for transplanting

# SAVING SEED

Saving seed of annuals and biennials, and occasionally perennials, is a simple and economical way of increasing your stock. The seeds of most species produce offspring almost exactly like the parent plant, but not all cultivars "come true" from seed. Collect seed from plants with good characteristics of their type, in dry conditions, since damp seeds may rot.

### ◁ COLLECTING SEED
*Seed should be collected when dry and just ripe. Keep a close eye on ripening seedheads (here, a hollyhock); the aim is to collect seeds just before they start to disperse.*

Unripe seedhead is still green and tightly closed

Seedhead splits open when ripe; collect the seed now before it is shed naturally

### SAVING CAPSULES ▷
*Some plants, like this Jacob's ladder (Polemonium), have seed capsules that explode at the moment they ripen; remove these seedheads on their stems as they turn brown. Place in a labelled paper bag; the seeds will then be shed into the bag when the capsule explodes.*

SEE ALSO: Increasing Border Plants, pp.162–163

# MAINTAINING ROSES

TO KEEP ROSES LOOKING GOOD, you will need to feed and mulch them after pruning. Bush roses benefit from an extra feed after the first flush of flower. Remove dead flowers and the unwanted basal growths known as suckers, and undertake some careful pruning. Different rose types require different pruning methods to give off their best. Roses are prone to a variety of ailments (*see pp.294–311*), especially if planted in numbers. To avoid this, control pests and diseases and prune in clear, dry, frost-free conditions. The main aims of rose pruning are to maintain the plant's health and vigour, and to maximize its flowering potential throughout the season.

## AUTUMN TRIM

Most roses will benefit from an initial shaping or trimming in autumn to help them survive winter and produce strong new growth in spring. To maintain an open centre, cut to outward-facing buds. On arching shoots, or if new shoots are needed to fill out the centre, cut to an upward- or inward-facing bud.

Long stems, if whipped by strong winds, may cause rocking and disturbance of the roots

Plump, healthy bud will develop new growth in the required direction

Correctly angled cut directs water away from the emerging new bud

Healthy stem with no signs of disease or discolouration

◁ **A PERFECT CUT**
*Make an angled cut, just above a bud, and sloping away from it. The bottom of the cut should align with the base of the bud.*

△ **BEFORE TRIMMING**
*In exposed sites and in cold climates, growth may be damaged and roots loosened in strong winds. A trim in autumn reduces these risks.*

△ **AFTER TRIMMING**
*Stems have been shortened by a half to a third of their height. After frost or strong winds, carefully firm the soil at the plant's base.*

## REMOVING SUCKERS

Suckers are unwanted growths that usually emerge during the growing season from the base of the plant, or sometimes a short distance away. Their leaves are frequently smaller, a different shape, or a different shade of green from those of the rest of the plant. They should always be removed as soon as they appear.

△ **HOW TO DESTROY SUCKERS**
*Gently scrape away the soil and trace the sucker back to its origin; this will be on the stem or root below the point where the graft was made. Wearing stout gloves, grip the sucker firmly and pull it away sharply. This may not be easy, but the sucker is less likely to regrow if pulled rather than cut, because pulling also removes any dormant buds.*

### TELL ME WHY

#### WHY REMOVE SUCKERS?

Most roses consist of one plant grafted onto the root system, or rootstock, of another; this is done to increase the vigour or longevity of the desired flowering plant. The rootstock is often more vigorous than the grafted plant and, if allowed to grow, its suckers will eventually overwhelm the grafted plant. Removing suckers will ensure that the vigour of the roots passes into the grafted plant.

## DEADHEADING

With roses that bear flowers in more than one flush, known as repeat-flowering roses, deadheading diverts energy from seed production into further flowering. With roses that flower only once, it stimulates strong new growth. Avoid deadheading roses that have decorative hips in late summer or autumn.

△ **A SINGLE BLOOM**
*Cut back faded, single blooms to a strong, outward-facing bud or shoot to encourage the production of a new flowering shoot.*

**FLOWER CLUSTERS** ▷
*In cluster-flowered roses, the central bloom fades first. Pinch or snip it out to display the remaining flowers to best effect.*

◁ **FADED CLUSTER**
*When all flowers in the cluster have faded, remove the entire cluster, cutting back to an emerging bud or fully formed shoot. If no buds are apparent, cut back to the desired height, which should stimulate a dormant bud into growth. If a stub is left above this new shoot, cut it away later.*

SEE ALSO: Initial Rose Pruning, p.151; General Border Maintenance, pp.152–153; Maintaining Shrubs, pp.156–157; Pruning Established Shrubs, pp.158–159

# PRUNING ESTABLISHED ROSES

For all roses, whatever their type, the first step when pruning is to remove dead, diseased, damaged, or weak growth. Patio, Polyantha and Miniature bush roses are treated like Cluster-flowered bush roses, only less so; their stems and sideshoots are shortened by one-third to a half. Prune ground-cover roses when not in growth; cut back long stems to outward-facing buds. To confine to an allotted space, shorten sideshoots if crowded and, to renew, remove one in four old stems.

To keep compact and encourage free flowering, cut back the tips of a proportion of the sideshoots at the edges of the plant

As growth becomes crowded and old stems less productive, cut 1 or 2 of the oldest stems out at the base, to an outward-facing bud

After removing weak stems, shorten remainder to within 25–30cm (10–12in) of ground level and sideshoots to within 2 or 3 buds of the main stems

## MODERN SHRUB ROSE

Most Modern shrub roses, including Hybrid Musks and Rugosas, are repeat-flowering. Prune when not in growth, preferably in early spring. Most need only light pruning to maintain shape. Shorten main stems by no more than one-third; sideshoots by a half to two-thirds; remove one in three old stems.

Make all cuts to outward-facing buds to maintain an open centre

## LARGE-FLOWERED BUSH ROSE

These bushes, also known as Hybrid Teas, flower throughout the summer and should be pruned hard while dormant, preferably in early spring. Retain three to five strong, healthy shoots; cut back to 20–22cm (8–9in) above ground level. Remove all spindly shoots that are of less than average thickness.

## CLUSTER-FLOWERED BUSH ROSE

The beauty of these roses, which are also known as Floribundas, lies in their massed flower clusters. In principle, they are pruned as for Large-flowered bush roses but, in order to retain more potential in the flowering shoots, the stems are not shortened so drastically; any sideshoots are shortened to two or three buds.

---

### ALWAYS REMEMBER

#### GET TO KNOW YOUR ROSES

Roses are classified into different groups, the major ones being Species, Modern, and Old Garden roses, the last two also with several sub-groups. They have different pruning needs, depending on growth and flowering habit and whether they bloom once or repeatedly. Check the label when buying; it will include the rose's group and so gives vital information on pruning needs.

---

# PRUNING OLD ROSES

Old Garden roses are noted for their grace and stature, and pruning aims to maintain these features. Most flower once a year only, in midsummer, and are pruned immediately after flowering in one of two ways, depending on their habit of growth. A few Old Garden roses — the Chinas, Bourbons, and Portlands — flower in repeated flushes throughout summer; prune these as for Modern shrub roses, when dormant, preferably in early spring.

△ ALBA, DAMASK, CENTIFOLIA, AND MOSS ROSES
*Open, free-branching, often gracefully arching shrubs. After flowering, reduce main stems and sideshoots by a third of their length, cutting back to a healthy, outward-facing shoot or bud. When mature, remove 1 in 4 of the oldest stems to encourage replacement growth. Shorten any long, whippy shoots in autumn to reduce wind damage.*

△ GALLICA ROSES
*Characteristically, Gallicas are dense, twiggy, free-branching roses with thorny stems. After flowering, thin growth by cutting back sideshoots by up to two-thirds of their length. Shorten any overlong shoots by up to a third. When mature, take out 1 or 2 of the oldest stems close to ground level, every 1–3 years.*

SEE ALSO: Roses, p.139; Roses, p.147; Maintaining Shrubs, pp.156–157

# INCREASING BORDER PLANTS

SOWING SEED AND DIVIDING mature plants are simple, inexpensive ways of increasing your stock of border plants. A few seeds need pre-treatment before they will germinate: for hard-coated seeds, like lupins, rub gently between two sheets of emery paper; for those with chemical inhibitors, like cyclamen, soak in clean water; and, for seeds that need chilling, sow outdoors in autumn or sow in spring after placing them in a refrigerator for a few weeks. Remember to always read the instructions on the seed packet and follow them closely. Division is a quick and easy method of increasing clump-forming perennials.

## SOWING SEED IN POTS

Most seeds are sown between late winter and early spring. Garden-collected seed of early to midsummer-flowering plants can be sown straightaway. A 9–13cm (3½–5in) pot or half-pot holds sufficient seedlings for most purposes. Cover seeds that need light for germination with a 5mm (¼in) layer of fine-grade vermiculite instead of compost. For most seeds, a temperature of 15°C (60°F) is ideal for germination. Hardy plants are best at about 10°C (50°F); half-hardy and frost-tender plants need a minimum of 15–21°C (60–70°F). Seedlings need bright light but not direct sun, which may scorch and kill them. When transplanting, handle seedlings only by their leaves; the vulnerable stems will rot if damaged.

### ALWAYS REMEMBER

One of the most common causes of failure when propagating from seed is when seedlings fall over, often with a brown ring at the stem base. This is known as damping off. It is caused by fungi that thrive in wet compost, poor light, and warm humidity. Crowded seedlings provide ideal conditions for their spread. To prevent damping off, use fresh compost, sow thinly, ventilate well, and provide good light.

### RAISING PLANTS FROM SEED

**1 PREPARE THE POT**
Fill a container, here a 13cm (5in) pot, with moist seed compost and firm it gently with a presser board to remove any air pockets. The finished surface should be no more than 1cm (½in) below the pot rim.

**2 SOW THE SEED**
Sow seed as thinly and evenly as possible on the surface of the compost by tapping it carefully from a folded piece of clean, smooth paper, or directly from the seed packet in which it came.

**3 COVER WITH COMPOST**
Cover the seed to its own depth with a layer of finely sieved compost or vermiculite. Label the pot, and water with a fine rose or by standing in a tray of water until the compost surface glistens. Allow to drain.

**4 COVER THE CONTAINER**
Place a sheet of glass or plastic kitchen film over the pot to minimize moisture loss. Place in good light, but out of direct sun, in a greenhouse, cold frame, or propagator. Remove the cover when germination occurs.

**5 TRANSPLANT SEEDLINGS**
When the seedlings have developed 2 seed leaves, use a widger to transplant the seedlings into individual pots. It is best to use biodegradable pots (see inset) for plants that dislike root disturbance.

**6 HARDEN OFF AND PLANT**
When the young plants have a good root system that almost fills the pot, first harden them off by placing the pot outside for increasing periods to accustom them to cooler conditions. Then plant them out in the border.

## FINE SEEDS

Some plants, like begonias, produce dust-fine seed that is difficult to sow thinly, increasing the risk of damping off. Mixing with fine sand allows them to be sown thinly. To prevent the seed being washed to one side, water from beneath by standing the pot in clean water until the top of the compost is uniformly moist.

### SOWING FINE SEEDS

**1 MIX WITH SAND**
Place a small quantity of fine, dry sand in a small plastic bag. Introduce the seeds and shake well. Using a folded piece of paper as a funnel helps to direct seed into the bag.

**2 SURFACE SOW**
Using a clean piece of folded paper as a funnel, place the mix of seed and sand in the crease, and sow onto the compost surface by tapping gently. Water the pot from beneath.

SEE ALSO: Establishing Plants in the Border, pp.148–149; Renovating Perennials, p.155; Saving Seed, p.155

# SOWING ANNUALS AND BIENNIALS

Sowing times for annuals and biennials differ, depending on hardiness. Outdoor sowing means in a seed bed or where the plants are to flower; indoors means in a greenhouse, cold frame, or propagator.

■ Sow hardy annuals outdoors in spring, when the soil has warmed up to at least 7°C (45°F), or in autumn.

■ Sow half-hardy or tender annuals outdoors after frosts have ended, usually in late spring or early summer. Indoors, sow in late winter or early spring, at 15–21°C (59–70°F) and plant out seedlings after the frosts have ended.

■ Sow biennials outdoors or in pots from late spring to midsummer. If sown in a seed bed, transfer to a nursery bed before planting out in autumn.

## SOWING SEEDS IN A BORDER

**1 PREPARE THE GROUND FOR SOWING**
*Rake the soil to a fine tilth. Sprinkle grit or sand onto the surface or score with a stick, to mark out areas or drifts for blocks of different plants. Sow seed thinly in shallow rows within each drift. For a natural effect, orientate the rows in different directions in adjacent drifts. Seedlings sown in rows are easier to identify and weed.*

**2 THINNING AND WEEDING**
*Label each drift and keep seedlings free of weeds. At this stage, they look regimented, but once thinned will form dense, informal drifts. Thin seedlings to recommended spacings when the soil is moist and the weather mild, in stages if necessary. Use any strong, thinned-out seedlings to fill gaps caused by poor or erratic germination.*

# DIVIDING PERENNIALS

Most perennials form clumps of shoots from growing points on spreading roots or rhizomes, making division an easy means of increasing stock. Plants are best divided when they are not in active growth, in autumn, winter, or early spring, and when conditions are neither dry nor freezing. In climates with cold winters, division is safer if delayed until spring. Spring or early-summer bloomers, such as epimediums, pulmonarias, and bearded irises, fare best if divided straight after flowering, and kept moist until well established.

△ **DIVIDING FIBROUS-ROOTED PERENNIALS**
*When dividing fibrous or fleshy-rooted plants, wash as much soil as possible off the roots and crown, so growth buds are visible and less susceptible to inadvertent damage. Insert two forks in the centre of the clump, back to back with tines close together and handles apart. Lever the handles gently back and forth to separate into sections.*

## HOW TO DIVIDE MATURE PERENNIALS

**1 LIFT THE CLUMP**
*Lift the entire clump with a fork, inserting it well away from the crown to avoid damaging roots. Shake off as much soil as possible and remove dead leaves and stems so that you can see the best places for division.*

**2 CHOP THE CLUMP**
*Many clump-formers develop new growth around the margins of the clump, with old, woody, and less productive growth at the centre. Chop the clump into sections, using a sharp knife or spade to sever woody portions of the clump.*

Avoid damaging the roots of vigorous young growth with the spade when dividing the clump

**3 TEASE OUT SMALL SECTIONS**
*Divide the sections into even smaller pieces, teasing them out by hand. This causes less damage to roots than cutting. Each piece should have a good root system and several shoots. Remove and discard old and woody growth.*

**4 REPLANT DIVISIONS**
*New divisions should be planted as soon as possible, at the same depth as they were before, in prepared soil. Firm in gently and water thoroughly. If there is any delay before replanting, keep roots moist and plants cool.*

SEE ALSO: Establishing Plants in the Border, pp.148–149; Renovating Perennials, p.155; Saving Seed, p.155.

# INCREASING SHRUBS

SMALL PIECES OF PLANT MATERIAL, known as cuttings, can be induced to form roots, and this is one of the best ways of propagating shrubs. Take stem cuttings from any current season's growth that is free of pests, diseases, and damage. Cuttings from vigorous young plants root most easily. Avoid thin, weak, or over-vigorous growth; choose stems of medium thickness for an individual shrub, with only a short distance between two sets of leaves. To prevent any fungal infection killing the cuttings, you should sterilize all your equipment. Hormone rooting compounds may also be used to encourage rooting. Simple layering is another reliable method of raising your own shrubs.

## HARDWOOD CUTTINGS

These are suitable for deciduous shrubs such as dogwoods and willows, as well as evergreens like escallonia. They should be taken from late autumn to midwinter, when the current season's wood is fully ripe and hard. Keep the cuttings weed-free and watered; refirm after frost if necessary. By the next autumn, they will be well rooted, and can be planted out.

### △ DECIDUOUS HARDWOOD CUTTINGS
*Trim off tips and cut stems into 20cm (8in) lengths. Make a horizontal cut just below a stem joint at the base and a sloping cut above, and angled away from, a bud at the top. Dip the base in hormone rooting compound. Insert them, 5cm (2in) apart, 5cm (6in) deep, in loam-based cuttings compost in pots either in a cold frame or outdoors.*

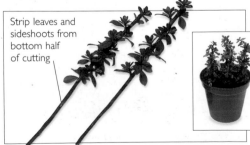

Strip leaves and sideshoots from bottom half of cutting

### △ EVERGREEN HARDWOOD CUTTINGS
*Cut shoots into sections, 20–25cm (8–10in) long. Trim just above a leaf base at the top and below another at the base. Strip leaves from bottom half of cutting. Insert 5–8 cuttings in a 15cm (6in) pot, so the foliage sits just above the surface. Label, and place in a propagator with bottom heat, or in a clear plastic bag. Rooting occurs in 6–10 weeks.*

## SEMI-RIPE CUTTINGS

A wide range of deciduous and evergreen shrubs may be increased from semi-ripe cuttings, from cotoneasters and mahonias to some lavenders. Take semi-ripe cuttings early in the day, when water reserves are at a maximum, in mid- to late summer, or early autumn. Most semi-ripe cuttings need a full growing season to root well. Harden them off gradually during the next spring and summer; apply a slow-release fertilizer in early summer. Pot up in autumn and grow on in a sheltered site.

Stem wood is firm but flexible

Wood is stiff and fully ripe

Stem is soft and sappy

Cutting is trimmed below a stem joint

TOO SOFT — CORRECT — TOO HARD

### △ DISTINGUISHING SEMI-RIPE WOOD
*The ideal semi-ripe cutting is taken from current season's growth that has begun to firm up; the base is quite hard, while the tip is soft and still actively growing. Such stems will offer some resistance when bent.*

### PROPAGATING A SHRUB BY SEMI-RIPE CUTTINGS

**1 TAKE A CUTTING**
*In mid- to late summer, select a healthy, semi-ripe shoot of current season's growth (here, Aucuba) and sever the cutting just above a stem joint with clean, sharp secateurs.*

**2 KEEP CUTTING MOIST**
*If the cutting is not to be used straightaway, place it in a clean plastic bag and label. Keep cool, out of direct sun for a couple of hours, or in a refrigerator for a few days.*

**3 TRIM THE CUTTING**
*Remove sideshoots from the stem with a sharp knife. Trim the stem to 10–15cm (4–6in), cutting just below a stem joint. Remove the soft tip and the lowest pair of leaves.*

**4 WOUND THE BASE**
*To stimulate rooting, cut a shallow sliver of bark, 1–2cm (½–¾in) long, from the base of the stem; do not expose the pith. This process is known as wounding.*

**5 ROOTING HORMONE**
*Dip the base of the cutting in hormone rooting compound. Make sure that the entire wound receives the thinnest possible, but even, coating, and shake off the excess.*

**6 INSERT CUTTINGS**
*Place cuttings 5–8cm (2–3in) apart in standard cuttings compost in a nursery bed outdoors (or in pots in a propagator). Label with name and date. Water and cover with a cloche.*

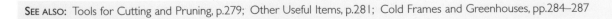

SEE ALSO: Tools for Cutting and Pruning, p.279; Other Useful Items, p.281; Cold Frames and Greenhouses, pp.284–287

# SOFTWOOD CUTTINGS

Softwood cuttings can root in as little as two or three weeks and are suitable for most deciduous shrubs. Such soft tissue is prone to wilt and rot, however. Use sharp, clean tools and good hygiene; prevent wilting by taking the cuttings early in the morning and placing them straight into a plastic bag. In dry weather, water the parent plant the night before. Handle cuttings gently; once rooted, harden them off, pot up, and grow on in a sheltered site.

◁ **SOFTWOOD CUTTINGS**
*Take softwood cuttings in spring and early summer from the new season's growth before it has begun to firm up. Choose vigorous, non-flowering shoots with 2 or 3 pairs of leaves, cutting just below a stem joint.*

**GREENWOOD CUTTINGS** ▷
*Take greenwood cuttings in late spring to midsummer, just as new stems begin to firm up. They are less prone to wilt and easier to handle than softwood, and root as readily. Treat them exactly as for softwood cuttings*

## PROPAGATING A SHRUB BY SOFTWOOD CUTTINGS

Remove the soft tip because it is vulnerable to rotting and scorch

Propagator vent will be opened gradually to harden off rooted cuttings

**1 TRIM THE CUTTING**
*Remove the soft tip just above a leaf joint, as well as the lowest pair of leaves. Cut large leaves in half to reduce moisture loss. Trim the base just below a leaf joint; the stem should be 4–5cm (1½–2in) long.*

**2 INSERT THE CUTTING**
*Fill a 13cm (5in) pot with cuttings compost. Make 2 or 3 holes around the edge and insert the cuttings so that the lowest leaves lie just above the compost surface and are not touching each other.*

**3 PLACE IN PROPAGATOR**
*After watering thoroughly with a proprietary fungicidal solution, label, and place pots in a closed propagator heated, if possible, at the base to 15°C (59°F). Keep in a shaded place, out of direct sun.*

**4 POT ON ROOTED CUTTINGS**
*Once cuttings have rooted, admit more air to harden them off. Knock out of the pot, tease apart, and pot up singly into 9cm (3½in) pots of potting compost. Pinch out growing tips to encourage bushy growth.*

# SIMPLE LAYERING

For climbers and shrubs that have flexible stems, such as clematis, honeysuckle, and rhododendrons, simple layering is a good method of producing a few new plants. It has the advantage that the layer remains attached to and is sustained by its parent until it has rooted. Layers can be made at any time of year, but autumn or spring are best. Find a low-growing, pliable stem that can be easily pegged down. Roots will form most readily at the point where one-year-old wood joins the older wood.

## PROPAGATING A SHRUB BY SIMPLE LAYERING

**1 SELECT A STEM**
*In autumn or spring, prepare the soil to make it friable. Choose a young, flexible stem from low down on the plant. Bend it to the ground and mark a position in the soil with a split cane, 22–30cm (9–12in) behind the stem tip.*

**2 PREPARE THE HOLE**
*Dig a hole, about 8cm (3in) deep in prepared soil, with a shallowly sloping side next to the parent plant and a near-vertical slope on the far side. Mix a little grit and organic matter into the bottom of the hole if soil is heavy.*

**3 WOUND THE STEM**
*Trim off sideshoots and leaves. At the point where the underside of the stem touches the soil, make a slanting cut through to the middle of the stem to make a "tongue" of bark, or remove a 2.5cm (1in) sliver of bark.*

**4 PEG THE LAYER DOWN**
*Dust the wound with some hormone rooting compound. Peg the stem down securely into the bottom of the hole using several U-shaped, galvanized wire pins or staples, placing them on either side of the wound.*

**5 FINISHING TOUCHES**
*Bend the stem tip up against the vertical side of the hole and secure with a stake. Backfill, firm, and water in. Keep weed-free and moist. A layer should be well rooted within a year; then sever it and plant out or pot up.*

**SEE ALSO:** Tools for Cutting and Pruning, p.279; Other Useful Items, p.281; Cold Frames and Greenhouses, pp.284–287

# CONTAINERS AND RAISED BEDS

## DESIGN AND POSITIONING

WHETHER YOU HAVE A GRAND GARDEN to rival that of a stately home or no more than a pocket-handkerchief backyard, containers can add another dimension to your outdoor space. Containers are tremendously versatile, allowing you to compose groups and rearrange plantings with relative ease. In a small garden, use them as lynch-pins of the design, to form focal points, flank a path or gateway, or accentuate an axis to enhance the garden's proportions. They can form a link between house and garden, combining hard materials with softer planting; stand them on the terrace or gathered by the door both to define and ease the transition from indoor to outdoor.

### CONTAINERS IN THE GARDEN

If you have only a patio or courtyard, roof terrace or balcony, you may need to garden exclusively in containers. But don't let this limit the planting – or your imagination: there is an enormous choice of plants, up to and including small trees, that will grow happily in a container. There are so many advantages to gardening in containers. You can create a flexible design with elements easily shifted or replanted. Containers provide instant impact even while you wait for plants to grow and spread out. They also add sculptural interest and – carefully sited – provide a framework, by repeating the same containers to help the overall design cohere.

Containers are useful in beds and borders too. Use them to fill gaps where herbaceous plants have died back or finished flowering. Use a dark pot if you want to minimize the impact of the container itself.

■ **Make a welcoming entrance** with pots by the front door, in either an informal cluster or formal pair. Include evergreens for year-round interest and bulbs to cheer the early days of spring.

■ **If you don't have wide windowsills,** affix sturdy metal brackets to the wall to support troughs; if you use plastic troughs, set the brackets low enough so that only the plants are in view when you look out. This also lets in more light.

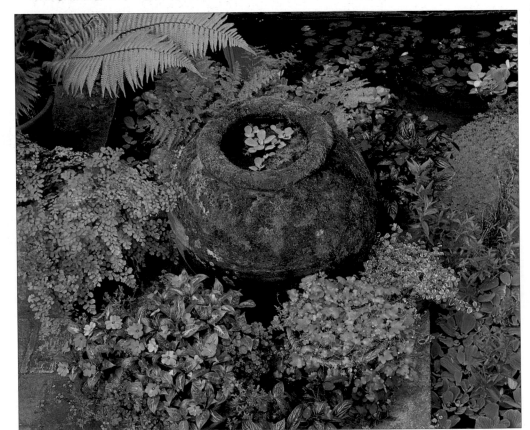

◁ A SHADY CORNER
*Pots filled with ferns and other shade-tolerant plants, like busy Lizzies and begonias, turn this awkward patio corner beside a pond into a lush haven.*

### POTS OF IDEAS

• Conceal an eyesore such as a dustbin, drain cover, or compost heap with a tiered display of pots planted with shrubs and trailing plants.

• Suspend a hanging basket at eye level or lower instead of overhead; you can see the flowers better and watering is easier.

• Improve a dull wall with plain clay pots filled with flowering and trailing plants. Circle pots with wire and suspend them from vine eyes knocked into the wall.

SEE ALSO: Container Planting Design, pp.172–175; Raised Beds, pp.180–181

# CREATING FOCAL POINTS

In any garden, having one or more focal points helps to give the garden definition and shape, setting up a series of views to be appreciated from different standpoints. This holds true for even the tiniest plot, but you may need no more than a single strongly planted urn or tub. Containers are invaluable in establishing key features in the garden or acting as focal points themselves – especially in a new garden, where plants that may later become more prominent are not yet established.

■ **Frame a view** out of the garden with containers on either side it or – more informally – to one side only. For a formal look, use a matching pair with a single, well-shaped specimen in each, such as clipped box or a fountain-like cordyline.

■ **In a long, narrow garden,** beware of accentuating the long axis by siting an ornamental container in the centre at the far end. Instead, site a group of pots of different heights and sizes about one-third of the way along and off-centre, which will improve the apparent proportions.

■ **Tiny garden or balcony?** Include one or two larger plants in generous pots to avoid an over-fussy effect. Check the sight line to your focal point container from the windows if you enjoy looking out onto the garden as much as being in it.

△ **ON A LEDGE**
*If your garden is limited in size, it is important to make the most of the space available. These pots bring colour to a narrow ledge, which would be bare if it were not for the versatility of container plantings.*

◁ **TRICK OF THE EYE**
*This colourfully planted trough has been cleverly placed on a windowsill on the sight line. Elevated to this level, the trough forms a link between the house and garden*

# CUSTOMIZED CONDITIONS

One of the benefits of container gardening is that you have a greater control over the growing conditions, so you can expand the range of plants you are able to grow. For example, if you have an alkaline soil in the open ground but yearn to grow lime-hating plants such as camellias or azaleas, cultivate them in containers using an ericaceous (lime-free) potting compost. Similarly, some plants, like many herbs and alpines, require good drainage; if the soil in your garden is heavy clay or boggy, you can improve its structure, but it is easier and more successful to grow such plants in pots or troughs, adding some fine grit or sharp sand to the compost and raising the containers on bricks so that excess water can drain away freely.

The portability of containers makes them an ideal home for tender plants that won't survive winter outdoors. Grow palms, cordylines, daturas (*Brugmansia*), cacti, and lemon trees in pots to bring an exotic feel to the garden in summer, then transfer the plants to a greenhouse, conservatory, or glazed porch before the first frosts. Potted houseplants usually benefit from a summer break outside too.

■ **Provide alpine and rock plants** with a gritty compost and grow in an old sink or shallow trough. Top-dress around the plants with a layer of coarse grit.

■ **Trees and shrubs** generally prefer a loam-based compost, such as John Innes No. 3, which is heavier and contains more nutrients than soilless potting composts.

**A CUSTOM-MADE DESERT** △
*To grow plants with special requirements or ones that don't suit your garden soil, recruit the services of a handy pot. This china bowl is now a miniature garden. Filled with very free-draining compost, it suits the needs of its resident succulents. Remember to provide drainage holes.*

SEE ALSO: Garden Styles, pp.122–123; Container Planting Design, pp.172–175; Planting in Containers, pp.176–177

# EASY DECORATIVE EFFECTS

If you want containers that are unique but not too expensive, it is simple enough to decorate cheap, plain pots and troughs yourself. You don't need special artistic talents to create attractive and impressive effects, just some time and basic materials.

■ **Paint:** prepare plastic pots and troughs by keying the surface first with sandpaper before painting. Look out for small sample pots of paint if you want to use several different colours, such as milky pastels in blue, mauve, and green, or rich, dark tones like deep green, burgundy, and navy. Finish off with a waterproof varnish.

■ **Stencils:** buy ready-made or design your own and cut out from thin card. Keep your motif simple and stylized for greatest impact. Repeat the stencil to make a decorative border. Apply the paint by sponging it on, then varnish to protect.

■ **Stain:** show off wooden tubs and planters with a natural or coloured stain that lets the wood grain show through.

■ **Beadings and mouldings:** add beading to a plain trough to create a panelled effect, or glue on simple mouldings such as fruits or leaves, available from DIY stores.

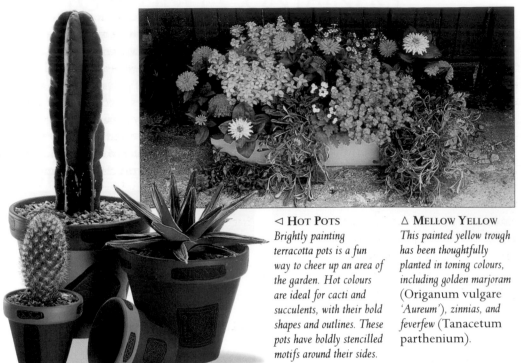

◁ **HOT POTS**
*Brightly painting terracotta pots is a fun way to cheer up an area of the garden. Hot colours are ideal for cacti and succulents, with their bold shapes and outlines. These pots have boldly stencilled motifs around their sides.*

△ **MELLOW YELLOW**
*This painted yellow trough has been thoughtfully planted in toning colours, including golden marjoram (Origanum vulgare 'Aureum'), zinnias, and feverfew (Tanacetum parthenium).*

■ **Mosaic and shells:** cover a plain container with small mosaic tiles or pieces of broken crockery laid crazy-paving style. Fix with all-in-one tile cement and grout or tile adhesive, depending on your materials.

You can buy coloured grout or pigment it yourself with a little acrylic paint. Instead of mosaic, you could use small seashells. If possible, work on the container in its final position as it will be heavy to move.

# ADAPTING EXISTING CONTAINERS

When looking for containers for the garden, there's no need to limit yourself to what the garden centre can offer. Keep an open mind and look out for other containers that could be recycled for garden use. These might be as basic as wooden fruit crates that you could paint or stain, or old galvanized metal buckets. Some people adapt metal wheelbarrows that are past their useful life or battered tin baths, water tanks, or feed troughs from farms. Tyres may be turned inside out, stacked, and painted.

Whichever kind of containers you find, remember that you will need to make holes to allow for drainage, and ensure that there will be enough depth of soil for the kind of plants you plan to grow. With degradable materials, such as basketware and timber, line the container with plastic and treat it with an exterior waterproof varnish to extend its life outdoors.

◁ **CROCK OF ROSES**
*Miniature rose Robin Redbreast fills this old bread crock. For drainage, holes have been drilled through the base, and broken pieces of the lid used to fill the bottom.*

▽ **A STAINED CRATE**
*An old, green-stained lemon crate makes an effective windowbox for these white, autumn-flowering cyclamen. Preservative was mixed with green wood stain and then painted on.*

Tall crock lifts this low-growing rose

Wood stain mixed with preservative extends life of crate

SEE ALSO: Fitting in with the Garden Style, p.168

# AGEING POTS

If you like your garden to have a settled, established look, you may find the raw brightness of new containers obtrusive. This is often especially true of terracotta, which may look very orange, and reconstituted stone or concrete, which may be almost white. One way of dulling down new terracotta is to sponge it with a light green wash (diluted paint). By the time this wears off, natural algae may be starting to take hold. Another method is to apply two colours of paint, then rub patches of the top layer away with wire wool. On concrete or terracotta moulded urns and troughs, replicate the effect of moss or algae by applying a little dryish green paint in the crevices of the mouldings – the areas where it would naturally tend to appear first.

If you want a more permanent solution, an alternative is to hasten the natural ageing process yourself. Simply brush containers with live yoghurt, sour milk, or chicken stock – anything that will encourage the growth of tiny plant organisms. Repeat after heavy rain.

## SPEEDING THE AGEING PROCESS

**1 PAINT ON YOGHURT**
Use live cultured yoghurt to paint the surface of a terracotta or stone pot. Some pots may take a few days to dry off.

**2 MOVE POT INTO LIGHT SHADE**
Place the container in a lightly shaded position. Plant with busy Lizzies and pelargoniums, which suit the conditions, and allow a month for the surface to age.

# MAKING A WOODEN TROUGH

Simple troughs made of weatherproofed wood can be directly planted up or used to hold pots or a plastic windowbox. This basic wooden trough is reasonably easy to make. You don't need to be a DIY expert, although you will need to be able to use an electric drill. The measurements here are for an average-sized windowbox, but of course you can adapt them to suit any window ledge or site; just make sure you have two matching end panels, two matching side panels, and a base panel that is the same length as the sides and the same width as the ends.

For this trough, you will need planed timber of about 2cm (¾in) thickness. Ask your timber supplier to cut it to size or saw it yourself. Use either metric or imperial measurements, but don't mix the two. Sand rough edges before you start.

The finished box can be treated with a wood stain, painted, stencilled, or decorated in any way you like. If it is to be used on a windowsill, make sure it is securely fixed in place so that it does not pose a danger to passers-by below. Stand the trough on shallow wedges or feet to allow drainage and slip a tray beneath it to catch surplus water if the windowsill is above a street. Troughs also look attractive simply raised on bricks or blocks on the ground, especially if filled with plants like rosette-shaped houseleeks (*Sempervivum*), which look good viewed from above.

## HOW TO MAKE A WINDOWBOX

### TOOLS AND MATERIALS

- 1 base panel (1m×17cm/3ft×7in)
- 2 identical end panels (17×20cm/ 7×8in)
- 2 identical side panels (1m×20cm/ 3ft×8in)
- Electric drill with 4mm (⅛in) drill bit

- Countersink
- 13mm (½in) drill bit
- Screwdriver
- Screws (5cm/2in long)
- Wood filler and sandpaper (*optional*)
- Exterior paint or stain and varnish

**1 MARK THE ENDS**
Lay the base flat on a table or workbench. Hold an end panel in position on the base panel, and mark along its inside edge on the base. Repeat for the other end panel. Now mark 3 spaced holes for screws at each end of the base within the marked-off areas.

**2 DRILL THE BASE**
Using the 4mm (⅛in) bit, drill the marked holes in the base. Rest the base on spare offcuts of wood to keep it level and protect the work surface from the drill. Use a countersink to make a shallow depression so that the screw head will lie below the surface.

**3 ASSEMBLE TROUGH**
Screw the end panels in place on the base, using the pre-drilled holes. Lay a side panel down flat and place the ends-and-base assembly on top to mark its position as you did with the ends. Mark holes around 3 edges of the side panels, keeping clear of the corners. Drill the holes.

**4 DRAINAGE HOLES**
Turn the trough upside-down and drill holes in the base for drainage, using the 13mm (½in) bit.

**5 LINE AND PROTECT**
Use wood filler to fill in the screw holes and cover the heads, if you like. Leave to dry; sand smooth. Paint or stain the box, then protect with exterior varnish. If it is to be filled directly with compost, line with plastic sheeting punctured for drainage.

SEE ALSO: Fitting in with the Garden Style, p.168; Which Material?, p.169

# CONTAINER PLANTING DESIGN

WHEN PLANNING PLANTING SCHEMES for containers, some of the same considerations apply as when designing beds and borders. Qualities such as shape and form, colour, texture, and scent may all be relevant, as well as the style and level of formality. Another important factor is position; a pot on a patio that will be enjoyed at close quarters might contain fragrant plants, like myrtle, and those with subtle textures, such as hostas. A pot sited at the far end of a path needs a plant of striking form or colour, perhaps a spiky cordyline. Containers provide you with great flexibility; you can design a planting in one pot, and it can stand alone or as part of a group.

## COMPOSING GROUPS

The relative portability of containers and the fact that they are self-contained means they can be moved to create different groups, changing the look of your garden as often as you like. Whether you want a formal or informal feel, your composition should have a sense of structure, both in the planting and in the arrangement of the containers. For example, for a strong centrepiece use a plant with a strong form, such as a New Zealand flax (*Phormium*) with fountain-like sprays of strappy leaves; then set smaller pots on bricks as tiers around it. Include trailing plants to spill over and soften the rigid lines of the containers and contrast with the sculptural silhouette of the architectural plant.

■ **Formal groups:** use containers that are identical or at least made of the same material. Keep planting simple, with just one type of plant per container. Try a row of pots filled with lilies to edge a pathway, or troughs, planted with auriculas, set on bricks in a stepped formation.

■ **Informal groups:** containers may be loosely clustered as if randomly grouped, but you still need to lay them out with care for a satisfying composition. Include plants of sprawling habit to fill the composition

△ **IN THE FRAME**
*The bold forms of these two agaves are used to frame an informal display of flowering container plants, which includes white lilies and pelargoniums.*

**A BRIGHT IDEA** ▷
*Pink petunias and silver senecio foliage in the same shimmering hues bring light to these steps, which would otherwise be dark and featureless.*

and soften the hard edges of pots. Perhaps add one or two strongly shaped specimens to bring definition and structure.

■ **Colour:** arrange a group of containers with plants in different hues of the same colour – blowsy pinks, fiery reds, or cool whites and creams. Or combine plants with a restricted range of colours; silver-grey foliage with white and pale pink blooms; lime-green with soft yellow and pure blue; bronze with purple and dark red. If you like the frisson of clashing colours, fine, but still limit the range for maximum impact. If you include every colour in the rainbow, the effect may look bitty and chaotic.

### TELL ME WHY

**CAN I GROUP PLANTS THAT NEED DIFFERENT GROWING CONDITIONS?**

Within any single container, you should combine only plants that have the same basic needs in terms of compost, water, and feeding. It is easier to grow one type of plant per pot. In a mixed group, plants need the same sort of environment (sun or shade). You can use large plants to provide shade for smaller plants beneath, if necessary.

SEE ALSO: Garden Styles, pp.122–123; Design and Positioning, pp.166–167; Planting in Containers, pp.176–177

# TOPIARY AND STANDARDS

△ **STYLE AND SYMMETRY**
*A period entrance is ideal for framing with standards in pots. Pictured here is a formal arrangement of two mop-headed privets underplanted with pelargoniums and ivy.*

Plants clipped into simple topiary shapes or trained as standards, with a clear stem like a miniature tree, are useful in containers to add height to any scheme or act as visual punctuation points. For a formal look, site a pair of standards either side of a doorway, to mark the start of a path or drive, or to flank a statue. They are not out of place in an informal setting either; use a clipped cone of box or a lollipop holly to contrast with tubs filled with casually sprawling lavender and daisy-like osteospermums.

To form a standard, choose a specimen with a strong central stem. Stake it, and gradually remove lower sideshoots over time. Cut the top off the main stem once at the required height to encourage growth of sideshoots and create a bushy head: pinch off the sideshoot tips each year.

## PLANTS AS STANDARDS

Many trees and shrubs may be trained as standards with a length of clear stem. They should be staked during their initial training, at the very least.

Bay (*Laurus nobilis*)
Box (*Buxus sempervirens*) **T**
Cherry laurel (*Prunus laurocerasus*)
Euonymus (eg *Euonymus fortunei* 'Silver Queen')
Fuchsia (eg 'Celia Smedley', 'Citation') **\***
Hibiscus (eg *Hibiscus syriacus* 'Blue Bird') **\***
Holly (*Ilex aquifolium*) **T**
Hydrangea (eg *Hydrangea macrophylla* 'Hamburg')
Laurustinus (*Viburnum tinus*)
Lemon verbena (*Aloysia triphylla*) **\***
Oleaster (eg *Elaeagnus* 'Quicksilver')
Pelargonium (eg zonal pelargonium 'Deacon Bonanza') **\***
Privet (e.g. *Ligustrum ovalifolium* 'Aureum') **T**
Yew ('*Taxus baccata*') **T**

**T** = plant may also be trained and clipped into dense topiary shapes, such as spheres or cones.
**\*** = not fully hardy.

---

# DISPLAYING SINGLE SPECIMENS

If you possess a star plant that you really want to show off, grow it as a single specimen in a container. The plant might be a particularly well-shaped shrub or small tree, or have especially fine flowers or foliage. Give it a prominent spot of its own to do it justice, in the natural line of sight from the house, for example, beside an ornamental garden bench, or raised on a small plinth, wall, or at the head of garden steps. Make sure its background forms a good foil; a plain wall, fence, or hedge is better than a confused mass of differently coloured plants.

Choose a container that complements the plant's good looks rather than over-competing with it for attention. You may like to opt for a container that has a similar style or mood to the plant, or prefer a distinct contrast between the two. For example, a succulent agave with spiky, sculptural stems would look at home in a plain terracotta pot, but growing it in a formal pedestal urn creates an element of surprise, which adds a touch of vitality to a garden. The container should also be in proportion to the plant in terms of height and width. Set the plant, still in its original pot, in the container to check the effect and balance before planting.

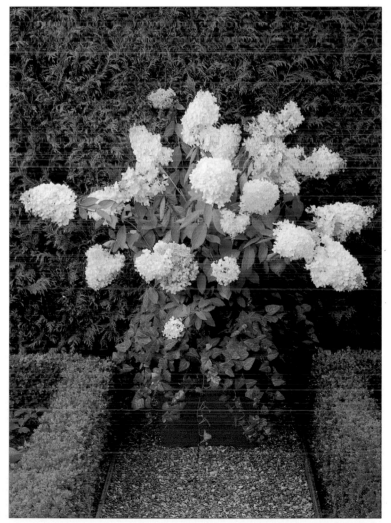

◁ **A FORMAL FAVOURITE**
*This white hydrangea looks simple, cool, and elegant in its nicely proportioned formal container. To make it into a prominent feature, the hydrangea is positioned against a thuja hedge at the end of a gravel path edged with clipped box.*

**SEE ALSO:** Garden Styles, pp.122–123; Maintaining Shrubs, pp.156–157; Design and Positioning, pp.166–167; Routine Care and Maintenance, pp.178–179

# PLANTING IN A SHADY SPOT

A shady area of the garden need not look dull or gloomy, and container plantings are a good way of turning an underused, dingy spot into a lush haven. One distinct advantage of using containers in shade is that the containers themselves add interest and colour. The gleam of glazed pots or the light tone of real or artificial stone can be especially welcome here. In a site in full sun, containers are often quick to dry out, whereas in shade they will be less thirsty.

Although few plants flower as prolifically in shade as they do in sun, there are some honourable exceptions, such as busy Lizzies (*Impatiens*) and begonias (Semperflorens group – the small, fibrous-rooted type, not the more flamboyant, tuberous kinds), both of which will bloom tirelessly until the first frosts.

Add impact with bold foliage plants like ferns, hostas, fatshederas, arums, and the immensely tolerant spotted laurel (*Aucuba japonica* 'Crotonifolia' has leaves densely flecked with golden yellow). Inclusion of variegated aucubas and ivies attractively splashed or margined with cream or yellow adds sparkle to a palette of mixed greens. To create a changing display and provide spots of light and colour, plant woodland bulbs, such as erythroniums and *Anemone blanda*, to flower in spring.

◁ **A GREEN CURTAIN**
*Pots and bowls of pastel-coloured busy Lizzies and begonias, mixed ferns, and ivy all grow well in this partly shaded spot against a dense, living curtain of evergreen shrubs.*

▽ **SIMPLE BEAUTY**
*This white, fibrous-rooted begonia in a small trough enjoys both the shade and the humidity of a watery location. The large, glossy waterlily leaves form a splendid backdrop.*

■ **Assess the amount of shade:** check if the area receives some sun in the morning or evening. Many plants will prosper with only an hour or two of sunlight each day.
■ **Dense shade** cast by trees or high walls is more restrictive, but painting a wall white reflects light. Try mahonias, hollies, ivies, bergenias, fatsias, and osmanthus.
■ **Dappled shade:** a wider range of plants thrive in partial shade. Many golden-leaved or variegated plants scorch in full sun, and they prefer a slightly shaded position.

# CONTAINERS IN EXPOSED SITES

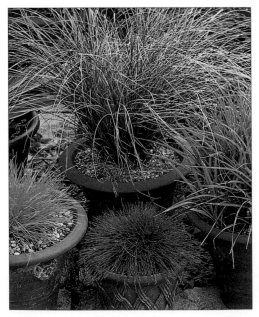

In exposed sites, such as roof terraces and balconies, your entire garden may consist of containers, while in hilltop and coastal gardens, tubs and troughs may be a key element of the planting scheme. There are two typical problems: temperature extremes and wind. The compost in containers tends to dry out more quickly in any case, so drying winds may make plants even more vulnerable.

In windy gardens, favour low-growing plants and those with small leaves, which are usually more tolerant of wind. If you want to include tall plants, opt for those

◁ **GRACEFUL GRASSES**
*Turn a problem into an opportunity by using a windy spot to grow grasses. They are more resistant to drying winds than broad-leaved plants and ripple gracefully in a breeze.*

with soft, pliable growth such as bamboos and phormiums rather than those with brittle stems. Alpines, rock plants, and dwarf bulbs – any plants that grow in exposed situations in the wild – are a good choice for windswept gardens. Minimize evaporation from the surface of the compost by mulching with stones or grit, and line clay pots and troughs with plastic sheeting to reduce moisture loss.

In coastal regions, choose plants that will tolerate salt-laden winds. Many shrubs will grow well in containers in these conditions and you can underplant them with low rock plants. Try prostrate and low-growing shrubs such as rosemary (*Rosmarinus officinalis* 'Benenden Blue') and tough-leaved seaside favourites like escallonias and olearias.

**SEE ALSO:** Mulching Materials, p.153; Design and Positioning, pp.166–167; Planting in Containers, pp.176–177; Routine Care and Maintenance, pp.178–179

# CONTAINER DISPLAYS FOR WINTER

In winter, when there is no competition from showy summer borders, container schemes come into their own. Planting is best done early to mid-autumn. Include conifers or broadleaved evergreen shrubs to form the core of a display, giving year-round interest and providing a strong framework around which to vary more transient elements such as spring bulbs and summer bedding for variety.

When choosing conifers, look for dwarf types so they don't outgrow their pot too quickly. Consider shape as well as colour; there are upright types shaped like a rocket or flame (such as *Juniperus communis* 'Hibernica'), rounded, cushion-like forms (*Pinus sylvestris* 'Nana'), as well as numerous conical and ground-hugging types. Foliage colours include gold, silvery-blue, bright green, and soft blue-green.

With broadleaved evergreens, seek out specimens with a good, well-balanced shape and handsome foliage. If you want winter berries, try cotoneasters, skimmias,

**BEAUTIFUL BERGENIAS** △
*Bergenias are handsome and hardy evergreen perennials with large leaves that look attractive in the depths of winter. They flower from midwinter to early spring.*

and hollies (with these last two, ask for female plants, but you also usually need a male pollinating plant nearby to ensure fruiting). Soften the slightly static look of many shrubs and conifers with ivies trailing over the sides of the container.

## PERFECT PARTNERS

Each pair of plants listed below includes a shrub or permanent plant plus another plant to grow beneath, around, or even through it. Each pairing will form a good display for winter although you can change the effect in other seasons by including spring bulbs or summer bedding plants, for example. There is a recommended particular species or cultivar in each case, just to inspire you, but a substitute of similar type will often work just as well. For example, almost any trailing ivy will look good as an underplanting.

Viburnum with snowdrops: *Viburnum farreri* + *Galanthus* 'Atkinsii'

Blue juniper with cyclamen: *Juniperus squamata* 'Blue Star' + *Cyclamen coum*

Hebe with winter pansies: *Hebe pimeleoides* 'Quicksilver' + *Viola* Floral Dance Series

Variegated euonymus with winter aconites: *Euonymus fortunei* 'Emerald 'n' Gold' + *Eranthis hyemalis*

Hellebore with variegated ivies: *Helleborus argutifolius* + *Hedera helix* 'Eva'

Elaeagnus with saxifrages: *Elaeagnus* × *ebbingei* 'Limelight' + *Saxifraga* × *urbium*

Bronze bergenia with purple-leaved ivies: *Bergenia cordifolia* 'Purpurea' + *Hedera helix* 'Glymii'

New Zealand flax with stonecrop: *Phormium* 'Dazzler' + *Sedum obtusatum*

# USING TRAILING PLANTS

When composing displays for containers, don't forget about plants that trail down as well as those that grow up. Deservedly popular for hanging baskets, where their pendent strands can move freely, trailing plants are also an asset for earth-bound tubs and urns, and wall planters. They break the rigid geometric outline of a pot or trough and add lightness and movement to a planting that is dense or architectural.

Use trailing plants to link a planted container with its immediate context. For example, a trough sited on a low wall or a pot at the top of garden steps can be visually anchored with trailers that blur the distinction between the container and its platform. There is no shortage of choice. As well as evergreens, such as ivies and periwinkle (*Vinca minor*), try the felted, silver-grey *Helichrysum petiolare* or its golden form 'Limelight' (best grown in dappled shade to prevent scorching) in the warmer months. Remember that many climbers, such as clematis, make attractive trailers if allowed to grow without a support.

△ **HANGING SPIDER**
*A spider plant cascades over* Pogonatherum saccharoideum *(left) and* Tolmeia menziesii *lending quiet colour to this shady doorway in summer.*

**GOLDEN BASKET** ▷
*Combine the trailing foliage of lysimachia and tradescantia with bright yellow oxalis and cosmos flowers to create this fresh green and yellow basket.*

SEE ALSO: Design and Positioning, pp. 166–167; Planting in Containers, pp. 176–177; Routine Care and Maintenance, pp. 178–179

# ROUTINE CARE AND MAINTENANCE

WHILE PLANTS IN THE OPEN GROUND can sometimes survive a degree of neglect or unsuitable conditions, those confined in containers are much more at your mercy and may well suffer or even die if you don't meet their individual needs. For this reason, it is definitely worth establishing a basic maintenance routine, including watering, feeding, deadheading, and clipping, as well as less frequent tasks such as repotting. Try to get into the habit of making a daily tour of your containers, especially if you have a balcony or courtyard and garden exclusively in pots, so that you keep your displays looking their best and any problems are picked up early and resolved.

## WATERING AND FEEDING

Even in wet weather, plants in pots may receive less water than you think; dense foliage may mean little rain reaches the compost. Don't leave pots sitting in water, however, as this impedes drainage and may lead to rotting of the roots. Flagging leaves or a suspiciously light pot usually indicates a need to water, but set up a routine rather than waiting until plants are in dire need. Periodically add a liquid feed when watering or use a controlled-release fertilizer during the growing season

There are irrigation systems, which also solve watering problems while you're away. These basically consist of a hose with holes that trickle water into each pot. Set the timer for evening or night-time to minimize water loss due to evaporation during the day.

△ **THIRSTY PLANTS**
*A good-looking arrangement will need to be densely planted, but this necessitates frequent watering, occasionally with a dilute liquid fertilizer.*

**PULLEY SYSTEM** ▷
*Watering is simple for hanging baskets attached to a pulley system.*

## MAINTAINING CONTAINER DISPLAYS

Provided that you water and feed your container plants appropriately, they should thrive, but to keep them looking their best you may also want to carry out a few other minor tasks.

With flowering plants, it is a good idea to deadhead them regularly; as well as looking tidier, this also encourages more flowers and so prolongs the display. Keep plants well shaped by pruning or pinching them out as necessary to encourage bushy growth. With topiaries or formally shaped specimens, you may need to clip them every few weeks during the growing season to maintain a well-defined outline. Climbing plants in pots should be regularly tied in, and the stems trained onto the support. To liven up a display that is starting to flag at the end of the season, replace two or three of the tired specimens with late-season plants; these will provide extra colour and interest.

▽ **SHAPELY PLANTS**
*These decorative container plants have been encouraged to grow into formal shapes by continual pruning and pinching out. It is simply a matter of confining all growth within the final shape; remove all leaves and stems that try to grow outside of these confines.*

CANARY ISLAND IVY
*Hedera canariensis* 'Gloire de Marengo'

Climbing evergreen growth must be tied in and trained over a frame

Strongly upright growth does not need to be supported by wire or stakes

BOX
*Buxus sempervirens*

Growth should be trimmed with scissors if it becomes straggly

△ **DEADHEADING**
*Cut off dead blooms at the stem joint to prolong the flowering season; leave them on the plant if you want berries or seedheads.*

BUSY LIZZIE
*Impatiens* 'Super Elfin Red'

SEE ALSO: Ways of Supporting Plants, pp.108–109; Maintaining Shrubs, pp.156–157; Topiary and Standards, p.173

# REPOTTING AND TOP-DRESSING

Thriving plants may soon outgrow their containers, so keep an eye out for tell-tale roots poking through drainage holes. Other indicators are loss of vigour or yellowing leaves. To check, lift the plant with its root ball from its pot. If the roots are crowded, or wound tightly round and round, it is time to repot. Very slow-growing plants also benefit from a change of compost even if they don't need more root room. Lift the plant and remove as much of the old compost as possible. Prune any damaged or diseased roots before repotting it back into the same pot using fresh compost.

For the first year or two, in spring repot long-term plants into a pot the next size up. With large or mature plants, you can top-dress them instead at the start of the growing season. Simply replace the top 5–8 cm (2–3 in) of the old compost with fresh compost of the same type, enriched with a balanced fertilizer. Top dressing is preferable to repotting for plants that dislike root disturbance or those that like their roots to be confined. In the case of surface-rooting shrubs, it is wiser to lift the plant and replace some of the compost beneath it instead.

## HOW TO REPOT A CONTAINER PLANT

**1 CHECK POT SIZE**
*To check the new pot is the correct size, slip the plant (here, Aucuba), still in its old pot, inside it. There should be a gap all round between the two pots of about 2.5cm (1in).*

**2 SOAK ROOT BALL**
*An hour or so before repotting, and keeping the plant in its original pot, soak in water. This reduces the impact of the move and helps to establish the roots in the new compost.*

**3 LOOSEN ROOTS**
*Encourage the roots to grow into the new compost by gently teasing out congested roots with your hands. Trim off damaged or dead roots with a sharp knife. Check for pests, and remove any you find.*

**4 REPOT**
*Place crocks in the base of the new pot. Add some compost, firm lightly, and position the plant. Check it is at the right level, with room to allow for watering. Fill around it with more compost, firming as you go.*

Use scissors or secateurs to remove dead or damaged growth

Fill pot with compost to within 2.5cm (1in) of the rim

**5 TRIM AND WATER**
*Trim off any dead leaves and straggly or damaged stems, add a controlled-release fertilizer plug, and water compost well. Add more compost if needed in any sunken spots.*

## TELL ME WHY

### WHY DO I HAVE TO REPOT MY LARGE, UNWIELDY PLANTS EVERY YEAR?

Although annual top-dressing (*see above*) may be sufficient, as it provides the compost with fresh nutrients, root pruning is most advisable, so it will still be necessary to lift the plant from its pot. Prune back about a quarter of the non-fibrous roots by up to two-thirds. Also prune the top-growth proportionally to reduce transpiration from the leaves, which could over-stress the plant. Replace the plant into its pot, or a new one of the same size, and add fresh compost to fill the space taken up by the pruned roots, making sure the soil level is the same as it was before.

# WINTER PROTECTION

One of the great benefits of container gardening is that you can grow tender plants outdoors in summer, then move them under cover for winter. Container plants are more vulnerable to freezing than those in open ground because the roots and compost are insulated only by the container. Some plants may need no more than moving to the shelter of a warm house wall, while some will survive in a cool greenhouse; others require a warmer spot, such as a well-lit room indoors or a heated conservatory. Before the onset of cool nights, make sure you know each plant's level of tolerance.

Containers that are too heavy to move must be protected outdoors; the level of protection depends on a plant's hardiness. In general, insulate the roots by wrapping the pot in plastic bubble-wrap or hessian packed with straw. Tie up strappy-leaved plants, like cordylines, to help protect the central growing point, and surround the top-growth in insulating fleece. Group plants together for mutual protection.

Tie in foliage of strappy-leaved plants before you move them

△ **DRAG ACT**
*To move a heavy pot, first tilt it so you can put a hessian or heavy-duty plastic sack beneath it, then drag it towards you.*

**FAKING IT** ▷
*Avoid having to heft heavy pots indoors by planting tender specimens in plastic pots to sit inside larger clay or stone pots. Add pebbles in the bottom for stability.*

SEE ALSO: Cold Frames and Greenhouses, pp.284–285; Dealing with Weeds and Plant Problems, pp.288–311

# RAISED BEDS: PLANTING AND MAINTENANCE

IF YOU HAVE BUILT a raised bed to create special conditions for growing certain kinds of plant, for example alpines or acid-lovers such as heathers and azaleas, it will probably be quite simple to formulate a planting scheme. For a general-purpose raised bed, however, you may wish to base your planting scheme on a theme, such as evening fragrances or a striking mix of summer colours. Trailing plants can be used to good effect around the edges, some even planted in wall crevices. Routine maintenance of raised beds — weeding, feeding, pruning, watering, and so on — is less arduous than with a normal border, since the soil and plants are within easy reach.

## COMPOSING PLANTING SCHEMES

Ask yourself about the primary function of your raised bed. Is it intended to provide architectural interest with a specimen plant? Do you want to create a scented garden for the visually impaired to enjoy? Would you like an oasis of colour in a place that otherwise would be drab in summer? Does a feature of vibrant evergreens to brighten up midwinter days appeal to you? Unless you have opted to create special conditions for certain plants (*see opposite, top*), it is also possible to combine some or all of the above elements.

When you have decided on a theme or combination of themes, you can start to look at the different plants that might be suitable. These range from trees and shrubs to rock plants, bulbs, and herbs.

■ **A specimen tree or shrub** might be used as a focal point in the centre of the bed, surrounded by low-growing plants. Miniature roses are ideal for small beds.

■ **Scented plants** include stocks, lavender, and herbs.

■ **Evergreens** for winter include evergreen cotoneasters, box, and dwarf conifers.

■ **Trailing plants,** useful for softening the hard outline of the bed, include alyssums, aubrietas, some clematis, and nasturtiums.

■ **Acid-loving plants** needing ericaceous compost range from azaleas and dwarf rhododendrons to heathers and camellias.

■ **Alpine and fleshy leaved plants** that relish the very good drainage of a raised bed include androsaces, cushion-forming saxifrages, sedums, and sempervivums.

### PERFECT PARTNERS

The following alpine plants are just some of the many that are ideal for growing in a raised bed.

*Androsace* (most species and hybrids)
*Antirrhinum molle, A. sempervirens*
*Campanula portenschlagiana, C. raineri*
*Daphne arbuscula, D. cneorum, D. petraea* 'Grandiflora'
*Gentiana acaulis, G. saxosa, G. verna*
*Papaver alpinum, P. miyabeanum*
*Phlox bifida, P. stolonifera*
*Sempervivum* (most species and hybrids)
*Saxifraga* (most species and hybrids)

△ **A THEMED BED**
*This formal bed features a horse chestnut as a central specimen tree, surrounded by clumps of lavender that provide scent in summer and foliage interest all year round.*

◁ **LEVELLING A SLOPE**
*One solution to the many problems associated with gardening on a slope is to create a series of level, raised beds for planting. The retaining walls help to keep the soil in place and prevent essential nutrients from being washed away.*

△ **SEASONAL PLANTS**
*Perennials such as lily-of-the-valley (Convallaria majalis) brighten up a raised bed in late spring or summer, but they will die right down during winter.*

**SEE ALSO:** Beds and Borders, pp.122–165; Establishing Plants in the Border, pp.148–151; Siting, Buying, and Planting Trees, pp.192–195

# CUSTOMIZED CONDITIONS

Alpines and succulent plants with fleshy leaves – both used to cold but not wet weather – and desert plants, which are especially adapted to exist in an arid environment, thrive only in very well-drained conditions. A raised bed is the ideal opportunity to create them.

For the best possible drainage, build the raised bed at least 25cm (10in) above ground level. Do not site it on a base of concrete or other impermeable material. Fill it with rubble or stones to at least one-third of the total height of the bed. For

alpines and succulents, it should be in bright sun and slightly sloping for better drainage. A free-draining compost is vital: add 1 part extra grit to 3 parts compost.

If your garden soil is neutral or alkaline (*see p.49*), a raised bed can also provide a home for acid-loving plants. It may be necessary to line the bed (*see p.181*) before filling it with ericaceous compost.

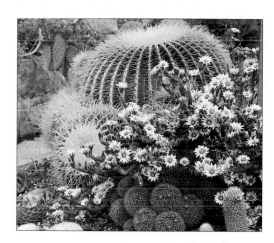

△ **CONTENTED CACTI**
*Cacti hailing from desert habitats are commonly perceived as dull, dusty plants, but given appropriate conditions and care, they can look lush and spectacularly colourful.*

# PLANTING IN WALLS AND CREVICES

Small plants may be grown in the gaps between stones or bricks in garden walls or in the sides of a raised bed. This will help to soften the rigid appearance and break up the monotony of the wall. It is very effective with some alpine plants, such as sempervivums and saxifrages, which

△ **CLOTHING A DRY-STONE WALL**
*For a gloriously informal, country-style look, try planting between the stones in a dry-stone wall. When established, colourful trailing plants will cascade down the side.*

have evolved to exploit natural crevices that occur in rocks, and they require little attention once established. Some trailing plants are also ideal for this purpose.

Fill the planting gaps or crevices with the appropriate soil or compost for the plant. Seedlings or small rooted cuttings are more likely to establish than large, mature plants. Ease the roots into the crevice, using a widger, and firm the plant in, adding more compost if necessary. Water the compost carefully, either through the top of the wall or with a mist spray

## HOW TO PLANT IN A CREVICE

**1 ADD COMPOST** Crevices in dry-stone walls or under steps (as here) and holes between bricks in raised beds can be planted. Fill the crevice with compost, and firm it in as much as possible.

**2 INSERT THE PLANT** Using a widger, make a small hole in the compost. With extreme care, place the plant in the hole, position it as required, and firm it in gently but securely.

**3 FINISH OFF** Use more compost to backfill beneath and around the plant until you are happy that it is not likely to become dislodged. Water, and keep an eye on the plant until established.

# ROUTINE MAINTENANCE

A properly constructed raised bed should not demand too much work to keep it looking attractive. Because of the good drainage, you will need to check regularly whether the soil or compost needs watering, especially around the edges where it may dry out and shrink away from the sides. If left, this could cause problems for the plants in frosty periods. Large beds may warrant the installation of an irrigation system. Before filling the raised bed with compost, lay a series of drip or trickle pipes and an inlet pipe.

Other routine care consists of weeding, feeding, pruning, replacing old or diseased plants, and renewing the top dressing or mulch. Feeding should not be required for some years if the original compost was correctly prepared. Thereafter, fork in a little bone meal mixed with a slow-release fertilizer around the plants in mid-spring, or remove the top-dressing and a layer of compost, replacing it with fresh compost and a new top-dressing of grit.

---

## GOOD IDEAS

• If possible, plan for any planting in walls before they are constructed, leaving niches at desired intervals in the top and sides.

• Choose plants that will thrive in the growing conditions provided by the wall.

• For alpines, use 3 parts loam to 2 parts coarse fibrous peat substitute or peat, to 1 or 2 parts sharp sand or grit, as the compost mixture.

• Wedge small stones around the plants to hold them and the compost in place.

---

## GOOD IDEAS

• Trim vigorous or invasive plants in early spring to keep the planting scheme balanced.

• Use gravel to generously mulch plants that are vulnerable to winter wet.

• Protect vulnerable alpines from winter moisture with cloches or sheets of glass or plastic; support these with a brick or wire frame fastened down to prevent them from being blown away. Make sure air can still circulate around the plants.

**SEE ALSO:** Soil and Drainage, p.19; Beds and Borders, pp.122–165; Raised Beds, pp.180–181

# ORNAMENTAL TREES IN THE GARDEN

## USING TREES AS DESIGN ELEMENTS

TREES ARE BREATHTAKING IN THEIR DIVERSITY, varying not only in height, shape, and form, but also in ornamental qualities, with a wonderful range of foliage, flowers, fruits, and even bark to suit any setting. The passing of the seasons provides ever-changing interest, as deciduous trees come into bright new leaf, flower, fruit, and finally shed their colourful foliage. Evergreens, however, keep up their show throughout the year. Even a single tree will add height and structural interest to a garden, however small; it acts as a living sculpture at the same time as introducing a sense of permanence. Trees also need little or no maintenance once established.

## TREES AS PART OF THE GARDEN DESIGN

Together with other long-term features, such as walls and paths, trees form part of the bones of a garden design, contributing greatly to its overall style and structure. In most gardens, small ornamental trees play a more important role than forest trees, which are only really suited to large gardens. It is vital to select and site a tree carefully so that it will become an asset rather than a problem – an ill-chosen or badly placed tree could obscure light and even annoy your neighbours. In some small gardens, coppiced or pollarded trees may be appropriate, and you can also train shrubs as single-stemmed standards (*see p.173*) to resemble small trees.

To decide on the right tree, picture its silhouette against the skyline, wall, or hedge. Bear in mind its increasing height and spread and how it will look at different times of year. Think about whether you want a single- or multi-stemmed tree in your design. Deciduous trees have a mass of foliage from spring to autumn, but bare branches in winter. Are you prepared to collect up all the fallen blossom, fruit, and leaves they will produce? Evergreen trees and conifers add welcome blocks of year-round texture and colour. If you have room for a number of trees, consider how they will work together as a composition, taking into account the shape and density of each, as well as leaves, flowers, or fruits.

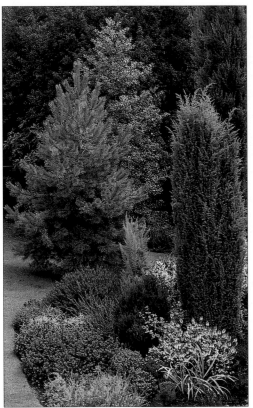

◁ **ADDING HEIGHT**
*A silver birch* (Betula utilis) *adds height and balances the informal mixed border on the opposite side of the path. The birch's autumn colours complement those of the fiery spindle bush and, as the leaves fall, its striking white trunk will come to the fore.*

△ **FITTING THE BILL**
*Here an upright, slow-growing juniper forms the focal point in a bed of low, mounded heathers, which provide winter colour to offset the tree's evergreen foliage. The tree is in good proportion to the design and will not outgrow its space for a considerable time.*

SEE ALSO: Seasonal Interest, pp.186–187; Features of Interest, pp.188–189; Coppicing and Pollarding, p.197

# GROUPING TREES AND SINGLE SPECIMENS

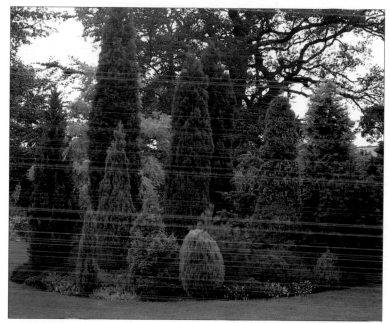

◁ **SCULPTURAL FORMS**
*This island bed of conifers, including cypress, juniper, thuja, and spruce, creates a harmony of repeated columnar and conical shapes. Subtle shifts in colour are achieved by juxtaposing grey-blue foliage with greens that range from light to dark.*

▽ **SPECIMEN MAPLE**
*A specimen tree does not have to look formal or be isolated in the middle of a lawn. This beautiful Japanese maple (Acer palmatum) rises from a sea of bluebells and long grass and is sited so that its leaves are lit up by the sun.*

Planting trees in groups can be highly effective visually. In an informal setting, try a relaxed grouping, designed to look like a natural copse, or a cluster of even just three or five trees such as maples (*Acer*) or birches (*Betula*). Odd numbers are always more pleasing to the eye than even numbers. If combining trees of different species, make sure that none will dominate, by checking their growing requirements and their potential height and spread before you buy, and that the differing forms complement each other. You could plant a pair of trees to support a hammock in later years.

If you have a small garden, with space for only one tree, think about its large-scale qualities first – eventual height and spread, silhouette, form, colour, mass – then consider its small-scale features such as flowers or fruits. Choose a tree to be in scale with its surroundings. To grow healthily and with a natural shape, all trees need adequate room, so check individual requirements before you buy. In larger gardens, growing a tree as a single specimen can create a dramatic effect. Select a tree with a strong shape or especially handsome foliage – beware the pitfall of choosing a tree for a brief display of spring blossom only to find it does little the rest of the year – and site it on its own where it can be enjoyed from a variety of viewpoints.

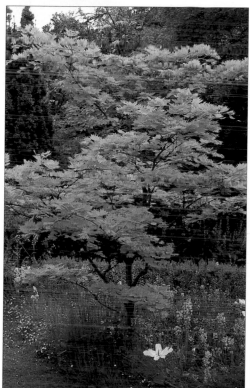

■ **For a small specimen tree**, try crab apples (*Malus*), rowans (*Sorbus*), Japanese maples (*Acer palmatum*), or trees that have colourful foliage such as the yellow-green false acacia (*Robinia pseudoacacia* 'Frisia').
■ **To edge a boundary**, choose trees that look good from a distance such as white poplars (*Populus alba*), small Irish junipers (*Juniperus communis* 'Hibernica'), or lofty Italian cypresses (*Cupressus sempervirens*).

# SHAPE AND FORM

A tree's shape and form dictate the effect of its initial impact – a columnar cypress forms a green pillar while a hawthorn tree in bloom resembles a lollipop. In general, trees with an upright habit and dense growth look more formal than those with an open-branched framework. Spreading trees, especially evergreens and conifers, create a wide area of shade, allowing less underplanting, but provide a cool retreat on hot days. As well as the tree's overall silhouette, think of the shape and growth pattern of its branches – which visually come to the fore in winter, especially in deciduous trees. Birches and Japanese maples, for example, have delicate, narrow branches, while ornamental fruit trees often have a more solid framework.

## BASIC TREE SHAPES

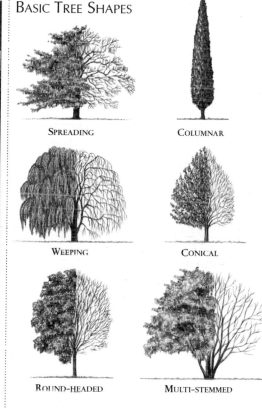

SPREADING

COLUMNAR

WEEPING

CONICAL

ROUND-HEADED

MULTI-STEMMED

## GOOD IDEAS

• To restrict the height of a tree in a small garden, change its natural single-stemmed shape by cutting it hard back (coppicing) or pruning to create a multi-stemmed tree.

• In a formal garden, try topiary – the art of clipping evergreen trees to create interesting shapes, such as birds, cones, or globes.

**SEE ALSO:** Topiary and Standards, p.173; Pruning to Form a Multi-stemmed Tree, p.196; Coppicing and Pollarding, p.197

# SEASONAL INTEREST

ONE OF THE PLEASURES of gardening is to observe how your living creation ebbs and flows throughout the year. Many trees have a marked seasonal cycle: in spring, the first signs of fresh growth emerge; in high summer, there is an abundance of foliage and flowers; autumn brings ripe fruits and dramatic leaf colours; and in winter skeletal branches may be iced with frost or displaying attractive textured bark. Many have more than one peak period, with spring blossom and autumn berries, for example. These changing effects can be set against a constant backdrop, such as the even colour and texture of an evergreen hedge, surrounding buildings, or the sky.

## SPRING

After a long winter, signs of spring as the first new leaves and flower buds appear are especially welcome. For a spectacular show of spring blossom, try flowering cherries and almonds (*Prunus*). Have a look, too, at hawthorns (*Crataegus*), crab apples (*Malus*), and rowans (*Sorbus*), many of which also bear attractive fruits in autumn.

Some of the earliest blossom appears on bare branches, for example *Prunus* 'Pandora', with clusters of pale pink flowers in early spring, or the weeping *Prunus × subhirtella* 'Pendula Rubra', which has deep pink blossom opening from ruby-red buds that grace the tree all winter. If the tree is to be sited near the house or by a path, look for one with fragrant flowers to enjoy as you walk beneath or past it. Do not forget foliage: the leaves of many trees are at their best and brightest in spring when young.

- **Spring flowers:** *Prunus* 'Shirofugen', *Prunus avium* 'Plena', *Malus* 'Lemoinei', *Cornus nuttallii*, *Pyrus calleryana* 'Chanticleer'.
- **Scent:** *Magnolia kobus*, *M. salicifolia*, *Prunus* 'Taihaku'.
- **Emerging leaf buds:** Whitebeam (*Sorbus aria* 'Lutescens') – pale green leaves, gleaming silver beneath, are spectacular as they emerge. Site it against a dark background for best effect. Golden honey locust (*Gleditsia triacanthos* 'Sunburst') – the emerging leaves are bright yellow, later turning to green. *Acer pesudoplatanus* 'Brilliantissimum' – the yellow-green leaves of this sycamore are a striking shrimp-pink when they first appear.

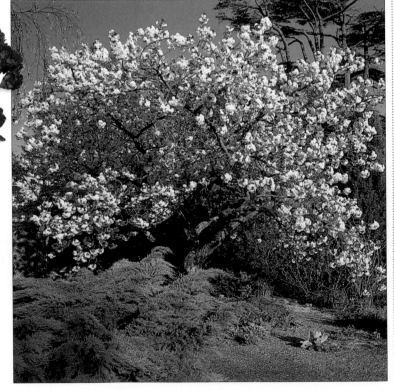

△ **SPRING SPLASH**
*The Midland hawthorn (*Crataegus laevigata*) 'Paul's Scarlet' is covered with vibrant pinkish red blossom – not scarlet – in late spring to early summer.*

**BURST OF BLOSSOM** ▷
*Few sights in spring are as instantly breathtaking as a flowering cherry (*Prunus*) in full bloom. Here, the profuse white blossom is offset by low-growing evergreens.*

## SUMMER

As late spring merges into early summer, the trees are fully in leaf and take on their characteristic shapes. Their foliage forms large blocks of uniform texture and colour, providing a backcloth or relief to bright summer flowers elsewhere in the garden. Many trees bloom during early summer, creating a smooth transition from spring; magnolias, laburnums, and – for large gardens – horse chestnuts (*Aesculus*) are all deservedly popular.

As the season progresses into mid- and late summer, some spring-flowering trees, such as rowans and crab apples, come into fruit, their colourful, bead-like berries anticipating the delights of autumn.

- **Summer blooms:** *Genista aetnensis* – yellow flowers, light canopy. For large gardens, the tulip tree (*Liriodendron tulipifera*) – green and yellow, tulip-shaped flowers.
- **Fragrance:** *Eucryphia glutinosa* – scented, white flowers; site a garden seat nearby.

△ **SUMMER SPLENDOUR**
*This* Cornus controversa *'Variegata' produces large, flattish heads of white flowers, in early summer, to complement its handsome, cream-variegated foliage.*

SEE ALSO: Plants for a Purpose, pp.38–41

# AUTUMN

This is the season when many deciduous trees are at their glorious, most colourful best, brightening up the garden when many border plants are past their peak. Most famous, maybe, are the maples, especially the many types of Japanese maple (*Acer palmatum*, *A. japonicum*), with the brilliant tints of their reddening foliage lit up by autumn sunlight. The stag's horn sumach (*Rhus typhina*) is one of the first to turn colour, with dazzling shades of yellow, orange, and red, but its display is brief and it is prone to suckering.

■ **Foliage colour:** Try the Japanese maple *Acer japonicum* 'Vitifolium', a beautiful specimen tree that thrives in dappled shade. Leaves turn rich crimson, orange, and purple in autumn. The Chinese tupelo (*Nyssa sinensis*) has fiery red, orange, and yellow leaf colours in autumn.

■ **Autumn fruits:** For berries and fruits, look at the thorns (*Crataegus*), rowans, and crab apples. *Sorbus* 'Joseph Rock' has yellow berries and good autumn leaf tints. Do not forget edible fruits, either, especially apple, pear, plum, and quince trees.

# CONTINUITY OF INTEREST

If you have space for only one tree, choose one that has something to offer all year — maybe an evergreen, or a deciduous tree with a graceful framework of branches. For continuous interest, look at slow-growing conifers as well as broadleaved evergreens.

■ **Evergreen:** Strawberry tree (*Arbutus unedo*); hollies (try *Ilex aquifolium* 'Silver Milkmaid').

■ **Deciduous:** Try crab apples (*Malus*), medlars (*Mespilus*), or rowans (*Sorbus*).

■ **Conifers:** Lace-bark pine (*Pinus bungeana*); Monterey cypress (*Cupressus macrocarpa* 'Goldcrest'); the cedar *Cedrus deodara* 'Aurea'.

◁ **AUTUMN FIRE**
*For large gardens only, scarlet oak (here Quercus coccinea 'Splendens') has sculptural leaves that turn deep red in autumn, bringing a blaze of colour to the garden on dull days.*

△ **BACKLIGHTING**
*Plant a tree chosen for its autumn foliage – this is a Japanese maple (Acer palmatum) – where you can view it with the sun behind so that the colours are at their most vibrant.*

CRAB APPLE
*Malus* 'Butterball'

**FLOWERS AND FRUITS** ▷
*Many of the crab apples (Malus) will provide at least 2 seasons of interest, with a fine show of white, pink, or red blossom in spring, followed by numerous brightly coloured fruits, which may last into winter.*

# WINTER

Unlike the more transient attractions of many herbaceous plants, trees provide interest right through the winter, whether from the pattern of their branches against the sky, from their evergreen foliage, or from precious flowers or bright persistent berries. Trees with attractive bark or stems are often now seen at their best, too. At this time of year, many conifers come to the fore; as well as every shade of green, there are types with blue-grey foliage, cheerful yellow-green, or gold. Always check their eventual height and spread as some will soon outgrow their space.

■ **Flowers:** *Prunus* × *subhirtella* 'Autumnalis'.

■ **Fruits:** *Arbutus*; *Photinia davidiana*; hollies (*Ilex*) – easy to grow, bright red berries, especially *I.* × *altaclerensis* 'Camelliifolia', and others have variegated foliage; Japanese rowan (*Sorbus commixta*).

△ **WINTER SHAPE**
*The graceful form against the sky and white bark of Himalayan birch (Betula utilis var. jacquemontii) are unequalled in winter.*

◁ **FROSTED ICING**
*The winter stems and bright red berries of this hawthorn (Crataegus laevigata) are decorated with a crisp layer of frost.*

**SEE ALSO:** Using Trees as Design Elements, pp.184–185; Features of Interest, pp.188–189

# FEATURES OF INTEREST

TREES ARE OFTEN RIGHTLY PRIZED for the sense of scale they bring to a garden, and for their architectural qualities of mass, silhouette, and form. Just like border plants, however, they also have individual ornamental features that make them worth growing. Many have especially good foliage, valued for its shape, colour, texture, or even the way it moves. Others may be grown for their flowers, or for their decorative or edible fruits, nuts, or cones. A lesser known, but no less desirable, quality is that of ornamental bark or stems, a distinctive feature of certain trees. Some trees may even have two or more special attractions that earn them a prime spot.

## FOLIAGE

Leaves provide colour and texture and help to determine the shape and mass of the tree canopy. Foliage also helps set the tone and style of the garden – from the exotic effect of the large, deeply lobed leaves of the fig tree, *Ficus carica*, to the airy feel of the aspen, *Populus tremula*, with its small leaves trembling on long leaf stalks. Evergreens, such as hollies, provide rich background colour all year round, and the leaves of some trees, both deciduous and evergreen, are brightly variegated with cream, white, or yellow. Conifers have needle- or scale-like leaves, each creating different textures, and some of the most colourful foliage, ranging from yellow-green to blue-grey.

When choosing trees for foliage, think about the overall effect. Look at the leaves' shape and size, which will influence the appearance of the canopy, and also their undersides – if felty or silvery, the leaves will shimmer in the breeze, providing a delightful colour contrast. Consider the site of a tree in relation to its foliage: trees with purple or bronze leaves may be overpowering in a small garden. Show off trees with silvery or glaucous blue foliage by siting them against a dark background.

**EXOTIC MOOD** ▷
*The narrow profile and dramatic, fan-shaped leaves of the Chusan palm* (Trachycarpus fortunei) *can bring a touch of the subtropics to temperate seaside and city gardens. This is the hardiest of the palms.*

◁ **GREEN AND GOLD**
*The large, golden, heart-shaped leaves of the Indian bean tree* (Catalpa bignonioides *'Aurea'*), *which is deciduous, form an impressive and wide-spreading canopy. This tree grows more slowly than the green-leaved species.*

△ **COLOUR MASS**
*The dense foliage of many conifers can make a good backcloth for other plants. The colour range includes greens, golds, and glaucous blue such as in this spruce,* Picea glauca *'Caerulea'.*

## FLOWERS

A tree in full bloom is a spectacular sight. Flowers vary hugely in shape and colour: they may be sculptural, such as the goblets of many magnolias, pendulous, such as the swaying yellow chains of laburnums, or borne in dense clusters like cherry blossom. Some, such as those of *Tilia × euchlora*, are also fragrant. Good deciduous choices for small or medium-sized gardens are dogwoods (*Cornus*), hawthorns (*Crataegus*), crab apples (*Malus*), flowering cherries (*Prunus*), and rowans (*Sorbus*). Alternatively, try the glorious evergreen bull bay (*Magnolia grandiflora*), which produces occasional, huge, cup-shaped, fragrant blooms throughout the year; it is best grown against a wall.

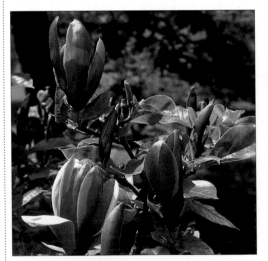

△ **WINE GOBLETS**
*Some magnolias, like this* Magnolia liliflora *'Nigra', produce upright, goblet-shaped flowers.*

◁ **BARE BEAUTY**
*The Judas tree,* Cercis siliquastrum, *bears flowers on the old stems before the leaves appear.*

SEE ALSO: Plants for a Purpose, pp.38–41

# FRUITS, NUTS, AND CONES

Trees exhibit an enormous range of fruits, which contain the seeds: there are berries and other fleshy fruits, including plums, mulberries, and other edible types, nuts, pods and winged seeds, catkins, and cones. Trees that bear berries or other bright fruits are ideal for encouraging wildlife: they provide food for birds, and windfalls are often picked up by small mammals, as are nuts and acorns.

For colourful fruits, consider hollies (*Ilex*), rowans (*Sorbus*), hawthorns (*Crataegus*), and crab apples (*Malus*), all good choices for a small garden. If you want berries that last through winter, choose a type with fruits that are persistent or less tempting to birds, such as the berries of *Sorbus cashmiriana*, which are pink ripening to white. Colour does not have to come from berries – many maples and sycamores (*Acer*) have winged seeds that may be tinged red in autumn.

Certain conifers have very fine cones, such as the violet-blue, cylindical fruits of the Korean fir (*Abies koreana*), which are borne even on young trees. Many have

cones that stay on the trees even after they have opened to disperse their seeds.

Bear in mind that some trees need to cross-pollinate if they are to bear fruit, while others are self-fertile, so check when buying. In hollies, for example, only female trees have berries, but a male holly must be in proximity for it to fruit. With apple trees, or any others where you plan to harvest the fruits, successful pollination affects the resulting yield, and it is often best to grow more than one tree.

◁ **BRILLIANT HARVEST**
*Many crab apples become covered with copious clusters of fruits that resemble bright beads. These may be cooked, and the strained juice used to make crab-apple jelly. The small, spreading trees reach a height of 6–8m (20–26ft), making them a good choice for a small garden.*

◁ **HOT COLOURS**
Euonymus europaeus 'Red Cascade', *has bright orange, fleshy seeds in bright reddish-pink capsules. It is toxic, however, so is unsuitable for gardens where children play.*

**EDIBLE HARVEST** ▷
*The sweet chestnut (*Castanea sativa*) has edible nuts that also appeal to foraging animals.*

---

# BARK AND STEMS

Coloured, patterned, or peeling bark and the bright growth of young stems are subtle attractions that are often overlooked. They are usually most noticeable in winter, when the tree's branches are bare of leaves. Some, such as silver birches (*Betula pendula* and others) with their ghostly white bark, are impressive even from a distance, while others, such as snake-bark maples (*Acer*) with their vertical stripes, are best enjoyed at close hand. The bark of the paper-bark maple (*Acer griseum*) peels off in strips, revealing fresh new, cinnamon-coloured bark beneath. Trees that have brightly coloured juvenile shoots, such as some forms of *Salix alba*, are sometimes cut right back at regular intervals, or coppiced, to stimulate this attractive new growth.

**APPEALING PEELING** ▷
*The glossy red-brown bark of paperbark cherry (*Prunus serrula*) continually peels off and renews itself. Position trees with attractive bark by a path where you can touch and enjoy the bark, but don't be tempted to peel it away.*

## BARK SELECTION

*Acer griseum*
Paper-bark
maple

*Betula utilis* var
*jacquemontii*
Himalayan birch

*Acer pensylvanicum*
A snake-bark
maple

*Acer capillipes*
A snake-bark
maple

*Eucalyptus pauciflora*
subsp. *niphophila*
Snow gum

**SEE ALSO:** Coppicing and Pollarding, p.197

# TREES TO SUIT YOUR SITE

BY FAR THE EASIEST APPROACH to gardening is to choose plants primarily on the basis of the growing conditions in your garden – that is, the climate, including temperature range and rainfall, and the soil type. If you try to grow certain plants regardless of their preferred conditions, gardening will rapidly become an uphill task. With trees, this is a particularly important consideration, because they are long-term plants. Whatever your site, you will still have plenty of choice, however. Whether you have a garden by the coast, on a windswept hillside, by a busy road, or in an inner-city oasis overshadowed by neighbouring buildings, there are trees that will thrive.

## CLIMATE AND LOCATION

The better you know your own garden and the conditions it has to offer, the easier it will be to choose plants that will thrive in it. First think about your local climate, including the temperature range and extremes and the average rainfall. Is there frost every winter or drought every summer, or any other problem such as extended snow cover or strong seasonal winds? With regard to the site, are you near the sea, for example, or at a high altitude? Is your garden in a built-up area, or exposed to winds on a hillside? It is important to identify key factors such as these that will affect your choice of tree.

To identify trees suited to your local conditions, observe what grows well nearby in woods, neighbouring gardens, and local parks and gardens open to the public. To blend well into the surrounding area, take into account any trees growing around or near your garden when you make your choice.

Remember that the garden itself may have sheltered areas and dry spots, as well as different aspects; bear in mind that what may grow vigorously in one part of the garden may do less well in another.

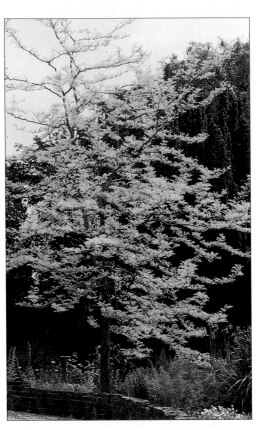

■ **Contact a local gardening club** if there is one and ask other members for advice.
■ **Be considerate:** if you plant a tree near a boundary, take care to choose one that will not restrict your neighbour's light, especially if it is dense or fast-growing. Think about your own light at the same time. Near boundaries, avoid trees such as sumachs (*Rhus typhina*) that produce suckers.
■ **Avoid root damage to house walls:** site trees with roots that vigorously seek out water, such as willows (*Salix*) and poplars (*Populus*), well away from houses.

◁ **SILVER BY THE SEA**
*Trees that withstand salty breezes are good for coastal gardens, or even inland ones where salt can be carried. The undersides of white poplar leaves show up well in the wind.*

◁ **SPLENDOUR IN THE CITY**
*Not all trees respond well to an urban environment, but the honey locust (Gleditsia triacanthos 'Sunburst') is especially tolerant of air pollution. It is a pretty tree with an open, airy habit and leaves that emerge golden yellow.*

### PLANT LIST

#### TREES FOR COASTAL GARDENS
While these trees will tolerate coastal winds, they will not stand up to being dowsed with salt spray.

Acer pseudoplatanus 'Brilliantissimum'
Hawthorn (*Crataegus monogyna*)
Highclere holly (*Ilex × altaclerensis*)
Mount Etna broom (*Genista aetnensis*)
Rowan, mountain ash (*Sorbus aucuparia*)
Strawberry tree (*Arbutus unedo*)
Whitebeams (*Sorbus aria*)

#### TREES FOR GARDENS IN EXPOSED OR WINDY SITES

Hawthorn (*Crataegus monogyna*)
Laburnums
Rowan, mountain ash (*Sorbus aucuparia*)
Silver birch (*Betula pendula*)
White birch, downy birch (*Betula pubescens*)
Whitebeams (*Sorbus aria*)

#### POLLUTION-TOLERANT TREES FOR URBAN GARDENS

Chinese privet (*Ligustrum lucidum*)
Common alder (*Alnus glutinosa*)
Common yew (*Taxus baccata*)
Dawn redwood (*Metasequoia glyptostroboides*)
Hawthorn (*Crataegus monogyna*)
Highclere holly (*Ilex × altaclerensis*)
Honey locust (*Gleditsia triacanthos* 'Sunburst')
Indian bean trees (*Catalpa bignonioides* and 'Aurea')
*Magnolia grandiflora*
*Pyrus salicifolia* 'Pendula'
Rowan, mountain ash (*Sorbus aucuparia*)

#### TREES THAT WILL TOLERATE DAMP SOILS

Alders (*Alnus glutinosa, A. incana*)
Medlar (*Mespilus*)
River birch (*Betula nigra*)
*Salix alba* 'Britzensis', *S. alba* subsp. *vitellina* (both should be coppiced for colourful stems)
*Salix babylonica* 'Tortuosa'
Kilmarnock Willow (*Salix × caprea* 'Kilmarnock')

SEE ALSO: Siting, Buying, and Planting Trees, pp.192–195; Coppicing and Pollarding, p.197

# SOIL TYPE AND CONDITIONS

The soil is the foundation of the garden and, as with climate, it is easier to work with its basic conditions rather than try to fight against them. The good news is that you do not need "perfect" soil in order to grow trees. What you do need is to choose your trees according to the soil you have, although you can also improve the soil to create better conditions.

Many soils fall between the extremes of clay and sandy, and may be silty or loamy (*see p.238 for how to assess your soil type*). Some soils may also be very stony. The addition of well-rotted organic matter, such as home-made garden compost or rotted manure, will improve the structure of most soils. Incorporate it carefully into the topsoil. The ideal soil in any garden is loam (*see p.142*), and most trees will grow happily in this.

Trees that are tolerant of heavy, clay soils include alders (*Alnus*), magnolias, and poplars (*Populus*). For sandy soils, try birches (*Betula*), *Robinia pseudoacacia* 'Frisia', or conifers such as junipers. The Mount Etna broom (*Genista aetnensis*) will grow well in either sandy or silty soil.

Remember that other factors can also affect a tree's rate of growth; for example, hot, dry conditions frequently keep trees such as the dawn redwood (*Metasequoia glyptostroboides*) smaller than they would be if they were growing in rich, moist soil.

△ GOOD FOR MOIST SOIL
*An excess of water in the soil can be just as damaging to some plants as a lack of soil water. Alnus glutinosa grows naturally on river banks, however, so it is perfectly suited to such conditions; it also tolerates heavy clay.*

△ GOOD FOR CLAY
*Clay soils are usually fertile, but their heavy texture provides poor drainage, which does not suit all trees. Magnolia × soulangeana is a magnificent specimen tree for clay soils, however.*

## AT-A-GLANCE GUIDE

Are you ready to make a shortlist of suitable trees for your garden? Use these quick reminders as a handy guide.

• **Climate:** Do you live in a temperate zone? Are there severe frosts? Periods of drought?

• **Local factors:** Do you live near the sea? In a city? At high altitude? Are there any other special factors specific to your garden?

• **Soil type:** Is your soil sandy or clay-based, silty, loamy, or stony? Does it drain freely?

• **Soil pH:** Is your soil acid or alkaline?

# SOIL pH

As well as knowing the type and structure of the soil in your garden, you should also know its approximate pH, or degree of acidity or alkalinity (*see below and p.238 for how to test soil pH*). This will affect which plants can flourish in your garden, and which are likely to struggle or fail.

■ **Look for indicator plants:** certain plants can provide a rough idea of the soil's pH. For example, heathers, foxgloves, and rhododendrons usually indicate acid soil, while rosemary, berberis, ash, and beech grow well in alkaline conditions.

■ **Test your soil:** you can buy soil-testing kits from most garden centres. Remember to take readings from more than one area of the garden, as conditions may vary.

■ **Trees and conifers for neutral to acid soil:** stewartias, firs (*Abies*), strawberry tree (*Arbutus unedo*), and spruces (*Picea*).

■ **Trees and conifers for alkaline soil (chalk and limestone):** Judas tree (*Cercis*), cherries (*Prunus*), *Robinia pseudoacacia* 'Frisia', hawthorns (*Crataegus*), junipers, and thujas.

△ ALKALINE CHOICE
*Many trees are happy in free-draining alkaline soils, which warm up quickly in spring. The Yoshino cherry (Prunus × yedoensis) has almond-scented blossom and is one of the earliest-blooming, most reliable of the flowering cherries.*

ACID LOVER ▷
*Like many other conifers, this white fir (Abies concolor 'Argentea') should grow well on acid soils, preferring moist but well-drained conditions.*

SEE ALSO: Preparing the Ground, pp.142–143; Get to Know your Soil, p.238; Soil Acidity and Alkalinity, p.238

# SITING, BUYING, AND PLANTING TREES

ONCE YOU HAVE ACCURATELY ASSESSED which trees are suitable for growing in a garden of your size and particular conditions, you can proceed to the next stage of the process. First select the most suitable site in the garden, and then prepare the ground thoroughly. When this has been done, you can finally buy and plant a healthy, strong young tree that will give you pleasure for a long time to come. Since trees are so long-lived, meticulous preparation and good initial aftercare are essential, in order to give them the best possible start.

## PREPARING THE SITE

Within a garden, there may be a range of conditions, including frost pockets and damp areas, so consider the specific site for your tree carefully. One part of the garden may be much more exposed than another, which will suit some trees but not others. If your garden is steeply sloping, bear in mind that a spot halfway down a slope tends to be warmer and more sheltered than either the top or the bottom.

Do not plant trees very close to walls or buildings where they will suffer from lack of moisture and light. Also some, such as willows (*Salix*) and poplars (*Populus*), have strong, moisture-seeking roots, which can damage foundations and drainage systems; these trees are best avoided unless sited well away. Never plant a tree in a place where it may interfere with overhead cables or power lines as it grows.

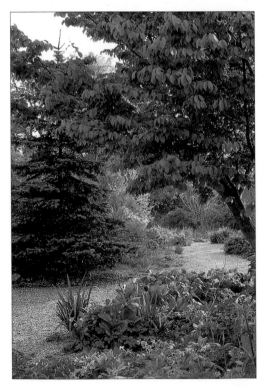

◁ **THE RIGHT SITE**
*Take care to select trees that will thrive in the specific conditions and microclimate of the planned planting site.*

△ **BLENDING IN**
*Trees can be used to link the artificial setting of the garden to its natural surroundings — this may influence your choice.*

It is advisable to prepare the planting site before buying the tree, because this will allow the soil to settle and means you can plant without delay after purchase.
■ **Choose a well-drained site**, unless the tree is a species that definitely tolerates damp conditions.
■ **Remove all vegetation** (turf, weeds, or ornamentals) in the immediate area which would compete for water and nutrients.
■ **Thoroughly dig the soil** throughout the chosen site, incorporating plenty of well-rotted organic matter.
■ **On an exposed, windy site**, protect a young tree until it establishes with a windbreak.

SEE ALSO: Preparing the Ground, pp.142–143

---

### TELL ME WHY

**WHEN IS THE BEST TIME OF YEAR TO PLANT A TREE?**

In general, it is best to plant trees in autumn or spring, depending on the type of tree, how it is sold, and the weather conditions. Autumn planting allows the roots to make some growth before winter, which helps the tree withstand dry spells in the following summer. In cold areas, planting in spring may be wiser, because this gives the tree more time to establish before the onset of winter. In all cases, do not plant during periods of sharp frost or drought.
**Container-grown trees**: plant out at any time, except during drought or frost.
**Bare-root deciduous trees**: plant in the dormant season from late autumn to early spring.
**Root-balled trees**: plant evergreens and conifers in mid-autumn in mild areas, or in mid- to late spring elsewhere; deciduous trees may be planted in winter.

# SELECTING A HEALTHY TREE

Garden centres usually stock a range of popular trees, but if you want something more unusual, need several trees, or want bare-root trees, visit a nursery; this may also be cheaper. Many trees for sale are grown in containers. Although usually quite expensive, they may be planted out at almost any time, and there will be less disturbance to the roots when planting – good for trees such as magnolias that dislike being transplanted. "Bare-root" trees, usually deciduous, are grown in open ground and only available from late autumn, when leafless. A good nursery will advise when a bare-root tree is ready.

Bear in mind that, although a semi-mature tree has more instant impact than a juvenile tree, young trees are much cheaper, and are more likely to transplant well and establish quickly.

## BUYING BARE-ROOT TREES

◁ **GOOD ROOTS**
*Look for well-developed roots that spread out evenly. Plenty of small, fine roots are a good sign, and suggest that the tree should grow well. Check that the roots do not look dried out, which indicates exposure to wind.*

◁ **POOR ROOTS**
*Avoid trees where the roots are wound in on themselves or with "hockey stick" roots where all the growth is on one side, as they will not establish well. Also make sure that the roots are free from damage or disease.*

**BUYING CONTAINER-GROWN TREES**

Check that the tree has a firm, straight trunk and a strongly growing central shoot

Look for a good, symmetrical shape with an even spread of branches

Check stems for die-back and foliage for browning or signs of disease

◁ **ASSESS THE TREE**
*Choose a tree that has a good root system, but is not pot-bound. Stand back to assess the tree's overall shape, then check closely for damage or disease.*

A good nursery will let you check the roots: lift the tree and the compost should mostly stay intact

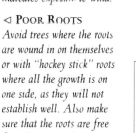

◁ **POT-BOUND ROOTS**
*Never buy a pot-bound tree, with a mass of tightly wound, congested roots, or one with thick roots poking through the drainage holes.*

# ROOT-BALLED TREES

Some trees for sale are described as "root-balled": these have been grown in open ground, but are lifted with soil around the roots and then wrapped in hessian or other material. Evergreens, especially conifers, are often available as root-balled trees, and deciduous trees over 4m (12ft) tall may also be sold this way. Root-balled trees have an advantage over bare-root ones in that the roots are less likely to dry out in the time between the tree being lifted and subsequently replanted.

Root-balled trees are usually sold direct from nurseries, often by mail order, so tend to be cheaper than container-grown trees, but are not generally available from garden centres. If buying from a nursery by mail order, choose a reputable or recommended one and try to plant the trees as soon as possible after delivery.

**CHECKING THE ROOT BALL △**
*When buying a root-balled tree, check that the root ball is firm — the soil should be clinging to the roots — and the wrapping intact. Watch out for any signs of damage or drying out of the roots, since these give an indication that the tree is less likely to establish successfully.*

# TREE STAKES AND TIES

If you are planting a tree in an exposed or very windy site, it is advisable to stake it, with the stake positioned on the side of the prevailing wind. This helps to support the tree until a strong root system has been developed. For whippy trees with flexible stems, use a tall stake, reaching to just below the crown. In the second year after planting, cut down the stake to about 50cm (20in) in height, and finally remove it altogether in the following year.

◁ **LOW STAKE**
*This allows the trunk some movement, helping the tree to grow strong roots. Before planting, drive in the stake so that about 50cm (20in) is above the ground.*

**ANGLED STAKE ▷**
*A low stake may be driven in clear of the tree's roots after planting. Knock it in firmly at an angle of 45°, making sure that it leans into the prevailing wind.*

SEE ALSO: Other Maintenance, p.197

# PLANTING A TREE

Once you have chosen an appropriate spot for your tree, and prepared the site, you are ready to buy and plant. You can dig the planting hole in advance to minimize the delay before planting once you have bought the tree — worth it for bare-root trees, which are vulnerable to drying out.

In order to give a tree a good start, mix the soil you dig out of the hole with some well-rotted organic matter such as garden compost. This improves the structure of the soil, and provides an ideal medium for the tree's roots to spread and grow strong.

Forking over the sides and base of the hole, particularly in areas with heavy, clay soil, will also make it easier for the roots to spread out and anchor the tree well. If planting in spring, add a little slow-release fertilizer (about 110g/4oz) to the topsoil mixture to encourage good growth.

When planting a container-grown tree, follow the basic procedure shown below. With a bare-root tree, prepare the site in the same way, but the hole must be large enough to take the tree's roots when fully spread out. Trim any damaged roots with secateurs, but take care not to damage the delicate-looking, fibrous roots through which the tree absorbs nutrients.

■ **If preparing the hole** in advance, backfill it loosely until you are ready to plant so that the soil remains warm, and cover with polythene or plastic sheeting.

■ **When using a stake,** knock it in either before or during planting (*see below*), or it may damage the roots of the tree.

A FAITHFUL FRIEND ▷
*Given a good start with careful planting and aftercare, a tree (here, a crab apple, Malus tschonoskii) should live to grace the garden for decades or even centuries.*

## HOW TO PLANT A CONTAINER-GROWN TREE

**1 DIG THE HOLE**
*Roughly mark out the area of the hole: about 3–4 times the diameter of the tree's root ball. Dig a hole to about 1½ times the depth of the root ball.*

**2 PREPARE THE HOLE**
*Fork over the base and sides of the hole. Mix the removed soil with organic matter, such as garden compost, and add some of it to the base of the hole.*

**3 CHECK THE PLANTING DEPTH**
*Set the tree — here a beech — in the hole and use a cane to check its depth (see box, facing page). The top of the root ball should be level with the soil surface: fill or dig out soil until it is level.*

**4 KNOCK IN THE STAKE**
*Taking care not to damage the root ball, insert a stake into the hole next to the tree, and knock it firmly into place with a mallet. The stake should be just off-centre on the side of the prevailing wind.*

**5 FILL WITH SOIL**
*Fill in around the root ball and the stake with the rest of the removed topsoil. Firm the soil gently as you go, with hammer or foot.*

**6 FIRM THE SOIL**
*Check the tree is still upright and finish by treading the soil gently until the surface is level, which also removes air pockets.*

**7 TIE THE STAKE**
*Attach the stake to the tree's young trunk with a plastic tree tie, taking care not to overtighten it — this would damage the stem.*

**8 WATER IN**
*Give your new tree a good drink of water to help it recover from planting. In the early stages, do not allow the roots to dry out.*

FINISHING TOUCHES ▷
*After watering, add a deep (5–8cm/2–3in) mulch, such as chipped bark, over the entire area of the hole, leaving a clear 5cm (2in) gap around the trunk. This helps retain moisture and suppresses weeds. Cut back any dead or damaged stems on the tree's crown, and prune any long sideshoots to create a balanced shape.*

SEE ALSO: Preparing the Ground, pp.142–143; Applying Mulch, p.152; Tree Stakes and Ties, p.193

# PLANTING A ROOT-BALLED TREE

The basic method is as for a container-grown tree (*see facing page*), although the hole can be only two or three times the width of the root ball. If staking the tree, use an angled stake, driven in clear of the root ball, or three guy-ropes secured to low stakes. In heavy, clay soil, plant the tree so that the root ball is slightly proud of the soil level, to assist drainage. Cover this exposed part with 5–8cm (2–3in) of a free-draining soil (such as topsoil mixed with organic matter), but leave a gap of about 5cm (2in) all around the stem.

**1 DIG THE HOLE AND POSITION THE TREE**
*Dig a hole 2 or 3 times the width of the root ball. Mix the soil with well-rotted organic matter. Set the tree in the hole – easier with two people – and untie the root ball.*

**2 REMOVE THE WRAPPING**
*Tilt the tree over to one side and roll the wrapping up under the root ball; then lean it the other way and tug the material out. Backfill, firm, and water well.*

# GROWING TREES IN CONTAINERS

You do not need a great expanse of open ground to grow a tree: there are many small and medium trees suitable for large tubs, pots, and planters placed on patios, balconies, or roof terraces. If you only have space for one tree in a container, choose one with more than one season of interest and a good silhouette. Using containers lets you cultivate trees that prefer a different soil type from that in your garden, and tender ones that can be placed under cover for the winter.

Make sure any container you use has drainage holes; cover with broken crocks, curved sides up, then a layer of coarse gravel. Use a good soil-based compost and incorporate a slow-release fertilizer. Water well in summer, and at other times as necessary, but keep on the dry side in winter. Mulch to minimize evaporation.

## TELL ME WHY

**WHY IS IT IMPORTANT TO PLANT A TREE SO THAT THE SOIL LEVEL IS THE SAME AS WHEN THE TREE WAS FIRST RAISED IN THE NURSERY?**

If a tree is planted too deeply, its roots may be deprived of oxygen, which may halt their growth or even kill them. On the other hand, if a tree is planted too shallowly, the roots may dry out. Always check the level carefully when planting: with a bare-root tree, look for the darker "soil mark" on the stem and lay a cane alongside the mark to ensure that the soil surface is at the same level as this, or is level with the top of the root ball for a container-grown tree.

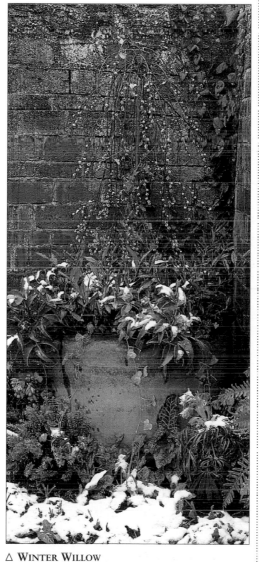

△ **WINTER WILLOW**
*The weeping branches and fat, furry catkins of the popular Kilmarnock willow (Salix caprea 'Kilmarnock'), are set off against the evergreen foliage of* Helleborus argutifolius *to make a charming feature in late winter.*

# TREE GUARDS

In many gardens, especially rural ones, you may need to protect newly planted trees from rabbits, deer, and rodents. You can buy proprietary tree guards from garden centres or tree nurseries, or make your own using wire mesh; whatever the type, make sure it will protect the whole height of the trunk. Fit guards at the time of planting, and check them regularly to ensure they are still in place. As a tree grows, the bark becomes tougher, so the guard may eventually be removed. In areas with deer, however, you may need to provide permanent protection.

△ **EXPANDABLE PLASTIC GUARD**
*This type of spiral, wrap-around plastic guard can expand as the tree grows. It is quick to use so is particularly suitable if you are planting a large number of trees. It should protect the bark from small animals such as rabbits.*

△ **WIRE GUARD**
*A barrier made from wire mesh or chicken wire is less intrusive visually than a proprietary tree guard, but more time-consuming to put in place. Make sure the supporting canes are pushed well down into the ground so that the barrier cannot be easily displaced.*

**SEE ALSO:** Routine Care and Maintenance, pp.178–179; Rabbits, p.298; Deer, p.301

# ROUTINE CARE

MOST ESTABLISHED TREES need little maintenance to keep them healthy and attractive. Routine tasks that will benefit your trees include replacing mulches, checking ties, harvesting fruit, removing fallen fruit and leaves, and watering in dry periods. Light pruning can sometimes be used to enhance the ornamental qualities of many trees, leading to more flowers or larger leaves, for example. Coppicing and pollarding are two types of hard pruning that may be used specifically to achieve special effects such as brilliantly coloured young stems or handsome foliage. Pruning can also help restore neglected trees, or create elegant, multi-stemmed shapes.

## LIGHT PRUNING

Most trees need very little pruning apart from removing any crossing, dead, or damaged branches. Overpruning may affect the growth and even health of the tree. If you do feel the need to prune, remember these simple principles: prune in the season appropriate for the type of tree; respect the habit of the tree and aim for a good all-round balance; remove any dead, damaged, or diseased branches, cutting back to healthy growth, or remove the entire branch if that makes for a well-balanced framework; take out weak or straggly growth and any crossing or congested stems – rubbing stems could encourage disease. Make pruning cuts just above a bud or pair of buds (*see below and pp.156–157*). If you are cutting back a mature branch, be sure to leave the branch collar, that is the slightly wider part close to the trunk, completely untouched.

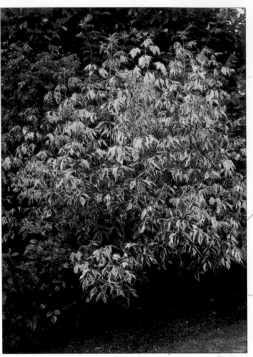

### CUTTING BACK A STEM

△ **REMOVING A MATURE BRANCH**
*To avoid a branch over 2.5cm (1in) thick tearing away from the trunk, remove it in two stages. When making the final cut to remove the stub, do not touch the branch collar.*

△ **ALTERNATE BUDS**
*Make a slanting cut about 5mm (¼in) above a bud. The sloping cut allows drops of rain, which might encourage rot or disease, to drain away from the bud.*

△ **OPPOSITE BUDS**
*Cut straight across above a pair of strong, healthy buds, keeping the secateurs as close above them as you can without grazing or damaging the buds.*

△ **PRUNING FOR FOLIAGE EFFECTS**
*This Acer negundo 'Flamingo' has been cut back to produce larger leaves and brighter variegation. Regular pruning of some trees will create strong, healthy foliage.*

## FORMATIVE PRUNING

When you buy a new, young tree, it may occasionally be necessary to carry out some formative pruning to encourage the tree to develop a well-balanced crown. Some trees, such as alders (*Alnus*), are naturally multi-stemmed; you can also create this effect on certain other species (not grafted cultivars), such as snakebark maples (*Acer davidii*), birches (*Betula*), or tupelo (*Nyssa sylvatica*), by cutting the main stem hard back (*see right*) so that several new stems develop. The resulting multiple trunks can be left clothed with foliage or the lower parts cleared to show off attractive bark.

### PRUNING TO FORM A MULTI-STEMMED TREE

**YEAR 1, WINTER** △
*Cut the main stem of a 2-year-old tree across at the desired height. Trim the wound so that there are no rough edges. The cut should stimulate low buds to shoot the following year.*

**YEAR 2, WINTER** △
*Select 3 or 4 strong, well-spaced shoots – preferably ones that are equally vigorous so that they develop evenly. Remove all other shoots, cutting them back to the base.*

**YEAR 3, WINTER** △
*Let sideshoots develop, only removing the lower ones if you want to have clear stems. Remove any new suckers that occur from the base; these may regrow later and should be cut out.*

SEE ALSO: Making Pruning Cuts, p.156; Why Prune?, p.157; Tools for Cutting and Pruning, p.279

# COPPICING AND POLLARDING

Traditionally, these techniques were used to produce regular supplies of new straight growth for firewood or charcoal, and fence- and basket-making. Coppicing and pollarding are now ways to grow trees in small gardens that would otherwise lack the required space. They are also used to enhance leaf colour or size, or to stimulate bright young shoots. Pollarding of large trees is a job for a professional as heavy branches must be removed, but pollarding of a young tree (see below) is not difficult. The new stems that appear are pliable and can be made into rustic plant supports, arches, or even garden sculptures.

■ **Coppicing:** in late winter or early spring, select a suitable tree, such as eucalyptus, paulownia, or willow, and cut it back almost to ground level, leaving the basal wood untouched.

■ **Pollarding:** a young standard tree is cut back to a clear stem of 1–1.8m (3–6ft) in late winter or early spring. Every second or third year, the young shoots are pruned back to their base. In-between times, thin out excess stems if you wish.

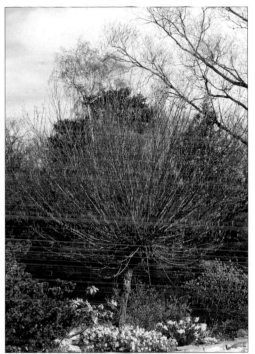

△ **BRIGHT YOUNG GROWTH**
*Some of the willows (Salix) that are known to produce colourful young growth make excellent candidates for pollarding. This is done on a main stem, about 1.5m (5ft) in height, to create an attractive crown of fresh and eye catching new shoots at a manageable height.*

# OTHER MAINTENANCE

For most trees to establish well, they need watering, feeding, and weeding during the first few years. Trees grown in containers need regular top-dressing and occasional repotting; they will also need to be watered and fed more frequently.

■ **Watering:** young or newly planted trees need a regular and plentiful supply of water throughout the growing season, especially if they are in light, sandy soil.

■ **Feeding:** most trees, especially newly planted ones and those that have been coppiced or pollarded, benefit from feeding. Apply an artificial fertilizer in mid-spring, strictly according to manufacturer's instructions, or an organic mulch such as well-rotted manure or compost in mid-autumn.

■ **Weeding:** keep the area beneath the tree canopy free of weeds (try mulching).

■ **Renewing mulches:** mulches, such as bark, laid to suppress weeds and conserve moisture should be renewed in late spring.

■ **Checking ties:** at the beginning and end of the growing season, check that the ties on staked trees have not become too tight around the trunk, restricting growth.

■ **Removing stakes:** when trees are established, remove all stakes and ties.

■ **Harvesting:** do not forget to pick any edible nuts or fruits, such as apples, when ripe and before they fall off the tree.

■ **Clearing up leaves and other debris:** rake up leaves and dead material as soon as you can as they may harbour disease.

# TREE SURGERY

All major tasks, such as removing large branches, crown thinning, and high-heading (having lower branches cut out to raise the canopy and so reduce shade), are best left to professional tree surgeons. These procedures could be dangerous if tackled yourself, and need experience to produce an aesthetically satisfying result. Seek professional advice, also, if you wish to fell a tree completely; there may be both safety and legal considerations.

SEE ALSO: Applying Mulch, p 152; Repotting and Top-dressing, p.179; Tree Stakes and Ties, p.193; Dealing with Weeds, pp.290–291

# WATER GARDENING

## WHY CHOOSE A WATER FEATURE?

THE USE OF WATER has long been valued for the added dimension it lends to a garden design; indeed, water is often considered the living soul of a garden. Water brings the ever-changing scintillation of reflected light and introduces the vitality of movement and sound to a garden in ways that no other single element can. A water feature greatly extends the range of plants that you can grow, from simple moisture lovers and bog plants to true deep-water aquatics. Such plant diversity not only adds to the gardener's pleasure, but it also contributes to an inviting habitat for wildlife that will bring interest and benefits to the garden as a whole.

## THE RIGHT STYLE

As with any component of garden design, you shouldn't be afraid to make your water garden express your individual taste, but remember that designs generally work best if they have a unified style that fits well with the immediate surroundings.

The first, most important, decision is whether you prefer a formal or informal style. This may also influence the possible choices of construction method, the types of plants you may grow, and the potential value of the finished feature for wildlife.

Formal features are characterized by crisp, geometric symmetry and strong, straight lines, framed with materials like stone or brick. Such hard edges often make access difficult for wildlife and may reduce potential for marginal plantings.

The informal style is expressed in natural irregularity, with soft outlines and sinuous curves. Informal pools are easier to meld into their surroundings with marginal planting, which incidentally provides cover for water fowl and amphibians alike.

### GOOD IDEAS

• Formal pools sit best in their surroundings if the hard materials used blend with those of the house and existing patios or paving.

• An informal feature looks best if placed in a low-lying area that might naturally have filled with water.

• Make a "wish list" to help you decide on a suitable style. If ease of installation, wildlife habitats, and maximum planting potential are priorities, an informal pool is best.

△ **CRISP GEOMETRY**
*The firm lines of this small formal pool echo the fence line beyond and are thrown into high relief by strong verticals provided by the upright leaves of basket-planted marginals. Softer plantings contrast and so emphasize the strength of the geometry.*

**SINUOUS IRREGULARITY** ▷
*An artfully random arrangement of stones enhances the sinuous outline of an informal pond. The margins are masked by a soft, naturalistic planting that extends into the shallows to provide safe shelter for fish fry, amphibians, and bathing or drinking birds.*

SEE ALSO: Water Features, pp.32–33, The Aquatic Environment, pp.214–215; The Transitional Zone, pp.216–217; The Moisture Lovers, pp.218–219

## SOUND AND MOVEMENT

Moving water in a design brings the visual excitement of glittering light and the soothing murmur of splashing water. Less obviously, it improves water quality by oxygenation to benefit plants and other living creatures, and it lends cool humidity to the surrounding air to refresh both gardener and moisture-loving plants alike.

Simply provide electricity to drive a circulating pump and you could create sparkling cascades, smooth, gleaming sheets over spill stones, or a gurgling fountain from a simple or ornate spout.

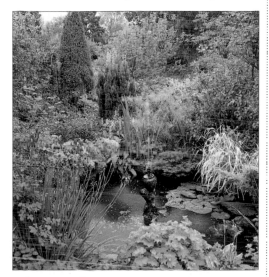

△ SPLASHING LIGHT
*A simple but elegant fountain head, powered by a low-voltage circulating pump, forms the focal point in this naturalistic pool. Dispersed jets of water catch the light as they fall, creating the sound of splashing raindrops while maintaining oxygen levels in the water.*

△ A ROCKY CASCADE
*Constructed on a gentle slope to provide the necessary fall, this cascade is lined with a waterproof membrane, which is disguised by thoughtfully sited planting and naturally disposed rocks and gravel. Such rapidly moving water is amply refreshed with oxygen as it traverses the cascade.*

## QUIET REFLECTION

A mirror-like surface of still, limpid water, undisturbed by splashing spouts, provides an air of tranquillity that is most valuable if you need a pool to be a focus for quiet contemplation. The play of light changes throughout the days and seasons, and a smooth surface presents an opportunity to reflect – and so more than double – the beauty of both plants and ornaments.

In this situation, a healthy aquatic environment relies heavily on a careful mixture of plants, including submerged oxygenators and shade-casting, floating-leaved plants, like water lilies, which will fail to thrive in splashing water.

△ MIRROR, MIRROR
*Typha latifolia and water irises create strong, vertical reflections, contrasting here with the curves of an Ali Baba pot. Flat paving accentuates the theme of tranquillity.*

## THE RIGHT PLACE

Before excavating, locate all utilities underground, such as pipes or cables. An ideal site has easy access to electricity (for pumps) and to water (for topping up, as necessary). Good access to the pond and surrounding plantings is also desirable.

Sunny sites are best, but avoid sun traps and provide wind shelter to minimize evaporation. Keep clear of frost pockets and of trees and shrubs, which cast shade and shed potentially polluting leaves.

Decide if you want a clear view of the feature from the house, or if a more secluded location is preferred – for your privacy or for the benefit of wildlife.

Avoid areas of deep shade, since water plants need high light levels to thrive

Avoid overhanging branches that may pollute water with falling leaves

A sunny site with shelter from wind is ideal – set a pool off-centre for more dynamic interest

△ FINDING THE PLOT
*Take time to observe the movement of sun and shade throughout the day before deciding on the final site. This will avoid mistakes that may be impossible to rectify later.*

## SAFETY FIRST

Parents should be aware of the fascination of water for small children and of the dangers it presents. Never allow small children unsupervised access to open areas of water. Converting a pond excavation into a sand pit is one option, but you might also choose a feature without open water, like a bubble fountain or a wall-mounted spout. These are also good choices if the garden is used by those less foot-sure or of restricted mobility.

If you still want a pond, consider installing a rigid, wire mesh barrier just below the surface, and think about using non-slip surfaces for the pond surrounds. Don't overlook the dangers of open water

to domestic pets and wild animals, like hedgehogs, who may come to drink. Give them safe access by including a gently sloping beach area or escape ramp.

### ALWAYS REMEMBER

**WATER AND ELECTRICITY DO NOT MIX**

Outdoor mains electricity at normal voltage is potentially hazardous. For small features, low-voltage equipment, with an indoor transformer to convert power to low voltage, is adequate and safe when used with waterproof connectors that are approved for outdoor use. Larger features may need mains electricity; for these, professional advice and installation are essential.

SEE ALSO: Container Pools, p.207; Installing a Fountain, pp.208–209; Moving Water in Small Spaces, pp.212–213

# BUYING A FLEXIBLE LINER

CALCULATING QUANTITIES for a liner, especially one of irregular shape, often confounds the novice, but the calculation is simple. Firstly, determine the maximum length, width, and depth of the pool. Liner length will be the maximum length plus twice the maximum depth, and liner width will be the maximum width plus twice the maximum depth. Finally, add 45cm (18in) to both length and width to allow for overlap. For circular ponds, substitute the diameter for length and width.

A liner is easier to work with if laid flat in the sun to warm up for half an hour or so, because warmth increases flexibility. Roll it up smoothly before laying.

## A SIMPLE POND WITH MARGINAL SHELF

Before excavating, dig a test hole in the centre of the site to establish the level of the natural water table. Usually, the water table will not be an issue, but if a liner is laid below the water table or in poorly drained soil, upward pressure of water causes it to balloon up – the "hippo effect". If you do discover poor drainage or a high water table, you may need to improve drainage. Alternatively, avoid the problem by making the pool a semi-raised feature, using excavated topsoil to build up the pool surround, which will bring the base above the water table.

Test hole helps differentiate between poor drainage and high water table

If water collects spontaneously at this level, suspect a high water table

△ DIGGING A TEST HOLE
*Dig a hole, 45cm (18in) deep and fill it with water. If it doesn't seep away, you have poor drainage or a high water table. Dig down a further 45cm (18in); if the hole begins to fill spontaneously, then you have a high water table.*

### TOOLS AND MATERIALS

- 10–12 pegs, for finding levels
- Lump hammer
- Spirit level
- Straight edge
- Shovel and spade
- Rake
- Sand or string, for marking out
- Soft sand or sifted soil for base
- Underlay
- Flexible liner
- Bricks or smooth, rounded stones to hold liner in place during filling

### MARKING OUT AND DIGGING

**1 LEVELLING THE POOL EDGES**
*Mark the pool outline with sand or string, then position marker pegs at equal intervals around it. With a lump hammer, spirit level, and straight edge, use the technique shown on p.206 to ensure that all the pegs are level, and the soil around them is horizontal.*

**2 EXCAVATING THE HOLE**
*Remove the turf to a depth of 5cm (2in) and retain for edging, if desired. Dig the entire area to 23cm (9in) deep, with the sides slightly sloping outwards, then rake the base. Mark the deep zone, leaving at least 30cm (12in) width for a marginal shelf.*

**3 PREPARING THE DEEP ZONE**
*Dig the deep zone to a further 38cm (15in). Rake over the base, removing all sharp and large stones, roots, or other projections. Spread a layer of sand or sifted soil, 2.5cm (1in) deep, over the base as an added precaution against punctures.*

### LAYING THE LINING MATERIAL

**1 ROLL OUT THE UNDERLAY**
*Remove any stones from the sides of the pool, then pat sand into the sides to make them smooth. Drape the underlay over the pool. Working from the centre outwards, press the underlay firmly into the contours of the hole, with as few creases as possible.*

**2 LAYING OUT THE LINER**
*Position the rolled-up liner on one side of the pool and unroll it gently. Don't pull the liner fabric, as this will stretch it and make it more vulnerable to puncture. Leave sufficient overlap around the margins and fold in the creases evenly.*

**3 FILLING WITH WATER**
*Use bricks to hold the liner in place temporarily. Fill slowly with water. The weight of water will settle the liner into the contours, so make adjustments, if necessary, by pleating creased areas and moving the bricks as the liner becomes taut.*

SEE ALSO: Bog Gardens, pp.204–205; Make it Level and True, p.206

# TURNING THE CORNER

If a pool is designed with broad, sweeping curves, little adjustment of the liner will be needed, but for more acute curves, careful pleating is necessary, especially around the marginal shelf. In pools with corners, the liner can be folded and excess tucked in.

Make pleats and folds as generous as possible to avoid over-stretching the liner and make as many adjustments as possible before filling with water; it's weight makes adjustment very difficult later on.

## ALWAYS REMEMBER

### A LINER IS A FRAGILE THING!

Although durable in use, flexible liners are relatively thin membranes that are especially vulnerable to punctures when laying. Never tread on a liner at any stage during construction. Make any adjustments when laying and filling by reaching in from the outside of the pond and resist all temptation to do it from within.

# TRIMMING THE LINER

Once the pool is full of water, the securing bricks can be removed, and the excess liner can be trimmed away. Never trim the liner right to the water's edge, but allow an overlap of about 10–15cm (4–6in). This prevents water seeping behind the liner, which can occur if the water level rises and the pool overflows after heavy rain. It also provides a good base for an edging of hard materials that are to be mortared in place.

◁ PLEATING
*To accommodate curves, gather the liner to form a series of pleats and hold them top and bottom with bricks until secured by the pressure of water on filling. Although both pleats and folds look unsightly, once compressed by water they become flattened and virtually invisible.*

◁ FOLD AND TUCK
*To make a neat corner, make a diagonal fold in the liner and tuck in the excess with one hand while securing the bottom of the fold with the other. Try to position the fold exactly in the corner for best effect. Hold in place with bricks until secured by the weight of water.*

◁ CUT TO FIT
*Using a pair of sharp scissors, trim away excess liner to leave an edge of 10–15cm (4–6in). Tread carefully around the margins of the pond so that you do not inadvertently kick stones into the water; they may cause punctures if they become lodged under planting baskets.*

# FINISHING OFF THE EDGES

For hard edging, or if earth is likely to subside beneath turf, install a concrete foundation. Lift the liner overlap and dig out a trench, 15–23cm (6–9in) deep. Roll the liner into the trench, lay a foundation on top, and mortar the edging in place. Keep mortar out of the water; it is toxic to fish and plants. If it does pollute the water, drain the pond and start again.

## GOOD IDEAS

• If edging with rocks, try to obtain from a local quarry. Distinctive sorts, like granite or slate, look misplaced when "out of habitat".

• Include a stone that slopes into the water as an escape route for frogs and hedgehogs.

• With hard edges, a slight overhang will cast shadows into the water that disguise the liner and protect it from direct light.

Pavers mortared onto liner are carefully levelled and set just below the turf to provide a mowing edge

Liner and underlay secured between foundation and bedding mortar are rendered invisible

Mortared brick edge and concrete foundation

Turves rolled back during construction of foundation

Once mortar has set, the void behind is backfilled with soil and the turves rolled back into place

Setts mortared onto

### FORMAL AND INFORMAL EDGINGS

There is a wealth of edging materials to choose from, ranging from naturalistic turf or rocks to setts and a wide range of paving slabs. Turf looks natural but becomes muddy under heavy traffic or from paddling domestic pets. Using rocks provides a firm edge with excellent niches to shelter toads and frogs. Hard paving makes an ideal surface for sitting on and enjoying the fruits of your labours.

PLANE DELIGHT ▷
*Rocks like granite have cleavage planes rather than strata. Align the rocks so cleavage planes are broadly parallel for the most natural effect, then mortar them carefully in place.*

ROCK STRATA ▷
*Sandstones and limestones have strata that look best set in overlapping diagonals, with strata lines running along the sides, rather than the top, to create the impression of an outcrop.*

△ ON THE BEACH
*For the most natural effect, lay rocks and stones in bands that gradually decrease in size as they get nearer the water. A smooth-pebbled beach is the perfect invitation for birds and small mammals to come to drink, and it is the ideal entry point for amphibians.*

SEE ALSO: On the Edge, p.207; Building a Stream with Waterfalls, p.211

# INSTALLING A FOUNTAIN

IN THE DAYS BEFORE ELECTRICITY, hydraulic technology relied on gravity, enormous reservoirs, and complex pumping systems. The advent of small, modern, submersible pumps has brought the possibilities of moving water to even the smallest spaces. Not only do fountains lend sound, movement, and sparkle to the garden, they refresh and de-ionize the air around them with cool humidity, and replenish oxygen levels in the water to the benefit of plants and fish. Given due regard to electrical safety, fountain installation is the essence of simplicity; nowadays, excellent fountain kits can be bought off the shelf from any good garden centre.

## CREATING SIMPLE FOUNTAINS

The mechanics are essentially simple. A fountain head is connected to an electric pump, which forces water through the head to create the spray. Height varies with pump power and a flow adjuster. Low-voltage pumps are capable of jet heights up to 1.2m (4ft), and submersible mains pumps, up to 2.2m (7ft). For higher jets, a mains surface pump is required.

> ### GOOD IDEAS
>
> • A spray width that is less than half that of the pool will fall entirely within its margins.
>
> • The finer the spray, the more water is lost by evaporation; to minimize losses, use a nozzle that produces a column of water rather than a fine, wide-arching spray.
>
> • Tap water is fine for topping up water losses by evaporation.
>
> • Place splash-sensitive plants, like waterlilies, beyond the splash zone.

**SIMPLE PUMP INSTALLATION ▽**
*The simplest type of fountain installation is powered by a low-voltage, submersible pump. A vertical discharge pipe connects the fountain head to the pump outlet.*

Fountain head emerges directly from outlet of pump, which is fixed to a plinth

Some plants, such as waterlilies, dislike moving water and so need to be placed beyond the immediate splash zone

An overhanging, stone slab edging hides the pump from view

Free-standing fountain head connected to pump outlet with a short length of delivery pipe

**◁ REMOTE PUMP**
*In larger pools, to bring the pump within easy reach for cleaning and maintenance, the pump is best sited near the edge. The fountain head is fed through a delivery pipe attached to the pump outlet.*

Submersible pump fixed to a plinth for stability. The electrical wiring is hidden beneath paving slab

**BUBBLE FOUNTAIN ▷**
*One of the safest ways of bringing the sight and sound of moving water to a small space is to install a bubble fountain. This one is supplied by a single pipe connected to a low-voltage pump hidden in a reservoir beneath the millstone.*

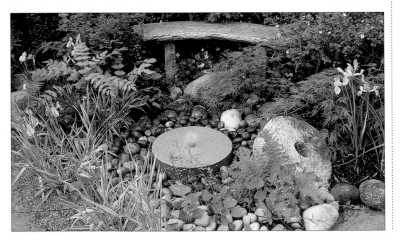

## SPRAY PATTERNS

Spray patterns are formed by the size and arrangement of holes in the fountain outlet nozzle. Simple nozzles, like those illustrated below, are attached directly to the outlet pipe of the pump.

Spray nozzles for more complex patterns need a special adaptor and may need a more powerful pump, depending on the height and volume of the spray.

**◁ A SINGLE SPRAY**
*Elegant in its simplicity, the single spray pattern suits ponds of simple design and is easily accommodated in small pools. The narrower the delivery pipe, the higher the elevation of the spray.*

**SINGLE-SPRAY NOZZLE**

**◁ TWO-TIERED SPRAY**
*Two concentric rings of holes in the spray nozzle provide a broader, two-tiered spray. Ideal for larger and more elaborate pools. The splash zone is larger, so in small pools, it may disturb plants like waterlilies.*

**DOUBLE-SPRAY NOZZLE**

**BELL-JET NOZZLE**

**△ BELL JET SPRAY**
*Bell jets produce a shimmering, hemispherical film of water that causes relatively little surface disturbance despite its relatively large splash zone. A Tiffany jet is a bell jet combined with a single-spray nozzle underneath, which gives the effect of a fountain within a fountain.*

**SEE ALSO:** Sound and Movement, p.199; Safety First, p.199

# PUMPS AND POWER SUPPLY

For most small water features, a low voltage pump is safe, adequate, and easy to install. For large features, a mains supply is needed and the hardware must be installed by a professional electrician.

If possible, buy from an aquatic specialist or a garden centre with a good aquatic department. They will happily advise; the best manufacturers also have telephone helplines or websites. Be prepared with your answers to the following questions:
■ Will the pump operate a watercourse, fountain, filter, or a combination of these?
■ What is the pool's volume?
■ What type of fountain spray is needed?
■ How high a spray do you want?
■ For water courses, you will also need to know the "head" height and "reservoir" pool volume (*see p.210*), and the width of the spillway or stream.

## USING MAINS ELECTRICITY

Mains systems are essential for large water courses or fountains in excess of 1.2m (4ft) in height. They are inevitably more costly as all equipment has high safety specifications and installation is a job for the professionals.

## USING LOW-VOLTAGE ELECTRICITY

Most small, moving water features, including fountains and cascades, can be driven by a low-voltage pump. Cost advantages are inherent in the scale and specifications of equipment used, in running costs and, not least, because it is a safe option for DIY installation.

Jets taller than 1.2m (4ft) need mains electricity to power the submersible pump

A transformer converts mains voltage to a low-voltage current and minimizes the risks of electrical shock

Earthed, mains supply switch must be turned off before handling any equipment

Waterproof connectors are essential

Armoured, waterproof cable

Circuit breaker (RCD) is vital for electrical safety outdoors

Plastic conduit is buried 60cm (24in) below ground

Small fountains, up to 1.2m (4ft) high, are adequately powered by low-voltage electricity

Submersible pump is kept stable by weight of attached plinth

Waterproof connector above water level also protects from penetrating damp

Plastic conduit provides permanent housing to carry cable safely beneath paving

# USING FILTERS

In the quest for crystal-clear water, filters are an important tool. They are fitted pre- or post-pump and may be submersible or located out of the water, depending on design. There are two main types – mechanical or biological – and they are often used in combination. Mechanical filters are simple strainers, usually using sponge-like foam to remove suspended particles. Effective as soon as switched on, they may be used intermittently.

Biological filters use colonies of beneficial bacteria to break down the nitrogenous waste of fish and other organisms. They take up to three weeks to take effect and, once switched on, must be kept running; the bacteria need a constant flow of oxygenated water to keep them active.

Inlet pipe with spray bar creates a spray of water to keep up oxygen levels for bacterial health

**ALL-PURPOSE FILTER** ▷
*This type of filter is located outside the pond. The inlet spray bar and foam sheets are easily accessible for cleaning. Bio-filter media should be cleaned only with pond water or non-chlorinated water.*

Water flows downwards through layers of open cell foam of increasing density

Bio-media of clay or glass provides large surface area for bacterial colonization

Outlet pipe incorporates overflow so filter is bypassed when blocked

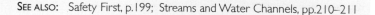

**SEE ALSO:** Safety First, p.199; Streams and Water Channels, pp.210–211

# STREAMS AND WATER CHANNELS

MOST GARDENS CAN ACCOMMODATE a small watercourse as an adjunct to a pool, whether it be a burbling stream, a rocky cascade, or more a formal water canal or rill. The basic requirements are a reservoir pool, a pump of sufficient power to raise the water through a delivery pipe to a header pool, and a sufficient difference in height (known as the head) between the header and the reservoir to ensure that gravity moves the returning water downhill along a totally watertight channel. If no incline exists naturally – and even a small head is adequate – a slope can easily be built up using soil from the excavation of the reservoir pool.

## THE ESSENTIAL ELEMENTS

A good specialist supplier will advise on a suitably powered pump for a watercourse, if given the following essential details:

■ **Measure the head** (the height of the header pool above the reservoir pool) and the length and width of the water stream.

■ **Calculate the volume** of the reservoir pool by multiplying maximum depth, by width, by length. The flow rate per hour must not exceed this volume.

Spill stone kept firm by mortaring to the liner; stiff mortar seals the gap between liner and bank

Backward-sloping header pool retains water should the pump fail; a safety feature for flora and fauna

Delivery pipe buried in trench beside stream and covered with soil, gravel, or small rocks for easy access

Pump lifts water from reservoir to header pool; the return flow is powered by gravity

Stream bed is formed with underlay and liner, which is disguised and protected from light by randomly laid pebbles

Changes in level create miniature waterfalls; the liner is pleated and mortared in place between two rocks

### A STREAM IN PROFILE
Whatever the style, a stream, in essence, comprises a channel cut through sloping ground; the channel may traverse changes in level to create waterfalls. The reservoir pool holds a pump and an ample volume of water to circulate via a delivery pipe and header pool.

## LINING A WATERCOURSE

Flexible liners come into their own in the creation of water courses, but to ensure a trouble-free, leak-proof channel for both formal and more naturalistic features:

■ **Take care to avoid punctures;** do not tread on the liner or drag it on the ground.

■ **Use an underlay** for added security.

■ **Ensure that the liner overlaps** the channel's sides by a generous margin.

■ **Protect the liner** from direct sunlight.

■ **Start at the bottom** with the reservoir, and work upwards to the header pool.

NATURAL ELEMENTS ▷
*Water glitters over the rocky cascade and gleams in a smooth sheet over a spill stone into the reservoir pool. A flexible liner forms a waterproof channel and is edged with artfully disposed rocks. Smaller stones of varying size disguise the base, while adding sound and sparkle.*

△ **A SIMPLE WATER CHANNEL**
*Bringing the gentle murmur of water to the garden, this simple channel is built from natural stone slabs mortared onto a plastic liner. A submersible pump circulates water through an in-pond filter; an ultra-violet filter and small header pool is hidden beneath the horizontal slab.*

SEE ALSO: Pumps and Power Supply, p.209; Using Filters, p.209; Moving Water in Small Spaces, pp.212–213

# BUILDING A STREAM WITH WATERFALLS

One of the beauties of creating streams with a flexible liner is that you can adapt the basic method to formal and informal style features, with or without waterfalls.

Lightweight butyl rubber or PVC are the most accommodating materials, especially for the beginner. Their flexibility allows them to be folded, tugged, and tweaked carefully into place in irregularly shaped channels. If you want the stream to meander gently along its course, be sure to make the liner wide enough to cover the maximum width with a generous overlap on both sides.

It is not essential that the stream and pool are constructed simultaneously – a watercourse can be added at a later date to complement an existing pond, which will then function as the reservoir pool. This is an ideal solution if you need to spread the costs of materials over more than one season, for example, or if you become bored with, or inherit, an existing pool. As your interest in water gardening grows, as it almost inevitably will, it also allows you to create yet more exciting possibilities for extending the scope of your waterside plantings.

## TOOLS AND MATERIALS

- Existing pool with marginal shelf
- Large rocks, for spill stones, foundation stone, and side walls, each weighing 20–50kg (55–110lb)
- Marker pegs and string
- Spade and shovel
- Rake
- Flexible liner and underlay
- Ready-mix mortar
- Watering can or hose
- Spirit level
- Submersible pump and delivery pipe
- Smaller rocks for hiding liner

## STREAM CONSTRUCTION WITH A FLEXIBLE LINER

**1 DIG THE HEADER AND STREAM**
*Mark out and excavate stream bed and backward-sloping header pool, and remove stones. Partly unroll liner, draping one end over existing reservoir pool. Ensure liner covers entire excavation with enough overlap at sides once it is pressed into contours.*

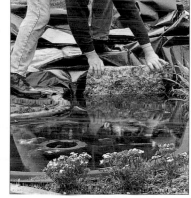

**2 LAYING THE FOUNDATION STONE**
*Place foundation stone on marginal shelf of reservoir pool, butted up hard against liner draped over pool edge. It is easiest if the stone is flat-bottomed, otherwise the pond must be drained and the stone laid level on a mortar bed on the marginal shelf.*

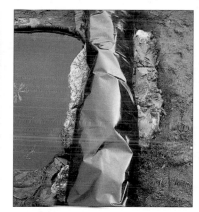

**3 SANDWICHING THE STONE**
*Pack stiff mortar between foundation stone and liner, then roll liner forwards over foundation stone, packing gap between liner and earth bank with mortar too. Sandwiched between two layers of mortar, the foundation stone will be stable and securely supported.*

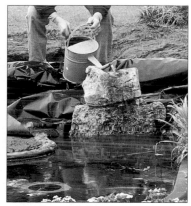

**4 SITING THE SPILL STONE**
*Partly unroll liner to expose foundation stone. Place spill stone on top of, and slightly overlapping, foundation stone. Check flow fall with a hose or watering can. Adjust until satisfactory, then mortar spill stone in place.*

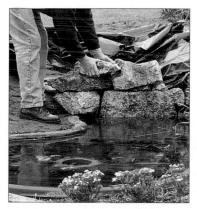

**5 BUILDING UP THE SIDE WALLS**
*Mortar first layer of side walls firmly in place on top of liner, then mortar subsequent layers onto previous layer. To prevent spillage, make sure all side wall rocks that flank the spill stone are higher than the spill stone itself.*

**6 PREVENTING WATER SEEPAGE**
*Use a can or hose to re-check water flow. To prevent water seepage, pull liner level with top of spill stone, then pleat and mortar liner behind spill stone. Wedge and mortar a second stone behind liner to secure it and protect it from light.*

**7 FINISHING STREAM AND HEADER**
*Unroll liner to cover rest of excavation. Build up side walls, arranging large rocks along stream margins and around header pool. Check levels as you work with a spirit level. Mortar a second spill stone in place at header pool outlet.*

**8 ADDING A SUBMERSIBLE PUMP**
*Lower submersible pump into reservoir pool and bury delivery pipe along one side of stream. Conceal delivery pipe where it enters header pool with a large, flat stone. Place smaller rocks of random sizes on stream bed to hide liner.*

**SEE ALSO:** Buying a Flexible Liner, pp.202–203

# MOVING WATER IN SMALL SPACES

THE PRINCIPLE OF CIRCULATING a relatively small volume of water in a small space is simple and is adaptable to a range of features. It can be used to create a rippling film of water over a millstone, a brimming urn, or a more substantial spout, such as an old-fashioned cast-iron hand pump. All have the great advantage of low maintenance and a small splash zone. As the recirculating water has little contact with sunlight, algal growth is minimized and potentially pump-blocking debris is excluded, since the reservoir pool is well covered. The largest maintenance job is regular replenishment of water to compensate for losses by evaporation.

## A WALL-MOUNTED FOUNTAIN

For patios, courtyards, or conservatories, where space is at a premium, a vertically mounted wall spout is the ideal solution. Wall-mounted spouts range from the traditional stone mask (or a less costly fibreglass facsimile) to metal sculptures in ultra-modern designs. All that is needed is a wall strong enough to take the weight of the spout, a reservoir pool (perhaps an old cistern or brick-built tank), and a circulating pump. The pump is installed in the reservoir or in a chamber to one side of it. If the fall is no more than 1.2m (4ft), a low-voltage model is perfectly adequate.

△ ADJUSTING THE WATER FLOW
*Ideally, the water issuing from the spout should fall into the centre of the reservoir pool without splashing over its sides. Adjust the flow rate as necessary using the flow adjuster on the pump outlet.*

### HOW TO INSTALL A MASK FOUNTAIN OUTLET

**1 DRILL HOLES FOR THE WATER PIPES**
*Drill 2 holes through the wall at a vertical distance apart of no more than 1.2m (4ft). This is easiest with a hammer-action drill fitted with a masonry bit of the same diameter as the copper pipe that will deliver the water. For the best visual effect, the top hole, from which the water emerges, should be just below eye level.*

**2 CUT COPPER PIPE FOR THE HOLES**
*Cut 2 lengths of copper pipe to fit the holes: the bottom length 5cm (2in) longer than the width of the wall, the top length 5cm (2in) longer than the width of the wall plus mask, with an angled cut at the outlet end. Thread them into their respective holes. The angled end of the top length of pipe will fit in the mouth of the mask.*

**3 CONNECT THE PIPES**
*At the back of the wall, fit elbow joints to each protruding copper pipe (the top joint turning down and the bottom one up). Attach an 8cm (3in) length of copper pipe to each joint, making push-fit connections watertight with plumbers' tape. Connect top and bottom pipes to one another with flexible hose and jubilee clips.*

**4 FIX THE MASK TO THE WALL**
*Mix the mortar to a stiff paste. Dampen the back of the mask to ensure good adhesion and apply mortar to the back surface, making sure that you avoid the mask's mouth opening. Spread mortar out evenly, keeping it well clear of the edges so that it does not ooze out from the margins when the mask is pressed into position.*

**5 CONNECT THE PUMP**
*Slide the mask over the upper pipe outlet, and press it firmly against the wall. Wipe away spilt mortar. The mortar takes about 36 hours to dry. Use a flexible delivery pipe to connect the pump outlet to the open end of the bottom pipe at the front of the wall, and secure it in place with jubilee clips. Site the pump in the reservoir.*

SEE ALSO: Sound and Movement, p.199; Safety First, p.199; Pumps and Power Supply, p.209

# MAKING A COBBLESTONE FOUNTAIN

The low cost and simple construction makes a cobblestone fountain an ideal project for the novice. It is one of the easiest ways of introducing moving water to the smallest space. To suit larger spaces, the scale can be increased by extending the cobbled area and its surrounds with imaginative planting. For added variety and interest, you can even adjust the cobbled area to suit the spray patterns of different fountain spouts.

## CONSTRUCTING THE FOUNTAIN

Sink a dustbin into a hole, its rim flush with the ground. Firm soil around the bin, and lay a plastic sheet over the prepared area; cut a central hole 5cm (2in) less than the bin's diameter. Introduce the pump, two-thirds fill the bin with water, and cover with mesh and cobbles.

*STYLE AND FOCUS ▷*
*A bubble fountain forms the focal point of this low-maintenance planting scheme. Plants of strong form are planted through landscaping fabric, which keeps down weeds, and a decorative shingle layer lends a stylish finish.*

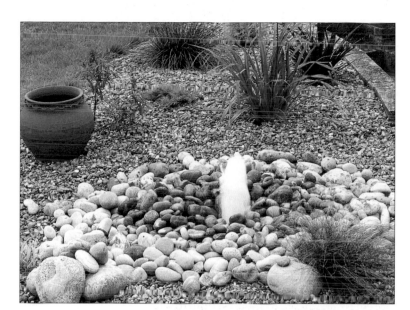

Plastic sheet catches falling water, channelling it back to the reservoir; ensure sheet extends over entire catchment area and slopes in gently towards the bin

Cobbles of varying size disguise the liner, protect it from light, and keep the outlet pipe upright

Watertight plastic dustbin forms the reservoir pool; make sure bin is level and secure by backfilling and firming down before filling with water

Galvanized wire mesh supports the cobbles, helps keep reservoir free from debris that might block the pump, and ensures a degree of safety for children and animals

The low-voltage submersible pump that powers the fountain jet is raised on a plinth to help prevent clogging by debris

### ALWAYS REMEMBER

#### COBBLES FROM THE BEACH?

In many localities, the removal of sea-washed pebbles and cobbles from the beach is both illegal and environmentally unacceptable, since it may contribute to erosion of the shore. A range of cobbles and pebbles suitable for this fountain is available from reputable builders' merchants.

# IN ORIENTAL STYLE

Japanese garden makers, the masters of simple but striking design, used natural elements of water, stone, and bamboo in ways that harmonize beautifully with living plants. The traditional plantings reveal a preference for subtlety, relying more heavily on myriad shades of green and textural contrast than on floristic brilliance. Use the diverse forms of bamboos, grasses, and ferns, perhaps with a seasonal flash of colour from evergreen azaleas, to lend unity and harmony.

## CONSTRUCTING A TSUKUBAI

The tsukubai is made simply from wood, bamboo, and a stone basin with a depression in the rim to channel outflow directly to the reservoir. A plastic sheet beneath it is all that is needed to direct any seepage to the reservoir.

*◁ SHISHI ODOSHI*
*A hollow bamboo tube is fixed with a pivot, so that the water's weight tips and empties it at regular intervals as it fills. Although now used as an elegant ornament, it functioned originally as a deer-scarer; the bamboo tube would strike a rock to make an intermittent clicking sound.*

Mesh to support cobbles and keep out debris. The water enters at a single point, so a plastic sheet beneath it is unnecessary

Hollowed-out wooden block accommodates bend in delivery pipe; vertical post and outlet are glued into drilled holes in wooden block

Delivery pipe hidden by cobbles where it exits the reservoir pool – it is then buried below ground, before entering the vertical post made of hollowed-out bamboo

Basin channels outflow through depression in rim

Low-voltage submersible pump is set on a brick plinth to avoid blockage by debris; the cable linking the pump to an electrical supply is threaded through a conduit pipe for added safety

Delivery pipe carries water from pump outlet to water outlet spout

SEE ALSO: Grasses, Bamboos, and Ferns, pp.140–141; Sound and Movement, p.199; Safety First, p.199; Installing a Fountain, pp.208–209

# THE AQUATIC ENVIRONMENT

A HEALTHY AQUATIC ENVIRONMENT, which can support fish, newts, tadpoles, and other water creatures, depends on the right balance of various types of plants that perform different functions. To keep water well oxygenated, a pool *must* have a sufficiency of submerged plants. To keep it clear and free from the algae that cause green water, it must include enough plants with floating leaves to cover at least one-third to a half of the water's surface. In any pool, it is only the moisture-loving plants that surround it that are chosen for their beauty alone. In the wild, however, moisture-loving plants mark the beginning of the transition from water to land.

## WHAT ARE AQUATICS?

An aquatic plant is any plant that can grow with its roots in water or in saturated soil. The term includes both floating-leaved plants and submerged oxygenators, as well as plants that are grown at the margins. Marginal plants are often those that are native to true bogs, such as marsh marigolds (*Caltha palustris*).

It is important to understand the distinction between true aquatics and moisture-loving plants. Many plants that are recommended for bog gardens or poolside planting are those that thrive in moist, but well-drained, soils. Unlike true aquatics, they are not adapted to function in saturated conditions. For successful plantings, the plants' needs and tolerances must be taken into account.

### TELL ME WHY

#### WHY MAKE THE DISTINCTION?

The roots of true aquatic plants are adapted to allow them to take up dissolved oxygen and nutrients from solution in water. Roots of moisture lovers, many of which also grow in ordinary garden soil, need higher levels of oxygen to function. Without access to the oxygen that is held in the spaces between soil particles, they will succumb to what is, in effect, death by drowning.

## FLOATING-LEAVED PLANTS

Floating-leaved plants can be grouped into two basic categories: those that need to root in soil (the muddy bottom or in planting baskets), such as waterlilies (*Nymphaea*), and the free-floating species, such as frogbit (*Hydrocharis morsus-ranae*).

Floating leaves shade out the sunlight that algae need to grow and proliferate. The roots, especially those of free-floating species, take up dissolved nutrients from the water, thus reducing levels available for algal growth. Floating leaves also give invaluable shade and shelter for fish, their fry, and other aquatic wildlife that forms an integral part of the aquatic ecosystem.

### OTHER RECOMMENDED SPECIES

*Aponogeton distachyos*, Cape pondweed. Deep water perennial with scented white flowers in summer.
*Azolla filiculoides*, Fairy moss. Floating perennial water fern, forming colonies of tiny, soft, pale green leaves that turn red in autumn. Useful for quick cover in new ponds, but may be invasive.
*Hydrocharis morsus-ranae*, Frogbit. Perennial floater; has heart-shaped leaves and white blooms in summer.
*Nuphar japonica*, Japanese pond lily. Rounded yellow flowers in summer above heart-shaped leaves.
*Persicaria amphibia*, Willow grass. Long, narrow, floating leaves and tiny pink flowers in summer.
*Stratiotes aloides*, Water soldier. Free-floating rosettes of semi-evergreen, spiky leaves, like pineapple tops.
*Utricularia vulgaris*, Greater bladderwort. Free-floating, bladder-like leaves trap insects; bears pouch-like yellow flowers in summer.

△ **YELLOW FLOATING HEART**
Nymphoides peltata *is a fully hardy, deciduous perennial, to 60cm (24in) across, with heart-shaped, floating leaves. Yellow flowers are held above the water throughout summer; suits depths of 15–45cm (6–18in).*

△ **WATER CLOVER**
Marsilea quadrifolia *is a fully hardy, creeping perennial with long, spreading roots. The leaves spread indefinitely across the water's surface in water up to 60cm (24in) deep; in shallow water the leaves will stand proud of the surface.*

## SUBMERGED PLANTS

Submerged plants are the workhorses of the aquatic environment; using the energy of sunlight to produce food, they release oxygen into the water as a by-product. They help clear water by competing with algae for nutrients and also process fish waste reducing the build-up of toxins.

Most submerged plants are so vigorous and easy to grow that they must be thinned out regularly. If unchecked, the pool and pump become rapidly clogged with growth, and floating-leaved plants fail to thrive against such tough competition. If floating-leaved plants succumb, algae proliferate. It always takes a little while to get the balance right, so be patient.

### PLANTS TO PROVIDE OXYGEN

| | |
|---|---|
| *Callitriche hermaphroditica* (Water starwort) | *Myriophyllum aquaticum* (Parrot feather) |
| *Ceratophyllum demersum* (Hornwort) | *Myriophyllum verticillatum* (Milfoil) |
| *Egeria densa* | *Potamogeton crispus* (Curled pondweed) |
| *Lagarosiphon major* (Curly water thyme) | |

SEE ALSO: The Moisture Lovers, pp.218–219; Planting Water Plants, pp.220–221; Caring for your Pond, pp.222–223; Water Gardens, pp.343, 353

# WATERLILIES

There are waterlilies (*Nymphaea*) to suit almost every size, depth, and style of pond. Although those described here are hardy, there are also many tropical species, for warmer climes or for conservatory pools in cold climates. Their exquisite blooms float on, or emerge just above, the water's surface, and their leaves, or pads, provide excellent shade, for clear, healthy water. Fish also appreciate their shelter.

All waterlilies need a sunny, sheltered position and water that is still, or almost so; site them well away from fountain jets or the inlets of cascades and streams.

Hardy species survive even if the surface water freezes; they die back in winter, and re-emerge in spring. Deadhead flowers and remove dying leaves regularly in the growing season. Lift, divide, and replant in late spring or early summer to avoid congestion, which reduces flowering.

△ *N.* ALBA
*With a spread of 2m (6ft) or more, the white waterlily is a vigorous species suited to a large pond 60–90cm (24–36in) deep. It has dark green pads, 30cm (12in) across, and bears many large, semi-double flowers of creamy white with golden stamens.*

△ *N.* 'AMERICAN STAR'
*Rounded, light green pads are purplish when young and red beneath. The salmon-pink flowers are star-shaped with golden orange stamens. With a spread of up to 1.5m (5ft), it thrives in depths of 30–45cm (12–18in).*

△ *N.* 'AURORA'
*This small lily bears flowers that are cream in bud, yellow on opening, and orange flecked with red when mature. With a spread of about 90cm (36in), less when confined in a barrel pool, it needs water that is 30–45cm (12–18in) deep*

△ *N.* 'ESCARBOUCLE'
*Semi-double flowers are borne amid dark green pads; the flowers have white-tipped outer petals surrounding vermilion-red inner ones and a boss of golden stamens. It will reach 1.2–1.5m (4–5ft) across, and thrives in depths of 30–60cm (12–24in).*

△ *N.* 'LAYDEKERI FULGENS'
*With large blooms of glossy burgundy red, borne from late spring though summer above dark green leaves, this adaptable waterlily is suitable for pools of any size, given a depth of 30–45cm (12–18in). Plants will reach up to 1.5m (5ft) across.*

△ *N.* 'PYGMAEA HELVOLA'
*With a spread of 60cm (24in) or less, and a need for only 15–23cm (6–9in) of water, this tiny lily is perfect for container pools. The small, semi-double, buttercup-yellow flowers are borne freely above neat, oval leaves that are heavily marked with purple.*

△ *N.* 'GONNÈRE'
*The globe-shaped, fully double flowers are a pristine, pure white and fragrant, borne above pea-green pads, which are bronzed when young. It is suitable for any size of pond, spreading to 1.2m (4ft) across, in depths of 30–45cm (12–18in).*

△ *N.* 'JAMES BRYDON'
*With a spread of 0.9–1.2m (3–4ft), this waterlily needs a depth of 30–45cm (12–18in) and is a favourite for barrels and small to medium pools. The bronze-green leaves set off double flowers of rich rose-pink to perfection.*

△ *N.* 'MARLIACEA CHROMATELLA'
*The soft yellow flowers are borne in abundance above olive-green leaves attractively mottled with purple-brown. A reliable performer for pools of any size, it spreads to 1.5m (5ft) across, in depths of 30–45cm (12–18in).*

△ *N.* 'ROSE AREY'
*Best rooted in a large planting basket or on the pool bottom, this lily reaches 1.5m (5ft) across. It bears semi-double, aniseed-scented pink flowers, above bronze-green pads, which are purple when young. Suits water 35–60cm (14–24in) deep.*

△ *N.* 'SUNRISE'
*Although hardy, this waterlily needs long, warm summers to bloom well. Semi-double, with long, narrow, bright yellow petals and clear green leaves mottled purple when young, it grows to 1.5m (5ft) across, in a water depth of 35–45cm (14–18in).*

△ *N.* 'VÉSUVE'
*In water 30–45cm (14–18in) deep, this elegant waterlily will bear its glowing, star-shaped, cherry-red blooms over very long periods above large, almost circular, dark green pads. The leaves will cover an area of about 1.2m (4ft).*

**SEE ALSO:** Planting Water Plants, pp.220–221; Caring for your Pond, pp.222–223; More Waterlilies, p.353

# THE TRANSITIONAL ZONE

UNDER NATURAL CONDITIONS, marginal plants occupy the shallow waters at a pool's edges. Many also grow with a foot in each camp, thriving equally well in water and saturated or permanently damp soil. This group of plants is invaluable for creating a seamless transition between land and water in informal pools, and giving valuable shelter for birds, amphibians, and insects. Marginals are often vigorous and sometimes invasive, but if necessary, they can be confined in planting baskets and positioned on a marginal shelf. In such a site, they can provide vertical contrast to the strong horizontal lines of more formal pools, breaking up their rigid outlines in pleasing way.

## MARGINAL PLANTS

To grow marginals successfully, it is essential to provide them with the depth of water that suits them best; some prefer as little as 2.5cm (1in) of water, others tolerate depths up to 30cm (12in), while many thrive in both wet soil and water. If they are planted in soil on the pond bottom, or in the wet soil margins, their spread into the pond will be limited by their depth tolerances. Since many are vigorous plants, however, their sideways spread can be considerable. If you choose not to use planting baskets, they may need regular thinning and cutting back.

When designing the planting scheme, try to match neighbouring plants for vigour; the rampant will rapidly out-compete less robust individuals. Large ponds will not be overwhelmed by drifts of marginals, but small ponds will be, so use planting baskets in these cases. Use strongly vertical plants, like water irises, for emphatic contrasts with horizontal ones that float on the open surface, like waterlilies.

### GOOD IDEAS

- Supplement shade cover at the pool's edges by using those with leaves that spill out across the water, like *Menyanthes trifoliata*.

- To create substantial, but confined, clumps of invasive marginals, use a large planting crate or build isolated planting beds.

- Some invasive species, like *Typha latifolia* (reedmace), have hard, pointed roots, which can pierce a pool lining. Confine them to planting crates to protect the liner.

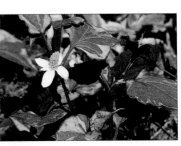

△ *ORONTIUM AQUATICUM*
Spreading by rhizomes in water up to 30cm (12in) deep, golden club is a hardy, deciduous perennial with blue-green leaves, which are silvery beneath. Flowerheads emerge above the water from late spring to midsummer. At 30–45cm (12–18in) tall by 60cm (24in) across, it is ideal for masking pool margins.

△ *HOUTTUYNIA CORDATA* 'CHAMELEON'
A spreading, hardy perennial with heart-shaped, green, pale yellow, and red leaves; its white flowers appear in spring. It is 15–60cm (6–24in) tall and thrives in both damp soil and in water 5cm (2in) deep, so it can spread indefinitely from pool margins to adjacent land. It may be invasive.

△ *ACORUS CALAMUS* 'ARGENTEOSTRIATUS'
The variegated sweet flag has iris-like leaves striped cream and green. It is hardy, thriving in water to 23cm (9in) deep. At 75cm (30in) tall, its strong, vertical lines contrast well with floating-leaved plants.

△ *MENYANTHES TRIFOLIATA*
Hardy, and thriving in wet soil or in water 15–23cm (6–9in) deep, the bog bean bears dainty, white spring flowers. Although only 23cm (9in) tall, the olive-green leaves spill out from the margins across the pool, so that land and water merge seamlessly.

△ *RANUNCULUS LINGUA* 'GRANDIFLORUS'
To 1.5m (5ft) tall, this hardy perennial flowers in early summer. Its rampant growth must be confined to a strong planting basket or it will spread indefinitely. It thrives in 15–23cm (6–9in) of still or moving water.

*MENTHA AQUATICA* △
Watermint roots in wet soil or in water to 15cm (6in) deep. An excellent soil binder at the margins of a wildlife pool, its rose-pink flowers are attractive to bees. Hardy, and up to 90cm (36in) tall and wide, it can be invasive, so thin regularly to control it.

SEE ALSO: Planting Water Plants, pp.220–221; Caring for your Pond, pp.222–223; Water Gardens, pp.343, 353

△ *LYSICHITON AMERICANUS*
*Emerging in spring, before the glossy, mid- to dark green leaves, the sculptural beauty of the bright yellow spathes is doubled when reflected in still water. Thriving in wet soil or 5cm (2in) of water, the clumps of skunk cabbage reach 1.2m (4ft) by 75cm (30in) across.*

△ *CALTHA PALUSTRIS* 'FLORE PLENO'
*In spring, the double-flowered marsh marigold bears waxy, buttercup-yellow flowers above dark green, kidney-shaped leaves. Forming clumps 25cm (10in) tall and wide, it is hardy and thrives in wet soil or very shallow water, but tolerates depths of 23cm (9in) for short periods.*

△ *PELTANDRA VIRGINICA*
*The elegant leaves of the green arrow arum form clumps up to 90cm (36in) tall. It is hardy and tolerates depths to 20cm (8in), and it makes an excellent soil binder for wet soils. Green flower spathes are borne in early summer, followed by spikes of green berries.*

△ *ZANTEDESCHIA AETHIOPICA* 'CROWBOROUGH'
*Dark green leaves and pristine summer spathes make this perennial an elegant candidate for a formal pool, growing to 1m (3ft) tall by 60cm (24in) across. At home in wet or dry soil, it is vulnerable to frost in the open garden, but hardy if submerged to 30cm (12in).*

## OTHER MARGINALS

*Acorus gramineus* 'Pusillus', Dwarf Japanese rush. Compact, evergreen perennial, to 10cm (4in) tall, with dark green leaves; ideal for container pools.
*Butomus umbellatus,* Flowering rush. Rose-pink flowers in second half of summer and very narrow, olive-green leaves; up to 1.2m (4ft) tall; best in 5–40cm (2–16in) of water in full sun, open soil or mud is more suitable than baskets.
*Cyperus longus,* Galingale. Upright stems, to 1.5m (5ft) tall, bear terminal tufts of narrow, bright green leaves and red-brown flower spikelets in late summer; grow in depths of 15–30cm (6–12in).
*Glyceria maxima* var. *variegata.* Sweet grass, Manna grass. Variegated water grass, 80cm (32in) tall, with narrow leaves, boldly striped in cream and green, sometimes flushed pink, and heads of green flowers in summer; grow in water to 15cm (6in) deep.
*Pontederia cordata,* Pickerel weed. Narrowly heart-shaped leaves and spikes of soft blue flowers in late summer; 75cm (30in) tall, in depths to 15cm (6in).
*Saururus cernuus,* Lizard's tail, Water dragon. Arching spikes of creamy white, fragrant flowers in summer above narrowly heart-shaped leaves; 23cm (9in) tall, in depths of 10–15cm (4–6in).

# WATER IRISES

Invaluable for their exquisite flowers and vertical form, water irises include *I. ensata, I. laevigata, I. pseudacorus, I. versicolor, I. virginica,* and their hybrids and cultivars. All need moist or wet soil, but most also thrive in water, 5–10cm (2–4in) deep. Site them in full sun to maximize flowering potential.

△ *IRIS PSEUDACORUS*
*Bright yellow flowers emerge from sheaves of sword-shaped blue-green leaves in summer. A vigorous, hardy colonizer of wet soils and shallow water, yellow flag makes a good soil binder for the margins of wildlife pools. Reaching up to 2m (6ft) tall, it is best used in larger features*

△ *IRIS LAEVIGATA* 'VARIEGATA'
*With soft purple-blue flowers in early summer, and fairly broad, white and green variegated leaves to prolong the show, this is an elegant specimen for the margins of a formal pool. It is hardy and grows to 80cm (32in) tall in either wet soil or water 8–10cm (3–4in) deep.*

SEE ALSO: Planting Water Plants, pp.220–221; Caring for your Pond, pp.222–223; Water Gardens, pp.343, 353

# THE MOISTURE LOVERS

THERE IS A HUGE RANGE of plants that positively thrive in damp soils. They include natural inhabitants of moist places, such as seasonally inundated meadows and stream banks, but there are many more that grow in drier soils elsewhere in the garden; given constant moisture and fertile soil, these plants grow with a vigour seldom achieved in open borders, remaining lush in summer heat. In ordinary soil, they may fade rapidly unless shaded – the reason why many border plants are classed as shade lovers. Although they play no part in the aquatic ecosystem, moisture lovers shelter wildlife and may prove a valuable food source for nectar-eating insects and seed-eating birds.

## PLANTS FOR BOG GARDENS AND POOL FRINGES

When buying moisture-loving plants, be aware that they are often described, and offered for sale, as bog plants. Only true bog natives thrive in saturated soil. All moisture lovers need drainage and will almost certainly perish in stagnant, waterlogged conditions.

Moisture lovers form the linking element between water and dry land. Formal pools may be surrounded by beds or borders and, if the soil is rich in organic matter, it will retain moisture well, so the plants will need additional water only in prolonged dry spells. If soil beds butt up to more informal, lined ponds, they often remain damp naturally, or soil can be kept moist in a specially created bog garden (see p.204).

Many moisture lovers are spreading, so adjacent clumps merge in a naturalistic way. Exploit this growth habit to create luscious schemes of contrasting textures, colours, and forms.

### OTHER MOISTURE LOVERS

*Astilbe.* Clump-forming perennials with divided leaves and plumes of white, pink, lilac, or red flowers in summer.
*Filipendula ulmaria,* Meadowsweet. Clump-forming perennial with fresh green, divided leaves and heads of creamy flowers in midsummer.
*Lobelia cardinalis,* Cardinal flower. Perennial with spires of luminous red flowers throughout summer.
*Matteuccia struthiopteris,* Ostrich fern, Shuttlecock fern. Tall, brilliant green "shuttlecocks" around a central clump of brown, fertile fronds.

△ *TROLLIUS EUROPAEUS*
The globeflower produces glossy, lemon- to mid-yellow flowers in spring above rounded, deeply divided leaves. A hardy and compact perennial to 60cm (24in) tall and 45cm (18in) across. It prefers heavy, fertile soils that never dry out, where it will thrive in sun or partial shade.

△ *MIMULUS CARDINALIS*
A hardy, creeping perennial with tubular scarlet flowers throughout summer above masses of light green foliage. It reaches 90cm (36in) in height by as much across. If it becomes untidy by late summer, cut back to encourage new growth. Grow in moist or dry soil, in sun or light shade.

△ *PERSICARIA BISTORTA* 'SUPERBA'
A vigorous, clump-forming, hardy perennial to 90cm (36in) tall, bearing dense, rounded spikes of soft pink flowers, which rise above large, ground-smothering leaves for long periods from early summer. It tolerates dry soil but romps away in moist ones and may be invasive. For sun or partial shade.

◁ *RHEUM PALMATUM* 'ATROSANGUINEUM'
A hardy architectural giant, 2m (6ft) tall, with large, deeply cut leaves, which are red-purple when young. The statuesque plumes of cerise-pink flowers arise in early summer. Best on deep, fertile, moist soils in sun or part-shade.

◁ *LIGULARIA PRZEWALSKII*
Dense, dark-stemmed spires of yellow flowers emerge above clumps of deeply cut, lobed leaves in mid- to late summer on this hardy perennial. It needs reliably moist soil, sun, and shelter from wind. Reaches 2m (6ft) in good conditions.

◁ *RODGERSIA PODOPHYLLA*
The jagged, rich green leaves, bronze when young, of this hardy perennial form bold clumps to 1.5m (5ft) tall. Creamy white flower plumes appear from midsummer. Needs reliably moist soil in sun; tolerates drier soils in partial shade.

SEE ALSO: Colour, Form, and Texture, pp.128–129; Improving Soil Types, p.142; Bog Gardens, p.p204–205

# HOSTAS

With hundreds of species and cultivars to choose from, hostas offer fabulously textured, subtly coloured foliage and bear often fragrant, bell-shaped flowers in tall, slender spikes in summer. They are hardy and thrive in deep, moist, fertile soils. Most prefer some shade, but the variegated ones usually colour best in sun. Their luscious leaves are a favourite with slugs and snails, so take steps to protect them (*see p.298*).

## OTHER RECOMMENDED SPECIES

*H.* 'Birchwood Parky's Gold' has heart-shaped, yellow-green leaves that mature to rich yellow.
*H.* 'Albomarginata' has pointed, ovate, deep green leaves margined with white.
*H. lancifolia* has ribbed, narrowly lance-shaped leaves of glossy dark green.
*H. undulata* var. *univittata* has twisted, undulating, matt olive green leaves with a central zone of creamy white.

### △ *H.* 'HADSPEN BLUE'
The mounds of heart-shaped and veined, grey blue leaves form clumps 25cm (10in) tall by 60cm (24in) wide. In summer, this hosta produces purple-stemmed spires of bell-shaped, mauve-grey flowers.

### △ *H. SIEBOLDIANA* VAR. *ELEGANS*
The bold clumps of large, heart shaped, deeply wrinkled, grey-blue leaves form mounds 1m (3ft) tall by 1.2m (4ft) wide. In summer, this hosta bears pale lilac-grey flowers in leafy spikes.

### △ *H. VENTRICOSA* 'AUREOMARGINATA'
This hosta bears tall spires of purple flowers in late summer above the deeply ribbed, glossy leaves; these are irregularly margined creamy white, and they form clumps 50cm (20in) tall by 1m (3ft) across.

### △ *H.* 'FRANCES WILLIAMS'
The blue-green leaves, broadly margined with yellow-green, are deeply puckered; they form clumps 60cm (24in) tall by 1m (3ft) wide. The elegant spikes of grey-white flowers are borne in early summer.

# PRIMROSES

There are approximately 400 primrose (*Primula*) species, some of which are native to damp meadows, streamsides, and bogs. They are ideal candidates for waterside plantings. All of them look particularly lovely in informal drifts at the poolside or on streambanks, while those with drumstick-type flowers or candelabra-like tiers of bloom also blend surprisingly well in more formal settings. They are hardy, moisture-loving perennials, but do need some drainage, since they will not tolerate stagnant conditions. A deep, fertile, neutral to acid soil enriched with organic matter is best, and although most thrive in partial shade, they grow well in sun provided that the soil never dries out completely. Many will self-seed where conditions suit, forming extensive colonies with time. All examples listed below are hardy to frost.

### △ *P. BEESIANA*
This species has basal rosettes of long, narrow, fresh green leaves and sturdy, white-mealy stems bearing whorls of red-pink, yellow-eyed flowers in summer. It is 60cm (24in) tall and may remain evergreen, or almost so, in winter, or it will die back to resting buds to re-emerge in spring.

### △ *P. BULLEYANA*
The basal rosettes of narrow, toothed, semi-evergreen leaves on this species give rise to stout and long-lasting candelabra-like spires of flowers. Individual flowers are crimson in bud and when newly open, but as they mature they fade to a rich, deep orange. To 60cm (24in) tall.

### △ *P. DENTICULATA* VAR. *ALBA*
The drumstick primulas are robust species and may self-seed where conditions are to their liking. The globular heads of small flowers are white in this variety, but the others come in many shades of purple and mauve. Flowers appear from spring to summer. To 45cm (18in) tall.

### △ *P. FLORINDAE*
The giant cowslip reaches 1.2m (4ft) in height in good conditions. It is one of the most elegant primroses, with strong, upright stems ending in a cluster of nodding, bell-shaped yellow flowers, which are fragrant and coated with a powdery white meal. The blooms appear in summer.

### △ *P. JAPONICA* 'MILLER'S CRIMSON'
The basal leaf rosettes of this primrose give rise to stout stems to 45cm (18in) tall, bearing whorls of dusky crimson flowers from late spring to early summer. The species has flowers of various shades from white to deep red-purple.

### △ *P. PROLIFERA*
A vigorous, rosette-forming species producing upright stems to 60cm (24in) tall with whorls of pale to golden yellow, occasionally dull violet flowers in early summer, clothed in a mealy, white powder. They are fragrant, and they look and smell fabulous when planted en masse.

SEE ALSO: Buying Good Plants, pp.146–147; Planting Perennials, p.148; Planting Water Plants, pp.220–221; More Hostas, p.322

# PLANTING WATER PLANTS

BY MID-SPRING, garden centres are usually well-stocked with aquatic plants and the weather – and water – is usually warm enough for them to establish without check. If planting in baskets, use specially formulated aquatic composts or, as second best, unfertilized garden soil. *Never* use ordinary potting composts, they are too rich and nutrients will leach into the water to feed algae. Unless you choose a fine-mesh basket, line baskets with hessian, so that soil does not fall out before rooting takes place. Always select a basket to suit the size of the plant; if too small, growth will be restricted and plants, especially taller marginals, may become top-heavy and unstable.

## PLANTING TECHNIQUES

Simply place free-floating plants directly onto the surface of the pond. For large pools, bundles of submerged oxygenators can be just dropped in, but in small pools, as with deep-water and marginal plants, they are more easily managed in containers.

Position containers by hand or, if you have a helper, thread two pieces of string through the basket rim and, standing on opposite sides of the pool, use the string as "handles" to lower the basket into place.

### A POND DESIGNED FOR PLANTS

The best design for a naturalistic pond includes levels of varying depth to accommodate the differing needs of aquatic and marginal plants. Soil beds or bog gardens butt up to the pool margin, allowing plantings to merge naturally with each other and to disguise the edges.

△ GOOD HYGIENE
*Before introducing new plants to the pond, rinse them in clean water and inspect them thoroughly. Look for and remove any jelly-like snail eggs and inspect any insects so that you do not introduce any harmful ones, such as great diving beetles, which may attack fish. Remove all dead and rotten material.*

DEEP-WATER PLANTS ▷
*Line the basket and fill three-quarters full with dampened soil or aquatic compost. Make a planting hole so that the buds sit 4cm (1½in) below the rim. Add more soil so the plant ends up at the same depth as it was in its original pot. Firm gently so as not to damage new shoots. Top with a 1cm (½in) layer of pea shingle.*

◁ OXYGENATORS
*Line the basket and fill to just below the rim with damp compost. Firm lightly and make evenly spaced holes, 5cm (2in) deep. Insert a plant bundle into each and firm in with your finger tips. Top with a 1cm (½in) layer of pea shingle. Trim off excess hessian. A 20cm (8in) basket will hold 5 plant bundles.*

As a watertight barrier prevents water moving into the surrounding soil, beds can be filled with ordinary soil to allow planting of a diverse range of non-moisture-loving plants

THE RIGHT DEPTH ▷
*Brick piers make invaluable depth adjusters. Leave permanently in place to bring marginal plants up to their preferred depth. For deep-water plants, remove bricks one-by-one to lower gradually to the specified depth as new leaves appear and stems elongate.*

Brick plinths are used as depth adjusters, either to bring deep-water plants up to their preferred depth, or as temporary measures to allow young deep-water plants to be lowered gradually to the appropriate depth as they grow

An alternative for adjusting planting depths is to incorporate brick-built planting beds; these are mortared in place onto the liner and filled with aquatic planting compost – plants are thus confined, but less restricted than in planting baskets

SEE ALSO: Bog Gardens, pp.204–205; The Aquatic Environment, pp.214–215; The Transitional Zone, pp.216–217; The Moisture Lovers, pp.218–219

△ THE PEA-SHINGLE TOPPING
*Top-dressing baskets with a layer of pea shingle or pebbles performs several functions. A 1cm (½in) layer will prevent soil drifting from the surface and muddying the water. It also prevents disturbance of the soil surface by fish. A 2.5cm (1in) deep layer adds weight and stability for top-heavy marginals and takes up less soil space than bricks or stones set at the bottom of the basket. It is also decorative.*

△ PLANTING IN MOIST OR WET SOIL
*Dig a hole in the soil bed large enough to accommodate the root ball comfortably. Slide the plant gently out of its pot, and place it in the hole so that it is at the same depth as it was in its container. Gently firm the soil around the roots with your fingers, taking care not to compact the soil or to damage any growing points or soft young growth. Thoroughly soak the entire area with water.*

# BUYING HEALTHY PLANTS

Aquatic plants are sold bare-rooted or in containers. Containerized plants are useful for instant effects, but in good conditions, smaller and less expensive, bare-rooted ones quickly catch up. It is often worth paying more for larger waterlilies to get flowers in the first year. Make sure that plants are clean, plump, and dense, paying special attention to roots and tubers; they must be fat and sound to nourish the young plant until it is well-established and able to make its own food. Keep plants cool and moist at all times, especially when transporting; double bagging will reduce the risk of leakage.

Plant is compact with lots of young leaves; foliage is glossy and dark green with no evidence of pests or diseases

△ CONTAINERIZED MARGINAL
*Buying containerized plants, here Caltha palustris, gives them a head start and avoids root disturbance, but make sure the container is large enough to allow for at least one season's growth, otherwise transfer to a larger pot before introducing to the pool.*

Small pockets of saturated soil can accommodate marginal plants, but for moisture lovers, the liner must be perforated to allow drainage

Moisture lovers suck water from the pond; for extensive bogs, or if large moisture lovers are grown, separate these areas from the pool to avoid excessive moisture loss by wicking (see p.204)

Marginal shelves can be created at depths to suit marginal plants (here, *Caltha palustris*); the shelves must be broad enough to keep planting baskets stable, and keep baskets within arm's reach, so lifting plants to tend or divide them is easy

Tubers are firm and plump with plenty of growth buds; new growth emerging from them is healthy and vigorous

GOOD EXAMPLE

BARE-ROOTED PLANTS ▷
*Bare-rooted plants are often sold as offsets, newly divided from their parent plant. If sound and healthy, they grow quickly in good conditions and are less costly than containerized plants. Make sure the root or tuber is plump with plenty of growth buds or young folded leaves emerging from them.*

Stems are limp and soggy, and leaves are badly discoloured with too few buds or emerging young leaves to replace them

POOR EXAMPLE

A deep zone provides a suitable niche for floating-leaved plants, like waterlilies, that thrive in the full depth of water; it may also provide a rooting zone for submerged oxygenators, which need the buoyancy of water to support their soft stems in order to function most efficiently

## TELL ME WHY

### IS IT A BASKET CASE?

Except in very large, informal ponds, baskets or crates make deep-water plants more manageable than in a layer of bottom soil. Baskets are invaluable for restricting the spread of vigorous plants and can be lifted, when necessary, to divide and re-pot plants as they outgrow their containers. Containerized marginals can be grouped and moved about easily until the desired effect is achieved.

SEE ALSO: The Aquatic Environment, pp.214–215; The Transitional Zone, pp.216–217; The Moisture Lovers, pp.218–219; Caring for your Pond, pp.222–223

# CARING FOR YOUR POND

REGULAR POND CARE is essential to maintain a healthy aquatic environment with clear, oxygenated water and thriving plants. Regular renewal of plants, by division in spring, will keep them healthy and trouble-free during summer, allowing them to play their part in controlling algal growth. Algae are the first species to proliferate in spring, and pond water will "green up" temporarily until the ecosystem resumes equilibrium. Try to complete any tasks involving entering the pond in one go, to minimize disturbance to the pond and its denizens, and take great care to remove decaying material during the season. Finally, take time to relax, observe, and enjoy!

## ROUTINE TASKS

Throughout summer, remove dying foliage and spent flowerheads before they can rot and pollute the water. Maintain the planting balance by thinning submerged and floating plants as necessary. Maintain vigorous growth of waterlilies and other containerized plants by feeding in late spring and midsummer with a slow-release, pond-plant fertilizer. These come in tablets or sachets, which avoid nutrients leaking into the water and promoting algae.

△ REMOVING BLANKET WEED
*This filamentous algae is an opportunist colonizer that deprives the water of oxygen and chokes other plants. The easiest way to remove it is simply to wind it around a stick; the filaments adhere firmly to the stick and each other.*

△ PROTECTING POND LIFE
*Excess oxygenators should be thinned as necessary by raking them from the surface. They form a niche for insect life and other beneficial creatures; drape thinned weed on the edge for a while, so they can escape back into the water.*

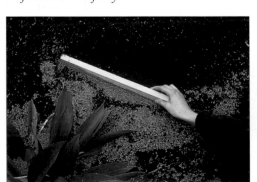

△ REMOVING SURPLUS FLOATING PLANTS
*Surplus floating plants, like duckweed, obscure the water surface, reducing light for submerged plants. Skim off with a piece of wood, held horizontally just below the surface. Dispose of duckweed carefully; it spreads like wildfire.*

△ REMOVING DECAYING LEAVES
*Decaying plant material affects water chemistry, and it may cloud the water and have detrimental effects on other pond life. Cut decaying material away with a sharp knife. If yellowing is excessive, lift and check the plant for disease.*

## PREPARING FOR WINTER

As the growing season draws to a close, lift tender and half-hardy plants, trim off any dead leaves, and store the plants in containers of damp sand in a frost-free place. Keep covered with a perforated plastic sheet so that air can enter and plants do not dry out. Treat any plantlets needed for propagation in the same way.

Take precautions to protect submerged plants and fish if water freezes over (*see below*). Bog plants and moisture lovers can be protected from freezing with a thick mulch of clean, dry straw in late autumn.

### ALWAYS REMEMBER

#### ICE FORCE ZERO

An ice sheet protects plants beneath it from freezing, but also places pressure on the pond sides as it expands and causes a build-up of noxious gases beneath it. Place floating balls on the surface to absorb expansion. Melt ice gently to allow gases to escape. Never smash ice; shock waves can kill fish.

△ NETTING PONDS IN AUTUMN
*Leaves falling from surrounding plants fall to the bottom and decompose, forming harmful by-products. Secure fine-mesh netting with bricks across the top of the pool to prevent this. Remove the netting every week or so, collect and compost fallen leaves, and replace the net securely.*

SEE ALSO: The Aquatic Environment, pp.214–215

# THINNING AND DIVIDING PLANTS

Water plants are propagated in several ways. Some, such as *Eichhornia crassipes*, produce plantlets from the rootstock or on runners, often detaching themselves and sinking to the bottom. They spend winter there as dormant buds, emerging in spring. Others, like waterlilies and irises, have roots, tubers, or rhizomes that must be physically separated. Provided that each division has a portion of root and a few shoots, they can grow independently of the parent plant.

For most water plants, the best time to do this is in late spring to early summer when the water warms up and plants resume active growth. Low water temperatures can cause newly divided plants to rot. When dividing, always discard the older growth in favour of the new; this rejuvenates plants and restores flowering potential, and there may be material left over to increase your own stock or give to friends.

## TELL ME WHY

### WHY SHOULD PLANTS BE DIVIDED?

Most water plants grow rapidly and, sooner or later, outgrow the site. This can happen in a single season in small pools, so division is necessary to relieve congestion. Overcrowded plants thrust leaves out of the water instead of floating on it, and flowering will also be impaired. Dividing and replanting only young growth renews productivity and restores pond health.

## THINNING OXYGENATING PLANTS

**1 SPRING AND AUTUMN**
*Thin oxygenating plants at the beginning and end of the growing season. Taking great care to avoid contact with the liner, rake out excess oxygenators. Lift out containerized oxygenators and trim back some stems with a knife.*

**2 LEAVE SUFFICIENT OXYGENATORS IN PLACE**
*To fulfil their oxygenating function, it is better to thin little and often, which makes it easier for the planting balance to resume equilibrium. Remember to drape weed on the side before removal — ideally to the compost heap.*

## REJUVENATING WATERLILIES BY DIVISION

**1 LIFT AND DIVIDE THE RHIZOME**
*Lift the plant and rinse off the soil. Trim off all opened leaves and cut the old, least productive sections of the rhizome away with a knife. Retain the youngest sections with plenty of emerging shoots, and discard the old.*

**2 REPLANT THE DIVISIONS**
*Trim long and coarse roots and replant with the crown just below soil level. Top with shingle and lower gradually into the pond. Large plants often yield 2 or more new plants; each division must have at least 2 or 3 growth buds.*

△ **SEPARATING PLANTLETS AND RUNNERS**
*In spring, separate vigorous young plantlets from the parent, either by snapping them off cleanly, as shown here with Eichhornia crassipes, or by severing the connecting runner (creeping stem) with a sharp knife. Floating plants can then simply be returned to the surface of the pool; they quickly generate a root system of their own. If plants are containerized, pot up the young plants in new soil and return to the appropriate depth.*

## DIVIDING OTHER RHIZOMATOUS PLANTS

**1 LIFT THE PARENT PLANT**
*Uproot the plant (here, Iris pseudacorus) and rinse the roots clean of soil. Clumps can be pulled or cut apart; separate out vigorous rhizomes, each portion with a number of fibrous roots, shoots, and strong young leaves.*

**2 TRIMMING THE RHIZOME**
*Neatly trim the rhizome with a sharp knife, removing any portions that do not have new shoot growth. Trim all top-growth back to 8–10cm (3–4in) so that when replanted, it will not form a "sail" and be unstable in the wind.*

**3 REPLANTING THE RHIZOMES**
*Trim roots so they fit comfortably in the new pot. Replant at the same depth as before; trickle soil around the roots rather than pressing them into a planting hole. Top-dress with shingle. Return to the pool with the trimmed top-growth just above water level.*

SEE ALSO: Dividing Perennials, p.163

# HERBS IN THE GARDEN AND THEIR USES

## CREATING A HERB GARDEN

HERBS HAVE BEEN PRIZED FOR THOUSANDS of years for their culinary, cosmetic, and curative uses, but many are equally valued for their ornamental qualities. While herbs are rarely showy plants, having pale or small flowers, plenty have handsome foliage and most are worth growing for their scent alone. Even in a tiny garden, it is worth including a few herbs – whether intermingled in a border, in pots tiered on garden steps, or ranked along a kitchen windowledge; or create your own dedicated herb garden with a collection of favourite herbs, perhaps laid out in a formal, geometric pattern of colour-themed beds, or in an informal, relaxed group.

### PLOTS DEVOTED TO HERBS

Making a dedicated herb garden may sound adventurous, but it can be as simple as you like; in fact, fussy or complicated designs are best avoided. For a formal plot, sketch out your plan on squared paper, then mark it out on the ground with pebbles or string. Low and creeping herbs are just right for formal plots, while shrubby and evergreen herbs, such as various forms of thyme, lavender, sage, and wall germander, provide year-round interest.

In an informal plot, the design comes from the plants themselves, but take care that informality does not slip into chaos, balancing plants of low or creeping habit, such as some thymes and mints, with more sculptural or upright shapes, such as bay or viburnum. There are fewer restrictions than in a formal layout, so include plants of varying heights and tall herbs such as fennel or angelica.

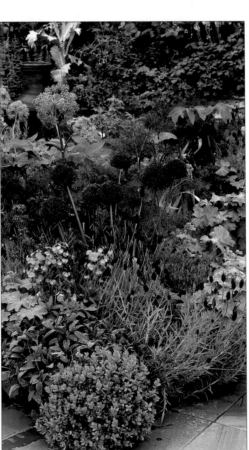

◁ FORMAL LAYOUT
*Even a small area will accommodate a simple geometric layout. Use low-growing herbs and repeat key plants to give emphasis to the overall design. Add height in the centre with a pedestal urn or large pot.*

△ INFORMAL DESIGN
*Herb gardens do not have to be formal, but they should be carefully planned: design your plant compositions as in other border schemes, considering echoes and contrasts of texture, form, and shape alongside colour.*

### COLOUR THEMING

As well as colour from flowers, many herbs have handsomely coloured foliage, which is an asset in a formal herb garden or a mixed border. Restricting the colour scheme creates a sense of cohesion and harmony, and highlights the shape and pattern of the herb-garden layout.

**PURPLE-BRONZE**
PURPLE BASIL
*Ocimum basilicum* 'Purple Ruffles'

**GOLDEN YELLOW**
GOLDEN MARJORAM
*Origanum vulgare* 'Aureum'

**SILVER-GREY**
COTTON LAVENDER
*Santolina chamaecyparissus*

### HERBS FOR COLOURFUL LEAVES

GOLDEN YELLOW
Golden lemon balm (*Melissa officinalis* 'Aurea')
Golden marjoram (*Origanum vulgare* 'Aureum')
Golden thyme (*Thymus × citriodorus* 'Aureus')
Gold-variegated sage (*Salvia officinalis* 'Icterina')

PURPLE-BRONZE
Bronze fennel (*Foeniculum vulgare* 'Purpureum')
Eau de Cologne mint (*Mentha × piperita* f. *citrata*)
Purple basil (*Ocimum basilicum* var. *purpurascens*)
Purple sage (*Salvia officinalis* Purpurascens Group)

SILVER-GREY
Cotton lavender (*Santolina chamaecyparissus*)
Curry plant (*Helichrysum italicum*)
Lavender (many: try *Lavandula* 'Sawyers')
Southernwood (*Artemisia abrotanum*)

SEE ALSO: Garden Styles, pp.122–123; Herbs and their Uses, pp.226–227

# GROWING HERBS IN MIXED BEDS AND BORDERS

Many herbs are ideal candidates for growing among other plants, in mixed or herbaceous borders, or in a kitchen garden. Include herbs with coloured leaves for dense hummocks of colour and shape: try purple sage (*Salvia officinalis* Purpurascens Group), blue-grey rue (*Ruta*), or gold-variegated ginger mint (*Mentha × gracilis* 'Variegata'). Some also have colourful flowers that are more than worthy of the border, such as the purple spikes of hyssop (*Hyssopus officinalis*) or the cheerful orange of pot marigolds (*Calendula officinalis*).

Tall herbs such as angelica and evening primrose (*Oenothera biennis*) provide vertical interest. Some herbs such as bay (*Laurus nobilis*) and lemon verbena (*Aloysia triphylla*) may even be trained as standards, adding a focal point at the centre of a bed.

In an open border, the play of light on and through foliage can be stimulating visually; watch to see how the light falls, especially at the beginning and end of the day, and site plants such as bronze fennel (*Foeniculum vulgare* 'Purpureum') or red bergamot (*Monarda didyma*), with its blood-red veined leaves, to take advantage of it.

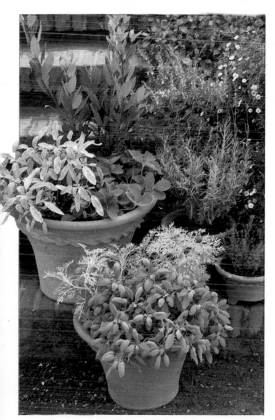

△ **BEAUTIFUL BORAGE**
*With its bright blue flowers and buds and stems haloed with fine hairs, borage (Borago officinalis) is a fine plant for the border. Plant it where the delicate hair-fringed heads will be lit by the sun from behind.*

◁ **BORDER WITH INTERMINGLED HERBS**
*Here, green and bronze fennel serve as a link, frothing in waves between the other plants and providing textural mass. A golden hop (Humulus lupulus 'Aureus') adds a bold splash at the back.*

# HERBS IN CONTAINERS

You don't need a grand garden or even a garden at all to grow herbs in containers: a small corner of a patio, balcony, or roof terrace is fine. For the herbs you like to use most often, site a strawberry planter (in which you can also grow mint, thyme, oregano, or marjoram), tub, or trough where it will be easily accessible.

Make your choices so that the plantings will be decorative as well as useful. Go for plants with coloured leaves rather than the plain green; the flavour is often just as good. Try using a bay tree (*Laurus nobilis*) trained as a standard to provide vertical emphasis as a focal point, or a prostrate rosemary (*Rosmarinus officinalis* 'Prostratus') to spread over the edge of a tub, releasing its scent as you brush past.

◁ **POTTED HERB GARDEN**
*A flight of steps hosts a simple group of terracotta pots containing a miniature herb garden, with sages, bay, rosemary, southernwood, and alpine strawberries.*

Growing herbs in pots allows you to provide varying conditions for a range of plants – separating herbs that enjoy sun and good drainage, for example, from those that prefer shade and moisture. Chervil, chives, parsley, rock hyssop, compact marjoram (*Origanum vulgare* 'Compactum'), and thymes will make good companion plants without the danger of one dominating the others.

## GOOD IDEAS

• If combining different herbs in a single container, make sure you choose those that require the same growing conditions.

• Add height to a collection of containers with a chimney pot planted with trailing nasturtiums or a cane wigwam covered with a climbing golden hop.

• Mint (*Mentha*) is always best grown alone in a pot because it is rampant and invasive.

SEE ALSO: Containers and Raised Beds, pp.166–183; Growing Requirements, p.228; How to Plant up a Strawberry Pot, p.230; Always Remember box, p.231

# HERBS AND THEIR USES

HERBS MAY BE ANNUALS, PERENNIALS, shrubs, or even trees, but what defines them as herbs and distinguishes them from other plants is their usefulness. Many herbs — the ones most people are familiar with — are invaluable for cooking, and some possess medicinal properties, which are exploited on a commercial scale as well as being used for home herbal remedies. Others are prized purely for their uplifting scents, whether produced in the garden or captured in a herbal pot-pourri to perfume the house. Some types of herb provide the basis for home-made cosmetic and beauty preparations, and yet others may be employed for a variety of household uses.

## A CULINARY PATCH

Fresh herbs are used in cuisines from all over the world to add an incomparable flavour to an enormous range of dishes. Adding herbs lends more taste to bland dishes and helps to reduce the need for salt in food. Certain herbs seem to be just made to go with particular foods: rosemary with lamb, basil with tomatoes, dill with salmon, coriander with curries.

If you have space, it is worth creating an area specifically for culinary herbs sited as near to the house as possible for ease of harvesting; if your culinary patch is too far away, you may well find you don't pick and use the herbs. Alternatively, you may prefer to include them as part of a kitchen garden, if you have one.

When planning your culinary bed, bear in mind which herbs you use in quantity — for example, you may want to allot more space for chives and parsley if you use them for garnishing as well as flavouring; either of these would make an attractive edging for a culinary patch.

A raised bed is ideal, reducing the need to bend for harvesting, and it is easy to provide the right conditions for your

plants. Alternatively, grow your most-used herbs in containers by the back door.

■ **Flavour comes first** for culinary herbs, but your herb patch can be decorative, too. Include golden, silver, and variegated forms of some herbs for extra colour and site shrubby herbs in key positions to provide structure and shape.

■ **Edible flowers** are an unusual addition to a conventional herb patch. Grow orange and yellow pot marigolds (*Calendula officinalis*) and nasturtiums (*Tropaeolum majus*) for flowers to brighten up a salad.

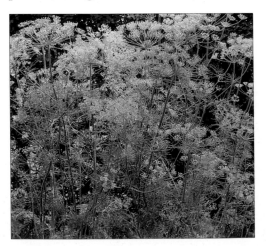

◁ **DANDY DILL**
*The striking form of dill in the border is only one of its attractions — both the leaves and the seeds are used in cooking. Dill is an annual, but it self-seeds easily in the open garden.*

**BOUQUET GARNI** ▷
*A bundle of herbs tied together and placed in soups, stews, or casseroles while cooking will lend extra flavour to the dish. This bouquet, for flavouring game, consists of rosemary, marjoram, lemon balm, and orange peel.*

◁ **CHEERY CHIVES**
*As well as providing tasty stems for using in salads or as a garnish, chives give a lift to the front of a summer border with their colourful, globular flowerheads.*

### HERBS FOR COOKING

If you have even a small sunny space in the garden, it really is worth growing your own herbs for use in the kitchen. As well as the ordinary species, look out for other forms that may be more visually attractive, for example those with variegated foliage, especially if growing herbs mixed in the border with other plants or in containers in a prominent position.

Basil (*Ocimum basilicum*)*
Bay (*Laurus nobilis*)
Chives (*Allium schoenoprasum*) and try garlic chives (*A. tuberosum*)
Coriander (*Coriandrum sativum*)
Dill (*Anethum graveolens*)
Fennel (*Foeniculum vulgare*)
French tarragon (*Artemisia dracunculus*)*
Lemon balm (*Melissa officinalis*)
Lovage (*Levisticum officinale*; this is a tall, dramatic plant good for the back of a border)
Marjoram (*Origanum vulgare*)
Mint (*Mentha spicata*, spearmint, is the classic culinary mint, but there are lots to choose from)
Parsley (*Petroselinum crispum*) also try the flat-leaved or continental parsley called 'Italian'
Rosemary (*Rosmarinus officinalis*)
Sage (*Salvia officinalis*)
Thyme (*Thymus vulgare* — lots to choose from)
Winter savory (*Satureja montana*) and try the less hardy summer savory (*S. hortensis*) which has a finer flavour

* not hardy

SEE ALSO: Raised Beds, pp.180–183

# AROMATIC HERBS

Culinary herbs usually have delicious fragrances as well as flavours, but there are other herbs that are valued for their scent alone. For example, the curry plant (*Helichrysum italicum*) is not used for making curries – although the leaves are mildly flavoured and may be added to rice – but its spicy, curry smell makes a good contrast to other aromatic herbs on a hot day.

Position scented plants by paths, gates, doors, and garden seats, where anyone passing will brush against them and be treated to a wave of scent: use lavender to form miniature hedges on either side of a path, or grow lemon balm in clumps by the front gate so that you can crush the leaves as you enter. For the ultimate in scented relaxation, grow aromatics such as lavender, rosemary, artemisia, and thyme near a hammock.

■ **Create a chamomile lawn**. The non-flowering *Chamaemelum nobile* 'Treneague' is often used (*see p.88*) because this form is naturally low-growing and there are no flowers which would otherwise need to be trimmed off. It is less hard-wearing than grass, so is not suitable for a main lawn.

■ **Remove a paving slab** or a few bricks to create a planting space in a patio for aromatic herbs, so you can rub the leaves between your fingers as you sit outside.

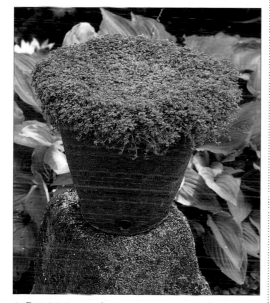

△ SCENT IN THE AIR
*The strongly scented Corsican mint (Mentha requienii) forms a low mound or mat; growing it in a container raised above ground will bring the aromas nearer to nose level.*

# MEDICINAL, COSMETIC, AND HOUSEHOLD USES

Herbs have been valued for their healing properties for thousands of years, yet it is only relatively recently that Western medicine is once again starting to recognize the benefits that herbs have to offer. In the pharmaceuticals industry, herbal derivatives are used frequently: the principal active constituent of one of the most used drugs in the world – aspirin – is salicylic acid, derived from willow (*Salix*).

For the knowledgeable, the herb garden can be a medicine cabinet containing home-made remedies to treat a number of minor ailments: mint, for example, is renowned for its antiseptic properties, but it is also a mild anaesthetic and helps to alleviate indigestion – try a cup of peppermint tea after a heavy meal to appreciate its effects.

Some herbs are used to make beauty preparations, such as skin lotions and shampoos. *Aloe vera* is grown commercially for its soothing, anti-inflammatory properties used in skin products. At home, there are many products you can make: infuse rosemary in hot water for a rinse to bring a shine to dark hair.

Many aromatic herbs have uses in the home. Strew artemisia in wardrobes to discourage clothes moths, and mint to

△ HEALING TROUGH
*If you don't have space for a herb garden, you can grow herbs just as well in containers, and even windowboxes. This trough contains a variety of medicinal plants*

deter mice. Lavender was used to scent linen and is still made into scented sachets.

■ **Tuck the dried leaves** of sweet woodruff (*Galium odoratum*) between sheets and linens to give it the scent of new-mown hay.

■ **Fix the fragrance** of pot-pourri with some powdered orris root (*Iris* 'Florentina').

■ **Don't suffer sleeplessness**: make a relaxing sleep pillow from muslin stuffed with dried hops and lavender.

▽ SOOTHING TEA
*Fennel and lemon balm may be infused together to produce a delicious and relaxing hot drink.*

SEE ALSO: Planting in Gravel, p.63; Alternative Lawns, p.88

# MAINTENANCE, HARVESTING, AND PRESERVING

ONE OF THE PLEASURES OF HERBS is that they do not, in general, rely on a constant round of watering, pruning, feeding, and mulching in order to thrive – quite the contrary, in fact, since many herbs hail from regions with low rainfall and poor soil. Certain routine tasks will help to keep them in good shape, however, but these are not too taxing. Harvesting your own home-grown herbs is a joy rather than a chore as you handle the aromatic foliage and snip fresh sprigs for cooking or use in the home. Enjoy them freshly picked or capture their scent and flavour for later use by preserving them in various ways – by drying, freezing, or infusing in oil or vinegar.

## ROUTINE CARE AND HARVESTING

The maintenance of herbs is generally straightforward and undemanding. Routine care largely consists of cutting back plants in spring and summer to encourage healthy growth, and tidying up dormant plants in winter. A herb's requirements depend partly on which type of plant it is – whether an annual, perennial, or shrub, for example.

■ **Annuals and biennials** (e.g. parsley and dill). These flower, set seed, and die all in the same year. You can harvest seed to sow the following season. Dill also self-seeds. Grow tender herbs raised annually, such as basil and coriander, under glass following instructions on the seed packet before planting them out.

■ **Perennials** (e.g. bergamot, or *Monarda didyma*, and mint). Regularly picking either leaves or sprigs for use will help to keep the plants shapely. Divide perennials periodically (*see p.231*) when the centre of the clump has become tired and unproductive. In summer, after rain, apply a mulch around plants that love moisture both to retain water and improve the soil.

△ **FRESH FROM THE GARDEN**
*This home-grown harvest includes bay, rosemary, parsley, basil, and sage, laid in a trug to prevent damage before preserving. Use scissors or secateurs to make clean cuts.*

■ **Shrubs** (e.g. lavender, rosemary, hyssop, and sage). As with perennials, regular harvesting both maintains a bushy shape and stimulates new growth. Trim off the flowerheads after flowering. Lavender will not regrow if you cut too hard back into old wood; prune in mid-spring, making sure some green growth remains on each stem. Picking of sprigs should be enough to keep thyme plants in shape.

■ **Do not take too much foliage** from a single plant at any one time. Have several plants of herbs you use in quantity, so you can pick here and there from the clumps.

■ **Angelica stems,** to be crystallized for cake decoration, should be cut while still young and tender, long before flowering.

■ **If picking rue,** wear gloves: for some people, the skin reacts badly to sunshine after contact with the plant.

## TELL ME HOW

### WHEN AND HOW SHOULD HERBS BE HARVESTED?

Pick herbs for using fresh as you need them. This is the process for most evergreen herbs, but in the case of bay some cooks prefer the stronger flavour of the dried leaves.

For preserving, harvest herbs on a dry, fine morning after the dew has evaporated, but before hot sun has burned off some of the essential oils. The oil content should be at its peak just before the herb comes into flower.

When collecting seed from dill, fennel, or coriander, loosely fasten paper bags over the flowerheads as they start to ripen, to make capturing the seed easier.

**FLAVOUR AT YOUR FINGERTIPS** ▷
*Growing herbs in pots on a well-lit windowsill ensures they are conveniently at hand whenever you need them. With care, potting up herbs can provide you with a winter supply.*

SEE ALSO: Maintaining Border Plants, pp.154–155; Increasing Border Plants, pp.162–163; Routine Care and Maintenance, pp.178–179; Increasing Herbs, p.231

# DRYING HERBS

Air-drying is the easiest way of preserving most herbs, although soft-leaved herbs such as mint are better frozen (*see box, below right*). Spread out sprigs, leaves, flowers, or seedheads in a single layer on a rack and leave in a warm, airy place to dry. Alternatively, tie sprigs or stems in small bunches and hang upside-down in a warm, dry – but not too sunny – spot. The drying process should take no more than 48 hours – if the leaves turn black or show any mould, the process has been too slow and the herb should be discarded.

Once completely dry, strip the leaves or the flowers (chamomile flowers, for example, may be infused to make herbal tea) from the stems and discard the stalks. Crush the leaves thoroughly between your hands and store them in airtight dark glass or ceramic containers (they will fade rapidly if kept in clear glass jars). Dried herbs will not keep their flavour indefinitely, so always start afresh the following season with a new batch.

◁ **AIR-DRYING**
*Spread out the herbs on a mesh-covered rack, and leave them in a warm place until dry. This should take 1 or 2 days. Alternatively, hang them up in bunches to dry.*

It is possible to control, and speed up, the drying process by placing the herbs in a microwave or in an oven heated to a very low temperature – 50–60°C (120–140°F). Microwave-drying should take about 2 or 3 minutes; oven-drying is really only suitable for underground plant parts that need lengthy drying, and may take 2 or 3 hours. The moisture content of herbs varies considerably, so you will need to experiment with timing for best results.

## HERBS FOR DRYING

The following list is just a selection of some of the most popular herbs that may be dried successfully. Most are culinary herbs while some, such as lemon balm and bergamot, are used to make herbal teas, and others, such as southernwood and lavender, are used in the home, in pot-pourri for example.

Alecost (*Tanacetum balsamita*)  L
Bay (*Laurus nobilis*)  L
Bergamot (*Monarda didyma*)  L  F
Chamomile (*Chamaemelum nobile*)  F
Chervil (*Anthriscus cerefolium*)  L
Coriander (*Coriandrum sativum*)  S
Cotton lavender (*Santolina chamaecyparissus*)  L  F
Dill (*Anethum graveolens*)  L  S
Fennel (*Foeniculum vulgare*)  S
Feverfew (*Tanacetum parthenium*)  L  F
French tarragon (*Artemisia dracunculus*)  L
Hyssop (*Hyssopus officinalis*)  L
Lavender (*Lavandula angustifolia*)  F
Lemon balm (*Melissa officinalis*)  L
Lemon verbena (*Aloysia triphylla*)  L
Lovage (*Levisticum officinale*)  L
Marjoram (*Origanum vulgare*)  L
Pot marigold (*Calendula officinalis*)  F
Sage (*Salvia officinalis*)  L
Southernwood (*Artemisia abrotanum*)  L
Summer savory (*Satureja hortensis*)  L
Sweet woodruff (*Galium odoratum*)  L
Thyme (*Thymus vulgaris*)  L
Winter savory (*Satureja montana*)  L

Key for parts of plants used:
L = leaves or sprigs  F = flowers  S = seeds

## FREEZING TIPS

Many soft-leaved herbs, such as basil and parsley, are better frozen than dried. For short-term storage, pack whole sprigs into plastic bags, label, and freeze until needed. For long-term storage, it is better to blanch the herbs first. Chop the leaves, then dip them in boiling water followed quickly by iced water. Pat them dry, bag up, and freeze.

• **Make herb ice cubes**: place single borage flowers or small mint leaves (try ginger mint) in ice-cube trays, add water, and freeze to make decorative ice for drinks. Use this technique also with herbs for cooking. Chop parsley or chives and half-fill an ice tray, topping up with water. To use, defrost in a sieve for garnish, or simply add as they are to soups and casseroles during cooking.

△ **FLOWERHEADS**
*Pick flowerheads when just opened (here, marigolds), and spread them on a tray lined with kitchen paper. Leave in a warm, dry place.*

△ **PICKING PETALS**
*With some herbs only the petals are used. Pluck the petals from the flower centres, and discard the latter. Marigold petals are used in pot-pourri, to flavour and colour foods such as rice, and for dye.*

# OILS AND VINEGARS

One way to preserve the flavour of fresh herbs is to steep them in oil or vinegar, which may then be used for cooking or in salad dressings. This works very well for a number of herbs such as French tarragon, oregano, thyme, and lavender.

■ **To make flavoured oil**, fill a clear glass jar with sprigs or leaves of the fresh herb, pour over a good, flavourless oil, such as sunflower, and seal. Leave the jar in a sunny spot for two weeks; shake or stir every day. Strain and bottle, adding a new sprig of the herb as identification. The oil is best stored in a refrigerator.

■ **To make flavoured vinegar**, crush the herb or herb mixture and put into a jar, then pour over a good wine or cider vinegar that has been slightly warmed, filling the jar to the brim. Proceed as for flavoured oil (*above*). Store in a refrigerator.

■ **For a sweet oil**, such as lavender, use almond oil as the base oil instead. This is usually available from herbalists, since it may also be used for massage.

■ **Preserve basil leaves** by packing them in jars of light olive oil. Make sure they are completely covered with oil, then seal and refrigerate. Use the oil for cooking or in salad dressings, and the leaves in sauces.

▽ **BOTTLED FLAVOURS**
*Once you have flavoured some oil with herbs in a jar, bottle it up, add fresh sprigs of the herbs, and seal with a stopper.*

SEE ALSO: Herbs and their Uses, pp.226–227

# THE EDIBLE GARDEN

## PLANNING THE EDIBLE GARDEN

THE FIRST STEP is to consider how much space you want to give over to vegetables and fruit. Growing your crops all in one place in an orderly fashion certainly makes practical sense, in that care and maintenance will be so much easier. However, in small, modern gardens, the traditional kitchen garden plot, separated from the ornamental part of the garden, may not fit the bill. You can, however, grow fruits and vegetables in beds and borders among ornamental plants, and in containers – perhaps not in the same quantity, but enough to ensure a few meals'-worth of favourites, fresh from the garden or patio, or even plucked from the windowsill.

## WHY GROW EDIBLE PLANTS?

Gardening with ornamental plants is, in a sense, its own reward, and you can choose how much work you want to put into it. Growing fruits and vegetables does commit the gardener to a certain amount of labour, but brings tangible, not to say edible returns. The flavour of home-grown produce is infinitely superior to shop-bought. Not only can varieties be selected for inherently better taste; the short interval between harvest and eating means that the fruits of your labours have higher levels of enzymes and vitamins than shop-bought. There is the heightened expectancy of waiting for crops to mature in their season, and intense satisfaction to be had from meals made with produce from your own plot. Finally, growing your own allows you the choice of whether to grow organically or not.

### GOOD IDEAS

• Don't grow things that nobody in your family really likes – it sounds obvious, but this mistake is surprisingly often made.

• "Maincrop" vegetables are always cheap to buy. Where space is limited, growing dearer or more unusual crops makes sense.

• Growing some crops, such as peas and strawberries, has great appeal for children.

## THE TRADITIONAL VEGETABLE PLOT

In a traditional kitchen garden, or in an allotment, vegetables and fruits are grown in neat rows or blocks in well-tended plots. That is not to say that flowers must be excluded; the traditional gardener well understands their value in attracting pollinating insects that ensure good crops. And cropping plants, well-grown and orderly, have their own charm too: this is an edible garden for those who find serenity in predictability, practicality, and productivity. But if you crave more obviously decorative plantings and only have a small garden, you may find this approach eats up too much space.

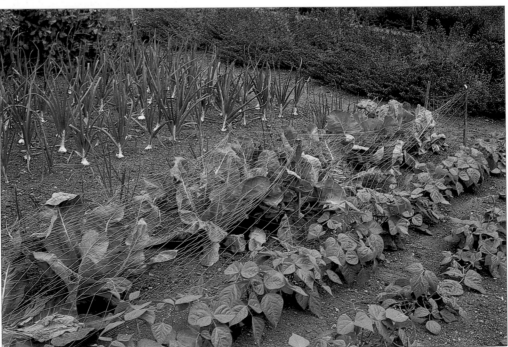

THE TRADITIONAL KITCHEN GARDEN ▷
*Well-ordered and weed-free rows of healthy vegetables are flanked by a band of aromatic, purple-flowered catmint (*Nepeta × faassenii*) to attract bees and other pollinating insects that ensure good crops.*

SEE ALSO: Planning and Practicalities, p.236; Rotating Crops, p.237

# Cottage Garden Style

The cottage garden was a place where time, not money, was spent: every inch of space was planted up with seed-raised crops and flowers. Although the effect, when well done, is of cheerful chaos, this approach takes quite a lot of upkeep, or the effect will not be one of random profusion, but of a mess. With little space "wasted" on evergreens, garden features and hard landscaping, this is perhaps the most delightful of styles for those who love to potter in the garden in spring and summer, but hibernate indoors in winter.

**THE COTTAGE GARDEN ▷**
*Feathery plumes of fennel flanked by parsnips and strawberries are interplanted with nectar-rich salvias and roses for cutting. Straw-strewn paths provide clean access and ground space for drying harvested shallots. Hazel wigwams and screens support runner beans or sweet peas.*

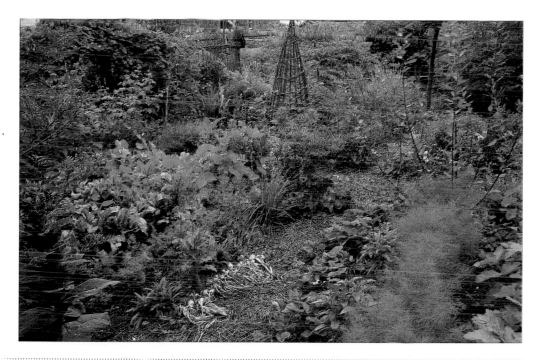

# The Ornamental Potager

As pretty as a knot garden or parterre, the potager combines formal beauty with productivity in an exuberant patchwork. Good design and strong permanent plantings are essential to "hold" the look when crops are harvested. The geometric beds must be carefully delineated, and paths straight, well-built and attractive; clipped edgings of box and lavender, and, as here, beautifully shaped standard bay trees and roses are key elements.

**EXUBERANT POTAGER ▷**
*Hard-wearing brick paths provide easy access and lend warm, mellow colour to a formal geometric framework that delineates highly productive beds. Colourful ribbons of nasturtiums attract hoverflies, whose larvae will feed on aphids, leaving frilly lettuce for their grower to savour.*

# Using Small Spaces

Container-grown crops can range from the utilitarian – peppers in a growbag, even potatoes in a bin bag – to a stunning wigwam of runner beans in a half-barrel planter. Even those with the tiniest of spaces can exploit hanging baskets, pots, and window boxes with salad leaves, bush tomatoes, or chillies. Interplant with marjoram, basil, or thyme, and summer salads will always be properly dressed.

**◁ URBAN LARDER**
*Here, lettuce, strawberries, and tomatoes thrive within arm's reach, using the tiniest space in the most productive way.*

**HANGING GARDEN ▷**
*Tumbling tomatoes share a hanging basket with French marigolds, grown here as a companion plant.*

**SEE ALSO:** Planting and Cultivating Herbs, pp.228–231; Tender Crops, pp.256–257

# NOURISHING YOUR CROPS

GOOD MANAGEMENT of the soil year on year is the key to productive plants. Different crops need different levels of nutrients such as nitrogen in the soil, so depending on what you grow, you may have to add specific compounds as well as a general feed. But if your soil does not have good texture, and you do not water when needed, feeding will be wasted: there must be air and moisture in soil for plant roots to absorb nutrients, and only well-textured soil holds both simultaneously. If growing crops in containers, fresh loam-based compost every year, with a slow-release general fertilizer, suits most crops – but check that, like tomatoes, they do not need a supplement.

## GET TO KNOW YOUR SOIL

Rub soil between your fingers, and you will get to know its texture, whether light or heavy. Unless you are very lucky and have something between the two (the perfect loam) you must improve the texture for crops to do well. The secret is to bulk up the soil with spongy, fibrous "organic matter" – anything derived from plants and animals. It will make heavy soil give up its water and nutrients more readily to plants, and make light soils hang on to them for longer. Never miss an opportunity to return organic matter to the soil in the vegetable plot – manure, mulches, leafmould, even spent potting compost (if the plants in it were healthy).

Sandy soil feels gritty and will not stick together

△ SANDY SOILS
*Light, sandy soils are based on large particles of stone, between which water, and any nutrients dissolved in it, drains through much too quickly (think of a beach as the tide retreats). In estuarine areas, silky-feeling river silt may also be present, helping the soil hang on to moisture.*

Clay soils form a more or less malleable ball that holds its shape when pressed

CLAY SOILS △
*Clay soils feel sticky, heavy, and cold when wet, and glue together in clods; when these dry out, they become rock-hard. Earthworms are a great ally on clay; they burrow through the clods, threading them with organic matter that they leave in their wake and making them crumble.*

## SOIL ACIDITY AND ALKALINITY

Most vegetables prefer neutral to slightly acidic soil, measured by pH (*see below and right*). Brassicas are an exception; not only do they like alkaline soil, but it protects them from the disorder clubroot. But for other crops, you will need to neutralize an alkaline (chalky or limy) soil, best done by regularly adding lots of farmyard or stable manure, which is acidic. If you have quite an acidic soil, or even mildly acidic to neutral and want to grow brassicas, you should add lime (*see right*) for success.

### TELL ME WHY

#### WHY IS pH IMPORTANT?

Soil pH affects the solubility of nutrients and hence their availability to plants. Alkaline soils may be deficient in manganese, boron, and phosphates; acid soils often lack phosphates and may contain harmful levels of aluminium and manganese. Soil pH also influences the incidence of soil-borne pests and diseases; clubroot thrives on acid soils, potato scab on alkaline ones.

## ADDING LIME

For safety, choose a less harsh liming agent such as calcium carbonate over traditional slaked lime. As a gentle way of neutralizing slightly acidic soil, use spent mushroom compost as a mulch; as you will see, it contains crumbs of chalk. Lime soil as well in advance of planting as possible; never less than a month before. Avoid contact with plants. Never apply lime and manure at the same time; they react to let useful nitrogen escape as a gas. If both are needed, apply them in alternate years.

**pH TESTING KITS** ▷
*Soil acidity or alkalinity is measured on the pH scale, which runs from 1 to14: below 7 is acid, 7 is neutral, and above 7 is alkaline. You can buy a simple kit that allows you to test your soil: colours are matched against a chart that will give you a numerical reading.*

After settlement, a yellow or orange colour indicates an acid soil

A small quantity of soil is shaken vigorously with a chemical indicator and allowed to settle

A brilliant green solution indicates a neutral soil

Dark olive green solution indicates an alkaline soil

◁ LIMING THE SOIL
*Choose a still day to apply lime and wear protective gloves and goggles. Spread on the soil surface with a spade, at the manufacturer's recommended rate. Rake, or fork in thoroughly. Do not overlime; you may induce nutrient deficiencies and affect plant growth.*

SEE ALSO: Improving Soil Types, p.142

## MANURE AND MULCHES

Manure is an ideal soil conditioner for the kitchen garden. While relatively low in nutrients (it is after all a waste product) it does wonders for the texture of the soil. There are two main ways of adding it.

The traditional way is to dig it in each autumn; spring is too late for many crops, which dislike or do badly on freshly manured soil. (Potatoes are an exception, and are a boon as a first crop if you have not been able to prepare a vegetable plot before the beginning of the season.) Then, in spring and early summer when the soil is warm and moist, apply an organic mulch – such as garden compost or leaf-mould – to the soil around crops to help keep down weeds, conserve soil moisture, and reduce soil temperature fluctuations. Do not use chipped wood or bark unless matured for two years, or it depletes soil nitrogen. Mulch after watering well, when planting out or when seedlings are at least 5cm (2in) tall. Apply a layer 2.5–7.5cm (1–3 in) deep, avoiding the crowns of the plants.

If you use deep, no-dig beds, you need to dig manure in once, during the initial deep cultivation in autumn. In subsequent years, apply it as a surface mulch in spring; worms and other soil-dwelling organisms will incorporate it during the growing season. Whichever method you use, all manure must be well rotted – otherwise it will scorch your plants. Add at least two 9-litre (2-gallon) buckets for each square metre/yard of soil; unlike fertilizers, you can never apply too much.

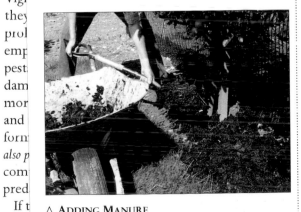

△ **ADDING MANURE**
*Well rotted farmyard or stable manure added to the soil is enjoyed by all crops, both fruits and vegetables. When applying it as a mulch, take care not to smother young plants or to let it touch the stems of more mature ones.*

## ADDITIONAL FEEDING

Briefly, plants take three major elements from soil for growth: nitrogen (chemical symbol N) for leaves, phosphorus (P) for fruits and flowers, and potassium (K) for roots. Only the legumes, such as peas, ever put anything back (nitrogen), so the gardener needs to replenish the soil with fertilizers. NPK are not applied neat (nitrogen, for example, is a gas) but in compounds that are more practical to apply or that plants find easier to use, for example nitrates for nitrogen, phosphates for phosphorus, potash for potassium. A general fertilizer, applied in spring (at the recommended rate – more is not better, and can be harmful), will supply balanced amounts of NPK, but some crops need more of one – tomatoes, for example, need plenty of potash to fruit well. Plants can also be given a growth boost in spring or early summer with a high-nitrogen fertilizer – no later unless it is a leafy crop, or the leaves will flourish instead of the edible parts. There are other elements needed in smaller quantities: calcium, magnesium, sulphur and, in tiny amounts, the "trace" elements: iron, manganese, molybdenum, boron. Good soil to which organic matter is regularly added usually contains enough of these. Any deficiency often shows up as specific symptoms (*see pp.296–309*); if you recognize them, you can use specific remedies: borax for boron, or Sequestrene for iron.

## TEMPORARY COVER

There will inevitably be gaps at times in the vegetable garden, but these are no bad thing, allowing soil to recover. You can also take the opportunity to improve soil, while stopping weeds from colonizing it. Either spread manure over it, then anchor down a sheet of polythene, and let the worms take it in; or, you can grow a living cover crop that will have the same effect. "Green manures" are increasingly available as seeds, and easy to use (*right*). Annuals such as mustard and phacelia for summer cover, and winter tares for winter, are most easily manageable for temporary use in a domestic garden.

## FERTILIZER NUTRIENT CONTENT

While bulky organic fertilizers contain few nutrients weight for weight, they provide vital trace elements, aid good root growth by improving soil structure, and increase water- and nutrient-holding capacities of the soil. Nutrient release by concentrated or slow-release fertilizers is dependent on soil pH, warmth and moisture.

| | % NITROGEN | % PHOSPHATE | % POTASH |
|---|---|---|---|
| **ORGANIC** | | | |
| ANIMAL MANURE | 0.6 | 0.1 | 0.5 |
| GARDEN COMPOST | 0.5 | 0.3 | 0.8 |
| BONE MEAL | 3.5 | 20 | |
| FISH, BLOOD AND BONE | 3.5 | 8 | - |
| HOOF AND HORN | 13 | - | - |
| SEAWEED MEAL | 2.8 | 0.2 | 2.3 |
| MUSHROOM COMPOST | 0.7 | 0.3 | 0.3 |
| ROCK POTASH | 5 | 8 | 10 |
| ROCK PHOSPHATE | - | 26 | 12 |
| WOOD ASH | 0.1 | 0.3 | 1 |
| COCOA SHELLS | 3 | 1 | 3.2 |
| **INORGANIC** | | | |
| GROWMORE | 7 | 7 | 7 |
| AMMONIUM NITRATE | 35 | - | - |
| TRIPLE SUPERPHOSPHATE | - | 42 | - |
| POTASSIUM CHLORIDE | - | - | 60 |
| POTASSIUM SULPHATE | - | - | 49 |

Never forget: if the soil dries out, plants cannot absorb nutrients. They also respond badly to sporadic watering, making nutrients available in fits and starts. You must water generously and regularly whenever soil is drying out.

△ **USING MUSTARD AS A GREEN MANURE**
*Sow seeds broadcast. A few weeks later, when seedlings are 15–20cm (6–8in) tall, chop them down with a spade and allow to wilt. Dig a series of shallow trenches, scrape green manure into the bottom of each and re-fill with soil.*

**SEE ALSO:** Preparing the Ground, pp.142–143; Applying Mulch, p.152; Sowing Annuals and Biennials, p.163.

# SOWING AND PLANTING OUTDOORS

MOST CROPS THAT YOU CAN raise from seed outdoors are sown *in situ*, where they are to grow. You either trickle the seeds along rows, then thin the young plants, or, with large seeds such as peas and beans, "space" sow one seed at every point that you want a plant. If you have germination failures, garden centres usually offer young plants with which to fill in gaps in spring, although there may not be much choice of varieties. Most seeds are sown in spring, not only after any frosts have passed but also after the soil has had time to warm up by a few degrees, and perhaps dry out a little; a blanket (*see p.240*) of fleece or, after a wet winter, polythene, can help you get ahead.

## BUYING VEGETABLE SEEDS

Because you harvest many vegetables before they flower, seed-saving is not an option, except with peas and beans. However, browsing through varieties in seed catalogues is one of the few jobs in gardening that can be done from a cosy armchair; moreover, when you buy seeds from a reputable source, either mail-order or from a garden centre, you also gain the knowledge that they conform to required standards of cleanliness, viability, and purity, and have been stored in the requisite cool, dry conditions at least up to point of sale (in garden centres, do always check the sell-by date; seeds lose viability with age and if stored in hot conditions).

Always read the packet to check that the seed can be sown outdoors in your locality (*if not, see pp.240–241 for what your options may be*). Follow the instructions on the packet, and take particular note of timings and temperatures for first sowings: most failures in germination occur because seed is sown in ground that is still too cold.

### THE RANGE OF SEEDS AVAILABLE

Untreated seeds are cheapest; choose these also if you garden organically and cannot get seed from an organic source. "Primed" seeds germinate quickly if you have missed sowing times; pelleted seeds are easy to handle; and dusted or coated seeds are useful if your seedlings often succumb to pest or disease problems.

Untreated, or natural, parsnip seeds, simply cleaned and dried after harvest

Mini-pelleted seeds make tiny seeds, like turnip, easy to handle

Pelleted parsnip seeds; the clay coat may include fungicide and insecticide

Coated cauliflower seeds are treated with a fungicidal dressing

Coated carrot seeds; wash hands after sowing coated or dusted seeds

Pea and bean seeds, here wrinkled peas, can be saved from your own crops

Primed carrot seeds are pre-treated to speed up germination

Coated cabbage seeds; coating is a protection against fungal diseases

Beetroot has clustered seeds that produce a clump of seedlings

Dusted seeds, here peas, are dusted with a fungicidal powder

## PREPARING THE VEGETABLE PLOT

Seeds need fine, crumbly soil, holding both moisture and oxygen in order to prime and soften the seed coat for germination. If you can, get your initial soil preparations – digging, manuring, and so forth – done in autumn, or at least by late winter. Then (in cool climates) the freeze–thaw action of any frosts will act to your advantage by cracking and breaking up clods still further.

In spring, in preparation for sowing, lightly fork over the soil and clear the plot of any weeds, especially perennial ones, that have germinated over winter; they are easily uprooted completely when still small. Apply a balanced fertilizer; if liming is necessary (*see p.238*), do it at least a month before sowing.

Just before sowing, choose a day when soil is neither excessively wet or bone dry, and rake down the soil to a fine tilth – a loose, crumbly, fine-grained surface. This allows seeds to be sown at a consistent depth. It also ensures that they make close contact with the soil and so can get the moisture needed for growth.

### GOOD IDEAS

• Try the stale seedbed technique. Prepare the seedbed a couple of weeks in advance of sowing and allow a crop of weeds to grow. Then hoe off shallowly (or in dry weather, flame-weed), just before sowing. The shallow cultivations bring very few weed seeds up to the light, so vegetable seeds get a head start.

• If you have been using cloches or polythene to warm the soil, remember that they will also have kept off any rain. You may need to water in the seeds (*see opposite*) if the soil has become very dry.

SEE ALSO: Preparing the Ground, pp.142–143; Adding Lime, p.238; Crop Protection, p. 240; Sowing Seeds in Containers, p.244

# SOWING IN DRILLS

Even when large seeds are going to be spaced individually, vegetable seeds are always sown along drills (troughs) of various depths, either in their final site, or in a seedbed for transplanting later. Seedbeds are used often for brassicas, which need a year to grow: you can grow them quite closely when young in a small patch, then plant out when room becomes available after harvesting another crop. Sowing in drills works even if you want vegetables in blocks rather than rows: you just make the drills closer together. Then you can tell exactly what are emerging seedlings, and what are weeds.

In general, the smaller the seed, the shallower the drill should be. Seed packets will indicate the required depth. Where this is quoted as a range, for example, lettuces may be sown at 1–2cm (½–¾in), the shallower depth is used for heavier soils and the deeper for light soils.

Most vegetables are sown in narrow drills; use broad drills for crops like peas, where a broad, dense row is needed, or for early carrots and cut-and-come-again crops that are harvested before maturity; as you harvest some plants, you will create space in which the remainder can grow.

## SOWING SEEDS IN A WIDE DRILL

**1 MARK OUT**
Mark out parallel drills, 15–23cm (6–9in) wide, and to the required depth, using a string line and pegs. Pull a draw hoe steadily towards you; keep the blade at a level depth, applying light, even pressure.

**2 SOW SEED**
Space-sow large seed at the required spacings given for the individual crop, or trickle small seed, along the base of the drill. Do not sow too thickly, or seedlings will be crowded and may rot, or fail to grow on well.

**3 COVER WITH SOIL**
Taking care not to move or dislodge seeds, cover them with soil, either with a draw hoe, a rake, or by drawing soil gently over the seeds with the foot. Water in well using a can or hose fitted with a fine rose.

**4 PROTECT SEEDS**
Protect the seeds from birds or foraging animals such as mice, if necessary, by pegging wire netting down over the row. Remove the netting after germination and before the seedlings are tall enough to grow through the mesh.

## SOWING SEEDS IN A NARROW DRILL (MOST VEGETABLE CROPS)

**1 MARK OUT**
Mark out the row with string line and pegs. Use the corner of a draw hoe or a trowel to draw out a small, even drill of the required depth for the individual seeds.

**2 SOW SEED**
Space sow, or trickle seeds thinly and evenly along the bottom of the drill. Cover over with soil carefully to avoid dislodging the seed and water in thoroughly.

---

# WET AND DRY SOIL

If sowing in wet soil is unavoidable, spread sand or vermiculite over the base of the drill before sowing. On deep beds, sow from surrounding paths; otherwise, use a board to protect soil from compaction. Water dry soils before you sow; press seeds lightly into the moist soil before covering.

△ **WET SOIL**
On heavy, slow-draining soils, sprinkle a layer of sand at the base of the drill before sowing. Stand on a board to avoid compaction.

△ **DRY SOIL**
Water the soil in the base of the drill before sowing. Use mains, not rain, water. Sow the seeds and then cover with dry soil.

# THINNING AND TRANSPLANTING

You must thin young seedlings to avoid overcrowding. Thin to final spacings in stages, to allow for losses. At each stage, aim to leave each seedling just clear of its neighbour. Move crops started in seedbeds, such as leeks or brassicas, as young as possible so that they re-establish quickly.

◁ **THINNING**
When seeds have germinated, thin while still small by pinching them out at the base of the stem between finger and thumb. This avoids disturbing the roots of remaining seedlings.

◁ **TRANSPLANTING**
Lift seedlings gently with as much soil as possible around the roots. Transfer seedlings to a clean plastic bag to avoid moisture loss; carry in a seed tray to avoid damage.

**REPLANTING** ▷
Replant at required spacing with the lowest leaves just above soil level. Planting too high exposes the stalk, which may not support the weight of the mature vegetable.

Firm the soil in very carefully with a fingertip around the delicate young stalk

SEE ALSO: Protecting against Problems, p.241; Catalogue of Vegetables, pp.246–257

# SOWING SEEDS IN CONTAINERS

SEEDS NEED TO BE RAISED under cover in pots or trays if temperatures outside are too low for germination. You may want to get ahead with hardy vegetables, especially in a cold spring; or, you may want to raise plants that need a longer growing season than your climate offers to germinate *and* grow to ripeness outside, as when growing sweetcorn in cool regions. These seedlings would be transplanted outdoors, but you might also want to raise crops to grow in a glasshouse, such as peppers. Whether you have a heated greenhouse or a simple propagator, raising from seed gives you unlimited choice of varieties compared to the range usually on offer as young plants.

## SOWING INDOORS OR UNDER GLASS

There is a wide range of containers that are used for sowing seeds under cover.

■ Pots and half-pots are adequate if only small numbers of seedlings are required, for expensive seeds that are sold in small quantities, and for single sowings of large seeds.

■ Trays and half-trays hold enough seedlings for the largest of plots; they are best for crops that tolerate transplanting.

■ Modular trays with individual pockets use less compost than trays or pots. Use them to sow directly, or to prick out seedlings germinated in trays or pots. Module-grown seedlings form a compact rootball that allows minimal disturbance on transplanting; it also allows root development to continue if conditions are unsuitable for planting out at the optimum time. Pelleted seeds can be sown singly in modules; others are sown 2–3 per cell and can be "singled", or thinned to the strongest seedling, later.

Once seedlings have germinated, keep them evenly moist but not wet, and place them in good light, but shade from bright sun that may scorch or kill them.

### GOOD IDEAS

• When sowing in containers, you nearly always produce more seedlings than you need, leaving spares to swap with gardening friends. If you organize a vegetable swap group, all members can extend their crop range with minimal cost and effort.

• After germination, most seedlings must be kept at a slightly lower temperature in light, well-ventilated, protected conditions. While a kichen windowsill suits germinating seeds, it may get too warm and stuffy for growing seedlings: move them to a cooler room, such a a spare bedroom.

### SOWING IN TRAYS

**1 PREPARE THE TRAY**
*Fill the tray with seed compost, mounding it up loosely above the rim. Tap the container to remove air pockets and level with a piece of wood. Firm gently so that the compost surface is about 1cm (½in) below the rim.*

**2 SOW SEED THINLY**
*Scatter seed thinly and evenly over compost surface and just cover by finely sieving more compost over them. Water in with a fine rose or from below by standing in a tray of clean water until the compost surface glistens.*

**3 COVER THE TRAY**
*Allow compost to drain thoroughly and cover tray with a sheet of glass or plastic kitchen film, or place in a propagator. Remove cover on germination. Keep seedlings in good light; prick out when they have 3–4 leaves.*

△ **BROADCAST SOWING IN POTS**
*This method is ideal if small numbers of seedlings are needed, or for seeds that germinate erratically. Fill a pot with standard seed compost; tap firmly to remove air pockets and firm the surface gently. Scatter seeds thinly and evenly over the compost surface. Cover seeds to their own depth with finely sieved seed compost. Water, label and cover with glass, or place in a propagator.*

△ **SOWING LARGE SEEDS**
*Large seeds, like courgettes, marrows, and cucumbers, are best sown on their sodes, one or two seeds to a 5–9cm (2–3½in) pot. On germination, the weaker of the two seedlings will be pinched out. Fill the pot with standard seed compost to within 2.5cm (1in) of the rim. Push in the seeds then cover with about 2cm (¾in) of seed compost. Water in, label, and place in a propagator.*

SEE ALSO: Nourishing your Crops, pp.238–239; Greenhouses, p.241

# PRICKING OUT

When seedlings have developed their first leaves, they must be "pricked out" to avoid the congestion that leads to damping off (*see p.300*), and also weak, leggy growth. Do this as soon as possible; if roots develop sufficiently to become entwined, seedlings are difficult to prick out without damage.

## PRICKING OUT SEEDLINGS

**1 LIFTING SEEDLINGS**
*Tap the tray on a hard surface to loosen compost. Handle seedlings only by their seed leaves; stems are very vulnerable to damage. Lift individual seedlings with a widger, keeping plenty of compost round the roots.*

**2 TRANSPLANTING SEEDLINGS**
*Prick out, well-spaced in a tray filled with standard potting compost, or, as here, modules. Make holes in the compost and place one seedling in each module. Push compost very gently up against the stem; do not press hard.*

# HARDENING OFF

Vegetable plants that are sown in a warm, protected environment must be hardened off gradually before planting outdoors, or the sharp drop in temperature will shock them too much. Ideally, transfer them to a cold frame, gradually opening the lid more over a period of about 7–10 days. Check the weather forecast and, if frost threatens, close down the frame and cover with insulation temporarily. Alternatively, place them in a sheltered spot outdoors for increasingly longer periods each day.

# TRANSPLANTING POT SOWINGS OUTSIDE

When the roots almost fill the pots, plants are ready for hardening off and transplanting. Before setting pot- or module-grown plants outdoors, water them thoroughly and set aside to drain. Each plant should then slide easily out of its pot with an entire root ball.

◁ **PLANTING OUT**
*Dig a hole with a trowel, large enough for the plant to be set a little deeper than it was in the pot. This ensures that the root ball does not dry out. Firm in and water well.*

# SOWING IN MODULES

Sowing in modules produces high quality plants that grow on well, since they can be planted out with little or no disturbance to the root ball. Seeds can be sown directly into modules, or seedlings can be pricked out into them. If sowing, sow 2–3 seeds in each cell and then thin to the strongest seedling after germination. Alternatively, use the multiblock sowing technique (*see below*).

## RAISING SEEDLINGS IN MODULES

**1 SOWING SEED**
*Fill the modules with seed compost and make a hole, 5mm (¼in) deep, in each cell. Sow one or two seeds per cell. Cover with sieved compost, label with the variety name and date, and water in with a fine rose.*

**2 PLANTING OUT**
*Remove each seedling from its module by pushing it out with a stick through the hole in the bottom. Make a hole to take the rootball. Place the plant in the hole with lowest leaves just above the soil surface. Water in well.*

# MULTIBLOCK SOWINGS

This method of sowing is useful for leeks, onions, turnips and beetroot – with root crops, it is ideal for growing tasty "baby" vegetables. Fill a modular tray with moist potting compost. Sow 3–5 seeds in each cell, cover to their own depth with compost, label, and water in. Put the tray in a warm, dry place; seedlings should germinate in 5–7 days.

◁ **PLANTING OUT**
*After germination, harden off. When two true leaves have formed, plant out at appropriate spacings.*

**HARVESTING** ▷
*Unthinned seedlings grow on to form clusters of small vegetables, here yielding a harvest of baby turnips.*

SEE ALSO: Crop Protection, p.240

# PEAS AND BEANS

VEGETABLES IN THIS GROUP, often referred to as legumes, are grown for their seed pods. Some are cooked and eaten whole, while others are grown for the seeds that are eaten cooked or raw. Most freeze well, and the seeds of some, like French beans, can be extracted and dried. Podded vegetables can be decorative as well as tasty; most have attractive blooms (traditional scarlet runners are the perfect cottage garden plant) and climbing types can be trained on wigwams, or used as screens in the kitchen garden. Remember that most peas and beans leave soil rich in nitrogen, ideal for a brassica crop to follow. After harvest, dig plants into the soil, or lift and compost them.

## FRENCH BEANS

French beans are sown from mid-spring to summer and harvested in summer to early autumn. You can expect about 4kg (8lb) of pods from a 3m (10ft) row, or a square metre (sq yd) block. You can sow seeds outdoors from mid-spring, buy young plants, or raise your own. There are both dwarf (bushy) and climbing varieties, with pods ranging from pencil-thick to the very fine "filet" types. Pods may be green, green flecked purple, red, purple, or yellow – yellow, wax-pod types have a waxy texture and fine flavour. The unusually-coloured beans look striking in the garden; the purple kinds turn green on cooking. Some varieties are especially good for growing for the beans, not the pods; they are shelled either when immature, for cooking and eating right away (when they are called flageolets), or for drying (haricots).

**SITE AND SOIL** No special preparations needed; erect supports (*see opposite*) before sowing or planting if growing climbers.

△ **EARTHING UP**
*French beans are planted shallowly, so once they have developed a few leaves, to prevent them from becoming top-heavy, it is a good idea to gently draw a little more earth up around their stems for extra support. Use a draw hoe to draw soil up around the stems almost to the depth of the lowest leaves. This will improve root anchorage.*

They grow well in containers in a loam-based compost, but you must water regularly and often.

**SOWING AND PLANTING** Never sow or plant outdoors until frosts are over. Sow 4cm (1½in) deep, *in situ* or individually in 8cm (3in) pots under glass, hardening off before planting out. Sow every 3 weeks until midsummer for successional crops.

■ The seeds will not germinate at low temperatures, so in a cold spring, either pre-warm the soil with cloches or plastic before sowing, or raise seedlings under cover; they need 12°C (54°F) for germination, if using a propagator.

■ You should see seedlings within 2 weeks. If the weather turns cold, cover the soil or young plants with fleece or a cloche.

**SPACING** Sow or plant dwarf types in staggered rows 23cm (9in) apart each way. Climbers grow 3m (10ft) or more tall. Grow in double rows, 60cm (2ft) apart, or on circular wigwams, 15cm (6in) apart.

**ROUTINE CARE** Earth up the stems of young plants for extra support (*see left*). Mulch well and never allow plants to dry out completely. If conditions are dry during flowering, water very generously – a couple of 2-gallon watering cans per plant, or equivalent.

**HARVESTING** Harvest after 7–13 weeks. Pick pods frequently while young and succulent and cook them fresh, or blanch and freeze. If you really cannot cope with a glut, just stop picking; they will stop making new pods while old ones are on the plant. To harvest haricots, pull up plants when the beans have swelled in the pods and hang upside down by the roots in a dry frost-free place. Shell beans when dry and store in airtight jars.

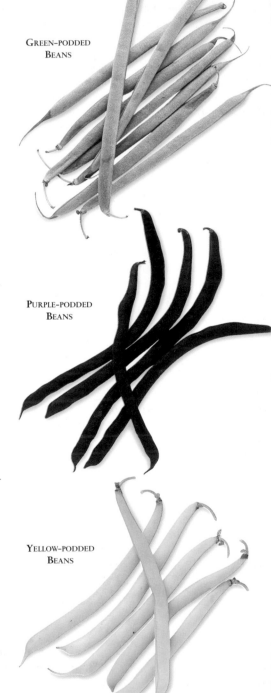

GREEN-PODDED BEANS

PURPLE-PODDED BEANS

YELLOW-PODDED BEANS

**SEE ALSO:** Rotating Crops, p. 237; Sowing in Containers, p. 245; Transplanting Pot Sowings Outside, p. 245; Hoes, p.278

# RUNNER BEANS

Runner beans are sown in mid-spring and harvested from midsummer. Young plants are usually widely available. They may be climbers, about 3m (10ft) tall, or dwarf, bushy plants, about 38cm (15in) tall. You can expect 1kg (2lbs) of pods per plant. They are pretty plants, with pink, red, white, or bicoloured flowers; you can grow sweetpeas among them for even more decorative appeal. Except in stringless varieties, "strings" along the sides of the pods must be removed before cooking.

**SITE AND SOIL** Erect supports for climbers before sowing or planting. Runner beans grow best in especially moisture-retentive soil. Make a trench along the row or around a wigwam, about a spade's-depth deep, and and fork lots of well-rotted garden compost into the base for best results: a layer of shredded, soaked newspaper is a traditional alternative. Runner beans grow well in containers in a loam-based compost, but you must water regularly and often.

**SOWING AND PLANTING** As for French beans, but sow 5cm (2in) deep.

**SPACING** Sow or plant 15cm (6in) apart.

**ROUTINE CARE** Mulch the young plants. If conditions are dry as flower buds form (they do so over quite a long period), water generously twice a week. Watch out for blackfly (*see black bean aphid, p.306*).

**HARVESTING** Usually ready for picking 13–17 weeks after planting. Pick pods when tender, before the seeds start to swell. Use fresh, or blanch and freeze.

## BEAN SUPPORTS

There are several ways to support climbing beans, depending on space. Plants may also be grown on a frame up strings or wire pegged into the ground. Do not use plastic-coated netting, since plants cannot cling on to it.

RUNNER BEANS

2.5m (8ft) canes are tied at the top or secured with a proprietary plastic wigwam support

△ **BEAUTIFUL BEANS**
*At maturity, climbing beans disguise their support completely. For more ornamental effects, try combining beans with flowering sweetpeas.*

Two rows of 2.5m (8ft) crossed canes tied at the top and secured with horizontal canes

10cm (4in) nylon net fixed to a softwood or recycled timber pole frame

**CROSSED CANE ROW**        **CANE WIGWAM**        **NETTING SUPPORT**

# PEAS

Peas are hardier than beans, and easier to raise from seed in cool climates. They do not cope with hot summers quite so well. You can start sowing hardy, early peas in late winter (in mild areas, you can even sow in autumn), continuing into spring to harvest from late spring through the summer. There is no need to raise plants under glass. Peas range from 45cm (18in) to over 2m (6ft) tall, and all benefit from the support of twiggy branches known as peasticks. Expect 5kg (10lbs) from a 3m (10ft) row, or a square metre (sq. yd) block.

Shelling peas, including tiny, sweet *petits pois*, are grown for fresh peas extracted from the pod. Mangetouts are eaten young, when still flat-podded; round-podded sugar or snow peas are used semi-mature. All can be eaten cooked or raw.

**SITE AND SOIL** No special preparations. Do not insert peasticks until the plants grow.

**SOWING AND PLANTING** Sow seeds 3cm (1¼in) deep; 5–8cm (2–3in) apart in blocks, or, for rows, 5cm (2in) apart in 23cm (9in) wide drills, 60–90cm apart.

■ Early and late sowings are less likely to be affected by pea moth (*see p.306*).
■ Make early spring sowings under a cloche or fleece to speed up germination; if firmly anchored, this should also keep birds and mice from taking the sown peas.
■ For successional crops, sow at 14-day intervals (avoid midsummer in warm areas), or sow "early" and later-maturing "maincrop" varieties at the same time.

**ROUTINE CARE** Cover sowings in open ground with netting to protect from birds. Remove it and erect supports (*see right*) when tendrils develop. Mulch when several leaves have formed to keep roots cool. If the weather is dry during flowering and as pods form, water generously once or twice a week.

**HARVESTING** Harvest early peas after 11–12 weeks; maincrops after 13–14 weeks. Use fresh, or freeze.

PEAS

MANGETOUT

**SUPPORTING PEAS** ▷
*When young plants have developed tendrils, push peasticks into the ground as nearly upright as possible, along the outside of the block or row. As peas grow, tendrils wrap around the twigs and draw plants up through them.*

**SEE ALSO:** Crop Protection, p. 240; Sowing Seeds in a Wide Drill, p. 243

# ONIONS AND ROOT VEGETABLES

BOTH OF THESE CROP GROUPS do best in light, well-drained soil. Stony ground is not suitable for them, as the roots will fork or bulbs distort where they meet stones; if you have stony soil, stick to spring onions and stubby or round carrot varieties. Many of these earthy stalwarts look good. The feathery foliage of carrots makes charming edging for a bed. Blue-green leeks planted with ruby chard (*see p.255*) is a stunning combination worthy of any border, and a few leeks allowed to flower will rival many an ornamental allium. Because onions need vertical space only, you can interplant them pleasingly with red looseleaf lettuces or cut-and-come-again salad leaves.

## ONIONS

Ordinary onions are not especially economical to grow, but unusual types and shallots are well worth giving space to. It is much easier to raise them from sets (small bulbs) than from seed. Onions store well if well-ripened and dry.
**PREPARATION** Do not grow on freshly manured soil. Apply a dressing of balanced fertilizer before planting.
**PLANTING** Plant onion sets in early spring 10–15cm (4–6in) apart, depending on the size of bulbs you want, in furrows 15–30cm (6–12in) apart, with the tips just above the soil. They may need protecting from birds. Shallot sets can be planted earlier, from midwinter (Boxing Day is a traditional planting day). Space them 18cm (7in) apart each way as they form a cluster of bulbs.
**ROUTINE CARE** Keep weed-free, especially when young. Water only in very dry spells. Watch for onion fly and rot (*see pp.306–307*).
**HARVESTING** Choose a dry spell, if possible, in late summer to harvest. Onions must be completely dry before storing, or they

**RED-SKINNED ONION**

**SHALLOT**

Thick, or "bull-necked", onions rot readily so use them first

◁ **STORING ONIONS**
*If you cannot dry off pulled onions outdoors, either because of the weather or lack of space, place them carefully in slatted boxes, no more than two layers deep, and keep in a dry, cool, airy place.*

will rot or start into growth, so lay them out on dry ground or if necessary under cover (*see above*) for 10–14 days after pulling, with the leaves intact. Either trim the leaves and store the bulbs in nets or slatted boxes, or leave on for stringing.

## SALAD ONIONS

Spring onions take only about 8 weeks to mature, and are a good choice for intercropping between rows of slower-maturing plants while these are young – including bulb onions. If you sow at intervals from early spring to mid-summer, you will have supplies from early summer right through the autumn. For a winter salad onion, sow some Welsh onions in spring or summer; they will not be ready until the autumn but they are evergreen and very hardy; you can harvest leaves right through winter. Sow both *in situ*, spring onions in rows 10cm (4in) apart, or in bands 8cm (3in) wide, 15cm (6in) apart. Sow Welsh onions in rows 30cm (12in) apart and thin to 23cm (9in). They need the same conditions and care as onions.

**SPRING ONIONS**

## GARLIC

Although store-bought garlic makes a cheerful crop for children to grow, for good kitchen supplies you need to buy specially prepared, virus-free cloves from an established nursery or seed firm. They need the same conditions and care as onions, and are vulnerable to the same problems. Plant individual cloves in mid-spring – or, if you have light, well-drained soil you can plant in autumn. Place cloves upright at twice their own depth, about 18cm (7in) apart each way. Bulbs for eating fresh should be ready by mid-summer; leave bulbs for storing to swell and ripen until the end of the season. Uproot as the leaves fade, and dry as for onions.

**GARLIC**

◁ **STORING GARLIC**
*Dry as for bulb onions and tie stems loosely together with raffia or plait them. Hang in a cool, dry place.*

△ **GARLIC IN MODULES**
*To give garlic the longest growing season to ripen, plant in autumn; if your soil is too cold and heavy, you can start the cloves off in modules, one clove per cell, in a cold frame. Plant out in spring when they have started to sprout.*

**SEE ALSO:** Adding Lime, p.238; Fertilizer Nutrient Content, p.239; Additional Feeding, p.239

# LEEKS

Although they can be sown outdoors in any climate, leeks must be transplanted so that you can set the young plants in much deeper holes, to ensure white stems. Sow in a seedbed or cold frame or, if space is limited, buy in young plants; set them out in early summer, and harvest from early autumn onwards; they can stand in the soil through winter to spring. Unlike onions, leeks enjoy ground manured the previous autumn, with a nitrogen-rich fertilizer added before planting.

**SOWING AND PLANTING** Sow between late winter and spring, 1cm (⅜in) deep, and transplant when 20cm (8in) tall, spacing them 10–23cm (4–9in) apart.

**ROUTINE CARE** Keep well-watered until established and weed-free at all times. Leeks need no additional water unless dry conditions are exceptionally prolonged.

△ **TRANSPLANTING**
*For white stems, transplant leeks into holes 15–20cm (6–8in) deep, 10–15cm (4–6in) apart. Trim very long leaves. Gently fill the hole with water so that soil will collect around stems.*

LEEKS

△ **TRANSPLANTING MODULAR SOWINGS**
*Raising leeks in modules, with up to 4 seeds per cell, is a simple and convenient technique. When seedlings have 3 leaves, each cell can be planted out in its entirety; thin by pulling baby leeks to give the remainder space to grow.*

# PARSNIPS

The stumpier varieties of parsnip are best if your soil is the least bit stony. The main problem with any parsnip is canker (*see p.309*), so look also for resistant varieties, and lime very acid soils (*see p.238*), which increase risk of canker. They are sown outside as early as possible, as they have a long growing season, and are ready to lift in autumn; however except in very harsh winters you can leave them in for longer, lifting as needed; frost improves the taste.

**SOWING AND PLANTING** Parsnip seed loses viability quickly, so always use fresh seed. Sow as soon as the soil is workable in early spring. Pre-warming soil with fleece or cloches improves germination, which is notoriously slow. Sow 2cm (⅜in) deep, in rows 30cm (12in) apart; thin seedlings to 10–15cm (4–6in) apart.

**ROUTINE CARE** Keep weed-free, especially when seedlings are growing, and water weekly in dry spells. Do not allow soil to dry out; parsnips tend to split if watered after a prolonged dry spell. Watch out for signs of attack by root aphids (*p.309*).

PARSNIP

# BEETROOT

Baby beetroots are ready 7–8 weeks after sowing outside, or you can leave them to grow larger, even through winter; though the roots become inedible, the leafy tops can be used as winter greens. Beetroot enjoys the same conditions, soil preparation and care as carrots; in addition, dress the soil with a nitrogen-rich fertilizer, once before sowing and again in growth.

**SOWING AND PLANTING** Sow at intervals once the soil reaches 7°C (45°F), either naturally or warmed with a cover. Choose bolt-resistant types for early sowing. Most "seeds" are clusters of 2–3, easy to handle: sow one every 8–10cm (3–4in) and wait to reduce each cluster to one until you can eat the thinnings as baby beets. "Monogerm" seeds make only one plant. Soak seed in warm water for 30 minutes before sowing, 2cm (⅜in) deep, in rows 30cm (12in) apart.

△ **HARVESTING BEETROOT**
*Grip the stems firmly and pull gently; the root should lift easily because beetroots are shallow-rooted. Twist off the leaves and cook the roots with the stalks still attached; the colour will bleed from any wound to the root.*

# CARROTS

Some varieties of carrot are best for eating very young; others improve in flavour as they grow larger, so grow a mixture of these "earlies" and "maincrops". They take about 2 and 3 months respectively before ready to eat, so if you make successional sowings, you can have fresh carrots for several months. Earlies freeze well if blanched. You should lift the last of the maincrops before frost; they will keep in boxes of damp sand in a cool room.

**SOWING AND PLANTING** Rake soil to a fine tilth and remove any stones. Start to sow earlies *in situ* when the soil reaches 7°C (45°F). Earlier sowings can be made under a fleece or cloche. Sow maincrops from late spring to early summer. Sow in drills, 1–2cm (½–¾in) deep, in rows 15cm (6in) apart. Try to sow thinly, to minimize thinning, which releases smells that attract carrot fly. Thin earlies to 8cm (3in) apart; maincrops to at least 4cm (1½in).

**ROUTINE CARE** Keep weed-free and water weekly in dry spells. Take precautions against carrot fly (*see p.309*) and watch out for damage by root and leaf aphids.

CARROTS 'FAVOURITE'

**SEE ALSO:** Sowing Seeds in a Narrow Drill, p.243; Thinning and Transplanting, p.243; Sowing in Modules, p.245

# CROPS FOR BLOCK PLANTING

IF YOU ARE USING small beds, you can easily devote a whole block to any of the crops described here. In warm regions, sweetcorn and squashes are often grown together, the corn shading the squashes from scorch, but in cooler areas squash fruits need all the sun they can get. While potatoes are not an attractive crop, rustling, ripening cornstalks are beautiful. Marrow and squash plants look attractive enough to grow with ornamental plants, but their smothering habit and the amount of water they need may not suit companions. They can be trained as climbers, provided that you support fruits individually: letting them trail over sunny banks also looks spectacular.

## POTATOES

While there are potato diseases that can, literally, blight a crop (see p.309), these are rare, and usually they are one of the most satisfying crops for the new kitchen gardener. If space is limited, remember that even organic maincrop or "old" potatoes are cheap; concentrate on early varieties ("new" potatoes) or waxy salad potatoes. If, conversely, you have more space than you can manage, maincrops are a useful filler, and growing and harvesting will improve the soil as you turn and manure it, and lift the crop. Potatoes like deep soil rich in organic matter, and newly dressed with manure. If your soil is thin, consider the no-dig method (p.237), or you can grow a small crop of new potatoes in a tub, or even a plastic sack.

**SOWING AND PLANTING** In late winter, you will see potatoes on sale at garden centres: you must use these "seed" potatoes rather than shop-bought ones; they are specially produced to make productive, disease-free plants. "Chit" them about 6 weeks before planting (above right). Plant (see above, far right)

Cool, light conditions result in plump, green shoots

△ **CHITTING SEED POTATOES**
*To sprout (chit) seed potatoes, set in a single layer in a box or tray (egg-boxes are ideal) with the end of the potato bearing the most "eyes" uppermost. Store in a well-lit, airy, frost-free place until sprouts have grown to about 2cm (¾in) in length. This usually takes about 6 weeks.*

when there is no risk of heavy frost; if the spring is cool, warm the soil with fleece before and after planting. A half-barrel-sized tub or feed sack on end will take three potatoes. Plant with the container half-full of compost, then add more to "earth up".
**ROUTINE CARE** If shoots emerge before risk of frost is over, cover with fleece. Once the foliage is growing well, apply a high-nitrogen fertilizer or liquid feed, and earth up the plants (see right). In dry conditions, water earlies generously every 10–12 days. Delay watering maincrops until tubers are at least marble-sized, then water really generously once. Watch for signs of blight (see p.309), which needs acting on quickly. If plants stop growing, unearth one to check for pests or other problems underground (see pp.308–311).
**HARVESTING** You can start lifting new potatoes when flowers open. Maincrops should be ready by summer's end, but you can leave them in, lifting as you need them, until mid-autumn, when you should harvest and store them (see right).

◁ **PLANTING POTATOES**
*Make a drill 8–15cm (3–6in) deep. Place seed potatoes in the bottom, sprouts uppermost. Cover them carefully with soil. Plant earlies 30cm (12in) apart, with rows 60cm (2ft) apart; maincrops 38cm (15in) apart in rows 75cm (2ft 6in) apart.*

△ **EARTHING UP**
*When stems are about 23cm (9in) high (or whenever frost threatens), earth up soil around them with a draw hoe. Earthing up ensures that the potatoes do not grow too near the surface, where light turns them green and unsafe to eat.*

FIRST EARLY POTATO 'Concorde'

MAINCROP POTATO 'Navan'

△ **HARVESTING**
*In mid-autumn, cut stem and leaves (the haulm) of maincrop potatoes with a sharp knife, 5cm (2in) above ground. Leave the crop in the ground for two weeks longer before lifting.*

△ **LIFTING, STORING**
*Lift potatoes with a fork, digging from the side of the ridge. Leave to dry for a few hours. Store blemish-free potatoes in a light-proof sack; use damaged ones immediately.*

SEE ALSO: "No-dig" Potatoes, p.237; Additional Feeding, p.239

# PUMPKINS, SQUASHES, MARROWS, AND COURGETTES

All of these need similar growing conditions: a warm, sheltered site in fertile, well-drained soil that is rich in organic matter and moisture-retentive. Courgettes, ready to eat about 8 weeks after planting, and the summer squashes are thin-skinned, and need picking and eating a few days after flowering. Courgette flowers are also edible. Marrows and winter squashes, a category that includes pumpkins, store well, provided that they have a long, warm growing season to ripen (up to 5 months for pumpkins). Most varieties are sprawling in habit and can be grown upwards over robust supports; generally, the neatest are courgettes, bush varieties of marrow.

**SOWING AND PLANTING** Sow seeds on edge, 2.5cm (1in) deep (*see p.244*) either *in situ* when risk of frost is over, or under glass in 8cm (3in) pots, at 15–18°C (59–64°F). Set out bush types 90cm (3ft) apart each way and trailing types 1.2–2m (4–6ft) apart.

**ROUTINE CARE** In cool areas, protect young plants with a cloche or fleece. Mulch after planting. Keep well-watered, but do not wet flowers or fruits; seephose is ideal. Apply a tomato fertilizer every two weeks from midsummer on. Watch out for slug damage.

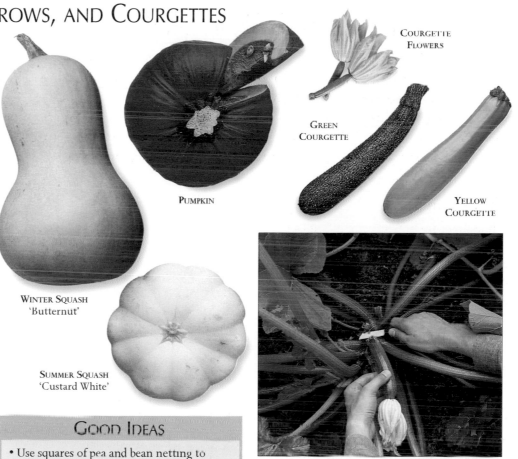

**COURGETTE FLOWERS**

**GREEN COURGETTE**

**YELLOW COURGETTE**

**PUMPKIN**

**WINTER SQUASH** 'Butternut'

**SUMMER SQUASH** 'Custard White'

### GOOD IDEAS

• Use squares of pea and bean netting to make "hammocks" for fruits on plants that are trained up or over supports.

• To store pumpkins, "cure" them first to harden the skins: leave in a dry sunny place for 10 days, or keep at 30°C (86°F) for 4 days

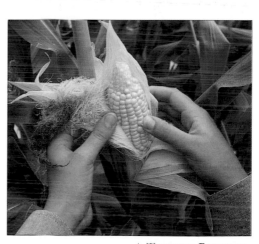

△ **HARVESTING COURGETTES**
*For the best flavour, courgettes are best cut when young, succulent and up to about 10cm (4in) long. Handle fruits carefully to avoid bruising and cut them away with a sharp knife, leaving about 1cm (½in) of stalk at the top of the fruit. Pick regularly to keep plants cropping.*

# SWEETCORN

In regions with long, warm summers, sweetcorn is sown and ripened outdoors with ease, but in cool climates it needs a head start by raising under cover, then planting out and hoping for a good long summer to ripen all the cobs. It cannot be grown in a greenhouse. You must grow it in blocks, rather than rows, so that it can be pollinated well by breezes. Expect 1–2 cobs per plant; although yields are not high, you can maximize use of space by interplanting with fast-growing salads.

**SOWING AND PLANTING** In cool areas, to raise your own plants sow seed at 15°C (59°F) in mid-spring, 2.5cm (1in) deep, in modules. Mice may take the seeds in greenhouses. Harden off and plant out, or buy young plants and plant them, when soil temperature reaches 13°C (55°F) and

any risk of frost is long gone. Plant in blocks of at least 9 plants, 30cm (12in) apart each way, to ensure good pollination. Cover with a fleece and remove it when plants have five leaves. In warm climates, seed can be sown *in situ* in a block pattern, 8cm (3in) apart, and thinned later; the seeds will need protection from birds.

**ROUTINE CARE** As with French beans (*see p.246*), give the stems more support by earthing up, to 13cm (5in). If conditions are dry at flowering or when grains are swelling, water generously once a week.

**SWEETCORN**

△ **TEST FOR RIPENESS**
*Once tassels turn brown, press a kernel with a thumbnail; if a milky liquid emerges, the cob is ripe; if watery, it is not ready; if doughy, it is overripe.*

SEE ALSO: Adding Lime, p.238; Crop Protection, pp.240–241

# LETTUCES AND OTHER LEAFY CROPS

ADEQUATE MOISTURE IS THE KEY to producing crisp, succulent salad and leaf crops. All the leafy salad crops thrive in moisture-retentive soils with plentiful organic matter and are ideally suited by deep beds, but you can plant them almost anywhere, in rows between other crops, in pots, as edging, or in patches to fill a potager bed. They are not just summer crops: by sowing different types at different times you can have salad leaves all year round. For cooking, although their flavour differs, Swiss chard and spinach beet are often used as substitutes for spinach. They are easier to grow, very decorative, and crop for a much longer period.

## LETTUCE

Lettuces grow much better in moderate climates, especially where nights are cool and fresh; in warm climates and hot spells they tend to bolt (flower and set seed), making them taste bitter. There are heat-resistant varieties for warm climates and for growing in high summer; siting summer sowings in partial shade can also help. Lettuces are either hearted (growing in a tight ball) or loose-leaved. Hearted lettuce are harvested once; with loose-leaved varieties, new leaves will sprout after you have cut the first crop (*see below*). Loose-leaves are easier to grow if you have difficulty getting cos, crisphead, or butter-head lettuces to "heart up", and because harvesting checks their development, they do not bolt. Never grow lettuces in ground manured within the previous year; it makes them rot at the crown.

**SOWING AND PLANTING** For a year-round supply, choose a mixture of varieties to sow at 2–3 week intervals between early spring and late summer. Germination is poor at temperatures over 25°C (77°F); avoid overheating by sowing in early evening. In autumn, sow hardy varieties under cover (such as a cloche) for a spring crop. Sow *in situ* or in modules, or sow in close rows and transplant thinnings. Later thinnings will probably be big enough to use in salads and garnishes. Transplant at the 5-leaf stage, when soil is moist, with leaf bases just above soil level. Space small varieties at 15cm (6in), larger ones at 30cm (12in). Shade young plants in hot weather until established. Sow cut-and-come-again lettuces thinly in wide bands.

**ROUTINE CARE** Apply a high-nitrogen fertilizer or organic liquid feed if plants are not growing well. Water generously in dry conditions; a critical period for hearted types is 7–10 days before maturity. In very hot spells, a fleece blanket or tunnel will shade crops and keep the leaves fresher. Protect autumn and early winter crops with cloches. Watch out for slug and other pest damage, and for rot in wet weather; trimming off leaves that touch the soil can help prevent rots spreading.

**HARVESTING** Begin harvesting loose-leaf lettuces 7 weeks after sowing. Cut leaves fresh as needed, as they do not store well. Cut butterheads after 10–11 weeks, cos and crispheads after 11–12 weeks; all of these keep well for a few days in the salad drawer of a refrigerator.

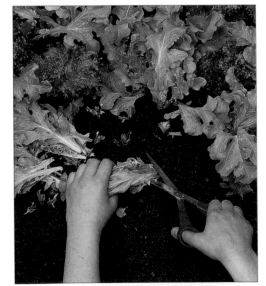

△ **HARVESTING LOOSE-LEAVED LETTUCE**
*Loose-leaved varieties of lettuce, like baby salad leaves (see opposite), can be grown as cut-and-come-again crops. When plants are 8–15cm (3–6in) high, cut just above the lowest leaves, leaving 3cm (1½in) of stem; it will soon sprout again. This can be repeated.*

**LOOSE-LEAF LETTUCE**
'Lollo Rosso'

**BUTTERHEAD LETTUCE**
'All the year round'

**SEMI-COS LETTUCE**
'Little Gem'

**COS LETTUCE**
'English Cos'

**SEE ALSO:** Types of Beds, p.237; Manures and Mulches, p.239

# CHICORY AND ENDIVE

Radicchio (red chicory) and curly endive (frisée type) have become so popular that seed and even young plants are readily available. They have much the same requirements as lettuces (*see opposite*), and take 8–12 weeks to mature; you can either pick off leaves, or cut the whole head. The older the leaves are, the more bitter they taste, especially in hot weather. Later crops usually taste sweeter than those that mature in high summer, though planting in light shade or with a fleece to shade plants, as with lettuces, can help. In cold weather, radicchio becomes crisper and the colour intensifies. For pale, sweet leaves at the centre of curly endive, blanch the middles by resting a sideplate on top of the plants when the leaves are dry for 10 days before harvesting.

**SOWING AND PLANTING** Sow seed in mid-spring for summer crops, and until mid-summer to crop from autumn into early winter, *in situ*, or in modules to transplant after 3–4 weeks. Thin or space to give plants 25–35cm (10–14in) each way, depending on the size of the variety.

**ROUTINE CARE** Keep well watered, especially in dry spells. Both crops are reasonably trouble-free, although slugs may take a fancy to endives.

RED CHICORY 'Cesare'

CURLY ENDIVE (BLANCHED)

# OTHER SALAD LEAVES

Baby leaf crops are easily grown from seed. Some have quite pungent flavours; others are blander. Spinach is much simpler to grow for young leaves than as a mature culinary crop, when it tends either to bolt or be badly pest damaged. Try different leaves to find ones that you like with different sowing and cropping times, so that you have something to pick through the year. Seed mixtures are available. Winter leaves are often the most peppery, and just a few will perk up a salad of shop-bought lettuce. These crops thrive in the humus-rich soil of a well kept vegetable plot, but will grow almost anywhere, as well as in containers; on light soils and in hot weather they tend to run to flower quite quickly. Follow the instructions on the packet for each crop. Water regularly and apply a high-nitrogen feed if plants need a boost. Leaves may be ready in as little as 3 weeks; cropping will continue for as long as you snip off leaves regularly, so that the plants do not mature. Pick off leaves that develop fungal leaf spots; you may also need to protect from birds. If flea beetles attack rocket, which they love, try sowing some more as far away as possible.

SPINACH      CORN SALAD      ROCKET

# SPINACH BEET AND CHARD

These leaf crops are used cooked like spinach, but tolerate higher temperatures, and are less prone to bolting and easier to grow. Spinach beet is also known as perpetual spinach. Red-stemmed chard is a striking crop, good in a border or potager. The broad, white leaf midribs of Swiss chard take longer to cook than the leaves and may be used as a separate vegetable.

**SOWING AND PLANTING** Sow in spring; sow spinach beet again in mid- to late summer for harvest through winter. Sow *in situ* in rows 38cm (15in) apart for spinach beet, 45cm (18in) apart for chard; thin early to 30cm (12in) apart. Alternatively, sow in modules and plant 30cm (12in) apart.

**ROUTINE CARE** Mulch after planting. Keep well watered and apply a high-nitrogen fertilizer during the growing season if plants are not developing well. Pick off any leaves that develop fungal leaf spots. You may find that birds eat the leaves in winter when other food is scarce.

**HARVESTING** Begin harvesting after 8–12 weeks; cropping continues for months as long as you pick leaves regularly.

SPINACH BEET

RED STEMMED CHARD

**SEE ALSO:** Thinning and Transplanting, p.243; Sowing Seeds in a Narrow Drill, p.243

# TENDER CROPS

IN WARM CLIMATES with long summers, these fruiting crops thrive outdoors, but in cool temperate regions, only some tomatoes reliably crop well without protection, and a heated greenhouse or propagator is certainly essential to raise young plants. Whether growing in a greenhouse or, say, on a sunny, sheltered patio, all do well in containers; growbags are ideal, ensuring that plants grow in fresh, disease-free compost each year. If your crops have been healthy, spent growbag compost can be added to the compost heap or even used to mulch ornamental plants – not crops, and certainly never potatoes, vulnerable to the same sorts of diseases.

## CHILLIES AND PEPPERS

Small chilli pepper bushes make lovely container plants for a patio; in cool areas you can grow them on under cover until fruits form, bring them out for summer display, then shelter them again once the evenings draw in. You can in theory do this with larger bell pepper plants, but they are unwieldy to move and stems may snap. Under glass or polythene peppers grow best at 21°C (70°F); you may need a greenhouse heater until summer.

**SOWING AND PLANTING** If you cannot give young plants the heat they need at first, wait until late spring to buy them. To raise your own, in late winter or early spring sow seeds 1–2cm (½–¾in) deep, in trays at 18–21°C (65–70°F). Prick out singly into 8cm (3in) pots when 5cm (2in) tall. When flowers form, plant two to a growbag, or singly in 20–25cm (8–10in) pots.

**ROUTINE CARE** Never move plants outside until any danger of frost is long past. Stake plants over 60cm (2ft) tall. Keep well watered, and damp down or mist in the greenhouse to maintain humidity. Feed every two weeks with a balanced fertilizer. In the greenhouse, watch out for red spider mite and mildews. If the last fruits stop ripening as days cool, uproot the plant and hang it upside-down, with the fruits still attached, in a warm place; they should colour up.

JALAPEÑO CHILLIES

CHILLI PEPPERS

PEPPER

## CUCUMBERS

Greenhouse cucumbers similar to the ones you buy in supermarkets are demanding and difficult plants. Outdoor, "ridge" cucumbers are much easier to grow, and less troubled by pests and diseases than the greenhouse kinds. Modern varieties are not bitter. Some have rough or bristly skin; peel before use. Each plant should yield about 15 fruits, from late summer to mid-autumn.

**SOWING AND PLANTING** In mid- to late spring, sow 2–3 seeds on edge in 8cm (3in) pots at 20°C (68°F); thin to the strongest. Plant out in early summer, two per grow-bag or 45cm (18in) apart in well-manured ground, on a slight mound to prevent rot, preferably under a cloche or fleece.

**ROUTINE CARE** Pinch out the growing tip after 6 leaves for a bushy plant, and mulch with straw or plastic to keep fruits clean. Train climbing varieties up canes, or string suspended from a frame. Water when dry; a watering system is ideal to maintain a regular supply. Once fruits develop, feed regularly with tomato fertilizer.

## AUBERGINES

In cool climates, a greenhouse heater may be needed for aubergines, especially when young; growth is checked below 20°C (68°F) and ideally they prefer 25–30°C (77–86°F). There are dwarf varieties, ideal to bring out into a sunny spot in summer, but if nights are chilly, it is worth protecting them with a fleece blanket.

**SOWING AND PLANTING** In late winter or early spring, sow seeds 1–2cm (½–¾in) deep, in trays at 18–21°C (65–70°F). Prick out singly into 8cm (3in) pots when 5cm (2in) tall. When the first flowers form, plant three to a growbag, or put dwarf types in 20cm (8in) pots. Pinch out the tip of the plant when about 38cm (15in) tall.

**ROUTINE CARE** As for peppers (*see above*), but use a tomato feed rather than a general fertilizer. To produce large aubergines, let only 4–6 fruits per plant develop. Watch plants under cover for greenhouse pests and mildews.

AUBERGINE

△ **HARVESTING AUBERGINES**
*Aubergines are ripe when the whole fruit is coloured and the skin is taut and shiny; once it loses its shine, or becomes wrinkled, the flesh will taste bitter. Cut the stalk at least 2.5cm (1in) away from the fruit.*

**SEE ALSO:** Sowing Indoors or under Glass, p.244

# TOMATOES

Tomato varieties come in different sizes, shapes, and colours, but their hardiness in your climate and their growth habit will have a greater influence on your choice. Bush tomatoes are largely self-supporting, but by far the wider choice of varieties is found among tomatoes with a sprawling habit, grown for convenience as supported single stems known as cordons. There are tomatoes of both habits that can be grown outdoors without protection in cool climates once plants reach a certain size, but you can virtually double yields, from 2 to 4kg (4–8lb) per plant, under glass.

**SITE AND SOIL** Before planting tomatoes in open ground, add organic matter and a balanced fertilizer to the soil, as tomatoes are sensitive to nutrient deficiencies. Under glass, use growbags or 25cm (10in) pots filled with fresh container compost.

**SOWING AND PLANTING** Young plants are easy to find in garden centres and markets; if you have a greenhouse, you can buy them early, ensuring the best choice of plants, or grow from seed. Sow seeds 2cm (¾in) deep, in trays or modules. Plants to be grown in greenhouses can be started in late winter, sowing at 15–18°C (59–64°F). Outdoor varieties will be ready to harden off and plant out in about 8 weeks, so time sowing of these so that this date will be after any danger of late frosts in your area. Pot on into 8cm (3in) pots at the 2–3 leaf stage and plant once flowers form. A fleece over new plants outdoors for the first week or two gets them off to a good start. Plant greenhouse tomatoes three to a growbag or one to a pot; outdoors, space cordons 45cm (18in) apart; dwarf and bush types 30 and 60cm (1 and 2ft) respectively.

**ROUTINE CARE** Mulch outdoor plants once the soil is warm. A plastic mulch under bushes will keep low fruits clean; white plastic also reflects the sun, aiding ripening. Never allow plants to dry out completely, or they may develop problems. Regular watering also prevents tough skins, uneven ripening, and split fruits (*see p.304*). A 2-gallon can of water per growbag per day may be needed in hot spells. After the first cluster (truss) of tiny fruits has developed from the flowers, feed weekly with high-potash tomato fertilizer, or an equivalent organic liquid feed. Cordons need support, either with canes, or with twine suspended from greenhouse rafters. They also need training to form a single, vertical stem (*see below*). Watch out for whitefly (*see p.299*); companion plants of French marigolds may help deter them.

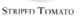

**STANDARD TOMATO**     **PLUM TOMATO**

**CHERRY TOMATOES**

**YELLOW TOMATO**     **STRIPED TOMATO**

## TRAINING CORDON TOMATOES

**1 PINCHING OUT SHOOTS**
*To train cordon tomatoes upwards, tie the main stem loosely to a cane, or to suspended twine, at intervals. Remove all leafy sideshoots that develop where leaves join the main stem, to concentrate energy into the fruits.*

**2 PINCHING OUT THE TOP**
*By late summer, when 4–6 trusses of fruits have formed (4 in cold areas, 6 in mild regions), stop more developing by pinching out the top of the plant – there will not be time for them to grow and ripen. Continue to pinch out sideshoots.*

△ **BETTER RIPENING**
*In cool climates, outdoor cordons will ripen their last fruits better if detached from their support, laid on a bed of clean straw and given the added warmth of a tunnel cloche. The roots stay in the ground to sustain the plant.*

---

### GOOD IDEAS

• Where space is limited, dwarf bush and trailing varieties are ideal for 25cm (10in) pots, or even hanging baskets (*see p.177*). The hardier varieties of cherry tomato provide a small but satisfyingly ripe crop and almost never develop blossom end rot.

• In cool climates, in most years the last fruits of the season will not ripen fully: pick green tomatoes and put them on a warm, sunny windowsill; the company of a ripe banana will help them colour up and ripen. Alternatively, use them for chutney.

**SEE ALSO:** Large Seeds, p.244; Sowing in Modules, p. 245

# STONE FRUITS

PLUMS, CHERRIES AND PEACHES are tree fruits known as stone fruits, because of their single seed kernel. They do not produce fruiting spurs and so pruning techniques differ to accommodate their fruiting habit. Unless they are grown in a special, trained form (most commonly a fan, which suits their growth and fruiting habit), they do not need a regular regime of pruning once established; you just need to use common sense to take out old, unproductive branches as necessary. Remember that unless you need to remove a damaged or diseased branch, which you should do straight away, stone fruits should be pruned in spring and summer, not winter.

## PLUMS

Grow plums, gages and damsons in moderately fertile, well-drained soil and a sunny, sheltered site; all flower early in spring, so for good fruit set need a site as frost-free as possible. In cool areas choose damsons and traditional, hardy varieties of plum such as 'Victoria'; even if the summer does not produce super-ripe fruits, they can be used for cooking. In mild areas, or on a sunny, sheltered wall, try dessert types. Many plums, including 'Victoria', are self-fertile, while others need a pollinator. Plums can be trained as bushes, pyramids or fans. The bush is a fairly compact form; it needs little pruning once established. 'Pixy' (dwarfing), or 'St Julien A' rootstocks make small- to medium-sized trees. Plant 4m (12ft) apart, in late autumn (no later than midwinter), as trees come into growth early. Mulch annually in early spring and, when trees reach flowering size, apply balanced fertilizer and a high-nitrogen feed, as for pears. In summer, after natural fruit drop, thin remaining fruit to 7–10cm (3–4in) apart, to yield better quality fruit and reduce risks of branch breakage. Plums may be affected by birds (see p.307), winter moth (Caterpillars, p.298), canker (p.300), and brown rot (p.304).

PLUM 'Marjorie's Seedling'

PLUM 'Coe's Golden Drop'

PLUM 'Victoria'

DAMSON 'Merryweather'

GREENGAGE 'Cambridge Gage'

△ PLUM IN FRUIT
*Trees in the plum group do not fruit on spur wood but at the base of year-old wood and all along two-year-old and older wood. Pruning must take account of this habit.*

### PRUNING A PLUM BUSH
Aim to produce a clear trunk of at least 75cm (2½ft). Once established, prune in early summer, to remove weak, dead, damaged, crossing or unproductive growth by cutting it back to its point of origin, or to a replacement shoot.

Shorten sublaterals by half, cutting back to a bud facing in a direction that will produce a balanced, open-centred crown

To keep the crown open and well-balanced, remove any over-vigorous new shoots that develop, and any that cross the centre or rub against main branches

With naturally spreading cultivars, like 'Victoria', make cuts to upward-facing buds or shoots. Horizontal branches will droop and may break under the weight of fruit

Cut lateral branches to outward-facing buds, or to upward-facing buds on horizontal shoots

◁ YEAR 1, EARLY SPRING
*Shorten 3–4 well-spaced laterals by two-thirds. Cut the leader back to the highest of the selected laterals, about 90cm (3ft) above ground. Shorten low laterals to 2 buds; pinch out subsequent growth to 2 leaves throughout the season.*

◁ YEAR 2, EARLY SPRING
*On each lateral, shorten 2–3 strong sublaterals by half. Remove completely any weak, badly placed or narrow-angled shoots. Remove low laterals that were pruned and pinched back the previous year. If further low shoots emerge, rub them off.*

◁ YEAR 3
*Delay pruning until spring or early summer. Prune branch leaders that are weak or growing horizontally by a quarter, cutting to a bud facing in a direction where new growth will fill in the branch framework.*

SEE ALSO: Planting Fruit Crops, pp.260–261; Pruning Fruit Trees, pp.262–263

# CHERRIES

Acid cherries will produce a culinary crop even in cold areas; in mild regions, or if you have a sunny, sheltered site, sweet cherries can be grown, although birds will fight you for them. Grow cherries in moderately fertile, well-drained soil and a sheltered site; acid cherries tolerate light shade. Most acid cherries and a few sweet cherries are self-fertile; both are most usually grafted onto the semi-vigorous rootstock 'Colt', on which a bush-trained tree will reach 4m (12ft) tall. In most gardens, there is seldom room for two trees of this size (to meet pollination needs) so select the self-fertile sweet cherry 'Stella' and acid cherry 'Morello'.

Cherries are commonly trained as bushes or fans. Sweet cherries fruit at the base of year-old shoots and all along older wood; they make excellent bushes, pruned and trained as for plums. Acid cherries fruit on the previous year's growth, so the aim of pruning is remove some fruited wood each year to make way for year-old wood. Mulch in early spring, also applying ammonium nitrate at 35g/sq m (1oz/sq yd) to acid cherries, but only to sweet cherries if growth is poor. Irrigate well in dry conditions. Fruit thinning is seldom necessary. Cherries may be affected by birds (see p.307), winter moth (Caterpillars, p.298), canker (p.300), and brown rot (p.304).

Cut back one in four fruited shoots to a replacement shoot near their base

Shorten to a sideshoot or leaf over-vigorous upright growth that will crowd the centre

Remove downward-pointing growth on lower branches

## PRUNING AN ACID CHERRY BUSH

Formative pruning is as for a plum bush, in spring. Acid cherries fruit on young growth produced the previous year. Once established, do the main pruning after fruiting. On older trees, also cut back one or two branches annually in spring to encourage new growth.

SWEET CHERRIES

ACID CHERRIES

# PEACHES AND NECTARINES

Peaches and nectarines do not ripen well in cool-summer climates unless given a favoured spot; here they are best fan-trained and need a 5m (15ft) wide wall space. An alternative is to grow a dwarf tree in a large container, and move it under cover for the winter. If you have a suitable wall, the easiest option is to buy a part-trained fan and plant in early winter. It will have two laterals, trained at 40° angles. Each of these needs two well-spaced shoots on the upper side and one below; tie in to canes lashed to wires as they grow, to form the ribs. Form new ribs by pruning main arms back by a third in

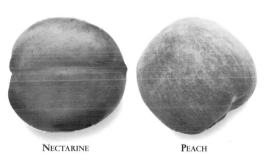

NECTARINE            PEACH

early spring, to produce laterals that are tied in during summer. Pinch out all unwanted shoots to one leaf. On established fans, both sideshoots and developing fruitlets need thinning, in order to maximize sun exposure on a small crop of fruits. Leave one sideshoot on each flowering shoot below the flowers, pinch out the rest to one leaf. Tip-prune this sideshoot when it reaches 45cm (18in) long and, after fruiting, cut each fruited shoot back to this replacement sideshoot and tie it in. Peaches are affected by peach leaf curl (see p.297), root knot eelworms (p.309), and canker (p.300).

## THINNING SHOOTS

**1 BEFORE THINNING**
If all the closely grouped shoots on this rib grow out, they will overcrowd the fan, produce too many small, poor quality fruits and shade them from ripening sun.

**2 AFTER THINNING**
Pinch out excess sideshoots at their point of origin to leave the remaining shoots at 10–15cm (4–6in) spacings, removing first any that grow into the wall.

THINNING FRUIT ▷
When the thinned fruits reach the size of walnuts, and some fruitlets have been shed naturally, they are thinned again to one every 15–22cm (6–9in) of branch. Loosely wrap ripening fruits in muslin to protect from birds.

SEE ALSO: Lashing Canes to Wires, p.261

# BUSH FRUITS

THESE ARE COOL-CLIMATE FRUITS, impossible to grow in hot countries; all tolerate some part-day shade. It makes sense to grow gooseberry and currant bushes together. It make it more convenient to give them all the well-rotted manure they love each spring, and also to enclose them with netting that will protect buds and fruits from birds.

Blueberries need very different conditions. If your soil has the acidity they need, you will almost certainly have limed the kitchen garden for other crops, and they will not grow there. Either grow these attractive shrubs in ornamental beds or in containers, also the solution if your soil is not acidic.

## GOOSEBERRIES

Gooseberries need cool summers; where summers are hot, site in light shade. They need shelter; the young shoots are quite brittle. Dig in well-rotted manure well before planting, and buy plants certified disease-free. Plant 1.2–1.5m (4–5ft) apart, in autumn or winter, then in late winter, prune by cutting back main stems by half; remove low shoots to form a short trunk, 15cm (6in) tall. Next winter, prune new shoots by half to an outward-facing bud. Prune shoots growing in- or downwards to one bud. Once established, gooseberries do not need regular pruning, although if the bush is widely spreading you should cut off any very low branches. As the bush ages fruits will get smaller and become more difficult to harvest amid crowded, spiny shoots, at which point you can take out an entire old branch or two (*see below*). Every spring, mulch with well-rotted manure and apply balanced fertilizer and 35g (1oz) of potassium sulphate per bush. Pick off leaves showing signs of mildew or leaf spot. Pick off caterpillars, probably sawfly larvae (*see p.298*); even if these get out of hand and strip bushes of leaves, the fruits should still be harvestable.

WHITE GOOSEBERRIES

RED GOOSEBERRIES

◁ **PRUNING A GOOSEBERRY**
*In late winter, remove oldest branches and shoots that cross the centre to prevent overcrowding and maintain an open centre. The pruned bush should have a crown of evenly spaced shoots pointing upwards or outwards (depending on how the variety grows).*

Remove all low-growing shoots to maintain a short trunk that keeps fruits clean by reducing soil splash

Three-year-old wood is darker brown with fruiting spurs. Older wood gradually becomes less fruitful

Second year wood bears fruit and is smooth and grey-brown

The newest, current season's growth has pale, yellow-green bark; fruit buds are not formed until the second year

◁ **FRUITING SHOOTS**
*Fruit-laden branches on gooseberries take three years to form. In the first year a shoot grows, in the second it bears fruits, and in the third the wood darkens, and begins to send out new sideshoots of its own to fruit the following year.*

## REDCURRANTS

Redcurrants grow and fruit in a very similar way to gooseberries (although they are not spiny). They tend to make taller, more upright bushes. The key difference is that the fruits need more sun to ripen, so you must prune them a little each year to let the light in.

Dig plenty of well-rotted manure into the soil before planting. In autumn or winter, buy young plants from a reliable supplier; there is no certification scheme for redcurrants that guarantees they are virus-free. Plant 1.2–1.5m (4–5ft) apart. Over the next two years, shape young bushes as for gooseberries (*see above*). When established, prune after fruiting or in autumn or winter; trim the tips from all of the main, leading branches, cutting to a bud, and cut back all of the sideshoots to one bud from the branch. Every spring, mulch with well-rotted manure and apply balanced fertilizer and 35g (1oz) of potassium sulphate per bush. Water in dry weather as the fruits develop, but not as they ripen; this causes skins to split. Be watchful for caterpillars, usually those of the winter moth (*see p.298*), and pick off any leaves with spots or mildew.

REDCURRANTS

SEE ALSO: Applying Lime, p.238

# BLACKCURRANTS

Although they are related to redcurrants, blackcurrants grow and fruit in quite a different way. Whereas redcurrants grow as a bush with a definite single trunk, blackcurrants send up shoots in a thicket from ground level. Once fully grown, they must be pruned each year to thin this thicket of growth, or the fruits will be shaded and smothered. Blackcurrants fruit best on wood made the previous season, so it is the oldest stems that need to be removed. You can expect crops two years after planting, modest at first but later around 5kg (10lb) per plant.

BLACKCURRANTS

Before planting, dig plenty of well-rotted manure into the soil. Always buy bushes from a reputable supplier that guarantees virus-free stock. Plant them more deeply than when in their containers, 1.2–1.5m (4–5ft) apart, in autumn or winter. Cut all the stems back to about 8cm (3in) from the soil, cutting to a bud; it sounds drastic, but will result in much better growth. In the next two winters, remove only any weak or downward-pointing shoots. From then on, prune each year before late winter as below. Every spring, mulch with well-rotted manure and apply a balanced fertilizer, and also 35g/1oz of potassium sulphate per bush. Water in dry weather but not as fruits ripen; this causes skins to split. Winter moth caterpillars (*see p.298*) and more rarely big bud mite (*see p.302*) are usually the only major problems.

**PRUNING A BLACKCURRANT ▷**
*Once the bush is established, pruning each winter consists of removing some stems close to the ground, and cutting other side branches back to where they join main stems. Concentrate on removing old wood, branches that sweep the ground, and those that cross the centre, crowding the bush.*

**THIN THE CENTRE ▷**
*Cut out at the base one in three or four of the stems, choosing the oldest and/or least productive (the ones with fewest young sideshoots). Use loppers for a good clean cut*

**◁ BRANCH TOO LOW**
*Cut back any branches that spread out over the ground; when laden with fruit they will brush the soil, and the fruits will get dirty or be eaten by mice and other pests.*

# BLUEBERRIES

Related to ornamental *Vaccinium* and to several wild, swamp- or moor-dwelling shrubs, blueberries only thrive in moist, ideally peaty, acidic soil. While their wilder relatives are mostly low-growing, the most attractive blueberries to grow are the highbush varieties, which make well-shaped, medium-sized shrubs, attractive in their own right; if you have suitable soil, they look good among rhododendrons and heathers, although you may lose fruits to birds this way. If you do not have acidic soil, you can mimic the conditions blueberries enjoy by using ericaceous compost in a container; it must be a good-sized tub, and you must water regularly to ensure the compost never dries out (you must use lime-free water; rainwater is ideal). Container-growing makes it easy to throw bird netting over the bushes. Each

spring, mulch them with well-rotted manure, or work a little bonemeal into container compost. Blueberries do not need regular pruning, but tolerate it, in winter, if they grow too large or become very congested. In the right conditions, blueberries are usually trouble-free; lime-induced chlorosis (*see general leaf-yellowing, p.296*) is the most common complaint.

BLUEBERRIES

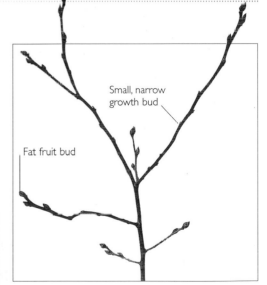

Small, narrow growth bud

Fat fruit bud

**◁ BLUEBERRY CROP**
*Blueberries ripen over a long season, so while you may need to pick over the bushes several times, there is not the problem of gluts, as with some other fruits.*

**△ WHAT TO PRUNE**
*Mature blueberries benefit from judicious pruning in winter. Fruit buds are quite distinctive, helping you identify the least productive branches for removal.*

**SEE ALSO:** Containers and Raised Beds, pp.166–183

# CANE FRUITS

RASPBERRIES, BLACKBERRIES, and hybrid berries are temperate climate crops, growing best where summers are not scorching and moisture is plentiful. They are susceptible to virus diseases, so buy stock certified free of disease and do not plant where cane fruits have grown before. They need slightly acid soil, around pH 6; if higher than pH 7, they may suffer from yellowing of the leaves at the margins and between the veins (*see p.296*). If this does occur, spray with liquid seaweed, or treat with a chelated form of iron and manganese. Equip yourself with a pair of stout gloves for pruning and training raspberries and prickly varieties of blackberry.

## RASPBERRIES

Raspberries grow as long, slender stems (canes) which, for the best crops, are cut down after they have fruited once. They need fanning out and tying in to a support system in a sunny, sheltered site to allow the fruits to ripen; they also need protection from birds. With summer-fruiting varieties, canes grow in one year and crop the next, in high summer; they are then cut out and the new young canes that have grown that year are tied in in their place (*see below*). With autumn-fruiting varieties, canes grow and fruit in the same season, cropping from late summer on, after which they are all cut down. Do not allow summer raspberries to crop in their first year (pinch out any flowers that appear); autumn-fruiters crop well the first year after planting. Before planting (*see p.261*), erect supports

RASPBERRIES

and prepare a area at least 90cm (3ft) wide for the rows, digging in plenty of well-rotted manure or compost; raspberries need fertile, moist but well-drained soil. Every spring, mulch ideally with well-rotted manure, or with leafmould (do not bury the canes), and apply a balanced fertilizer to the soil at least 60cm (2ft) either side of the row, at 100–140g per metre (3–4oz per yd). Keep weed-free and well-watered. To keep the plants manageable, remove canes that emerge from the soil more than 22cm (9in) from the main row. Each year, after fruiting, prune back the canes after you have picked the last fruits, and tie in the new ones as they grow. Watch out for signs of raspberry beetles (*see p.305*), grey mould (*p.305*), and viruses (*p.305*).

△ SUPPORTS FOR RASPBERRIES
*Install post and wire supports (top picture) as described on p. 261. An easy alternative method is to guide canes between posts and nylon string (shown viewed from the top, above). Loop nylon string 45cm (18in) above ground between two 2m (6ft) posts; with a second loop at 1.2m (4ft). Add connecting ties at intervals between the parallel strings to stop canes slumping or being blown about.*

△ FIRST SEASON AFTER PLANTING
*In spring, new canes will grow in a cluster from ground level around the original single stem. Space them out evenly and tie them in to their supports as they grow upwards. In midsummer, remove the old, original cane by cutting it right back to its base.*

## PRUNING AND TRAINING SUMMER-FRUITING RASPBERRIES

**1 AFTER FRUITING**
*Cut out all of the fruited canes at the base immediately after harvesting. Leave the new, pale-stemmed canes that have not borne fruit.*

**2 SPACING CANES**
*Tie in or space out the new canes to the supporting wires at 10cm (4in) apart. Here, continuous lacing with twine is used, vbut you can tie them in indidually; use figure-of-eight knots so that the canes do not chafe against the wires..*

**3 TIP-PRUNING**
*At the end of the growing season, loop over the tips of canes that are taller than the wires and tie them into the top wire, to stop them thrashing about in winter winds. In spring, before growth begins, tip prune all canes to a healthy bud, about 15cm (6in) above the top wire.*

SEE ALSO: Planting Cane Fruits, p.261

# BLACKBERRIES AND HYBRID BERRIES

Blackberries and their hybrids, such as loganberries, boysenberries and tayberries, fruit in late summer on long, slender stems (canes) produced the previous year. Thornless cultivars are less vigorous than prickly ones, but are easier, or at least more comfortable, to train and harvest. They need the same growing conditions as raspberries, so prepare the site and maintain them in the same way. Provide support wires, spaced 30cm (12in) apart, as described on p. 261.

Plant during winter. If the weather or soil conditions are very cold and wet, delay planting until late winter or early spring. Some varieties are more susceptible to cold damage than others and may be killed in very cold areas; seek advice from a local supplier. Training methods vary (see below), but all aim to separate the current year's fruiting canes from newly developing ones that will fruit in the following year. As the fruits develop, they will need protection from birds. After cropping, cut out the fruited canes at ground level. Retain the new canes that have developed during the current season and tie them in to the support. Remove any that are weak or damaged at the base. In early spring, tip prune any canes that show die-back as a result of frost damage. Harvest regularly, leaving in the central core of the fruits.

Blackberries and hybrid berries may be affected by raspberry beetles (see p.305), grey mould (p.305), and viruses (p.305).

CULTIVATED BLACKBERRIES

TAYBERRIES

LOGANBERRIES

△ PRUNING, SPRING AFTER PLANTING
*Blackberries and hybrid berries, like raspberries, are usually bought as a single stem (cane), planted in late winter or early spring. Once you see new shoots growing strongly from ground level around the original plant, the old stem can be cut back.*

Cut back to 10–13cm (4–5in) from the ground

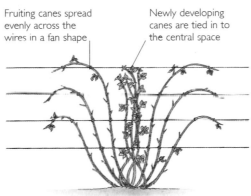

Fruiting canes spread evenly across the wires in a fan shape

Newly developing canes are tied in to the central space

△ FAN-TRAINING METHOD
*This is an ideal method for less vigorous cultivars and suits those with more rigid canes. The fruiting canes are splayed out and tied in across the fan on either side of the centre. New canes are tied into the central space as they grow and lowered and tied into place after fruited canes are cut out.*

Fruiting canes woven together and tied in to horizontal wires

New canes tied in to central space and along top wires as they grow

△ ROPE-TRAINING METHOD
*This is a good method for vigorous cultivars with many flexible canes. Fruiting canes are twisted loosely together and tied along the lower wires, new canes up the middle and, if necessary, along the top. When fruited canes are cut out, the new ones are divided between the lower wires.*

△ TYING IN NEW SHOOTS
*Use soft twine and make a figure-of-eight knot to secure the cane firmly to the wire (this is easiest with thornless cultivars, like 'Oregon Thornless'). Space the canes evenly across the support so that each cane receives its share of sunlight and good air circulation is maintained.*

All fruited canes are cut back to ground level, near the base of the stem

Newly developed canes can be bundled gently and carefully together during pruning and spaced out when pruning is complete

◁ PRUNING AFTER FRUITING
*Once established, annual pruning is done immediately after harvest. Here, new canes have been tied in a central bundle to separate new from old. Cut all fruited canes out at the base. Tie new canes securely to horizontal wires according to the system used. Continue tying in as the canes grow during the season.*

SEE ALSO: Ways of Supporting Plants, pp.108–109; Planting Cane Fruits, p.261

# OTHER FRUITS

A STRAWBERRY BED ranks highly among the delights of summer, although for healthy, heavy crops it requires a certain amount of care and attention. If you are not committed to a full-scale kitchen gardening, a few plants can be grown attractively in containers, however, and alpine strawberry plants will grow happily in the front of a border, and look good too. Rhubarb is also a handsome perennial, although as it needs regular manuring you might not want to give it too prominent a site; beside the compost heap is traditional. Grape vines score highly on looks too, a bonus in cool climates where heavy, ripe crops are not assured outdoors.

## STRAWBERRIES

There are three types of strawberry: summer-fruiting, which crop over 2–3 weeks in summer; perpetual-fruiting, which crop in summer and again in autumn, and alpine varieties, which bear a long succession of small, piquant fruits. These are often grown as ornamentals and make attractive edging, but the heavier-cropping varieties are best grown and cared for all together in a strawberry patch or container; the specially-made urn-shaped pots with planting pockets make lovely patio ornaments.

Buy plants that are certified virus-free in late summer and early autumn, to crop the next summer. They should crop well for four years or more. Grow in a warm, sunny site in fertile, preferably slightly acid, moist but well-drained, well-manured soil, or good-quality loam-based compost. In beds, plant 45cm (18in) apart in slightly raised rows 75cm (30in) apart, with the base of the central crown at soil level. On sandy or chalky soils, apply a balanced fertilizer before planting.

Keep weed-free and well-watered. Protect flowers from night frosts with fleece; lift it in the day for pollination. Protect fruits from birds and from contact with the soil, to guard against rot and slug damage. Remove runners, the creeping stems on which young plantlets develop; they take energy from the fruits. This runnering habit is useful, however, for raising your own plants (right), easy to do and ideal to perpetuate a variety that crops well for you, with a good flavour.

Harvest every other day when fully ripe, complete with stalks. After harvest, clear away surplus runners, weeds, straw and old foliage. Apply a balanced fertilizer.

EARLY-FRUITING STRAWBERRIES

ALPINE STRAWBERRIES

△ **USING PLASTIC MULCH**
*Planting through crosswise slits in a plastic sheet mulch reduces weeding, retains soil moisture and encourages early cropping by warming the soil; it also helps keep fruit clean.*

△ **REMOVING RUNNERS**
*Remove excess runners by pinching them out carefully close to the parent plant. If left in place, they divert the plant's energy away from ripening fruits and reduce yields.*

△ **KEEPING FRUIT CLEAN**
*Strawing down is the traditional way of keeping fruits clean; strawberry mats may also be used. Pack a thick layer of straw beneath plants when in flower or when fruits are forming.*

### RAISING YOUR OWN STRAWBERRY PLANTS

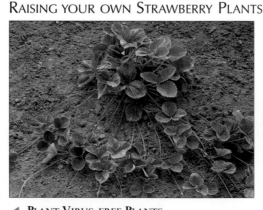

**1 PLANT VIRUS-FREE PLANTS**
*Plant one or two virus-free plants each year for new stock. Remove all flowers. As runners form, spread them out evenly around the parent; let them root into the gound, or pin them down into small pots sunk into the ground.*

**2 SEVER THE ROOTED RUNNERS**
*Once the runners have rooted, and are making new growth, lift the plantlet or the pot carefully and sever the runner from the parent plant. Transplant to well-prepared soil, or move them into larger pots for planting out later.*

SEE ALSO: Rotating Crops, p.237; Nourishing your Crops, pp.238–239

# RHUBARB

Rhubarb is a trouble-free, very hardy perennial that may be productive in good conditions for twenty years. It is a temperate climate crop and does not thrive in warm conditions. Rhubarb grows in a wide range of soils provided that they are fertile and well-drained. Dormant plants, known as crowns or sets, are available to buy in autumn or winter.

Before planting, prepare the soil by digging in copious amounts of well-rotted manure or garden compost. Plant crowns between autumn and spring, 75–90cm (2½–3ft) apart. Mulch plants heavily each year in autumn or early spring. Apply 45–55g (1½–2oz) of a high-nitrogen fertilizer per plant at first, increasing to 110g (4oz) when mature. Water thoroughly in dry weather. Remove any flowering stems. Divide plants (*above right*) when they become very crowded.

For forced stems, more tender and ready for harvest about three weeks earlier than

**RHUBARB**

unforced stems, cover dormant crowns with a 10cm (4in) layer of clean, dry straw in late winter, and cover with a forcing pot, or a 45cm (18in) deep bucket. Watch out for signs of crown rot (*see p.304*); rhubarb may also be affected by honey fungus (*p.301*).

## DIVIDING RHUBARB

**1 LIFT OR EXPOSE THE CROWN**
*Once the leaves have died back in autumn, lift or expose the crown. Cut through the crown with a spade, taking care not to damage buds. Ensure that there is at least one good growth bud on each section.*

**2 REPLANT THE SECTIONS**
*Prepare the soil by digging in manure. Replant the sections 75–90cm (2½–3ft) apart, with the crown bud just above the soil. Firm in gently, water in, and rake the soil level around the plant.*

◁ **HARVESTING RHUBARB**
*Harvest stems in spring and early summer. Grasp the stem firmly and twist slightly while pulling upwards and outwards. Do not harvest, or harvest only very lightly, in the first year so plants establish well. Once established, harvest heavily until early to mid-summer, then stop.*

# GRAPES

Whereas in warm winemaking regions, vines are grown on open supports of posts and wires so that air can circulate around them, in cooler climes a sunny, sheltered wall – equipped with horizontal wires every 30cm (12in) – will help the fruits to ripen. Even so, in a poor summer the crop may not be up to much, but the beauty of the vine is some compensation. Buy a young vine (most likely a two- or three-year vertical stem) in late autumn to early winter, and plant against the wall as for any climber (*see p.110*). This central stem,

once it reaches the top wire, is kept cut back to that height. The aim is to allow horizontal side branches to grow out every year, tying them into the wires. After they have borne fruit, they are cut back hard to the central stem (*see below*), which will become increasingly knobbly and gnarled. Water whenever dry, reducing as fruits ripen. Apply tomato fertilizer every 2–3 weeks once shoots develop; stop as fruits start to ripen. Prune in summer (*see below*). Grapes may be affected by mildew (*see p.296*) and grey mould, as on strawberries (*p.305*).

**WHITE MUSCAT GRAPES**

**BLACK GRAPES**

**SUMMER-PRUNING▷**
*Once all the sideshoots are tied in, summer-pruning aims to control vigorous leafy growth, concentrating energy into a few, choice bunches of grapes. Prune side branches without fruit bunches to 5–6 leaves, and ones with fruits to 2 leaves beyond the last bunch. If there are lots of fruit clusters, thin them to one every 30cm (12in). Pinch back sideshoots to one leaf.*

**WINTER-PRUNING ▷**
*In midwinter, prune all the side branches back to one bud if the bud looks strong, or two buds, if not. Where the central stem is becoming very knobbly and congested, use a pruning saw to saw off the oldest sections. Cut back the central stem to a bud just below the top wire. Untie it and bend to the horizontal to encourage shoots to break evenly lower down.*

Tie leader to the horizontal in midwinter and retie to the vertical as buds break in spring

**SEE ALSO:** Ways of Supporting Plants, pp.108–109; Preparing the Ground, pp.142–143; Preparing a Vegetable Garden, pp.236–237

# LOOKING AFTER THE GARDEN

## MAKING THE MOST OF YOUR GARDEN

WHEN YOUR GARDEN IS ESTABLISHED, you will want to keep it looking as good as possible. To do this, you will need some basic tools and other items of equipment, as well as somewhere to store them. A garden shed is the obvious answer, if you have room, but there are other choices. Sheds and storage areas can be attractively integrated into the garden design. Maintaining a garden produces a lot of waste material, but there are a number of ways of recycling this to produce organic matter for feeding your plants and soil. If you intend to propagate from your own plants, or grow some tender ones, protection in the form of cold frames or a greenhouse will be necessary.

### STORING TOOLS

You will soon start to acquire a variety of implements useful in the garden, whatever its size. If your garden already has a shed, no doubt you will make use of this for storage. If not, consider all the options before purchasing one.

In small gardens, there may not be room for a shed, so think about whether the tools could be stored in the garage, inside the house or conservatory, or in some sort of weatherproof storage chest outside. An important consideration is whether you can gain quick and easy access to an item when it is required. If you decide on a shed, there are several shapes and sizes to choose from; your choice will largely be dependent on whether you need room for large items, such as lawnmowers and bicycles, as well as for smaller tools.

**A TIDY SHED** ▷
*Not only will your tools and equipment be easier to find if neatly stored inside a shed, but it will also be a safer place. Large tools with handles may be hung up on nails or hooks, as shown here, and smaller ones placed on shelves or in labelled boxes or drawers.*

△ **AN INTEGRAL FEATURE**
*A shed need not be purely functional, but can be seen as a feature in its own right, chosen to blend in with the style of the surrounding garden. Climbing plants may later be enticed to grow up the sides of the shed, softening its outline and providing seasonal colour. Access to the shed should always be kept free, however, so that its contents may be easily reached and moved to other areas.*

◁ **PURPOSE-BUILT STORAGE RACK**
*For extra neatness and safety, attach a metal hanging rack to the inside wall of your shed; it is dangerous to leave rakes and forks lying around or entwined with wires, cables, and other tools.*

SEE ALSO:   Storage Areas, pp.276–277;  Tools and Equipment, pp.278–281

# RECYCLING WASTE

Gardens create a lot of waste in the form of grass and hedge clippings, prunings, and fallen autumn leaves. Because this is all organic matter, it is a shame to throw it away. Instead, it may be recycled in a compost heap or wormery, together with suitable kitchen scraps, to make a rich, fertile garden compost that can be dug into the soil to improve it. Leafmould can also be spread around plants as a nutritious mulch and soil improver. The waste must be allowed to rot thoroughly before it is ready for use. Although this process can take some time, depending on the time of year and the material, it is usually worth the effort. If you have room, it is a good idea to have two compost heaps: one to be used, after rotting, and the other to be filled up. In this way, you should have a continuous supply of compost, saving you money.

**HOME-MADE HEAP ▷**
*Although you can buy purpose-made compost boxes or frames, it is possible, as shown here, to contain a compost heap with any suitable materials that you have handy, such as old fence panels, wooden posts, and chicken wire.*

# PROTECTING PLANTS

In warm climates, gardeners do not have to worry about providing frost protection for their plants, but in cooler areas this can be quite a problem if you wish to grow tender or exotic species, or to create your own stock of new plants from seeds or cuttings. There are many fully hardy plants that will withstand low winter temperatures, and these will not require any protection. Half-hardy or frost-tender plants, however, will need to be grown under glass for at least some of the time.

The simplest way to provide some protection is to use a cold frame, which is suitable for small numbers of plants. You will need a greenhouse if you have a large number to protect, or you wish to create a display. Greenhouses can also be heated to a specific temperature to accommodate the needs of particular plants.

**◁ BLENDING IN**
*This simple wooden greenhouse forms an integral and decorative garden feature in its own right, as well as providing a protective environment for young and tender plants.*

**▽ GROWING EXOTICS**
*A greenhouse is the best place to grow a collection of exotic plants that require special growing conditions, particularly if some or all of them are frost tender. This show of carnivorous plants includes some pitcher plants; they digest insects that have fallen into a pool of liquid inside the pitcher.*

**A FINE SHOW ▷**
*Sections of a greenhouse may be used to produce a spectacular display of flowering plants that require frost-free, dry, or other particular conditions in order to thrive.*

SEE ALSO: Making Compost, p.236; Greenhouses, p.241; Garden Compost, pp.282–283; Cold Frames and Greenhouses, pp.284–287

# WATERING EQUIPMENT

Some plants will grow quite happily in the garden requiring no water other than that supplied by rainfall, but new plants will need watering until they are established, especially in dry areas. Plants grown in pots or containers, and those in the greenhouse, will need a regular water supply.

The simplest method is to use a plastic or metal watering can, usually with a perforated sprinkler head, called a rose, on the end of the spout. Fill the can from a water butt, from an outside tap if you have one, or from the kitchen tap. For large gardens, you will need a hose, for which an outside tap is probably essential. Hoses may be rigid or flat when empty; the latter takes up less space on a reel when not in use.

Sprayers are useful for mist-spraying plants and for applying pesticides and fertilizers. Sprinklers are an option for lawns and large borders. Always check whether there are any restrictions on the use of hoses or sprinklers in your area.

### WHICH ROSE?

• Use a fine rose for seeds and seedlings because the gentle spray will neither damage them nor wash the compost away.

• For more established plants, a coarse-spray rose delivers water more quickly.

• Brass roses are more expensive than plastic ones, but they are more durable. They tend to give a finer spray.

• A dribble bar on a watering can is more accurate than a rose for applying weedkiller.

**HOSE REEL** ▷
*A reel with a handle, or one with wheels, is easy to move around. Make sure the hose is long enough to reach all parts of the garden.*

△ **HOSE-END ATTACHMENT**
*A trigger-action hose nozzle may be connected to the end of the hose to water large numbers of plants. Adjust it to give a jet or a spray.*

**KNAPSACK SPRAYER** ▷
*When mist-spraying large areas of plants, use a knapsack sprayer that sits neatly on your back. The spray is pumped up by the lever.*

▽ **GREENHOUSE WATERING CAN**
*The long spout reaches plants at the back of a bench, and the reversible rose has both fine and coarse faces.*

**PLASTIC CAN** ▷
*A plastic watering can is lighter than a traditional metal one but just as hardwearing. Choose one that feels comfortable to hold.*

**WATER BUTT** ▷
*To collect and store rainwater from a house or greenhouse roof, install a water butt in a suitable place. The butt should have a tap and a lid, which keeps out debris. You may have to raise the butt up on bricks to allow a watering can to fit beneath the tap.*

# WHEELBARROWS

There are times in the garden when you need to move bulky or heavy plants, soil, compost, or other material from one place to another. The least back-breaking way to do this is to put it in a wheelbarrow. These may be made of metal or plastic, but metal is more durable.

Traditional barrows are less stable on newly dug or rough ground than ball-wheeled barrows. Builder's barrows have an inflatable tyre to cushion the load and are suitable for heavy work. Never overload the barrow; distribute the contents so that the greatest weight is at the front.

△ **BALL-WHEELED WHEELBARROW**
*For use on rough ground, or for very heavy loads, a wheelbarrow with a ball wheel, or one with an inflatable tyre, will be much easier to manoeuvre. This one has a plastic bin, which, although lightweight, may split.*

△ **TRADITIONAL WHEELBARROW**
*This type of barrow has a single, solid wheel and a shallow bin that is deeper at the front in order to allow more weight to be carried. The galvanized metal is more expensive than plastic, but it should last well before any rust appears.*

**SEE ALSO:** Watering a Lawn, p.84; Watering Techniques, p.152; Storing Tools, p.274; Chemicals for Weed Control, p.290

# OTHER USEFUL ITEMS

What other items you will need will depend on how you use your garden. If you have a greenhouse, and intend to use it for raising plants, then pots, saucers, trays, modules, and labels will be essential. In the open garden, plant stakes and ties, carriers, gloves, and sieves may all make life easier. For sowing and planting, widgers and dibbers come in handy; a dibber is a pencil-shaped tool used for making planting holes, and a widger is a narrow spatula for lifting seedlings.

### POTS AND PANS ▷

*Plant containers come in all shapes and sizes. The larger, ornamental ones are excellent for growing specimen plants and may be moved around the garden. Smaller pots and shallow pans are ideal for cuttings and young plants. Pots and pans are made of clay or plastic. Clay is porous, so the compost tends to dry out more quickly.*

### ◁ TRAYS AND MODULAR SYSTEMS

*These are useful for individual seeds and cuttings. A rigid outer tray holds a single-use flexible module consisting of plastic cells, which are filled with compost. Seedlings and young plants may be separated with minimal damage to the roots.*

### PLANT STAKES ▷

*Some perennials may need support, in the form of stakes, to give of their best. Ring stakes are best for clump forming plants, and link stakes are suitable for tall ones.*

RING STAKE

LINK STAKE

Bamboo cane

Rose stake

Green bamboo cane

Split cane

WOODEN TRUG

### △ WIRE-MESH SIEVE

*Garden sieves are used for separating out stones and other coarse material from soil or potting compost before sowing or planting. Wire mesh is more long-lasting than plastic.*

### △ COTTON-FABRIC GARDENING GLOVES

*Fabric or leather gloves will protect your hands against thorns as well as keeping them clean. Some have vinyl grips for extra protection and comfort.*

### CARRIERS ▷

*A trug is handy for carrying flowers or fruit after picking. Plastic sheets and bags are ideal for moving light but bulky waste, such as hedge clippings. Bags should have strong handles.*

CARRYING SHEET AND BAG

## LOOKING AFTER TOOLS

• Clean off any soil, grass clippings, or other garden material immediately after use.

• After cleaning, wipe all metal parts with an oily rag to prevent rust developing.

• Store neatly in a dry place, such as a garden shed; remember that you should never leave tools out in the rain.

• Regularly remove and sharpen the blades of pruning and cutting tools.

• Tools that will not be required at all over the winter period should be especially well oiled before storing them away.

CORNUS KOUSA

### PLANT TIES △

*Use plastic ties to secure plants to their supports. The tie should not constrict the stem.*

### LABELS AND MARKERS △

*There is a wide variety of labels and markers available for garden use. They should be durable, weather-resistant, and large enough to contain all relevant information.*

### PLANT SUPPORTS ▷

*Standard roses require sturdy stakes. Bamboo or split wooden canes are fine for other single-stemmed plants.*

SEE ALSO: Ways of Supporting Plants, pp.108–109; Supporting and Staking, p.151; Sowing Seed in Pots, p.162; Storing Tools, p.274

# GARDEN COMPOST

CREATING YOUR OWN garden compost is an excellent way of recycling garden and kitchen waste and returning it as organic matter to enrich the soil. This improves aeration and aids the retention of moisture and nutrients. You will need to be patient, since composting can be quite a slow process. The presence of worms in the waste, however, accelerates decomposition and creates an even better end-product. Dead leaves that have fallen onto the lawn or borders can also be recycled either by turning them into leafmould or by adding them to the compost heap.

## THE COMPOST HEAP

To create a successful compost heap, you must put in a mixture of "wet" material, such as grass clippings or other soft, leafy material, and "dry" material, like shredded paper, bark, or straw. Add any vegetable waste, but *never* add meat or cooked foods (it attracts rats), perennial weeds, or woody stems (unless shredded). Also add manure, but not from cats and dogs. The heap must reach a high temperature for bacteria to thrive; for this to happen, the heap must be at least 1 cubic metre (1 cubic yard) in volume. It takes about three months to mature in summer, longer at lower temperatures. Turning the heap helps speed up the process. Only use the compost when extremely well rotted – it should be dark, crumbly, and sweet-smelling.

◁ **LAYERS OF COMPOST**
*Start with a thick layer of twiggy material, then build up the heap in 10–15cm (4–6in) layers. Add a little manure on top of each layer.*

## USING A WORMERY

Brandling, or tiger worms can be of great benefit in the garden, because they quickly break down organic matter through their digestive systems. They can be introduced into a normal compost heap, or kept in a purpose-built wormery. The worms work upwards from the bottom of the heap, and a wormery is designed to take advantage of this by allowing you to remove the bottom layer of finished compost. The worms will feed on most vegetable matter from the kitchen or garden, as long as you do not overload the bin. They prefer warm temperatures, so cover the bin in winter.

### GOOD IDEAS

• Place the wormery in a sunny, sheltered part of the garden – the optimum temperature for the worms is 20–24°C (68–75°F).

• Remember to mix together the different types of waste to be added.

• Never add more than a few centimetres of waste material at any one time.

• Wait for the worms to digest one layer before adding the next.

• Add small amounts of animal manure or partially rotted compost on top of each new layer. Manure may be added on its own.

## LEAFMOULD

Leaves take even longer than other waste vegetable matter to decompose, because the process involved is different – they are broken down by fungi rather than by bacteria. It is best, therefore, to keep them in a separate heap. When they do rot down, after about a year or more, the resulting leafmould is well worth the wait. It can be used as a mulch or to improve the soil, but is also good enough to use as a seed or potting compost.

Find a little-used corner of the garden where there is plenty of light and the heap can be left undisturbed. Make a simple container out of wire and stakes (*see below*). Place fallen leaves in the container, and firm them down each time. Add a little water in hot, dry periods.

**1 ATTACHING THE CHICKEN WIRE**
*You will need 4 wooden stakes, driven 30cm (12in) into the ground, and a length of chicken wire. If your cage is to be next to a fence or wall, first staple the wire to 2 of the stakes with a hammer. Otherwise, attach the wire after inserting the stakes.*

**2 COMPLETING THE WIRE CAGE**
*Attach the 2 cut ends of the chicken wire firmly to the last stake by hammering in staples. It is a good idea to wear gloves at this stage to avoid cutting your hands on the sharp edges.*

**3 THE FINISHED CONTAINER**
*The leafmould cage should be square and reasonably low and broad to allow for easy access to the middle. You will need to be able to compact the leaves after putting them in, either by treading on them or by firming with a rake, broom, or other suitable tool.*

**SEE ALSO:** Applying Mulch, p.152; Making Compost, p.236; Recycling Waste, p.275

# MAKING A COMPOST BIN

You can make garden compost in a free-standing heap, but a container of some sort will keep the compost tidy and moist right through. Ready-made plastic or slatted wood containers are only sufficient for small amounts of compost. Larger containers may be constructed at home from various recycled materials, such as posts and wire, bricks, wood, or plastic fruit barrels, but bricks should only be used if the heap will never be moved.

It is quite simple to make your own wooden compost bin (see right and below). The sliding front panels make removal of the well-rotted compost much easier. If you have space, consider having two bins on the go, using the second when the first is full.

## TOOLS AND MATERIALS

- 4 × 1m (3ft) lengths of 5×10cm (2×4in) wood for uprights
- 19 × 1m (3ft) planks of wood for sides
- Strong nails
- Wooden spacer, 1cm (½in) wide
- 4 × 75cm (30in) battens
- 2 small bits of wood
- 5 × 75cm (30in) lengths of wood for front panels
- Wood preservative
- Thick nylon string

THE FINISHED BIN, READY FOR USE

## CONSTRUCTING THE FRAME

**1 MAKING THE SIDES**
Put 2 of the uprights on the ground, 75cm (30in) apart, and lying parallel to each other. Using 4 nails per plank, nail 1 of the side planks securely into position, 8cm (3in) from the bottom of each of the uprights.

**2 COMPLETING A SIDE**
Nail 5 more side planks to the uprights, using the wooden spacer to keep them 1cm (½in) apart. They should be parallel to each other and at right angles to the uprights. Repeat for the opposite side.

**3 MAKING THE BACK**
Stand the 2 sides parallel to each other, 75cm (30in) apart, and at right angles to a wall. Nail 2 strips of wood across the top of each of the opposite uprights to keep them stable. Attach 6 side planks to the back.

**4 PREPARING THE FRONT**
Remove the stabilizing strips, and turn the bin around so that the back is flush against the wall. Nail just 1 side plank across the front of the uprights, 8cm (3in) up from the bottom.

**5 ATTACHING BATTENS**
Place 2 battens on the side edge of each of the front uprights, making sure that the front panels can easily slide between them. Attach the battens with nails, then nail a small bit of wood across the bottom of each batten, which will keep the panels in place.

**6 FITTING THE FRONT PANELS**
Try sliding each of the front panels in-between the battens to make sure that they fit well. If necessary, cut them down to the required length.

**7 PAINTING THE BIN**
Coat the entire bin, including all the cut edges and the front panels, with a water-based wood preservative, and then leave it until completely dry.

**8 FINISHING THE BIN**
Slide all the front panels into position. Finally, tie a length of thick nylon string or rope across the top of the container so that the sides will not start to bulge out when the bin is filled with compost.

SEE ALSO: Recycling Waste, p.275

# COLD FRAMES AND GREENHOUSES

IN COOLER CLIMATES, where there are winter frosts, only fully hardy plants will survive in the open garden. You can still grow half-hardy and frost-tender ones, however, if you provide them with some form of protection. This means growing them under glass, either in a cold frame or in a greenhouse. For certain tender plants, such as ones that originate in the tropics, you will need to maintain a minimum level of heat and humidity in the greenhouse. Cold frames and greenhouses are also ideal for raising cuttings, seedlings, and young plants.

## USING COLD FRAMES

Cold frames can be used throughout the year to grow a wide range of crops. In spring, they are useful for hardening off plants raised in a greenhouse, and in winter they protect winter-flowering plants, autumn-sown hardy annual seeds, and alpine plants that are susceptible to wet weather. The framework is made of wood or metal, and it is fitted with glass or clear plastic at the top and sometimes also the sides. The top panels are called lights, and they should be hinged, sliding, or removable to give easy access.

### GOOD IDEAS

• To be practical, a cold frame should be at least 120cm×60cm (48×24in), but you can use whatever space you have.

• For plants in pots or tall vegetable seedlings, raise the frame temporarily on loose bricks to increase its height.

◁ **INEXPENSIVE, LIGHTWEIGHT COLD FRAME**
*The clear plastic panels at the top of this cold frame slide back to provide extra light and ventilation for plants during the day when they need less protection. The aluminium struts make it relatively long-lasting.*

◁ **WOODEN FRAME**
*Traditional timber frames retain heat well. Before planting directly in the frame, cover the base with a thick layer of drainage material, such as broken crocks or coarse gravel. Then add a 15cm (6in) layer of good garden soil or compost. Plants may also be grown in the frame in individual pots or in trays.*

△ **SLIDING LIGHTS**
*Lights that slide open to allow air to enter and circulate inside the frame are not as vulnerable as hinged lights to sudden gusts of wind, but heavy rain will get inside.*

△ **HINGED LIGHTS**
*These may be held open on hot, sunny days to provide ventilation, but may not stand up to a gust of wind. To harden plants off, eventually remove the lights completely.*

## WHY A GREENHOUSE?

If you have the room and the money, do not be afraid to invest in a greenhouse – it will give you an all-weather place for carrying out routine tasks, and will vastly increase the variety of plants you are able to grow. An unheated greenhouse will help to extend the growing season of hardy and half-hardy plants, but a heated one allows a far greater range of plants to be grown, including frost-tender species, and provides a suitable environment for raising plants. The greenhouse can also form an attractive garden feature.

◁ **CREATING YOUR OWN NEW PLANTS**
*Using the greenhouse to propagate from your own garden plants, or to raise new plants from seed, will not only save you money in the long run, but will also give you a great deal of pleasure and satisfaction.*

**SEE ALSO:** Protecting Plants, p.275; Crop Protection, pp.240–241

# CHOOSING A GREENHOUSE

A great variety of shapes and sizes of greenhouses are on offer, from conventional span or lean-to greenhouses to specialist houses for certain types of plant, such as alpines or decorative shapes, like domes or polygons. To decide on the best type of greenhouse for your garden, think about how you intend to use it.

■ A traditional span (*see below right*) or Dutch light greenhouse is best for functional purposes, such as growing border plants or propagation. A Dutch light has sloping sides and allows in maximum sunlight.

■ For displaying tropical or semi-tropical plants, an attractively shaped greenhouse, perhaps with room for central staging, will form an eye-catching feature.

■ A lean-to greenhouse (*see below*) is ideal for conserving heat and creating a "garden room" next to the house.

■ Alpine houses are designed specifically for protecting alpine plants from winter rain – they are not heated and are closed only in the very coldest weather.

△ **METAL FRAME**
*Aluminium alloy frames are light but very sturdy. They also require very little maintenance.*

△ **TIMBER FRAME**
*For the more traditional look, a durable hardwood such as cedar is a good, low-maintenance option.*

## POINTS TO LOOK FOR

There are so many different types of greenhouse to choose from that it is advisable to have a good idea of what you are looking for before you go to buy one. The most important considerations are rigidity, access, height, and ventilation. The greenhouse should have a firm base and a rigid structure to withstand strong winds. Doors should be at least 60cm (24in) wide. The height at the eaves should be at least 1.35m (4½ft). Roof ventilators are often inadequate as supplied; the total ventilation area should equal one-sixth of the floor area.

Doors may be hinged or sliding – the latter are easily adjusted for ventilation – and should fit closely

Ridge height should be at least 1.7m (5ft 6in)

So that they can be easily replaced, glass panels should be of a standard size such as 60cm (24in) square

A kick panel at the foot of the door reduces the risk of breaking the glass

Gutters and downpipes help to stop water cascading from the roof and damaging nearby plants – channel water into a water butt

A base may be an optional extra – most timber-framed greenhouses need one – but a step may prove a problem for access

Side ventilators allow free circulation of air; louvre vents must close tightly

◁ **LEAN-TO GREENHOUSE**
*Where space is limited, or a mainly decorative show-house is preferred, a lean-to greenhouse is an excellent choice. Some resemble conservatories, and they may be used as a garden room. It is cheaper and easier to provide power and water supplies for a lean-to because it is nearer the house, and the house wall may help to conserve heat and provide extra insulation.*

**TRADITIONAL SPAN GREENHOUSE** ▷
*This free-standing greenhouse has vertical sides and a span roof, giving ample growing space as well as headroom. A traditional span greenhouse is ideal for growing border plants and raising seedlings, providing good use of space for relatively little cost.*

**SEE ALSO:** Greenhouses, p.241; Protecting Plants, p.275

# ERECTING A GREENHOUSE

Before you erect a greenhouse, take some time to choose the right spot. A free-standing greenhouse should be sited in an open position where it will receive good light but is sheltered from strong winds. If there is no natural protection, you can construct a windbreak. Which way your greenhouse should face depends on its use. If it is intended mostly for summer displays, its longer axis should run north to south. For raising young plants in spring or overwintering tender species, an east to west orientation of the longer axis provides reasonable light for much of the day.

The greenhouse should be erected on solid foundations, such as brick or concrete built in advance to the correct dimensions, as for a shed (see p.277).

This lies in the path of a possible wind funnel and is too close to the hedge

This greenhouse is sited in an ideal, open position, away from the shade cast by buildings and trees

GOOD POSITION

POOR POSITIONS

A line of tall trees serves to provide shelter from the prevailing wind

Shade cast in summer

Shade cast in winter

This lies in the shade of the tree and may be affected by falling leaves in the autumn

A wind funnel may be created between 2 adjacent buildings

◁ SITING THE GREENHOUSE
*It is important to make sure that the greenhouse will not be affected by shade, cold winds, or falling leaves.*

# CONTROLLING THE ENVIRONMENT

Your greenhouse represents an oasis in the garden — a place where you are in control of the environment. Instead of choosing plants to suit the conditions available, you can now alter the conditions to suit the plants you want to grow.

It is vital to achieve a balance in the conditions, however. Insulation to retain heat and keep out draughts must be considered together with the need for thorough ventilation. Atmospheric humidity may be a requirement of the plants, and this is provided either by a special humidifier or by damping down the paths with water from a can or hose. For a heated greenhouse, choose an efficient and reliable, economic heater. In summer, shading (see opposite) is essential to prevent plants overheating. In low light conditions, a growing lamp (see below) may be necessary.

## TELL ME WHY

### WHY HEAT THE GREENHOUSE?

Heat in the greenhouse gives you more options for growing different and exciting plants than either an unheated greenhouse or a cold frame. Such plants include frost tender ones that cannot normally survive over winter in cool climates. It also provides ideal conditions to create new plants from seeds and cuttings early in the season.

GROWING LAMP ▷
*This supplies additional light to stimulate or improve plant growth when light levels are low. It should be secured directly over the plants, if possible.*

△ FROST ALARM
*If you have tender plants, a frost alarm is a useful safeguard against a power failure or heater breakdown. The bell will alert you to near-freezing temperatures.*

WATERING SYSTEMS
*Automatic irrigation systems employ an overhead reservoir that feeds water to plants either by means of capillary matting underneath the plants or through small-bore trickle tubes that supply water to individual pots.*

CAPILLARY SYSTEM

TRICKLE SYSTEM

SEE ALSO: Laying Concrete, pp.60–61; Protecting Plants, p.275; Siting the Shed, p.277; Choosing a Greenhouse, p.285

# USING THE GREENHOUSE

When you start to use the greenhouse, you will soon discover the need for good organization within it. The various elements required for creating the right environment must all be correctly positioned and accessible. You will need some benches, known as staging, to work on. To maximize the space available for pots and plants, you may also need shelves or hanging-basket brackets. Shade-loving plants can be placed beneath the staging.

◁ **FIXED STAGING**
*Permanent, purpose built staging is often supplied with the greenhouse. This should be fitted during initial construction.*

◁ **FREE-STANDING STAGING**
*These benches are movable, and therefore allow for greater flexibility within the greenhouse.*

◁ **SLATTED STAGING**
*Attractive wooden slats allow more air to circulate around the plants, but they are not suitable for a capillary watering system.*

**A TIDY LAYOUT ▷**
*The greenhouse will be easier to work in if all the elements are sensibly and neatly organized. This well-planned layout for a lean-to greenhouse makes best possible use of a limited amount of space.*

Overhead reservoir supplies water to the plant tray beneath

Thermometer for monitoring temperature

Heated propagator

Shelf for displaying flowering plants

Seedlings and cuttings growing in trays

Fixed staging

Pots sunk into sand underneath staging

Slatted staging

Heater to regulate temperature

# SHADING AND VENTILATION

In summer, when the sun is hot, you will need to provide some shading in your greenhouse, in the form of roller blinds, a shading wash, or plastic mesh. Remember not to block out too much light, however, as this will inhibit plant growth. Remove the shading in late summer.

Good air circulation, even in winter, is vital, so make sure the greenhouse is fitted with vents. Hinged roof vents should open wide, to an angle of about 45°, to allow maximum airflow while preventing gusts of wind from entering. They should also be staggered, or air will simply blow across. Louvre vents allow air in at just above ground level. Fit automatic vent openers to at least some of the hinged or louvre vents. A mechanically driven fan ventilation system is another option.

△ **SHADING**
*A shading wash should be applied to the outside of the greenhouse at the beginning of the sunny season. This stops the temperature inside rising too high, without greatly reducing light. Wash off in late summer.*

△ **FLEXIBLE MESH**
*Plastic mesh netting can be cut to size and used for shading greenhouse plants.*

△ **AUTOVENT OPENER**
*This automatically opens a vent when the temperature rises above a certain level.*

△ **HINGED VENTS**
*These are normally fitted in the roof. They should open widely and securely.*

△ **ROLLER BLINDS**
*Hardwearing blinds provide a versatile way of shading the greenhouse.*

△ **LOUVRE VENTS**
*These are fitted in the side just above ground level to improve internal air flow.*

SEE ALSO: Increasing Border Plants, pp.162 163; Protecting Plants, p.275; Choosing a Greenhouse, p.285

# DEALING WITH WEEDS AND PLANT PROBLEMS

## WEEDS IN THE GARDEN

THERE ARE PEOPLE who actually enjoy weeding, but the majority of us find it a real garden chore. Weeds must be dealt with, however, if the plants that you do want in your garden are to stay healthy. There are a number of ways to prevent and control garden weeds, which fall into two basic categories: annual and perennial weeds.

Annual weeds are opportunists, seeding themselves into any welcoming gap among ornamental plantings. If they are removed before they flower, they cannot perpetuate themselves. Perennial weeds are much more insidious, persisting in the soil all year round and coming up not only around but among the roots of ornamental plants.

## WHAT IS A WEED?

A weed is not so much "a plant in the wrong place", it is a plant growing where it is not wanted. Traditionally, wild plants and flowers were viewed as weeds, while cultivated garden varieties were prized, but the range of plants that we grow, and reasons why we grow them, is much wider today, and many native wild plants are now valued. For some gardeners, the term "weed" is reserved for plants that can be invasive, so even cultivated plants can "become" weeds or "be weedy" – a bugle planted for ground cover that runs riot, for example, or a buddleja that self-seeds to the point of nuisance.

## WHY WEED?

Even the most informal meadow planting of wild flowers needs careful management if weeds are not to overtake it. Weeds are most often fast growing and invasive, competing with cultivated plants for food, water, light, and air, usually emerging as the victors. Plants crowded by weeds will grow small and weak, and will not flower or crop as freely as they should; they will also be more vulnerable to pests and diseases, for which weeds may act as hosts. Clear the ground before you plant. Even though it will not eliminate annual weed seeds, it is just as important as controlling any weeds that subsequently appear.

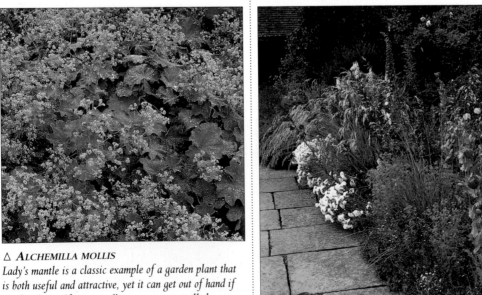

△ ALCHEMILLA MOLLIS
*Lady's mantle is a classic example of a garden plant that is both useful and attractive, yet it can get out of hand if its abundant self-sown seedlings are not controlled.*

◁ FORMAL BORDER
*Weeds will spoil the look of a carefully planted border and guzzle soil moisture; close planting will minimize areas of free soil space that they can colonize.*

△ WANTED WEEDS
*Impoverished soil and regular mowing allow wild flowers to flourish among grass in this less manicured area of the garden.*

SEE ALSO: Lawns with Added Interest, p.75; Controlling Weeds, p.87; Naturalistic Effects, p.89

# USEFUL WEEDS

As managed meadows and hedgerows disappear from the farmed landscape, the gardener has an opportunity to restore the balance in favour of local wildlife by introducing some less controlled areas into the garden. Ivy, for example, should be allowed to grow bushy and fruit; if it is kept cropped close to a wall, it loses almost all of its value as a food source and nesting site for birds. Some annual wild flowers have great ornamental charm as well as being beneficial to wildlife, and they are easily prevented from seeding too profusely. Moreover, many insects have marked preferences for native food plants. Retain a clump of "weeds" in an out-of-the-way spot where they can be left alone and undisturbed; the weedy patch may actually lure harmful garden creatures, such as voracious butterfly and moth caterpillars, away from more valuable plants, minimizing damage.

**COMMON IVY ▷**
*Ordinary forms of garden plants, such as ivy, are often preferred by local birdlife over more unusual cultivated varieties.*

**◁ FIELD POPPY**
*Soil cultivation in any rural area is likely to bring poppy seeds to the surface to sprout; keep them not only for their looks, but also to attract hoverflies and insect-eating birds.*

**SOIL IMPROVER ▷**
*Some weeds, such as this black medick and other clover species, actually enrich garden soil by adding nitrogen through their roots. These plants can be dug in and are frequently used as a green manure (see The Edible Garden, p.239).*

# PREVENTING WEEDS

One of the key factors in preventing weed growth is really effective ground clearance before planting. The subsequent growth of weeds will then be much easier to control by hand weeding, and the need for chemical weedkillers will be greatly reduced or completely unnecessary.

Organic gardeners set great store by preventive measures. The guiding principle behind most preventive measures is light deprivation; without light, the weeds are simply unable to grow. You can exclude light from the soil surface by mulching either with organic materials applied in a really chunky layer, or with a thick dressing of gravel, or with sheet mulches (see below). Sheet mulches have the added advantage of keeping new weed seeds from entering the soil.

Close planting, especially with ground-hugging plants, also creates a dark canopy over the soil. Fast-growing ground cover can be a real boon in a new garden, particularly in problem areas, but do ensure that the plant you choose for ground cover will not become a "weed" itself. Plants such as *Vinca major*, the greater periwinkle, can metamorphose from solution to problem very rapidly. Clump-forming perennials are more manageable in a mixed planting; planted close, they can always be lifted and divided. Herbaceous kinds are especially valuable where spring bulbs are planted, because their foliage will grow to cover the bare patches left as bulb leaves die down.

# TOOLS OF THE TRADE

Applying chemical weedkiller requires a certain amount of paraphernalia (see p.290), but for hand weeding a good, strong hand fork that will not bend is the most useful tool; if you loosen the soil before pulling up a weed, you are much less likely to leave the roots behind. There are special tools for weeding lawns and paving, but an old kitchen knife is just as effective. Sheet mulches for suppressing weeds are now very widely available.

**△ TRUSTY FRIEND**
*Invest in a quality hand fork for years of service. Those with a separate hasp and handle are usually strongest; wood is warm and comfortable to hold.*

**SHEET MULCH ▷**
*This porous material may also be referred to as landscape fabric, geotextile, or planting membrane. It is usually bought off a roll in a range of widths.*

**SEE ALSO:** Ground Cover, p.75; Preparing the Soil, p.78; Creating Effective Ground Cover, p. 88

# DEALING WITH WEEDS

HOW YOU CONTROL WEEDS is determined by whether or not you wish to use chemical weedkillers. Often, the use of weedkillers can be avoided only by putting in long hours of clearing weeds by hand, but there are alternatives if you are willing to make certain compromises. There is no doubt that chemical weedkillers save time and work, and they are sometimes the only practical way of turning around really badly neglected patches of land. For effective control, you must also match the methods you use to the type of weeds you are contending with, whether annual or perennial, so learning to recognize common weeds is time well spent.

## CHEMICALS FOR WEED CONTROL

There are a great many proprietary weedkillers on the market, and they work in different ways. They do not prevent seed germination. You must ascertain exactly what you want a weedkiller to do, and then select an appropriate product; it is worth asking for advice when you buy.

**Contact weedkillers** destroy any plant material that they touch and are often used on paths and paving. They will kill annual weeds completely, but only kill the top-growth of perennial weeds, which usually reshoot from the roots. Contact weedkillers do not affect the soil.

**Systemic weedkillers**, sprayed or dabbed with special "spot" applicators onto leaf and stem surfaces, are absorbed by the plant and taken down into the roots, where they kill the plant. They are sometimes called translocated weedkillers because they are transported around the plant. Systemic weedkillers eradicate both annual and perennial weeds, although more than one application may be needed for the latter. These weedkillers do not affect nearby plants provided that the chemical does not touch them during application, and they do not persist in a harmful way in the soil.

**Soil-acting weedkillers** are absorbed by plant roots, then they move up the plant to kill it. They are also known as residual weedkillers and are useful for clearing infested ground, but they can remain active in the soil for many months so you will have to wait out the manufacturer's stated time lapse before you can plant. **Selective weedkillers** usually kill broadleaved plants, but not grasses. They are used in lawns mainly and are also called broadleaved weedkillers.

### APPLYING CHEMICALS

Methods of application vary according to the size of the problem. In a small garden, especially for isolated weeds in beds, lawns, or paths, spot or touch applicators, or small, ready-mixed hand-sprays are ideal. For a larger area, unless you are using a soil-acting granular product, you will probably need to mix up quantities of dilute chemical, and safety here is paramount. A watering can with fine rose or spray bar is not an ideal dispenser except on gravel, driveways, unplanted ground, or lawns, as you will not be able to control the amount or direction of the flow well enough. A pump-action sprayer with wand is a good investment, especially in larger gardens; it makes it much easier to direct the weedkiller where you want it. Accurate spraying is essential when you are killing weeds among garden plants, as any drifting or splashing will damage and can kill the plants. A useful tip is to cover cultivated plants carefully with supermarket plastic bags or bin bags while you spray; wear gloves when removing the bags after spraying and dispose of them safely. Then wash your hands.

## SAFETY FIRST

The corrosive and toxic potential of any garden chemical means that it must be used with extreme care.
- Choose the right product for the job, reading all labelling before you buy.
- Follow the manufacturer's instructions carefully, especially for rates for dilution, which must be strictly adhered to.
- Keep completely separate equipment for chemicals, rinsing thoroughly after use.
- Wash your hands after use.
- Always dispose of unused dilute weedkiller; read labels carefully before you buy if you are not on mains drainage. Never pour diluted or undiluted weedkiller down drains – if you have old products to get rid of, take them to a council dump or ring your local authority. Pour small amounts left over on an out-of-the-way patch of vacant ground.
- Keep products in their original containers, out of reach of children and animals, preferably in a locked overhead cupboard. Tape over labels if necessary to keep instructions intact and readable.

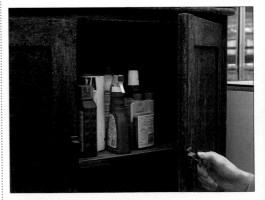

△ SAFETY WITH CHEMICALS
*A cool, dark cupboard keeps products in good condition, prevents labels mouldering or fading, and can be locked to keep them safe from children. Give it a good clear out periodically, so that you do not hoard obsolete chemicals.*

---

### ALWAYS REMEMBER

#### NEVER SPRAY ON A WINDY DAY

Always spray in calm, still weather, otherwise you risk spray drifting onto neighbouring valued plants and onto any beneficial insects hovering nearby. Spray may also be blown over your clothing and face. Always check out the instructions for accidental skin contact before you start mixing and spraying, so you know what to do straight away should a mishap occur.

---

SEE ALSO: Controlling Weeds, p.87; Using the Shed, p.277

# ALTERNATIVES TO CHEMICALS

There is much more scope for controlling annual weeds without using chemicals than perennial weeds. Annuals can be dug into the soil, rather than dug out, and are easily removed by hand or hoe. They can also be smothered or burnt off.

Annual weeds grow, flower, set seed, and die within one year. Although they do not persist, their seeds arrive continuously, either on the wind or borne by birds and animals. They are fast-growing, and several generations may appear in one growing season; in a mild winter, autumn-germinated weeds, especially chickweed, may survive to create a year-round nuisance. They appear most often on regularly cultivated land, such as vegetable plots, where the soil is regularly turned over to expose more seeds. Although chemicals can be used to clear infested areas, annual weeds are just as easily dug or rotavated into the ground, provided that they have not set seed (if so they should be dug out and destroyed). Established plantings can usually be kept weed-free by hoeing and hand pulling, but the difficulty arises among juvenile or seedling plants, as annual weeds are faster growing and will smother them. Instead of repeatedly hoeing rows of young crops, some vegetable gardeners put down polythene or carpet to smother and prevent weeds, planting through it as for a sheet mulch. This works well as long as provision is made for watering; plastic and synthetic-backed carpet may keep rain off the soil, but they also keep moisture in, so ensure the ground is wet before the mulch is laid. Where annual flowers are grown from seed, it can be difficult to tell them from weed seedlings; sowing in rows rather than broadcasting helps.

On patios, paths, and gravel, where hand weeding is awkward, a small garden flamethrower is an ideal tool for burning off annual weeds, with one exception: it must not be used if the hard landscaping is laid over plastic or geotextile.

## ALWAYS REMEMBER

### CATCH WEEDS BEFORE THEY SEED

If you don't have the time or aren't in the mood for a proper weeding session, you can still help control weeds by nipping off their top-growth or flowering heads before they set seed and multiply. Repeated removal of top-growth will weaken perennial weeds considerably. If you get into this habit, you can save yourself a great deal of work in the future.

▽ ANNUAL MEADOW GRASS
*Poa annua*

◁ GROUNDSEL
*Senecio vulgaris*

▽ HAIRY BITTERCRESS
*Cardamine hirsuta*

▽ COMMON CHICKWEED
*Stellaria media*

**ANNUAL WEEDS**
*If the ground is not too wet and not too dry, most annual weeds can be pulled up quite satisfyingly, with their roots in a single clump. If there is room between plants, hoe them up onto the surface to wither and die. Provided that they have not set seed, you need not gather small weeds up, especially in dry weather, although you may prefer to do so for aesthetic reasons. If there is lots of debris, however, it is advisable to clear it up, as it will create a haven for pests and diseases.*

SHEPHERD'S PURSE ▷
*Capsella bursa-pastoris*

FAT HEN ▷
*Chenopodium album*

SEE ALSO: Controlling Weeds, p.87; Perennial Weeds, pp.292–293; Sowing in Drills, p.243

# PERENNIAL WEEDS

Some perennial weeds are imported garden plants that have run wild, like Japanese knotweed, but most are native plants of field and woodland that really relish the good soil and relative lack of competition they find in a garden. If you are prepared to put in the time, and the soil is free of weeds before you plant, then odd perennial weeds can be removed immediately or kept weak by persistent hand pulling, so that they never really get a grip. Alternatively, a dab-on systemic weedkiller, which kills only the weed and will not last in the soil, is a real boon. Infestations of perennial weeds are, however, a more serious problem.

## DEALING WITH OVERGROWN PERENNIAL WEEDS

If you inherit or decide to tackle a patch of ground infested with perennial weeds, getting rid of them takes time and planning. Moreover, it is near impossible to eliminate perennial weeds growing strongly in and around plants by hand. On herbaceous (leafy) weeds, you can carefully apply a systemic weedkiller (glyphosate is the most popular). On weeds with extensive root systems, repeat applications may be needed. The best time to apply glyphosate is midsummer, when the weeds are growing strongly, but check labels for timing as well. Leave enough time for the weedkiller to do its job; if you lift wilting weeds too early, you run the risk that the chemical will not have travelled down to the root tips.

If the infestation is so bad that there are more weeds than ornamental plants, it is better to lift the ornamentals and treat the whole area, especially if woody weeds, such as brambles and tree seedlings, have taken hold. For these, a soil-acting weedkiller

△ **LESSER CELANDINE**
*Ranunculus ficaria*

▽ **COUCH GRASS**
*Elymus repens*

◁ **HEDGE BINDWEED**
*Calystegia sepium*

**HORSETAIL** ▷
*Equisetum arvense*

◁ **PERENNIAL STINGING NETTLE**
*Urtica dioica*

△ **FIELD BINDWEED**
*Convolvulus arvensis*

◁ **GROUND ELDER**
*Aegopodium podagraria*

SEE ALSO: Controlling Weeds, p.87; Weeds in the Garden, pp.288–289; Dealing with Weeds, pp.290–291 like ammonium sulphamate is needed. Do not replant any ornamental without hosing its roots thoroughly to check that no weed root fragments are present.

Clearing ground infested with perennial weeds without the use of chemicals is a challenge. Every scrap of weed root must be forked out by hand; rotavators are no good as they simply chop roots up to produce many new weeds. The alternative, if you are prepared to wait at least a year before you can use that part of the garden, is to totally smother the soil with an impenetrable material such as black polythene sheeting, old carpet, or a thick layer of newspapers or cardboard weighted down with bricks. Be prepared also to sink plastic barriers at least 45cm (18in) deep into the soil at the garden boundaries if you know that weeds like ground elder are spreading from neighbouring land. Grassing over is another long-term remedy for very persistent weeds such as horsetail, but you must keep the turf closely mown for several years.

△ JAPANESE KNOTWEED
*Fallopia japonica*

## TELL ME WHY

### WHY CAN'T YOU KILL WEEDS IN WINTER?

Many perennial weeds are evergreen, and while the quiet winter months may seem the ideal time to apply weedkiller for the gardener, treatment will not be effective. Although the plants are in leaf, they are not growing (or only growing very sluggishly) and systemic weedkillers will not be transported around their systems to do their work.

DOCK ▷
*Rumex*

BRAMBLE ▷
*Rubus fruticosus*

◁ DANDELION
*Taraxacum officinale*

△ CREEPING THISTLE
*Cirsium arvense*

◁ WILLOW HERB
*Epilobium angustifolium*

SEE ALSO: Controlling Lawn Weeds, p.87; Weeds in the Garden, pp.288–289; Dealing with Weeds, pp.290–291; Manure and Mulches, p239

# FRUIT AND FRUITING VEGETABLES

DAMAGE TO FRUITLETS and to ripening fruits takes away the whole *raison d'être* of some plants. Make sure you identify the real cause of the problem: rots often enter only because there is damage to fruit skins through frost crack or scab, for example; and earwigs are often blamed when they colonize fruits via holes made by wasps. Many pests are drawn by the high sugar content of ripening fruit, and traps and lures can be very effective. Tomatoes have their own specific problems, but when grown under glass they and other crops also become prey to greenhouse pests, attracted not so much by the plants as by the warm, sheltered conditions.

## TREE FRUITS

### BITTER PIT

A disorder of apples that causes brown speckling on the skin and through the flesh of the fruit, tainting the flavour. It is caused by calcium deficiency, either because it is lacking in the soil or because the soil is dry and the tree cannot extract it. (A deficiency of boron causes the same symptoms in pears; *see p.308*.)
■ Mulching and regular watering helps prevent bitter pit, and you can spray developing fruits with a calcium nitrate solution to overcome it. This chemical can damage some varieties, so read instructions carefully.

### BROWN ROT

This fungal rot develops distinctive rings of white pustules (*see below*) that rupture to spread spores onto other fruits.
■ Pick off and destroy affected fruits promptly. If the whole fruit has been affected and remains on the tree, looking mummified, prune out the spur it is attached to as well. Bird pecks and wasp damage most commonly cause the wounds through which the fungus enters, so control measures for these pests will help limit brown rot.

### CODLING MOTH

The caterpillars of this moth are the pest that causes maggotty apples. A very characteristic sign is their crumbly excreta around the eye end of apples; the damage inside (*see below*) can be considerable.
■ You must act before caterpillars bore into the fruits; use a pheromone trap to detect when the adult moths are about and laying eggs, then use an insecticide, following the timing instructions. On isolated apple trees, the trap itself may catch enough moths to limit damage.

### PEAR MIDGE

Blackened pear fruitlets are a sign that this small fly's whitish orange larvae are feeding within. Whole crops can be lost.
■ Trees can be sprayed at white bud stage (just before flowers open); the non-chemical alternative is to pick off affected

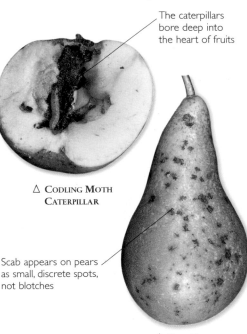

The caterpillars bore deep into the heart of fruits

△ CODLING MOTH CATERPILLAR

Scab appears on pears as small, discrete spots, not blotches

△ PEAR SCAB

fruitlets to prevent the larvae pupating in the soil when the fruits drop, resulting in fewer flies the next year.

### SCAB

Apples, crab apples, and pears (*see below left*) can develop scabby patches which, if extensive, can deform and crack the fruits, creating entry points for rots. The leaves also show grey-brown patches.
■ Rake up and dispose of fallen leaves, and prune out and destroy scabby shoots, to stop the fungus overwintering. Spray with a fungicide. There are resistant varieties.

### SPLITTING OF FRUITS

Splits in apples and pears usually callus over and can be tolerated, but in other fruits with soft flesh and thin skins, such as plums, grapes, and tomatoes, splits can ruin them. The cause is uneven watering; a lot of water after a dry spell causes a growth spurt that can rupture the fruits.
■ Keep trees regularly watered and mulch soil around them when moist to reduce drying out.

### WASPS

Wasps damage ripe fruits leaving holes prey to secondary problems, such as rots and invasion by earwigs.
■ If you have only a few, choice fruits (for example, on a peach fan) you can enclose them in muslin bags; or, to make a wasp trap, fill a jam jar with beer, or coat it inside with syrup or jam. Make a paper lid and pierce a wasp-sized hole in it, then hang it from a branch (*see p.294*). If you can locate the nest, there are chemical preparations to deal with it, but it may be safer to call in your local authority.

△ BROWN ROT

SEE ALSO: Silver Leaf, p.297; Canker, p.300; Birds, p.302

# BERRIES AND CURRENTS

## AMERICAN GOOSEBERRY MILDEW

An infection causing whitish grey fungal growth and, in bad cases, distorted shoot tips. Infected fruits turn brown on cooking but are still edible.
■ Crowding and soft growth encourage it, so prune well and do not overfeed bushes with nitrogen. 'Invicta' and 'Greenfinch' have good resistance. Prune out affected branches and use a fungicidal spray.

## GREY MOULD ON STRAWBERRIES

Fuzzy grey growth on softening fruit (*see below*) is a fungal infection encouraged by damp, often entering wounds made by other pests. It persists in the soil.
■ Keep fruits clean and dry on straw or similar (*see p.272*) and tidy plants regularly. Do not water from above. A fungicidal spray at flowering time protects them. Destroy affected fruits promptly.

## RASPBERRY BEETLES

Dried-up patches at the stalk end of raspberries, blackberries, and hybrid berries are the work of beetle larvae.
■ Spray with derris when beetle larvae are newly hatched; exact timing varies with the type of fruit.

*Other berry and currant problems include: sawfly larvae (eaten gooseberry leaves), p.298, big bud mite, p.302*

Dried-up area around the stalk caused by feeding larvae

△ RASPBERRY BEETLE DAMAGE

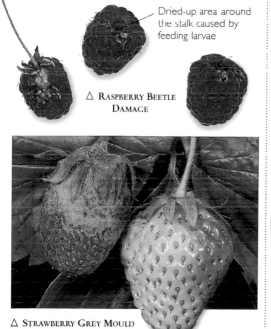

△ STRAWBERRY GREY MOULD

# TOMATOES, PEPPERS, COURGETTES, AND CUCUMBERS

## BLOSSOM END ROT

Tomatoes and peppers may be affected by this disorder, in which dark patches appear at the base of developing fruits; these gradually sink and rot (*see below right*). The cause is not a disease, but dry soil around the roots that prevents the plant taking up the mineral calcium.
■ Regular watering is the key to saving the rest of the crop (discard affected fruits) and preventing the deficiency from recurring. Plants growing in small containers are more vulnerable, as the soil or compost will dry out quicker. Small-fruited tomatoes are less prone to this deficiency.

## TOMATO BLIGHT

Brown patches develop on leaves, which dry and curl; stems may blacken. Fruits develop brown discoloration and shrink (*see below left*), then rot. Uproot and destroy affected plants, and check any potato crops nearby; this is the same fungal infection as potato blight (*see p.309*).
■ Several fungicides can be used for preventive spraying on both crops; copper-based mixtures, acceptable to some organic gardeners, can be used on tomatoes.

## UNEVEN RIPENING OF TOMATOES

Unripe patches on tomatoes fall into two categories. A regular ring of green, leathery tissue around the stalk end of the fruit is a condition called greenback, to which some varieties are genetically prone, while others are not. The exact cause is not known.

Affected areas of flesh start to sink

Tomato skin turns leathery as fruits ripen

△ TOMATO BLIGHT

■ Adequate shading of fruits from hot sun (do not remove too much foliage), good greenhouse ventilation, and ensuring plants get enough potash and phosphate help prevent greenback. General uneven patches of unripeness on tomatoes are a symptom of inadequate care, probably a deficiency of potassium exacerbated by inadequate or uneven watering and high temperatures; the same preventive measures as for greenback can be used.

## VIRUSES

All these crops are vulnerable (*see also pp.297 and 303*), especially to mosaic viruses, which cause mottled leaves and sometimes curled or distorted, stunted foliage.
■ There is no cure; infected plants should be destroyed immediately, and all other plants at the end of the season. Many varieties show good resistance, including the tomato 'Shirley'; cucumbers 'Jazzer' and 'Bush Champion'; courgettes 'Badger Cross' and 'Defender'; and marrow 'Tiger Cross'. Control aphids and other sap-feeding pests, as they spread viruses. Some viruses are transmitted by handling.

*Other tomato, pepper, courgette, and cucumber problems include: grey mould (courgettes are especially prone), see left; fruit splitting (tomatoes), see facing page.*

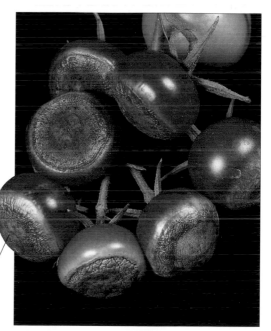

△ BLOSSOM END ROT

SEE ALSO: Protecting Crops, p.240; Greenhouses, p.241

# SOIL AND BULBS

THERE ARE SOME PESTS that, if infesting the soil, may cause concern even when, like ants and woodlice, they are merely a disruptive presence rather than actually eating plant roots. In the kitchen garden, crop rotation is critical in preventing any pest or disease that affects particular plants, or group of plants, building up; this applies to the problems detailed on pp.308–309 as well as to some of the soil-based pests described here. Soil-dwelling pests are difficult to eradicate because they can migrate unseen from an area that has become inhospitable. Many are larvae (immature stages), and some controls rely on preventing adult pests from laying eggs near to plants.

## PESTS VISIBLE IN THE SOIL

### ANTS

Ants need controlling only if they become a real nuisance. They do not eat plant material at all, but they can mine in and around plant roots to form their nests; the soil disruption can prevent the plants from thriving, especially if they are young. Ants also "farm" aphids for their honeydew, fighting off aphid predators to protect their stock. Eliminating individual ants is no good; you need to treat the nest.
■ There are many preparations on the market for ant trouble, including dusts and poisoned baits. Organic gardeners may use pyrethrum, although this may harm other, beneficial insects.

### CHAFER GRUBS

Chafer grubs curl into a C-shape when exposed, which helps to identify them (*see facing page, below*). The larvae of various beetles, they have three pairs of legs at the front of their bodies. They eat roots, making plants wilt suddenly. In flower beds, if you identify the problem swiftly, you may be able to dig up all the grubs and squash them; there may not be very many. However, populations commonly build up in lawns unseen, causing widespread yellow patches. Digging in lawns by foxes, badgers, rooks, magpies, or crows, all of which relish the grubs, is usually confirmation of their presence.
■ There is currently no chemical or biological control available to amateur gardeners for dealing with pests in lawns. Good cultivation of the grass will make the turf more vigorous and more tolerant of pest damage.

### CUTWORMS

Cutworms cause the same sort of damage as wireworms (*see facing page*), eating through the stems of seedlings just below soil level or into root vegetables, but they also emerge above ground at night to eat foliage. However, they look very different, and are the larvae of a number of moths. Often they are present only in ones and twos, so if you can find the culprit in the soil and squash it, you may solve the problem.
■ You can dust planting holes and rows with an insecticide, as for wireworms, to protect against the young larvae, but older cutworms resist chemical controls.

### FLATWORMS

The Australian and New Zealand flatworms are chiefly of concern to gardeners because they prey on earthworms, which have a critical role to play in soil health. In the United Kingdom, however, they have not yet become the major problem that early predictions forecast, but populations are growing in certain areas. They look very like leeches, but are completely smooth: leeches have fine lines running across their bodies defining their segments, and also have a sucker underneath their bodies at the rear. The New Zealand flatworm is reddish brown, up to 15cm (6in) long; the Australian flatworm is orange-brown, up to 10cm (4in) long.
■ There is no chemical control. As with vine weevils, be careful not to introduce flatworms into your garden via new plants. Inspect root balls carefully, both for the worms and for their shiny black egg capsules. Immersing the root balls in water for a couple of hours often encourages any flatworms to emerge.

### LEATHERJACKETS

These are mainly a lawn pest, causing yellow-brown patches where they eat through the grass stems below ground. The larvae of the crane fly (daddy-long-legs), which lays its eggs in late summer, they are greyish brown, tubular, up to 4.5cm (1¾in) long, with no obvious head.
■ Treatment is as for chafer grubs (*see left*). You can also bring leatherjackets to the surface and pick them off by covering areas of grass with black polythene sheeting overnight, or after heavy rain or a good watering.

Wireworms move slowly, a characteristic of plant eaters

Cutworms are soil-coloured for camouflage

◁ WIREWORMS     △ CUTWORMS     △ VINE WEEVIL LARVAE

SEE ALSO: Problems At and Below Soil Level, pp.308–309

## MILLIPEDES

Millipedes feed mainly on decaying matter on the soil, but sometimes damage seedlings and are a particular nuisance when they attack strawberry fruits.

■ Lifting strawberry fruits up onto straw helps protect them, and dusting seedling rows with lindane dust may also deter millipedes. If you find them in potatoes, they are not the real culprits: they get in through holes made by slugs, so if you deal with these, you should solve the problem. Millipedes have two pairs of legs on each segment of their bodies; do not confuse them with centipedes (see p.295), which only have one pair, since these are very useful pest predators.

## VINE WEEVIL LARVAE

Adult vine weevils, which are distinctive beetles (see p.299), nibble foliage – but this is harmless to plants compared with the damage the larvae can do underground to roots. They are often first seen only once the root ball of a purchased plant is removed from the container, as fat white grubs with brown heads (see facing page, below). If you find one, destroy it and rinse the roots off thoroughly to expose any more. Inspect all other plants purchased from the same source. (The root balls of container-grown plants are likely to contain pellets of slow-release fertilizer that are sometimes mistaken for vine weevil larvae. If in doubt, squeeze between the fingers – larvae will readily squash.) Once vine weevils have been introduced to the garden they are difficult to get rid of. In open ground they may not damage any

Chafer grubs curl into distinctive C-shape

△ CHAFER GRUBS

one particular plant too badly, but in containers they can be devastating, and any plant that is faring poorly for no apparent reason should be lifted out of its pot and the roots given a thorough investigation.

■ Imidacloprid, applied as a drench or purchased pre-mixed in potting compost, gives good control of the grubs. There are also biological controls, which are effective in containers and on confined areas of warm, light but moist soil. Always destroy adult weevils – each is female and can lay many hundreds of eggs into the soil throughout the summer.

## WIREWORMS

These click beetle larvae are especially common where planting areas used to be grassed over, and the problem usually subsides after a few years if the soil is kept cultivated. They feed on any roots, but the chief damage they cause is to seedlings, as they eat through the stems below ground, and to root crops, into which they tunnel. They are orange-brown segmented creatures (see facing page, below), up to 2.5cm (1in) long, with three pairs of legs at the front end.

■ If you identify wireworms in your soil, avoid growing potatoes and carrots in it for a few years if possible; if not, growing early varieties and lifting crops as soon as they are mature should prevent too much damage. Seedlings can be protected by dusting planting rows with lindane dust.

## WOODLICE

Woodlice (sometimes referred to as pillbugs) do no real harm to plants, except possibly to seedlings, in confined areas where populations can build up, since their activities can disturb soil around roots.

■ If woodlice become troublesome in greenhouses, a tidy-up and spring-clean, removing any debris or other matter that provides them with hiding places, should encourage them to move elsewhere. Saucers of water under greenhouse staging legs will stop them climbing up and onto benches.

# BULBS AND CORMS

## NARCISSUS BULB FLY

A relative of horseflies, the larvae eat out the centre of narcissus (daffodil) and hippeastrum bulbs (see below).

■ It cannot be treated with chemicals, but you can protect valuable spring bulbs after flowering by mounding soil around their bases and even covering with fleece blankets to prevent the fly laying eggs at the base of the plant. Leave the protection in place until midsummer. Bulbs planted in shade or windy sites are less vulnerable.

## EELWORMS

Some eelworms feed on roots (see p.309) but some attack bulbs of narcissi and also onions, producing stunted growth; when narcissus bulbs are cut across, brown rings can be seen. There is no treatment.

■ Always buy onion sets and narcissus/daffodil bulbs from reputable suppliers. Crop rotation should eliminate an infestation of onion eelworm. Narcissus eelworm is difficult to eradicate and can ruin naturalized plantings, but there is no effective option other than to lift and destroy bulbs.

## MICE AND OTHER RODENTS

Crocus corms are a favourite food of mice, as are pea, bean, and sweetcorn seeds, which mice can locate even before they have had a chance to germinate. Nibbled green shoot tips on the ground where crocuses and crops are growing is the more common scenario, however.

■ There are several types of humane trap if you are not keen on the traditional variety, but a mouse can find its way back over distances of up to a mile, so disposal may be rather a chore. Press soil down firmly over crocus corms to make it more difficult for mice to locate them. Chicken-wire over the soil can deter them, but it must be very fine mesh.

Core of bulb is eaten away and destroyed by bulb fly larvae

△ NARCISSUS BULB FLY

SEE ALSO: Problems At and Below Soil Level, pp.308–309

## PART THREE

# WHAT LOOKS GOOD WHEN

# GOOD YEAR-ROUND 1

## STRUCTURE PLANTS

### *SASA VEITCHII*
✿✿✿ ↕1–2m (3–6ft) ↔ indefinite

This hardy bamboo has strongly upright stems with white-margined leaves. It is useful for very shady areas, but keep it in a container in the ground to restrict its spread.

### *SAMBUCUS NIGRA* 'GUINCHO PURPLE'
✿✿✿ ↕↔ 6m (20ft)

This dark-leaved elder is a fast-growing deciduous shrub. The broad, flat clusters of white flowers in early summer develop into glossy round fruit. Effective for structure in a wild garden.

### *BETULA PENDULA* 'TRISTIS'
✿✿✿ ↕25m (80ft) ↔ 10m (30ft)

Silver birches are graceful trees with unusual peeling bark, yellow-brown catkins in spring, and pretty foliage colours in autumn. On 'Tristis', the peeling bark remains white underneath.

### *BERBERIS THUNBERGII* 'RED PILLAR'
✿✿✿ ↕↔ 1.5m (5ft)

This deciduous, densely leaved shrub makes an excellent hedge with attractive red-purple foliage. The shape opens out as the shrub matures. For better autumn colour, grow in a sunny spot.

### *COTINUS COGGYGRIA* 'NOTCUTT'S VARIETY'
✿✿✿ ↕↔ 5m (15ft)

This smoke bush is a dense deciduous shrub with fuzzy-looking, purple-pink flowers in summer, which give the plant a distinctive texture. Red-purple leaves provide good colour contrasts.

### *CRYPTOMERIA JAPONICA*
✿✿✿ ↕to 25m (80ft) ↔ to 6m (20ft)

The Japanese cedar grows into a tall, conical tree, valued for its red bark and decorative cones. It tolerates a variety of garden conditions and requires little pruning to keep in shape.

### *PHORMIUM* 'BRONZE BABY'
✿✿ ↕↔ 60–80cm (24–32in)

Good in a coastal garden or in large pots, New Zealand flaxes form a focal point with their evergreen, blade-like leaves. 'Bronze Baby' is a dwarf variety with rigidly upright, bronze-coloured leaves.

## FATSIA JAPONICA
✻✻ ↕↔ 1.5–4m (5–12ft)

This evergreen shrub suits a container or mixed
border in a sheltered courtyard or town garden.
It is loved for its large, shiny leaves and autumn
flowers. Brings structure to a shady corner.

## ACER NEGUNDO 'FLAMINGO'
✻✻✻ ↕ 15m (50ft) ↔ 10m (30ft)

This fairly fast-growing, deciduous maple tree
produces large, multi-coloured leaves in spring.
It loves a sunny position and can be kept small
by regular pruning.

## AUCUBA JAPONICA 'CROTONIFOLIA'
✻✻✻ ↕↔ 3m (10ft)

This tough evergreen shrub is ideal for all kinds
of difficult sites, such as full shade, polluted areas,
and places exposed to sea winds. 'Crotonifolia'
produces red berries in autumn.

## PRUNUS PENDULA 'PENDULA RUBRA'
✻✻✻ ↕↔ 8m (25ft)

This pretty cherry tree has a weeping habit. It comes
into its own from spring, when dark pink flowers
emerge on the slim branches before the leaves. The
deciduous leaves turn yellow in autumn.

## MALUS × ROBUSTA 'RED SENTINEL'
✻✻✻ ↕↔ 7m (22ft)

One of the crab apples, grown as much for its
fragrant flowers as the long-lasting autumn fruits,
which mature to glossy dark red. An excellent
specimen tree for smaller gardens.

### MORE CRAB APPLES

MALUS BACCATA VAR. MANDSCHURICA
*Rounded tree; scented blossom in spring*

M. FLORIBUNDA
*Popular and reliable crab apple; pink spring flowers*

M. HUPEHENSIS
*Vigorous; fragrant white flowers in spring*

M. 'JOHN DOWNIE'
*Edible crab apples in autumn; white spring blossom*

M. × MOERLANDSII 'PROFUSION'
*Purple-pink spring blossom*

M. TORINGO 'PROFESSOR SPRENGER'
*White spring blossom*

M. TORINGO SUBSP. SARGENTII
*Long-lasting, dark red autumn fruit*

M. × ZUMI 'GOLDEN HORNET'
*Small yellow crab apples persist into winter; large, pink-
flushed white flowers in late spring*

# GOOD YEAR-ROUND 2

## MORE STRUCTURE PLANTS

*LIGUSTRUM OBTUSIFOLIUM*
✻✻✻ ↕ 3m (10ft) ↔ 4m (12ft)
Most familiar as a hedge, privet can also be grown
as a spreading shrub. Its flowers, which can have
an unpleasant scent, are followed by round black
berries in autumn. Good for chalky soil.

*YUCCA GLORIOSA*
✻✻ ↕↔ 2m (6ft)
With its dagger-shaped evergreen leaves, this yucca
makes an excellent architectural plant for a large
pot basking in full sun. Its flowers appear from
late summer to autumn.

*SKIMMIA JAPONICA* 'BRONZE KNIGHT'
✻✻✻ ↕↔ to 6m (20ft)
Ideal in a shrub border, this evergreen bears dark
red buds in winter and glossy leaves all year
round. It prefers shade, but is tolerant of
most conditions and needs no attention.

*COTONEASTER FRIGIDUS* 'CORNUBIA'
✻✻✻ ↕↔ 6m (20ft)
This vigorous, semi-evergreen shrub makes a good
hedge, bearing white summer flowers, which
develop into masses of red berries. Some leaves
turn bronze in winter. Cut back hard to rejuvenate.

*TAXUS BACCATA* 'REPENS AUREA'
✻✻✻ ↕↔ 1–1.5m (3–5ft)
Yews are tolerant of difficult growing conditions,
including dry soils and polluted areas. This cultivar
has gold-bordered leaves, yellow shoots, and red
fruits in autumn. A good hedge or specimen tree.

*ACER PALMATUM* VAR. *DISSECTUM*
DISSECTUM ATROPURPUREUM GROUP
✻✻✻ ↕ 2m (6ft) ↔ 3m (10ft)
These Japanese maples are small, round deciduous
shrubs with red-purple, finely dissected leaves,
turning gold in autumn. Shade from hot sun.

### PYRACANTHA 'MOHAVE'
✷ ✷ ↕ 4m (12ft) ↔ 5m (15ft)

Often called firethorn for its showy, long-lasting, bright red berries, this vigorous, spiny shrub can be grown either in a border or on its own. Easy to grow, it is a good barrier hedge for warding off intruders.

### SORBUS SARGENTIANA
✷ ✷ ✷ ↕↔ 10m (30ft)

The pretty ornamental leaves and flowers of this mountain ash make it an asset in any small garden. It is an upright tree, which tolerates pollution and likes to grow in moist but well-drained soil.

### CRATAEGUS LACINIATA
✷ ✷ ✷ ↕↔ 6m (20ft)

Hawthorns are good specimen trees tolerant of most situations, including exposed and coastal sites. This species bears bunches of late spring flowers, followed by round, orange-red berries.

### ILEX AQUIFOLIUM 'PYRAMIDALIS AUREOMARGINATA'
✷ ✷ ✷ ↕ 6m (20ft) ↔ 5m (15ft)

Best in a sunny spot, this holly makes a shrub or small tree with green leaves bordered with gold. Plenty of bright red berries appear in autumn.

## MORE HOLLIES

*ILEX X ALTACLERENSIS 'BELGICA AUREA'*
*Upright shrub; yellow-margined leaves*

*I. X ALTACLERENSIS 'LAWSONIANA'*
*Compact shrub; yellow-splashed leaves*

*I. AQUIFOLIUM*
*Common holly; suitable for hedging*

*I. AQUIFOLIUM 'FEROX ARGENTEA'*
*Slow growing; very spiny; cream-margined leaves*

*I. AQUIFOLIUM 'MME BRIOT'*
*Tall shrub, good as a windbreak; dark green leaves with gold margins; bright red berries from autumn to winter*

*I. CORNUTA 'BURFORDII'*
*Rounded shrub; plenty of red berries in autumn*

*I. CRENATA 'CONVEXA'*
*Dense, broad shrub; black berries in autumn*

*I. MESERVEAE BLUE PRINCESS*
*Dark greenish blue leaves*

### PYRUS SALICIFOLIA 'PENDULA'
✷ ✷ ✷ ↕ 5m (15ft) ↔ 4m (12ft)

This weeping pear almost has the look of a small willow, with its slim, grey-green leaves and gracefully hanging branches. It tolerates pollution and is good on its own on a small garden lawn.

### SEMIARUNDINARIA FASTUOSA
✷ ✷ ✷ ↕ to 7m (22ft) ↔ 2m (6ft) or more

This tall, upright bamboo is ideal for providing height in a display, in a woodland garden, or on its own. The young canes in particular have purple-brown stripes. It may be invasive.

### CORDYLINE AUSTRALIS 'VARIEGATA'
✷ ↕ 3–10m (10–30ft) ↔ 1–4m (3–12ft)

This New Zealand cabbage palm is a dramatic plant with cream streaks on its long, spiky leaves. Excellent in a courtyard or cool conservatory. Bring it inside for winter in frost-prone areas.

# LONG FLOWERING SEASON

| SUN | SUN OR SHADE |

*CERASTIUM TOMENTOSUM*
✿✿✿ ↕ 5–8cm (2–3in) ↔ indefinite
This plant, known as snow-in-summer, is rather
useful in dry, sunny sites, such as on a garden wall,
in a rock garden, or as ground cover. The flowers
appear in profusion from late spring.

*ANTHEMIS* 'GRALLAGH GOLD'
✿✿✿ ↕↔ 60–90cm (24–36in)
Golden marguerites are excellent in a mixed border,
flowering over a long summer season, and they last
well when cut. Cut this cultivar back hard after
flowering to preserve vigour for the following year.

*AJUGA REPTANS* 'BRAUNHERZ'
✿✿✿ ↕ 15cm (6in) ↔ 60–90cm(24–36in)
Bugle is an evergreen perennial valued as colourful
and easy ground cover for shaded areas. It will
tolerate most soils as long as they are moist. The
flowers appear from spring to summer.

*CAMPANULA CARPATICA*
'BRESSINGHAM WHITE'
✿✿✿ ↕ to 15cm (6in) ↔ to 60cm (24in)
This bellflower is a low-growing, spreading plant
with large flowers from summer to autumn. It is
useful on a sunny bank or wall.

*ALCHEMILLA MOLLIS*
✿✿✿ ↕ 60cm (24in) ↔ 75cm (30in)
Good as ground cover, lady's mantle also makes an
appealing cut flower. It is useful for shade, but self
seeds freely and may take over. It flowers over a
long summer season.

*VINCA MINOR* 'ARGENTEOVARIEGATA'
✿✿✿ ↕ 10–20cm (4–8in) ↔ indefinite
This periwinkle flowers best in sun from mid-
spring to autumn amid cream-margined leaves.
Useful ground cover, but cut it back in early spring
to stop it taking over. Tolerates partial shade.

*PERSICARIA AMPLEXICAULIS* 'FIRETAIL'

✿✿✿ ‡↔ to 1.2m (4ft)

Knotweed likes moist soil and would be ideally placed in a bog garden. Its flowers emerge on tall stalks from clumps of leaves in summer and early autumn. Suitable for full sun or partial shade.

*PHYGELIUS × RECTUS* 'MOONRAKER'

✿✿ ‡↔ to 1.5m (5ft)

This upright, evergreen shrub flowers over a long period in summer and into autumn. The shrub may spread widely by its suckering shoots. It is usually grown as a border perennial in frosty areas.

*TIARELLA WHERRYI*

✿✿✿ ‡ to 20cm (8in) ↔ to 15cm (6in)

Generally, tiarellas prefer moist, shady conditions, although they tolerate a range of soils. This species is slow growing with flowers emerging from spring. Good ground cover under trees and shrubs.

*GERANIUM MACRORRHIZUM* 'BEVAN'S VARIETY'

✿✿✿ ‡ 50cm (20in) ↔ 60cm (24in)

Useful ground-cover for shade, this geranium has small flowers and scented leaves, which colour in autumn. Good for a woodland or wild garden.

*SYMPHYTUM CAUCASICUM* 'GOLDSMITH'

✿✿✿ ‡↔ 60cm (24in)

Comfrey is a good ground-cover plant for a shady area, with variegated leaves. Nodding, pale blue, cream, or pink flowers appear in spring from red buds. It can be grown under a hedge.

*NEPETA* 'SIX HILLS GIANT'

✿✿✿ ‡ to 90cm (36in) ↔ 60cm (24in)

Masses of flower spikes are borne throughout summer on this vigorous plant, commonly known as catmint because the scent attracts cats. Nepetas are ideal for mixed herbaceous borders.

## MORE GERANIUMS

G. 'ANN FOLKARD'
*Continuous magenta flowers from midsummer to autumn*

G. CLARKEI 'KASHMIR WHITE'
*Large and white, pink-veined flowers throughout summer*

G. HIMALAYENSE
*Blue flowers until autumn, most profuse in early summer*

G. NODOSUM
*Useful for ground cover in dry shade; purplish pink flowers from late spring to autumn*

G. × OXONIANUM 'WARGRAVE PINK'
*Vigorous; bright salmon-pink flowers from spring to autumn*

G. PSILOSTEMON
*Brilliant magenta flowers throughout summer*

G. SANGUINEUM 'ALBUM'
*Pure white flowers all through summer*

G. SANGUINEUM VAR. STRIATUM
*Compact; pink flowers in profusion throughout summer*

*EUPHORBIA PALUSTRIS*

✿✿✿ ‡↔ 90cm (36in)

A robust perennial with slim leaves that turn yellow and orange in autumn. The plant likes a sunny spot with reliably moist soil; it is good beside water. Cut back in spring to keep it compact.

*LAMIUM ORVALA*

✿✿✿ ‡ to 60cm (24in) ↔ 30cm (12in)

The toothed leaves of this clump-forming dead nettle make an effective foil for the flower spikes, which appear from late spring into summer. Good as ground cover.

# ALL-SEASON FOLIAGE INTEREST 1

## VERTICAL INTEREST

### HUMULUS LUPULUS 'AUREUS'
✿✿✿ ↕↔ 6m (20ft)
This vigorous, twining climber is a bright gold-leaved version of the hop used in brewing. The small summer flowers are are overshadowed by the large leaves, which colour best in full sun.

### HEDERA HELIX 'ANNE MARIE'
✿✿ ↕↔ 1.2m (4ft)
This self-clinging climbing ivy is valued for its grey-green, cream-edged foliage. It is not fully frost hardy, so it is best grown against a sheltered, sunny wall. It does not need support.

### ACTINIDIA KOLOMIKTA
✿✿✿ ↕↔ 5m (15ft) or more
This twining climber bears scented white flowers in early summer. The deciduous, dark green leaves are purple-tinged on young plants, maturing to white and pink. Grow against a wall or through a tree.

## BEDS AND BORDERS

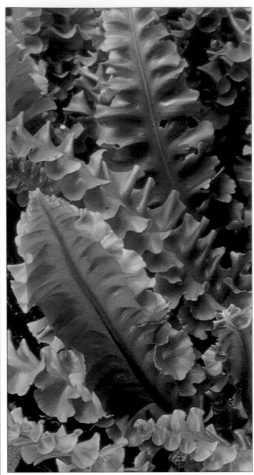

### ASPLENIUM SCOLOPENDRIUM CRISPUM GROUP
✿✿✿ ↕ 45–70cm (18–28in) ↔ 60cm (24in)
This group of evergreen ferns are best in a moist, shaded spot, such as a woodland garden. The long leaves are strongly crinkled, which gives them a striking appearance in a border of mixed foliage.

## MORE FERNS

*ADIANTUM PEDATUM*
Deciduous, fishbone-like fronds on wiry stalks

*ASPLENIUM TRICHOMANES*
Slender, black-stalked evergreen fronds with neatly paired divisions; a delicate-looking, but tough little fern

*DRYOPTERIS AFFINIS*
Bright green, deeply divided, semi-evergreen fronds; forms a shuttlecock-like shape; tolerates alkaline soil

*ONYCHIUM JAPONICUM*
Finely divided, bright green fronds on slender, wiry stalks; elegant growth forms dense clumps

*POLYPODIUM CAMBRICUM*
Fronds remain fresh and green until late winter

*POLYSTICHUM SETIFERUM DIVISILOBUM GROUP*
Finely divided, rich green fronds; for well-drained soil

*WOODSIA POLYSTICHOIDES*
Deeply divided, pale green fronds; forms small clumps, ideal for walls or rock crevices

### ELAEAGNUS × EBBINGEI 'GILT EDGE'
✿✿✿ ↕↔ 4m (12ft)
A popular, rounded or spreading evergreen shrub that grows well in exposed sites. The insignificant autumn flowers are followed by berries. Full sun is best, and the plant tolerates quite dry soil.

### ARTEMISIA 'POWIS CASTLE'
✿✿ ↕ 60cm (24in) ↔ 90cm (36in)
The feathery foliage of this shrubby perennial makes an excellent backdrop in a herbaceous border. Take cuttings in autumn, just in case outdoor plants die during a very severe winter.

### RHEUM PALMATUM 'BOWLES' CRIMSON'
✿✿✿ ↕ to 2.5m (8ft) ↔ to 1.8m (6ft)
This ornamental rhubarb has large, imposing leaves, and the dark red flowers appear in early summer. It is best near water or in a woodland garden, needing deep, moist soil.

*CYNARA CARDUNCULUS*
✳ ✳ ✳ ↕ 1.5m (5ft) ↔ 1.2m (4ft)
The cardoon is a tall, elegant, thistle-like perennial, which creates an imposing presence in a mixed border. The autumn flowerheads are purple and make good cut flowers either living or dried.

*ATRIPLEX HORTENSIS* VAR. *RUBRA*
✳ ↕ 1.2m (4ft) ↔ 30cm (12in)
A spinach-like annual grown for its blood-red or purple-red foliage, very effective used as a contrast colour in a summer border, especially against grey and silver. The flowering spikes are deep dark red.

*FOENICULUM VULGARE* 'PURPUREUM'
✳ ✳ ✳ ↕ 1.8m (6ft) ↔ 45cm (18in)
A slender-stemmed perennial, this fennel has finely cut, aniseed-flavoured, bronze-purple foliage. Flat heads of tiny yellow flowers appear in summer. Grow in well-drained soil in full sun.

*MELISSA OFFICINALIS* 'AUREA'
✳ ✳ ✳ ↕ 60–120cm (24–48in) ↔ 30–45cm (12–18in)
This drought-tolerant perennial is known as lemon balm from the smell of the crushed leaves. The leaves are splashed with yellow. Cut back in early summer to promote new growth.

*STACHYS BYZANTINA* 'SILVER CARPET'
✳ ✳ ✳ ↕ 45cm (18in) ↔ 60cm (24in)
This non-flowering foliage shrub has rosettes of silvery grey, thick and wrinkled leaves. It may be susceptible to mildew. Grow in a sunny part of the garden; also ideal as hedging or ground cover.

# ALL-SEASON FOLIAGE INTEREST 2

## MORE BEDS AND BORDERS

### BRACHYGLOTTIS 'SUNSHINE'
✳✳✳ ↕ 1.5m (5ft) ↔ 2m (6ft)
This spreading bush has white-hairy evergreen
foliage with scalloped edges. Bright yellow, daisy-
like blooms appear against this background from
summer to autumn. Good for coastal sites.

### HOSTA 'GOLDEN TIARA'
✳✳✳ ↕ 30cm (12in) ↔ 50cm (20in)
Hostas are suited to moist, shady sites, like woodland
or bog gardens, but the attractive foliage needs
protecting from slugs and snails. Spikes of deep
purple flowers appear on this cultivar in summer.

### GUNNERA MANICATA
✳✳✳ ↕ 2.5m (8ft) ↔ 3–4m (10–12ft)
This large perennial is grown for its immense
and spreading leaves, up to 2m (6 ft) across. It is
splendid at the side of a pond or stream, needing
moist soil and plenty of room. Protect from frost.

### ORIGANUM VULGARE 'AUREUM'
✳✳✳ ↕ 30–90cm (12–36in) ↔ to 30cm (12in)
Golden marjoram forms dense, low-growing pads
of aromatic yellow leaves. Pink flowers emerge in
clusters in late summer. Also makes a decorative
addition to a herb garden.

### CAREX ELATA 'AUREA'
✳✳✳ ↕ to 70cm (28in) ↔ 45cm (18in)
This splendid perennial tufted sedge forms a clump
of arching, grass-like leaves. Flowers emerge in late
spring, but the plant is usually valued for its rich
yellow foliage. Grow in sun or partial shade.

## MORE HOSTAS

*H. 'BLUE ANGEL'*
*Bluish grey leaves, 40cm (16in) long; white flowers*

*H. CRISPULA*
*Deep green leaves irregularly margined with white*

*H. FORTUNEI VAR. AUREOMARGINATA*
*Deeply veined leaves with yellow margins*

*H. 'FRANCEE'*
*Very puckered, blue-green leaves with green-yellow margins*

*H. 'GOLD STANDARD'*
*Green-yellow leaves; lavender-blue flowers in summer*

*H. PLANTAGINEA VAR. GRANDIFLORA*
*Wavy leaves; fragrant flowers in late summer*

*H. 'SUM AND SUBSTANCE'*
*Yellow-green to yellow leaves; for sun or partial shade*

*H. VENUSTA*
*Dark green leaves; violet flowers in summer and autumn*

*H. 'ZOUNDS'*
*Thick golden leaves*

### BALLOTA PSEUDODICTAMNUS
✳✳✳ ↕ 45cm (18in) ↔ 60cm (24in)
An evergreen shrub with yellowish, grey-green
leaves that will tolerate the driest of soils, and it
flowers in late spring. It makes good ground cover
in a border; cut it back in spring to keep it bushy.

### PACHYSANDRA PROCUMBENS
✳✳✳ ↕ 20cm (8in) ↔ indefinite
Grown mainly for its luxuriant, textured foliage,
this semi-evergreen perennial is an attractive
ground-cover plant, ideal for a shaded part of
the garden. Cut back each year to keep it tidy.

## CONTAINERS

*SALVIA OFFICINALIS* 'TRICOLOR'
✻✻✻ ‡ to 80cm (32in) ↔ 1m (3ft)
A decorative version of the herb sage with grey-green, aromatic leaves with cream and pink to purple shading. The colour is most noticeable in a sunny site. Lilac-blue flowers appear in midsummer.

*SEMPERVIVUM TECTORUM*
✻✻✻ ‡ 15cm (6in) ↔ 50cm (20in)
The rosettes of this common houseleek form evergreen mats of spine-tipped leaves. These rosettes die after producing red-purple flowers, but new rosettes follow. Good for troughs or sinks.

*HEDERA HELIX* 'SPETCHLEY'
✻✻✻ ‡↔ 15cm (6in)
This ivy is very compact. It has very small, dark green leaves and looks effective as a houseplant or in a mixed container. It is also useful for evergreen ground cover.

*OSMUNDA REGALIS*
✻✻✻ ‡ 2m (6ft) ↔ 4m (12ft)
The deciduous royal fern is suited to damp soil. The bright green fronds – up to 1m (3ft) long – are joined by distinctive, tassel-tipped brown fronds in summer. Keep roots moist at all times.

*AEONIUM* 'ZWARTKOP'
❀ ‡↔ to 2m (6ft)
Dramatic rosettes of fleshy leaves spring from base shoots on this succulent plant. In late spring, yellow flowers emerge from the centres of the rosettes. Grow in a pot and bring indoors over winter.

*LYSIMACHIA NUMMULARIA* 'AUREA'
✻✻✻ ‡ to 5cm (2in) ↔ indefinite
Also known as golden creeping Jenny or golden moneywort, this yellow-leaved evergreen is very vigorous and forms carpets of foliage. Bright yellow, cup-shaped flowers are seen in summer.

*HELICHRYSUM PETIOLARE* 'LIMELIGHT'
✻ ‡ to 50cm (20in) ↔ 2m (6ft) or more
Excellent in a hanging basket or container, the bright lime-green leaves of this shrub make an effective foil against deep colours, such as violet or dark blue. Often grown as a half-hardy annual.

*SENECIO CINERARIA* 'SILVER DUST'
✻✻ ‡↔ 30cm (12in)
Lacy, white-grey felted leaves are the main feature of this evergreen shrub. Yellow flowerheads are produced in the second year if the plant survives the winter. Good for a warm, sunny corner.

# WINTER TO EARLY SPRING 1

| WALLS | BEDS AND BORDERS |
|---|---|

### JASMINUM NUDIFLORUM
✳✳✳ ↕↔ 3m (10ft)

Useful for splashes of winter colour, this deciduous winter jasmine bears its small flowers through winter. It can be trained against a wall, even a north-facing one, and cut back after flowering.

### CLEMATIS ARMANDII
✳✳ ↕ 3–5m (10–15ft) ↔ 2–3m (6–10ft)

This vigorous evergreen climber keeps its glossy green leaves through winter, and once established, flowers abundantly in spring. Provide shelter by growing against a sunny wall. Pruning Group 1.

### GARRYA ELLIPTICA
✳✳ ↕↔ 4m (12ft)

This evergreen shrub comes into its own in winter, when tassel-like, long grey catkins appear. Garryas are either male or female; the catkins are more showy on males. Very good against a wall.

### ERANTHIS HYEMALIS
✳✳✳ ↕ 5–8cm (2–3in) ↔ 5cm (2in)

Winter aconites prefer a damp woodland site, so to ensure winter flowering do not let the soil dry out in summer. Once established, aconites can form a carpet of winter bloom under deciduous trees.

### SALIX ACUTIFOLIA 'BLUE STREAK'
✳✳✳ ↕ 10m (30ft) ↔ 12m (40ft)

This slender, arching willow is grown for its colourful winter shoots. Cut it back hard every few years to ensure good colour and to keep the plant small.

### LONICERA × PURPUSII 'WINTER BEAUTY'
✳✳✳ ↕ 2m (6ft) ↔ 2.5m (8ft)

This honeysuckle forms a shrub and may be deciduous or semi-evergreen. The very fragrant flowers, white with yellow anthers, are produced throughout winter and early spring.

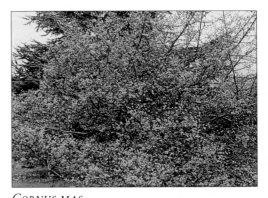

### CORNUS MAS
✳✳✳ ↕↔ 5m (15ft)

The Cornelian cherry is a deciduous shrub or small tree, which flowers on the bare branches in winter. In autumn, the dark green leaves turn red-purple. Grow at the back of a border; it tolerates most sites.

## MORE CORNUS

*C. ALBA 'AUREA'*
Dark red winter shoots; yellow leaves

*C. ALBA 'ELEGANTISSIMA'*
Red winter shoots; grey-green leaves with uneven white margins

*C. ALBA 'SPAETHII'*
Red winter shoots; yellow-margined leaves

*C. 'ASCONA'*
Purple winter shoots; green flowers; colourful autumn leaves

*C. MAS 'AUREA'*
Yellow flowers in late winter; leaves yellow when young, maturing to green

*C. MAS 'VARIEGATA'*
Compact shrub; abundant yellow flowers in late winter followed by red fruits; white-margined leaves

*C. STOLONIFERA 'FLAVIRAMEA'*
Vigorous shrub; yellow-green winter shoots; white flowers in late spring; leaves redden in autumn

*BERGENIA* × *SCHMIDTII*

❋❋❋ ↕ 30cm (12in) ↔ 60cm (24in)

This vigorous perennial forms rosettes of leathery leaves and bears its flowers in late winter. Good ground cover for moist soil in partial shade; the plant may attract slugs and snails.

*CYCLAMEN COUM* F. *ALBISSIMUM*

❋❋❋ ↕ 5–8cm (2–3in) ↔ 10cm (4in)

This perennial thrives in a well-drained, partly shaded site. White flowers with dark carmine red throats appear on slender stems above heart-shaped, silver-patterned leaves in winter and early spring.

*VIBURNUM* × *BODNANTENSE* 'DAWN'

❋❋❋ ↕ 3m (10ft) ↔ 2m (6ft)

From late autumn to spring, clusters of fragrant, dark pink flowers that mature to pinkish white are borne on the bare branches of this deciduous shrub. The young leaves are bronze, later green.

*SARCOCOCCA HOOKERIANA* VAR. *DIGYNA* 'PURPLE STEM'

❋❋❋ ↕ 1.5m (5ft) ↔ 2m (6ft)

An undemanding shrub with very fragrant, pink-tinged, white winter flowers followed by black berries. The young shoots are dark purple-pink.

*MAHONIA AQUIFOLIUM*

❋❋❋ ↕ 1m (3ft) ↔ 1.5m (5ft)

The Oregon grape is a robust and versatile shrub and will tolerate a variety of sites. It is grown for its spiny, glossy evergreen foliage, which turns red-purple in winter. Yellow flowers follow in spring.

# MID-SPRING 1

| WALLS | BEDS AND BORDERS IN SUN OR PARTIAL SHADE |

*CHAENOMELES × SUPERBA* 'NICOLINE'
✿✿✿ ↕ 1.5m (5ft) ↔ 2m (6ft)
The flowering quince produces an abundance of vivid scarlet flowers on its spiny branches from early spring. Train against a wall or grow on a bank. A sunny site improves flowering.

*CLEMATIS ALPINA* 'FRANCES RIVIS'
✿✿✿ ↕ 2–3m (6–10ft) ↔ 1.5m (5ft)
This delicate, spring-flowering clematis also bears fuzzy seedheads in late summer. A sunny, sheltered site with well-drained soil suits this climber best. Pruning Group 1.

## MORE CLEMATIS

*C. ALPINA* 'PINK FLAMINGO'
*Freely produces semi-double, pale pink flowers from spring to early summer. Pruning Group 1*

*C. ARMANDII* 'APPLE BLOSSOM'
*Pinkish white spring flowers. Pruning Group 1*

*C. CIRRHOSA*
*Evergreen clematis; cream flowers from late winter; seedheads follow. Pruning Group 1*

*C. MACROPETALA* 'MARKHAM'S PINK'
*Sugar-pink flowers from spring to early summer; silver seedheads follow. Pruning Group 1*

*C. MONTANA* F. *GRANDIFLORA*
*Very vigorous, ideal for covering a large, featureless wall; big, white spring flowers in abundance. Pruning Group 1*

*C. MONTANA* 'ELIZABETH'
*Scented, pale pink flowers in spring. Pruning Group 1*

*C. MONTANA* 'TETRAROSE'
*Satiny pink flowers from spring. Pruning Group 1*

*MAGNOLIA × SOULANGEANA* 'LENNEI ALBA'
✿✿✿ ↕↔ 6m (20ft)
This magnolia gives a magnificent display of goblet-shaped, fragrant flowers in mid- and late spring. It tolerates heavy clay soils and also makes a good specimen tree on a lawn.

*MUSCARI ARMENIACUM* 'BLUE SPIKE'
✿✿✿ ↕ 20cm (8in) ↔ 5cm (2in)
This bulbous perennial is also known as grape hyacinth. It is a vigorous plant that spreads easily, so it may need to be kept in check. The dense flower spikes are borne in spring amid fleshy leaves.

*CAMELLIA JAPONICA* 'COQUETTII'
✿✿✿ ↕ 9m (28ft) ↔ 8m (25ft)
In spring, this slow-growing shrub bears a profusion of lovely deep red flowers on downward-sweeping branches. An elegant addition to a border or woodland garden; it also looks effective in a container.

*CHIONODOXA FORBESII* 'PINK GIANT'
✿✿✿ ↕ 10–20cm (4–8in) ↔ 3cm (1¼ in)
This slug-resistant, bulbous perennial bears pretty pink, star-shaped flowers in early spring from clumps of upright leaves. Under deciduous shrubs or trees, this perennial should naturalize freely.

*CROCUS TOMMASINIANUS*
✿✿✿ ↕ 8–10cm (3–4in) ↔ 2.5cm (1in)
This bulbous perennial bears small, slender-petalled flowers from late winter to spring. Grow in drifts under trees or at the front of a border. It self seeds in suitable conditions.

**SALIX HELVETICA**

✳✳✳ ↕ 60cm (24in) ↔ 40cm (16in)

The Swiss willow is a graceful tree with slim, grey-green leaves. In early spring, silver-grey catkins appear from little golden yellow buds. Suitable for a shrub border; dislikes poor, chalky soil.

## MORE WILLOWS

*SALIX BABYLONICA 'TORTUOSA'*
Fast-growing; yellow-green catkins in spring; curiously twisted shoots give structural interest in winter

*S. CAPREA 'KILMARNOCK'*
Weeping habit; good for small gardens; grey spring catkins

*S. DAPHNOIDES*
Silky grey catkins in spring; purple young shoots

*S. ELAEAGNOS*
Slender green catkins in spring; grey shoots turn red-yellow

*S. EXIGUA*
Grows well on sandy soils; grey-yellow catkins in spring

*S. GRACILISTYLA 'MELANOSTACHYS'*
Bushy shrub; black catkins with red anthers in spring

*S. HASTATA 'WEHRHAHNII'*
Shrubby growth; silvery grey catkins in spring

*S. PURPUREA 'NANA'*
Compact, suitable for a hedge; silvery green spring catkins

**CHOISYA 'AZTEC PEARL'**

✳✳✳ ↕↔ 2.5m (8ft)

Choisyas are grown for their evergreen leaves and star-shaped spring flowers. Excellent and easy to care for in a shrub border. The flowers may reappear in autumn.

**OSMANTHUS × BURKWOODII**

✳✳✳ ↕↔ 3m (10ft)

This dense, rounded evergreen shrub also works well as a hedge and can be trained into different shapes. The tubular white flowers are fragrant and appear in mid- and late spring.

**KERRIA JAPONICA 'PLENIFLORA'**

✳✳✳ ↕↔ 3m (10ft)

This shrub is especially vigorous with double yellow flowers in mid- to late spring. Easy to grow, although the long green shoots may need support. Also suitable for a woodland garden.

**FRITILLARIA MELEAGRIS**

✳✳✳ ↕ to 30cm (12in) ↔ 5–8cm (2–3in)

The broadly bell-shaped, spring to early summer flowers of this bulb are purple, pinkish purple or even white. Like crocuses, fritillaries look good in drifts and can be naturalized in grass.

# MID-SPRING 2

## MORE BEDS AND BORDERS IN SUN OR PARTIAL SHADE

## BEDS AND BORDERS IN SHADE

*FORSYTHIA × INTERMEDIA* 'ARNOLD GIANT'
✿✿✿ ↕↔ 1.5m (5ft)
This shrub is grown for its deep yellow spring
flowers, which appear in early and mid-spring
before the leaves. Like other forsythias, this
cultivar can also be grown as hedging.

*ERYSIMUM ALLIONII*
✿✿✿ ↕ 50–60cm (20–24in) ↔ to 30cm (12in)
This bright orange wallflower with a curiously
spicy scent is ideal for the front of a sunny border
or a raised bed. The spring flowers are produced
in the second year. A short-lived perennial.

*DORONICUM ORIENTALE* 'FRÜHLINGSPRACHT'
✿✿✿ ↕ to 40cm (16in) ↔ 90cm (36in)
Sometimes labelled 'Spring Beauty', this yellow
double daisy makes a bright splash of colour in a
border. It flowers from mid-spring, bearing blooms
on slender stems, and it is also good for cutting.

*TULIPA* 'KEES NELIS'
✿✿✿ 25–40cm (10–16in)
The single flowers of this spring-flowering tulip
are blood red with lighter, orange-yellow margins.
As well as being an effective bedding plant, it is also
good as a cut flower. Best planted in clumps.

### MORE TULIPS

*T.* 'ANCILLA'
*Soft pink spring flowers with red throats*

*T. CLUSIANA* VAR. *CHRYSANTHA*
*Clusters of yellow flowers from early spring*

*T.* 'KEIZERSKROON'
*Broadly yellow-margined scarlet flowers in mid-spring*

*T. LINIFOLIA*
*Slender habit; bowl-shaped red flowers from early spring*

*T.* 'PRINSES IRENE'
*Unusual, orange and purple flowers in mid-spring*

*T. TARDA*
*Clusters of yellow spring flowers with white petal tips*

*T. TURKESTANICA*
*Clusters of up to 12 star-shaped, white spring flowers*

*T.* 'ZAMPA'
*Primrose-yellow spring flowers with bronze and green bases;
leaves marked dark bluish maroon*

*ANEMONE BLANDA* 'WHITE SPLENDOUR'
✿✿✿ ↕↔ 15cm (6in)
The tubers of this spreading perennial produce
prettily toothed leaves and large and open, white
spring flowers, pink-tinged beneath. It should
naturalize well and form large clumps quickly.

*EPIMEDIUM × VERSICOLOR* 'SULPHUREUM'
✿✿✿ ↕ 30cm (12in) ↔ 1m (3ft)
This perennial tolerates fairly dry soils, forming
clumps of divided evergreen leaves with dark
yellow flowers in mid- and late spring. Also
good for ground cover.

*ERYTHRONIUM DENS-CANIS*
❄❄❄ ‡ 10–15cm (4–6in) ↔ 10cm (4in)
The dog's tooth violet is a bulbous perennial also good under deciduous trees or in a rock garden. The white, pink, or lilac spring flowers have backward-curving petals. Keep stored bulbs slightly damp.

*PRIMULA VULGARIS* SUBSP. *SIBTHORPII*
❄❄❄ ‡ 20cm (8in) ↔ 35cm (14in)
The spring flowers on this yellow-centred primrose vary from rose-pink or purple to red or white. Good at the front of a border or under trees and shrubs.

*BRUNNERA MACROPHYLLA* 'DAWSON'S WHITE'
❄❄❄ ‡ 45cm (18in) ↔ 60cm (24in)
Useful for ground cover in a woodland garden or shady border, this perennial is grown for its white-margined foliage and bright blue spring flowers, which are similar to forget-me-nots.

*PULMONARIA SACCHARATA*
❄❄❄ ‡ 30cm (12in) ↔ 60cm (24in)
This pulmonaria bears red-violet or violet flowers from late winter to late spring on a background of white-spotted leaves. One of the earliest perennials to flower, it is also attractive to bees.

*OMPHALODES CAPPADOCICA* 'CHERRY INGRAM'
❄❄❄ ‡ to 25cm (10in) ↔ to 40cm (16in)
This perennial is similar to the forget-me-not, bearing deep blue flowers from clumps of evergreen leaves. Grow in a woodland garden or use as ground cover in a shady border.

*RIBES SANGUINEUM* 'BROCKLEBANKII'
❄❄❄ ↔ 1.2m (4ft)
This yellow-leaved version of the familiar flowering currant is a thornless, deciduous shrub, which bears pale pink, tubular flowers in spring, followed by black berries. The leaves pale slightly in summer.

*SCILLA SIBERICA*
❄❄❄ ‡ 10–20cm (4–8in) ↔ 5cm (2in)
This pretty woodland plant is grown for its bowl-shaped, deep blue spring flowers. Grow under trees or shrubs, or naturalize in grass. There is no need to water scillas once they have finished flowering.

*HYACINTHOIDES HISPANICA*
❄❄❄ ‡ 40cm (16in) ↔ 10cm (4in)
The Spanish bluebell is a vigorous bulbous perennial, which suits woodland gardens or sites under tall shrubs. The bell-shaped flowers emerge from among the strap-shaped leaves in spring.

# MID-SPRING 3

## ACID SOIL

*RHODODENDRON* 'BEETHOVEN'
✳✳✳ ↕↔ 1.3m (4½ft)
This spring-flowering evergreen dwarf azalea is a suitable shrub for a site with dappled shade. The showy flowers have a deep mauve mark inside each petal; they may be damaged by late frosts.

*RHODODENDRON* 'CÉCILE'
✳✳✳ ↕↔ 2.2m (7ft)
Large, trumpet-shaped flowers are borne on this vigorous deciduous azalea in mid- and late spring, the buds opening to dense trusses of salmon-pink blooms. A large shrub that needs plenty of space.

### MORE RHODODENDRONS

R. 'HINOMAYO'
*Dense, dwarf evergreen azalea; pink flowers from mid-spring*

R. LUTEUM
*Large deciduous azalea; scented yellow flowers into summer*

R. 'MAY DAY'
*Low-growing evergreen; scarlet flowers in mid-spring*

R. 'MRS G.W. LEAK'
*Good large shrub for clay; pink spring flowers*

R. 'NARCISSIFLORUM'
*Compact; scented yellow flowers; leaves bronze in autumn*

R. 'STRAWBERRY ICE'
*Medium shrub for full sun; pale pink flowers from spring*

R. 'SUSAN'
*Vigorous, compact, pollution-tolerant shrub; mauve, mid-spring flowers fade to white*

R. YAKUSHIMANUM
*Popular, medium-sized evergreen; pink spring flowers*

## CONTAINERS

*ARABIS CAUCASICA* 'VARIEGATA'
✳✳✳ ↕ 15cm (6in) ↔ 50cm (20in) or more
The fragrant spring flowers of this perennial emerge against green leaves with striking, pale yellow margins. Also grows well in a rock garden or as ground cover; needs sunny, fast-draining soil.

*BELLIS PERENNIS* TASSO SERIES
✳✳✳ ↕↔ 5–20cm (2–8in)
A cultivar of the ordinary daisy, but with double, quill-petalled flowers in pink, white, or red. It is most often grown as spring bedding, but it grows easily in containers in full sun or partial shade.

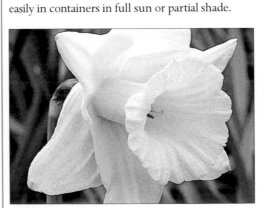

*NARCISSUS* 'EMPRESS OF IRELAND'
✳✳✳ ↕ 40cm (16in)
One of the largest trumpet daffodils, 'Empress of Ireland' has creamy white spring flowers, with a single trumpet on each stem. It also makes an effective display in a shrub border.

*RHODODENDRON* 'IROHAYAMA'
✳✳✳ ↕↔ 60cm (24in)
This compact, evergreen dwarf azalea has small leaves and small clusters of funnel-shaped, lilac-edged white flowers in spring. It likes a sunny spot and is also effective in a massed planting.

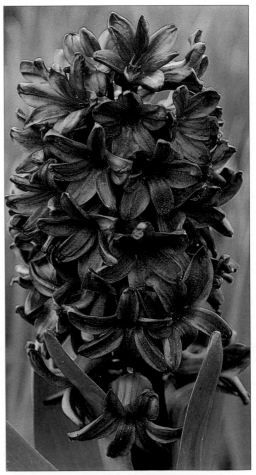

*HYACINTHUS ORIENTALIS* 'BLUE JACKET'
✳✳✳ ↕ 20–30cm (8–12in) ↔ 8cm (3in)
Hyacinths are excellent for spring colour, whether grown in pots or used in bedding displays, and they are easy to look after. The waxy, fragrant blooms of 'Blue Jacket' are intense navy to purple-blue.

## WATER GARDENS

***PRIMULA PULVERULENTA* 'BARTLEY STRAIN'**
❀❀❀ ↕ to 1m (3ft) ↔ 60cm (24in)
A candelabra primula with whorls of tubular,
shell-pink flowers with red eyes on upright stems
until early summer. It prefers a permanently moist,
shady spot, ideally in a bog garden or by a stream.

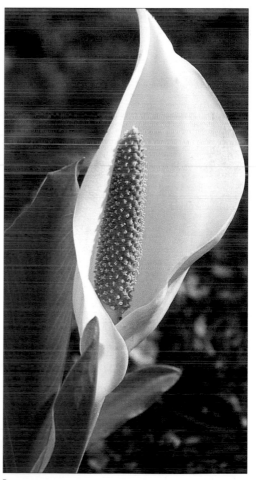

***PRIMULA PROLIFERA***
❀❀❀ ↕↔ 60cm (24in)
The spring blooms of this candelabra primula vary
from creamy white to golden yellow. The basal
leaves form a rosette. Grow in a bog or woodland
garden, so long as the soil is permanently moist.

***HOUTTUYNIA CORDATA* 'CHAMELEON'**
❀❀❀ ↕ to 15–30cm (6–12in) or more ↔ indefinite
Use houttuynias as part of a damp border or at the
side of a pond. 'Chameleon' is grown for its bright,
variegated leaves, which are coloured green, pale
yellow, and red. Slugs and snails may be a problem.

***CALTHA PALUSTRIS***
❀❀❀ ↕ 10–40cm (4–16in) ↔ 45cm (18in)
Calthas, also known as marsh marigolds, are
best grown at the edge of water, although they
can survive in a border if kept very moist. This
species has waxy yellow flowers, like a buttercup.

***LYSICHITON CAMTSCHATCENSIS***
❀❀❀ ↕↔ 75cm (30in)
The white skunk cabbage is a marginal aquatic
perennial grown for its glossy green leaves and
striking, usually pointed white spathes, which
appear from early spring and have a musky scent.

# LATE SPRING TO EARLY SUMMER 1

## WALLS IN SUN

**CALLISTEMON VIMINALIS 'ROSE OPAL'**
�֍ ↕1.5–2m (5–6ft) ↔ 1.5–4m (5–12ft)
This shrub is known as a bottlebrush because of its brush-like flower spikes from late spring, which are made up of numerous tiny flowers with long stamens. Grow against a warm, sunny wall.

**ABUTILON VITIFOLIUM VAR. ALBUM**
✖✖ ↕5m (15ft) ↔ 2.5m (8ft)
A fast-growing deciduous shrub suited to a sunny, sheltered, well-drained site. It produces showy white flowers on long stalks in early summer. Prune in late winter or early spring.

**FREMONTODENDRON 'PACIFIC SUNSET'**
✖✖ ↕↔ 2m (6ft)
A good evergreen shrub for the back of a sheltered border as well as a sunny wall, with large, saucer-shaped yellow flowers over a long period from early summer. The shoots and leaves may irritate skin.

**WISTERIA SINENSIS 'ALBA'**
✖✖✖ ↕9m (28ft) or more
Chinese wisteria is a vigorous climber, which will twine itself around a supporting framework or into a tree. Very long fronds of fragrant white flowers appear in late spring and early summer.

**SOLANUM CRISPUM 'GLASNEVIN'**
✖✖ ↕6m (20ft)
Vigorous and scrambling, this climber is ideal for rapid cover of a wall or shed. Decorative blue-purple flowers appear from early summer until autumn, followed by yellowish white fruits.

## WALLS IN SUN OR PARTIAL SHADE

**JASMINUM HUMILE**
✖✖ ↕2.5m (8ft), sometimes to 4m (12ft) ↔ 3m (10ft)
Usually, but not always fragrant, this jasmine forms a bushy shrub and is valued for its delicate yellow flowers from late spring and bright green leaves. Prune in autumn, once flowering has finished.

**ROSA 'MME GRÉGOIRE STAECHELIN'**
✖✖✖ ↕to 6m (20ft) ↔ 4m (12ft)
A vigorous, arching climbing rose with a good covering of dark green leaves, forming a backdrop for the fully double, red-flushed pink roses in early summer. Large, round red hips follow.

### MORE ROSES

*R. BANKSIAE*
*Thornless climber, best if protected from frost; rosettes of violet-scented, double white flowers in late spring*

*R. BANKSIAE 'LUTEA'*
*Thornless climber that needs a sheltered wall; double yellow flowers in late spring*

*R. CITY OF YORK*
*Climber; clusters of scented, semi-double, creamy white flowers in early summer*

*R. 'GRANDIFLORA'*
*Vigorous upright rose; scented, single, flat to cup-shaped, creamy white, early summer flowers with yellow stamens*

*R. 'MAIGOLD'*
*Strong climber; scented, bronze-yellow, early summer flowers, may bloom again in autumn*

*R. XANTHINA 'CANARY BIRD'*
*Arching shrub; musk-scented, single yellow flowers in late spring, may bloom again later in season*

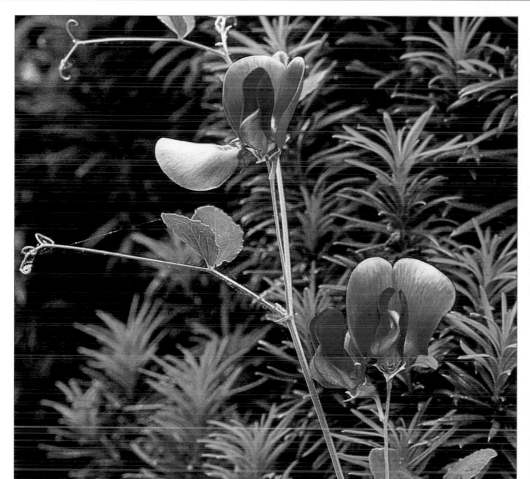

**LATHYRUS GRANDIFLORUS**
✳✳✳ ↕1.5m (5ft)

The everlasting pea will, if supported, climb up
a wall or through shrubs and small trees. From
early summer, pink-purple and red, pea-like
flowers emerge in a showy display.

**CLEMATIS 'WILLIAM KENNETT'**
✳✳✳ ↕2–3m (6–10ft) ↔ 1m (3ft)

In early summer, this deciduous climber bears
large, single, pale lavender-blue flowers with dark
red anthers. They appear on the previous year's
growth. Pruning Group 2.

**LONICERA JAPONICA 'HALLIANA'**
✳✳✳ ↕10m (30ft)

This delightful twining climber is a very vigorous
Japanese honeysuckle, bearing fragrant, pure white
flowers from late spring to late summer, which
mature to dark yellow. Blue-black berries follow.

**AKEBIA QUINATA**
✳✳✳ ↕10m (30ft)

The pretty leaves, which tinge purple in winter,
make the chocolate vine an attractive climber
even without its spring flowers, which are brown-
purple and vanilla-scented. It is very vigorous.

**HYDRANGEA ANOMALA SUBSP. PETIOLARIS**
✳✳✳ ↕15m (50ft)

The climbing hydrangea clings to a framework by
means of aerial roots. The flowers emerge from
early summer and the leaves yellow in autumn.
Shelter from cold, drying winds; slow to establish.

# LATE SPRING TO EARLY SUMMER 2

## BEDS AND BORDERS HOT AND DRY

### HELIANTHEMUM 'FIRE DRAGON'
✼✼✼ ‡ 20–30cm (8–12in) ↔ 30cm (12in)

This spreading, sun-loving shrub is ideally suited to a rock garden or raised bed. The bright flowers or this sun rose are carried over a long period from late spring to midsummer. Easy to look after.

### LOBULARIA MARITIMA 'LITTLE DORRIT'
✼✼✼ ‡ to 10cm (4in) ↔ 20–30cm (8–12in)

Most cultivars of sweet alyssum are useful bedding plants from early summer on. They grow well just about anywhere, including crevices between paving stones. This one has white flowers.

### ARMERIA MARITIMA 'VINDICTIVE'
✼✼✼ ‡ to 20cm (8in) ↔ to 30cm (12in)

This cultivar of sea thrift has profuse rose-pink flowerheads from late spring to summer and stiff, upright stems. It forms clumps and prefers a dry and sunny, open site; a rock garden is good.

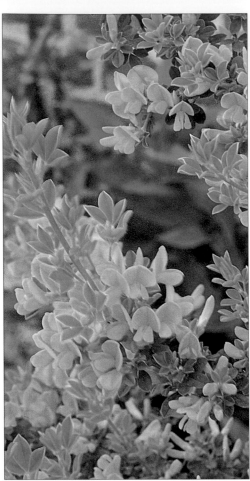

### CYTISUS 'PORLOCK'
✼✼ ‡↔ 3m (10ft)

This broom is a vigorous, semi-evergreen shrub. The late spring, pea-like flowers are very fragrant, and they are followed by downy seed pods. Tolerates all but very chalky soil.

### LINUM NARBONENSE
✼✼✼(borderline) ‡ 30–60cm (12–24in) ↔ 45cm (18in)

The saucer-shaped flowers of this Mediterranean perennial are borne continuously in the first half of summer. It prefers full sun and needs protection from winter wet. Ideal for a rock garden.

### CISTUS × CYPRIUS
✼✼ ‡↔ 1m (3ft)

This shrub bears small clusters of white flowers from early summer. Each bloom lasts only a day, but they are soon replaced. It is unsuitable for very chalky soil, but is easily grown in a container.

### IRIS 'SILVERADO'
✼✼ ‡ to 1m (3ft)

The large, beautifully ruffled flowers of this tall bearded iris are a pretty pale silver-blue and appear from mid-spring. The broad leaves appear in a fan-shape. For a mixed or herbaceous border.

## MORE IRISES

*I. BUCHARICA*
Fast-growing; up to six golden yellow to white flowers per stem in mid- and late spring

*I. 'EARLY LIGHT'*
Fragrant bearded iris; lemon-flushed, cream and yellow flowers in mid- and late spring

*I. FOETIDISSIMA*
Dull purple flowers in early summer followed by attractive seed capsules for autumn display

*I. GRAMINEA*
Plum-scented, rich purple-violet flowers borne among the bright green leaves in late spring and early summer

*I. INNOMINATA*
Beardless, Pacific Coast iris; early summer flowers range from bright yellow to cream, and purple to pale blue

*I. PALLIDA 'VARIEGATA'*
Large and scented, soft blue flowers in late spring and early summer; bright green leaves with yellow stripes

## BEDS AND BORDERS IN SUN OR PARTIAL SHADE

### CEANOTHUS 'CONCHA'
✿✿ ↕↔ 3m (10ft)
In late spring, the reddish purple buds of this evergreen shrub open to a profusion of dark blue flowers. Most ceanothus cultivars grow to twice their normal height when trained against a wall.

### POTENTILLA 'WILLIAM ROLLISON'
✿✿✿ ↕ to 45cm (18in) ↔ 60cm (24in)
Potentilla flowers provide good colour over a long season. This clump-forming perennial produces its flowers from early to late summer. It is useful for late colour in a mixed border.

### ERYSIMUM 'JOHN CODRINGTON'
✿✿✿ ↕ 25cm (10in) ↔ 30cm (12in)
This evergreen perennial wallflower adds colour to any border or raised bed in full sun with its late spring flowers. Also good against a wall; trim after flowering.

### EXOCHORDA GIRALDII VAR. WILSONII
✿✿✿ ↕↔ 3m (10ft)
This pretty flowering shrub needs a well-drained site, but it is otherwise very easy to look after. New leaves are pinkish green, maturing to pale green. A profusion of white flowers appear in late spring.

### LABURNUM × WATERERI 'VOSSII'
✿✿✿ ↕↔ 8m (25ft)
A spreading tree grown for its hanging chains of flowers, which proliferate in late spring. Unsuitable for a family garden as all parts are toxic if eaten.

### DIANTHUS 'PIKE'S PINK'
✿✿✿ ↕ 15cm (6in) ↔ 20cm (8in)
An alpine pink for the rock garden, raised bed with good drainage, or border edge. The double, pale pink flowers are clove-scented and bloom from early summer.

### ROSA 'CHARLES DE MILLS'
✿✿✿ ↕↔ 1.2m (4ft) or more
This dense and arching, thornless shrub rose has mid-green foliage and can also be grown as a hedge. Pink buds appear from early summer, opening to fully double, fragrant, mulberry-coloured flowers.

### MORE SHRUB ROSES

R. 'BLANCHE DOUBLE DE COUBERT'
*Dense, spreading habit; semi-double, fragrant white flowers with yellow stamens from early summer to autumn*

R. 'BUFF BEAUTY'
*Rounded habit; large clusters of lightly fragrant, fully double apricot flowers from early summer*

R. CONSTANCE SPRY
*Arching habit that will climb if supported; fully double, myrrh-scented pink flowers from early summer*

R. GLAUCA
*Vigorous species; single, reddish pink flowers with gold stamens from early summer; red hips in autumn*

R. GRAHAM THOMAS
*Arching habit; fully double, fragrant yellow flowers continue from early summer until autumn*

R. 'WILLIAM LOBB'
*Arching, prickly stems may need support; double, scented, purple to lavender-grey flowers from early summer*

# LATE SPRING TO EARLY SUMMER 3

## MORE BEDS AND BORDERS IN SUN OR PARTIAL SHADE

**WEIGELA 'LOOYMANSII AUREA'**
✱✱✱ ↕↔ 1.5m (5ft)
This slow-growing, spreading deciduous shrub
suits partial shade, with flowers that appear in late
spring and early summer. Useful at the back of a
border; trim to size, but do not cut into old wood.

**CENTAUREA CYANUS**
✱✱✱ ↕ 20–80cm (8–32in) ↔ 15cm (6in)
An upright annual, the cornflower has dark blue
flowerheads from late spring to midsummer,
which are attractive to bees and butterflies.
Grow in well-drained soil in full sun.

**THALICTRUM AQUILEGIIFOLIUM**
✱✱✱ ↕ to 1m (3ft) ↔ 45cm (18in)
Suited to a wild or woodland garden, this upright
perennial produces fluffy clusters of flowers with
bright purple-pink stamens in early summer. Take
care not to damage dormant plants in spring.

**COREOPSIS GRANDIFLORA 'SUNRAY'**
✱✱✱ ↕ 50–75cm (20–30in) ↔ 45cm (18in)
The double, deep yellow flowers of this annual
will brighten up a sunny border display. Borne
on long stalks, the flowerheads attract bees.
Coreopsis flowers are splendid for cutting.

**SALVIA × SYLVESTRIS 'BLAUHÜGEL'**
✱✱✱ ↕ 50cm (20in) ↔ 45cm (18in)
This perennial forms clumps of wrinkled,
scalloped leaves. Tall stems of bright blue flowers
emerge in early summer, which provide brilliant
colour for a bedding display.

**PAEONIA LACTIFLORA**
**'DUCHESSE DE NEMOURS'**
✱✱✱ ↕↔ 70–80cm (28–32in)
This perennial peony is grown for its large and
fragrant, early summer flowers. Stake the flowers
for support, and do not move once established.

**CAMASSIA LEICHTLINII**
✱✱✱ ↕ 60–130cm (24–54in) ↔ 10cm (4in)
A bulb to grow in a wildflower meadow or border.
Star-shaped, creamy white flowers appear in late
spring; as they fade, the flower segments twist
together. Do not let them become waterlogged.

**SYRINGA VULGARIS 'MRS EDWARD HARDING'**
✱✱✱ ↕↔ 7m (22ft)
Large sprays of double, fragrant, purple-red flowers
appear in late spring and early summer on this
shrubby lilac tree for a sunny site. Grow in a shrub
border or on its own; needs light pruning only.

*DELPHINIUM* 'BLUE BEES'

❀ ❀ ❀ ↕ 1.7m (5½ft) ↔ to 75cm (30in)

Delphiniums are the classic cottage garden perennial. The tall, wiry flower stems will need staking if exposed to wind. Cut down to ground level in autumn. Blooms appear in early to late summer.

*ROSA* JUST JOEY

❀ ❀ ❀ ↕ 75cm (30in) ↔ 70cm (28in)

A large-flowered bush rose of open, branching habit. Rounded, fully double, fragrant, copper-pink flowers with wavy-margined petals are borne from early summer until autumn.

## MORE BUSH ROSES

*R.* INTRIGUE
Compact, cluster-flowered bush with dark red double flowers from early summer to autumn

*R.* 'PRINCESSE DE MONACO'
Vigorous, large-flowered bush; fragrant white flowers from early summer to autumn

*R.* REMEMBER ME
Large-flowered bush; wide sprays of copper-orange flowers from early summer to autumn; glossy leaves

*R.* SUPER STAR
Large-flowered bush; rounded, fully double, lightly scented, pale scarlet flowers from early summer to autumn

*R.* 'THE QUEEN ELIZABETH'
Vigorous, cluster-flowered bush with rounded, double pink flowers on long stems from early summer to autumn

*R.* VALENCIA
Large-flowered bush with an open habit; fragrant, double, amber-yellow flowers from early summer to autumn

*PHILADELPHUS* 'VIRGINAL'

❀ ❀ ❀ ↕ 3m (10ft) or more ↔ 2.5m (8ft)

The mock orange is popular shrub with strongly orange-blossom scented flowers in the first half of summer. Establishes easily in a shrub border or woodland garden, and it makes a good screen.

*DEUTZIA GRACILIS*

❀ ❀ ❀ ↕↔ 1m (3ft)

A bushy shrub with bright green leaves for a shrub border or as a specimen plant. Many fragrant, star-shaped white flowers are produced from spring to early summer. It is happiest in a sunny site.

*ANCHUSA AZUREA* 'LODDON ROYALIST'

❀ ❀ ❀ ↕ 90cm (36in) ↔ 60cm (24in)

The bright deep blue flowers of this sturdy perennial appear in early summer. It should not need staking, but deadhead after the first flush of flowers to promote further flowering.

# LATE SPRING TO EARLY SUMMER 4

| MORE BEDS AND BORDERS IN SUN OR PARTIAL SHADE | SHADE |

### SPIRAEA 'ARGUTA'
✽✽✽ ↕↔ 2.5m (8ft)

Also known as bridal wreath because of the foamy, white spring flowers, this slender, arching shrub makes a dense, rounded bush. It prefers a site in full sun. Prune after flowering.

### ALLIUM HOLLANDICUM 'PURPLE SENSATION'
✽✽✽ ↕ 1m (3ft) ↔ 7cm (3in)

This bulb, an ornamental cultivar of the onion family, does well in sun and gives impact in a border. Large, round heads made up of many star-shaped flowers appear from early summer.

### LUZULA NIVEA
✽✽✽ ↕ to 60cm (24in) ↔ 45cm (18in)

The snowy woodrush is a grass-like evergreen perennial, which is good for ground cover in shady or damp areas. Clusters of shiny, brownish white flowers are produced from early summer.

### GLADIOLUS CALLIANTHUS
✽ ↕ 70–100cm (28–39in) ↔ 5cm (2in)

In summer, this perennial bears loose spikes of very fragrant flowers, which arch gracefully on long, slim tubes and are suitable for cutting. Plant in groups for best effect; will not survive cold winters.

### TROLLIUS PUMILUS
✽✽✽ ↕ to 30cm (12in) ↔ to 20cm (8in)

This yellow-flowered perennial has pretty, glossy, toothed basal leaves and cup-shaped, late spring flowers, similar to buttercups. Moist, heavy soil is best, such as a bog garden.

### NIGELLA DAMASCENA 'PERSIAN JEWELS'
✽✽✽ ↕ to 40cm (16in) ↔ to 23cm (9in)

The showy summer flowers of this slender-stemmed annual are followed by green seed pods, which can be dried for flower arrangements. Grow love-in-a-mist at the front of a border.

### KOLKWITZIA AMABILIS 'PINK CLOUD'
✽✽✽ ↕ 3m (10ft) ↔ 4m (12ft)

This cultivar of the beauty bush produces masses of bell-shaped pink blooms from late spring. Each flower has a yellow-flushed throat. It is a deciduous shrub, suitable for a sunny border.

### MYOSOTIS SYLVATICA 'VICTORIA ROSE'
✽✽✽ ↕ to 25cm (10in) ↔ to 15cm (6in)

A cultivar of the common forget-me-not with large, bright pink flowers in spring to early summer. Vigorous and upright, this is a useful biennial for spring bedding. Protect from slugs.

### SMILACINA RACEMOSA
✳ ✳ ✳ ‡ to 90cm (36in) ↔ 60cm (24in)
A good perennial for a shady border or woodland garden that bears creamy white, sometimes green-tinged flowerheads in mid- and late spring. The leaves turn to yellow in autumn.

### DICENTRA SPECTABILIS
✳ ✳ ✳ ‡ to 1.2m (4ft) ↔ 45cm (12in)
Known as bleeding heart or dutchman's breeches for the unusual shape of the hanging flowers from late spring, this perennial is ideal for woodland, tolerating some sun if the soil stays moist.

### CONVALLARIA MAJALIS
✳ ✳ ✳ ‡ 23cm (9in) ↔ 30cm (12in)
Lily of the valley is a perennial with arching clusters of bell-shaped, strongly scented, waxy white flowers in late spring. It makes good ground cover in a damp and shady border.

### DIGITALIS PURPUREA EXCELSIOR GROUP
✳ ✳ ✳ ‡ 1–2m (3–6ft) ‡ 60cm (24in)
These are pastel-coloured cultivars of the common foxglove with early summer spikes of creamy yellow, white, purple, or pink flowers. They make excellent cut flowers. Grow from seed each season.

### POLEMONIUM CAERULEUM
✳ ✳ ✳ ‡ 30 90cm (12–36in) ↔ 30cm (12in)
Jacob's ladder is a perennial grown for its early summer flowers. It grows well in grass and prefers moist but well-drained soil. Deadhead regularly to promote flowering.

### POLYGONATUM × HYBRIDUM
✳ ✳ ✳ ‡ to 1.5m (5ft) ↔ 30cm (12in)
Common Solomon's seal is a perennial for moist soil in full or partial shade. Its leaves turn yellow in autumn, and its greenish white flowers hang from arching stems in late spring. Black berries follow.

### AQUILEGIA 'MAGPIE'
✳ ✳ ✳ ‡ 60cm (24in) ↔ 45cm (18in)
An unmistakable perennial with attractive, fern-like foliage and striking, black, dark purple, and white flowers from late spring. Easy to grow in light shade, or in sun if the soil remains moist.

# HIGH SUMMER 5

## MORE CONTAINERS

### FELICIA AMELLOIDES 'READ'S WHITE'
❄ ↕↔ 30–60cm (12–24in)

Felicias are grown for their long-lasting, daisy-like blue flowers from summer to autumn. This white-flowered form becomes quite bushy if the growing tips are pinched out regularly. Protect from frost.

### BEGONIA NON STOP SERIES
❄ ↕↔ 30cm (12in)

The double flowers of these tuberous begonias come in many bright colours, making them really excellent plants for a long-lasting summer display. They need good light, but not direct sun.

### AGAPANTHUS 'BLUE GIANT'
❄❄❄ ↕ 1.2m (4ft) ↔ 60cm (24in)

The striking flowerheads of this perennial appear from midsummer, emerging on long stems from clumps of strap-shaped leaves. The flowers are suitable for cutting. Mulch in winter in cold areas.

### VERBENA × HYBRIDA 'NOVALIS'
❄ ↕ to 25cm (10in) ↔ 30–50cm (12–20in)

This bushy perennial bears flowers from summer to autumn in rose-pink, deep blue, and scarlet. It suits containers in sunny sites and can also be used as edging. Provide protection in winter.

### DIMORPHOTHECA PLUVIALIS
❄ ↕ to 40cm (16in) ↔ 15–30cm (6–12in)

An attractive, upright annual with white summer flowerheads, which close in dull weather – it needs full sun. They have violet-brown centres and are deep violet-blue below. Deadhead regularly.

### FUCHSIA 'PRESIDENT MARGARET SLATER'
❄ ↕ 30–45cm (12–18in) ↔ 45–75cm (18–30in)

This pretty fuchsia bears flowers throughout summer and autumn. It is a good trailing shrub for a hanging basket. Keep moist and avoid full sun; provide protection in winter.

### PLATYCODON GRANDIFLORUS
❄❄❄ ↕ to 60cm (24in) ↔ 30cm (12in)

In the second half of summer, clusters of balloon-like buds open up to bell-shaped flowers on this perennial balloon flower. Good for cutting; grow in a container or at the front of a border.

### HELIOTROPIUM ARBORESCENS 'MARINE'
❄ ↕ to 45cm (18in) ↔ 30–45cm (12–18in)

Heliotropes are short-lived shrubs grown for their sweetly scented, slightly flattened flowerheads in summer. This cultivar is quite compact. An excellent container or summer bedding plant.

## WATER GARDENS

### NUPHAR LUTEA
✽✽✽ ↔ 2m (6ft)

This aquatic bears bright yellow, almost ball-shaped flowers in summer above spreading, leathery, floating leaves. It is also known as the yellow pond lily. The scent of the flowers can be unpleasant.

### NYMPHAEA 'JAMES BRYDON'
✽✽✽ ↔ 0.9–1.2m (3–4ft)

Rounded, bronze-green leaves form a backdrop to the bright rose-pink summer flowers of this waterlily. Grow in undisturbed water in sun and feed with aquatic fertilizer when in growth.

### MORE WATERLILIES

NYMPHAEA 'BLUE BEAUTY'
*Star-shaped, fragrant, mid-blue summer flowers; wavy-margined leaves; growth is frost tender*

N. 'CAROLINIANA NIVEA'
*Star-shaped, fragrant, ivory white flowers with yellow stamens; pale green leaves; fully hardy*

N. 'FROEBELII'
*Cupped, then star-shaped, burgundy-red flowers with orange-red stamens; pale green leaves; fully hardy*

N. 'GLADSTONEANA'
*Star-shaped white flowers in summer; rounded, wavy-margined, dark green leaves; fully hardy*

N. 'ODORATA SULPHUREA GRANDIFLORA'
*Very large, star-shaped, bright rich yellow flowers held slightly above water; marbled, dark green leaves; fully hardy*

N. 'PYGMAEA HELVOLA'
*Slightly fragrant, vivid yellow flowers; heavily mottled, purple-marked leaves; withstands all but heavy frost*

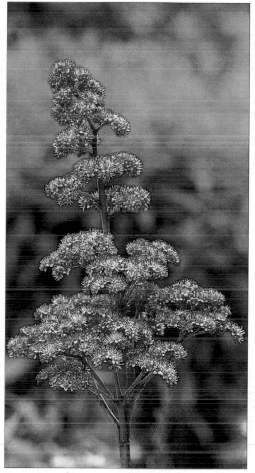

### RODGERSIA PINNATA 'SUPERBA'
✽✽✽ ↕ to 1.2m (4ft) ↔ 75cm (30in)

Grow this perennial near water at a woodland margin or in a bog garden. It has glossy dark green leaves, which are purplish bronze when young. The mid- to late summer flowers are bright pink.

### BUTOMUS UMBELLATUS
✽✽✽ ↕ to 1.5m (5ft) ↔ 45cm (18in)

A decorative perennial with delicate, fragrant flowers from midsummer. Grow in full sun in shallow water at a pond margin or in a bog garden. The leaves emerge bronze-purple as they extend.

### SAGITTARIA LATIFOLIA
✽✽✽ ↕ 45–90cm (18–36in) ↔ 90cm (36in)

An excellent plant for the margin of a wildlife pool, as the tubers attract birds. The flowers are borne in summer. Trim back spreading growth in late summer.

### MIMULUS LUTEUS
✽✽✽ ↕ 30cm (12in) ↔ to 60cm (24in)

The yellow monkey flower is a vigorous, spreading perennial, which self seeds freely. It suits a damp border or a bog garden, but it can be grown in water to 7cm (3in) deep.

### GLYCERIA MAXIMA VAR. VARIEGATA
✽✽✽ ↕ 80cm (32in) ↔ indefinite

This vigorous, aquatic grass is grown for its foliage, which is striped cream, green, and white. It spreads easily in water up to 15cm (6in) deep, making it good for cover in a large pool.

# LATE SUMMER TO EARLY AUTUMN 1

## WALLS IN SUN

### MAGNOLIA GRANDIFLORA 'GOLIATH'
✳✳ ↕ 6–18m (20–60ft) ↔ to 15m (50ft)
A particularly striking evergreen magnolia with
blooms up to 30cm (12in) across from late summer
and broad, slightly twisted leaves. The tree can be
trained against a warm wall; it tolerates dry soil.

### CAMPSIS × TAGLIABUANA 'MME GALEN'
✳✳ ↕ 10m (30ft) or more
This woody climber is vigorous with long stems of
leaflets and trumpet-shaped, orange-red flowers,
which appear from late summer to autumn. It
may take two or three years to establish.

### LAPAGERIA ROSEA VAR. ALBIFLORA
✳✳ ↕ 5m (15ft)
Grown for its showy, elongated flowers, which
appear from summer to late autumn, this
evergreen twining climber is best against a
sheltered wall. Provide a winter mulch.

## WALLS IN SHADE

### CLEMATIS 'PAUL FARGES'
✳✳✳ ↕ 7–9m (21–28ft) ↔ 3m (10ft)
This vigorous deciduous climber carries a
profusion of small flowers from midsummer
through to autumn. They appear on the current
year's shoots. Pruning Group 3.

## MORE CLEMATIS

C. 'ALBA LUXURIANS'
*Small white flowers from midsummer. Pruning Group 3*

C. 'BILL MACKENZIE'
*Lantern-like yellow flowers in abundance from midsummer.
Pruning Group 3*

C. 'ETOILE VIOLETTE'
*Small and nodding, violet-purple flowers until late autumn.
Pruning Group 3*

C. FLAMMULA
*Star-shaped white flowers into autumn. Pruning Group 3*

C. 'PERLE D'AZUR'
*Azure blue blooms from midsummer. Pruning Group 3*

C. 'POLISH SPIRIT'
*Deep purple-blue flowers from midsummer. Pruning Group 3*

C. REHDERIANA
*Scented yellow flowers until late autumn. Pruning Group 3*

C. VITICELLA 'PURPUREA PLENA ELEGANS'
*Purplish mauve flowers to late autumn. Pruning Group 3*

### CELASTRUS ORBICULATUS
✳✳✳ ↕ 14m (46ft)
Train this deciduous climber up a wall, fence,
pergola, or into a tree. Plant males with females so
the small, green summer flowers are followed by
yellow fruits, which split to reveal pink seeds.

### BERBERIDOPSIS CORALLINA
✳✳ ↕ 5m (15ft)
This woody evergreen climber blooms from
summer to early autumn, some flowers hanging
and others in clusters. Let it twine through a
support in partial shade. Protect in winter.

## BEDS AND BORDERS HOT AND DRY

### *ECHINOPS RITRO*
✿ ✿ ✿ ↕ to 60cm (24in) ↔ 45cm (18in)
Globe thistles are easy to look after and grow in almost any soil. This perennial species has round, metallic blue flowerheads in late summer. They are suitable for cutting and drying.

### *PEROVSKIA* 'BLUE SPIRE'
✿ ✿ ✿ ↕ 1.2m (4ft) ↔ 1m (3ft)
Tall, grey-white stems support a profusion of flowers in late summer and early autumn on this shrub. Grow in a mixed border; cut back hard in spring to promote flowering and compactness.

### *ZAUSCHNERIA CALIFORNICA* 'DUBLIN'
✿ ✿ ✿ ↕ to 25cm (10in) ↔ to 30cm (12in)
Also known as the Californian fuchsia, this deciduous perennial bears bright red, funnel-shaped flowers over a long season from late summer. Excellent for late season colour.

### *CROCOSMIA* 'BRESSINGHAM BLAZE'
✿ ✿ ↕ 75–90cm (30–36in) ↔ 8cm (3in)
The spikes of brilliant orange-red, funnel-shaped flowers of this perennial make a hot splash of colour at the edge of a mixed border. It flowers in late summer and is excellent for cutting.

### *SEDUM SPECTABILE* 'ICEBERG'
✿ ✿ ✿ ↕↔ to 60cm (24in)
In early autumn, this fleshy-leaved perennial bears flat flowerheads of white flowers. Grow at the front of a mixed border or in a rock garden; it is attractive to beneficial insects. It tolerates light shade.

### *TAMARIX RAMOSISSIMA* 'PINK CASCADE'
✿ ✿ ✿ ↕↔ 5m (15ft)
This graceful shrub has arching, red brown shoots and rich pink flowers on new growth in late summer and early autumn. Particularly good for an exposed coastal garden.

# LATE SUMMER TO EARLY AUTUMN 2

| BEDS AND BORDERS HOT/DRY | BEDS AND BORDERS IN SUN OR PARTIAL SHADE |

### GAILLARDIA PULCHELLA 'RED PLUME'
�֍ ✖ ✖ ‡↔ 30cm (12in)
From summer to autumn, double flowerheads are borne on this upright annual. Gaillardias have a long flowering period, and they are also good for cutting. Deadhead regularly.

### GAURA LINDHEIMERI
✖ ✖ ✖ ‡ to 1.5m (5ft) ↔ 90cm (36in)
This graceful, bushy, clump-forming perennial has slender stems and star-shaped flowers, which open from late spring to early autumn. It is unsuitable for very dry soils.

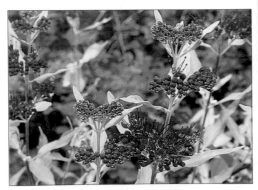

### CARYOPTERIS × CLANDONENSIS 'WORCESTER GOLD'
✖ ✖ ✖ ‡ 1m (3ft) ↔ 1.5m (5ft)
This deciduous shrub has warm yellow leaves and aromatic, lavender-blue flowers in late summer and early autumn. Best against a sunny wall.

### ECHINACEA PURPUREA
✖ ✖ ✖ ‡ to 1.5m (5ft) ↔ 45cm (18in)
Also known as cone flower for the distinctive, cone-shaped centre of the daisy-like flowerhead, this perennial flowers from midsummer. It is very popular for mixed or herbaceous borders.

### GALTONIA VIRIDIFLORA
✖ ✖ ‡ to 1m (3ft) ↔ 10cm (4in)
This bulbous perennial with broad and very long, lance-shaped leaves bears compact clusters of flowers in late summer. Best in a sunny border; it will need protection from severe frosts.

### TRADESCANTIA × ANDERSONIANA 'KARMINGLUT'
✖ ✖ ✖ ‡↔ 40–60cm (16–24in)
From summer to autumn, carmine-red flowers appear on this perennial amid the tufts of leaves. Cut back after flowering to encourage more blooms.

### RUDBECKIA HIRTA 'BECKY MIXED'
✖ ✖ ✖ ‡ to 25cm (10in) ↔ 30–45cm (12–18in)
This dwarf rudbeckia is usually grown as an annual in borders or summer beds. Its abundant summer to early autumn, daisy-like flowers are good for cutting.

### CERATOSTIGMA WILLMOTTIANUM
✖ ✖ ✖ ‡ 1m (3ft) ↔ 1.5m (5ft)
This spreading and deciduous shrub is grown for its pretty blue flowers and for its autumn leaf colour. Best in a sunny, sheltered spot; good as ground cover in a mixed border.

### *LEYCESTERIA FORMOSA*
✿✿✿ ↕↔ 2m (6ft)

The Himalayan honeysuckle is a thicket-forming shrub with bamboo-like young shoots. Flowers appear in summer and early autumn, followed by purple-red berries. Prune hard in spring.

### *ASTER AMELLUS* 'VEILCHENKÖNIGIN'
✿✿✿ ↕ 30–60cm (12–24in) ↔ 45cm (18in)

Asters can be found for most garden sites, and this violet-purple cultivar (also sold as 'Violet Queen') prefers a well-drained, open and sunny position. In late autumn, after flowering, cut back and mulch.

## MORE ASTERS

**A. x FRIKARTII 'MÖNCH'**
*Tolerant of air pollution; long-lasting, lavender-blue flowerheads with yellow-orange centres from late summer*

**A. LATERIFLORUS 'HORIZONTALIS'**
*Widely spreading branches; pink-tinged white flowerheads with darker pink centres from midsummer to mid-autumn*

**A. 'LITTLE CARLOW'**
*Large clusters of violet-blue flowerheads with yellow centres in early autumn; excellent for cutting and drying*

**A. NOVAE-ANGLIAE 'ANDENKEN AN ALMA PÖTSCHKE'**
*Vigorous, strong-stemmed growth; sprays of bright salmon-pink flowerheads with yellow centres from late summer*

**A. NOVI-BELGII 'CARNIVAL'**
*Very bright pink, yellow-centred flowerheads in late summer*

**A. NOVI-BELGII 'LITTLE PINK BEAUTY'**
*Semi-double, soft pink flowerheads from late summer*

**A. NOVI-BELGII 'MARIE BALLARD'**
*Double, pale blue flowerheads from late summer*

### *HELIANTHUS DECAPETALUS* 'TRIOMPHE DE GAND'
✿✿✿ ↕ to 2m (6ft) ↔ 1.2m (4ft)

This perennial cultivar of the classic sunflower has large flowerheads. Provide plenty of sun, and support the stems to prevent them from breaking.

### *HEBE* 'PURPLE QUEEN'
✿ ↕↔ 1.5m (5ft)

Hebes are versatile evergreen shrubs. This cultivar has large, late summer flowers and dark green leaves. Suitable for a container. In cold climates, it will need shelter from frosts.

### *ANEMONE × HYBRIDA* 'SEPTEMBER CHARM'
✿✿✿ ↕ 60–90cm (24–36in) ↔ 40cm (16in)

In mid- to late summer, this upright perennial bears branched stems of flowers. Grow in moist, fertile soil, adding a mulch in spring and late autumn in colder areas. A popular cottage garden flower.

# LATE SUMMER TO EARLY AUTUMN 3

## MORE BEDS AND BORDERS IN SUN OR PARTIAL SHADE

*NERINE BOWDENII* 'MARK FENWICK'
✳✳✳ ↕ 45cm (18in) ↔ 8cm (3in)

This bulbous perennial carries open clusters of pink autumn flowers on top of upright, dark green stalks. Plant bulbs in early spring in well-drained soil in sun. Water freely during active growth.

*PHYSALIS ALKEKENGI*
✳✳✳ ↕ 60–75cm (24–30in) ↔ 90cm (36in) or more

Chinese lantern is a vigorous, spreading perennial with bell-shaped flowers from midsummer. Grown for its papery, lantern-like red calyces surrounding the fruits. Suitable for cutting and drying.

*HELENIUM* 'BUTTERPAT'
✳✳✳ ↕ 90cm (36in) ↔ 60cm (24in)

This upright perennial has bright, rich yellow flowerheads from midsummer with yellow-brown centres. They are attractive to bees and are suitable for cutting. A colourful addition to a flower border.

*SOLIDAGO* 'GOLDENMOSA'
✳✳✳ ↕ to 75cm (30in) ↔ 45cm (18in)

Called golden rod for its tall, bright yellow flowerheads from late summer to autumn, this bushy perennial is suitable for natural gardens, because the flowers attract bees and butterflies.

*ACONITUM CARMICHAELII* 'ARENDSII'
✳✳✳ ↕ to 1.2m (4ft) ↔ 30cm (12in)

Monkshood is a good upright perennial with rich blue flowers in autumn, which are suitable for cutting. Ideal for a woodland garden or mixed border; it may need staking.

*ANGELICA GIGAS*
✳✳✳ ↕ 1–2m (3–6ft) ↔ 1.2m (4ft)

This short-lived perennial is grown for its striking flowers, which are carried on tall stems and appear in late summer and early autumn. Grow in full or partial shade. This is not the edible angelica.

*PHYSOSTEGIA VIRGINIANA* 'VIVID'
✳✳✳ ↕ 30–60cm (12–24in) ↔ 30cm (12in)

The obedient plant is named for its unusual flower spikes, which remain in a new position if bent or twisted. This cultivar is a clump-forming perennial that flowers from midsummer; suitable for cutting.

*HIBISCUS SYRIACUS* 'DIANA'
✳✳✳ ↕ 3m (10ft) ↔ 2m (6ft)

This excellent deciduous shrub bears particularly large flowers, to 12cm (5in) across, from late summer to mid-autumn. It needs a hot summer to flower really well.

| BEDS AND BORDERS IN SHADE | CONTAINERS |
|---|---|

*LIRIOPE MUSCARI*

✵✵✵ ↕ 30cm (12in) ↔ 45cm (18in)

An evergreen perennial with long, pointed leaves. It flowers in autumn, producing bright purple flowers, followed by black berries. It makes good ground cover, and is tolerant of dry sites.

### SCENTED-LEAVED PELARGONIUMS

P. 'AROMA'
Small, sweet-smelling, grey-green leaves; white flowers

P. 'ATOMIC SNOWFLAKE'
Large, yellow-variegated leaves with a lemon scent

P. 'ATTAR OF ROSES'
Rose-scented leaves; clusters of mauve summer flowers

P. 'CLORINDA'
Cedar-scented, lobed leaves; clusters of rose-pink flowers

P. CRISPUM 'VARIEGATUM'
Cream-margined, lemon-scented leaves; pale mauve summer flowers

P. 'FAIR ELLEN'
Deeply lobed, very spicy leaves; purple-pink flowers

P. 'FILICIFOLIUM'
Fern-like leaves with a balsam scent; pale mauve flowers

P. 'FRAGRANS'
Pine-scented, grey-green foliage; white summer flowers

P. 'LADY PLYMOUTH'
Eucalyptus-scented, silver-margined leaves; lavender-pink summer flowers

P. 'MABEL GREY'
Strongly lemon-scented leaves; purple summer flowers

P. 'OLD SPICE'
Spicy-scented leaves; white flowers throughout summer

P. 'PRINCE OF ORANGE'
Small, orange-scented leaves; clusters of mauve flowers

P. 'ROYAL OAK'
Spicy-scented leaves shaped like oak leaves; clusters of mauve flowers in summer

P. TOMENTOSUM
Peppermint-scented leaves, white flowers; trailing stems

*FUCHSIA MAGELLANICA*

✵✵ ↕ to 3m (10ft) ↔ 2–3m (6–10ft)

This upright, shrubby fuchsia produces red and purple flowers with long red tubes throughout summer. It will grow in a variety of sites; partial shade is best, and do not let the soil get too dry.

*GENTIANA ASCLEPIADEA*

✵✵✵ ↕ 60–90cm (24–36in) ↔ 45cm (18in)

The willow gentian looks effective grown with shade-loving ferns and grasses. It is a clump-forming perennial with trumpet-shaped blue flowers in the second half of summer.

*CEANOTHUS × PALLIDUS* 'PERLE ROSE'

✵✵✵ ↕↔ 1.5m (5ft)

A pink form of a traditionally blue-flowered shrub. It is bushy and deciduous, and it flowers from midsummer through to autumn. Grow in a shrub border or against a sunny wall. Prune annually.

*HYDRANGEA PANICULATA* 'UNIQUE'

✵✵✵ ↕ 3–7m (10–22ft) ↔ 2.5m (8ft)

This vigorous shrub bears large conical heads of white flowers in late summer and early autumn, which can be dried for indoor display. A large shrub best on its own or in a large border.

*PELARGONIUM* 'GRAVEOLENS'

❀ ↕ 45–60cm (18–24in) ↕ 20–40cm (8–16in)

The leaves of this vigorous perennial have a strong lemony aroma, and pale mauve flowers appear in summer. Also good as border edging.

# AUTUMN TO WINTER 1

| WALLS | BEDS AND BORDERS |
|---|---|

### COTONEASTER HORIZONTALIS
✤✤✤ ‡1m (3ft) ↔ 1.5m (5ft)
A rigid shrub that will grow flat against a sunny wall or strong fence in a fishbone pattern. Bees visit the tiny spring flowers, and the autumn berries are fed on by birds. The leaves turn red before they fall.

### CLEMATIS TANGUTICA
✤✤✤ ‡5–6m (12–20ft) ↔ 2–3m (6–10ft)
A twining climber with beautiful, bell-shaped yellow flowers from midsummer to autumn. Its seedheads persist among ghostly grey stems into winter. Provide support. Pruning Group 3.

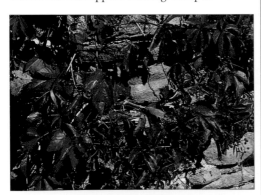

### PARTHENOCISSUS QUINQUEFOLIA
✤✤✤ ‡to 15m (50ft) or more
The Virginia creeper is best on large, featureless walls where it climbs without support. Its leaves turn a brilliant red in autumn. Do not let the vigorous growth interfere with guttering.

### VIBURNUM OPULUS 'XANTHOCARPUM'
✤✤✤ ‡5m (15ft) ↔ 4m (12ft)
This yellow-berried guelder rose is a deciduous shrub with lacecap-like heads of white flowers in summer. The leaves redden before they fall. Allow plenty of room.

### CALLICARPA DICHOTOMA
✤✤✤ ‡↔ 1.2m (4ft)
This dense deciduous shrub bears extraordinary purple berries, which follow the pale pink summer flowers. The fruits are not attractive to birds, so they persist long after the leaves fall.

### GAULTHERIA PROCUMBENS
✤✤✤ ‡15cm (6in) ↔ to 1m (3ft) or more
A creeping evergreen shrub for ground cover, with leathery leaves gradually turning red as the days grow colder. The pinkish white summer flowers are followed by berries. Unsuitable for alkaline soil.

### RUBUS COCKBURNIANUS
✤✤✤ ‡↔ 2.5m (8ft)
This ornamental bramble is deciduous and has red stems with a white bloom. The summer flowers are deep purple, and the fruits are inedible. Cut back hard in spring for good winter stem colour.

### COLCHICUM 'WATERLILY'
✤✤✤ ‡12cm (5in) ↔ 10cm (4in)
This autumn crocus looks good if the bulb-like corms are planted in drifts under deciduous trees. The unusual, feathery double flowers are lilac-pink. Also suitable for a container.

*IRIS UNGUICULARIS* 'MARY BARNARD'
✿✿✿ ‡30cm (12in)

A very low growing evergreen perennial with
fragrant, almost stemless flowers in midwinter.
It soon forms clumps in a sunny, sheltered spot.
Avoid slug-infested areas.

*CHRYSANTHEMUM* 'SALMON FAIRIE'
✿✿✿ ‡30–60cm (12–24in) ↔ to 60cm (24in)

A beautiful florists' chrysanthemum with
pompon-shaped, salmon-pink flowerheads, 4cm
(1½in) across, in late autumn. Apply a balanced
liquid fertilizer weekly for the best display.

## MORE CHRYSANTHEMUMS

*C.* 'BRONZE FAIRY'
Short cultivar, to about 60cm (24in) tall; pompon-style
autumn flowerheads in a rich seasonal shade

*C.* 'GEORGE GRIFFITHS'
Deep red flowerheads in autumn with backward-
curving petals

*C.* 'MADELEINE'
Sprays of pink autumn flowerheads with backward-
curving petals

*C.* 'PENNINE ALFIE'
Sprays of light bronze autumn flowerheads; all of the
"Pennine" chrysanthemums make a fine garden show

*C.* 'SALMON MARGARET'
Sprays of pale peach-pink flowerheads in autumn with
backward-curving petals

*C.* 'YVONNE ARNAUD'
Reddish purple autumn flowerheads to 14cm (5½in)
across with backward-curving petals

*FOTHERGILLA GARDENII*
✿✿✿ ‡↔ 1m (3ft)

The witch alder is a dense, bushy shrub with
spikes of fragrant white flowers in early spring.
It dislikes alkaline soil. Particularly good for its
vibrant autumn colour.

*RUSCUS ACULEATUS*
✿✿✿ ‡75cm (30in) ↔ 1m (3ft)

Planted in groups, butcher's broom makes a spiny,
subshrubby evergreen ground cover that thrives
in dry shade. Vivid red berries appear on female
plants from autumn to winter.

*CORNUS* 'EDDIE'S WHITE WONDER'
✿✿✿ ‡6m (20ft) ↔ 5m (15ft)

Beautiful most of the year, this small and spreading
deciduous tree has orange, red, and purple foliage
in autumn and inconspicuous flowers surrounded
by creamy bracts in spring. Needs a sunny site.

# AUTUMN TO WINTER 2

## MORE BEDS AND BORDERS

*BERGENIA* 'BALLAWLEY'
✳ ✳ ✳ ↕ 60cm (24in) ↔ 45–60cm (18–24in)
Good for colourful late-season ground cover when the leaves of this perennial turn bronze-purple in winter. Crimson flowers appear in mid- and late spring. A sheltered site is preferable.

*SYMPHORICARPOS × DOORENBOSII* 'WHITE HEDGE'
✳ ✳ ✳ ↕ 1.5m (5ft) ↔ indefinite
This snowberry is a useful deciduous shrub for most areas. Good for a city garden as it tolerates pollution. Also used for informal hedging.

*CROCUS SPECIOSUS* 'OXONIAN'
✳ ✳ ✳ ↕ 10–15cm (4–6in) ↔ 5cm (2in)
Plant drifts of this crocus out in late summer for a beautiful display of autumn flowers, which are violet-mauve with dark violet bases. It prefers sunny, well-drained soil that is not too rich.

*MAHONIA × MEDIA* 'BUCKLAND'
✳ ✳ ✳ ↕ to 5m (15ft) ↔ to 4m (12ft)
This evergreen shrub is grown for its spiky foliage and fragrant, bright yellow flowers on arching stems from late autumn to late winter. An easy shrub to grow; it makes a good barrier.

### MORE ROSES FOR HIPS

*R.* 'FRU DAGMAR HASTRUP'
*Small shrub; large and single, pink summer flowers; huge, tomato-red hips in autumn*

*R. MOYESII*
*Tall, arching rose; scarlet or pink flowers in summer; large, flagon-shaped hips in autumn*

*R. PIMPINELLIFOLIA*
*Spreading, prickly shrub; white, early summer flowers; round, purplish black hips in autumn*

*R. PRIMULA*
*Tall rose; pale yellow spring flowers; brownish maroon hips*

*R. ROXBURGHII*
*Stiffly growing shrub; unusual, spiny autumn fruit*

*R.* 'SCHARLACHGLUT'
*Can be trained as a climber; scarlet autumn hips*

*R.* 'SCHNEEZWERG'
*Dense bush; flat, scented white flowers from summer to autumn; tomato-shaped, orange-red hips follow*

*ROSA RUGOSA*
✳ ✳ ✳ ↕↔ 1–2.5m (3–8ft)
The Japanese rose has very prickly stems and makes a useful barrier hedge. It is grown for its fat, glossy red hips from autumn into winter. Purple-red flowers and unusual foliage extend the display.

## ACID SOIL

*EUONYMUS OXYPHYLLUS*

❀❀❀ ↕ 2.5m (8ft) or more ↔ 2.5m (8ft)

Glowing autumn leaf colour distinguishes this deciduous spindle tree from the well-known evergreens. It useful in a shrub border or for impact on its own.

### MORE EUONYMUS

**E. ALATUS**
*Dark green leaves turn brilliant red in autumn; spherical, reddish purple fruit appear from autumn; deciduous shrub*

**E. BUNGEANUS**
*Pale green foliage turns to yellow and pink in autumn; yellow-white winter fruit; graceful deciduous shrub*

**E. EUROPAEUS 'RED CASCADE'**
*Foliage turns red in autumn; red fruit in autumn and winter; deciduous shrub with conical shape*

**E. FORTUNEI 'EMERALD 'N' GOLD'**
*Bright green leaves with broad, bright yellow margins, tinged pink in winter; compact, evergreen shrub*

**E. FORTUNEI 'SILVER QUEEN'**
*White-margined, dark green leaves, margins tinged pink in winter; bushy and upright evergreen shrub*

**E. VERRUCOSUS**
*Foliage turns yellow or red in autumn; deeply lobed, yellow-tinged red fruit from autumn; rounded deciduous shrub*

*DISANTHUS CERCIDIFOLIUS*

❀❀❀ ↕↔ 3m (10ft)

This rounded deciduous shrub is grown for its autumn leaf colour, which turns to yellows, oranges, reds, and purples – all displayed at once. Plant alone for maximum impact.

*VACCINIUM ANGUSTIFOLIUM*
VAR. *LAEVIFOLIUM*

❀❀❀ ↕↔ 10–60cm (4–24in)

The lowbush blueberry is a spreading deciduous shrub with white spring flowers. It is grown for its blue-black, edible berries. Good autumn colour.

*CALLUNA VULGARIS* 'ANNEMARIE'

❀❀❀ ↕ 50cm (20in) ↔ 60cm (24in)

From midsummer to late autumn, this heather forms long spikes of flowers, which are good for cutting. All heathers are good as ground cover; cut back in spring for next year's flowers.

## PART FOUR

# WHAT
# TO DO
# WHEN

# HOW TO USE THIS SECTION

All gardens, even low-maintenance ones, require some care throughout the year to keep them looking their best and the plants healthy and thriving. When you think about jobs to be done, remember that they are opportunities to go into the garden and enjoy it, rather than chores.

Working in amongst the plants in your garden will bring you close to them and allow you to appreciate the textures of foliage, the flourish of a tiny flower, the chattering song of birds in the hedge, or a sweet perfume floating on the air. Whether weeding a border or planting a tree, take time to stop and look about you at the fruits of your labours and at how the garden changes through the seasons.

### WHAT NEEDS TO BE DONE WHEN?

To enable you decide easily what needs to be done in the garden and at what time of year, this section comprises listings largely distilled from previous chapters in the book. Individual, one-off projects are suggested on the facing page. The season-by-season listings in the rest of this chapter serve as brief reminders of routine tasks that you might need to carry out during the gardening year. Use the Index to Seasons (*see right*) to find a season and the appropriate task list.

---

## KEEPING CLIMBERS TO SIZE

■ **If a climber outgrows** its allotted space on the house, or any other, wall, spring is the time to cut it down to size.

■ **Cut back overlong shoots** with secateurs, cutting just above an upward- or downward-facing bud.

■ **Trim the shoots to irregular** lengths, within the desired outline of the plant, for a natural look.

CUTTING BACK IVY

---

### USING THE SEASONAL LISTINGS

Most seasons are split into month-long slots, for example "Early spring", "Mid-spring", and "Late spring", because the timing of garden tasks depends on the growing conditions, not the calendar month. There is also a category for tasks such as cleaning tools that are not dependent on the season ("Anytime").

■ Within the seasons, the tasks are further divided into columns for different areas of the garden, for example "Herbs" or "Beds and Borders", to remind you which areas of the garden are likely to need your attention.

■ Within quieter seasons such as winter, there may be no listing covering some areas of the garden, if there is little to do at that time of year.

■ Possible tasks are allocated to the part-season or season in which it is best to carry them out. Some tasks may be carried out in more than one season, so appear wherever relevant.

■ To enable you to prioritize work in the garden, essential tasks are highlighted at the top of each column. These include activities that may cause problems later if not done at the recommended time, such as watering new lawns, and others that can be done only at the indicated time, for example taking cuttings.

■ Bear in mind however that the listings *should be taken only as a guide*, not as rules to be followed slavishly. If you live in a warm climate or the weather is unusually mild, you may be able to start some tasks earlier and finish later; if in a cold region, you may have to delay them. Every garden is unique: its site (sheltered or exposed) and soil type (wet, dry, heavy, or light) affect the rate at which plants grow and the time when various activities are best carried out.

### ADDITIONAL INFORMATION

■ Cross-references lead you from the listing to more detailed information on how to carry out the task in appropriate chapters of the book.

■ The listing also features tips boxes with additional information (*see example, left*), ideas, or lists of relevant plants.

---

# GARDEN PROJECTS FOR ANY TIME OF THE YEAR

As well as tasks that are dependent on the seasons or on the plants in the garden (*see following pages*), there are other, usually one-off, projects which affect the garden's permanent structure (*see below*) to be done at any time, as long as the soil is not sodden or frozen. Some may be necessary to keep the garden looking tidy and functioning efficiently, such as laying paths or erecting a tool store, but most are projects to be undertaken as and when you wish, to enhance your own enjoyment of the garden.

Projects involving construction or major changes to the garden layout may involve more effort than routine tasks, but can have a great impact in the garden and be very rewarding.

Before embarking on a project, it pays to spend a little time in planning – consider how the new feature will fit into the garden layout, if you have all the materials and tools you need, delivery times of materials, how much time the job will take, if you need any help, and if any plants need to be prepared in advance.

## PATHS AND PAVING
- **Lay a patio** (*see pp.56–59*) to provide a link between the house and garden and a space for outdoor living.
- **Use concrete or gravel** to create a path, driveway, or area of hard surfacing (*see pp.60–63*). For a softer look, introduce planting pockets (*see p.63 and p.72*) with tough, low-level herbs or grasses, or alpine plants.
- **Install decking** to provide a patio, sitting area, or walkway (*see pp.64–65*). Leave it in natural tones to weather and blend in with the garden or paint it in bright colours for an original, contemporary look.
- **Make or renew a path** with hard surfacing, such as brick or crazy paving, or soft materials, such as bark chips (*see pp.66–67*).
- **Build some steps** to create a point of interest or to link different levels of the garden (*see pp.68–69*).
- **Extend the possibilities** of the garden by installing lighting (*see pp.70–71*), to allow use of it at night and to highlight the hidden beauty of favourite plants.
- **Jazz up the patio** by introducing plants in containers, a water feature, barbecue, or patio furniture (*see pp.72–73*).

POINTED CEMENT PAVING SLABS

## BOUNDARIES AND DIVISIONS
- **Erect fencing** such as wooden larchlap (*see p.94*) and picket fencing (*see p.95*) to enclose or divide up the garden. Paint it with wood preservative in natural tones or in bright colours for a contemporary look.
- **Put up trellis** to support plants (*see p.95*) and enable them to clothe walls and buildings or as a divider between areas of the garden.
- **Create an arch** to entice the eye along a path – assemble a ready-made one (*see p.99*) or build your own.

- **Build a pergola** on which to grow climbers for a charming shady retreat. You can assemble the pergola from a kit (*see p.101*). Alternatively, construct a simple one out of plain timber or from rustic poles, or employ someone to build it for you.

## BEDS AND BORDERS
- **Create a gravel bed** to provide ideal growing conditions for alpine and drought-tolerant plants as well as an attractive feature in the garden (*see p.132*). You could also plant it with herbs (*see p.229*).
- **Mark out a new border** to increase the space for planting (*see p.145*).

## CONTAINERS AND RAISED BEDS
- **Brighten up windows** – fix brackets to the wall so that you can add a splash of colour or touch of greenery with a windowbox (*see p.166*).
- **Make a windowbox** or planter out of wood – a good way of obtaining unique containers while saving money (*see p.171*).
- **Build a raised bed** with bricks or wooden railway sleepers (*see p.181*). You can fill them with plants that need special soil conditions, such as acid-soil lovers like azaleas and heathers, or that are small and better appreciated at close hand, such as alpine plants.
- **Customize your containers:** paint or decorate them (*see pp.169–170*), or age new terracotta and stone planters to give them a weathered look (*see p.171*).

## WATER GARDENING
- **Build a pond**, using a preformed pond unit (*see p.201 and p.206*) or a flexible pond liner (*see pp.201–203*). It will form a focal point in the garden, attract wildlife, and increase the range of plants you can grow, and if it is big enough, you can also keep a few fish.
- **Introduce the sound** of running water by installing a fountain – in a pool or a pond (*see pp.208–209*), on a wall or in a ground-level feature (*see pp.212–213*). For a unique feature, try recycling an old sink, watering can, or piece of scrap metal as a base for the fountain.

BARREL POOL

- **Make a bog garden** (*see pp.204–205*) as a specialized planting area or to complement and extend an existing water feature.
- **Prepare containers** such as wooden barrels or earthenware pots for use as small ornamental pools (*see p.207*).

## THE HERB GARDEN
- **Create a herb garden**, as a decorative feature in a formal or an informal style (*see p.224*), or a simple culinary patch near the house to supply the kitchen (*see p.226*).

## THE EDIBLE GARDEN
- **Plan a vegetable plot**, fruit bed, or ornamental potager, taking account of sowing and cropping times, yields, and soil needs (*see pp.234–237*), for a year-round harvest. Then mark out and prepare the beds, at least a month before sowing or planting them.

## GARDEN STRUCTURES
- **Erect a tool store** (*see p.276*), garden shed (*see pp.276–277*), or greenhouse (*see p.286*). If you want to grow tender plants in a cool or cold climate or to raise your own plants, a greenhouse can be invaluable.
- **Make a compost bin** (*see p.283*), create a leafmould bin, or set up a wormery (*see p.282*). You can use these to recycle garden waste into homemade compost; thereby enriching your soil and saving money.

# EARLY SPRING

| LAWNS | BOUNDARIES AND DIVISIONS |

## ESSENTIAL TASKS

■ **Control moss in lawns** if necessary (*see p.87*).

■ **Cut meadow grass** before flowering plants are too far into growth (*see p.89*).

■ **Sow seeds in containers** of herbs and similar plants to create a non-grass lawn (*see p.88 and p.162*).

## SOWING AND PLANTING

■ **Lay turf for a new lawn** (*see p.77 and pp.80–81*) as soon as the weather permits, so that the grass has time to establish before summer. Keep well watered.

■ **Prepare the soil and site** (*see p.78*) for spring sowings of grass seed.

■ **Plant plugs or sprigs** for a new lawn in warm climates (*see p.81*). Keep well watered.

■ **Plant divided sections** of herbs (*see p.231*) to create a non-grass lawn (*see p.88*).

## ROUTINE CARE

■ **Begin mowing established** lawns, as soon as weather permits, at appropriate intervals for the lawn type (*see p.82*); set the mowing height to maximum.

■ **Tidy up lawn edges** by recutting them (*see p.83*).

■ **Trim non-grass lawns** to remove dead or straggly growth (*see p.88*).

## ESSENTIAL TASKS

■ **Plant bare-root** rambler or climbing roses against walls, fences, or trees (*see p.110*) before they start into growth.

■ **Prune Groups 2 and 3 clematis** (*see p.114*).

## PLANTING

■ **Plant shrubs** against walls, fences, or trees (*see p.110*). Train stems into formative shapes (*see p.113*).

■ **Plant clematis** against walls, fences, or trees; tie stems into desired shape (*see p.111*).

■ **Plant hedges** (*see p.120*).

## ROUTINE CARE

■ **Feed and mulch climbers** and wall shrubs. Use a general-purpose fertilizer, according to the manufacturer's instructions. Rambler or climbing roses are hungry feeders and do well if given specialized rose fertilizer.

■ **Feed and mulch evergreen** hedges to prepare them for renovation pruning in mid-spring (*see p.121*).

## PRUNING AND TRAINING

■ **Prune established** climbers and wall shrubs that flower on the current season's shoots (*see pp.112–113*). These include bignonias, trumpet vines (*Campsis*), the Chilean bellflower (*Lapageria*), *Solanum crispum*, and stephanotis among climbers; abutilons, forsythias, lavateras, perovskias, and *Spiraea japonica* among shrubs.

■ **Renovate evergreen climbers** if needed, before they start into growth (*see p.115*).

■ **Prune hedges,** if they include plants such as *Fuchsia magellanica* and *Lonicera nitida* (*see chart, p.117, and p.121*).

## KEEPING CLIMBERS TO SIZE

■ **Climbers growing up house walls** can cause damage if allowed to grow into gutters and window frames or under roof slates and tiles.

■ **If a climber outgrows** its allotted space on the house, or any other, wall, spring is the time to cut it down to size.

■ **Cut back overlong shoots** with secateurs, cutting just above an upward- or downward-facing bud.

■ **Trim the shoots to irregular** lengths, within the desired outline of the plant, for a natural look.

**CUTTING BACK IVY**

## BEDS AND BORDERS

### ESSENTIAL TASKS

■ **Divide peonies** before they start into growth. Use a knife to cut the soft, fleshy roots into sections, each with 2 or 3 buds, taking care to avoid bruising them. Dust the cuts with fungicide, and replant the pieces so that the buds are just below the soil surface. (*See also p.135.*)

■ **Cut back tender grasses** and bamboos to the ground, before they start into growth, but after the frosts have abated.

■ **Water newly planted** plants regularly, if the weather is dry (*see p.152*).

■ **Pruning established** deciduous shrubs that flower on the current season's growth (*see p.158*).

■ **Finish pruning bush roses**, including modern bush roses, and China, Bourbon, and Portland old roses (*see p.161*).

### PLANTING

■ **Plant hardy perennials** (*see p.148*), summer-flowering bulbs (*see p.149*), grasses (*see p.140*), and shrubs, except containerized ones (*see p.150*). Buy good, healthy plants (*see pp.146–147*) for the best results. Give shrubs an initial prune after planting (*see p.151*) and stake if necessary (*see p.150*).

■ **Plant bare-root roses** (*see p.151*). Buy good, healthy plants (*see p.147*) for the best results. Give the roses an initial prune after planting (*see p.151*).

■ **Prepare light, sandy soils** for planting by forking in well-rotted organic matter to help the soil hold moisture (*see p.142*).

### ROUTINE CARE

■ **Feed plants in gravel beds**, if they have not grown well in the previous season (*see p.133*).

■ **Tidy gravel beds**: renew the top-dressing and remove any dead or damaged shoots from the plants (*see p.133*).

■ **Deadhead** spring-flowering plants, such as camellias (*see p.158*), bulbs, and alpine plants, as soon as the flowers fade. Leave the foliage on bulbs to die down naturally.

■ **Feed and mulch roses** after pruning. A specialized rose fertilizer is best.

■ **Mulch beds and borders**, if not done in autumn (*see pp.152–153*).

■ **Apply slow-release** fertilizer before the plants have begun to grow away (*see p.153*).

### PRUNING AND TRAINING

■ **Carry out initial pruning** for shape (*see p.157*) and restorative (*see p.159*) pruning of deciduous shrubs.

■ **Prune** hydrangea hybrids and shrubs with cane-like stems that flower in summer, such as Himalayan honeysuckle (*Leycestera formosa*) and *Kerria japonica* (*see p.159*).

■ **Prune dogwoods** (*Cornus*) grown for winter stems and shrubs such as *Cotinus* grown for bright young foliage (*see p.159*).

### RAISING YOUR OWN PLANTS

■ **Sow seed outdoors** (*see p.149 and p.163*) of hardy annuals.

■ **Sow seed indoors** of tender and half-hardy annuals and of perennials (*see p.162*).

■ **Divide perennials** (*see p.163*).

■ **Take softwood cuttings** from shrubs (*see p.165*).

■ **Layer shrubs** (*see p.165*).

## CONTAINERS AND RAISED BEDS

### ESSENTIAL TASKS

■ **Water containers** if needed – check regularly (*see p.178*), even if it has been wet.

■ **Pinch-prune** plants such as coleus, chrysanthemums, and fuchsias in containers (*see p.173 and box, p.381*).

### PLANTING

■ **Plant in containers** (*see p.176*), shrubs, bush or miniature roses, hardy perennials, hardy annuals and biennials, summer-flowering bulbs, and spring-flowering alpines.

■ **Cut back hard invasive** or vigorous plants in raised beds.

### ROUTINE CARE

■ **Feed or renew** compost of any established raised beds and top-dress or mulch (*see p.183*). Replace any exhausted or diseased plants.

■ **Repot or top-dress** permanently planted climbers; shrubs, bulbs, and alpines in containers, except spring-flowering ones. Root-prune if needed (*see p.179*).

PRIMROSE

# EARLY SPRING

| ORNAMENTAL TREES | WATER GARDENING | HERBS |
| --- | --- | --- |

## ESSENTIAL TASKS

■ **Finish coppicing and pollarding** trees (*see p.197*).

## PLANTING

■ **Prepare the soil** (*see p.192 and pp.142–143*) for mid-spring plantings of container-grown, bare-root, or evergreen root-balled trees.

■ **Plant bare-root** trees (*see p.194*) of hardy deciduous species. When filling in the planting hole, make sure there are no air pockets in-between the roots by gently shaking the stem up and down.

## ROUTINE CARE

■ **Top-dress or repot** trees in containers before they start into growth. To top-dress, replace the top 5cm (2in) of compost mixed with slow-release fertilizer. Water well, and mulch with gravel or bark chippings.

■ **Watch out for suckers** and water shoots growing from tree trunks or roots and remove them before they get too big and spoil the tree (*see p.197*).

TREE TOPIARY

## ROUTINE CARE

■ **Thin oxygenating plants** to clear out old growth in preparation for the growing season (*see p.223*).

### CLEANING WATER PUMPS

■ **Why do I need to clean the pump?** All pumps have filters to stop debris from the pond entering the pump. If the filter becomes silted up, the water flow will be impeded and the pump may be overloaded and break down.

■ **When does a pump need cleaning?** It depends on the model: follow the manufacturer's advice – some models need to be cleaned up to once a week in summer. It is also advisable to get pumps serviced once a year.

■ **How do I clean a pump?** Always disconnect the pump from the electric supply first. Lift out the pump and detach the filter, or strainer; sluice reusable filters with clean water and replace disposable filters.

## ESSENTIAL TASKS

■ **Prepare the soil** (*see p.228*) for spring plantings of moisture-loving herbs.

## ROUTINE CARE

■ **Lift invasive herbs** planted in sunken containers (*see p.231*), divide, and repot in fresh soil, compost, or a mixture of both.

■ **Cut off old growth** on perennial herbs, in cool climates.

■ **Discard or plant out** herbs that were potted up for winter use (*see p.231*).

■ **Top-dress or repot** perennial herbs grown in containers. To top-dress, replace the top 2.5–5cm (1–2in) of compost. Water well, and mulch with gravel or pea shingle.

## PRUNING AND TRAINING

■ **Cut back shrubby herbs** hard to encourage bushy new shoots.

## RAISING YOUR OWN PLANTS

■ **Sow seed outdoors** (*see p.149 and p.163*) of hardy annual herbs, such as chervil, coriander, and dill.

■ **Sow seed indoors** (*see p.162*) of tender and half-hardy annual herbs, such as basil.

■ **Rejuvenate tired shrubby** herbs by mound layering (*see p.231*).

■ **Divide large shrubby** or clump-forming herbs (*see p.231*), if not done in early autumn.

## THE EDIBLE GARDEN

### ESSENTIAL TASKS

- **Water newly planted vegetables** and fruit crops if needed (*see box, p.236*).

- **Dig in green manures** that were sown in the previous autumn (*see p.239*).

- **Finish sprouting seed potatoes** to prepare them for planting (*see p.252*).

- **Plant early seed potatoes** (*see p.252*).

- **Finish planting bare-root fruit trees** and cane fruits (*see pp.260–261*).

- **Protect newly planted or sown** crops from frosts in cool climates under cloches, fleece, or, with strawberry plants, sheets of newspaper.

### SOWING AND PLANTING

- **Sow seed of vegetables indoors** in containers (*see p.244*), such as:
Aubergines, chillies, and peppers (*see p.256*)
Calabrese (*see p.248*)
Greenhouse tomatoes (*see p.257*)
Lettuce (*see p.255*), in a cold frame
Sprouting broccoli (*see p.248*), in a cold frame.

- **Sow hardy vegetable seed outdoors** (*see p.242*), under cloches in cold areas, such as:
Beetroot (*see p.251*)
Bulb and spring onions (*see p.250*)
Calabrese (*see p.248*)
Early carrots (*see p.251*)
Hardy lettuce (*see p.255*)

Hardy peas, under netting to keep off birds and mice (*see p.247*)
Leeks (*see p.251*)
Parsnips (*see p.251*)
Salad leaves (*see p.255*)
Spinach beet and Swiss chard (*see p.255*)
Spring onions (*see p.250*)
Sprouting broccoli (*see p.248*)
Summer kale (*see p.248*)
Summer radish (*see p.249*)
Welsh onions (*see p.250*).

- **Sow seed of green manures** – to cover empty soil temporarily during the growing season (*see p.239*).

- **Protect vegetables outdoors** from frosts, if necessary, under cloches (*see p.240*).

- **Plant onion and shallot sets** (*see p.250*).

- **Plant rhubarb** (*see p.273*).

### ROUTINE CARE

- **Feed vegetable beds** (*see p.239*), and fork over and weed the soil in preparation for planting or sowing.

- **Warm the soil** in cooler regions by placing cloches (*see p.240*) or fleece over it, to prepare it for sowing.

- **Feed fruit trees**, bush and cane fruits, strawberries, and rhubarb (*see pp.264–273*).

- **Erect supports** (*see p.247*) for peas and climbing beans.

### PRUNING AND TRAINING

- **Prune young plum** (*see p.266*) and acid cherry trees (*see p.269*), once the buds have opened.

- **Prune off the cane tips** of summer-fruiting raspberries, blackberries, and hybrid berries, before growth begins (*see p.270*).

- **Re-tie leaders of grape vines** as the buds appear (*see p.273*).

### HARVESTING

- **Pick winter vegetables, such as**:
Beetroot (*see p.251*)
Calabrese (*see p.248*)
Kale flower shoots (*see p.248*)
Leeks (*see p.251*)
Parsnips (*see p.251*)
Spinach beet (*see p.255*)
Sprouting broccoli (*see p.248*)
Turnip tops (*see p.249*)
Winter cabbages (*see p.249*)
Winter lettuce (*see p.255*).

---

### GREEN MANURES

Sow these in empty patches of soil to protect the soil from drying out and to lock nutrients into the soil. Choose fast-growing types in spring and summer that are dug in before they flower and hardy types to occupy beds over winter.

**SPRING- AND SUMMER-SOWN**
Bitter lupin
Borage
Essex red clover
Mustard
*Phacelia tanacetifolia*
Rape

**AUTUMN-SOWN**
Bitter lupin
Comfrey
Grazing rye
Winter field beans
Winter tares

**SOWING SEED IN CONTAINERS**

# MID-SPRING

| LAWNS | BOUNDARIES AND DIVISIONS |

## ESSENTIAL TASKS

■ **Water new lawns** (*see p.84*) regularly in dry weather, so that they establish properly.

■ **Sow seed for a new lawn** (*see p.77 and p.79*) on prepared, moist ground, so that the grass has time to establish before summer. Keep the plot well-watered.

![Sowing grass seed with a neat edge]

SOWING GRASS SEED WITH A NEAT EDGE

## SOWING AND PLANTING

■ **Plant plugs or sprigs** for a new lawn in warm climates (*see p.81*).

■ **Prepare the soil and site** (*see p.78*) for late-spring planting of seedlings to create a non-grass lawn.

## ROUTINE CARE

■ **Mow established lawns** at appropriate intervals for the lawn type (*see p.82*); set the mowing height to maximum. Trim the edges (*see p.83*).

■ **Repair damaged patches** in lawns (*see p.86*) and reseed or returf if necessary.

---

### LIVING TAPESTRY

If the lawn area is not used frequently, why not make it more decorative by planting it with different, low-growing plants to form a tapestry quilt of contrasting textures and colours.

■ **Mark out the planting area** with a simple pattern: a chequerboard grid is easy to plant and very effective. You could also try stripes or swirls, but avoid anything complex – it will look fussy. Then plant with small plants as for a non-grass lawn (*see p.88*).

■ **Good plant choices** are creeping mints or thymes, mind-your-own-business (*Soleirolia soleirolii*), or green and black cultivars of the grassy perennial, *Ophiopogon planiscapus*. Make sure that you choose plants that grow at roughly the same rate for a balanced effect.

■ **Use paving or timber slabs** in a chequerboard pattern, alternating with squares of chamomile, herbs, or a even a meadow mixture, for a more hardwearing non-grass lawn.

---

## PLANTING

■ **Plant shrubs or climbers**, including clematis, against walls, fences, or trees (*see pp.110–111*). Train stems into the desired shape (*see p.113*). Plant hedges (*see p.120*).

## PRUNING AND TRAINING

■ **Prune evergreen climbers** and wall shrubs (*see pp.112–113*), after frosts are over.

■ **Renovate evergreen climbers** (*see p.115*) and hedges, if necessary (*see p.121*). Feed and mulch them afterwards.

■ **Prune evergreen flowering hedges** of *Garrya elliptica*, lavender, and pyracantha (*see chart, p.117, and p.121*).

---

### RAISE A NEW CLIMBER

■ **Many climbers root readily** from their stems to produce a new plant, if given the opportunity. Some even have aerial roots, such as ivies (*see p.108*).

■ **The best time to start** a new plant is in mid-spring or autumn.

■ **Choose a long, low stem** and peg onto the soil (layering). Nicking the stem where it touches the soil helps it root. Bury 15cm (6in) of the stem. Keep it watered until new shoots appear; usually about a year. Dig up the stem, detach from the plant, and pot up.

LAYERING A CLIMBING HYDRANGEA SHOOT

## BEDS AND BORDERS

### ESSENTIAL TASKS

■ **Water newly planted** plants regularly, if the weather is dry (*see p.152*).

■ **Finish initial pruning** for shape (*see p.157*) and restorative (*see p.159*) pruning of deciduous shrubs before they start into growth.

■ **Finish pruning** hydrangea hybrids (*see p.159*).

### PLANTING

■ **Plant hardy perennials** (*see p.148*), summer-flowering bulbs (*see p.149*), grasses (*see p.140*), and evergreen and container-grown shrubs (*see p.150*). Buy good, healthy plants (*see pp.146–147*) for the best results. Give shrubs an initial prune after planting (*see p.151*) and stake if necessary (*see p.150*).

### ROUTINE CARE

■ **Feed plants in gravel beds**, if they have not grown well in the previous season (*see p.133*).

■ **Tidy gravel beds**: renew the gravel and remove any dead or damaged shoots from the plants (*see p.133*).

■ **Thin perennials** that form clumps, while they are still small, to guarantee bigger and better flowers later in the season (*see p.154*).

■ **Deadhead** spring-flowering plants, such as camellias (*see p.158*), bulbs, and alpine plants, as soon as the flowers fade. Leave the foliage on bulbs to die down naturally.

■ **Mulch beds and borders**, if not done in autumn (*see pp.152–153*).

■ **Apply slow-release fertilizer** before the plants have begun to grow away (*see p.153*).

■ **Stake perennials and biennials** that might flop over when fully grown (*see p.154*).

### PRUNING AND TRAINING

■ **Prune evergreen shrubs**, both newly planted (*see p.157*) and established (*see p.158*) shrubs. Wait until all danger of frost is passed, to minimize damage to new shoots.

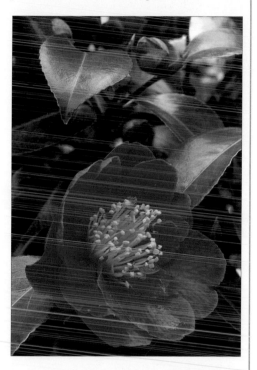

*CAMELLIA JAPONICA 'ALEXANDER HUNTER'*

■ **Prune shrubs** with cane-like stems that flower in summer, such as Himalayan honeysuckle (*Leycestera formosa*) and *Kerria japonica* (*see p.159*).

■ **Trim lavender bushes** to stop them becoming straggly and sparse (*see p.155*).

### RAISING YOUR OWN PLANTS

■ **Sow seed outdoors** (*see p.149 and p.163*) of hardy annuals.

■ **Divide oriental poppies** if the plants are large enough (*see p.135 and p.163*).

■ **Take softwood cuttings** from shrubs (*see p.165*).

■ **Layer shrubs** (*see p.165*).

## CONTAINERS AND RAISED BEDS

### ESSENTIAL TASKS

■ **Pinch-prune** plants such as coleus, fuchsias, and chrysanthemums in containers (*see p.173 and box, p.381*).

■ **Water containers** when necessary — check them regularly (*see p.178*), even if it has been wet.

### PLANTING

■ **Plant in containers** (*see p.176*) climbers, shrubs, bush or miniature roses, hardy perennials, hardy annuals and biennials, summer-flowering bulbs, and succulents.

### ROUTINE CARE

■ **Deadhead** regularly (*see p.178*) and keep plants well-shaped by removing any tired, diseased, or straggly foliage.

■ **Repot or top-dress** permanently planted climbers, shrubs, and alpines in containers, unless they are spring-flowering ones. Root-prune if needed (*see p.179*).

■ **Feed or renew compost** of any established raised beds and top-dress or mulch (*see p.183*). Replace any exhausted or diseased plants.

■ **Regularly weed** raised beds.

■ **Discard or plant out** bulbs that have been grown in containers.

### PRUNING AND TRAINING

■ **Regularly clip over** established topiary and standard plants (*see p.178*).

■ **Prune woody plants** in raised beds once risk of frost is past (*see p.156–161*).

■ **Trim lavender bushes** to stop them becoming straggly and sparse (*see p.155*).

# MID-SPRING

| ORNAMENTAL TREES | WATER GARDENING | HERBS |
|---|---|---|

## ORNAMENTAL TREES

### PLANTING

- **Prepare the soil** (*see p.192 and pp.142–143*) for late-spring plantings of container-grown, hardy evergreen bare-root, or evergreen root-balled trees.

- **Plant root-balled evergreen** trees (*see p.195*).

### ROUTINE CARE

- **If you use artificial fertilizers,** now is the time to feed established trees with a liquid or granular feed (*see p.197*).

- **Check tree ties** and stakes (*see p.193*) and remove or loosen them as necessary to avoid their chafing and damaging the tree bark.

- **Check tree guards** (*see p.195*) are still in place.

ROOT-BALLED
LEYLAND CYPRESS

- **Watch out for suckers** and water shoots growing from tree trunks or roots and remove them before they get too big and spoil the tree (*see p.197*).

## WATER GARDENING

### ESSENTIAL TASKS

- **Divide overcrowded plants,** except waterlilies, soon after they start into growth, to rejuvenate them (*see p.223*). Mature plants can be increased by division.

DIVISIONS OF JAPANESE RUSH
(*ACORUS GRAMINEUS*)

### PLANTING

- **Plant** (*see pp.220–221*) all water garden plants.

### ROUTINE CARE

- **Thin oxygenating plants** to clear out old growth in preparation for the growing season (*see p.223*).

## HERBS

### ESSENTIAL TASKS

- **Transplant seedlings** of biennial herbs such as angelica and caraway (*see p.149*) to their final positions.

- **Prune lavender** (*see p.232*) once all danger of frosts is past.

### PLANTING

- **Plant container-grown** perennial or shrubby herbs in beds, in paving, or in pots and hanging baskets (*see pp.228–231*).

- **Plant rooted cuttings** or small plants in-between paving (*see p.229*).

- **Plant divided sections** of herbs (*see p.231*) to create a non-grass lawn (*see p.88*).

### ROUTINE CARE

- **Lift invasive herbs** planted in sunken containers (*see p.231*), divide, and repot in fresh soil, compost, or a mixture of both.

### RAISING YOUR OWN PLANTS

- **Sow seed outdoors** (*see p.149 and p.163*) of hardy annual herbs.

- **Rejuvenate tired shrubby** herbs by mound layering (*see p.231*).

## THE EDIBLE GARDEN

### NEW HERBS FROM OLD

There are several fairly easy ways of growing your own herbs (*see below*). All annuals and biennials, and in cool climates many tender perennials, have to be raised from seed.

DIVISION
Chives, fennel, French tarragon, horseradish, lemon balm, lovage, mint, oregano, sorrel, thyme.

MOUND LAYERING
Artemisia, cotton lavender, lavender, rosemary, sage, thyme, winter savory.

CUTTINGS
Hyssop, lemon balm, mint, oregano, rosemary, sage, thyme.

VARIEGATED SAGE
(*SALVIA OFFICINALIS* 'TRICOLOR')

SEED
Angelica, basil, borage, caraway, chervil, coriander, dill, hyssop, parsley, sweet marjoram.

### ESSENTIAL TASKS

■ **Water newly planted vegetables** and fruit crops if needed (*see box, p.236*).

■ **Plant early seed potatoes** (*see p.252*).

### SOWING AND PLANTING

■ **Sow seed of green manures** to cover empty soil temporarily during the growing season (*see p.239*).

■ **Plant container-grown** vegetables. If necessary, protect the plants from frosts under cloches or fleece (*see p.240*).

■ **Sow seed of vegetables indoors** in containers (*see p.244*), such as:
Chicory and endive (*see p.255*)
French beans (*see p.246*)
Lettuce (*see p.255*)
Runner beans (*see p.247*)
Sprouting broccoli (*see p.248*)
Pumpkins, squashes, marrows, and courgettes (*see p.253*)
Ridge cucumbers (*see p.256*)
Sweetcorn (*see p.253*)
Tomatoes (*see p.257*).

■ **Sow hardy vegetables outdoors** (*see p.242*), under cloches in cold areas, such as:
Beetroot (*see p.251*)
Calabrese (*see p.248*)
Early carrots (*see p.251*)
Hardy lettuce (*see p.255*)
Leeks (*see p.251*)
Parsnips (*see p.251*)
Peas, under netting to keep off birds and mice (*see p.247*)
Red cabbage (*see p.249*)
Salad leaves (*see p.255*)
Spring onions (*see p.250*)
Summer radish (*see p.249*)
Spinach beet and Swiss chard (*see p.255*)
Sprouting broccoli (*see p.248*)
Summer turnips, under cloches (*see p.249*)
Welsh onions (*see p.250*).

■ **Plant out garlic cloves** or plants started earlier in modules (*see p.250*).

■ **Plant rhubarb** (*see p.273*).

### ROUTINE CARE

■ **Feed vegetable beds** (*see p.239*) and fork over and weed the soil in preparation for planting or sowing.

■ **Dig in green manures** that were sown in the previous autumn or in early spring (*see p.239*).

■ **Warm the soil** in cooler regions by placing cloches (*see p.240*) or fleece over it, to prepare it for sowing.

■ **Mulch vegetables and fruit** crops, while the soil is warm and moist (*see p.239*).

■ **Erect supports** (*see p.247*) for peas and climbing beans. Support young peas by sticking peasticks – strong, twiggy stems left over from pruning – into the ground around them (*see p.246*).

■ **Feed bush fruits** (*see pp.268–269*).

■ **Check ties and stakes** (*see p.193*) on fruit trees and remove or loosen them as necessary to avoid them chafing and damaging the bark.

### PRUNING AND TRAINING

■ **Thin out sideshoots** on peach trees (*see p.267*).

■ **Cut back blackberry** and hybrid berry canes after winter planting (*see p.271*).

### HARVESTING

■ **Pick winter and early vegetables,** such as:
Calabrese (*see p.248*)
Leeks (*see p.251*)
Spinach beet (*see p.255*)
Spring cabbages (*see p.249*)
Spring onions (*see p.250*)
Sprouting broccoli (*see p.248*)
Winter lettuce (*see p.255*).

■ **Pick early fruit crops, such as:**
Forced rhubarb (*see p.173*).

# LATE SPRING

| LAWNS | BOUNDARIES AND DIVISIONS | BEDS AND BORDERS |
| --- | --- | --- |

## ESSENTIAL TASKS

■ **Water new lawns** (*see p.84*) regularly in dry weather, so that they establish properly.

## SOWING AND PLANTING

■ **Plant plugs or sprigs** for a new lawn in warm climates (*see p.81*).

■ **Plant out seedlings** for a non-grass lawn (*see p.88*).

## ROUTINE CARE

■ **Begin mowing new grass** once it is 5cm (2in) tall (*see p.79, p.80, and p.82*). Set the mower to maximum height.

■ **Mow established** lawns at appropriate intervals for the lawn type (*see p.82*); set the mowing height to maximum. Trim the edges (*see p.83*).

■ **Apply lawn fertilizer** to grass lawns (*see p.84*) or general fertilizer to non-grass lawns (*see p.88*).

## ESSENTIAL TASKS

■ **Keep an eye out for pests** and diseases such as aphids and blackspot and take steps to stop them taking hold (*see p.111*).

## PLANTING

■ **Plant shrubs or climbers,** including clematis, against walls, fences, or trees (*see pp.110–111*). Train stems into the desired shape, for example a fan (*see p.113*).

■ **Plant hedges** (*see p.120*).

## ROUTINE CARE

■ **Deadhead plants** to prolong flowering.

## PRUNING AND TRAINING

■ **Train climbers** (*see pp.108–109*) and roses (*see p.115*) into supports as they grow. Check old ties.

■ **Thin overgrown Group 1 clematis** (*see p.114*).

■ **Prune hedges,** if they include plants such as box, *Forsythia* x *intermedia*, and Leyland cypress (*see chart, p.117, and p.121*).

■ **Prune recently planted hawthorn** and privet shrubs into shape (*see p.120*).

### BEATING APHIDS

**LADYBIRD LARVA**

■ **Squash aphids** by gently running your fingers up and down affected stems.

■ **Wash them off** with a tight spray from the hose, or a spray with a solution of insecticidal soap.

■ **Only use pesticides** that allow the aphid predators like ladybird larvae to do their work.

## ESSENTIAL TASKS

■ **Finish planting** summer-flowering bulbs (*see p.149*), container-grown and all evergreen shrubs (*see p.150*), and grasses (*see p.140*). Buy healthy plants (*see pp.146–147*) for the best results. Give shrubs an initial prune after planting (*see p.151*) and stake them if necessary (*see p.150*).

■ **Finish mulching** beds and borders, if not done in autumn (*see pp.152–153*), onto moist soil; water it beforehand if necessary.

■ **Water new and established** plants as necessary (*see p.152*).

■ **Stake perennials and biennials** that might flop over when fully grown, before they become too big to stake without spoiling their appearance (*see p.154*).

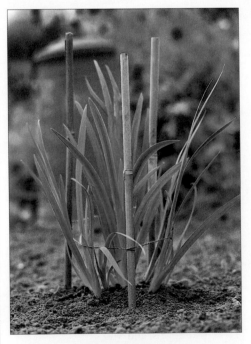

**CANE AND TWINE SUPPORT**

■ **Finish pruning shrubs with cane-like** stems that flower in spring, such as Himalayan honeysuckle (*Leycestera formosa*) and *Kerria japonica* (*see p.159*).

■ **Finish thinning perennials** that form clumps, while they are still small, to guarantee bigger and better flowers later in the season (*see p.154*).

- **Sow seed outdoors** (*see p.149 and p.163*) of hardy, half-hardy, and tender annuals for flowers in mid to late summer.

## PLANTING

- **Plant perennials** (*see p.148*). Buy good, healthy plants (*see p.146*) for the best results.

- **Plant out plug plants** (seedlings with sturdy root balls that are available mail-order or from plant centres) of hardy annuals and biennials, for an early show of flower in the garden.

## ROUTINE CARE

- **Tidy gravel beds**: renew the top-dressing and remove any dead or damaged shoots from the plants (*see p.133*).

- **Deadhead** bulbs, perennials (*see p.155*), alpine plants, and flowering shrubs, such as rhododendrons (*see p.158*), as soon as the flowers fade. Leave the foliage on bulbs to die down naturally.

- **Lift tulips**, once their leaves are yellow and faded, and store in a warm, dry place in a paper (not plastic) bag over summer or discard them.

- **Feed plants in gravel beds**, if they have not grown well in the previous season (*see p.133*).

- **Give an extra feed** to any plants that need a boost, if necessary (*see p.153*).

- **Nip off the shoot tips** ("stopping') of flowering sideshoots of those perennials that produce them, such as dahlias, chrysanthemums, and Michaelmas daisies, to increase the number of flowers (*see p.154*).

## PRUNING AND TRAINING

- **Prune established** deciduous shrubs that flower on the previous year's growth (*see p.158*).

- **Prune evergreen shrubs**, both new (*see p.157*) and established (*see p.158*) plants, once all danger of frost is passed.

PRUNING COTTON LAVENDER (*SANTOLINA*)

## RAISING YOUR OWN PLANTS

- **Plant out seedlings** of tender annuals that were sown earlier in the year

- **Sow seed of biennials** in rows in a spare patch of soil or seedbed (*see p.149*).

- **Take softwood cuttings** from shrubs and perennials; take greenwood cuttings from shrubs (*see p.165 and p.381*).

- **Layer shrubs** (*see p.165*).

## CONTAINERS AND RAISED BEDS

### ESSENTIAL TASKS

- **Water containers** when necessary – check them regularly (*see p.178*), even if it has been wet.

- **Finish repotting** or top-dressing permanently planted climbers; shrubs; and alpines in containers, unless they are spring-flowering ones. Root-prune if needed (*see p.179*).

- **Finish feeding or renewing** compost of any established raised beds and top-dress or mulch (*see p.183*). Replace any exhausted or diseased plants.

- **Pinch-prune** plants such as coleus, fuchsias, and chrysanthemums in containers (*see p.173 and box, p.381*).

- **Finish pruning woody** plants in raised beds once all risk of frost has passed (*see p.196*).

### PLANTING

- **Plant in containers** (*see p.176*) climbers, shrubs, bush or miniature roses, perennials, hardy annuals and biennials, and cacti and succulents.

### ROUTINE CARE

- **Regularly deadhead** and keep plants well-shaped by removing any tired, diseased, or straggly foliage (*see p.178*).

- **Weed raised beds** regularly.

- **Lift and divide** perennials in raised beds, keeping new healthy growth and discarding old, tired parts (*see p.155*).

- **Discard or plant out** bulbs that have been grown in containers.

### PRUNING AND TRAINING

- **Clip established** topiary and standards regularly (*see p.178*).

# LATE SPRING

## ORNAMENTAL TREES

### ESSENTIAL TASKS
■ **Water if needed,** especially trees planted in the last 2–3 years. A couple of canfuls of water every so often is better than frequent but light sprays (*see p.197*).

### PLANTING
■ **Plant** container-grown, hardy evergreen bare-root, or evergreen root-balled trees.

### ROUTINE CARE
■ **In cold or cool climates,** move tender trees, such as citruses, in containers (*see p.195*) from their winter shelters into the open garden for the summer.

■ **Mulch** around trees with organic material such as bark chippings (*see p.197*).

FLOWERING CHERRY *PRUNUS* 'KANZAN'

■ **Check tree ties** and stakes (*see p.193*) and remove or loosen them as necessary to avoid chafing and damaging the bark.

■ **Check tree guards** (*see p.195*) are still in place.

■ **Watch out for suckers** and water shoots growing from tree trunks or roots and remove them before they get too big and spoil the tree (*see p.197*).

## WATER GARDENING

### ESSENTIAL TASKS
■ **Divide overcrowded plants,** including waterlilies, soon after they start into growth, to rejuvenate them (*see p.223*). Mature plants can also be divided to yield several new plants.

DIVIDING JAPANESE RUSH (*ACORUS CALAMUS*)

### PLANTING
■ **Plant** (*see pp.220–221*) all water garden plants.

### ROUTINE CARE
■ **Thin oxygenating plants** to clear out old growth in preparation for the growing season (*see p.223*).

■ **Give the first feed** of the season to water lilies and other container-grown plants (*see p.222*).

■ **Cut back or thin out** (by division, *see p.223*) overcrowded or straggly marginal plants.

■ **Clean out neglected ponds** if necessary. Siphon off most of the water; remove container-grown plants; move floating plants and fish to holding containers. Scoop out the mud; clean the liner and make any necessary repairs; then replant and refill the pond.

## HERBS

### ESSENTIAL TASKS
■ **Finish sowing seed outdoors** (*see p.149 and p.163*) of hardy annual herbs.

■ **Sow seed outdoors** (*see p.149 and p.163*) of half-hardy and tender annual herbs.

### PLANTING
■ **Prepare the soil** (*see p.228 and pp.142–143*) for summer plantings of moisture-loving herbs.

■ **Plant container-grown** perennial or shrubby herbs in beds, in paving, or in pots and hanging baskets (*see pp.228–231*).

■ **Plant** rooted cuttings or small plants in-between paving (*see p.229*).

■ **Plant divided sections** of herbs (*see p.231*) to create a non-grass lawn (*see p.88*).

### ROUTINE CARE
■ **Move tender herbs in containers** from their winter shelters into the garden (*see p.195*) for the summer.

■ **Water herbs** in containers.

### RAISING YOUR OWN PLANTS
■ **Rejuvenate tired shrubby** herbs by mound layering (*see p.231*).

■ **Plant out seedlings** of tender annual herbs that were sown earlier in the year.

■ **Sow seed of biennial herbs,** such as angelica and caraway, in rows in a spare patch of soil or seedbed (*see p.149*).

### HARVESTING
■ **Cut angelica stems** for crystallizing (*see p.232*).

## THE EDIBLE GARDEN

### ESSENTIAL TASKS

- **Water newly planted vegetables** and fruit crops if needed (*see box, p.236*).

- **Protect your carrot crop** against the carrot fly by erecting a barrier around the plot (*see p.241*) before the first generation of flies begins to lay eggs.

- **Plant maincrop seed potatoes** (*see p.252*).

- **Finish planting out garlic** started earlier in modules (*see p.250*).

- **Earth up early potato plants** to stop the tubers going green (*see p.252*).

- **Thin peach fruitlets** under glass to obtain good sized fruits later (*see p.267*).

### SOWING AND PLANTING

- **Sow green manures** to cover empty soil temporarily during the growing season (*see p.239*).

- **Sow seed of vegetables indoors** in containers (*see p.244*), such as:
Autumn and winter kale (*see p.248*)
Ridge cucumbers (*see p.256*)
Sprouting broccoli (*see p.248*).

- **Sow seed of vegetables outdoors** (*see p.242*), such as:
Autumn and winter kale (*see p.248*)
Beetroot (*see p.251*)
Calabrese (*see p.248*)
Chicory and endive (*see p.255*)
French beans (*see p.246*)
Leeks (*see p.251*)
Lettuce (*see p.255*)
Maincrop carrots (*see p.251*)
Peas, under netting to keep off birds and mice (*see p.247*)
Pumpkins, squashes, marrows, and courgettes (*see p.253*)
Red cabbage (*see p.249*)
Runner beans (*see p.247*).
Salad leaves (*see p.255*)
Spring onions (*see p.250*)
Spinach beet and Swiss chard (*see p.255*)
Sprouting broccoli (*see p.248*)
Summer radish (*see p.249*)
Summer turnips, under cloches (*see p.249*)
Winter cabbages for using fresh (*see p.249*)
Welsh onions (*see p.250*).

- **Plant out young plants of:**
Aubergines, chillies, and peppers (*see p.256*)
French beans (*see p.246*)
Rhubarb (*see p.273*).
Runner beans (*see p.247*).
Sweetcorn (*see p.253*)
Tomatoes, under cloches or glass (*see p.257*).

### ROUTINE CARE

- **Feed vegetable beds** (*see p.239*) and fork over and weed the soil in preparation for planting or sowing.

- **Dig in green manures** that were sown in the previous autumn, or earlier in spring (*see p.239*).

- **Mulch vegetables and fruit** crops, while the soil is warm and moist (*see p.239*).

- **Feed bush fruits** (*see pp.268–269*).

- **Remove flowers from strawberry** plants that were planted late (*see p.272*).

### GREENHOUSE SHADING

- **The greenhouse in summer** can get very hot: plants can wilt or be scorched.

- **As soon as the weather** warms up, shade the greenhouse.

- **Greenhouses can be shaded** with a wash, roller blinds, or plastic mesh.

- **A greenhouse wash** is cheap, but must be cleaned off again in late summer, when the light levels fall.

### PRUNING AND TRAINING

- **Cut back pear tree leaders** (*see p.264*).

- **Cut back older acid cherry** trees to encourage new fruiting branches (*see p.267*).

- **Tie in fruit canes** of blackberries and hybrid berries (*see p.271*) and of raspberries (*see p.270*) to supports.

### HARVESTING

- **Pick winter and early vegetables,** such as:
Calabrese (*see p.248*)
Leeks (*see p.251*)
Salad leaves (*see p.255*)
Spinach beet (*see p.255*)
Spring cabbages (*see p.249*)
Spring onions (*see p.250*)
Sprouting broccoli (*see p.248*)
Summer radish (*see p.249*)
Winter lettuce (*see p.255*).

- **Pick early fruit crops, such as:**
Forced rhubarb (*see p.273*).

### STICKY TRAPS

- **What insects do they catch?** Whitefly, thrips, and fungas gnats.

- **How do they work?** The bright colour attracts the insects and they stick to the non-drying glue.

HANGING UP A STICKY TRAP

# EARLY SUMMER

## LAWNS

### ESSENTIAL TASKS

■ **Water new lawns** (*see p.84*) regularly in dry weather, so that they establish properly.

### SOWING AND PLANTING

■ **Plant plugs or sprigs** for a new lawn in warm climates (*see p.81*).

### ROUTINE CARE

■ **Mow lawns** at appropriate intervals for the lawn type (*see p.82*); the mowing height may be reduced. Trim the edges (*see p.83*).

■ **Apply lawn fertilizer**, if not done in late spring (*see p.84*).

■ **Look out for weeds** and keep under control (*see p.87*).

■ **Mow spring-flowering meadows** once the flowers have safely set seed for next year.

## BOUNDARIES AND DIVISIONS

### ESSENTIAL TASKS

■ **Keep an eye out for pests** and diseases such as aphids and blackspot and take steps to stop them taking hold (*see p.111*).

■ **Prune climbers and wall shrubs**, that flower on the previous year's shoots, immediately after flowering (*see pp.112–113*).

■ **Water if needed**, especially recently planted or young plants.

■ **Prune rambler roses** immediately after flowering (*see p.115*).

### ROUTINE CARE

■ **Deadhead** plants, as needed, to prolong flowering, unless you want seeds later.

### PRUNING AND TRAINING

■ **Train climbers** (*see pp.108–109*) and roses (*see p.115*) into supports. Cut out any dead or diseased shoots and check ties.

**TYING IN A CLEMATIS**

■ **Thin overgrown Group 1 clematis**; prune Group 3 clematis (*see p.114*).

■ **Prune hedges,** if they include plants like *Berberis* x *stenophylla* (*see chart, p.117, and p.121*).

## BEDS AND BORDERS

### ESSENTIAL TASKS

■ **Water new and established** plants as necessary (*see p.152*).

■ **Give an extra feed** to any plants that need a boost, if necessary (*see p.153*).

■ **Finish stopping perennials** that produce flowering sideshoots, to increase the number of flowers (*see p.154*).

■ **Finish sowing seed outdoors** (*see p.149 and p.163*) of half-hardy and tender annuals.

■ **Stake perennials and biennials** that might flop over when fully grown, before they become too big to stake without spoiling their appearance (*see p.154*).

### PLANTING

■ **Plant autumn-flowering bulbs** (*see p.149*). Buy good, healthy bulbs (*see p.146*) for the best results.

■ **Plant out plug plants** (available mail-order or from plant centres) of hardy annuals and biennials, for an early show of flower in the garden.

### ROUTINE CARE

■ **Lift tulips**, once their leaves are yellow and faded, and store in a warm, dry place over summer or discard them.

■ **Deadhead** bulbs, perennials (*see p.155*), annuals and biennials, alpine plants, roses, and flowering shrubs, such as rhododendrons (*see p.158*), as soon as the flowers fade. Leave the foliage on bulbs to die down naturally.

### PRUNING AND TRAINING

■ **Prune deciduous shrubs** that flower on the previous year's growth (*see p.158*).

### RAISING YOUR OWN PLANTS

■ **Sow seed of biennials** in rows in a spare patch of soil or seedbed (*see p.149*).

## CONTAINERS AND RAISED BEDS

■ **Collect seed** of early-flowering perennials as they ripen (*see p.155*) and sow (*see p.162*) immediately for the best results.

■ **Divide spring-flowering** perennials (*see p 163*) once the flowers fade.

■ **Take softwood cuttings** from shrubs (*see p.165*), greenwood cuttings from shrubs, and softwood cuttings from perennials.

### CUTTINGS OF PERENNIALS

■ **When do I take cuttings?** As soon as the plant produces suitable shoots.

■ **What are the best shoots?** Look for strong, healthy shoots from this season's growth, with closely spaced leaves, that are still soft and pliable (softwood).

*KEEPING CUTTINGS MOIST*

■ **How do I take a cutting?** Choose the top 8–13cm (3–5in) of a stem, and cut it off just below a leaf joint.

■ **How do I prepare a cutting?** Trim off all but the top 2 or 3 leaves; don't leave any snags or remove the stem tip. Insert the cuttings in pots of compost, and treat in the same way as shrubby cuttings (*see p.165*).

### ESSENTIAL TASKS

■ **Water containers** regularly – check them daily (*see p.178*).

■ **Water** raised beds if necessary (*see p.183*).

■ **Pinch-prune** plants such as coleus, fuchsias, and chrysanthemums in containers (*see p.173 and box, below*).

### PINCH-PRUNING

■ **Why do you do it?** To train shrubby plants into standard plants (with a single stem and round, tree-like canopy) or simple shapes, or to make them bushy.

■ **When do you do it?** From when the plant starts into growth until 2 months before flowers are needed or, if the plant is grown for its foliage, until the end of the growing season.

■ **How do you do it?** Use your forefinger and thumb to nip off soft new shoot tips repeatedly to shape the plant and encourage it to produce dense, bushy growth.

■ **What shapes can you make ?** Try a standard, ball, cone, pillar, fan or poodle – several balls, one above the other

■ **Will the plant flower?** The flowers should all open at the same time, 6–8 weeks after the last pinch-prune.

### PLANTING

■ **Plant in containers** hardy deciduous climbers, bush or miniature roses, perennials, annuals and biennials, summer-flowering alpines, and cacti and succulents.

### ROUTINE CARE

■ **Feed containers** 6–8 weeks after planting (*see p.178*) at regular intervals, if a slow-release fertilizer was not used. Foliar or liquid feeds are most convenient.

■ **Regularly deadhead** and keep plants well-shaped by removing any tired, diseased, or straggly foliage (*see p.178*).

■ **Weed raised beds** regularly.

■ **Lift early spring-flowering** bulbs once the leaves die down to store over summer. Clean off the bulbs; lay on a tray to dry; and store in a paper (not plastic) bag.

### PRUNING AND TRAINING

■ **Clip established** topiary and standards regularly (*see p.178*).

■ **Tie in climbing plants** to supports (canes or trellis) as they grow (*see pp.108–109*). Support tall annuals or perennials in pots before they become top-heavy and floppy; string twined around some canes is ideal. As the plants grow, they will hide the canes.

*SUPPORTING SALPIGLOSSIS*

# EARLY SUMMER

## ORNAMENTAL TREES

### ESSENTIAL TASKS

- **Water if needed,** especially trees planted in the last 2–3 years. A couple of canfuls of water every so often is better than frequent but light sprays (*see p.197*).

GALVANIZED STEEL WATERING CAN

### ROUTINE CARE

- **Watch out for suckers** and water shoots growing from tree trunks or roots and remove them before they get too big and spoil the tree (*see p.197*).

### PRUNING AND TRAINING

- **Prune deciduous trees** that flower in spring if necessary (*see p.196*).

## WATER GARDENING

### ESSENTIAL TASKS

- **Divide overcrowded plants** soon after they start into growth, to rejuvenate them (*see p.223*). Mature plants can also be divided to yield several new plants.

- **Remove blanketweed** at regular intervals (*see p.222*).

- **Thin floaters,** oxygenators, and duckweed at regular intervals (*see p.222*).

### PLANTING

- **Plant** (*see pp.220–221*) all water garden plants.

### ROUTINE CARE

- **Regularly remove** spent flowers and dying foliage to avoid polluting the water (*see p.222*).

---

### KEEPING A POND HEALTHY

- **Remove spent flowers** and dying foliage promptly before they rot and sour the water.

- **Control choking algae,** such as blanketweed, by removing it at regular intervals throughout the summer.

- **If the water level falls** in hot weather, fish and plants can suffer from lack of oxygen. Keep the pond topped up with a slowly trickling hose.

- **If the plants cover** more than half the surface, thin or cut them back to let sunlight penetrate the water below.

- **Remember to clean pumps** – as often as recommended by the manufacturer: a clogged filter may stop the pump working effectively.

- **Don't overfeed fish** – uneaten fishfood will decompose, pollute the water, and encourage algae.

---

## HERBS

### ESSENTIAL TASKS

- **Water and feed** herbs in containers.

- **Finish sowing seed outdoors** (*p.149 and p.163*) of half-hardy and tender annual herbs.

### PLANTING

- **Plant container-grown** herbs in beds, in paving, or in containers (*see pp.228–231*).

- **Plant** rooted cuttings or small plants in-between paving (*see p.229*).

### ROUTINE CARE

- **Pick and deadhead** plants regularly.

- **Mulch moisture-loving** herbs with bulky organic matter, after rain or a thorough watering.

### RAISING YOUR OWN PLANTS

- **Sow successive** batches of regularly used herbs such as basil and parsley (*see p.243*) outdoors every 2–4 weeks.

- **Sow seed of biennials** in rows in a spare patch of soil or seedbed (*see p.149*).

### HARVESTING

- **Pick sprigs and flowers** as they mature for drying, freezing, or infusing (*see p.233*).

MINT

- **Cut angelica stems** for crystallizing (*see p.232*).

## THE EDIBLE GARDEN

### ESSENTIAL TASKS

- **Water crops** as needed outdoors and water any in growbags, containers, or in greenhouses regularly, so they grow strongly and consistently (*see box, p.236*).

- **Damp down the greenhouse floor** and increase ventilation in hot weather to help prevent the crops overheating and deter red spider mite (*see p.296*).

- **Finish mulching around crops** – water the soil well beforehand (*see p.236*).

MULCHING WITH WELL-ROTTED MANURE

- **Regularly feed vegetables** in containers and growbags, and of greenhouse crops, including tomatoes (*see p.257*), according to their needs.

- **Earth up potato plants** to stop the tubers going green (*see p.252*).

- **Thin fruits on apple and plum trees** (*see p.265*) and on peach trees (*see p.267*).

- **Summer-prune grape vines** (*see p.273*) regularly, to avoid tangled shoots. Tie in to supports.

### SOWING AND PLANTING

- **Sow green manures** to cover empty soil temporarily during the growing season (*see p.239*).

- **Sow summer vegetables outdoors** (*see p.142*) in successive batches for a prolonged harvest, as well as seed of winter vegetables, such as:

Beetroot (*see p.251*)
Calabrese (*see p.248*)
Chicory and endive (*see p.255*)
French beans (*see p.246*)
Lettuce, in cool of evening (*see p.255*)
Maincrop carrots (*see p.251*)
Runner beans (*see p.247*)
Peas, under netting to keep off birds and mice (*see p.247*)
Pumpkins, squashes, marrows, and courgettes (*see p.253*)
Salad leaves (*see p.255*)
Spring onions (*see p.250*)
Summer radish (*see p.249*)
Welsh onions (*see p.250*).

- **Plant out** winter brassicas, container-grown vegetables, and tender vegetables.

- **Plant out young plants of:**
Aubergines, chillies, and peppers (*see p.256*)
Kale (*see p.248*)
Leeks (*see p.251*)
Lettuce (*see p.255*)
Ridge cucumbers (*see p.256*)
Sprouting broccoli (*see p.248*)
Sweetcorn (*see p.253*)
Tomatoes (*see p.257*).

### ROUTINE CARE

- **Mulch vegetables and fruit** crops, once the soil is warm and moist (*see p.239*).

- **Water the compost heap** in dry weather to keep it moist and rotting down.

- **Dig in green manures** that were sown earlier, before they flower (*see p.239*).

- **Give a boost to vegetables** with a high-nitrogen fertilizer if needed (*see p.239*).

- **Pinch out tomato sideshoots** (*see p.252*) to keep cordon plants growing tall and upright and make it easier to pick off the fruits. Tie the stems into canes.

- **Pinch off flowers** of first-year summer-fruiting raspberries, to give the plant time and energy to establish (*see p.270*).

- **Net strawberries** to protect the ripening fruits from pests (*see p.272*). Remove surplus runners from plants. Place straw beneath fruits to keep them clean.

### PRUNING AND TRAINING

- **Summer-prune** formally trained stone-fruit trees (*see p.263*).

- **Prune newly planted pear** trees (*see p.264*).

- **Prune established plum** and sweet cherry trees (*see p.266*) in warm, dry weather.

- **Tie in raspberry canes** to supports and cut back weaker canes (*see p.270*).

- **Tie in fruit canes** of blackberries and hybrid berries to supports (*see p.271*).

### RAISING YOUR OWN PLANTS

- **Root strawberry runners** of selected plants (*see p.272*).

### HARVESTING

- **Pick vegetables, such as:**
Beetroot (*see p.251*)
Early carrots (*see p.251*)
Early potatoes (*see p.252*)
Lettuce (*see p.255*)
Peas (*see p.247*)
Salad leaves (*see p.255*)
Spinach beet and Swiss chard (*see p.255*)
Spring onions (*see p.250*)
Summer kale (*see p.248*)
Summer radish (*see p.249*)
Summer turnips (*see p.249*).

- **Pick early fruit crops, such as:**
Gooseberries from thinning, for cooking (*see p.268*)
Rhubarb (*see p.273*)
Strawberries (*see p.272*).

# MIDSUMMER

| LAWNS | BOUNDARIES AND DIVISIONS | BEDS AND BORDERS |

## ESSENTIAL TASKS

■ **Water new lawns** (*see p.84*) regularly in dry weather, so that they establish properly.

## SOWING AND PLANTING

■ **Plant bulbs in grass** to flower the next autumn (*see p.89*) as soon as the bulbs are available – bulbs planted when fresh are most likely to thrive.

## ROUTINE CARE

■ **Mow lawns** at appropriate intervals for the lawn type (*see p.82*); the mowing height may be reduced. Trim the edges (*see p.83*).

■ **After spring-flowering** bulbs (*see p.82*) have died down, make the first mowing of long grass.

■ **Look out for weeds** and keep under control (*see p.87*).

**DIGGING OUT PERENNIAL WEEDS**

## ESSENTIAL TASKS

■ **Water if needed,** especially recently planted or young plants.

■ **Keep an eye out for pests** and diseases such as aphids and blackspot and take steps to stop them taking hold (*see p.111*).

■ **Prune established** climbers and wall shrubs, that flower on the previous year's shoots, immediately after flowering (*see pp.112–113*).

■ **Prune established wall shrubs** that readily bleed sap, eg *Prunus* (*see p.112*), and prune flowering quinces (*see p.113*).

■ **Prune rambler roses** immediately after flowering (*see p.115*).

## ROUTINE CARE

■ **Deadhead** plants, as necessary, to prolong flowering, unless you want seeds later.

■ **Feed ramblers and climbing** roses; specialized rose fertilizer is easiest.

## PRUNING AND TRAINING

■ **Train climbers** (*see pp.108–109*) and roses (*see p.115*) into supports as they grow. Cut out any dead or diseased shoots and check ties.

■ **Prune formal hedges,** if they include plants such as *Berberis thunbergii*, hornbeam, and yew (*see chart, p.117, and p.121*).

## ESSENTIAL TASKS

■ **Water new and established** plants as necessary (*see p.152*).

■ **Finish lifting tulips,** once their leaves are yellow and faded, and store in a warm, dry place over summer or discard them.

■ **Finish planting** autumn-flowering bulbs (*see p.149*). Buy good, healthy bulbs (*see p.146*) for the best results.

■ **Feed and mulch** roses. A specialized rose fertilizer is best.

**CLUSTER-FLOWERED BUSH ROSE, *ROSA* 'PLAYBOY'**

■ **Finish taking greenwood cuttings** from shrubs (*see p.165*).

## ROUTINE CARE

■ **Deadhead** bulbs, perennials (*see p.155*), annuals and biennials, alpine plants, roses, and flowering shrubs as soon as the flowers fade. Let bulb foliage die down naturally.

## PRUNING AND TRAINING

■ **Prune established deciduous** shrubs that flower on the previous year's growth (*see p.158*).

## RAISING YOUR OWN PLANTS

■ **Sow seed of biennials** in rows in a spare patch of soil or seedbed (*see p.149*).

■ **Collect the seed** of early-flowering perennials (*see p.155*), and of annuals and

## CONTAINERS AND RAISED BEDS

biennials, as they ripen. Sow seed of the perennials immediately (*see p.162*) and store that of annuals and biennials for an autumn or spring sowing (*see pp.162–163*).

■ **Divide perennials that** flower in early summer (*see p.163*), once the flowers fade.

■ **Take semi-ripe cuttings** from shrubs (*see p.164*).

■ **Take softwood cuttings** from perennials (*see p.165 and p.381*).

### WATERING TIPS

■ **Watering is best done** in early morning and evening to minimize wasteful evaporation.

■ **Try to water thoroughly** or not at all – water one part of the garden thoroughly rather than giving the whole garden a brief soaking which may cause roots to grow up to the surface and be scorched.

■ **If plants need watering** during the day, avoid wetting the leaves, because they may scorch under hot midday sun. Water onto the soil or compost instead.

■ **Apply a thick mulch** to keep soil moist, but make sure that the soil is thoroughly moist first.

■ **If there is a water shortage,** concentrate on watering newly planted plants and containers.

### ESSENTIAL TASKS

■ **Water containers** regularly – check them daily (*see p.178*).

■ **Water raised beds** if necessary (*see p.183*).

■ **Pinch-prune** plants such as coleus in containers (*see p.173 and box, p.381*).

### PLANTING

■ **Plant in containers** (*see p.176*) hardy deciduous climbers, perennials, annuals and biennials, autumn-flowering bulbs, and alpines.

### ROUTINE CARE

■ **Regularly deadhead** and keep plants well-shaped by removing any tired, diseased, or straggly foliage (*see p.178*).

■ **Weed raised beds** regularly.

■ **Feed containers** from 6–8 weeks after planting (*see p.178*) at regular intervals, if a slow-release fertilizer was not used. Foliar and liquid feeds are most convenient.

■ **Lift spring-flowering** bulbs once the foliage has died down and store over summer. Clean off the bulbs; lay on a tray to dry; and store in a paper (not plastic) bag.

### PRUNING AND TRAINING

■ **Clip established** topiary and standards regularly (*see p.178*).

■ **Tie in climbing plants** to supports (canes or trellis) as they grow (*see pp.108–109*)

### RESCUING A DRIED-OUT CONTAINER

■ **Soak the container** in a large bowl of water to rewet the compost.

■ **Once the surface** of the compost is moist, take out the container and place in a shady spot until the plants recover.

■ **Nip off any withered** flowers or leaves before putting the container back in position.

RE-SOAKING A DRIED-OUT BASKET

# MIDSUMMER

| ORNAMENTAL TREES | WATER GARDENING | HERBS |
|---|---|---|

## ESSENTIAL TASKS

- **Prune flowering cherries**, peaches, plums, and apricots (*Prunus*), if necessary (*see p.196*), to minimize the risk of silver leaf and other diseases.

- **Water if needed**, especially trees planted in the last 2–3 years. A couple of canfuls of water every so often is better than frequent but light sprays (*see p.197*).

## ROUTINE CARE

- **Watch out for suckers** and water shoots growing from tree trunks or roots and remove them before they get too big and spoil the tree (*see p.197*).

## HARVESTING

- **Gather any edible nuts** and fruits when ripe (*see p.197*).

## ESSENTIAL TASKS

- **Regularly remove** spent flowers and dying foliage to avoid polluting the water (*see p.222*).

- **Remove blanketweed** at regular intervals (*see p.222*).

- **Thin floaters**, oxygenators, and duckweed at regular intervals (*see p.222*).

## PLANTING

- **Plant** (*see pp.220–221*) oxygenating, marginal, and bog plants, and deep-water plants.

## ROUTINE CARE

- **Feed water lilies** and other plants in containers (*see p.222*).

## ESSENTIAL TASKS

- **Water and feed** herbs in containers.

**HERBS IN A TIERED CONTAINERS**

- **Collect seed** from annual and biennials as soon as it is ripe. Clean the seed and store in paper packets in a cool, dry, dark place.

- **Finish sowing** seed of biennial herbs, such as angelica and caraway, in rows in a spare patch of soil or seedbed (*see p.149*).

## ROUTINE CARE

- **Pick and deadhead** plants regularly.

## RAISING YOUR OWN PLANTS

- **Take cuttings** from perennial and biennial herbs (*see box, p.381*).

- **Sow successive batches** of regularly used herbs such as basil and parsley (*see p.243*) outdoors every 2–4 weeks.

## HARVESTING

- **Pick sprigs and flowers** as they mature for drying, freezing, or infusing (*see p.233*).

## THE EDIBLE GARDEN

### ESSENTIAL TASKS

■ **Water crops** as needed outdoors and water any in growbags, containers, or in greenhouses regularly, so they grow strongly and consistently (*see box, p.236*).

■ **Damp down the greenhouse floor** and increase ventilation in hot weather to help prevent the crops overheating and deter red spider mite (*see p.296*).

■ **Regularly feed vegetables** in containers and growbags, and of greenhouse crops, including tomatoes (*see p.257*), according to their needs.

■ **Shade young salad plants** (*see p.255*) in hot weather.

■ **Thin pear and apple fruits** (*see p.261*).

■ **Summer-prune grape vines** (*see p.273*), to avoid tangled shoots. Tie into supports.

### SOWING AND PLANTING

■ **Sow green manures** to cover empty soil temporarily in the growing season (*see p.239*).

■ **Sow summer vegetables outdoors** (*see p.142*) in successive batches for a prolonged harvest, and winter vegetables, such as:
Beetroot (*see p.251*)
Carrots (*see p.251*)
Chicory and endive (*see p.255*)
Lettuce, in cool of evening (*see p.255*)
Peas, under netting to keep off birds and mice (*see p.247*)
Salad leaves (*see p.255*)
Spring onions (*see p.250*)
Sweet corn (*see p.253*)
Spinach beet (*see p.255*)
Summer radish (*see p.249*)
Welsh onions (*see p.250*)
Winter turnips (*see p.249*).

■ **Plant out** winter brassicas, container-grown vegetables, and tender vegetables.

■ **Plant out young plants of:**
Autumn and winter kale (*see p.248*)
Leeks (*see p.251*)
Lettuce (*see p.255*)
Sprouting broccoli (*see p.248*)
Winter cabbages for storing (*see p.249*).

### ROUTINE CARE

■ **Water the compost heap** in dry weather to keep it moist and rotting down.

■ **Dig in green manures** that were sown earlier, before they flower (*see p.239*).

■ **Give a boost to vegetables** with a high-nitrogen fertilizer, if needed (*see p.239*).

■ **Wrap ripening peaches** loosely in muslin to keep off birds (*see p.267*).

■ **Remove surplus runners** from strawberry plants (*see p.272*). Place straw beneath fruits to keep them clean. Tidy up plants that have finished fruiting.

■ **Gather up and burn** rotten fruit that has fallen from fruit trees and bushes, to stop diseases spreading.

### PRUNING AND TRAINING

■ **Summer-prune** formally trained stone-fruit trees (*see p.263*).

PRUNING A
PLUM TREE
(*PRUNUS*)

■ **Cut out original raspberry canes** of new plants (*see p.270*).

■ **Tie in fruit canes** of blackberries and hybrid berries to supports (*see p.271*).

■ **Prune pyramid pear trees** (*see p.264*).

■ **Pinch out tomato sideshoots** (*see p.252*) to keep cordon plants growing tall and upright and make it easier to pick off the fruits. Tie the stems into canes.

### RAISING YOUR OWN PLANTS

■ **Root strawberry runners** on selected plants (*see p.272*).

### HARVESTING

■ **Pick vegetables, such as:**
Beetroot (*see p.251*)
Calabrese (*see p.248*)
Chicory and endive (*see p.255*)
Early carrots (*see p.251*)
Early potatoes (*see p.252*)
French beans (*see p.246*)
Garlic (*see p.250*)
Indoor tomatoes (*see p.257*)
Leeks (*see p.251*)
Lettuce (*see p.255*)
Peas (*see p.247*)
Pumpkins, squashes, marrows, and courgettes (*see p.253*)
Runner beans (*see p.247*)
Salad leaves (*see p.255*)
Shallots (*see p.250*)
Spinach beet and Swiss chard (*see p.255*)
Spring onions (*see p.250*)
Summer cabbages (*see p.249*)
Summer kale (*see p.248*)
Summer radish (*see p.249*)
Summer turnips (*see p.249*)
Sweetcorn (*see p.253*).

■ **Pick fruit crops, such as:**
Blackcurrants (*see p.269*)
Blueberries (*see p.269*)
Dessert gooseberries (*see p.268*)
Sweet cherries (*see p.267*)
Peaches (*see p.267*)
Redcurrants (*see p.268*)
Rhubarb (*see p.273*)
Summer-fruiting raspberries (*see p.270*)
Strawberries (*see p.272*).

# LATE SUMMER

| LAWNS | BOUNDARIES AND DIVISIONS | BEDS AND BORDERS |
|---|---|---|

## ESSENTIAL TASKS

■ **Water new lawns** (*see p.84*) regularly in dry weather, so that they establish properly.

■ **Finish planting bulbs** in grass to flower the next autumn (*see p.89*) as soon as the bulbs are available.

## SOWING AND PLANTING

■ **Prepare the soil and site** (*see p.78*) for autumn sowings of grass seed or laying of turf.

■ **Prepare the soil and site** (*see p.78*) for autumn planting of a non-grass lawn.

## ROUTINE CARE

■ **Mow lawns** at appropriate intervals for the lawn type (*see p.82*); the mowing height may be reduced. Trim the edges (*see p.83*).

■ **Apply autumn fertilizer** formulated for lawns (*see p.84*).

■ **Look out for weeds** and keep under control (*see p.87*).

■ **Trim non-grass lawns** to remove dead or straggly growth (*see p.88*), if not done in early spring.

## ESSENTIAL TASKS

■ **Water if needed,** especially recently planted or young plants.

■ **Keep an eye out for pests** and diseases such as aphids and blackspot and take steps to stop them taking hold (*see p.111*).

■ **Prune established** climbers and wall shrubs, that flower on the previous year's growth, immediately after flowering (*see pp.112–113*).

■ **Prune rambler roses** immediately after flowering (*see p.115*).

## ROUTINE CARE

■ **Deadhead** plants, as needed, to prolong flowering, unless you want seeds later.

*CLEMATIS 'ROUGE CARDINAL'*

## PRUNING AND TRAINING

■ **Train climbers** (*see pp.108–109*) and roses (*see p.115*) into supports as they grow. Cut out any dead or diseased shoots and check ties are not too tight.

■ **Summer-prune** established wisterias (*see p.111*).

■ **Prune formal hedges,** if they include plants such as beech, hornbeam, and holly (*see chart, p.117, and p.121*).

■ **Prune hawthorn and privet** shrubs that were planted last winter into a good shape (*see p.120*).

## ESSENTIAL TASKS

■ **Water new and established** plants as necessary (*see p.152*).

## PLANTING

■ **Plant** spring-flowering bulbs (*see p.149*), including tulips (*see p.137*). Buy good, healthy bulbs (*see p.146*) for best results.

■ **Prepare the soil** in beds or borders – except on light, sandy soil – to improve their condition and ready them for planting up (*see pp.142–143*) or improve a patch of soil (*see p.150*).

## ROUTINE CARE

■ **Deadhead** bulbs, perennials (*see p.155*), annuals and biennials, alpine plants, roses, and flowering shrubs as soon as the flowers fade. Leave the foliage on bulbs to die down naturally.

## PRUNING AND TRAINING

■ **Prune established deciduous** shrubs that flower on the previous year's growth (*see p.158*).

■ **Prune most old garden roses** once they have flowered (*see p.161*).

## RAISING YOUR OWN PLANTS

■ **Collect seed** of summer-flowering perennials (*see p.155*), and annuals and biennials, as they ripen. Store them for an autumn or spring sowing (*see pp.162–163*).

■ **Take semi-ripe cuttings** from shrubs (*see p.164*).

■ **Take softwood cuttings** from perennials (*see p.165 and p.381*).

## CONTAINERS AND RAISED BEDS | ORNAMENTAL TREES

### LILIES FROM BULBILS

■ **What are bulbils?** Some lilies, such as *Lilium bulbiferum, L. leichtlinii, L. sargentiae, L. chalcedonicum,* and *L. × testacum,* form what look like small dark berries at the bases of their leaves. They provide an easy, if somewhat slow, way of growing new lilies.

■ **How do I collect them?** If the bulbils are ripe, they should come away easily.

■ **How do I grow them?** Treat them like large perennial seeds and sow them in pots (*see p.162*) or trays.

■ **When do I plant them out?** Plant out the entire pot of "seedlings" in the following autumn.

COLLECTING LILY BULBILS

CACTI AND SUCCULENTS IN METAL CONTAINERS

### ESSENTIAL TASKS

■ **Water containers** regularly – check them daily (*see p.178*).

■ **Liven up summer containers** by replacing a few spent plants with late-flowerers such as asters, Japanese anemones, and pansies.

■ **Water raised beds** if necessary (*see p.183*)

■ **Pinch-prune** plants such as coleus in containers (*see p.173 and box, p.381*).

### PLANTING

■ **Plant in containers** (*see p.176*) hardy deciduous climbers and autumn-flowering alpines.

### ROUTINE CARE

■ **Feed containers** from 6–8 weeks after planting (*see p.178*) at regular intervals, if a slow-release fertilizer was not used. Foliar and liquid feeds are most convenient.

■ **Regularly deadhead** and keep plants well-shaped by removing any tired, diseased, or straggly foliage (*see p.178*).

■ **Weed raised beds** regularly.

### PRUNING AND TRAINING

■ **Give a last trim to** established topiary and standards (*see p.178*).

■ **Tie in climbing plants** to supports (cane or trellis) as they grow (*see pp.108–109*).

### ESSENTIAL TASKS

■ **Water if needed,** especially trees planted in the last 2–3 years. A couple of canfuls every so often is better than frequent but light sprays (*see p.197*).

### ROUTINE CARE

■ **Watch out for suckers** and water shoots growing from tree trunks or roots and remove them before they get too big and spoil the tree (*see p.197*).

### PRUNING AND TRAINING

■ **Prune evergreen trees** if necessary (*see p.196*). Don't cut back conifer shoots too far; most will not regenerate from old wood.

### HARVESTING

■ **Gather any edible nuts** and fruits when ripe (*see p.197*).

# LATE SUMMER

| WATER GARDENING | HERBS |
|---|---|

## ESSENTIAL TASKS

■ **Finish planting** (*see pp.220–221*) deep-water plants.

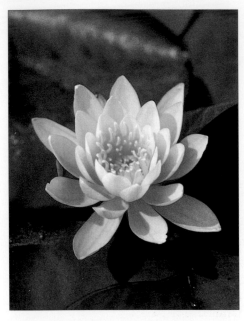

WATERLILY (*NYMPHAEA* 'FIRECREST')

## ROUTINE CARE

■ **Remove the last of** the spent flowers, dying foliage, blanketweed, floaters, and duckweed, to avoid polluting the water (*see p.222*).

■ **Thin oxygenating plants** at regular intervals (*see p.222*).

## ESSENTIAL TASKS

■ **Water and feed** herbs in containers.

■ **Collect seed** from annual and biennial herbs as soon as it is ripe. Clean the seed and store in paper packets in a cool, dry, dark place.

■ **Finish taking cuttings** from perennial and biennial herbs (*see box, p.381*).

## PLANTING

■ **Take rooted shoots** from mound-layered herbs (*see p.231*) and repot or replant them or plant in crevices in paving (*see p.229*).

## ROUTINE CARE

■ **Pick and deadhead** plants regularly.

## HARVESTING

■ **Pick sprigs and flowers** as they mature for drying, freezing, or infusing (*see p.233*).

### KEEPING HERBS IN TRIM

■ **Pick leaves or sprigs** regularly throughout the growing season of all herbs to keep the plants neat and vigorous.

■ **Deadhead any herbs** grown for their foliage to encourage plenty of strong, new shoots.

■ **Removing flowerheads** of shrubby herbs as soon as they fade prevents the plants wasting energy on seed production.

■ **Watch out for** plain green shoots on variegated herbs; if they are not removed, the entire plant will revert to plain green.

■ **Second-year biennial** herbs will last longer if regularly picked and deadheaded.

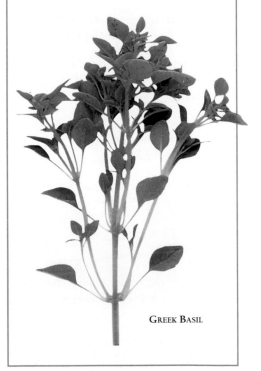

GREEK BASIL

## THE EDIBLE GARDEN

### ESSENTIAL TASKS

- **Water crops** as needed outdoors and water any in growbags, containers, or in greenhouses regularly, to keep them growing strongly and consistently (*see box, p.236*).

- **Damp down the greenhouse floor** and increase ventilation in hot weather to help prevent the crops overheating and to deter red spider mite (*see p.296*).

- **Remove shading wash** from the greenhouse, if you have used one. Don't leave it on into autumn because the light levels will be too low for healthy growth.

- **Regularly feed vegetables** in containers and growbags, and of greenhouse crops, including tomatoes (*see p.257*), according to their needs.

- **Shade young salad plants** (*see p.255*) growing outdoors in hot weather.

- **Finish pruning new pear trees** and established pear pyramids (*see p.264*).

- **Finish summer-pruning** of formally trained stone-fruit trees (*see p.263*); summer-prune formally trained apple trees (*see p.263*).

- **Prune established acid cherry** trees after fruiting (*see p.267*).

- **Finish summer-pruning grape** vines (*see p.273*) regularly, to avoid tangled shoots. Tie into supports.

### SOWING AND PLANTING

- **Sow green manures** to cover empty soil temporarily during the growing season (*see p.239*).

- **Sow summer vegetables outdoors** (*see p.142*) in successive batches for a prolonged harvest, as well as seed of winter vegetables, such as:
Bulb and spring onions (*see p.250*)
Salad leaves (*see p.255*)
Spinach beet (*see p.255*)
Spring cabbage (*see p.249*)

Summer radish (*see p.249*)
Welsh onions (*see p.250*)
Winter turnips (*see p.249*).

- **Plant out** winter brassicas, container-grown and tender vegetables.

- **Plant strawberry plants** (*see p.272*). Apply a fertilizer to sandy or chalky soils before planting.

### ROUTINE CARE

- **Dig in green manures** that were sown earlier, before they flower (*see p.239*).

- **Water the compost heap** in dry weather to keep it moist and rotting down.

LAYERS OF COMPOST IN THE BIN

- **Give a boost to vegetables** with a high nitrogen fertilizer if needed (*see p.239*).

- **Pinch out tops of cordon tomatoes** (*see p.252*) to encourage the last fruits to ripen.

- **Clean up** strawberry plants that have finished fruiting (*see p.272*).

- **Gather up and burn** rotten fruit that has fallen from fruit trees and bushes, to stop diseases spreading.

### PRUNING AND TRAINING

- **Cut back summer-fruiting** raspberry canes, after fruiting, and tie in strongest canes to supports (*see p.270*).

### RAISING YOUR OWN PLANTS

- **Root strawberry runners** of selected plants (*see p.272*).

### HARVESTING

- **Pick vegetables, such as:**
Aubergines, chillies, and peppers (*see p.256*)
Beetroot (*see p.251*)
Bulb onions (*see p.250*)
Calabrese (*see p.248*)
Chicory and endive (*see p.255*)
French beans (*see p.246*)
Garlic (*see p.250*)
Lettuce (*see p.255*)
Maincrop carrots (*see p.251*)
Maincrop potatoes (*see p.252*)
Peas (*see p.247*)
Pumpkins, squashes, marrows, and courgettes (*see p.253*)
Ridge cucumbers (*see p.256*)
Runner beans (*see p.247*)
Salad leaves (*see p.255*)
Shallots (*see p.250*)
Spinach beet and Swiss chard (*see p.255*)
Spring onions (*see p.250*)
Summer radish (*see p.249*)
Sweetcorn (*see p.253*)
Tomatoes (*see p.257*).

- **Pick fruit crops, such as:**
Acid cherries (*see p.267*)
Apples (*see p.265*)
Blackberries and hybrid berries (*see p.271*)
Blueberries (*see p.269*)
Raspberries (*see p.270*)
Peaches (*see p.267*)
Plums (*see p.266*)
Strawberries (*see p.272*).

# EARLY AUTUMN

| LAWNS | BOUNDARIES AND DIVISIONS | BEDS AND BORDERS |

## ESSENTIAL TASKS

■ **Plant rooted shoots** of mounded herbs (*see p.231*) to create a non-grass lawn (*see p.88*).

■ **Plant bulbs in grass** to flower in spring (*see p.89*) as soon as the bulbs are available.

## SOWING AND PLANTING

■ **Lay turf for a new lawn** (*see p.77 and pp.80–81*), if not done in spring, once the weather cools.

■ **Sow seed for a new lawn** (*see p.77 and p.79*), if not done in spring, if the soil is moist.

## ROUTINE CARE

■ **Mow lawns** at appropriate intervals for the lawn type (*see p.82*); set the mowing height to maximum. Trim the edges (*see p.83*).

■ **Scarify, aerate, and top-dress** grass lawns to keep them in condition (*see p.85*).

■ **Apply autumn fertilizer** formulated for lawns, if not done in late summer (*see p.84*).

## PLANTING

■ **Plant shrubs or climbers** against walls, fences, or trees (*see p.110*), including clematis (*see p.111*). Train stems into the desired shape, for example a fan (*see p.111 and p.113*).

■ **Plant hedges** with container-grown trees and shrubs (*see p.120*).

## ROUTINE CARE

■ **Deadhead** plants to prolong flowering.

## PRUNING AND TRAINING

■ **Check supports for climbers,** wall shrubs, and roses and renew them if necessary; finish tying in any stray shoots; check old ties (*see pp.108–109*).

■ **Prune climbing roses** once flowering is finished (*see p.115*).

■ **Prune evergreen hedges,** such as Lawson cypress, *Lonicera nitida*, and *Thuja plicata* (*see chart, p.117, and p.121*).

### CHECKING PLANT TIES

■ **Why must ties be checked?** As the stem grows and thickens, old ties bite into the bark and cause wounds which may girdle and kill the stem, allow disease to enter, or weaken the stem so that it snaps in the wind. Check ties when pruning, and at least twice a year.

**STEM DAMAGED BY OVER-TIGHT TIE**

## ESSENTIAL TASKS

■ **Water new and established** plants as necessary (*see p.152*).

■ **Divide peonies** (*see p.135*) before the soil gets too cold. Use a knife to cut the fleshy roots into sections, each with 2 or 3 buds. Try to avoid bruising the soft roots. Dust the cuts with fungicide, and replant the pieces with the buds just below the surface.

■ **Finish taking semi-ripe cuttings** from shrubs (*see p.164*).

■ **Finish taking softwood cuttings** from perennials (*see p.165 and p.381*).

## PLANTING

■ **Plant spring-flowering bulbs** (*see p.149*), including tulips, daffodils, and lilies (*see p.137*). Buy healthy bulbs (*see p.146*) for good results.

■ **Prepare the soil** in borders – except on light, sandy soils – to condition them and ready them for planting (*see pp.142–143*) or improve a patch of soil (*see p.150*).

■ **Plant perennials** (*see p.148*) and root-balled and container-grown shrubs (*see p.150*). Buy good healthy plants (*see p.146*) for best results. Give shrubs an initial prune after planting (*see p.151*) and stake if needed (*see p.150*).

## ROUTINE CARE

■ **Deadhead** late-flowering plants, particularly perennials (*see p.155*) and annuals and biennials.

■ **Mulch beds and borders,** if not done in spring (*see pp.152–153*). Make sure that the soil is moist; water it beforehand if needed.

■ **Cut down** perennials to clear away dying, untidy growth, except in cold regions (*see p.155*). Clear away dead and dying annuals and biennials.

■ **Lift begonia, dahlia, and gladioli** rootstocks to store over winter (*see p.397*).

## CONTAINERS AND RAISED BEDS

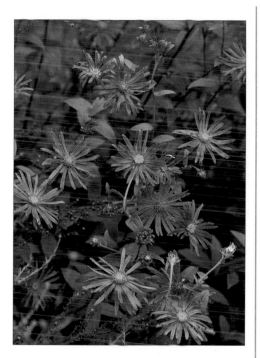

ASTER

### PRUNING AND TRAINING

- **Cut back** tall rose bushes to prevent winter winds rocking the bush and working loose the roots (*see p.160*).

### RAISING YOUR OWN PLANTS

- **Transplant biennial seedlings** to their final flowering position (*see p.149*).

- **Collect seed** of summer-flowering perennials (*see p.155*), and annuals and biennials, as they ripen. Store them for autumn or spring sowing (*see pp.162–163*).

- **Sow seed outdoors** (*see p.149 and p.163*) of hardy annuals, for an early show of flower next year. In cold regions, protect seedlings over winter with cloches or fleece.

- **Divide perennials** (*see p.163*), except in regions with cold winters.

- **Plant out rooted shrub cuttings** taken the previous year from shrubs (*see p.164*), whether hardwood or semi-ripe, or grow them on in pots.

### ESSENTIAL TASKS

- **Water containers** as necessary – check them regularly (*see p.178*).

- **Give final feeds** to plants in containers before the end of the growing season (*see p.178*), if slow-release fertilizer was not used.

- **Pinch-prune** plants such as coleus in containers (*see p.173 and box, p.381*).

### PLANTING

- **Plant in containers** (*see p.176*) hardy climbers, shrubs, and spring-flowering bulbs for next year.

- **Plant containers for winter** with small conifers, evergreen shrubs and climbers, and spring-flowering bulbs. Add winter-flowering pansies for bright colour.

### ROUTINE CARE

- **Regularly deadhead** to prolong the display and keep plants well-shaped by removing any tired, diseased, or straggly foliage (*see p.178*).

- **Repot or top-dress** spring-flowering climbers and alpines in containers; root-prune if necessary (*see p.179*).

- **Give raised beds** a final weeding.

- **Lift and divide perennials** in raised beds, keeping new healthy growth and discarding old, tired parts (*see p.155*), if not done in spring.

### PRUNING AND TRAINING

- **Tie in climbers** to supports such as canes or trellis (*see pp.108–109*).

### RAISING YOUR OWN PLANTS

- **Sow seeds of hardy annuals** in pots, trays, or modules (*see p.162*) to grow on for planting out next spring.

- **Layer shrubs** (*see p.165*).

### STORING SEEDS

- **Make sure the seeds are dry** before storing them; otherwise they may rot and die. If collecting them, choose a sunny day and lay the seeds on a tray in a warm, airy place to dry.

- **Clean the seeds** by sorting them from the chaff – sift the seeds in a sieve.

- **Place the seeds in paper bags** – black photographic film containers are good alternatives. Remember to label them with the plant name and the date.

- **Store the seeds** in a cool, dry, dark place, or the bottom of a refrigerator, for up to a year.

STORING SEEDS IN FILM CONTAINERS

# EARLY AUTUMN

| ORNAMENTAL TREES | WATER GARDENING | HERBS |
| --- | --- | --- |

## PLANTING

- **Prepare the soil** (*see p.192 and pp.142–143*) for mid-autumn plantings of container-grown, hardy bare-root, or, in mild areas, evergreen root-balled trees.

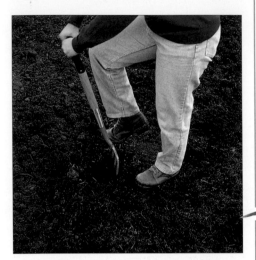

FORKING IN ORGANIC MATTER

## ROUTINE CARE

- **Watch out for suckers** and water shoots growing from tree trunks or roots and remove them before they get too big and spoil the tree (*see p.197*).

- **Gather up fallen fruit,** leaves, and other debris that has fallen from trees and place on the compost heap. Burn any rotten fruit, to stop diseases spreading.

## HARVESTING

- **Gather any edible nuts** and fruits when ripe (*see p.197*).

## ESSENTIAL TASKS

- **Net ponds to catch** falling leaves and gather up the leaves regularly (*see p.222*).

SILVER MAPLE LEAVES
(*ACER SACCHARINUM*)

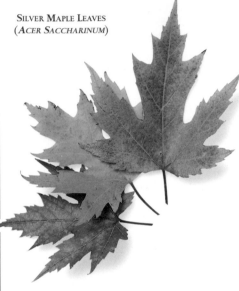

## ROUTINE CARE

- **Rejuvenate marginals** and bog plants by dividing them, if not done in spring (*see p.223*).

- **Thin oxygenating plants,** removing excess growth and debris that might rot over winter (*see p.223*).

## ESSENTIAL TASKS

- **Take rooted shoots** from mound-layered herbs (*see p.231*) and repot or replant them or plant in crevices (*see p.229*).

## ROUTINE CARE

- **Pot up for winter use** herbs such as chives or mint (*see p.231*).

## RAISING YOUR OWN PLANTS

- **Plant out seedlings of biennial** herbs into their final positions (*see p.149*).

- **Sow seeds** (*see p.149 and p.163*) outdoors of hardy annual herbs, for an early spurt of growth the next year. In cold regions, protect the seedlings over winter with cloches or fleece.

- **Divide large shrubby** or clump-forming herbs after flowering (*see p.231*), if not done in early spring.

## THE EDIBLE GARDEN

### ESSENTIAL TASKS

■ **Water crops** as needed outdoors and water any in growbags, containers, or in greenhouses regularly, so they grow strongly and consistently (*see box, p.236*).

■ **Feed tomatoes** regularly to avoid diseased or sparse fruits (*see p.257*).

### SOWING AND PLANTING

■ **Dig over vegetable beds** (*see p.239 and pp.143–143*) to enrich and condition the soil.

■ **Sow green manures** to cover empty soil through winter and dig in ones that were sown earlier, before they flower (*see p.239*).

■ **Plant out garlic cloves** or plants raised in modules in well-drained soil (*see p.255*).

■ **Sow vegetable seed indoors**, such as:
Winter lettuce (*see p.255*)
Salad leaves, such as rocket
Spinach beet (*see p.255*)
Summer radish (*see p.249*).

■ **Sow hardy vegetable seed outdoors**, such as:
Early peas (*see p.247*)
Salad leaves (*see p.255*)
Summer radish (*see p.249*)
Winter lettuce, under cloches (*see p.255*).

■ **Plant bush and cane fruits** and container-grown fruit trees (*see pp.260–261*), except plums.

■ **Plant strawberry** plants (*see p.272*) and rhubarb (*see p.273*).

### ROUTINE CARE

■ **Lay outdoor cordon tomatoes** down on beds of straw or pick them and put on a windowsill, to ripen more quickly (*see p.257*).

■ **Earth up winter cabbages** (*see p.249*) and sprouting broccoli (*see p.248*) and remove any rotting leaves. Stake tall broccoli.

■ **Clean up strawberry plants** that have finished fruiting (*see p.272*).

■ **Mulch rhubarb**, if not done in early spring (*see p.273*).

■ **Gather up and burn** rotten fruit that have fallen from fruit trees and bushes, to stop diseases spreading.

■ **Check ties and stakes** (*see p.193*) on fruit trees and remove or loosen them as needed to avoid them damaging the bark.

### PRUNING AND TRAINING

■ **Cut back blackcurrants** on planting (*see p.261*) to above soil level.

■ **Prune established redcurrants** (*p.268*).

■ **Cut back summer-fruiting** raspberry canes, after fruiting, and tie in strongest new canes to supports (*see p.270*). Do the same with blackberries and hybrid berries (*see p.271*).

### RAISING YOUR OWN PLANTS

■ **Split mature rhubarb** plants into new sets (*see p.273*), once the leaves die down.

### HARVESTING

■ **Pick vegetables, such as:**
Aubergines, chillies, and peppers (*see p.256*)
Autumn kale (*see p.248*)
Beetroot (*see p.251*)
Bulb onions (*see p.250*)
Chicory and endive (*see p.255*)
Calabrese (*see p.248*)
French beans (*see p.246*)
Leeks (*see p.251*)
Lettuce (*see p.255*)
Maincrop carrots (*see p.251*)
Maincrop potatoes (*see p.252*)
Peas (*see p.247*)
Pumpkins, squashes, marrows, and courgettes (*see p.253*)
Ridge cucumbers (*see p.256*)
Runner beans (*see p.247*)
Salad leaves (*see p.255*)
Spinach beet and Swiss chard (*see p.255*)
Spring onions (*see p.257*)
Summer radish (*see p.249*)
Sweetcorn (*see p.253*)
Tomatoes (*see p.257*)
Welsh onions (*see p.250*).

■ **Pick fruit crops, such as:**
Apples (*see p.265*)
Autumn-fruiting raspberries (*see p.270*)
Pears (*see p.264*)
Perpetual-fruiting and alpine strawberries (*see p.272*)
Plums (*see p.266*).

---

### HARVESTING VEGETABLES

■ **Root vegetables:** leave in the ground or layer in boxes of slightly moist sand.

■ **Peas and beans:** Hang uprooted plants, eg haricot varieties of French beans, upside-down to dry, then shell and store the beans in airtight jars.

■ **Pumpkins and squashes:** cure, or ripen, by leaving them in a warm, dry place that is exposed to the sun, such as the greenhouse bench, for a few weeks.

■ **Cabbages and onions:** Hang up in net bags, or place on wooden slats or in boxes, in a cool, dry, frost-free place.

**STORING ONIONS**

# MID-AUTUMN

| LAWNS | BOUNDARIES AND DIVISIONS | BEDS AND BORDERS |
|---|---|---|

## LAWNS

### ESSENTIAL TASKS

- **Plant bulbs** in grass to flower in spring (*see p.89*) as soon as the bulbs are available.

### SOWING AND PLANTING

- **Lay turf for a new lawn** (*see p.77 and pp.80–81*), if not done in spring.

### ROUTINE CARE

- **Mow lawns** at appropriate intervals for the lawn type (*see p.82*); set the mowing height to maximum. Trim the edges (*see p.83*).

- **Clear dead leaves** from the lawn by sweeping or raking them; compost the leaves for leafmould in a wire netting bin or in black plastic bags.

- **Repair damaged patches** in lawns (*see p.86*) and reseed or returf if necessary.

---

### WORM BINS

Here are a few tips for keeping the worms in your bin happy.

- **Brandling worms hate acidity:** don't put in much citrus fruit at one time and add a little dried calcium now and again to keep the mix alkaline.

- **If the compost looks soggy,** add a layer of shredded newspaper.

- **Remember to tap off the liquid** that collects at the bottom of the worm bin regularly – before it drowns the compost and the worms. It makes a good liquid feed when diluted in water.

- **Wrap the worm bin** in some insulating material for the winter (*see p.282*) in cool climates so the worms remain warm and active.

---

## BOUNDARIES AND DIVISIONS

### PLANTING

- **Plant shrubs or climbers** against walls, fences, or trees (*see p.110*). Train stems into the desired shape (*see p.111 and p.113*).

VIRGINIA CREEPER
(*PARTHENOCISSUS TRICUSPIDATA* 'VEITCHII')

- **Plant clematis** against walls, fences, or trees; train stems into shape (*see p.111*).

- **Plant hedges** with container-grown trees and shrubs (*see p.120*).

### PRUNING AND TRAINING

- **Prune climbing roses** once flowering is finished (*see p.115*).

- **Cut back Group 3 clematis** plants that are outgrowing their bounds (*see p.114*).

- **Prune flowering hedges,** such as *Cotoneaster lacteus*, escallonia, and hawthorn (*see chart, p.117, and p.121*).

---

## BEDS AND BORDERS

### PLANTING

- **Plant spring-flowering bulbs** (*see p.149*), including tulips and daffodils (*see p.137*). Buy healthy bulbs (*see p.146*) for good results.

- **Prepare the soil** in beds or borders – except on light, sandy soils – to improve their condition and ready them for planting up (*see pp.142–143*) or improve a patch of soil (*see p.150*).

- **Plant perennials** (*see p.148*) and root-balled and container-grown shrubs, (*see p.150*). Buy good, healthy plants (*see pp.146–147*) for the best results. Give shrubs an initial prune after planting (*see p.151*) and stake if needed (*see p.150*). Water the roots of each plant well before planting – soak the pot in a bucket for about an hour.

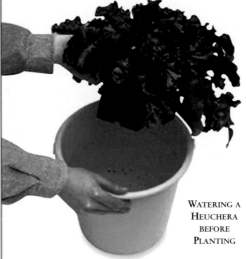

WATERING A HEUCHERA BEFORE PLANTING

### ROUTINE CARE

- **Deadhead** late-flowering plants, particularly perennials (*see p.155*).

- **Mulch** beds and borders, if not done in spring (*see pp.152–153*).

- **Renew top-dressing** or mulch on established gravel beds (*see p.133*).

- **Lift begonia, dahlia, and gladioli** rootstocks to store over winter. Trim back the foliage and clean off excess soil and any dead or dying material; leave on a tray to dry for a few weeks; then pack loosely,

## THE EDIBLE GARDEN

### ESSENTIAL TASKS

■ **Water crops** as needed outdoors and water any in growbags, containers, or in greenhouses regularly, so they grow strongly and consistently (*see box, p.236*).

■ **Feed tomatoes** regularly to avoid diseased or sparse fruits (*see p.257*).

### SOWING AND PLANTING

■ **Dig over vegetable beds** (*see p.239 and pp.143–143*) to enrich and condition the soil.

■ **Sow green manures** to cover empty soil through winter and dig in ones that were sown earlier, before they flower (*see p.239*).

■ **Plant out garlic cloves** or plants raised in modules in well-drained soil (*see p.255*).

■ **Sow vegetable seed indoors**, such as:
Winter lettuce (*see p.255*)
Salad leaves, such as rocket
Spinach beet (*see p.255*)
Summer radish (*see p.249*).

■ **Sow hardy vegetable seed outdoors**, such as:
Early peas (*see p.247*)
Salad leaves (*see p.255*)
Summer radish (*see p.249*)
Winter lettuce, under cloches (*see p.255*).

■ **Plant bush and cane fruits** and container-grown fruit trees (*see pp.260–261*), except plums.

■ **Plant strawberry** plants (*see p.272*) and rhubarb (*see p.273*).

### ROUTINE CARE

■ **Lay outdoor cordon tomatoes** down on beds of straw or pick them and put on a windowsill, to ripen more quickly (*see p.257*).

■ **Earth up winter cabbages** (*see p.249*) and sprouting broccoli (*see p.248*) and remove any rotting leaves. Stake tall broccoli.

■ **Clean up strawberry plants** that have finished fruiting (*see p.272*).

■ **Mulch rhubarb**, if not done in early spring (*see p.273*).

■ **Gather up and burn** rotten fruit that have fallen from fruit trees and bushes, to stop diseases spreading.

■ **Check ties and stakes** (*see p.193*) on fruit trees and remove or loosen them as needed to avoid them damaging the bark.

### PRUNING AND TRAINING

■ **Cut back blackcurrants** on planting (*see p.261*) to above soil level.

■ **Prune established redcurrants** (*p.268*).

■ **Cut back summer-fruiting** raspberry canes, after fruiting, and tie in strongest new canes to supports (*see p.270*). Do the same with blackberries and hybrid berries (*see p.271*).

### RAISING YOUR OWN PLANTS

■ **Split mature rhubarb** plants into new sets (*see p.273*), once the leaves die down.

### HARVESTING

■ **Pick vegetables, such as:**
Aubergines, chillies, and peppers (*see p.256*)
Autumn kale (*see p.248*)
Beetroot (*see p.251*)
Bulb onions (*see p.250*)
Chicory and endive (*see p.255*)
Calabrese (*see p.248*)
French beans (*see p.246*)
Leeks (*see p.251*)
Lettuce (*see p.255*)
Maincrop carrots (*see p.251*)
Maincrop potatoes (*see p.252*)
Peas (*see p.247*)
Pumpkins, squashes, marrows, and courgettes (*see p.253*)
Ridge cucumbers (*see p.256*)
Runner beans (*see p.247*)
Salad leaves (*see p.255*)
Spinach beet and Swiss chard (*see p.255*)
Spring onions (*see p.257*)
Summer radish (*see p.249*)
Sweetcorn (*see p.253*)
Tomatoes (*see p.257*)
Welsh onions (*see p.250*).

■ **Pick fruit crops, such as:**
Apples (*see p.265*)
Autumn-fruiting raspberries (*see p.270*)
Pears (*see p.264*)
Perpetual-fruiting and alpine strawberries (*see p.272*)
Plums (*see p.266*).

---

### HARVESTING VEGETABLES

■ **Root vegetables:** leave in the ground or layer in boxes of slightly moist sand.

■ **Peas and beans:** Hang uprooted plants, eg haricot varieties of French beans, upside-down to dry; then shell and store the beans in airtight jars.

■ **Pumpkins and squashes:** cure, or ripen, by leaving them in a warm, dry place that is exposed to the sun, such as the greenhouse bench, for a few weeks.

■ **Cabbages and onions:** Hang up in net bags, or place on wooden slats or in boxes, in a cool, dry, frost-free place.

STORING ONIONS

# MID-AUTUMN

| LAWNS | BOUNDARIES AND DIVISIONS | BEDS AND BORDERS |

## ESSENTIAL TASKS

- **Plant bulbs** in grass to flower in spring (*see p.89*) as soon as the bulbs are available.

## SOWING AND PLANTING

- **Lay turf for a new lawn** (*see p.77 and pp.80–81*), if not done in spring.

## ROUTINE CARE

- **Mow lawns** at appropriate intervals for the lawn type (*see p.82*); set the mowing height to maximum. Trim the edges (*see p.83*).

- **Clear dead leaves** from the lawn by sweeping or raking them; compost the leaves for leafmould in a wire netting bin or in black plastic bags.

- **Repair damaged patches** in lawns (*see p.86*) and reseed or returf if necessary.

---

### WORM BINS

Here are a few tips for keeping the worms in your bin happy.

- **Brandling worms hate acidity:** don't put in much citrus fruit at one time and add a little dried calcium now and again to keep the mix alkaline.

- **If the compost looks soggy,** add a layer of shredded newspaper.

- **Remember to tap off the liquid** that collects at the bottom of the worm bin regularly – before it drowns the compost and the worms. It makes a good liquid feed when diluted in water.

- **Wrap the worm bin** in some insulating material for the winter (*see p.282*) in cool climates so the worms remain warm and active.

---

## PLANTING

- **Plant shrubs or climbers** against walls, fences, or trees (*see p.110*). Train stems into the desired shape (*see p.111 and p.113*).

VIRGINIA CREEPER
(*PARTHENOCISSUS TRICUSPIDATA* 'VEITCHII')

- **Plant clematis** against walls, fences, or trees; train stems into shape (*see p.111*).

- **Plant hedges** with container-grown trees and shrubs (*see p.120*).

## PRUNING AND TRAINING

- **Prune climbing roses** once flowering is finished (*see p.115*).

- **Cut back Group 3 clematis** plants that are outgrowing their bounds (*see p.114*).

- **Prune flowering hedges,** such as *Cotoneaster lacteus*, escallonia, and hawthorn (*see chart, p.117, and p.121*).

---

## PLANTING

- **Plant spring-flowering bulbs** (*see p.149*), including tulips and daffodils (*see p.137*). Buy healthy bulbs (*see p.146*) for good results.

- **Prepare the soil** in beds or borders – except on light, sandy soils – to improve their condition and ready them for planting up (*see pp.142–143*) or improve a patch of soil (*see p.150*).

- **Plant perennials** (*see p.148*) and root-balled and container-grown shrubs, (*see p.150*). Buy good, healthy plants (*see pp.146–147*) for the best results. Give shrubs an initial prune after planting (*see p.151*) and stake if needed (*see p.150*). Water the roots of each plant well before planting – soak the pot in a bucket for about an hour.

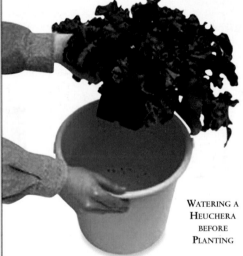

WATERING A
HEUCHERA
BEFORE
PLANTING

## ROUTINE CARE

- **Deadhead** late-flowering plants, particularly perennials (*see p.155*).

- **Mulch** beds and borders, if not done in spring (*see pp.152–153*).

- **Renew top-dressing** or mulch on established gravel beds (*see p.133*).

- **Lift begonia, dahlia, and gladioli** rootstocks to store over winter. Trim back the foliage and clean off excess soil and any dead or dying material; leave on a tray to dry for a few weeks; then pack loosely,

## CONTAINERS AND RAISED BEDS

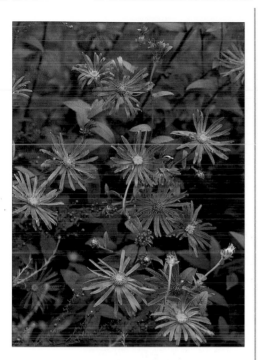

ASTER

### PRUNING AND TRAINING

■ **Cut back** tall rose bushes to prevent winter winds rocking the bush and working loose the roots (*see p.160*).

### RAISING YOUR OWN PLANTS

■ **Transplant biennial seedlings** to their final flowering position (*see p.149*).

■ **Collect seed** of summer-flowering perennials (*see p.155*), and annuals and biennials, as they ripen. Store them for autumn or spring sowing (*see pp.162–163*).

■ **Sow seed outdoors** (*see p.149 and p.163*) of hardy annuals, for an early show of flower next year. In cold regions, protect seedlings over winter with cloches or fleece.

■ **Divide perennials** (*see p.163*), except in regions with cold winters.

■ **Plant out rooted shrub cuttings** taken the previous year from shrubs (*see p.164*), whether hardwood or semi-ripe, or grow them on in pots.

### ESSENTIAL TASKS

■ **Water containers** as necessary – check them regularly (*see p.178*).

■ **Give final feeds** to plants in containers before the end of the growing season (*see p.178*), if slow-release fertilizer was not used.

■ **Pinch-prune** plants such as coleus in containers (*see p.173 and box, p.381*).

### PLANTING

■ **Plant in containers** (*see p.176*) hardy climbers, shrubs, and spring-flowering bulbs for next year.

■ **Plant containers for winter** with small conifers, evergreen shrubs and climbers, and spring-flowering bulbs. Add winter-flowering pansies for bright colour.

### ROUTINE CARE

■ **Regularly deadhead** to prolong the display and keep plants well-shaped by removing any tired, diseased, or straggly foliage (*see p.178*).

■ **Repot or top-dress** spring-flowering climbers and alpines in containers; root-prune if necessary (*see p.179*).

■ **Give raised beds** a final weeding.

■ **Lift and divide perennials** in raised beds, keeping new healthy growth and discarding old, tired parts (*see p.155*), if not done in spring.

### PRUNING AND TRAINING

■ **Tie in climbers** to supports such as canes or trellis (*see pp.108–109*).

### RAISING YOUR OWN PLANTS

■ **Sow seeds of hardy annuals** in pots, trays, or modules (*see p.162*) to grow on for planting out next spring.

■ **Layer shrubs** (*see p.165*).

### STORING SEEDS

■ **Make sure the seeds are dry** before storing them; otherwise they may rot and die. If collecting them, choose a sunny day and lay the seeds on a tray in a warm, airy place to dry.

■ **Clean the seeds** by sorting them from the chaff – sift the seeds in a sieve.

■ **Place the seeds in paper bags** – black photographic film containers are good alternatives. Remember to label them with the plant name and the date.

■ **Store the seeds** in a cool, dry, dark place, or the bottom of a refrigerator, for up to a year.

STORING SEEDS IN FILM CONTAINERS

# EARLY AUTUMN

| ORNAMENTAL TREES | WATER GARDENING | HERBS |
| --- | --- | --- |

## PLANTING

■ **Prepare the soil** (*see p.192 and pp.142–143*) for mid-autumn plantings of container-grown, hardy bare-root, or, in mild areas, evergreen root-balled trees.

FORKING IN ORGANIC MATTER

## ROUTINE CARE

■ **Watch out for suckers** and water shoots growing from tree trunks or roots and remove them before they get too big and spoil the tree (*see p.197*).

■ **Gather up fallen fruit,** leaves, and other debris that has fallen from trees and place on the compost heap. Burn any rotten fruit, to stop diseases spreading.

## HARVESTING

■ **Gather any edible nuts** and fruits when ripe (*see p.197*).

## ESSENTIAL TASKS

■ **Net ponds to catch** falling leaves and gather up the leaves regularly (*see p.222*).

SILVER MAPLE LEAVES
(*ACER SACCHARINUM*)

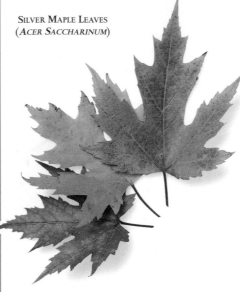

## ROUTINE CARE

■ **Rejuvenate marginals** and bog plants by dividing them, if not done in spring (*see p.223*).

■ **Thin oxygenating plants,** removing excess growth and debris that might rot over winter (*see p.223*).

## ESSENTIAL TASKS

■ **Take rooted shoots** from mound-layered herbs (*see p.231*) and repot or replant them or plant in crevices (*see p.229*).

## ROUTINE CARE

■ **Pot up for winter use** herbs such as chives or mint (*see p.231*).

## RAISING YOUR OWN PLANTS

■ **Plant out seedlings of biennial** herbs into their final positions (*see p.149*).

■ **Sow seeds** (*see p.149 and p.163*) outdoors of hardy annual herbs, for an early spurt of growth the next year. In cold regions, protect the seedlings over winter with cloches or fleece.

■ **Divide large shrubby** or clump-forming herbs after flowering (*see p.231*), if not done in early spring.

## THE EDIBLE GARDEN

### ESSENTIAL TASKS

■ **Water crops** as needed outdoors and water any in growbags, containers, or in greenhouses regularly, so they grow strongly and consistently (*see box, p.236*).

■ **Feed tomatoes** regularly to avoid diseased or sparse fruits (*see p.257*).

### SOWING AND PLANTING

■ **Dig over vegetable beds** (*see p.239 and pp.143–143*) to enrich and condition the soil.

■ **Sow green manures** to cover empty soil through winter and dig in ones that were sown earlier, before they flower (*see p.239*).

■ **Plant out garlic cloves** or plants raised in modules in well-drained soil (*see p.255*).

■ **Sow vegetable seed indoors**, such as:
Winter lettuce (*see p.255*)
Salad leaves, such as rocket
Spinach beet (*see p.255*)
Summer radish (*see p.249*).

■ **Sow hardy vegetable seed outdoors**, such as:
Early peas (*see p.247*)
Salad leaves (*see p.255*)
Summer radish (*see p.249*)
Winter lettuce, under cloches (*see p.255*).

■ **Plant bush and cane fruits** and container-grown fruit trees (*see pp.260–261*), except plums.

■ **Plant strawberry** plants (*see p.272*) and rhubarb (*see p.273*).

### ROUTINE CARE

■ **Lay outdoor cordon tomatoes** down on beds of straw or pick them and put on a windowsill, to ripen more quickly (*see p.257*).

■ **Earth up winter cabbages** (*see p.249*) and sprouting broccoli (*see p.248*) and remove any rotting leaves. Stake tall broccoli.

■ **Clean up strawberry plants** that have finished fruiting (*see p.272*).

■ **Mulch rhubarb,** if not done in early spring (*see p.273*).

■ **Gather up and burn** rotten fruit that have fallen from fruit trees and bushes, to stop diseases spreading.

■ **Check ties and stakes** (*see p.193*) on fruit trees and remove or loosen them as needed to avoid them damaging the bark.

### PRUNING AND TRAINING

■ **Cut back blackcurrants** on planting (*see p.261*) to above soil level.

■ **Prune established redcurrants** (*p.268*).

■ **Cut back summer-fruiting** raspberry canes, after fruiting, and tie in strongest new canes to supports (*see p.270*). Do the same with blackberries and hybrid berries (*see p.271*).

### RAISING YOUR OWN PLANTS

■ **Split mature rhubarb** plants into new sets (*see p.273*), once the leaves die down.

### HARVESTING

■ **Pick vegetables, such as:**
Aubergines, chillies, and peppers (*see p.256*)
Autumn kale (*see p.248*)
Beetroot (*see p.251*)
Bulb onions (*see p.250*)
Chicory and endive (*see p.255*)
Calabrese (*see p.248*)
French beans (*see p.246*)
Leeks (*see p.251*)
Lettuce (*see p.255*)
Maincrop carrots (*see p.251*)
Maincrop potatoes (*see p.252*)
Peas (*see p.247*)
Pumpkins, squashes, marrows, and courgettes (*see p.253*)
Ridge cucumbers (*see p.256*)
Runner beans (*see p.247*)
Salad leaves (*see p.255*)
Spinach beet and Swiss chard (*see p.255*)
Spring onions (*see p.257*)
Summer radish (*see p.249*)
Sweetcorn (*see p.253*)
Tomatoes (*see p.257*)
Welsh onions (*see p.250*).

■ **Pick fruit crops, such as:**
Apples (*see p.265*)
Autumn-fruiting raspberries (*see p.270*)
Pears (*see p.264*)
Perpetual-fruiting and alpine strawberries (*see p.272*)
Plums (*see p.266*).

---

### HARVESTING VEGETABLES

■ **Root vegetables:** leave in the ground or layer in boxes of slightly moist sand.

■ **Peas and beans:** Hang uprooted plants, eg haricot varieties of French beans, upside-down to dry; then shell and store the beans in airtight jars.

■ **Pumpkins and squashes:** cure, or ripen, by leaving them in a warm, dry place that is exposed to the sun, such as the greenhouse bench, for a few weeks.

■ **Cabbages and onions:** Hang up in net bags, or place on wooden slats or in boxes, in a cool, dry, frost-free place.

**STORING ONIONS**

# MID-AUTUMN

| LAWNS | BOUNDARIES AND DIVISIONS | BEDS AND BORDERS |

## ESSENTIAL TASKS

■ **Plant bulbs** in grass to flower in spring (*see p.89*) as soon as the bulbs are available.

## SOWING AND PLANTING

■ **Lay turf for a new lawn** (*see p.77 and pp.80–81*), if not done in spring.

## ROUTINE CARE

■ **Mow lawns** at appropriate intervals for the lawn type (*see p.82*); set the mowing height to maximum. Trim the edges (*see p.83*).

■ **Clear dead leaves** from the lawn by sweeping or raking them; compost the leaves for leafmould in a wire netting bin or in black plastic bags.

■ **Repair damaged patches** in lawns (*see p.86*) and reseed or returf if necessary.

---

## WORM BINS

Here are a few tips for keeping the worms in your bin happy.

■ **Brandling worms hate acidity:** don't put in much citrus fruit at one time and add a little dried calcium now and again to keep the mix alkaline.

■ **If the compost looks soggy,** add a layer of shredded newspaper.

■ **Remember to tap off the liquid** that collects at the bottom of the worm bin regularly – before it drowns the compost and the worms. It makes a good liquid feed when diluted in water.

■ **Wrap the worm bin** in some insulating material for the winter (*see p.282*) in cool climates so the worms remain warm and active.

---

## PLANTING

■ **Plant shrubs or climbers** against walls, fences, or trees (*see p.110*). Train stems into the desired shape (*see p.111 and p.113*).

**VIRGINIA CREEPER**
(*PARTHENOCISSUS TRICUSPIDATA* 'VEITCHII')

■ **Plant clematis** against walls, fences, or trees; train stems into shape (*see p.111*).

■ **Plant hedges** with container-grown trees and shrubs (*see p.120*).

## PRUNING AND TRAINING

■ **Prune climbing roses** once flowering is finished (*see p.115*).

■ **Cut back Group 3 clematis** plants that are outgrowing their bounds (*see p.114*).

■ **Prune flowering hedges,** such as *Cotoneaster lacteus*, escallonia, and hawthorn (*see chart, p.117, and p.121*).

---

## PLANTING

■ **Plant spring-flowering bulbs** (*see p.149*), including tulips and daffodils (*see p.137*). Buy healthy bulbs (*see p.146*) for good results.

■ **Prepare the soil** in beds or borders – except on light, sandy soils – to improve their condition and ready them for planting up (*see pp.142–143*) or improve a patch of soil (*see p.150*).

■ **Plant perennials** (*see p.148*) and root-balled and container-grown shrubs, (*see p.150*). Buy good, healthy plants (*see pp.146–147*) for the best results. Give shrubs an initial prune after planting (*see p.151*) and stake if needed (*see p.150*). Water the roots of each plant well before planting – soak the pot in a bucket for about an hour.

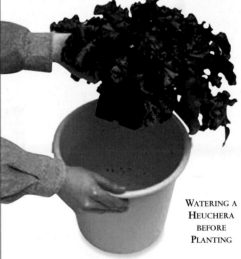

WATERING A
HEUCHERA
BEFORE
PLANTING

## ROUTINE CARE

■ **Deadhead** late-flowering plants, particularly perennials (*see p.155*).

■ **Mulch** beds and borders, if not done in spring (*see pp.152–153*).

■ **Renew top-dressing** or mulch on established gravel beds (*see p.133*).

■ **Lift begonia, dahlia, and gladioli** rootstocks to store over winter. Trim back the foliage and clean off excess soil and any dead or dying material; leave on a tray to dry for a few weeks; then pack loosely, roots downwards, in coir or vermiculite; keep in a dry, frost-free place. Don't forget to label them!

■ **Cut down perennials** to clear away dying, untidy growth, except in cold regions (*see p.155*). Clear away dead and dying annuals and biennials.

■ **Cut back grasses** and bamboos to the ground, unless they are tender plants or decorative in winter. Store cut bamboo canes for use as garden stakes next year.

## PRUNING AND TRAINING
■ **Carry out initial pruning** for shape (*see p.157*) or restorative pruning (*see p.159*) of deciduous shrubs.

■ **Cut back** tall rose bushes to prevent winter winds rocking the bush and working loose the roots (*see p.160*).

## RAISING YOUR OWN PLANTS
■ **Plant out seedlings of biennials** to their final flowering position (*see p.149*).

■ **Collect seed** of late-flowering perennials (*see p.155*) as they ripen. Sow immediately or store them for sowing next year (*see pp.162–163*).

■ **Sow seed outdoors** (*see p.149 and p.163*) of hardy annuals, for an early show of flower next year. In cold regions, protect seedlings over winter with cloches or fleece.

■ **Divide perennials** (*see p.163*), except in regions with cold winters.

■ **Layer shrubs** (*see p.165*)

# CONTAINERS AND RAISED BEDS

## ESSENTIAL TASKS
■ **Water containers** as necessary – check them regularly (*see p.178*).

## PLANTING
■ **Plant containers for winter** with small conifers, evergreen shrubs and climbers, and spring-flowering bulbs. Add winter-flowering pansies for bright colour.

WINTER PLANTING OF JUNIPER AND WINTERGREEN

## ROUTINE CARE
■ **Deadhead** and remove any tired, diseased, or straggly foliage (*see p.178*) to keep the plants well-shaped.

■ **Repot or top-dress** spring-flowering climbers and alpines in containers; root-prune if necessary (*see p.179*).

■ **Renew mulch** on established raised beds (*see p.183*).

■ **Lift and divide** perennials in raised beds, keeping new healthy growth and discarding old, tired parts (*see p.155*), if not done in spring.

■ **Protect tender plants** in containers (*see p.179*) and tender plants in raised beds (*see p.183*) against winter cold, if necessary.

■ **Lift summer-flowering bulbs** once the foliage has died down and store over winter. Clean off the bulbs; lay on a tray to dry; and store in a paper (not plastic) bag.

# ORNAMENTAL TREES

## ESSENTIAL TASKS
■ **Check tree ties** and stakes (*see p.193*) and remove or loosen them as necessary to avoid chafing and damaging the bark.

## PLANTING
■ **Prepare the soil** (*see p.192 and pp.142–143*) for late-autumn plantings of container-grown trees.

■ **Plant hardy evergreen** root-balled trees (*see p.195*), except in cold regions.

## ROUTINE CARE
■ **Mulch established trees** with a 5–8cm (2–3in) layer of well-rotted manure or compost. Keep the mulch away from the trunk. Mulch 3–4m (10–12ft) out, or to the edge of the canopy of a young tree.

■ **Check tree guards** (*see p.195*) are still in place.

■ **Watch out for suckers** and water shoots growing from tree trunks or roots and remove them before they get too big and spoil the tree (*see p.197*).

■ **Move tender trees** in containers under cover for the winter in cool or cold climates before the first frosts.

■ **Gather up fallen fruit,** leaves, and other debris that has fallen from trees and place on the compost heap. Burn any rotten fruit, to stop diseases spreading.

## HARVESTING
■ **Gather any edible nuts** and fruits when ripe (*see p.197*).

# MID-AUTUMN

| WATER GARDENING | THE EDIBLE GARDEN |
|---|---|

## ESSENTIAL TASKS

- **Gather fallen leaves** regularly from netting over ponds (*see p.222*).

- **Protect container pools** (*see p.207*) from winter cold by bringing them under cover or sinking them into the soil.

- **Lift tender and half-hardy** plants in cold climates for storage overwinter (*see p.222*) before the first frost.

## ROUTINE CARE

- **Thin oxygenating plants,** removing excess growth and debris that might rot over winter (*see p.223*).

- **Cut back or thin out** (by division, *see p.223*) overcrowded or straggly marginal plants and clear out any rotting material from the water.

---

### RAISING YOUR OWN HERBS

- **Plant out seedlings of biennial** herbs to their final positions (*see p.149*).

- **Sow seed outdoors** (*see p.149 and p.163*) of hardy annual herbs, for an early spurt of growth next year. In cold regions, protect the seedlings over winter with cloches or fleece.

---

## ESSENTIAL TASKS

- **Cover tender crops** and root vegetables in the ground with cloches (*see p.89*) to protect them over winter in cool climates.

## SOWING AND PLANTING

- **Plant out garlic cloves** or plants raised in modules in well-drained soil (*see p.255*).

- **Sow green manures** to cover empty soil through the winter (*see p.239*).

- **Dig over vegetable beds** (*see p.239 and pp.143–143*) to enrich and condition the soil.

**DIGGING OVER A DEEP BED**

- **Sow hardy, over-wintering vegetables** (*see p.242*) outdoors, such as:
Salad leaves, under cloches (*see p.255*)
Summer radish, under cloches or fleece (*see p.249*)
Winter lettuce, under cloches or fleece (*see p.257*).

- **Plant bush and cane fruits** and container-grown fruit trees (*see pp.260–261*), except plums.

- **Plant rhubarb** (*see p.273*).

## ROUTINE CARE

- **Gather up and burn** rotten fruit that have fallen from fruit trees and bushes, to stop diseases spreading.

- **Check ties and stakes** (*see p.193*) on fruit trees and remove or loosen them as needed to avoid their damaging the bark.

---

- **Clean up strawberry plants** that have finished fruiting (*see p.272*).

- **Mulch rhubarb,** if not done in early spring (*see p.273*).

## PRUNING AND TRAINING

- **Cut back blackcurrants** on planting (*see p.261*) to one strong bud on each stem.

- **Prune established redcurrants** (*see p.268*).

## RAISING YOUR OWN PLANTS

- **Split mature rhubarb** plants to obtain several new sets (*see p.273*), once the leaves die down.

## HARVESTING

- **Pick vegetables, such as:**
Aubergines, chillies, and peppers (*see p.256*)
Autumn kale (*see p.248*)
Beetroot (*see p.251*)
Bulb onions (*see p.250*)
Chicory and endive (*see p.255*)
Early peas (*see p.247*)
Leeks (*see p.251*)
Lettuce (*see p.255*)
Maincrop carrots (*see p.251*)
Maincrop potatoes (*see p.252*)
Parsnips (*see p.251*)
Red cabbages (*see p.249*)
Ridge cucumbers (*see p.256*)
Salad leaves (*see p.255*)
Spinach beet and Swiss chard (*see p.255*)
Spring onions (*see p.250*)
Tomatoes (*see p.257*)
Welsh onions (*see p.250*)
Winter turnips (*see p.249*).

- **Pick fruit crops, such as:**
Apples (*see p.265*)
Autumn-fruiting raspberries (*see p.270*)
Pears (*see p.264*).

- **Cut down haulms (top-growth)** of maincrop potato plants two weeks before lifting the crop (*see p.252*).

# LATE AUTUMN

| LAWNS | BOUNDARIES AND DIVISIONS | BEDS AND BORDERS |
|---|---|---|

## ESSENTIAL TASKS

■ **Finish planting bulbs** in grass to flower in spring (*see p.89*) as soon as the bulbs are available.

■ **Mow lawns for the last time** before the onset of winter; set the mowing height to maximum (*see p.82*). Trim the edges (*see p.83*).

## SOWING AND PLANTING

■ **Lay turf for a new lawn** (*see p.77 and pp.80–81*), if not done in spring.

## ROUTINE CARE

■ **Clear dead leaves** from the lawn by sweeping or raking them; compost the leaves for leafmould in a wire netting bin or in black plastic bags.

■ **Cut summer-flowering meadows** once flowering plants have safely set seed for next year (*see p.89*).

## ESSENTIAL TASKS

■ **Feed and mulch deciduous** hedges to prepare them for renovation pruning in midwinter (*see p.121*).

## PLANTING

■ **Plant shrubs or climbers** against walls, fences, or trees (*see p.110*), including clematis (*see p.111*). Train stems into the desired shape, for example a fan (*see p.111 and p.113*).

PLANTING A CLEMATIS BY A WALL

■ **Plant bare-root rambler** or climbing roses against walls, fences, or trees (*see p.110*).

■ **Plant hedges** (*see p.120*).

## PRUNING AND TRAINING

■ **Prune climbing roses** once flowering is finished (*see p.115*).

■ **Cut back Group 3 clematis** plants that are outgrowing their bounds (*see p.114*).

■ **Prune hedges,** if they include plants such as box and *Cotoneaster lacteus* (*see chart, p.117, and p.121*).

## ESSENTIAL TASKS

■ **Finish planting bulbs** that flower in spring (*see p.149*), including tulips and daffodils (*see p.137*). Buy healthy bulbs (*see p.146*) for good results.

■ **Finish mulching** beds and borders, if not done in spring (*see pp.152–153*), before the ground becomes too cold.

■ **Finish planting out biennial** seedlings to their final flowering positions (*see p.149*).

■ **Finish sowing seed outdoors** (*see p.149 and p.163*) of hardy annuals, for an early show of flower next year. In cold regions, protect the seedlings over winter with cloches or fleece.

## PLANTING

■ **Prepare the soil** in beds or borders – except on light, sandy soil – to improve their condition and ready them for planting up (*see pp.142–143*) or improve a patch of soil (*see p.150*).

■ **Plant perennials** (*see p.148*) and shrubs, except containerized and evergreen ones (*see p.150*). Buy good, healthy plants (*see pp.146–147*) for the best results. Give shrubs an initial prune after planting (*see p.151*) and stake if necessary (*see p.150*).

■ **Plant bare-root roses** (*see p.151*), except in cold regions. Buy good, healthy plants (*see p.147*) for the best results. Give the roses an initial prune after planting (*see p.151*).

## ROUTINE CARE

■ **Cut back grasses** and bamboos to the ground, unless they are tender plants or decorative in winter. Store cut bamboo canes to use as garden stakes next year.

■ **Cut down perennials** to clear away dying, untidy growth, except in cold regions (*see p.155*). Clear away dead and dying annuals and biennials.

*(Continued overleaf.)*

# LATE AUTUMN

| BEDS AND BORDERS (CONT.) | CONTAINERS AND RAISED BEDS | ORNAMENTAL TREES |
| --- | --- | --- |

## PRUNING AND TRAINING

- **Carry out initial pruning** for shape (*see p.157*) and restorative (*see p.159*) pruning of deciduous shrubs.

- **Cut back** tall rose bushes to prevent winter winds rocking the bush and working loose the roots (*see p.160*).

## RAISING YOUR OWN PLANTS

- **Collect seed** of late-flowering perennials (*see p.155*) as they ripen. Sow immediately or store for sowing next year (*see pp.162–163*).

- **Divide perennials** (*see p.163*), except in regions with cold winters.

- **Take hardwood shrub cuttings** (*p.164*).

- **Layer shrubs** (*see p.165*).

---

### TAKING ROOT CUTTINGS

Some perennials are easy to propagate from pieces of their fleshy roots. Try taking root cuttings at this time of year from oriental poppies, sea hollies (*Eryngium*), and verbascums.

- **Dig up a healthy plant** and gently wash the soil off the roots. Look for roots of average thickness and cut them off close to the plant. Take no more than a third of the roots; replant the plant.

- **Cut up the roots** into pieces 8cm (3in) long. So you know which way up the cuttings should be, cut a slant at the downward tip and straight across at the top end of each piece.

- **Fill a pot with cuttings compost**, and insert the cuttings vertically, so that the straight top is level with the surface. Top with coarse sand or grit and label.

- **Keep in a sheltered** place and keep just moist until new shoots and roots appear in spring. Grow on and plant out in autumn to flower the following year.

---

## ESSENTIAL TASKS

- **Water containers** as necessary – check them regularly (*see p.178*).

- **Check that terracotta or ceramic** containers of hardy plants are raised on bricks or "feet" to avoid frost damage (*see p.169*) in cool climates. Group the containers together in a sheltered spot.

- **Protect tender plants** in containers (*see p.179*) and tender plants in raised beds (*see p.183*) against winter cold, if necessary.

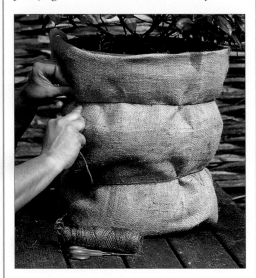

**INSULATING A CONTAINER WITH HESSIAN**

- **Shield alpines** in raised beds from winter wet (*see p.183*).

## ROUTINE CARE

- **Lift and divide perennials** in raised beds, keeping new healthy growth and discarding old, tired parts (*see p.155*), if not done in spring.

- **Lift summer-flowering** bulbs once the foliage has died down and store over winter. Clean off the bulbs; lay on a tray to dry; and store in a paper (not plastic) bag.

---

## ESSENTIAL TASKS

- **Move tender trees** in containers under cover for the winter in cool or cold regions.

## ROUTINE CARE

- **Watch out for suckers** and water shoots growing from tree trunks or roots and remove them before they get too big and spoil the tree (*see p.197*).

- **Gather up fallen fruit**, leaves, and other debris that has fallen from trees and place on the compost heap. Burn any rotten fruit, to stop diseases spreading.

## PLANTING

- **Prepare the soil** (*see p.192 and pp.142–143*) for winter plantings of container-grown, hardy deciduous bare-root, or deciduous root-balled trees.

- **Plant bare-root trees** (*see p.194*) of hardy deciduous species, except in cold regions. When filling in the planting hole, make sure there are no air pockets in-between the roots by gently shaking the stem up and down.

## HARVESTING

- **Gather any edible nuts** and fruits when ripe (*see p.197*).

| WATER GARDENING | HERBS | THE EDIBLE GARDEN |

## ESSENTIAL TASKS

■ **Protect container pools** (*see p.207*) from winter cold by emptying them, bringing them inside or sinking them into the soil.

■ **Mulch bog plants and** moisture-loving marginals (*see p.222*) to insulate them against severe cold, which could kill them.

■ **Clear leaves** from netting over ponds (*see p.222*).

## ROUTINE CARE

■ **Thin oxygenating plants,** removing excess growth and debris that might rot over winter (*see p.223*).

■ **Cut back or thin out** (by division, *see p.223*) any overcrowded or straggly marginal plants and clear out any rotting material from the water.

---

### END-OF-SEASON CLEAR-UP

■ **Clean and oil tools** before putting them away for the winter (*see p.281*) to prevent them rusting.

■ **Clean empty containers** to get rid of any disease or pests that could infect fresh compost or plants. Scrub the pots and trays thoroughly with horticultural disinfectant or household bleach.

SCRUBBING POTS WITH
DETERGENT

---

## ESSENTIAL TASKS

■ **Move tender or half-hardy** herbs in containers under cover (*see p.230*) for the winter in cool climates before the first frost.

■ **Finish planting out biennial** herb seedlings to their final positions (*see p.149*).

■ **Finish sowing seed outdoors** (*see p.149 and p.163*) of hardy annual herbs, for an early spurt of growth next year. In cold regions, protect the seedlings over winter with cloches or fleece.

## ROUTINE CARE

■ **Cut off old growth** on perennial herbs, in mild climates.

■ **Remove dead leaves** or other debris from low-growing evergreens to avoid fungal rot attacking them.

---

## ESSENTIAL TASKS

■ **Cover tender crops** and root vegetables in the ground with cloches (*see p.89*) or fleece to protect them over winter in cooler climates.

## SOWING AND PLANTING

■ **Dig over vegetable beds** (*see p.239 and pp.143–143*) to condition the soil.

■ **Sow green manures** to overwinter (*p.239*).

■ **Sow hardy vegetables outdoors,** such as: Hardy peas, under netting (*see p.247*).

■ **Plant out garlic cloves** or plants raised in modules in well-drained soil (*see p.255*).

■ **Plant bare-root fruit** trees (*see pp.261–261*), bush and cane fruits and container-grown fruit trees (*see pp.260–261*), and grape vines in early winter (*see p.273*).

## ROUTINE CARE

■ **Mulch rhubarb,** if not done in early spring (*see p.273*).

■ **Gather up and burn** fallen rotten fruit and nuts, to stop diseases spreading.

## PRUNING AND TRAINING

■ **Cut back blackcurrants** on planting (*see p.261*). Prune redcurrants (*see p.268*).

■ **Tie in cane tips of** summer-fruiting raspberries to avoid winter damage (*see p.270*).

## HARVESTING

■ **Pick vegetables, such as:**
Cabbages (*see p.249*); chicory and endive (*see p.255*); early peas (*see p.247*); kale (*see p.248*); leeks (*see p.251*); lettuce (*see p.255*); maincrop potatoes (*see p.252*); parsnips (*see p.251*); salad leaves (*see p.255*); spinach beet and Swiss chard (*see p.255*); spring onions (*see p.257*); summer radish (*see p.249*); Welsh onions (*see p.250*); winter turnip (*see p.249*).

■ **Pick fruit crops, such as:**
Apples (*see p.265*).

# EARLY TO MIDWINTER

| BOUNDARIES AND DIVISIONS | BEDS AND BORDERS | ORNAMENTAL TREES |

## ESSENTIAL TASKS

■ **Finish planting bare-root** rambler or climbing roses against walls, fences, or trees (*see p.110*) before it becomes too cold.

## PLANTING

■ **Plant hedges** (*see p.120*).

## PRUNING AND TRAINING

■ **Renovate deciduous climbers** and hedges, if necessary (*see p.115 and p.121*).

■ **Prune established** vines and wall shrubs that are grown for foliage (*see pp.112–113*).

*ELAEAGNUS PUNGENS* 'MACULATA'

■ **Winter-prune wisteria** in midwinter (*see p.111*).

■ **Prune flowering hedges** of *Cotoneaster lacteus*, hawthorn, and sloe or blackthorn (*see chart, p.117, and p.121*).

■ **Prune young hawthorn and privet** shrubs into a good shape (*see p.120*).

## ESSENTIAL TASKS

■ **Finish planting bare-root roses** (*see p.151*), except in cold regions, in early winter. Buy good, healthy plants (*see p.147*) for the best results. Give the roses an initial prune after planting (*see p.151*).

## PLANTING

■ **Plant containerized shrubs** and container-grown ones (*see p.150*). Buy good, healthy plants (*see p.147*) for the best results. Give the shrubs an initial prune after planting (*see p.151*) and stake if necessary (*see p.150*).

## ROUTINE CARE

■ **Cut back grasses** and bamboos to the ground by early winter, unless they are tender plants or decorative in winter. Store cut bamboo canes for use as garden stakes next year.

■ **On light, sandy soils**, spread a thick 8–13cm (3-5in) layer of well-rotted organic material over the surface, and leave until early spring to dig in.

## PRUNING AND TRAINING

■ **Carry out initial pruning** for shape (*see p.157*) and restorative (*see p.159*) pruning of deciduous shrubs.

## RAISING YOUR OWN PLANTS

■ **Divide perennials** (*see p.163*), except in regions with cold winters.

■ **Take hardwood cuttings** from shrubs (*see p.164*).

## ESSENTIAL TASKS

■ **Stop snow weighing** down conifer branches by brushing it off immediately or tying the tree with twine to preserve its shape.

■ **Formative prune** young trees for shape (*see p.196*).

HOLLY (*ILEX X ALTACLERENSIS*)

## PLANTING

■ **Plant hardy bare-root** trees (*see p.194*), except in cold regions.

■ **Plant root-balled deciduous** trees (*see p.195*). When filling in the planting hole, make sure there are no air pockets in-between the roots by gently shaking the stem up and down.

## WATER GARDENING

### ESSENTIAL TASKS

■ **In very cold weather**, don't forget to protect pond surfaces from freezing over (*see p.222*), especially if you have fish.

## THE EDIBLE GARDEN

### ESSENTIAL TASKS

■ **Finish planting grape vines** in early winter and prune for shape (*see p.273*).

■ **Winter-prune grape vines** (*see p.273*) when sap bleeds less readily.

### SOWING AND PLANTING

■ **Sow seed of hardy vegetables** indoors (*see p.211*) in midwinter.

■ **Plant fruit trees**, except pears, and cane fruits (*see pp.260–261*). Tie in cordons to supports (*see p.261*).

■ **Plant bush fruits**, if soil and weather are suitable (*see p.261*).

■ **Plant rhubarb** (*see p.273*).

■ **Plant shallot sets** (*see p.250*).

### ROUTINE CARE

■ **Cover the compost heap** or bin with old carpet or plastic sheeting to keep it warm and active over winter.

### PRUNING AND TRAINING

■ **Cut back blackcurrants** on planting (*see p.261*); prune established blackcurrants and redcurrants (*see p.268*).

■ **Winter-prune fruit trees**, such as apples and pears (*see pp.262–265*).

■ **Cut back blackberry** and hybrid berry canes after planting (*see p.271*). Thin blueberries, if needed (*see p.269*).

### HARVESTING
■ **Pick winter vegetables**, such as:
Beetroot tops (*see p.251*)
Chicory and endive (*see p.255*)
Leeks (*see p.251*)
Parsnips (*see p.251*)
Red cabbage (*see p.249*)
Salad leaves (*see p.255*)

Spinach beet and Swiss chard (*see p.255*)
Welsh onions (*see p.250*)
Winter cabbages (*see p.249*)
Winter kale (*see p.248*)
Winter lettuce (*see p.255*)
Winter turnips (*see p.249*).

### PLANNING FOR NEXT YEAR

■ **While away the long evenings** of winter by ordering seed catalogues and making up a list of crops to purchase for sowing in the new year.

■ **Plan out the vegetable plot** for next year, and consider how much room each crop will need and how long it will occupy the soil, in order to work out how many seeds to buy.

■ **If you have collected** your own seeds, plan to sow them a little more thickly than purchased seeds.

LARGE SEEDS

FLAT SEEDS

FINE SEEDS

# LATE WINTER

| LAWNS | BOUNDARIES AND DIVISIONS | BEDS AND BORDERS |
| --- | --- | --- |

## SOWING AND PLANTING

- **Prepare the soil and site** (*see p.78*) before in early spring laying turf or planting divided herbs for a non-grass lawn, or, in warm climates, for plantings of plugs or sprigs.

## ROUTINE CARE

- **Clean and service lawnmowers** and other equipment.

---

### DOGS IN THE GARDEN

- **Avoid yellow patches** developing on the lawn, where a pet bitch urinates, by throwing a bucket of water over the spot immediately afterwards if possible.

- **Protect tree trunks** from the attentions of the dog by surrounding the base with a prickly "collar" of straw.

---

## ESSENTIAL TASKS

- **Finish pruning established** vines and wall shrubs that are grown for foliage (*see pp.112–113*).

IVY (*HEDERA HELIX* 'GOLDHEART')

- **Winter-prune** flowering quince (*p.113*).

## PLANTING

- **Plant hedges** (*see p.120*).

## PRUNING AND TRAINING

- **Prune established climbers** and wall shrubs that flower on the current season's shoots (*see pp.112–113*).

- **Thin overgrown Group 1 clematis;** prune Groups 2 and 3 clematis (*see p.114*).

- **Renovate deciduous climbers** (*p.115*).

- **Check supports** and renew them if necessary (*see p.109 and p.115*).

- **Prune flowering hedges,** such as *Cotoneaster lacteus*, hawthorn, and sloe or blackthorn (*see chart, p.117, and p.121*).

## ESSENTIAL TASKS

- **Finish planting** containerized and container-grown shrubs (*see p.150*). Give shrubs an initial prune after planting (*see p.151*) and stake if needed (*see p.150*).

## ROUTINE CARE

- **Cut back hardy grasses** and bamboos that have been left over winter to the ground, before they start into growth.

- **On light, sandy soils,** spread a thick 8–13cm (3-5in) layer of well-rotted organic material; leave until early spring to dig in.

## PRUNING AND TRAINING

- **Prune deciduous shrubs** for initial shape (*see p.157*) and for restoration (*p.159*).

- **Prune established deciduous** shrubs that flower on new shoots (*see p.158*).

- **Prune bush roses,** including modern bush roses, and China, Bourbon, and Portland old roses (*see p.161*), in mild climes.

## RAISING YOUR OWN PLANTS

- **Sow seed indoors** of tender and half-hardy annuals and of perennials (*see p.162*).

- **Divide perennials** (*see p.163*), except in regions with cold winters.

WINTER ACONITE (*ERANTHIS HYEMALIS*)

| ORNAMENTAL TREES | THE EDIBLE GARDEN |
|---|---|

## ESSENTIAL TASKS

■ **Finish planting root-balled** trees of deciduous species (*see p.195*).

■ **Stop snow weighing** down conifer branches by brushing it off immediately or tying the tree with twine to preserve its shape.

## PLANTING

■ **Prepare the soil** (*see p.192 and pp.142–143*) for early-spring plantings of container-grown or hardy deciduous bare-root trees.

■ **Plant bare-root trees** (*see p.194*) of hardy deciduous species, except in cold regions, when conditions are good. When filling in the planting hole, make sure there are no air pockets in-between the roots by gently shaking the stem up and down.

## PRUNING AND TRAINING

■ **Prune deciduous trees** that flower in late summer — except cherries, plums, peaches, and apricots (*Prunus*) — if necessary (*see p.196*).

■ **Coppice and pollard** trees (*see p.197*).

## ESSENTIAL TASKS

■ **Sprout early seed potatoes** to prepare them for planting (*see p.252*).

■ **Finish planting bush fruits** (*see p.261*), if soil condition and weather are favourable.

■ **Plant peach trees** (*see p.260*).

■ **Finish winter-pruning fruit trees** (*see pp.262–265*), such as pears and apples.

■ **Force rhubarb into growth** for an earlier spring crop (*see p.273*).

SOWING VEGETABLE SEED

## SOWING AND PLANTING

■ **Sow seed of tender vegetables** in containers indoors (*see p.244*), such as:
Aubergines, chillies, and peppers (*see p.256*)
Greenhouse tomatoes (*see p.257*).

■ **Sow hardy vegetable seed outdoors** (*see p.242*), under cloches in cold areas, such as:
Leeks (*see p.251*).

■ **Plant fruit trees** and cane fruits (*see pp.260–261*), except pears and plums.

■ **Plant rhubarb** (*see p.273*).

## ROUTINE CARE

■ **Warm the soil** in cooler regions by placing cloches (*see p.240*) or fleece over it, to prepare it for sowing.

## PRUNING AND TRAINING

■ **Cut back blackcurrants** on planting (*see p.261*).

■ **Prune redcurrants** and gooseberries (*see p.261 and p.268*).

■ **Cut down autumn-fruiting** raspberry canes (*see p.270*).

## HARVESTING

■ **Pick winter vegetables**, such as:
Beetroot tops (*see p.251*)
Calabrese (*see p.248*)
Leeks (*see p.251*)
Parsnips (*see p.251*)
Spinach beet and Swiss chard (*see p.255*)
Sprouting broccoli (*see p.248*)
Welsh onions (*see p.250*)
Winter cabbages (*see p.249*)
Winter kale (*see p.248*)
Winter lettuce (*see p.255*).

# ANYTIME

| HERBS | THE EDIBLE GARDEN | GENERAL MAINTENANCE |
|---|---|---|

## PLANTING

- **Plant container-grown** perennial or shrubby herbs in beds, pots, or hanging baskets (*see pp.228–231*), except in drought, frosty, or waterlogged conditions.

ROSEMARY

- **Make a gravel garden** in which to plant herbs (*see p.229*) or build raised beds.

## PLANTING

- **Lime the soil** if necessary (*see p.238*) at least one month before planting any vegetables.

- **Prepare the soil** at least two months before planting any fruit (*see p.260*).

- **Plant container-grown fruit** trees (*see p.260*), except when the ground is frozen, dry, or waterlogged.

## ROUTINE CARE

- **Remove weeds** regularly to stop them competing with the crops (*see pp.288–293*).

---

### BALLERINA ARCH

- **Make a living arch** out of ballerina apple trees (developed to grow as a single stem with short fruiting spurs).

- **Plant two ballerina trees,** one each side of a path. They should be of the same cultivar so that they grow at the same rate.

- **Train the tips to join up,** once the trees have grown taller than 2m (6ft). Do this by twining heavy-duty wire loosely around the stem tips while they are still pliable and bending them towards each other.

- **Adjust the wire every season,** until the tips meet across the arch, then remove it.

## STRUCTURES

- **Re-treat wooden sheds,** tool stores, or cold frames with preservative, and make any repairs, as necessary.

- **Keep greenhouse glass clean** so that plants within receive the maximum light.

---

### RUST-FREE TOOLS

- **Garden tools** will function better and last longer if regularly cleaned and oiled (*see p.279*).

- **Clean small tools** by rubbing them with an oily cloth or with a handful of oily sand.

- **Clean large tools** by plunging them several times into a bucket of sand, into which a little oil has been added.

PLUNGING A FORK INTO OILED SAND

# GLOSSARY

**Acid** (of soil) With a pH value of less than 7. See also *alkaline* and *neutral*.

**Alkaline** (of soil) With a pH value greater than 7. See also *acid* and *neutral*.

**Annual** Plant that grows, flowers, sets seed, and dies in a single growing season.

**Biennial** Plant that produces leafy growth in the first year after germination and flowers, sets seed, and dies in the second. See also *annual* and *perennial*.

**Blind** Of a shoot that fails to produce a flower.

**Bolt** To produce flowers and set seed prematurely.

**Brassica** Member of the cabbage *family*.

**Broadcast** To scatter fertilizer or seed over the ground rather than in *drills*.

**Cloche** Small, generally portable, structure made of clear plastic, glass, or horticultural fleece on a supporting framework. Used to warm the soil and/or protect crops in open ground.

**Cold frame** Box-like structure, made from brick, metal, timber, or plastic, with a hinged or removable glass or clear plastic lid. Used to protect seeds, seedlings, and other plants from excessive cold.

**Compost** *Organic* material formed by the decomposition of plants or other organic matter. Used as a soil improver or mulch. See also *potting compost*.

**Cultivar** (abbr. cv.) Variant of a *species* selected or artificially bred for a special characteristic, such as its flower or foliage form or colour (for example *Helianthus atrorubens* 'Monarch').

**Deadhead** To remove faded flowers or flowerheads so as to prevent self-seeding.

**Division** Method of increasing plants by dividing them into pieces, each with its own roots and growing point.

**Dormancy** Pause in active plant growth, usually in winter.

**Drill** Straight furrow in soil used for sowing seeds or transplanting seedlings.

**Earth up** To draw up soil around the base of a plant so as to encourage its stems to produce roots, to blanch the stems, or to reduce wind rock.

**Family** Group of several *genera* that share some common characteristics. For example *Bellis* and *Helianthus* both belong to the daisy family, Compositae.

**Forma** (abbr. f.), **Subspecies** (abbr. ssp. or subsp.), **Varietas** (abbr. var.) Naturally occurring variants of a *species*. For example, *Helianthus debilis* subsp. *cucumerifolius* is a shorter variant of the species *Helianthus debilis*, and also has larger flowerheads.

**Frost pocket** Area of ground, often a hollow or beside a solid structure, in which cold air accumulates and where frosts may be severe and/or prolonged.

**Genus** (pl. genera) Group of related plant *species* linked by several common characteristics (for example *Helianthus*); the rank of plant classification between species and *family*.

**Graft** To join artificially one plant part to another. See also *rootstock* and *scion*.

**Harden off** Gradually to acclimatize plants that have been raised in a protected environment to outdoor growing conditions.

**Hardy** Of a plant that is able to withstand a wide range of climatic conditions, including frost, year-round. See also *tender*.

**Herbaceous** Non-woody plant with top-growth that dies back at the end of the growing season.

**Humus** Chemically complex, gel-like residue of decayed *organic* matter in soil.

**Hybrid** Offspring of two genetically distinct plant parents. Indicated by the symbol "×" in the Latin name (for example, *Helianthus × multiflorus*).

**Mulch** Material applied to the soil surface to suppress weeds, conserve moisture, or insulate roots. Can also be used to add *organic* matter to the soil.

**Neutral** (of soil) With a pH of 7; neither *acid* nor *alkaline*.

**Nursery bed** Soil bed for germinating seeds or growing on young plants until transferred to their permanent site.

**Organic** (1) Of carbon-based matter of natural plant or animal origin. (2) Of cultivation without the use of synthetic or non-organic materials.

**Perennial** Plant that lives for three or more seasons. Is usually applied to *herbaceous* plants even though the term in fact also includes woody perennials, that is shrubs and trees.

**pH** Measure of acidity or alkalinity on a scale of 1–14. See also *acid*, *alkaline*, and *neutral*.

**Pinch out** To remove the growing tip on a plant so as to stimulate growth of sideshoots lower down the stem, or the formation of flowerbuds.

**Potting compost** (also called potting medium, potting mix) Mix of loam, sand, peat substitute (or peat), and nutrients in varying proportions. Used for growing container-grown plants. Soilless mixes are usually made of peat (or substitute) and nutrients; they contain no loam.

**Prick out** To transfer young seedlings from their germination site into a pot or *nursery bed*.

**Propagator** Structure that provides a protected environment for raising seeds and rooting cuttings.

**Rootstock** (1) Root system of a plant. (2) Plant that provides the root system for a *grafted* plant.

**Sheet mulch** Sheet of artificial material, for example geotextile membrane or plastic, used as a *mulch*.

**Species** Group of plants that breed naturally to produce offspring with similar characteristics (for example, *Helianthus debilis*); the rank of plant classification between *genus* and *forma*, *subspecies*, and *varietas*.

**Subsoil** Layer of soil that is less fertile and of poorer texture and structure than the *topsoil* above it.

**Subspecies** (abbr. ssp. or subsp.) See *forma*.

**Sucker** Shoot arising from a plant's roots or underground stem, or from the *rootstock* of a *grafted* plant.

**Systemic** Of a pesticide or fungicide that is absorbed throughout a plant when put on its foliage or planting site.

**Tender** Of a plant that is vulnerable to frost damage. See also *hardy*.

**Top-dress** To apply *compost*, decorative dressing (for example, grit or pebbles) fertilizer, or fresh soil, to the soil surface around a plant or on a lawn.

**Topsoil** Topmost, usually most fertile, layer of soil. See also *subsoil*.

**Varietas** (abbr. var.) See *forma*.

# INDEX

# ACKNOWLEDGMENTS

**Publisher's Acknowledgments**
Dorling Kindersley would like to thank all staff at the RHS, in particular Susanne Mitchell, Barbara Haynes, and Karen Wilson at Vincent Square, and staff at the RHS Garden Wisley. Grateful thanks also to the following people for their invaluable contributions to this book: Lee Griffiths and Mary-Clare Jerram for their support and faith in the book production team. Jane Simmonds, Lin Hawthorne, and Pamela Brown for developing the original synopsis; Louise Abbott, Lynn Bresler, Pamela Brown, Alison Copland, Annelise Evans, and Lesley Riley for expert and patient editorial help; Frances Hutchison and Ray Rogers for commenting on the picture selection; Louise Abbott, Murdo Culver, Stephen Josland, and Wesley Richards for organizing and helping with new photography; Murdo Culver, Ursula Dawson, Clive Hayball, Wesley Richards, and Alison Shackleton for additional design assistance; Richard Dabb for help with sourcing pictures from the Dorling Kindersley picture library; Andrea Hill for additional DTP assistance; Barry Prescott for help with administration. David Joyce (contributor, Part One) and the publisher wish to thank Andrew Lawson for the material that provided the basis for the garden illustrated and described on pages 52–53.

**Commissioned Photography**
Peter Anderson

**Illustrations**
Gill Tomblin, pages 50, 51, 52; Karen Gavin, lighting illustrations page 71

**Agency Picture Credits**
The publisher would like to thank the following for their kind permission to reproduce their photographs:

(Key: a=above; c=centre; b=below; l=left; r=right; t=top)
**1 Garden Picture Library:** John Glover c
**2 Clive Nichols:** Anthony Noel
**5 Scotts of Stow**
**6 Garden Picture Library:** Juliette Wade
**8–9 Garden Picture Library:** Clay Perry
**10 Marianne Majerus: Designer:** Jon Baillie bl; **Steve Wooster: Designer:** Anthony Paul c
**11 Jerry Harpur:** tl, bc; **Clive Nichols: Designer:** Keeyla Meadows bl
**12 Garden Picture Library:** Ron Sutherland tr; **Jerry Harpur:** bl; **Steve Wooster: Designer:** Piet Oudolf c
**13 Jerry Harpur: Designer:** Christopher Masson tr; **Anne Hyde:** br; **Clive Nichols:** Clive & Jane Nichols bl; **Steve Wooster:** Hannah Deschar Gallery c
**14 Jerry Harpur:** cl, c
**15 Jerry Harpur:** bl
**14–15 Jonathan Buckley:** Designer Penny Smith
**16 Elizabeth Whiting & Associates:** bl
**17 Garden Picture Library:** Michael Howes b **Elizabeth Whiting & Associates:** tl
**16–17 Clive Nichols:** Clive & Jane Nichols
**18 Greenworld Pictures Inc.:** Mick Hales bl
**19 Garden Picture Library:** Eric Crichton bl; **Jerry Harpur:** br; **Marianne Majerus:** tr
**18–19 John Glover**
**20 Andrew Lawson:** bl
**21 John Glover:** br; **Jerry Harpur:** bc
**20–21 Andrew Lawson**
**22 Garden Picture Library:** Ron Sutherland bl; **Clive Nichols:** The Priory, Kemerton, Worcs c
**23 Garden Picture Library:** Steven Wooster b
**24 Garden Picture Library:** Eric Crichton tc; John Baker bc; Ron Sutherland br
**24 Jerry Harpur:** tr; **Clive Nichols: Designer:** Vic Shanley bl

**25 Garden Picture Library:** Rowan Isaac bc; **Andrew Lawson:** tc, tr, br; **Steve Wooster:** tl
**26 Derek Fell:** tl; **John Glover:** bc; **Jerry Harpur:** tc; **Anne Hyde:** tr; **Andrew Lawson:** York Gate, Leeds bl; **Steve Wooster:** br
**27 John Glover:** br; **Andrew Lawson:** tr; Designer: Ryl Nowell, Wilderness Farm bl; **Clive Nichols:** tl; Designer: Anthony Noel bc; **Steve Wooster:** tc
**28 Garden Picture Library:** Gary Rogers br; John Baker bc; **The Interior Archive:** Herbert YPMA tr; **Elizabeth Whiting & Associates:** tc, bl
**29 Garden Picture Library:** Jerry Pavia tl; Rex Butcher bl; **Andrew Lawson:** tc; Designer: Lynden Miller cra; **Elizabeth Whiting & Associates:** bc, br
**30 Garden Picture Library:** Marijke Heuff bc; Tommy Candler bl; **John Glover:** Bosvigo 968 tc; **Andrew Lawson:** Designer: Sir Miles Warren tr; **Marianne Majerus:** tl; **Elizabeth Whiting & Associates:** br
**31 Jonathan Buckley:** cr; **Garden Picture Library:** Steven Wooster bc; **Jerry Harpur:** bl; **Anne Hyde:** tl; **Andrew Lawson:** tc, tr; **Elizabeth Whiting & Associates:** br
**32 Garden Picture Library:** Marie O'Hara bl; **John Glover:** tr, bc; **Marianne Majerus:** Design: Lesley Rosser br; **Steve Wooster:** tc
**33 Garden Picture Library:** Ron Sutherland bc; **John Glover:** tr; **Clive Nichols:** Andrew & Karla Newell tl; Lambeth Horticultural Society bl; Little Coopers, Hampshire br; **Steve Wooster:** tc
**34 Garden Picture Library:** Juliette Wade tc; **John Glover:** tr; **Jerry Harpur:** bl; **Clive Nichols:** Paula Rainey Crofts br; **Derek St Romaine:** bc
**35 Emap Active:** tr, bc; **Garden Picture Library:** John Miller tc; **Jerry Harpur:** bl; **Elizabeth Whiting & Associates:** tl
**36 Garden Picture Library:** Brian Carter tr; Gary Rogers tc; Steven Wooster bl; **John Glover:** bc; **Clive Nichols:** br
**37 Garden Picture Library:** Lamontagne bc; Mel Watson tr; **John Glover:** tl, tc; **Andrew Lawson:** Designer: Penelope Hobhouse br; **Derek St Romaine:** bl
**38 Clive Nichols:** tr, br; Chenies Manor, Bucks bl; **Steve Wooster:** bc
**39 Anne Hyde:** tl, bl
**40 Jerry Harpur:** The Priory, Hatfield Peverel, Essex tc; **Clive Nichols:** Parnham House, Dorset bc; The Anchorage, Kent br; **Steve Wooster:** tr
**41 Jerry Harpur:** br; Design: Edwina Von Gal bl; **Andrew Lawson:** tl, bc; **Clive Nichols:** Bassibones Farm, Bucks tc; Designer: Elisabeth Woodhouse tr
**42 Jerry Harpur:** Neil Diboll, Wisconsin bc; **Clive Nichols:** Chenies Manor, Bucks tr
**43 Garden Picture Library:** Vaughan Fleming br; **Andrew Lawson:** tr; **Clive Nichols:** Designer: Anthony Noel bc; Designer: Jill Billington tl
**44 Jerry Harpur:** c; **Clive Nichols:** Designer: Sarah Hammond bl
**46 Jerry Harpur:** Designer: Simon Fraser c; **Anne Hyde:** bl
**47 Andrew Lawson:** Designer: Penelope Hobhouse cl; **Clive Nichols:** Designer: Jill Billington bc
**48 John Glover:** bc; **Jerry Harpur:** crb; Diana Ross, London tr
**49 Andrew Lawson:** tc, c
**50 Andrew Lawson:** tr, br
**51 Andrew Lawson:** tr
**52 Andrew Lawson:** tr, cla, clb, bl, br
**53 Andrew Lawson:** tl, cl, bl
**54–55 Garden Picture Library:** Janet Sorrell
**61 Jerry Harpur:** br
**63 Clive Nichols:** bc
**65 Garden Picture Library:** Ron Sutherland br
**70 Emap Active:** cl
**71 Clive Nichols:** Garden & Security lighting cr; **Clive Nichols:** Andrew & Karla Newell cr

**73 Clive Nichols:** cr
**74 Eric Crichton Photos:** c; **Garden Picture Library:** Brigitte Thomas bc; **Clive Nichols:** Hilary Macpherson br
**75 Garden Picture Library:** Brian Carter cra; JS Sira bl; Juliette Wade tc; **Jerry Harpur:** Designer: Wesley & Susan Dixon cr; **Clive Nichols:** Bassibones Farm, Bucks br
**76 John Glover:** br; **Jerry Harpur:** P. Hickman, Thames Ditton bl; **Andrew Lawson:** clb
**81 Garden Picture Library:** Jacqui Hurst bl; Jane Legate clb; **Clive Nichols:** White Windows, Hampshire cr
**82 Garden Picture Library:** Howard Rice bl
**87 Garden Picture Library:** Chris Burrows bcr
**88 John Glover:** bl; **Garden Picture Library:** John Glover bc
**89 Eric Crichton Photos:** tr
**90 Steve Wooster:** bl
**92 Garden Picture Library:** Howard Rice br
**95 Eric Crichton Photos:** bl
**96 Jerry Harpur:** br
**97 John Glover:** c
**98 Garden Picture Library:** Howard Rice c
**100 John Glover:** bl; **Jerry Harpur:** bc
**103 Steve Wooster:** tr, cr
**106 Garden Picture Library:** Mayer/Le Scanff tr
**122 Garden Picture Library:** Gil Hanly bl
**139 Garden Picture Library:** Howard Rice bcl
**172 Garden Picture Library:** Steven Wooster cr
**174 Garden Picture Library:** Juliette Wade bl
**176 Jo Whitworth:** br
**180 Garden Picture Library:** Brian Carter bl; Gary Rogers c; **J S Sira:** br
**181 Andrew Lawson:** bc
**183 Garden Picture Library:** Ann Kelley cl
**184 Eric Crichton Photos:** bc; **Jerry Harpur:** cr
**186 Steve Wooster:** bc
**187 Steve Wooster:** tc
**189 Garden Picture Library:** Stephen Jury bc; **Steve Wooster:** tr
**190 Steve Wooster:** c
**195 Andrew Lawson:** c
**224 Eric Crichton Photos:** bl
**228 Garden Picture Library:** John Glover c
**232 Neil Campbell-sharp:** br
**274 Garden Picture Library:** John Glover bl; **Scotts of Stow:** bc
**275 John Glover:** c
**276 Scotts of Stow:** ac
**280 Garden Picture Library:** Howard Rice crb
**292 Oxford Scientific Films:** Colin Milkins cl
**295 Holt Studios International:** Nigel Cattlin bl
**296 Holt Studios International:** Nigel Cattlin clb, bl, bcr
**297 Holt Studios International:** Nigel Cattlin bcl, bcr, bcrr
**299 The Garden Magazine:** Tim Sandell bcl; **Holt Studios International:** Nigel Cattlin br, bcl
**300 Holt Studios International:** Nigel Cattlin br
**301 A-Z Botanical Collection:** bcr; **RHS Wisley:** J. Maynard abc
**302 Heather Angel:** br; **Holt Studios International:** Nigel Cattlin bcl
**304 Holt Studios International:** Nigel Cattlin bl, bcl, bcr
**305 Holt Studios International:** Nigel Cattlin bl, br
**306 Holt Studios International:** Nigel Cattlin bl; **RHS Wisley:** K.M. Harris bcl
**307 Holt Studios International:** Nigel Cattlin c; **RHS Wisley:** crb; A.J. Halstead br; P. Becker cr
**308 Holt Studios International:** Nigel Cattlin bl, bcl, bcr
**310 The Garden Magazine:** Tim Sandell bl; **Holt Studios International:** Nigel Cattlin bcr; **RHS Wisley:** P. Becker bcl
**311 The Garden Magazine:** Tim Sandell br
**312–313 Garden Picture Library:** Clive Nichols
**362 Garden Picture Library:** JS Sira br
**364–365 Garden Picture Library:** Juliette Wade
**Jacket: Jerry Harpur:** back acr